GW00733361

# LOVE AND WAR

## by

## Martin Allen

The Naval & Military Press Ltd

*Published by*

## The Naval & Military Press Ltd

Unit 5 Riverside, Brambleside
Bellbrook Industrial Estate
Uckfield, East Sussex
TN22 1QQ England

Tel: +44 (0)1825 749494

www.naval–military–press.com
www.nmarchive.com

© Martin Allen 2024

Cover design by James Kingston-Stewart

# Author's note

When my father, Stanley, died in 2013 – my mother, Peggy, having died two years earlier – I discovered a collection several hundred of their letters spanning the years from 1936 to 1946.

Stanley was born on 24th February 1918, at the moment of the major German First World War offensive which threated to bring them victory, the offensive eventually being halted, the allied counter offensive proving decisive, bringing the war to an end that November.

Peggy was born on 15th February 1919, three months after the end of the war, and nine months before the ill-fated Treaty of Versailles which paved the way for the resurgence of Germany under Hitler.

Stanley's father, William Allen, was vicar of the Good Shepherd church in Dyke Road, Brighton, where Stanley and his brother Michael (eight years his junior) were brought up with his mother, Meg, and the family housekeeper, the elderly, kindly Mrs Christian.

Peggy's father, Arthur, was a Brighton estate agent and land surveyor. At the start of, and throughout much of the period of the correspondence, Peggy lived with her father and mother, May, and her elder brother, Tom, Arthur being closely involved with the Church. Completing the household, was the family housekeeper, Florrie.

Although it is not known when Stanley and Peggy first met, they knew each other, probably through church related social activities, when they were both at school (Stanley at Brighton College and Peggy at Brighton & Hove High School), or possibly even when they were children.

It is clear that Stanley had fallen for Peggy by the time the letters begin in 1936, when he was 18, there being reference to her attending a school dance with him. It seems, however, that it took him a year or more, to "win" her, their courtship developing through the year or so before the start of the war.

Stanley started his articles with a solicitors' practice soon after he left school, and by the time of signing up in 1939, he had taken, but failed, his final exams.

Peggy started nursing at St Bartholomew's Hospital ('Bart's') in 1938, her nursing career having to be curtailed towards the end of 1940, shortly before marrying Stanley, married women not being allowed as hospital nurses.

They were married on 6th January 1941.

For the next year or so, Peggy had various nursing roles as well as working for a few months at Dover Castle, as a clerk to Post Office telephone engineers.

Stanley signed up in April 1939 as a Territorial Army volunteer, his Army Record referring to him as being a driver, being called up on the outbreak of war at the beginning of September and, presumably after an initial period of training, becoming "embodied" (accepted into the Army) towards the end of that month, then being assigned to the Royal Army Service Corps as a private.

He became commissioned, as a Second Lieutenant, on 4th January 1941.

For the remainder of his time with the Home Forces, until June 1944, he was with the 43rd Wessex Division (the "Wyverns"), comprising regiments from across the South. For most of that time, he was based in Kent, the county closest to, and with most similar terrain to, Normandy, it being known, probably as early as 1940, after Dunkirk, that if Britain survived the threat of German invasion, the British Army would return to Europe, with an inevitable campaign in Northern France.

Throughout those years, Stanley's letters vividly portray the frustration, and often, the boredom, of endless training. However, when the 43rd Division was eventually deployed in Normandy, it quickly established itself as one of the best trained and most effective divisions within the Allied invasion force.

After the first, gruelling phase of the campaign, the bloody battle for Normandy, the 43rd Division spearheaded the crossing of the Seine, then, as part of the 2nd Army, driving across France and the Low Countries. It suffered its most serious setback as part of the ill-fated attempt to thrust into Germany at Arnhem, Stanley spending two days cut off at Nijmegen by encircling German forces.

At the beginning of November 1944, Stanley, then a Captain, was transferred to the 51st (Highland) Division, and promoted to Major.

The 51st (Highland) Division having won fame as part of Montgomery's 8th Army, defeating Rommel at the Battle of El Alamein, took part in the Allied invasion of Normandy, landing the day after D-Day. However, its performance in the Normandy campaign was considered disappointing, particularly by Montgomery, with the result that a new Commanding Officer was appointed, Major General Tom Rennie, leading to a strengthening of the Division in terms of morale, effectiveness and personnel. It appears that Stanley's transfer was part of this process, the Division's reputation being fully restored by its role in the subsequent campaign as the Allies moved towards Germany.

With the 51st, Stanley took part in the Ardennes battle – "The Battle of the Bulge" – containing the major German offensive that, at one stage, threatened the entire Allied campaign, the Division also being selected to spearhead the fiercely contested crossing of the Rhine.

As part of Montgomery's 2nd Army, and General Sir Brian Horrocks's XXX Corps, the 51st Division moved through Belgium and Holland, before the Rhine crossing, ending the war in Northern Germany.

Having to play an important part in the logistics of the German surrender, and of the subsequent administration of both military and civilian populace, Stanley participated in the surrender negotiations, encountering certain of the senior German officers.

At the time of the surrender, on 7th May 1945, the Division was in the area of Bremerhaven, Stanley being present at the victory parade through the town on 12th May.

In early 1946, while he was still stationed in Germany as part of the occupying army, then known as the British Army of the Rhine (BAOR), Stanley was awarded the MBE. The citation states: "In every operation in which the Division has been engaged he has displayed a very high sense of duty in times which severely tested the whole Divisional RASC".

Following their marriage in January 1941, Stanley and Peggy lived apart for more than 5 years. Until June 1944, Stanley being stationed mainly in Kent, they were able to see each other quite frequently although Stanley's periods of leave were generally limited to 48 hours with an occasional 7 days. It seems, however, that he was also able to make regular trips to meet Peggy, these often being fleeting visits, sometimes unannounced, and for just a few hours.

Until the outbreak of war, when Peggy was nursing at Barts in London, most of the hospital's patients and staff then being relocated to St Albans where she remained until her marriage. After that she lived at the family home in Hove, albeit spending some periods away for her subsequent nursing and other jobs, including some months in Canterbury.

After Stanley's departure for France in June 1944, they did not see each other until January 1945, which was his only leave before the end of the war. Thereafter, his periods of leave were a week in July and another in November 1945, and about two weeks compassionate leave in December.

When they were married, their temporary home, referred to as "the hut", was a wooden chalet in the church grounds originally serving as a temporary church hall when the church had been built in the early 1920s.

Except when Stanley was home on leave, however, Peggy remained living with her parents, remaining with mother after her father's death early in 1945.

Their first child, Anthony was born on 23rd December 1943. The fact that Peggy was living at home enabled her to rely on her mother for a good deal of support and baby-sitting, and was thus able to enjoy a good deal of socialising.

Stanley saw Anthony only during his short periods of leave, the child being 2 years and 3 months when Stanley was finally released from the Army.

During my initial exercise of reading and transcribing the letters, it became increasingly apparent that they told only part of the story. In deciding to try to fill in the extensive gaps, I realised that I would need to strike a careful balance between being faithful to the story that they, themselves, were narrating, and the imagining of the lives they were living through such a dramatic period of history.

What was remarkable was that they continued to write to each other so frequently, particularly when Stanley was in Europe when they were both writing almost daily, it being even more remarkable that he was able to do so even when he was engaged in the most intensive periods of fighting.

Stanley often complains about the postal service, letters sometimes taking several days. What is truly surprising, however, is that the postal service was so effective throughout the campaign.

Many names feature in the correspondence, including family and close friends. The cast of Stanley's army colleagues frequently changes, it often proving difficult to identify, let alone to give personality, even to those who become his closest comrades, such characters, therefore, sometimes requiring a degree of imaginative construction.

During Stanley's lifetime (he lived to 95), he rarely recounted his experiences during the European campaign, other than a handful of often repeated anecdotes, generally the lighter moments such as his encountering Monty in his staff car when Stanley was in a vehicle loaded with "liberated" champagne, Monty's response to being told of the vehicle's contents being a simple "Carry on!"

The only account of action that I can recall him giving, was of the Rhine crossing, which, as is vividly recounted in one of his letters, he was not only present at, but which prompted him to admit to fear.

It was when reading the letters, that I learned that he had been present at the trial of those who ran the Belsen concentration camp, including its infamous commandant, Josef Kramer, the "Beast of Belsen", and the sadistic young female, Irma Grise, the "Beautiful Beast", something he never spoke about.

Both of the Divisions in which Stanley served, sustained heavy losses during the campaign, the 43rd suffering 13,500 casualties including 3,000 killed, and the 51st over 19,000 casualties including more than 3,000 killed.

Undoubtedly the most striking feature of the correspondence is not only the fact that Peggy and Stanley wrote to each other so frequently throughout their long separation, but that their emotions, and the compelling story of their love and devotion to each other, are so vividly in the spotlight of this remarkably graphic personal history, leaving one, perhaps more than anything, with a sense of gratitude.

In these current troubled times, when it is easy to forget what Peggy and Stanley, and so many millions of their, and their parent's, generation lived through, their story provides a timely and salutary reminder of the consequence of the escalation of international rivalries, and why the peace which the two of them prayed for with such desperation, is so precious – and so precarious.

**Martin Allen**

*Dedicated to my sadly missed elder brother, Anthony, who features in this story and who told me that he remembered sitting in his pram, watching formations of bombers flying over.*

# ONE

He watched as a man in dirty overalls and cloth cap lifted the thick rope from the mooring bollard, the rope sliding from the quay, splashing into the water, two crew members on the deck guiding it, glistening and dripping, onto the capstan.

Along the side of the ship the throng of men, officers and troops, peered down at the dock as the ship began to move, the deck vibrating with the thrumming of the engines, expressions pensive, each man's thoughts his own, the common realisation being that they were finally on their way.

As the stern rope was released, the bulk of the liberty ship, *Fort Rae*, Canadian built, but with the American Stars and Stripes fluttering from its mast high above them, edged out into the Thames Estuary, joining the procession of similar vessels making their way slowly towards the open sea.

Beyond the quay stretched the faceless sprawl of Purfleet, merging with the huge encampment, far larger than the town, thousands of tents in their geometric grids, the barbed wire perimeter giving the camp its nickname, *Stalag*, the network of roads and tracks congested with vehicles, predominantly lorries, but with many cars and myriad other types – personnel carriers, armoured cars, some odd looking things with specialised engineering devices mounted on them – all uniform army khaki, queuing, waiting their turn to be lifted aboard the ships ready to ferry them to their destination.

Stanley was conscious of the tightening in the pit of his stomach and a sudden spasm of emotion, fearing for a moment, that he was going to let the side down and allow tears to form in his eyes. He breathed deeply, regaining control.

"Here we go then, sir," a private, standing beside him, hands clasping the metal parapet, said, glancing up at the tall captain, reading the tension on his good natured features.

"Good to be on our way," he replied, forcing a smile. "After all that hanging about."

It seemed an age ago that they had made their early morning departure from the Kent village which had been their base for the past year, their convoy processing north, every road it seemed, filled with the great confluence of army vehicles, progress becoming even slower, the roads merging as they ground through the London suburbs crawling towards the Purfleet embarkation encampment.

The three days they had spent in the camp were particularly uncomfortable and frustrating, much of their time queuing - for food, latrines, and the meagre facilities for ablutions – and when they weren't queuing, chatting, the group of officers playing endless games of bridge and Monopoly, the one positive thing about his fellow captain, Mead, a man who, having co-existed with him for nearly three years, he utterly detested, being his Monopoly set which somehow he had managed to fit into his kit-bag.

All they wanted now, was to get going, to get the job done. For nearly five years his division, the 43rd – the Wessex Wyverns - had been training, driven by their autocratic tyrant of a CO, Major-General Ivo Thomas, a seasoned soldier, a gunnery officer in the Great War, decorated and twice wounded, highly respected by officers and men alike – a "very difficult man" as corps commander, Lieutenant General Brian Horrocks described him - the division's morale fluctuating, dropping to rock-bottom during the periods of intense boredom when they were kicking their heels at their camps and billets, with endless square-bashing, PT, lectures, and weapons training, alleviated by visits to the local pubs where they were able to guzzle beer, chat to the villagers, and ogle the village girls, the occasional trips into Canterbury or Ashford offering them the delights of cinema and a few shows.

The exercises, tough as they were, both physically and with their often grim conditions of cold, wet and fatigue, nevertheless, broke the monotony, taking them ranging around the countryside and sometimes further afield, once as far as Yorkshire. And with the exercises came the realisation that they were not only learning the business of warfare which, at some point, they knew they would have to put into practice, but acquiring a self-belief, that the Wyverns were a force to be reckoned with. They were acutely aware, however, that even the live ammunition exercises, daunting as they were at times, were far removed from the reality, of pitting themselves against the fearsome, battle-hardened opponents whom, all too soon, they would encounter.

After a couple of miles, the noise of the ship's engines suddenly diminished, the vessel losing way, the rattle of the anchor chains reverberating through the decks.

Several of the troops who, after they had cast off, had been herded down into their quarters below decks, reappeared, looking around, enquiring of the officers the reason for their stopping, the officers shrugging.

"What's going on?" another officer, a pink faced young captain shouted to one of the crew who was standing at the bow, peering over the side, watching the anchor chain become taut.

The man glanced at the soldiers, ignoring the question, instead looking up at the bridge with a thumb's up gesture before sauntering back along the deck, shouldering his way through the khaki clad men and disappearing through a door which clanged shut behind him.

"Thanks mate!" the pink faced officer said sarcastically, looking around for approval.

As darkness began to fall, the troops having returned to their quarters, Stanley and his fellow officers selected their places on the deck, the desultory conversation tailing away as some of them managed to sleep, others absorbed in their own wakeful thoughts.

Stanley pulled his blanket, one having been issued to each of them, over him in an attempt to keep warm, the metal deck beneath him cold and unforgiving, his thoughts, yet again, taking him to that last parting with his beloved Peggy, three weeks previously, when he had managed to get away for just long enough to make the trip down to Brighton, borrowing one of the division's motorcycles. This time he had not forewarned her, uncertain until the last minute that he would be able to make it, knowing that the "confined to barracks" order was imminent.

It had been a difficult few hours, the tension between them making them awkward and oddly formal. Anthony, their six month old infant, had been asleep when he arrived, and as Peggy's mother had been there, they had been able to go out for a walk, down to the park where they had sat on a bench, his arm around her, her head on his shoulder, words redundant as they both knew that this was their last time together.

And when it had been time to leave, he had given Anthony, then wide awake, warily eyeing this large alien figure, a gentle kiss on the forehead, handing the child to his wife, his throat tightening as he did so, pecking her on the cheek and turning quickly away, determined not to look back as he kicked the motorcycle into life, accelerating away.

It has been a mistake, he knew, to telephone her from the camp, but he could not help himself, that earlier parting filling him with an all consuming sadness which he felt that speaking to her again might somehow assuage. For more than an hour he had queued, waiting for one of the phones in the tent serving as a temporary telephone centre and post office for the tens of thousands of troops passing through the camp, and when he had got through to her, he instantly regretted his decision.

"I just wanted to say goodbye, my darling girl. I'm sorry. I know we said it the other day, but...." He could hear his voice becoming tremulous. "I won't be able to speak to you again for....for quite a long time."

"I know," she replied, her voice, for a moment sounding resolute. "I knew when you left."

She had been unable to contain the sob which suddenly tore at his heart.

"I love you, my dearest darling. I'll be thinking of you every minute of the day and night. And I'll write to you as often as I can."

"I love you too," she said, regaining her self control. "We both love you."

He could picture those innocent little eyes looking up at him, uncomprehending, as he had kissed his beloved son. "See you soon, old chap," he had whispered as he had handed the infant back to Peggy.

"I must go," he said, conscious of the grumbling in the line of men behind him.

"Look after yourself," Peggy said. "I want you back safely."

As he had wandered back through the lines of tents he had felt nothing but numbness, retreating into the tent he was sharing with several fellow officers, shaking his head to tell them that he was in no state to talk to them.

Unable to sleep, he walked across to the side of the deck, stepping over several somnolent bodies, looking across the wide estuary, the dark silhouette of the Kent coast a couple of miles away, and closer, the structure of one of the anti-aircraft platforms which had been built to try to protect London from enemy planes using the Thames estuary as a safer line of approach than the land routes, with their numerous ack-ack batteries.

As he watched, the battery suddenly came to life, the percussion of the guns tearing through the calm of the night, lines of tracer lacerating the dark, the officers on the deck leaping to their feet.
"Must be another of these buzz-bombs," a voice near him suggested as the

16

unfamiliar engine sound approached from over the land. "Look, there!"

He could just make out the dark shape, moving at speed.

"Go get it, matey!" someone else shouted as a Spitfire appeared from the opposite direction, looping round behind the shape. The burst of gunfire found its target, the shape erupting in a ball of flame, plummeting downward, hitting the water a mile or so from ship to uproarious cheering from the men now crowding the deck, many of the troops having emerged from below.

As the sky was beginning to lighten with the approach of dawn, he was awoken from his fitful sleep by the restarting of the engines, followed by shouted exchanges between members of the crew, their American accents straight out of the Hollywood films which had become a major part of their entertainment over the last few years, chain clattering as the anchor was lifted, the ship slowly gaining way, moving further out into the stream.

Several of the officers were standing at the side of the deck, all of them quite still, dark, mute, cut-out shapes, the only movement the lifting of arms as cigarettes were briefly brought to life, tips glowing like fire-flies, opaque exhalations of smoke brushed away by the movement of the ship, those men on the left side – "port" as the sailors referred to it, watching the land to the north receding as they emerged from the estuary, now many miles wide, the ship following the Kent coast.

When the sun rose, the scene it presented was one of a perfect summer's day, the water quite calm although they encountered a slight swell as they reached the open sea, the low angled rays igniting the tops of the rounded waves. Ahead and astern of them, the other ships in the convoy, stretched as far as one could see in both directions, grey hulls illuminated by the low angled sun, some of the vessels ahead, silhouetted, functional shapes – high sided, central funnels and superstructure, masts and derricks – the guns mounted on bow and stern the only indication of the military intent. During the night, several naval ships, as far as he could make out, four destroyers and two frigates, had joined them, shepherding their convoy as they approached more dangerous waters.

"Like being on a cruise," a voice beside him said, Stanley leaning on the parapet, studying the coast, the end of the North coast of Kent drawing near.

He glanced at the man beside him, Atkins, a fellow captain, "Tommy", inevitably, although his first name actually was Thomas. Stanley had got to know and like

Atkins over the year of so since they had been together, part of the same RASC officers' mess. He was a gentle, softly spoken chap with a dry sense of humour, easy to get along with both when they were working closely together in the sometimes frantic organisation of exercises, and when they were out together, in town or the local pubs, generally with a few others. He had remarked to Peggy that he felt lucky that, despite his endless grumbling, about boredom, and army life generally, and invariably about the dreadful Mead, and, of course, "the old man", their sour-natured CO, his was a good mess, rubbing along together well, having plenty of laughs, most of them sharing his passion for bridge, the endless sessions punctuated by games of Monopoly, money changing hands on both.

"Margate," Stanley said, pointing towards the line of grand seafront buildings and the prominent church tower on the hill behind. "Peggy and I had a day out there a few months back."

Atkins sucked on his pipe, the fragrant smell of his tobacco prompting Stanley to reach into his pocket, taking out his own pipe, extracting a pinch of tobacco from his pouch, tapping it into place with his finger before striking his Swan Vesta match, shielding the flame from the wind, sucking rhythmically until he was able to draw the warm smoke into his mouth, the first few draws always the best.

"Strange to think how we hated Kent, all that time we spent there," Atkins said, "when it looks so lovely now."

Stanley snorted a laugh of agreement. "Who'd have thought we would actually want to go back there? God, I wish we could be there now."

At 8 o'clock the order was given for all the officers and men who wished to take communion, to assemble on deck, the majority doing so, trust in the Almighty having never been so prevalent as it was now, virtually every man mouthing a personal prayer for his own survival.

How peculiar the setting, Stanley thought, the padre, his dog-collar so incongruous with his battledress, the pips on his shoulders signifying his officer status, having climbed up onto the forward gun platform from where he could look down on the several hundred men crammed into the confined deck space, heads uniformly bowing as he intoned the prayers, raising his voice over the noise of the engines.

And when it came to the partaking of the communion, the padre descended to the deck and with two officers assisting, administering the wafers and wine, forgoing the requirement to kneel, each communicant standing, bowing his head.

As they rounded North Foreland, now heading south, the wind increased, the swell rising, the ship beginning to pitch, causing the men to stagger as they moved around.

Towards the stern, troops were taking advantage of their allotted time for a spell on their area of deck, smoking and chatting, the frequent laughter forced, disguising the apprehension they all felt.

Stanley, finding himself a place to sit, leaning against the housing of one of the large vents, close to the winches, took out his small writing pad and the fountain pen which Peggy had bought for him, handing it to him as she had extracted his solemn promise to write to her, "not every day, I'm sure you'll be far too busy, but when you can."

He studied the nib, still unstained, saved for use on his "adventure", the thought occurring to him, whether his single bottle of ink would last until it was all over.

*18.6.44*
*166179 Capt S R Allen HQ RASC 43 Div APO England*
*My darling*
*Tommy says we might be 'the secret weapon' so I can't tell you where we are at the minute. I don't think it is a breach of security to say we are on a boat – as Tommy again says – the good ship Venus. Although somewhat uncomfortable we are at least fairly cheerful - in fact very cheerful and today everyone is getting sunburnt. It feels like a cruise! Unfortunately we cannot go bathing though it looks very tempting.*
*The wind is fairly stiff & I think we may get a rough sea later – I hope not because it is quite uncomfortable enough already.*
*I am very worried about you and these bloody 'buzz bombs' – I do hope so much that you are safe – they certainly are a complete menace. One day I'll be able to tell you of all our adventures in the past few days. At the moment I can only tell you, my beloved, that I am safe & well and happy & very much in love with my darling.*
*As there is no chance of posting this until we arrive in France, I'll continue it later.*
*Keep safe my darling and love to all at home.*
*Your ever loving husband*
*Stanley*

He read the letter, his writing even worse than usual, Peggy having often chided him for his scrawl, the interpretation of some of his least legible words a running joke between them, this time his valid excuse being the movement of the ship, becoming even more pronounced as they headed south towards South Foreland and the entrance of the Dover Straits.

He wondered when there would be an order requiring them to change their address on their letters, and if they would be allowed to say where they were, or even which country they were in. Much of the recent mess conversation had been about the speed of their prospective advance across Europe and how soon the war would be over, any doubts subsumed by the shared need for optimism.

After the chill of their first night at sea, the officers having to sleep on deck, making do with their single blankets and a limited supply of tarpaulins, much of the grumbling being about the hardness of the deck, they passed the day lounging around, the deck more crowded again now, the men filling their area in the back half of the ship. Many dozed in the warm sun, the parapet around the side of the deck offering shelter from the now stiff breeze, faces soon reddening with sunburn, several groups immersed in conversation, or games of bridge or poker, a couple of chess sets having also appeared.

"Christ Almighty!" Atkins muttered, returning from a visit to the latrines, a row of what were in effect, large buckets positioned between the hold cover and the base of the central mast, the duty men having the job of tipping full buckets over the side of the ship, a couple of hoses provided both for flushing them out and for ablutions. "Those are the worst bloody lats I've ever come across."

"I do like a good private crap," Stanley mused, "with a Woodbine and the paper."

"None of that here," Atkins said with a snort of laughter. "All shitting in a line."

By the end of the day, complaints about the state of the latrines and the ridiculously inadequate ablution facilities had become a good deal more vociferous, one of the officers, Wilson, a major who, although of average height, had something in his breadth of shoulder and bearing which suggested he was not to be messed with, was deputed to speak to the Captain, the handful of crew they encountered, meeting enquiries as to use of the ship's facilities with surly shrugs and American mutterings which, although largely indecipherable, were undeniably unfriendly.

When Wilson returned, his announcement that the officers were be allowed to use the crews' latrines and showers, prompted a cheer, tempered by his adding that there was nothing which could be done for the men, who would have to make to with the similarly basic facilities on their part of the deck.

"How did you manage to persuade him?" someone asked, Wilson's face creasing into a smirk.

"I didn't even have to threaten bodily injury," he said, the smile broadening. "Well not in so many words. It's not great down below," he added. "Only been 24 hours and it's pretty bad. Quite a few men have been sick as well."

When it was Stanley's turn, he squeezed into the small latrine compartment, closing the door, lighting his pipe, luxuriating in the privacy for just a few minutes before voices from outside the door and a banging fist told him his time was up.

That night, they decided to try sleeping on the hold cover, reckoning that its wood and canvas would make for a better mattress than the metal deck, he, Doc, their MO, and Mead sharing a tarpaulin, and while this worked to the extent that they did not suffer the numbing discomfort of lying on cold metal, the tarpaulin seemed to have a mind of its own, endlessly sliding off them, or at times covering them completely, Stanley waking several times feeling he was suffocating, pulling the heavy fabric off his head, breathing the cool night air.

Each time he woke, Mead was sound asleep, his snoring just one of the catalogue of the man's habits which Stanley found so intensely annoying. But it wasn't just his habits, it was the man himself; he just grated with him. "Chemistry," Peggy has suggested when he had been complaining to her about having to live and work in proximity to "such a repellent specimen".

The day dawned with a covering of cloud, the grey of the sea broken by white crests, the wind now strong, blowing from the north, the pitching motion of the ship increasingly unpleasant although, as yet, he had not seen any of the officers succumbing to seasickness. A couple of times he had climbed down the steep metal steps to the deck where the men were packed in, his first impression being one of shock, the scene being more that of a slave ship than a modern army being transported to participate in the greatest crusade the world had ever known. The smell was almost overpowering, although he was able to resist the temptation to put his hand over his face, the stench being a cocktail of latrines, vomit and sweat, tempered by the fug of tobacco, the density of the smoke adding to the picture of a visit to a sort of maritime Hades. He was met with a surprisingly cheerful greeting, the sarcasm – "nice and sunny up there is it, sir?"

– good natured, the fact that the men were able to take their turns on deck going some way to mitigate the conditions.

Towards the end of the afternoon, two members of the crew they hadn't seen before, wearing rather shapeless navy blue uniforms and tin helmets, threaded their way through the officers, virtually all now either seated in groups, absorbed in their interminable games, or prone, dozing or just staring at the sky. The two men climbed up to the gun platform, taking positions at the gun.

"Expecting trouble?" someone shouted up to them.

"Watch out Jerry battleships!" another added to ripple of approving laughter.

The crewmen ignored the ribaldry, putting the gun through a few practice movements, rotating it to the side and raising the barrel to its maximum elevation.

As the convoy was making its wide arc, turning to the west as it entered the Channel, keeping as close as possible to the English coast, the white cliffs just a few miles away, the heavy "whump" of gunfire from the French coast, now clearly visible, prompted many of the officers to get to their feet, several of them moving to the port side.

"Fucking hell!" Atkins, close beside Stanley, exclaimed quietly, all of them seeing the small group of projectiles, passing over them at such speed it was almost impossible to keep track of them. And a few seconds later, somewhere inland, well beyond the white cliffs, they could hear the soft thump as the German shells found their targets.

"Bastards!" Stanley said through his teeth. "Just wait till we get our hands on them."

With no more excitement, they settled down again, Stanley extracting his notepad, unscrewing the top of his pen, the nib poised as he tried to assemble his thoughts.

*19.6.44*
*My sweetheart darling*
*After lunch on a very windy afternoon and we are all quite well though rather cold & uncomfortable. We spend our time playing endless bridge, chess, telling stories and watching our surroundings. The weather isn't all it might be but at least it isn't raining. I wonder*

*how you are darling. All I can tell you is that we are somewhere at sea and that we are going to somewhere in France where I shall be able to post this.*

*Our ship is an American one & the conditions are very bad, especially the latrines and sleeping. The Master & Mate of the ship have been very unhelpful about the former and as far as we can make out we are not expected to do anything but sitting down from sailing to disembarkation. However it is a large ship & fairly steady at the moment.*

*I sleep on the floor above the hatch, under a tarpaulin. Doc is on one side of me and P.Mead on the other. The nights are just too bloody for words.*

*The food isn't too bad – 14 man Compo-Packs.*

*The padre is organising a concert tonight which should be quite fun although somewhat draughty.*

*I wonder what you are doing at the moment my sweetheart. Like me I expect you are wondering how many weeks will elapse before we meet again. Not too many I hope. I shall have such a lot to tell you, to fill in the gaps which cannot be put into telephone conversations & letters. Doesn't it seem ages since that phone conversation. You sounded so sad my poor sweet darling that I hated having to tell you rather brutally that we must say goodbye.*

*I am horribly dirty and long for a bath & change of clothing. You probably wouldn't recognise me as I have quite a fair sized whisker, dirty somewhat brown face, filthy battle dress, a lifebelt and a pipe.*

*Our convoy is a very impressive sight, just like the ones you see in the films, with a grand naval escort. It is a pity one can't get photos of this never to be forgotten cruise. I don't think I'll ever want to go on a ship again!*

"Getting a bit busy." Doc sat down beside him, leaning against the side of the hold. "Lot of traffic now."

Stanley stood up, climbing up onto the hold cover, scanning the sea ahead, several other convoys making their way in both directions, one passing them on its return to collect its next load of men and equipment, naval escorts winking their signals to each other. He could see that they were now moving away from English coast, heading further out into the Channel. The horizon was obscured by a dark fog, the product, he realised, of the huge numbers of ships as well, he presumed, of naval guns, the sound now reaching them, like an approaching summer thunderstorm, the rolling thunder more frequent than any storm he had experienced.

"Writing to Peggy?" Doc asked. "Tough, isn't it, particularly with the little'uns. Yours is just a baby, isn't he?"

"Anthony. Yes, six months. Broke my heart to leave him. Both of them. It's still giving me a lump in the throat. Yours are a bit older, aren't they?"

"Seven and five," Doc replied pensively. "Girls. I left all three of them sobbing their eyes out. I managed to keep it together until I was out of sight when, I don't mind admitting, I had to dab my eyes."

Stanley looked at him, the creases at the side of his pale blue eyes, giving one the impression of kindliness and humour, his face round and open but with a slightly care-worn appearance, his time in a London hospital at the peak of the Blitz having deeply affected him. Stanley noticed his hands, the fine fingers intertwined, as if undecided whether to clasp together in prayer, the hands beautifully formed, like a sketch Peggy had shown him in one of her art books. Durer was the name that came to him.

He felt oddly comforted that this man should ask him about his beloved Peggy; a man several years his senior, and one who had experience of the harsh realities of life in time of war far beyond Stanley's own, his couple of instances of being close to falling bombs, and once, a crashing German plane, frightening as they were at the time, a long way removed from the unimaginable awfulness of having to tend to scores of those brought into hospital with grievous injuries, many of them whom he was unable to save.

"It's hard, leaving them behind, isn't it," Doc said, as if sharing the pain of parting would somehow help to come to terms with it. "Particularly when they don't know if they'll see us again."

They remained sitting side by side on the hold cover, their view down the Channel ever more congested, the sound of heavy gunfire now seeming to come both from the sea, somewhere in the murk ahead of them, as well as the land, several dark smudges of what at first seemed low cloud beyond the coast, now taking shape as thick columns of smoke.

"Sorry, Stanley," Doc said, breaking their silence, "I interrupted your writing. You'd better get on with it. I'm sure she'll be interested to hear about our leisurely cruise!" The creases deepened momentarily, the smile which Stanley was going to become familiar with, once again lighting the MO's face.

It was not until the next afternoon that he resumed the letter, a lengthy series of games of bridge, as well as one of Monopoly at which, most gratifyingly, he won two and six, having intervened, justifying the delay on the basis that he would not be able to post the letter until they were in France.

*June 20th*
*Darling, I am able to tell you a bit more about our voyage which will end this evening. I will then get this rather disjointed letter posted.*
*Since Saturday we have been plodding steadily along, all being well except for one or too excitements last night. The sea is now rough but so far none of the officers has been sick despite the frightful conditions at night. At times it has been like a pleasure cruise. We played bridge on the deck most of the morning and are now sprawled out on a lovely afternoon in the sun on the boat deck. The ship is rolling & pitching a lot but the strong NE wind seems to have gone down a bit.*
*We don't' get on at all well with the crew; today thanks to a threat of bodily violence by Donald Wilson, we are able to use the shower, bathe (very luxurious) and the lats.*
*We had a last view of England about 2.30 this afternoon & now at 4.30 we're about mid channel.*

As the convoy continued its slow progress, the French coast now noticeably closer than England, the afternoon light, during the short intervals when the smoke cleared, tinting the famous white cliffs ochre, many of the troops, officers and men, were on their feet, lining both sides of the ship, awe-struck at the spectacle they were witnessing, the sheer scale of it almost beyond comprehension.

As hundreds of vessels plied back and forth to the coast, they passed through the line of naval ships, stretching as far to the west as one could see, raised guns unleashing repeated salvoes, their targets now many miles inland. With an almost deafening roar, the battleship, *HMS Rodney,* little more than a mile from them, its massive 18 inch guns at maximum elevation, fired a full salvo, the tongues of flame spurting from the barrels like a cluster of angry dragons, black smoke rolling out across the water.

Overhead, matching their maritime partners below, an armada of aircraft, bombers, fighters and transports, filled the sky, passing in both directions, outward, to drop their loads of high explosive on the enemy, the fighters keeping the depleted, yet still active Luftwaffe at bay, the returning flights, less regimented in their formations, but no less impressive in the huge numbers.

As they drew closer to the coast, they could also now make out the beaches, and the ominous shapes of wrecked vessels, some sticking out of the shallow water, broken hulls and superstructure, others further out, a few still afloat, one naval vessel, Stanley guessed a destroyer, on its side, its propeller partly visible.

It was mid morning when word reached them from the Captain, via a couple of senior officers who had been in close discussion with him on the bridge, that it was too rough for them to disembark, and that they had no choice but to anchor and to wait for the wind to drop.

Throughout the afternoon, they wallowed in increasingly steep waves rolling in from the north east, the motion of the ship, now at anchor, far more unpleasant than when they had been under way, the hours punctuated with the sound of retching, dejected men leaning over the rail, throwing up into the grey sea, white crests surging along the hull, carrying the contents of many stomachs towards the beach.

At one point, a startlingly loud siren alerted the men to the approaching danger of enemy aircraft, everyone lying down on the deck, pressing against each other as they sought the limited protection of the thin metal parapet.

Raising his head cautiously, Stanley could see a single plane, approaching from the east in a wide arc, guns from several ships, including their own screen of destroyers, opening up, the plane, appearing to be coming straight towards him, low over the sea. A moment after it had released a single bomb, the splash rising high in the air several hundred yards away, the plane, which he could now identify as a twin engine Messerschmitt, bucked in the air as it was hit, emitting a puff of smoke, one of its engines bursting into flames, the plane suddenly dipping one wing, dropping down, the wing tip hitting a wave, the plane cartwheeling, breaking in half, carving through the wave, and quickly disappearing.

The cheer which went up was half hearted, this, for many of those watching, their first encounter with the death of an enemy apart from the planes they had witnessed shot out of the sky in the endless aerial battles over Kent which, somehow, seemed more distant and remote than this shockingly vivid incident, the cockpit of the doomed aircraft clearly visible.

"How long do you reckon we're going to be here?" Mead asked, his question addressed to no one in particular, everyone – officers, and the men taking advantage of their allotted time to come up from below - now huddled on the deck, the afternoon having turned cold, adding to the unpleasantness of the ship's pitching.

"How the hell should we know," Wilson replied tetchily. "Until it's calm enough for us to get ashore. Be thankful for the respite, Mead. We'll all to soon be in the thick of it." He raised his arm, gesturing towards the coast, the almost incessant rumble of gunfire, a sort of undercurrent to the salvoes from the naval ships, a constant reminder of where they were heading.

After another chilly and disturbed night, the navy keeping up their unrelenting gunnery, they woke to a dawn of heavy cloud, the sky in every direction, leaden grey, the smoke seeming to be trapped between sea and cloud, the wind swirling it in patterns, daubed across the apocalyptic scene.

*June 21st 11.15am*
*We dropped anchor off the French coast at about 8.30 last night. The scene is really remarkable. As far as the eye can see in all directions there are ships of all sizes and descriptions – battleships, cruisers, destroyers, corvettes, transports, hospital ships and the rest. Unfortunately the weather is still terrible. A gale blew all night & we just pitched and rolled at our anchorage. This morning is like mid winter. There is a very big sea running, the skies are leaden and the scene is very grim, yet awe-inspiring & magnificent. Off loading is impossible but we have had a service & prayed for calm weather. Despite the conditions we are still OK, though many are sick and some of the troops are very ill. One feels that one will be able to put up with any conditions after this trip. The food is alright but exactly the same every day – breakfast - tea, biscuits, 'Prem', jam; lunch - bully, self heating soup, plum pudding tinned; tea – tinned salmon; supper - bully, tinned veg. The worst part is that our cars, where all our clothes & forks and things are, are in the hold and we can't get at them. But I have got my jerkin which really has saved my life.*
*The finest example of Anglo American cooperation was the remark of the mate who said that as far as they were concerned we were just like a herd of animals and they have certainly treated us accordingly though now we have got the concession of showers and latrines.*
*We are longing to get ashore – never did dry land seem so dear, but the chief thought on the minds of all is the fact that there should be several days mail for us and we shall know if any of our loved ones have suffered in recent raids. It seems a pity that we can't direct some of the buzz-bombs to USA!*

"That's where we're going, as soon as we get off this bloody hulk," Atkins said, his voice, as so often, quiet, his ability to bellow at the men when called upon to do so, so unexpected from one so softly spoken. The two of them were leaning on the rail, the evidence of the raging battle – the gunfire and palls of smoke – just a few miles inland, out of sight, leaving the visualising of it to their imaginations.

Stanley, once again, felt fear clutching at the pit of his stomach, but managed a wry response. "They're obviously waiting for us to get into it so that we get Jerry on the run."

They both looked up as a squadron of Hurricanes, flying in perfect echelon, came low over their heads, watching them as they headed inland, peeling away from their formation just before they were lost to view in the smog of battle.

As the day passed, the wind increased, reaching gale force, the motion of the ship, straining at its anchor, making it impossible to walk even a short distance without clutching the rail or some other suitable hand-hold, men cursing as they stumbled into one another.

The officers had agreed a duty rota to go below to see the men, to try to prevent their morale from plummeting to even greater depths, the mood when he took his turn first thing that morning, having become both angry and despairing. At least they had managed, against the crews' orders, to open a couple of portholes, allowing fresh air to lessen the stench, albeit at the cost of water, every now and again, gushing in, the crests of some of the waves now up to the height of the hull.

On deck, the officers sat huddled in their blankets, most of them grouped under tarpaulins, their faces now sunburned, with three days of stubble, shaving being impossible, the games their only means of passing the time, several having to be curtailed as players had to break away, hurrying unsteadily to the side to throw up, the sick men lying, supine, the universal desire being to get ashore, the prospect of going into battle a far lesser evil than having to remain on the hellish vessel.

Thankful that he still felt well, the involuntary exposure to fresh air certainly helping him avoid sickness which he had experienced on a previous occasion when he and his father had gone on a fishing holiday, travelling by ship to Scotland, the passage from London Docks to Aberdeen having involved a day of stormy conditions in the North Sea, when, having emptied his stomach repeatedly until there was nothing left to expel, he had lain on his bunk in a state of utter misery, until they had come into harbour, the marvel being that within an hour of doing so, he was ravenously hungry, tucking into a hearty meal.

Sitting now on the deck, watching the bow rising, and then, as it dipped, opening up the view of the coast and the grimness beyond, he found himself immersed in his thoughts, picturing Brighton seafront, one of his favourite places, when, as so often before the war, he and several friends, Peggy often included, would go swimming, lying in the sun to dry off, before walking slowly back through the town, crossing Hove Park, making his way back to vicarage on Dyke Road, leaving Peggy at her family home, just a couple of hundred yards away, in Hove Park Road. On a few occasions she had asked him in for tea, which, whilst allowing him to spend a bit more time with her, also meant having to be in the company of her mother, a rather stern woman who, he felt, was always looking at him with a critical eye, his sense being that she considered him not quite suitable. There had been a few times also, when Peggy's father had been there, putting Stanley even more on his guard. He was very familiar with the man, Mr Arthur Wing, who was closely involved with the church, frequently attending meetings with his own father, who, as vicar, presided over certain church committees. To Stanley, however, Mr Wing was an intimidating man, his expression always dour, his thankfully infrequent and brief conversations with the vicar's eldest son, suggesting disdain.

When had he realised that Peggy was to be the love of his life? They had known each other from childhood, but it was during his late teenage years that he had come to see her as someone special, thus starting the long and, at times, painful process, of winning her, which was only truly accomplished when, on a cold, snowy January day, three years ago, he had walked out of the church with her as his wife.

How longingly now, he looked back, particularly to that golden year, 1939, when, despite his ever present, gnawing insecurity, her being away nursing at Bart's, inducing bouts of deep anxiety, he knew, deep down, that she had finally accepted him, their love blossoming as the storm clouds of approaching war darkened the horizon. Indeed, through the prism of the growing certainty of imminent cataclysm, their courtship induced an almost euphoric intensity, heightened by the brevity of their times together.

That summer of such contrasting emotions, when he had to buckle down to study for his law finals, his application, always a struggle, tested by his constant thoughts about her as well as the expectation that probably within weeks, he would be called up, now filled his memory, like a vista of some imaginary magical land. God how he loved her; how he longed for her.

For a while the sense of dejection weighed upon him. If only they could get ashore and get on with the necessary business. Just sitting here, waiting, listening to the sounds of the battle they were soon to join, was becoming intolerable.

"You OK, Stanley?" Doc sat down beside him. Stanley was grateful to him for the moment of intimacy, Doc rarely using first names, having told him during one of their conversations over the past three days, that he had learned to use formality as a sort of safety screen, to try to limit his tendency to become too involved with people, a lesson hard learned during the Blitz.

"Lost in my thoughts," he replied. "Same for all of us though."

The next day, although the wind had abated slightly, the sea was still too rough for them to disembark, meaning another long, miserable day, mitigated minimally by the lifting of the previous day's blanket of cloud, the sun now breaking through at intervals.

For some time he sat with the unfinished letter in front of him, reading what he had already written, gathering his thoughts. Dejected though he felt, he suddenly found himself picturing her, his beloved Peggy, the last time he had been home on twenty four hours leave – a couple of weeks before that awful, final fleeting visit. They had spent the night in "the hut" as they fondly referred to it, the wooden chalet constructed in the vicarage garden which had served as the temporary, and rather restricted church hall when the church had been built in the early twenties, fitted out, when they were married, with basic amenities to make it habitable. Although Peggy continue to live with her parents when Stanley was away, when he was home, the hut became their own home, Anthony being with them, Stanley experiencing the delight, and the pride, of being with his family.

Their all to short stays in the hut were also the time of their love making, on several occasions, mainly on his brief visits, the two of them spending just a few hours there, Peggy's mother looking after Anthony, Stanley feeling acutely embarrassed at her awareness of the reason they had asked her to do so.

Once in the hut they would pull down the blinds, putting a record on the record player, dancing, kissing, and making passionate love, Stanley now picturing Peggy naked, the sun filtering through the blinds, laughing as she disported herself provocatively in front of him. It amazed him that, not so long ago, he had thought her to be slightly prudish, assuming that she had acquired a measure of her parents' starchy Victorian propriety. How wrong he had been, her passionate nature, when unleashed, whole-hearted, her appetite seeming to match his own.

*June 22nd*
*My darling, I wonder how you are and how life in Brighton is. I do hope and pray you haven't had too many buzz-bombs. We are still lying off the French coast as it is still too rough to disembark. Yesterday was the roughest day of all & a gale blew all day. Today is actually a lovely day but there is still a stiff breeze and too high a sea for us to get off this stinking boat. Still there is always plenty to watch and if it wasn't for the lousy food and*

*appalling conditions we shouldn't mind. It would do some of the folks who grouse &*
*grumble at all the little discomforts at home good to spend just a couple of hours at night*
*on this tub!*
*Discomfort makes one dream of home. And everyone is feeling very randy, darling! It is a*
*week since we saw a woman and God knows how long since we spoke to one. How*
*blissfully happy the thought of my lovely, slim, red lipped darling, & Anthony cooing in*
*his cot, & the hut & meals together & the gramophone.*

When he looked back on that long and uncomfortable week on the ill-equipped liberty ship with its hostile crew, those last two days were the worst, the boredom compounding their sinking morale, the stubbled, sun-burnt faces, their bodies reeking of sweat, the ship itself, stinking like a huge, floating sewer, relieved only by the miasma of tobacco smoke.

Finally, on 24th June, six days after they had sailed, the sea having become almost calm overnight, the order came to ready themselves for disembarkation, the men forming orderly queues as the crew fixed scrambling nets, waiting for the landing craft to take them ashore.

Patiently, they stood, watching the endless activity, the troops now with their packs hoisted onto their backs, most of them, even RASC men, carrying rifles. Stanley, seated on the side of the hold cover, decided there was time, before his turn to disembark, for a final instalment of the letter which he had been writing for so many days.

*Saturday June 24th*
*Darling we are just about to get off this ship & we are all very glad as the last days have*
*been extremely uncomfortable – and the food supplies are running very low. The weather*
*is grand now and we are all in good spirits. It will be grand to get ashore & have a change*
*of underclothing & be able to get at some of the things that have been in the hold for a*
*week. Also, we might get a peaceful nights sleep!*
*I heard on the news today of more buzz-bomb raids & felt extremely worried about you.*
*It is a dreadful feeling being entirely out of touch with you for nearly 10 days now.*
*I had a piece of bread last night with a slice of ham which we got from the crew. I have*
*never tasted anything so delicious or welcome.*
*The American crew are frightful & after unloading had been held up for 2 days because*
*of the weather, they worked for half an hour then knocked off.*
*I must stop now my beloved sweet darling wife & go ashore.*
*Ever your adoring husband*
*Stanley*

The landing craft pulled alongside the concrete jetty, Stanley and the others on board climbing ashore, grateful that, contrary to their expectation, their briefings having told them that they would be wading ashore, they arrived dry shod.

The scene on the wide beach was, at first glance, one of apparent chaos, with lines of men threading their way across the sand, heading to their destinations inland, others, including beach marshals, engineers and military police, directing, shouting, trying to make themselves heard above the noise of the engines of numerous vehicles being disgorged from landing craft; lorries bouncing ashore, armoured cars, jeeps, several staff cars. A few ships alongside the arms of the Mulberry harbour were unloading vehicles with their derricks, swinging them precariously onto the narrow jetties, the lines of disembarked traffic merging on the beach, following the "roads", some slatted wood, others some form of fabric unfurled from giant spools, drivers peering at the array of signs, most of them able simply to follow those ahead of them.

Stanley and several other officers gathered their men together at the back of the beach, waiting for others to be ferried ashore in the relay of landing craft. For over an hour they sat on the sand, most of the men happy to lie in the late afternoon sun, the day pleasantly warm after the chill of the last days at sea. Many of them laughed at the odd sensation, as if the beach was moving, it taking sometime for the motion of the sea to fade.

Busy with his role, overseeing several platoons, readying them for the imminent move to their first base, hoping that as soon as they arrived there they would be able to send their mail, he took out the pad, the cumulative letter now covering several pages. As he was about to add a final instalment, Atkins arrived, having been off to liaise with the officers assembling their convoy, to announce that they were now ready.

Hastily, Stanley scrawled a short postscript.

PS  *Landed in France OK 4.15 Sat 24th*

# TWO

As they headed north out of Brighton, taking the London road through Patcham, he was unable to remove the grin which he realised was stuck on his face, or to stop glancing, every few minutes, across to the passenger seat at Peggy, leaning back, staring out of the window, wrapped in the pleasure of the countryside, resplendent in its mantle of fresh May green, commenting on sights which caught her eye; a field of sheep, lambs now half grown, but still gambolling with spasms of joyful energy; a field full of haymakers, cutting by hand, swinging their long scythes.

Stanley had been driving now for two years, since his seventeenth birthday, his father surprisingly generous in allowing him the use of the Wolseley, his, the Reverend William Allen's use of it, limited to trips to those of his parishioners at the outer reaches of his parish, stretching as it did across a swathe of Hove and part of Preston, the quarter of Brighton, once the first area of downland one came to when heading inland from the sea, sloping up from the London Road to Dyke Road, which, once one was past the affluent section, bordered by some of the area's largest houses, took one up to the Devil's Dyke with its magnificent views across the Weald.

It was on the Dyke that, a few months earlier, Peggy has stood with her father and her brother Tom, witnessing the destruction of the famous Crystal Palace, the glow of the fire which reduced it to a ruin of tangled metal and shattered glass, clearly visible in the late November afternoon from forty miles away, as a dull red glow, tinting the base of the low clouds.

When, over lunch the previous Sunday, choosing his moment, knowing that his father, "Pop", tended to be at his most affable when he had finished his morning's duties and was enjoying a glass of claret with the Sunday roast, he had asked him if he might use the Wolseley the following Wednesday, his apprehensiveness was not as to Pop's assent, which he knew was a formality, his father being due to conduct a special service that day to mark the new King's coronation; it was how he was going to answer the question which would inevitably follow, probably from his mother.

He had rehearsed his response, a casual statement that he was going to London to see the coronation and that Peggy would be going with him. But each time he repeated the statement, in his mind and a few times aloud in the confines of his bedroom, any semblance of casualness failed abysmally in the face of the excitement which seemed to have a hold on his entire body and mind.

Having known Peggy for many years, as part of the lively social circle which revolved around the church, crossing over with tennis and rugby clubs, and, increasingly, outings to dance halls, theatres and cinemas, his feelings towards her had, over the previous year or so, transmuted into the seeds of something he now recognised had been sown long before; something which he was realising was what he had yet to label as "love", testing instead, the terms which prefaced the full declaration; "fondness"; "deep affection".

The previous summer, when she had accepted his invitation to accompany him to his school, Brighton College, Commemoration Day, was the day when, looking back, he realised that he had found the love of his life. The afternoon they had spent walking around the school playing field, watching the various activities put on for visiting families and friends, and taking tea outside the catering marquee. And in the evening at the "Commem Ball", they had danced all evening, his dancing skills a good deal less polished than hers, his clumsiness a source of laughter, she promising to teach him.

It was also the day of their first kiss.

As everyone on the crowded dance floor dutifully stood quite still when the band rounded off the ball with the National Anthem, he felt the gentle touch of her hand, her little finger linking with his.

They had caught the train from Kemp Town Station, close to the school, changing at Brighton for the one further stop to Preston Park, walking hand in hand up the steep hill to Dyke Road, stopping at the top where, in a pool of darkness, they embraced, the kiss, the first of real intent for both of them, filling Stanley with a sense of liquidity, as if he was dissolving in ecstasy.

"I must go," she had whispered, suddenly breaking from his encircling arms, smiling back at him as she crossed the road, leaving him staring after her for several minutes before she had disappeared into Hove Park Road. Eventually he walked slowly in the opposite direction, the short distance to the vicarage, his parents, thankfully in bed, the housekeeper, Mrs Christian, an amiable old soul who doted on him, but whose affection was sometimes manifest by way of scolding, even now, when he was on the brink of manhood, waiting up, fussing, insisting on making him a cup of Ovaltine before he retired to bed.

He lay on his bed, the image of Peggy in her simple, pale blue summer dress, floating before him, a mirage of indescribable beauty, her eyes, grey blue, her skin, already lightly tanned from her regular sessions on the tennis court, her hair thick and slightly wavy, cut in a sort of bob but, when away from the immediate attention of her hairbrush, tending to become rather shapeless, her face strong boned but with something oddly vulnerable behind her ready smile. Her sense of fun was only one of her many attributes which contributed to the wonderful whole, the person who had come to fill his thoughts.

It was his last term at the College, his articles, to Thomas Eggar, solicitors with offices in Brighton and London, due to start in just a few short weeks. The fact that he was about to embark on his career, as yet, had scarcely dawned on him, the approaching holidays offering the prospect of a summer of delights, Peggy featuring in every planned activity, his father having agreed that, in addition to the family holiday along the Sussex coast at West Wittering (from which, as it meant two valuable weeks apart from her, he had vainly sought leave of absence), he should be allowed two weeks "to prepare yourself" before donning the suit which his mother had bought for him, and acquiring the status of Articled Clerk.

"If you're taking Peggy with you to the coronation," his mother said across the Sunday lunch table, his cheeks warming as he endeavoured to go on eating, avoiding her quizzical look, "you had better make sure you get her home on time."

"Of course I will, Mother," he replied, relieved that he had not been required to make the announcement he had been practising, that he would only be taking Peggy with him, having managed, with a certain degree of guile, to arrange for the couple of other friends who had been going to accompany them, to travel separately. "Has her mother mentioned it?"

"They both did, as we were coming out of church," his mother replied. "They were still in two minds about allowing her to go, but I assured them you were a very safe driver and a responsible young man." She smiled her warm smile, his father's face remaining impassive.

"You don't want to get on the wrong side of Mr and Mrs Wing," his father warned. "Not if you are thinking of walking out with Peggy on a regular basis."

Again, Stanley felt his face reddening.

And now they were on their way, the dreary weather of the last few days having given way to intermittent sunshine, although the forecast was for rain later in the day.

The approaches through south London had been busy, traffic converging on the city for the great occasion, although having decided to walk the last couple of miles, they easily found a place to park not far from Waterloo Station from where they crossed Westminster Bridge, joining the flow of humanity towards the route of the procession.

They were in good time, having resolved that, even if it meant having to wait several hours, it would be worth it to guarantee a vantage point close to Piccadilly Circus where they settled down, sitting on the pavement until it became too crowded to do so. Time passed quickly, the excitement of the crowd creating a festive atmosphere.

An hour or so after they arrived, they could hear cheering some way off, telling them that the procession was en route from Buckingham Palace to Westminster Abbey, the service itself expected to last two hours before the return procession which was due to meander through central London, ensuring that as many people as possible could catch a glimpse of the newly crowned monarch.

Quite apart from the palpable anticipation of the crowd around them, and the realisation that they were part of such a magnificent occasion, Stanley had to pinch himself to realise that he was really here with Peggy, just the two of them, his scheming having included omitting to arrange a rendezvous with their friends.

Since the Commemoration Ball, he had seen her regularly, their relationship now having reached the point of it being known that they were "stepping out", holding hands when they were walking together, albeit not when their parents or any of their various relatives were present, with the exception of Stanley's younger brother Michael, 8 years his junior, whom they would occasionally take with them on daytime outings, and Tom, although they both tended to find that Peggy's elder brother was a bit too much a cut off her father's block, with his tendency to censoriousness. On a few occasions they had been for walks alone together in the country, taking a picnic, which, when polished off, was the opportunity for them to lie together, embraced, kissing and exchanging endearments.

Yet, as the months has passed, rather than becoming more secure in their still young relationship, he felt increasingly uneasy. It was as if she was holding back, reticent about committing herself. They skirted around that word, "love". He was desperate for her to utter it, as if this would be the true declaration that she was his. He would plead his affection, trying to elicit a response. It felt as if he had to devise strategies, scenarios about their future, to finesse her acknowledgment that it was to be shared – that she was to be with him, always.

To compound his growing insecurity, he was worried that other suitors continued to sniff around, one in particular, Charles, a good friend of his, and one of their regular circle, being very obviously keen on her. What was most galling was the way Charles seemed to make her laugh, her cheeks flushed and her eyes shining when she enjoyed his jovial manner and his endless supply of jokes and anecdotes.

One day, just a few weeks earlier, when he had decided to call for her, as he did from time to time in the early evening after his day at his office, for the two of them to go for a walk usually down to the park, he stopped in his tracks at the top of her road when he saw Charles's car (his father's car which, like Stanley, he had licence to make regular use of) parked outside her house. As he stood, undecided as to whether to turn around, her front door opened, the two of them emerging, laughing, clearly sharing some joke, Peggy following Charles out onto the pavement as he opened the car door. For a dreadful moment, he thought they were going to kiss, their closeness, and their obvious comfort in each other's company, indicating intimacy, his heart thumping in his chest as he stepped back, peering round the corner, unable to tear himself away.

His relief, when Charles climbed into the car, no kiss having taken place, was tempered by burning jealousy. He was tempted to stride the short distance to her house, to remonstrate angrily with her, yet something stopped him. What would she think if she knew he had been watching, spying on them. Instead, he stepped nonchalantly out into the road, crossing over towards her, feigning normality.

She greeted him with her usual warmth, smiling brightly, with not a hint of the guilt he was looking for.

"You just missed Charles," she said, disarming him with such admission. "He came to deliver an invitation to the Tennis Club dance on Whitsun Saturday. He said he was just off to drop yours into the vicarage."

The surge of relief made him want to laugh out loud although he could not rid himself of the picture of the two of them, standing so close together, something in Charles's manner, and in his flirtatious, self satisfied grin, making it obvious that the delivery of the invitation had been a pretext for him to call to see her. Good friend though he was, Stanley was becoming increasingly wary of the jovial, chubby faced chap, but he decided to say nothing more.

The approach of the coronation procession was announced by the roar of the crowd lining the route, the pavements packed, the weight of humanity retained by the line of soldiers and police, every window above filled with faces, the cheering seeming to roll along the grand streets of central London, rising to a crescendo as the royal coach, gleaming gold, pulled by eight horses, flanked by footmen hurrying to keep up with the pace of the horses, swept into view, hands, newspapers, a few flags, waving wildly, many of those at the back of the crowd watching through periscopes, vendors of the devices having enjoyed an excellent day's trade.

As the coach drew level with them, for just a split second, Stanley saw the face of the king, hand raised in a sort of fixed wave, his face unsmiling, the impression to Stanley, in that instant, of sadness, instead of the joy one would have expected on day of his coronation.

And yet, one could understand that this was the man who, rather than having been born to be king, had had the crown forced upon him by the abdication, just a year before, of his elder brother, the brief reign of Edward VIII having ended abruptly when, to the opprobrium of so much of the nation, he chose his American divorcee, Wallis Simpson, ahead of his country and his Empire.

One had the impression, from the little one knew about this new king, that he had taken on the mantle, ascending the throne, with reluctance, his retiring nature being quite out of kilter with the role now thrust upon him. It was also known that the unfortunate man suffered a dreadful stutter, a grievous curse for someone whose daily business was that of public speaking.

As the king and queen passed them, Peggy took hold of Stanley's arm, her eyes shining with child-like excitement at the sight of the fairy-tale golden coach, reciting names as she identified the occupants of several of the concourse of following carriages, Stanley's own surge of pleasure as much the wonder of being here with her, clutching at his arm, as the occasion itself.

"The little princesses! How sweet they are!" she exclaimed, turning briefly to him, her face alight with the smile which made him want to lean towards her and kiss her beautiful lips.

For the best part of an hour the procession continued, great phalanxes of marching soldiers, others on horseback, representatives from every corner of the Empire, Stanley feeling an immeasurable sense of pride, that here they were, in the heart of the greatest city in the world, witnessing the coronation of the monarch who still ruled over a third of the world's nations.

As soon as the final formation of soldiery had passed, the crowd spilled into the road, relieved to be able to move around after the hours of standing.

"Come on," Peggy said, taking his hand and leading him through the milling throng, "let's go to the Palace."

Much of the crowd was moving in the same direction, allowing them to be carried along, Peggy's impatience every now and again prompting her to weave her way forward, Stanley hanging onto her hand as if his life depended on it.

When they reach the Mall, the crowd became increasingly dense, but still Peggy managed to find a way through, meandering from one side of the road to the other, gauging where there was a narrow gap. Finally, when they were some two hundred yards from the railings in front of the Palace, she turned to him, beaming with satisfaction that they had managed to find such a good place, hemmed in though they quickly became, which entirely suited him, Peggy being compelled to press tightly against him. She leaned her head back against his shoulder as they looked expectantly up at the balcony, the doors open, shadowy figures moving about inside.

When the king and queen emerged, resplendent in their ermine gowns, crowns perched on their heads, the eruption of cheering was almost deafening, Peggy herself, emitting a shrill sound, more scream than cheer, Stanley's acclaim a more restrained "hurrah!".

With the two young princesses beside them and a handful of senior royals in the background, they remained for some minutes, waving to the vast crowd. As the noise was beginning to subside, Queen Mary, appeared, taking centre stage, the cheer rising to a fresh crescendo, the revered matriarch of the Royal Family, widow of the late George V, and the woman who had been the anchor of the monarchy through the hiatus of her elder son's infamous abdication, representing, more than any other, the solidity and continuity of the institution which was the cornerstone of the country's greatness.

With her familiar, stiff handed wave, as if stirring the air around her head, she acknowledged the acclamation, the king and queen, and all members of the family, seeming somehow to lessen around her.

After the family retreated back into the Palace, the crowd seemed reluctant to disperse, hoping, perhaps, for an encore, but the doorway to the balcony remained empty.

Slowly, Stanley and Peggy made their way back along the Mall, pausing under Admiralty Arch as if sensing the echoes of the thousands of marching feet, the horses and the wheels of the carriages which, just a short time ago, had passed through it, before crossing Trafalgar Square, still crowded with revellers, many determined to prolong the day's celebration, pubs everywhere filled to capacity.

They were surprised to be able to find a table in the Lyons Cornerhouse in the Strand, tucking hungrily into a high tea of egg on toast, followed by a celebratory slice of cake, lingering over their cups of tea before wandering across Waterloo Bridge, keeping pace with the traffic crawling slowly over the river.

When they set off for the return drive to Brighton, for the first few miles the traffic continued at a crawl, it being after eight o'clock when they reached the suburbs, even then, the traffic remaining heavy. To Stanley's alarm the garage he had been aiming to stop at, was closed, the next one, he knew, being some way. He drove slowly, the needle on the petrol gauge precariously close to empty, praying that there was enough in the tank to cover the remaining miles. Thankfully, the garage was open, but the combined result of the traffic and the shortage of fuel meant that by the time they reached Brighton it was approaching eleven, his promise to Peggy's parents having been to be home by ten, a promise he had repeated to his own mother and father.

The next morning Peggy made her way downstairs to breakfast with a good deal of trepidation, her father having waited up for her the night before, her parents generally retiring to bed by ten, greeting her with a curt "What time do you call this, young lady?", informing her, without allowing any response, that "I will speak to you in the morning."

She took her place at the breakfast table, the family routine, as set by her father, requiring both Tom and Peggy to be dressed and at the breakfast table by eight, the housekeeper, Florrie, well practised in presenting each member of the family with their egg and bacon, placing the plates on the table in the order of priority, their mother first, father second, and Tom, as the elder sibling, taking precedence to Peggy as both the youngest, and a girl, thus, on both counts, being the lowest member of the hierarchy.

For several moments her father remained hidden behind his *Telegraph*, before folding it, laying it in its customary position beside his place, lowering his head, each of the others following suit as he said grace, the brief breakfast version, the lunch and dinner grace somewhat more extensive.

"For what we are about to receive, may the Lord make us truly thankful."

"Amen," they muttered in quiet unison.

They ate their breakfast in silence, Tom, without awaiting his father's instruction, then standing up. "If you'll excuse me father," he said. "I must get ready." Having joined his father's surveying and estate agency practice the year before, he took immense pride in his professional persona, his tweed suit matching that of his father as the two of them went on their regular trips around the Sussex countryside, valuing farms, estates and rural properties.

"Perhaps you would care to explain yourself," her father said, Peggy sitting, hands on her lap, readying herself for what she hoped would be no more than the dressing down with which she was familiar, particularly over the months since she had left school the previous summer, several of the beratings she had received being for breaching the curfew which her father had laid down. She had realised by now, from previous instances, that pleading that the breach was merely by a margin of twenty or thirty minutes, or that the film had been longer than expected, and on one occasion that she was now eighteen years old, was not only fruitless by way of mitigation, but would inflame the situation.

"We hold Stanley principally responsible," her mother said, Peggy wondering for a second if the censure was thus diminished by the casting of blame upon Stanley, the possibility quickly dashed by her father's retort.

"Which in no way exonerates you, my girl." He looked at her, his brown eyes seeming to examine her to see if he could discern any remorse, his cheeks, with their small tufts of hair retained as a sort of token of respect for the great Victorian era, the passing of which he so bemoaned, flushing, his jaw slowly working, the sign she recognised of the anger which, although rarely vented, seemed to smoulder inside him. "Your mother and I will consider what sanction we should impose upon you. Whilst you remain under our roof, as a member of this family, you would do well to remember that you will abide by our rules."

Realising that she was duly dismissed, she left the room, her father seeming relieved to be able to disappear once again behind his newspaper.

As she crossed the hall, making for the stairs, she passed Florrie who gave her a

41

smile of sympathy. "Don't worry, my love," she said in a confidential whisper, "it'll soon be mended.

For an hour she lay on her bed, trying to read, her concentration thwarted by her exasperation. Not for the first time she pondered her possible escape, the routes available to her in terms of occupation which would have any prospect of gaining parental approval, precious few. And of those which would allow her to depart the family home, she had only come up with one possibility, the thought of nursing increasingly taking shape in her head.

Her grievance at the morning's dressing down was, however, insufficient to do more than moderately tarnish the pleasure of the trip to London. The sights and sounds of the day continued to revolve vividly through her memory as she ran through each part of it. The thrill of the moment when the golden coach had come into view; the glimpse, past the king, of the queen, her face turned away, but the sense that unlike her husband, there was a smile on her face; a smile that later, even from so far away in the crowd in front of the palace, seemed to light up the day, contrasting with the regally austere expression of Queen Mary, which one could fully understand, the poor lady having had to go through so much, with the loss of her husband, and then the dreadful business of the abdication. Yes, one could forgive her the seriousness with which she viewed the proceedings.

And how she had enjoyed being with Stanley. Dear Stanley, he had become so much more than a friend although she found it difficult to work out how she really felt about him. She felt so comfortable in his company, his easy manner, although she had noticed, in recent months, his tendency to become slightly irritable if she went out somewhere without him, apart from shopping or doing errands for her mother.

She loved the way he would become excited about music – the music he appreciated, dance bands and the popular music of the day, ever adding to his collection of records, sitting her down to listen to his latest acquisition, nodding to the rhythm, sometimes insisting they dance around the vicarage drawing room, his large frame moving in a slightly ungainly way, his clumsy feet frequently treading on her toes. Over six foot tall, with long, gangling legs and arms, an open face with a ready grin, the brown eyes alert, his hair, these days centre parted, the waves repressed by copious quantities of Brylcreem, he was undoubtedly a handsome young man with a lively interest in the world around him and a thirst for knowledge translating into a habit of spouting facts at her, bubbling with boyish enthusiasm.

He loved his gadgets; gramophone, camera, barometer – which he would regularly tap, pronouncing his prediction of the weather in store for them. Indeed, he had a fascination for matters meteorological, remarking on cloud patterns and what they signified, changes in the wind direction presaging "a front coming in" or, with an easterly, "a settled spell".

She had, undeniably, loved being with him on such a memorable day. He made her feel so safe. Even when he became anxious and cross with himself as they drove at a snail's pace, fretting about being nearly out of petrol, she had not felt in the least bit worried that they might not get home, apart from the consequences of breaching curfew.

She enjoyed kissing him, and, when they went on their walks, lying on the picnic rug, there was something oddly exciting about the sensation of his body against hers, and the hardness in his trousers when he would press himself urgently against her, his heart thumping in his chest, his muttered endearments so delightfully tender.

Always, however, he was trying to get her to say what, in a way, she wanted to say, but did not feel ready for. She had to make something of herself, if only for a few years before committing to a life of domesticity and motherhood. Part of it, she knew, was her determination to defy her parents, her place in life, as she was so often reminded by both her father and mother, being to prepare herself, to ensure that when the time came, she would be a good, capable wife.

But it was more than that. She was, as yet, unsure of her feelings. She was only eighteen, it being the norm, for girls of her age, and of her class, to move from schooling to marriage with scarcely a gap in between. But she had to see something of the world, to enjoy a spell of independence, and to do something worthwhile.

The ticking off was still smarting, and she was concerned that Stanley's parents, although a good deal more liberal than hers, when, as was inevitable, her parents spoke to them, would feel compelled to censure him. Why did they have to be so unreasonable? In her fit of pique she almost felt that they begrudged her her enjoyment of the grand occasion.

Through the ensuing months, much against his nature, Stanley knew he had to buckle down to work, being due to sit his first set of law exams in June, his love of summer, this year, so wonderfully enhanced by his love for Peggy, tempered by the lengthening shadow of the impending test of his resolve, and indeed, his ability, to make the grade, and thus to move on to the next stage on the arduous route to qualification.

Although she had mentioned, several times, that she had been giving some thought to the possibility of becoming a nurse, he did not, initially, take it seriously, assuming it to be no more than fanciful musing as to what she might do to keep herself occupied through what he earnestly hoped would be a relatively short period before she would become his wife, as he was convinced she would.

When, at the beginning of June, she had told him that she was intending to apply to St Bartholomew's – Bart's - Hospital to become a trainee nurse, it felt like a body blow. He reacted angrily, revealing to her a side of his character she had not seen before, but which, in the years ahead she would be become familiar with, and learn how to manage.

"How am I going to manage without you?" he pleaded. "How will I survive?"

He took it so personally, her explanation, that they had their lives ahead of them, and that she wanted to do something worthwhile, just for a few years, failing to mitigate his obdurate resistance.

It also revealed a facet of her own character; her stoicism as well as her determination, as she sympathised with him whilst remaining set in her plan.

When she asked his father to provide the requisite reference, if there had been any doubt in his mind as to her intention, it was now dispelled.

Whenever the subject came up, which it did virtually every time they were together, their meetings now being every weekend and two or three weekday evenings, either for a walk, sometimes for an outing to the cinema or theatre, or to sit in the vicarage drawing room, listening to his records and dancing around the room, he would, like a cracked record, repeat his pleading for her to reconsider, her response, patiently, reiterating the same explanation, only allowing her exasperation occasionally to surface, telling him, firmly, that her mind was made up.

The only solace for Stanley was that it was by no means certain that Bart's would accept her, her alternative being to try to find an opening elsewhere, possibly even locally.

Even with this uncertainty, and the likelihood that if she were to be accepted it would be some months before she started, the thought of her going off to London cast a long shadow over the summer, a shadow darkened by his failing his exams.

Those months, of autumn and winter, emerging into the bright spring of 1938, were, unbeknown to them, the last they would spend together for many years, even though such togetherness was a matter of the slow evolution of their relationship.

For Stanley, his experience of failing his exams motivated him to greater efforts for his second attempt. However, what truly convinced him that he must pass, and thus set himself on the road to his finals, and to qualification, was the knowledge that as a member of the legal profession, highly esteemed as it was in the eyes of Mr Arthur Wing, his prospects of winning Peggy's hand, with the requisite parental consent, would be greatly enhanced.

Impatient by nature, Stanley had a tendency to self-pity, a product of a somewhat spoilt childhood, particularly by his mother who, having come to motherhood a good deal later than was usual for the time, channelled her natural generosity of spirit towards her first born son, Mrs Christian also, behind her stern exterior, doting on the boy, her discipline, skin-deep as it was, readily giving way to acquiescence to whatever her young charge desired.

He had realised, however, that with Peggy, he had to learn the art of patience, to woo her by constancy, their common interests, in theatre and cinema, in dancing and socialising, and in the enjoyment of nature and the outdoor world, bringing them ever closer.

And yet, hanging over them – over him – was the Sword of Damocles in the form of her impending departure, to begin her nursing training, his residual hope that she might not be accepted, steadily draining away, such was her own certainty. Although she was not due to start until June, the months seemed to rush past, as if intent upon hastening the dreaded moment.

He did his utmost to avoid what he had learned to be a subject she was wary of; their future together. But despite his best intentions, lapses occurred. In one instance, when they were sitting together in the vicarage drawing room, he told her that he had written her a letter that he had not had the courage to send as he was worried that she might not want to read it. He felt he was in the confessional, divulging some heinous sin, that of speaking from the heart.

At her insistence he showed her the letter, watching anxiously, and with an odd feeling of relief as she read it. What he had written was as close as he had ever come to both a declaration of his everlasting love, and, albeit not in express terms, a proposal, skirting around the actual question with allusions to "Fate having brought us together," reckoning that the avoidance of directness would be less likely to evoke the reaction he had encountered previously, of a sort of vague, non-committal "too soon", "I've got too much I want to do first."

Whilst venturing into the minefield of such matters of the heart, he concluded that he might as well throw in, not for the first time, his grievance at her decision to choose nursing before him, stopping short, however, of saying aloud what was filling his head; that by going away, she was risking their future. Self-pity quickly took over as he deployed the threat which he knew, full well, to be entirely hollow, but nevertheless, was indicative of the depth of his unhappiness; that if she was intent on adhering to her decision, so bereft would he be without her that he might look for a position abroad, in some part of the colonies.

"It's a lovely letter," she said quietly, giving little away, her expression pensive. "I'll need to think about it before I reply."

With such non-committal reaction, she left him to the agony of uncertainty throughout the next day, which was the first day of his exams – his second attempt, having had to leave early to catch the train to London, as to whether she had written to him as she had promised, and what she was going to say, his turbulent thoughts making it all the more difficult to focus his mind of the exam papers.

As soon as he arrived home, his heart leaped with joy at the sight of the letter on the hall table, seizing it and racing upstairs, two at a time, inserting the paper knife with some trepidation.

*15.3.38*
*4 Hove Park Road*
*Dear Stanley*
*I am so glad you let me read your letter. It was a very sweet one – but in some things I do not agree with you. Fate has certainly brought us together & holds both our futures in her hands – but I think it is more truly God than fate. May He grant happiness to us both if it is his will.*
*Although nursing is probably a noble career yet I am afraid it was not with the high ideal of relieving suffering humanity that I took it up, it was merely the only thing that I seemed capable of doing. I don't think your objections to my going to London were selfish really.*

*I am afraid I then had to harden my heart to keep to my determination.*

*I also wish that you may be happy in your work. I think it best if we both 'follow our secret heart'. That is I am sure how the best things in life are found. If we both do as we have determined we shall have seen more of the world & will certainly know our own minds then. We shall be able to see perhaps whether 'absence makes the heart grow fonder' or 'out of sight, out of mind'. I hope with all my heart it will be the former.*

*I hope you can gather the thread of my thought from these not very clear sentences but I am tired although my heart is very full – too I send you also my love or the nearest I have ever got to that.*

*Peggy*

Sitting on his bed, he read the letter three times, unsure whether he was relieved or saddened, finally, hanging onto her hope that absence would make their hearts grown fonder, and her final sentence, which came closer than ever before, to the declaration he so longed for.

Increasingly, their conversations would touch upon what was going on in the world, Europe in particular, the growing feeling, certainly amongst their friends, being that at some point, Hitler was going to have to be confronted. Stanley was an avid newspaper reader, his habit being to have a preliminary look at the sports pages of his father's *Telegraph*, time permitting, before breakfast, and before his father claimed possession of it, Stanley sometimes buying a *Times* on his way to the office, reading it during his lunch hour.

The news, during those days of March, made particularly grim reading, reports each day describing the "Anschluss", the term coined by the Nazis for the invasion of Austria. Even more depressing was the fact, if the reports were to be believed – and the *Times* was the one newspaper whose reports one could assume to be factual and unbiased – the Austrians were welcoming the invader with open arms, the photographs of Austrian guards with smiling faces, helping German soldiers to dismantle border barriers, symbolic of the once great county becoming a mere vassal of its all powerful neighbour, and the scenes of celebration on the streets of Vienna, graphic evidence of the what they all now believed to be Hitler's remorseless ambition.

"It's partly our fault," Stanley said one evening, when, in sombre mood, they were discussing the situation, the room having fallen quiet after the record they had been listening to, Artie Shaw's *Begin the Beguine,* had finished, Stanley lifting the stylus, putting the record back in its sleeve, deciding not to put on another one. "The terms we imposed on them after the war, at Versailles, were so obviously going to backfire. God Almighty, how could they have been so short sighted?"

"You can understand them wanting some sort of recompense," Peggy said, her own knowledge of the terms of the Treaty limited to what she had picked up from her father, and from Tom, who shared the opposing view, that Germany needed to be punished for the suffering it had caused, both the death toll to the Allied fighting men, and to the Allies' economies. "The desire for retribution is only human."

He had looked at her, her comment revealing, not for the first time, what he thought to be her slightly simplistic view of the world, her tendency to see things in such black and white terms, irritating him. It was, however, a minor blemish in the overall perfection, and one which he would pass over with some dismissive comment, unaware of her recognition of his sometimes condescending manner.

"It was bound to lead to festering resentment," he added as gently as he could. "And what has happened, with Hitler and the Nazis, was inevitable."

"When Tom went there," Peggy said, the fact that her brother had actually been to Germany being a card she would play when she felt she needed to offer some resistance to Stanley's assertiveness, "he said that what they were doing there was quite incredible." Tom's visit, on an exchange, had given him the opportunity to travel around a certain amount, the high point of his visit, in terms of his understandably frequent recounting of it, being taken by the family he was staying with, to one of Hitler's Nuremberg rallies, his pen-friend, now his host, being a member of the Hitler Youth, Tom, in company with the pen-friend's parents, having seats in a stand as the side of the square. "He certainly didn't like much of what was going on, but he said that the rally was unlike anything he'd seen before. Really impressive. And the reception they gave Hitler was quite ecstatic."

"Mm, I'm not sure I would want a Prime Minister I felt ecstatic about," Stanley said, tempted to tell her that this was about the fourth time she had mentioned Tom's experience. When, just a few years later, he, and most of the British people, came to revere Churchill as a similarly heroic figure, he will have almost forgotten his dismissiveness of Tom's awe-struck account of the huge, regimented rally, filling the vast square, the images which he, Stanley, had seen on *Pathe News* showing Hitler at the podium, the backdrop, the monumental triple swastika banners and, at each end of the curve of the building, the two towering eagles, the square itself, filled with ranks of soldiers and Hitler Youth, in perfect formations, all, in unison, raising their arms in the straight armed salute to their Fuhrer.

A few weeks later, when Stanley called for her, as they set off for one of their regular walks, this time heading up Dyke Road towards the Downs, she seemed unusually subdued. It was only when they sat down, facing the wide vista of the channel, the dark contours of the Isle of Wight clearly visible against the later afternoon sun, the reason became clear.

"This came today," she said, handing him a typed letter which he unfolded. As he instantly recognised the address, he felt a pang in his stomach.

27.4.38
*St Bartholomew's Hospital, London EC1*
*Miss P Wing*
*Dear Madam*
*May I remind you that arrangements are being made to receive you at the Preliminary Training School, 24 Kings Square, Goswell Road, London EC1 on Monday June 13th 1938 between the hours of 4 and 6pm.*
*The fee of £6-6-0 for the Course is payable in advance and should be sent to the Clerk to the Governors, St Bartholomew's Hospital before May 13th.*
*May we have your vaccination and dental certificates, and also a certificate from your doctor stating that you are still in good health and fit to commence your training.*
*I am, yours faithfully*
*Delia Day*
*Matron and Superintendent of Nursing*

"You've definitely made up your mind then," he said, handing the letter back to her. By implicit agreement between them, the subject having prompted the only real arguments of their courtship, for the previous couple of months they had treated it as a sort of taboo, its only mention having been when they had been in company, particularly with Peggy's closest friends, Paddy and Barbara, both of whom voiced their admiration for Peggy's courage in taking such a step, both the decision to take up nursing, and, even more so, to have to go to live in London. It was as if she had resolved to go on an adventure in a foreign land, the fact that it was merely an hour's train journey failing to lessen their praise for her bravery.

"Yes," she replied with more conviction than she was feeling. "I've made up my mind. You know that." She took his hand, looking at him, his face a picture of dejection. "We'll still be able to see each other regularly. I'll be home whenever I have time off, and you can come and meet me in London."

Those last weeks seemed to fly past with cruel speed, the day arriving all too soon when they spent the evening together knowing that, first thing the following morning, she would be catching the train to London, having declined his offer to drive her, preferring to make her own way. It was a solemn occasion, their conversation over their dinner at *Jimmy's*, one of their favourite restaurants, stilted, Stanley finding it difficult to maintain the brave face he had determined to show, Peggy's attempt at jollity foundering on his mood.

They stood for several minutes on the corner of Hove Park Road, far enough away from her house not to be seen should her parents happen to be looking out of the window, it still not being fully dark, the June evening warm with the promise of imminent high summer, Stanley holding her tightly in his encircling arms until she eventually prized herself away, blowing him a kiss as she hurried towards her house.

While Peggy quickly settled into her new existence, getting to know the other trainee nurses, particularly those living in the same nurses' home, and becoming immersed in both the practical training at the hospital and the not inconsiderable amount of study they were set, Stanley drifted through that summer in a state of constant misery, alleviated only by occasional outings with a few of his friends, and by an absorbing Ashes series, with the legendary Don Bradman performing his usual magic, with three centuries in three tests, a feat eclipsed by Len Hutton's record breaking 364 in the final test, England amassing and extraordinary 903 runs, trouncing the Australians by an innings and 579 runs. Disappointing as it was that the series was drawn, Stanley could see some justice in such outcome, neither of such exceptional teams deserving to lose such a series.

Peggy's letters were, as she had promised when she had been trying to console him on that sad evening before her departure, frequent and full of her news, his, by contrast, flat and, as he was only too well aware, uninteresting. Often he would find himself with pen poised over notepaper, searching for news which might be of interest to her, his mundane accounts of the goings on in his office, or of his application to his studies, dreadfully dull, although serving the purpose of at least giving him something to spread across the pages.

The ever present rumblings of Germany's seemingly insatiable appetite for expansion, at the expense of its neighbouring countries, meant that the threat of war was an incessant background. Indeed, when, in July, the government announced the issuing of gas masks to the general public, it seemed to escalate the threat to a higher level, conversations invariably turning not just to the likelihood of war, but how soon it would occur and what it would be like, the fear being that this time there would be dreadful new weapons, bringing the war to towns and homes, civilians being at as much risk as the soldiers.

The combination of being kept busy and, by the end of the day, feeling tired enough to want to retire to her bed, helped Peggy to shrug off the homesickness which, nevertheless, she knew to be ever present, just once or twice, when her guard was down at the end of a particularly demanding day, reducing her to a bout of tears, which, with a stern reprimand to herself, she would quickly curtail. She found that sharing such emotions with her co-trainees helped a good deal, instilling a sort of camaraderie which she came to value, sowing the seeds of a few lasting friendships.

One of the first she met, on the day she arrived, Brewster, was a girl with a distinct trace of cockney, a throaty laugh, and, as Peggy was to discover instantly, a bawdy sense of humour.

Staff being referred to by their titles – "Sister", "Matron" – or their surnames, Christian names were reserved for off duty times, although for some reason, Brewster remained "Brewster", her Christian name, Daisy, seeming rather inappropriate for this earthy, lively girl, who Peggy took to. She was such a contrast to her friends at home, her obsession with, and, as Peggy soon discovered, her considerable experience of, sex, while at first quite shocking, soon became a subject which Peggy thoroughly enjoyed, Brewster's scurrilous accounts of her escapades, some with the array of young doctors at the hospital, exciting Peggy's keen interest, a fact which set her wondering what Stanley would think if he heard Brewster recounting one of her licentious assignations, in graphic detail, reducing her audience, sometimes just Peggy, but more often, a handful of the open mouthed trainees, to fits of squeamish laughter.

By contrast with chatty, saucy Brewster, Bubby – known generally by her nickname apart from when she was on duty, very few knowing that her name was in fact, Beryl – was a rather quiet, well spoken girl, who, as Peggy soon discovered, had hidden depths, sharing Peggy's enjoyment of Brewster's risqué anecdotes, the two of them, Peggy and Bubby, having in common a love of literature and theatre, both of which Brewster admitted, were way above her head.

The friendship which the three of them developed in those early weeks, endured for much of Peggy's time at Bart's, supporting one another during the difficult times each of them were to face.

It was when, in August, the country was sweltering in a heatwave, that she realised how much she missed the sea air, such a contrast with the weight of heat and grimy air which were special to London. There were times when she longed to be on the beach, her love of swimming and of lying in the sun, sacrificed for her determination to pursue her ambition. As the sun beat down, she would sometimes go to one of the London parks, hoping to find a bit of relief but in fact, encountering the opposite, the air stultifyingly torpid, the thought of walking across the shingle and immersing herself in the sea, like a mirage, her thirst remaining unquenched.

The fact that she had her first set of exams in the middle of the heatwave, did little to lessen her longing for home.

In those early months of her new career, Brewster also became Peggy's confidante, describing to her her meetings with Stanley, holding nothing back, revelling in the re-living of their kissing and his sometimes almost lyrical profession of his undying love, Brewster invariably lowering the tone.

"Did you get your hand down his trousers?" she would ask, with a staccato laugh. "What's his old fella like? Good sized handful is it?"

At moments, Peggy would find herself blushing as she thought about the hardness in his trousers which she had become familiar with as they embraced, but the notion of touching it with her hands, even through the fabric, let alone, of sliding her hand inside, quite shocked her.

"When are you going to let him have his wicked way with you then, Peg?" she asked, Brewster being the only one of the trainees using the diminutive. She looked at Peggy intently for a moment, her lively blue eyes searching her friend's. "You want to give it a go before he gets a ring on your finger, in case it doesn't measure up." The serious moment rapidly ended with another bark of throaty laughter.

Having sailed through her first set of exams, Peggy met up with Stanley for a night out, enjoying a meal and several drinks in a pub before going their separate ways, he having to hurry to Victoria to catch the train back to Brighton, she just managing to get back to the nurses' home before the 10.30 lights out, which, in reality, was the time they were required to be safely indoors, windows often being peppered with handfuls of gravel as latecomers announced their return, doors being quietly opened to admit them.

With the probationary exam under her belt, Peggy achieved the formal status of trainee nurse, taking up proper duties on the wards.

It was over her first weekend home that something changed. She felt almost light headed with the pleasure of breathing the sea air, the two days a whirl of activity with Stanley at his most charming and entertaining, his mood positively jovial, apart from the moments of quiet tenderness. As they sat at their table at *Jimmy's*, his brown eyes looking intently into hers, he reached for her hand, taking it in his, examining it as he gathered his courage.

"You know what I want to say, don't you?" The skin of his palm was slightly damp as he gave her hand a gentle squeeze. "I'm sorry. I know you don't like me saying this sort of thing. But I've just got to. Before I go off to Scotland next week."

Due to depart for a two week fishing trip with his father, this weekend felt to him, to be another moment of parting, engendering in him a determination, finally, to speak his mind.

"Yes, I know," she replied, returning the pressure on his hand, lifting it slightly, as if in encouragement. "And I don't mind."

"I can't ever imagine my life without you. I love you so very much."

He felt his heart pounding, but at the same time, a sense of achievement, and of descending calm as she held his gaze, a faint smile fixed on her face.

"I think we probably shall," she replied, confusing him for a moment. "Be together," she added quickly. "But I must go on with my nursing. Just for a time. A few years."

In a doorway in the narrow cul-de-sac leading to *Jimmy's*, they held each other in an embrace which, to each of them, felt equally meaningful, as if they were acknowledging a new certainty, neither wanting to break the spell, Peggy eventually reminding him of the time.

Sitting on the train, after he had waived her off, walking to the end of the platform, keeping up with her, blowing kisses, oblivious of the fact that she was in a compartment filled with other passengers, she could not help herself from smiling with a feeling of happiness which she had not known before. Although this was not the wondrous falling in love that she had sometimes dreamed about, what she could now see to have been steadily evolving, had finally taken root, with a solidity that she recognised as what she truly wanted. Yes, she could now say to herself that she did love him.

There were moments during that long summer when Peggy felt unexpectedly exhilarated, revelling in her freedom, becoming increasingly familiar with the great city, her early doubts about her determined choice of career, dispelled by a new feeling of confidence.

The work was hard, both on the wards and the study which seemed unrelenting, and yet, despite the fatigue which, if they – she and her fellow trainees - allowed it to do so, would prompt them to take gratefully to their beds, they would regularly use their limited free time to go out on the town, getting to know the places where they could get good food reasonably cheaply, taking full advantage of the benefits which were often available through the hospital, including theatre tickets.

At times, she had pangs of conscience that she was out enjoying herself so much when Stanley was working away at his articles, studying for his next set of exams. She decided to give him a full account of everything she did, valuing the honesty which they had committed to.

She also felt sufficiently confident, occasionally, to go out by herself.

*20.8.38*
*Tottenham Court Road Brasserie*
*Dear Stanley*
*As you see I am now at the Brasserie having a meal. I am having this dish called 'Opera' made of mushrooms & liver on toast, a coffee ice & some iced cider.*
*I hope you are having a good time. I think of you so often & wonder how you are enjoying yourself. I am very happy & hope you are too.*
*I have now dragged myself away from the music & am very glad as it is a glorious evening. The sky is very blue and schooned with little soft clouds that all have caught some of the light from the setting sun – which is a lovely golden pink. It is so bright that the statues on the domes of the National Gallery are all silhouetted. I am now sitting in Trafalgar Square having walked down Charing Cross Road. All the world around here seems happy & people are hurrying about to theatres & on various errands & the hundreds of birds in the trees around here on St Martins in the Fields & all chirping together so that it seems like a grand chorus of birds' songs. It seems as though all the world is thanking God for such a wonderful day. That is what I am doing tonight, thanking Him also for work to do, health, friends, home, your love & life itself.*

*With love & kisses*
*Peggy*

As summer slowly declined, a spell of warm weather, with much talk of an Indian summer, giving way to a more familiar equinoctial pattern, of showers and cool westerly winds, talk of war took centre stage, the Prime Minister, Neville Chamberlain making great play of his determination to find a route to maintaining peace.

When she met Stanley, the threat of war took on an even greater intensity, they both knowing that Stanley would have to fight, a prospect which filled Peggy with dread. As always, however, she put on a brave face.

*I pray that there will be peace, yet if there is not, we will find a still harder task to do. We should have to keep our spirits & help the many more who need our aid. Still I hope this won't happen. Though I sympathise with Chamberlain I don't think his way will prove the best way to peace.*
*My love*
*Peggy*

On the day that Chamberlain was sitting down with Hitler, his paltry negotiating skills, and his feeble hand, no match for the guile and obduracy of his protagonist, Stanley and Peggy strolled across St James' Park, savouring the last of their few hours together.

"I do hope they can come to their senses," Peggy said, their mood subdued, partly because of their imminent parting, she insisting on cutting short their day, a backlog of study pricking her conscience, she and the other girls having spent too many of their off duty hours going "into town", a term which encompassed their range of activities, Stanley having to make his way to Victoria, but also sharing the general mood of apprehension.

"He may be able to put off the evil hour," Stanley replied, his opinion of the Prime Minister, shared by many others, being of a man in whom one could have little faith. "But I don't think it'll be any more than that."

As she made her way back to the nurses' home, catching the bus to Oxford Street and then walking the rest of the way to Bloomsbury, London seemed to share their anxiety.

*When I was on the bus heading for Oxford Street, the guns in Hyde Park rather impressed the feeling of anxiety, also the people standing outside Selfridges watching the news.*

*Everybody on the ward was especially nice last night, probably because war seemed so near. It is amazing how people's characters are shown when working with them especially when things are serious.*

*War does seem so inevitable and there is such a feeling of foreboding. They have started dumping sandbags round this block. Now two aeroplanes have just flown over towing a sign saying 'Join the Auxiliary Fire Service'.*

*With much love*

*Peggy*

Chamberlain returned from his Munich meeting with Hitler, brandishing what was to become his infamous "piece of paper", proclaiming his achievement that Hitler had agreed that "our two peoples will never go to war with one another again". It was, the Prime Minister insisted, "peace with honour", despite the fact that for the avoidance of war he had offered up Czechoslovakia as a sacrifice to annexation, Germany, the following week, occupying Sudetenland and, soon after, the remainder of Czechoslovakia.

"Peace for our time," Chamberlain crowed, his words greeted with relief albeit, tempered with a large measure of scepticism. "Go home and get a nice quiet sleep", he said, concluding his speech with an attempt to give paternal comfort to the nation.

Despite the lingering doubts as to the duration of the vaunted peace, the nation breathed a sigh of relief that if there was to be a war, it had been put off to another day. Life went on, almost as normal, Peggy and Stanley having settled into the pattern of their courtship, their meetings in London usually being for an afternoon or sometimes a full day and an evening, Stanley occasionally staying the night in a hotel, where he would manage to sneak her into his room, their passion threatening the bounds of the constraint which, by implicit propriety deeply embedded through their upbringing – hers somewhat more than his - and the mores of their class and time, nevertheless held firm.

She would get back home whenever she could, usually for weekends off or sometimes just for the day. Much as she enjoyed being back in Brighton, and seeing Paddy, Barbara, and other friends, and the outings that Stanley arranged, often as a group, with the arrival of winter, the town did not have the draw of the summer months. It almost became her preference to remain in London, the city seeming to take on its winter mantle with relish. With the approach of Christmas, the fragile peace seemed to infuse the season with a determination to enjoy it to the full, the shops donning their festive attire, the pubs and restaurants enjoying bumper trade.

It was in December that Peggy had her first period of night duty, experiencing the strange sensation of observing the somnolent city. As she sat, staring out of the window, pondering what to say to Stanley, she felt a moment of melancholy. Perhaps it was the thought of Christmas away from home, and from him, knowing how miserable he would be, as he had already made very clear to her when he had vainly pleaded with her to see if she could change her duty to allow her to get home even for part of the day.

Peggy was no longer shocked by Brewster's accounts of her exploits as she had been initially. Rather, she found them strangely stimulating; most definitely far beyond her own experience, but nevertheless, playing rather too vividly in her imagination. It was as if she was getting some vicarious pleasure from the re-telling of each assignation, there being something quite liberating about the idea of having sex, purely for the physical pleasure.

Brewster clearly relished her reporting, usually to the two of them, Peggy and Bubby, Bubby's wide-eyed, open mouthed attentiveness concealing a dilemma which she wrestled with, her sense of what was decent far more deeply seated even than Peggy's. Peggy would sometimes encourage Brewster, partly through her own curiosity, but also as she rather enjoyed seeing the shock registering on Bubby's face. To Peggy also, it was a sort of education in matters carnal, such sex education as she had had, being in the form of a couple of talks at her school, one of the mistresses using allusions to acts and body parts so obscure that the girls were left to decode the sessions amongst themselves. What she knew, or thought she knew until she met Brewster, came largely from conversations with her group of closest school friends and a few she knew through church circles. Between them – Paddy, Barbara, Sally and Bubbles – they would conjecture and speculate, testing theories, often dissolving into fits of giggles.

"What's it like?" she asked Brewster one afternoon when the three of them were sitting, heads close together at the Lyon's Cornerhouse table, enjoying tea and cake. "I mean doing *it*?" She registered Bubby's startled expression at the audacity of the question.

"What, getting a good seeing to from a fella? Bloody lovely, when they take a bit of time." Her laugh sounded more a snort of derision. "Trouble is, most of the time, it's in, waggle it about a bit, and they're done before you've even got going! But when they do keep going, blimey, girls, it's like your whole body's melting. One of the doctors – no, don't ask me to tell you which one, or you'll want a go with him – well, I can tell you, has he got staying power! Left me wrung out for a week!" This time the laugh was full throated.

"I mean," Peggy continued tentatively, "when they put it…You know. What's it feel like?"

"Depends how big it is, Peg, my love. Some of them, the littluns, you hardly know it's in. But my special doc, what a whopper! It's like he's going to split you up the middle. Bloody nice way of being impaled though!"

Peggy looked again at Bubby, her cheeks now flushed, her eyes appearing ready to pop out of her face.

"I think I'm going to wait until I'm married," Bubby said quietly. "I want to be truly in love with the man I…"

"Well, I recommend giving it a go first," Brewster replied, her own face now pink with the delight she always found in such conversations. "But I guess you two are set on going as virgins to the altar. Something to be said for it, I suppose. Makes it a bit special when it happens. Provide it works OK. Might take a while to really get in the swing of it. Like riding a bike: bit wobbly at first until you get the hang of it. Then you can pedal to your heart's delight!"

Sometimes when Peggy was with Stanley, she would think of some the things Brewster had said, almost feeling herself blushing, as if Stanley could see inside her thoughts. She could not help herself from wondering what it would be like, to make love with him, to feel his large frame on top of him, and for that hardness, the shape of which she felt she almost knew, so often did she feel it pressing against her, to be inside her.

Quickly she would start talking about something, to try to push such thoughts out of her mind.

# THREE

On a cold, dank London morning, Stanley sat at the breakfast table in his digs, a large house in Kensington Gardens Square, reading the *Telegraph,* the main news being of the Spanish Civil War, clearly now drawing to a close with Franco's capture of Barcelona, at the heart of Catalonia, once the bastion of the Republican's, whose remnants were now scattered through the region, many retreating over the border into France, little expecting that a year later, those who had not managed to get away from the refugee camps would be compelled, by the Vichy regime, to return to face whatever fate Franco's newly installed Falangist regime saw fit to meet out.

At the beginning of January, Stanley had started his course at Gibson and Weldon, the privately run college, accredited by the Law Society to run the training courses for articled clerks, Stanley now being in what, hopefully, would be the last stage, sitting his finals in the summer.

He knew that the course was going to be tough, the two previous ones having proved severely testing of both his academic ability and his application. This time, however, there was one big difference, with both a huge advantage and a worrying drawback: his proximity to Peggy. He would be able to see her far more often than over the previous six months when their meetings had been, at best, once a week, and then often only for a few hours. The disadvantage was that being so close to her, he would give in to the temptation to spend time with her when he should be at his books.

His new found motivation, to qualify, so that he would achieve the status to persuade her father to allow them to marry, was, however, the perfect incentive.

It remained the general view that, despite Chamberlain's bowing to Hitler's ambition, he had done no more than to buy some time, putting off the inevitable. Indeed, the prospect of war cast an ever lengthening shadow, heightening the determination to enjoy the time of peace while it lasted.

The guns which, prior to Munich, had appeared in Hyde Park, had been removed, although it was noticeable that the emplacements in which they had been located, dug into the turf, ringed with sandbags, remained, ready to accommodate the guns should they need to be re-deployed.

Having spent Christmas and the New Year apart, Peggy and Stanley did their best to make up for it by having a day together, January 2$^{nd}$, going to see the film of *War of the Worlds*, Peggy's hand gripping Stanley's as the alien creatures wreaked their havoc to Earth and mankind. After the film, they had dinner at Tottenham Court Road Brasserie, where they treated themselves to "Gin and It" and a bottle of wine, time briefly suspended until she suddenly realised that it was nearly "lights out", resulting in a hurried departure, Stanley accompanying her as they caught the bus along Holborn, then running the last few hundred yards to the nurses' home, parting after a hasty kiss.

Adding to the anxiety about Germany, for a while the threat from the IRA became almost more worrying, with several bombings in London and elsewhere in the country. Although the bombs themselves were small, apparently amateurish devices, they were far too close for comfort, with one going off at Tottenham Court tube station, one of Stanley and Peggy's rendezvous points.

As if this wasn't enough to heighten the mood of apprehension, in early February, in response to Hitler's continued sabre rattling, Chamberlain, appearing to recognise the extent to which he had been duped by the German *Fuhrer*, and feeling it necessary to show his strength, made a statement to the House that any attack on France would be regarded as an attack on Britain, a declaration which, whilst welcomed as an attempt to stand up to Hitler, was greeted with a certain amount of scepticism, not least because of a widely shared sentiment, that, despite the fact that we had fought at their side throughout the Great War, the French were not our natural allies.

With the swirling undercurrent of unease, the young couple's courtship seemed to take on a greater intensity. Having a longer than usual break, of three whole days, Peggy decided that, after spending the afternoon with Stanley, she would return home for two days, catching an evening train.

She now felt entirely at home in London, and was enjoying her work, both the practical side, and, to a lesser extent, the challenge of the academic. However, it was when she returned after a visit home that she again felt an expected touch of homesickness. She loved the clean sea air, the sound of the seagulls which was so much the soundtrack to the town, as well as the comfort of home. Although her parents were still their rather stiffly formal selves, overt affection never having been part of their manner with their children, their delight at her being back with them was palpable, not least by their insisting on taking her out, when time allowed, for restaurant meals.

She found also, that with her emotions slightly unsettled by the enjoyment of seeing her old friends, and then having to leave them behind, the train journeys back to London became a time of pensiveness. Often, also, her thoughts turned to her relationship with Stanley, now a wonderfully solid foundation to her life, her love for him still surprising her, her own delight at times, catching her unawares, giving her a glow of contentment.

Having more time to spend together, both being in London, the intimacy between them evolved, the fact that they would, one day, become man and wife – something both of them were certain of despite the fact that they had not yet become engaged, encouraging them to delve ever deeper into facets of their relationship which, for the time being, they were only able to explore in their minds, and their fantasies. Their agreement that they would resist the temptation to make love until they were married, added a tension to their physical relationship, the fervour of their clinching heightened by their repressed eagerness, their conversation becoming more overt as they explored their feelings.

Stanley, in particular, clearly found such discussions stimulating, sexual matters aired, sometimes through a thin veil of faux philosophising, but in reality, learning more about each other, and about the desires and idiosyncrasies of the opposite sex.

Stanley was deeply devoted to his parents, taking for granted his mother's insistence, when he was a child, and still now, on spoiling him, sweets and new toys now replaced by a pound note, and occasionally, a fiver, inside a letter, or permission to buy new clothes on her account at Cobleys or Hanningtons. His father, Pop, was a slightly remote figure, spending much time in his study, dealing with parish correspondence or composing his sermons, although when Stanley would have reason to interrupt, quietly opening the door to the dim, dusty room, heavy with the aroma of pipe tobacco, books and old leather ( in the form of the worn top of his large desk, his old fishing shoes, and several holders for rods and fishing equipment), his father often seemed to be immersed in a book, in the evenings, a glass of whisky beside him on the desk, his posture always relaxed, leaning back in the creaking, upholstered revolving chair.

Reverend William Allen's benevolence to his parishioners was certainly deeply felt, and yet, Stanley felt, looking back in later years, more intellectual than emotional, his empathy rather at arm's length. On a few occasions his father had taken him with him on visits to ailing members of his flock, his ministering being a sort of endowment of his ecclesiastical presence, contact being limited to a brief, light, laying of his long fingered hand on shoulder or arm as he concluded a bedside prayer.

For all his remoteness, Stanley was devoted to Pop, respectful of his great esteem in the parish, but also sharing a deep affinity, all the more valued for its infrequent airing, manifest with a shared taste for dance band music and operetta, the two of them having passed many hours singing along to the melodies of Gilbert and Sullivan.

Michael, Stanley's brother, being eight years younger, was very much the baby of the family, and indulged as such, spoiled even more than Stanley, the evidence being the poor child's fatness, which he only managed to shed when, just at the end of the war, he started his national service, joining the Navy.

To their mother's delight, despite the age gap, Stanley and Michael appeared to be remarkably close, Stanley content to play frequent games of cricket with his young brother in the vicarage garden, his superior craft enabling him to dominate each game, moderation though kindness notwithstanding, hammering Michael's benign bowling around the garden, the tubby bowler, red faced and sweating as he rushed around to retrieve the ball.

One late afternoon, showing off his prowess with the bat, Stanley struck a full blooded drive, the ball arching towards the church which marked one boundary to the playing area. As the brothers watched the flight of the ball, to their horror, it hit a stained glass window, punching a hole through some coloured saintly figure, the ball, it was reported to Stanley during his subsequent dressing down, landing, mid evensong, in the aisle, compelling his quick thinking father, seamlessly, to adapt the prayer he was reciting, improvising, "the perils which He rains down upon us".

"Clearly a very fine six!" his father opined, to conclude the mild reprimand.

The twenty-fourth of February 1939, Stanley's twenty first, was, of necessity, a day of study, although, as he went into the dining room for his breakfast, he was greeted with a slightly restrained rendition from his fellow lodgers, of "Happy Birthday". He was also deeply touched by the letter from his father.

*My dear Stanley*
*We send you our best love and all good wishes for a very happy day tomorrow, your twenty-first birthday. Our thoughts go back to the early hours of the morning of Feb 24th 1918 when you first made your debut into this somewhat strange world and of course we cannot but think of what the future holds in store for you. We feel sure that if you do your duty and try to please God in everything, you can't go far wrong and that your heart will be full of peace which passeth understanding.*

*"As the days are so shall thy strength be" is a favourite text of mine and I pass it on to you and hope you will always keep it in mind for it will bring you much comfort and strength both in joy and sorry.*
*God bless you and prosper your undertakings.*
*Your loving Dad*

After Germany had occupied Czechoslovakia, effectively gifted to Hitler by the Munich agreement, he then turned his sights on Poland, and in particular, the Danzig corridor, the small Baltic area which was both strategically important to the resurgent Germany, as well as a focus of the festering humiliation of Versailles.

At the end of March, Chamberlain, continuing his efforts to recast himself as the strong man, after his abysmally feeble showing at Munich, once again made his mark in the sand, his statement to the Commons this time, that "in the event of action which clearly threatened Polish independence, His Majesty's Government would feel themselves bound at once to lend the Polish Government all support in their power", the commitment which, within a matter of months, would lead to war.

As Stanley continued to wrestle with his studies, the distraction offered by Peggy's proximity was compounded by the uncertainty as to whether he would be called up, the Government having introduced a Military Training Bill, which, when passed by Parliament, would require all men between the ages of twenty and twenty-two, to undergo preliminary military training.

"I sometimes wonder whether there is any point in going on with the exams," he told Peggy, her response being a resolute insistence that he must do so.

"There's still a chance it might not happen," she said without conviction. "That Hitler will finally see sense."

Rather than wait until called up, Stanley decided to volunteer, joining the Territorial Army, taking the bus from Bayswater Road to Chelsea where he joined a queue of young men, filing into Chelsea Barracks, the interview with a red faced Sergeant-Major, taking a few minutes, followed by a medical examination with a bored Medical Officer who looked at his throat, tapped his chest, told him to identify a few letters on a wall chart, ordered him to cough as he cupped his balls, and gave a nod of acknowledgment that he would do, the whole process complete by midday when he found himself back in his digs, the possessor of a uniform, a booklet telling him what was expected of him, and a postcard bearing the royal coat of arms and his acceptance certificate, which he read with a mixture of pride and unease, his affirmative answer to the question of whether he held a driver's licence resulting in his designation as "Driver".

**This is to certify that *Driver, S.R.Allen* has been accepted for Service in the Territorial Army**
**Station – Chelsea**
**Unit – 514**
**Date 18/4/39**
**Signed – Officer Commanding**

What he did not see was the full record of his enlistment which was placed in his newly opened Army file.

## IDENTIFICATION OF S.R.ALLEN ON ENLISTMENT

**STANLEY ROWLATT ALLEN**
**Personal Number 166180**
**Date of birth 24.2.18**
**Apparent Age 21 years 2 months**
**Height 6ft 2ins**
**Weight 12st 5lbs**
**Girth 38 ins    Range of expansion 2 ins**
**Eyes Brown**
**Hair  Brown**
**Father - William Joseph Rowlatt Allen**
**Mother – Mary Emma Gertrude Allen (Brewer)**
**Good Shepherd Vicarage, 172 Dyke Road, Brighton, Sussex**
**"I have examined the above named recruit and find that he does not present any of the causes of rejection specified in the Regulations. He can see at the required distance with either eye: his heart and lungs are healthy; he has free use of his joints and limbs; and declares that he is not subject to fits of any description.**
**I consider him fit for the Territorial Arm.**
**18.iv.39    Medical Officer"**

**Special knowledge experience:**
**Brighton College 1ˢᵗ XV & Water Polo Team**
**School Certificate 1935 – 5 Credits**
**OTC**
**Law Student (articled to Thomas Eggar and Son Solicitors of**

**Westminster)**
**Passed Law Society Intermediate Examination Nov 1938**

**18.4.39 Signed up Territorial Army**
         **Service in Ranks**
         **Attested driver**
         **1st London Div PET Coy – 514 Coy RASC**
**Chelsea**

Stanley felt a little disappointed that the training was a good deal less onerous – and less time consuming – than he had expected, allowing him ample time to continue with his studies. His application, however, became increasingly wayward as he was overtaken by a sort of fatalism; that before he was going to be able to make his way in the world of law, there were military matters with which he was going to be preoccupied.

His real concern, however, was that donning the King's uniform, particularly as a Territorial reservist of lowly rank, would leave him very far adrift from the status he knew he would have to acquire to have any prospect of obtaining Peggy's father's consent to giving him his daughter's hand.

As spring passed into summer, he drifted in the uncertainty which hung over his future – indeed, which hung over the future generally. While he plodded along with studies, his recalcitrant brain ever less willing to absorb the mass of statute and precedent which was deemed the necessary grounding to convert an articled clerk into the fully fledged solicitor, his love for Peggy was all consuming, illuminating his days and filling his nights with dreams and, from time to time, with nightmares about losing her, scenarios and images blurring, engendering a panic from which he would wake, sweating, fearful, but quickly remembering that for the time being at least, they were close together, able to enjoy the plentiful pleasures which London had to offer.

Having brought his wireless with him to his digs, he would have it switched on when he was pouring over his books and notes, the music programmes soothing but not helping his concentration.

It was one evening, when labouring over a particularly obscure passage on jurisprudence, that, for the first time, he heard Billie Holiday's *Strange Fruit*, the gritty, mournful account of a lynching, instantly powerful, striking him like a physical blow. There was something in the song's melancholy which attuned to his own anxiety.

When he bought the record and played it to Peggy, she listened with a solemn expression, sitting in silence for some moments after it finished.

"Why are people so horrid?" she asked sadly, not expecting an answer. "Why can't they just get on. Look where it's taking us."

Noticing the tears brimming in her eyes, he cradled her head against his shoulder, holding her tightly against him until she sat up straight, dabbing her eyes with her handkerchief.

"Haven't you got anything more cheerful?"

To Glen Miller's *Little Brown Jug*, they danced around his small room, their mood instantly lifting.

"I do love you, Stanley," she said as the tune ended.

When she was back at the nurses' home, she felt quite elated, their love seeming to become more real, and more delicious each time they were together. She sat with Sally, a trainee nurse who she had recently got to know, to two of them instantly hitting it off and becoming close friends. Brewster and Bubby were such good chums to chat to and to go out with, but with Sally, she was truly able to confide, divulging the closest matters of the heart.

"I still have to pinch myself," she said, her eyes shining and her cheeks flushed with excitement. "I had often imagined falling in love, but I never thought it could creep up on me like this. I've known him for ages, and always liked him. But it was as if my eyes were suddenly opened and I saw him differently. Sally, I just love him!"

When she was back in her room, she sat down at her table, feeling a need to put something into words while the moment of ecstasy had hold of her.

*Darling*
*I just had to write to tell you that I have fallen in love tonight. You can't possibly guess what he is like – he is rather like a lamppost, not quite – he has hair that is rather inclined to wave a reddish nose & two laughing brown eyes with little wrinkles round, that laugh too.*
*Why I am writing at this hour is because I have done the impossible – I was 'too much in love to say goodnight'. Darling, I wanted to tell you that I loved you so much tonight. The world is a wonderful place isn't it really?*

*I would like to still be with you though I really think it better for me here as it is about time I bid the world goodnight.*
*My love to you*
*Peggy*

In early August they were able to arrange a weekend when they were both at home with their respective families at the same time. The fact that the news was becoming ever more grim made them determined to shake off their anxiety, just for a short while, the mood when they went out with a party of friends - Paddy and her newly betrothed fiancé, Alan; Barbara with her boyfriend, Bill; and Peggy's cousin Marjorie – positively merry.

Paddy, always a girl to enjoy life, had found a perfect match in Alan, a chap several inches smaller than her, a jovial character who had the capacity to liven up any occasion, usually with the aid of liquor and dry sense of humour. Having started the evening in a pub, Peggy drinking gin and lime, her new favourite which Alan had introduced her too, they then went to see *Jimmie Hunter's Follies* on the Palace Pier. And with several more drinks at the end of the show, they meandered unsteadily back through the town, singing snatches of the songs from the show, laughing aloud as they remembered some of the comedy lines.

In between the music programmes, and the occasional play, Stanley, like much of the population, listened to the BBC news, the sombre tones of the news readers, most notably Alvar Lidell who was to become so much the voice of the war, issuing from wireless sets in virtually every household, adding to the grim mood. But with the inevitability came the conviction that if there was to be war, the nation was ready for the test, fearful though, that this time round it would be even worse than the last time, with new weapons and technology promising dreadful horrors.

Stanley and Peggy would discuss it, in their own hushed tones, needing to come to terms with the likelihood of long periods of separation. On one occasion he felt compelled to raise the question of his own survival.

"If I don't make it…" he began, hesitating, his imagination taking him to some vaguely perceived battlefield, images of the trenches of the Great War playing in his mind.

"You will come through it," she interrupted, holding tightly to his hand. "I just know it. God will protect you, if we pray hard enough for Him to do so."

Religion, to both of them, was part of their way of life, an unquestioned, solid, necessary foundation to their existence. For Peggy, perhaps more than Stanley, faith also evoked a deep emotional belief, that the beauty of the world was impossible to conceive without the hand of the Deity, although the capacity of mankind for malevolence would sometimes cause her to frown as she struggled with the concept, as regularly addressed by those wise men in their pulpits, of evil being part of God's means of testing mankind, necessarily laying upon his beloved creation, the dilemma of choice. Only by having the freedom to choose evil could man truly discover the path of righteousness.

Stanley, at times, felt the same firm conviction, although there were also moments when doubt, and reason, seeped into his vexed intellect. He was able, however, to brush such wavering aside, knowing that, in the times ahead, he would need the solace of belief that his prayers would be heard.

Towards the end of August, coming like a veritable kick in the teeth, Russia, until that moment, an ally by virtue of the old maxim than "my enemy's enemy is my friend", although always of questionable reliability, Stalin known to be an arch schemer never to be fully trusted, signed a non-aggression pact with Germany, respective foreign ministers, Molotov and Ribbentrop appearing in newspapers and newsreels, their expressions, as they shook hands, giving away little other than, perhaps, a mutual suspicion, pragmatism having trumped the fact that the regimes they represented were, on the face of it, polar opposites, the Communist and the Fascist, although in truth, it was a play by two equally dangerous dictators.

The implication, instantly recognised, was that having effectively neutralised any threat in the East, Hitler would be able to focus his attention, and when necessary, his forces, on the West.

Peggy, in the common room of the nurse's home, listened to the news with the same feeling of betrayal.

"That's it then," Brewster said, serious for once. "Them bloody Bolshies. Can't trust them as far as you can throw them.

Peggy hurried to her room, wishing Stanley had been there to talk to, but having to make do with putting her thoughts on paper.

*Darling*
*The news looks pretty grim doesn't it? We are all prepared really. When the reality of it*

*does come near to you it is dreadful isn't it? We were thinking that all the people who had been cured here would probably be being shot at & wounded & return much 'iller' than they were before & others fit & well would be brought to just as bad condition. It is pretty ghastly isn't it?*
*I will write again possibly before Monday. Some things in the world – the best things are still OK so keep cheerful.*
*My love to you darling*
*Peggy*

For the next few days, whilst events in Europe were moving rapidly towards the point of no return, time seemed in suspense, as if the nation – the world – was holding its breath.

With Stanley having finished his exams, and Peggy having a few days off, his parents took them for a short, three day holiday, to Bexhill, leaving the young couple very much to their own devices.

They would remember it as a rather curious time, their love now in full bloom, but infused with a desperation, knowing only that what lay ahead was impossible to discern beyond the inevitability of parting and pain.

On the last day of August, it was announced that Parliament was about to order the introduction of conscription.

The same day, Bart's Hospital began moving the majority of its patients and nurses out of London, most to Hill End Hospital in St Albans, others to the nearby Cell Barnes Hospital. The move continued for the next three days, the nurses helping patients onto the convoys of vehicles, ambulances and coaches, transporting them from London, many of them confused by the sudden upheaval, the convoy including several lorries filled with hospital equipment.

At the end of the first day of the move, despite her exhaustion, having been unable to sleep when, at the Ward Sister's insistence, she had had a break for a couple of hours, she had wanted to telephone Stanley, feeling the need to speak to him, but not knowing where he was, she sat down to write to him.

*Darling*
*I have heard the news tonight & according to that it seems that you must have been called up. In case I don't hear from you or see you tomorrow I thought I must write.*
*It seems we shall have to part for a while in service of our country – hoping it won't be for long.*

*I hope you don't feel too lost tonight, darling. I can sympathise fully with your feelings this morning after having spent a sleepless half day thinking very much of you. It was dreadfully depressing getting up, but I feel much more cheerful now. The people on this ward are grand & only 12 patients, all going tomorrow.*

*The night seems to have gone quite quickly although being high up on the third floor, I have seen a lot of this wonderful night above the roofs of the square.*

*The dawn is just breaking now in a lightening blue sky, the moon & stars are fading in this first day of September. I hope & pray it won't bring with it a war for the world.*

*Peggy*

The following day, as she returned from the postbox, enjoying the early morning stroll before breakfast, intent then of trying to get a few hours sleep, never having been able to adjust to daytime sleeping, tending to wake after three or four hours, taking a nap in the afternoon, the radio was on in the crowded dining room. As she entered the room, her impression was of everyone having frozen, as if in a photograph, such was the absolute silence, apart from the voice of the news reader.

*Germany has invaded Poland and has bombed many towns.*

After the headlines, the clatter of cutlery resumed, a few hushed voices exchanging comments as the news continued, informing them that Parliament was being recalled for later that day and that the King had ordered a general mobilisation of the armed forces.

Peggy stared at the radio, the implication of the term "general mobilisation" instantly clear, her assumption, the previous day, that Stanley would now be called up, beyond any doubt.

She turned to Sally, across the table, as her friend reached out and took her hand, the two of them looking at each other, as if needing to find some mutual comfort in their friendship, and in their realisation that what they were hearing was personal to them, Sally's fiancé, David, like Stanley, having joined the TA some months earlier.

Peggy had little appetite, forcing herself to eat her egg and toast, and despite her gratitude for Sally's gesture, wanting only to be alone with her thoughts. She found a bench in the hospital yard, sitting in the sun for half an hour before returning to the bedroom, lying down in a vain attempt to sleep, eventually drifting off for a few hours, sleep fractured with images of planes and injured soldiers.

For the first time that night, the blackout came into force, and although they been instructed how to fit the window boards, where for some reason a window could not be covered, they were required to fit special bulbs which had been issued which gave off a dim, blue light.

Fortunately, with many of the wards now empty and in darkness, the impact of the blackout was less than would otherwise have been the case.

On the morning of 2nd September, it being her day off, she had arranged to meet Stanley in London, their rendezvous this time for some reason which Stanley hadn't explained, in Euston Square, his voice, on the telephone the evening before, sounding strained.

The previous afternoon, having heard then news of the German invasion of Poland, with the permission of the partner who was his principal, he left the office early, they both realising that his articles were about to be curtailed. He had only been back in the office for a few days since he completed his exams, and, if he passed, would be into the last phase of his articles.

"I've been lent a flat," he told her when they met. "I thought it would be best if we could be by ourselves today. As we might not be seeing each other for a while."

For a moment she had looked at him, his awkwardness unlike him.

"A chap from the firm's London office lives there, but he's just going off to the Navy, and he said, well, I could borrow it if I wanted a place to stay."

"A place to stay?" she repeated. "I've got to get up to St Albans this evening."

The flat was in a narrow road, not far from Oxford Street. He led her up three flights of stairs, the décor of the hallway and landings stained, the wallpaper peeling. The flat itself, though small, was in slightly better condition than the rest of the building, the living room window facing the street, the morning sunlight streaming in, illuminating the anonymous furniture and worn carpet.

Peggy having poured them coffee from the flask she had brought with her, finding cups in the narrow kitchen, they sat on the sofa, conversation stilted, both of them acutely aware of the tension.

"It'll probably be tomorrow," he said. "War. There's no turning back now they've invaded Poland."

He turned towards her, tears rolling down her cheeks, putting his arm around her, pulling him towards him, her head resting on his shoulder.

"We could go to a flick this afternoon," he said, trying, unsuccessfully, to sound light hearted. "They'll probably close them all down soon," he added, not realising that his flippancy anticipated the imminent reality.

She looked up at him, managing a weak smile. The kiss was gentle, tentative at first, but quickly becoming more urgent, their arms around each other.

Without saying anything, he stood up, pulling her by the hand towards the flat's only bedroom. At the door, he felt her resist, holding back before relenting, lying down beside him.

"We may not see each other again," he said, his voice thick. "For some time."

Their faces a few inches apart, she looked at him, aware of what his was suggesting.

"We don't know what will happen. If we'll ever…" He allowed the unspoken thought to tail away.

She kissed him again, her body pressing into his, his hand stroking her back, venturing downward, grasping her buttock, pulling her towards him, the hardness in his trousers, pushing against her, only the fabric of their clothing separating it from her – from where she suddenly, desperately wanted to feel it.

She began to stroke his side, her fingers digging into his flesh, working cautiously down to his hip, causing him to emit a slight grunt as her finger tips squeezed between them, gently massaging his hip bone.

"It's alright," he whispered, feeling her withdrawing her hand, returning it to the back of his shoulders. "We might never get another chance."

"I love you," she said, pulling her face away from his again. "Very much, darling. But we mustn't. We must wait."

"There may not be another time." His face had become flushed and she could see the exasperation in his expression. "I may be sent off to fight any day."

"I know. I want to. But I can't. It's against everything I believe in. And everything I want."

He knew her well enough by now to realise that argument would be pointless. For the rest of the morning, they lay together, embraced, kissing, whispering their eternal love for each other, but with the tension now removed.

They helped themselves to some Sherry, finding the bottle in a kitchen cupboard, the liquor lifting their mood for a short while.

When the time came for them to leave, they lingered inside the flat door, reluctant to open it, knowing that once they were outside, they would be stepping into a world fraught with anxiety and uncertainty.

Determined as she was, to be strong, as they paused on the pavement, before going their separate ways, his face such a picture of dejection, feeling her eyes pricking, she kissed him, quickly turning away, hurrying to the end of the road, glancing back as she came to Oxford Street, seeing him still standing where she had left him, giving him a hasty wave before crossing the road towards the bus stop.

The next morning, her emotions feeling a little less turbulent, Brewster called her to come down to the common room to listen to Chamberlain's broadcast. She joined the group of her fellow trainees, one of them twiddling the knob on the radio, finding the Home Service.

"This is London." The announcer's voice seemed vested with even greater solemnity than usual. "You will now hear a statement by the Prime Minister."

She always felt there was something insubstantial about Chamberlain's voice, which, even at such a grave moment, sounded wooden, the intoning lacking any expressiveness.

"I am speaking to you from the Cabinet Room at 10 Downing Street. This morning, the British ambassador in Berlin handed the German government a final note, stating that unless we heard from them by eleven o'clock, that they were prepared, at once, to withdraw their troops from Poland, a state of war would exist between us."

She caught Sally's eye, Sally giving a sort of half smile, half grimace.

"I have to tell you now, that no such undertaking has been received and that consequently, this country is at war with Germany."

Back in her room, she stared out of the window, the pavement wet, the sky leaden grey, her mind numb, her one thought being that she wanted Stanley to be with her. During wakeful spells in the night, she had been filled with regret that she had not agreed to their making love. But there was something, deeply embedded in her, an obdurate propriety, which she knew she could not overcome.

*My Darling*

*War – at last, darling. Isn't it ghastly. We all heard Chamberlain this morning sitting in our common room with a sinking feeling in our hearts & grim awe at this thing we had heard such dreadful things about but never experienced, thinking of those lads so very dear to us, not knowing where they might be. Darling, I am just longing to hear from you to know where you are. It is worse this war now that it has really come (not that we have experienced much yet, but just the dread feeling) than I ever thought it would be. The grim silence after the Premier's speech, even though we expected what he said, from people who would usually make quite a lot of noise was enough.*

*The bombers that have been flying overhead make one realise it & our preparations that have been going on all day.*

*I love you so very much so look after yourself for this little girl's sake, my darling little (?) soldier.*

*With all my love*

*Peggy*

# FOUR

*4.9.39*
*Good Shepherd Vicarage, Brighton*
*My dear Stanley*
*Well now we know where England really stands – firm against the cruel and beastly tyranny of Nazism. In my soul I have loathed even knowing about the regime.*
*I am truly sorry your career is so interrupted but have faith and courage and pray God the clouds will roll by in due time & the sun of peace shine again. The scenes outside here are truly memorable today but outwardly it looks like a picnic with all the helpers basking in sunshine on the Hall lawn.*
*Keep us informed of your movements so far as you are allowed for we shall have our minds fixed on your welfare above all else. "Flee from evil and do the thing that is right".*
*Michael seems supremely calm & collected about it all & in many ways has been very useful – phone messages etc & taking his radio in the Hall for them to hear the news.*
*Some silly ass sounded a raid signal at 11.20.*
*God bless and keep you safe.*
*Love from Dad*

Stanley sat on his bed in a dormitory of some 20 cadets, the last of the evening sunlight slanting through the high windows, offering a glimmer of illumination in the dim, featureless room, the cadets, some sitting, like him, reading the post which had only just been distributed, others lounging or milling around, a few chatting, all awaiting the order to put up the blackout panels.

After two days of what felt like mainly hanging around, queuing for registering, the issuing of kit, and for food, he had at least got started on the instruction for his designated role, as a driver, having spent the afternoon with a group of other cadet drivers being introduced to an army lorry, a conducted tour of its engine followed by their taking turns at driving it around a small circuit within the confines of the barracks, their first venture onto the roads of London due for the following morning.

Reading his father's letter stirred up the emotions which, since his parting from Peggy, he had been trying to contain, the activity, until that moment, keeping him occupied.

As he had eventually turned and walked away from her, having stood for several minutes after she had disappeared around the corner of the street, he came as close to tears as he had ever done, since childhood. Having become used to parting from her over the past year, partings having become so much a part of their courtship, this time it was different, the sadness so raw, the new element, of fear, overlaying the usual dejection.

His father, as one would expect from someone whose business was preaching and of giving counsel and comfort, had a way with words, his letters, infrequent though they were, always touching a particular soft spot in his eldest son, infused as they were with something almost poetic. Always, also, the paternal was combined with something wider; an allusion to God's purpose and man's place in His domain, the effect on Stanley being to reinforce his own faith which, whilst resting on a solid foundation, was nevertheless, less than resolute in its practice.

With his easy manner and readiness to chat to people, Stanley never found it difficult to make friends, something which, over the years ahead would prove testing when, as was an inevitable part of the life of an army at war, friends were compelled to go in different directions. He was also to learn, much later, the bitter experience of friends being killed and wounded.

After those first few days, life settled into a routine, driving now being more purposeful as their initial convoy practice became real, their missions taking them initially around London, and then further afield, often out into Kent and Essex, mainly ferrying supplies and equipment, and occasionally men.

The highlights were his meetings with Peggy, usually brief, having to fit in with their respective duty times, and her letters which arrived every two or three days, making him feel guilty at his less frequent writing, excused by the long hours of work and the resulting weariness, an excuse which, in her kindly way, she would scoff at, his work, if anything, a good deal less arduous than hers.

At the end of the initial four weeks training, cadets were "embodied", thus becoming part of the rapidly expanding army.

There was much talk about where they were likely to be going, the assumption being that they would probably be heading across the Channel for the impending confrontation with the Germans, the first contingent of British troops, designated the British Expeditionary Force, having already been deployed, joining the French army to protect their borders, the French having surprised everyone by immediately going on the offensive and advancing into the German territory of Saar, meeting negligible resistance, and halting their advance after just a few miles.

What characterised those early months of the war, however, was the absence of any significant military action in Europe, the period later becoming known as the "Phoney War". It was as if having declared war on each other, the protagonists were having second thoughts, although nobody seriously believed that it was going to end before it had really begun.

With the lack of any engagement between opposing armies, the few other incidents which did take place made the headlines, reminders that the country was indeed at war.

Barely two weeks after the outbreak of the war, there was the first devastating news; the aircraft carrier, HMS Courageous, being torpedoed and sunk by a U-Boat, with the loss of over 500 men. A month later, a U-Boat penetrated the Royal Navy base at Scapa Flow, sinking the battleship, HMS Royal Oak, with loss of 835 men. Over the years ahead, whilst never becoming inured to bad news, it became something one learned to bear; the harsh reality of war.

It was not until mid December that these first grievous losses were avenged, when the German "pocket" battleship, Admiral Graf Spee, was engaged in the South Atlantic by a group of Allied cruisers, each far inferior to the German ship, but mustering sufficient fire power between them to inflict substantial damage, the battleship retreating into Montevideo harbour for emergency repairs. When it emerged the next day, its stay in port being limited due to Uruguay's neutral status, believing it was about to encounter a larger enemy force, the Admiral Graf Spee's captain took the decision to scuttle his ship, the Allied crews watching in disbelief, and with immense relief, as a series of explosions were heard from the German ship, which quickly capsized and sank.

For Stanley, the routines of army life quickly became known, the hardships, in terms of regimented hours, lack of privacy, hard beds and the heavy hand of discipline, being offset by his having taken readily to the world of soldiering. No longer did he have to worry about exams or to wrestle with the vexed issues of probate and equity, the business of military transport, and even the square bashing and physical training, being quite acceptable, and at times, particularly when he was part of a convoy ranging around the region, positively enjoyable.

Always, however, there was Peggy, filling his mind with love, and with nagging anxiety. The fact that she had declared herself his seemed to anchor him, secure in the knowledge that, patient as he knew he had to be, she was the one with whom he was going to spend his life. The anxiety, however, stemmed, in part, from something within him, perhaps a facet of a spoilt childhood, too readily having his own way. And here was the thing he wanted more than anything before in his life, and he had to wait. Patience was not his greatest virtue.

Part of his unease was also the knowledge that she was mixing with so many other people – young men, including hospital doctors whose notoriety, in his mind, stemmed mainly from the tales Peggy had recounted to him, largely recycled versions of Brewster's accounts, with certain of the more salacious elements edited out.

At times, particularly during the nights, he would awake almost in a panic, convinced that she was playing around with other men, terrified that she would come across one who would carry her off, the absence of his own ring on her finger meaning that she was still free to do what she chose; to be with whoever she chose.

It was her letters which, to a large extent, served to allay his fears. Although he did not see it in such terms, there was a cycle to his volatile emotions, the low points – those sweating spells of insomnolent worry – assuaged by a letter, and then, the high points, his meetings with her, when almost all residue of uncertainty was swept away, until the next trough crept up on him.

By another stroke of luck, it transpired that one of his fellow cadets, Hunter, who came from a well-healed family, had his own flat in Hampstead which his father had bought for him before the war, Hunter having joined his father's stock-broking business.

"You're very welcome to use it," he offered one evening when they were discussing their respective girlfriends, "if you and Peggy want to…you know… have a bit of hanky-panky". It proved to be considerably larger and better appointed than the flat off Oxford Street.

Having promised to respect Peggy's insistence on "waiting till we're married", secretly hoping, nevertheless, that she might soon relent and recognise that "everything is different now", being the basis of his argument that they should no longer be expected to adhere to the morality instilled into them by their upbringing, the flat became their meeting place, other than when they had time and reason – a play or film – to go into town.

When, in a brief telephone call, she had not only told him that she had "24 hours" the following week, which coincided with his off duty day, but suggested that they spend the night at the flat which he had, very cautiously mentioned to her he was able to borrow, the intervening days passed in a mist of almost unbearable anticipation.

"You will be good, though, won't you," she had added, his assurance being far more resolute than his lingering hope that she would change her mind.

When they met, as arranged, at Hampstead tube station, he immediately sensed her apprehension, her manner rather stiff. As they walked the short distance to the flat, which he had been to an hour earlier, to make sure that it was suitably tidy, and also, he decided, having passed a florist near the station, to put a bunch of flowers on the kitchen table, it was as if she was holding back, walking deliberately slowly.

"I've got a bottle of sherry," he told her, looking pointedly at his watch to indicate that "the sun was over the yard arm", as she was having a quick inspection of the flat.

A large glass of sherry seemed to do the trick, as she became more relaxed, suddenly giggling like a naughty school girl.

"What would Mummy and Daddy say? If they knew we were spending the night together?" She shivered at the thought.

"I'd probably be cast out and forbidden from ever seeing you again," he said, similarly alarmed at the notion of their finding out. "But they'll never know!"

Having bought fish and chips for their supper, and with the bottle of sherry left empty on the kitchen table, they spent their first night together, Stanley in a state of considerable agitation, arms entwined, bodies pressed together, blood pumping through his unsatiated veins. Several times during the night he awoke from his fraught sleep, unsure whether he was awake or still immersed in a sexually charged dream, conscious only of the thinnest veil of fabric – his pyjamas and her cotton nightie – between his painfully persistent erection and the wonders of her body.

With the first light of dawn, he awoke again to find her face close to his, her eyes open, a loving smile greeting him.

"Thank you," she whispered, kissing him. "For being good," she added, his expression momentarily confused.

Needing to be back at the barracks by eight, having tried, unsuccessfully, to get out of bed without waking her, she reached her arm out to him, summoning him for a bleary kiss, leaving her as she curled back to sleep, he sat on the tube feeling light-headed from the lack of sleep and the exhilaration of having spent the night with her, the fact that they had not made love, subsumed by his conviction that their relationship had moved to a different level, the tendrils of insecurity, whilst still prone to resurface from time to time, lessened. Indeed, in the darkness of the tube tunnel, seeing his rather smug smile of satisfaction reflecting in the glass, he contrived his best poker face as he made his way up the steps and out into the London morning.

Towards the end of October, Stanley and his fellow cadets, having completed their initial period of training, were told where they were being sent. There had been much speculation, in particular, as to whether they would be going "abroad", to join the British Expeditionary Force in France, although they were also aware of some deployments further afield, to parts of Africa and the Far East.

When Stanley received his orders, that he was to report to a unit in Kent, and that he had been assigned to the Royal Army Service Corps - RASC, the part of the army which worked behind the front line, supplying almost everything the fighting troops required including food, ammunition and fuel - he felt disappointed, although having started his military life as a driver, it did not come as a total surprise that he was not going to be a front line soldier.

When he told Peggy, having expressed a modicum of sympathy as his disappointment, she was palpably relieved that he would be facing less danger. "I want you to be as safe as possible," she said. "We've got the rest of our lives to think of."

Thus it was that Stanley found himself billeted in an outhouse of a stately home, Calehill Park, close to the Kent village of Little Chart, not far from Ashford. It soon became clear that Kent was, to a large extent, being taken over by the army, the troops assuming this to be because of the county's proximity to France, the most obvious staging post for getting across the Channel, although they were to learn later that it was also selected as the most effective training area due to the similarity of the terrain to the parts of France which, one day, the Allies would have to fight their way through, the notorious *bocage*, a battleground which would see some of the bloodiest fighting of the war.

He was to learn also a harsh fact of army life that friendships tended to be transitional, the endless cycles of reorganisation and redeployment requiring men to change units and locations, his first such experience being his separation from his two pals, Cheesman and Hunter, although within his first few days at Calehill he had made a handful of new friends, one in particular, Harris, a thin, wiry chap of about his own height, his reserved manner disguising an acerbic wit, becoming a good pal over the ensuing months, he and Stanley sharing a love of dance band music as well as enjoying a pint of beer.

Although Stanley did not realise it at first, notwithstanding the number of wireless sets amongst the men, and the availability of newspapers, life in the army was a world apart, even the regular visits to the local pubs, invariably being in their own company, giving them only limited contact with local civilians. Whilst they all followed what was happening from the military point of view, it tended to be when he was with Peggy, and from her letters, that he picked up more about the impact of the war generally. Indeed, although there had been a good deal of mention on the BBC news of children being evacuated from London and other cities, when Peggy referred to children from Brighton being included, it brought the reality home to him.

His letters to her reflected his immersion in his new world of the military.

1.11.39
*A Section 514 Coy RASC, Calehill Park, Little Chart, Nr Ashford, Kent*
*My sweetheart darling*
*First of all my very hearty congratulations again on passing your exam. I think it probably pleased me as much as you!*
*Quite a lot has happened since I last wrote. We have been busy all the time. Yesterday we went to London in convoy. We left here at 12 & got to Olympia at 3. We were escorted through London (12 lorries) by the London police and it was great fun to go past all the lights etc without having to stop. We had to sleep on the grass last night as our lorries were full but it wasn't bad except for the beetles & things.*
*Today has been quite exciting, as we have at last had our final interviews and have reached the top rung in the ladder to OCTO (Officer Cadet Training Officer).*
*Goodnight my darling.*
*Yours ever*
*Stanley*

With the onset of winter, Stanley discovered that although Kent was the neighbouring county to his beloved Sussex, its climate was noticeably different, particularly when the wind was in the east, gusting relentlessly, laden with bitter air drawn from Siberia, dampened in transit by the chill waters of the North Sea.

With regular drills and exercises, the hard-hearted senior officers paying no heed to the conditions, the less than luxurious billets proved to be veritable sanctuaries, surpassed only by the cosiness of the pubs, and, when they could get into Ashford, the warmth of the cinema.

There were times when the men became bored, although fatigue, rigid discipline and just sufficient distractions prevented them from becoming unduly restless.

And always there were rumours about where they might be going. Still the war had failed to really get going, mutterings of frustration that they were being denied the chance "to get at them" adding to the undercurrent of grumbling. There was a sense, however, that this tense stand-off could not last, particularly with the news that Germany was threatening Belgium and Holland.

As if to stir things up even more, Russia, that most untrustworthy and turncoat of nations, invaded and annexed Finland, a move which put Norway and Sweden in jeopardy, Germany fearing that the British might occupy the remainder of Scandinavia to prevent it from falling into German hands, Sweden opting to keep out of danger by declaring neutrality.

*6.11.39*
*Hill End, St Albans*
*Darling*
*I have been thinking of you on guard tonight. It is such a wonderful night that I think I would rather be outside.*
*I should think by the news that you will probably be moved soon. Do you think it will make any difference to you? It really proves the Germans have some spirit doesn't it? But it is also pretty grim that Holland & Belgium are threatened. They haven't had a very peaceful existence during the last half century. Even Switzerland is preparing I think & it will soon be world war.*
*Goodbye for the present sweetheart.*
*Keep smiling*
*My fondest love*
*Peggy*

On a bitingly cold late December afternoon, Peggy and Stanley emerged from the grand Leicester Square Theatre, Peggy clutching his arm as they walked quickly across the square, making their way to the Corner House in Shaftesbury Avenue, having allowed themselves an hour for tea and a bun before going their separate ways.

In silence they walked, heads down into the wind as it whipped along the street, both feeling emotionally drained from the epic *Gone With The Wind*, Stanley's only comment, as they left the cinema, being "Blimey! That was quite something"!

As they drank their tea, they began to recount various of the film's scenes, stunned by the spectacle of the sweep of American history and the heart-wringing tragedy of the story, brought so vividly to life by the brilliance of the cast. Indeed, as they became more animated in their recollections, they laughingly disagreed about the best performance, Peggy having no doubt that Clark Gable had stolen the show, Stanley, like much of the male population, most of which, within the next few months would have seen the film, quite besotted by the gorgeous Vivien Leigh.

When they said their farewell, holding onto each other on the street corner, oblivious of the passers-by stepping past them, their heightened emotions seemed to vest their parting with even greater sadness than usual, Peggy unable to prevent the tears from running down her cheeks, reaching for her handkerchief, still damp from copious use during the film.

With the dawning of 1940, little changed with the "Phoney War", the British Expeditionary Force still arrayed with the French along their eastern frontier, facing the impending threat of attack from the formidable German army, expecting that, with the end of winter, the months of inactivity must come to an end, yet secretly hoping that some accommodation might be arrived at without the need to resume the carnage which, they now knew, 1918 had merely suspended. In reality, however, it was generally accepted that as Hitler had repeatedly demonstrated, his troops progressively swallowing adjoining territory, the days of persuasion were past, meeting force with force being the only thing he would understand.

As training continued, much to Stanley's delight, for several weeks, he was required to attend a special vehicle training course in Eastbourne, back in Sussex and, more importantly, within easy reach of Brighton. For several weeks, he and Peggy worked their arrangements so that they could both be home at the same time, although when it came to it, allowing for travelling time and the dictates of duty, their time together tended to be limited to a day or occasionally two.

Peggy had learned to gauge his moods, knowing almost instantly, whether she was getting the jovial, chatty, enthusiastic version, or the doleful, "poor me" one, the variations seeming to alternate. With the former, she would allow him to recount the goings on in his army world, the conversation flowing freely, with only limited contribution from her. The art she had acquired, however, was to deal with the bouts of gloom, sometimes punctuated with bursts of anger, at the stupidity of those in authority, or the pointlessness of endless square bashing and physical training. She would listen, responding with soothing words, at moments, having a gently dig at him for his self-pity, comparing his lot with her own.

Invariably, the gloomy calls would be followed by a bright one, as if he had picked himself up, his opening being his apology at being "such a misery".

She knew also, that pervading their conversations, both over the phone and when they were together, the subject of their getting engaged was becoming an issue with him, her attempts to side step it, or to respond with an assurance which would give him the comfort of knowing that she was his for life, whilst avoiding committing until the time was right, increasingly met with an insistence which, if she did not love him as she did, his moods and at times rather demanding nature being part of him, she would have seen as rather petulant.

"You know why I can't get married," she would say, restating what, to her, was so obvious. "Nurses can't be married."

His response was, on the face of it, entirely logical. "We don't need to name the day. We can have a long engagement. Long enough for you to become fully qualified."

For this was her ambition, to see it through; to become a proper nurse, even if she had then to curtail her career to become a wife and mother.

The fact that Paddy and Alan had become engaged, only served to fuel his determination.

"We could make it a double celebration," he suggested. "We could get engaged at the same time."

"You know why not," she replied, hearing her own sigh, the repeating of the same argument becoming rather wearing. She had little doubt that if she relented, and they became engaged, he would then turn his pressurising to the naming of the day.

They both knew also, that other factors came into play, quite apart from her aspiration, to become a qualified nurse. He had made no secret of the fact that he would prefer her to be back at home, as his wife, waiting for him, possibly doing some suitable part time work locally. After all, there was plenty of call for people with medical knowledge, even if they were not fully qualified.

The predominant obstacle, however, which they were both only too aware of – and which she was able to cite to support her stance – was her father's consent, which, even though not yet sought, would certainly not be given until he was in a position to provide for her.

It was abundantly clear to him also, that it was not simply a matter of money, it being as much to do with status. A lowly soldier serving in the ranks as a driver, would never be deemed suitable for the daughter of Arthur Wing, middle class professional gentleman of unshakeably rigid views.

For Stanley also, there was a nagging feeling that Peggy's parents did not really approve of him. When he was with them, he was always on his very best behaviour, avoiding frivolity – her father having an often aired his low opinion of popular music, his taste for which Stanley had, on an earlier occasion, rashly acknowledged – their demeanour towards him, however, always being courteous. He sensed that had it not been for the fact that he was the son of the vicar for whom they had a great deal of respect - albeit with some minor concerns, only mentioned in the confines of their home, as to what they discerned as a hint of liberalism, and a tendency to dilatoriness manifest by his lack of attention to detail in matters such as reading minutes to Parish Council meetings which Arthur would always study assiduously - his prospects of winning their daughter's hand would have been greatly diminished.

"I fear it may be a family trait," Arthur remarked one evening to his wife, as they were sitting by the fireside, the meagreness of the fire due to Arthur's parsimony and his belief in the virtue of frugality in all things. Even in the depths of winter, they would counter the chill of the house by "rugging up warm".

She had come to notice how often he had colds. Everyone had their fair share, particularly in winter, but he seemed to have one every few weeks, preceded by a sore throat and an almost flu-like day or two of fever.

It would be two years later that his health issues escalated, threatening his life.

With the proximity of Eastbourne, it was also easy for her to visit him when she was home and he was able only to get a few hours off, their favourite pastime being to catch the bus to Beachy Head and to walk along the cliffs, the English Channel spread before them, Stanley's added pleasure being the vantage point to spot the ships passing up and down the Channel, identifying the occasional battleship, usually screened by a bevy of smaller ships, destroyers and corvettes.

"We are a little disappointed that, when you are home, you spend so little time with us," her mother complained as Peggy was about to set off for the station to catch the train to Eastbourne, having arrived from St Albans only an hour earlier, similar complaints having been simmering for some while although, until now, not overtly expressed. "Your father and I would like to enjoy your company, just occasionally. I know you are wanting to see your friends, but do think of us as well."

Peggy had stood in the hall with her coat on, conscious of the time, knowing that she had to walk down to Preston Park station to get to Brighton to make the connection for Eastbourne.

"I promise to be back in good time," she replied, determined to spend an evening with them.

"And I know you always want to be with Stanley," her mother added as a parting dig, Peggy picking up the trace of derogatory emphasis of the name.

They had lain on the grass near the cliff edge, the red and white striped Beachy Head lighthouse far below them, the afternoon sun pleasantly warm with a soft breeze wafting up the cliff face.

"I wish we could stay here forever," he said, his voice taking on the hoarse tone which, as she had come to recognise, indicated impending seriousness. At some point during most of their meetings, he needed to have his solemn moment, expressing his love for her in terms which, she sometimes felt, he always wanted to be new and fresh, his words tending to become muddled. It was as if he could never quite get hold of what it was he really wanted to say, or rather, how he wanted to say it, yet the substance ever the same. She would respond with the reassurance she realised he needed, restated each time, sustaining him through their periods of separation, mitigating his underlying insecurity which drove his yearning for them to be married.

Why was it that when he was with her he could never quite get to the point of saying what he was wanting to say, either because something was holding him back or what actually came out was more convoluted than he had meant. In his letters, however, he would sometimes be more overt in expressing his doubts, even going as far as questioning her motives for choosing to take up nursing, his questioning revealing the depth of his anxiety.

18.3.40
*Good Shepherd Vicarage, 172 Dyke Road, Brighton*
*My beloved darling*
*I am home for the evening but I am longing very much for you and am remembering that 24 hours ago we were together. Darling, I think I can explain what I was saying yesterday better than I did then. You see, darling, the flame of love is always burning but when we are away it is as if it has to be turned down a bit although it always burns. But when we meet it gradually flares up & by the end of last evening it was a bright as ever & darling I was very happy when we parted.*
*Darling I've got some good news – I am now getting proficiency pay – 17/6 a week – so as from March 3ʳᵈ I get some back pay. A step nearer that happy ending – or rather, beginning maybe.*
*As I'm not a fatalist, I won't say like some people that I <u>know</u> that I won't be bumped off, but I'll say this – that I feel, somewhere deep in my heart, that God has ordained that we shall be happy together for all time. Oh God please make this true.*
*Till my next letter darling. Goodbye. I return many loving kisses: the memory of your sweet soft lips is always with me, & when I send you kisses by post, I live all over again those moments so divine when your lips touch mine. (poetry not intended!).*
*Yours with a heartful of love.*
*Stanley*

Not having had a letter back from her, his one phone call to her being brief and unsatisfactory, she telling him that she only had a few moments as she was about to be on duty, anxiety returned, taking hold of him, compelling him to write again. As he wrote, notwithstanding his desire to censure her for the absence of a reply, he resolved to appear light-hearted.

1.4.40
*Compton Court, Dittons Road, Eastbourne*
*My own darling*
*I'm in great need of your soothing company, smiles & kisses.*
*Please write soon, darling & tell me you love me. Just to read it is so marvellously cheering in these days when events are too swift for the liking of any of us.*
*Harry Lauder is on and is lousy – all flat in 'Rocket in the Cradle'.*
*Story:- A young doctor was visiting the ward of a maternity hospital and went up to one of the beds & asked the occupant when she was expecting her baby. "June 10ᵗʰ" was the*

*reply. He went to the next bed and got the same answer. Seeing that the occupant of the next bed was asleep he asked the second expectant mother when this third woman was expecting hers. "I don't know" was the answer. "You see, doctor, she wasn't at the picnic". "That's not very funny" I can see you saying!*

*I expect by the time I see you again I shall be half immune from typhoid as I've had the first jabs.*

*Harry Lauder is ending up well though telling us "To keep right on to the end of the road". "Though you yearn for the best things you love…". How very true of you my sweetheart darling.*

*Darling, <u>please</u> marry me at the earliest moment that our present jobs are done & I have the means to support you. I know your answer is that you will but I just have to repeat how this burns inside me.*

*I'll bid you a very very loving goodnight – my kisses be with you.*

*Yours till death us do part, & ever after that.*

*Stanley*

She allowed herself a sigh as she folded the letter, placing it in the drawer with all his previous letters, all but the last few in bundles neatly tied up with string. She had hoped that, after their last conversation, when she had been rather more forceful than was her habit, in trying to get the message across to him that although she had set her heart on marrying him, she was more determined than ever to become a fully qualified nurse, her determination now even greater with the new sense of duty.

"There's not a lot that we girls can do," she had said. "It's easy for you chaps, because you join up and are able to fight for King and country. But I want to do my bit as well."

"You will be doing more than "your bit" by providing a home and, I hope, a family, for this particular soldier," he had responded, doggedly trotting out one of his stock arguments, although, he realised, not one of his stronger ones.

"That's a bit unfair," she said, coming perilously close to a show of anger, something which, she liked to think, was not part of her nature, her firm belief being that disagreements were seldom resolved by ill temper.

What vexed her also, was her own equivocation. She loved the idea of being engaged – and of being married. She truly wanted to spend her life with him, the prospect of waiting, possibly for a few years, difficult to come to terms with now that she was certain that he was the one for her. What was even more difficult for her to acknowledge, was that there was a part of her that longed to be back home; to give up nursing; to admit it had been a means of getting away. But then she would pull herself together, draw breath, and reassert her conviction, that she was doing the right thing for herself and her country.

Why then, when she put pen to paper, did she allow herself to accede to his plea? How muddled she sometime felt, her resolution when she started writing, wilting the following morning when she longed for his company and to feel his long arms around her.

*Darling heart*
*Don't you realize when all circumstances permit I will marry you – but hope that it may be peace time if possible. At any rate & for all time my heart is yours darling, so please don't be miserable.*
*Darling it would be rather grand to be engaged wouldn't it? Then we could start collecting things for the little house we hope to have one day couldn't we – at least we could save some cash.*
*May God bless you and keep you.*
*Peggy*

But any hope she might have harboured that forthrightness, together with what she deemed her provisional agreement to become engaged, would persuade him to allow the subject to rest, at least for the time being, proved vain when, just a few days later, she received his next letter, written when he had a couple of days leave and, clearly, too much time to ruminate.

*My darling dearest Peggy*
*I was so happy to receive so sweet a letter this morning. It would be marvellous and so lovely to be 'officially' engaged. I personally, would like to tell the world as soon as I could that I had won the love of the loveliest & dearest girl in the world. Why keep such a happy thing secret in a world full of sadness?*
*This morning we had a very funny lecture by Peter Candler on first aid on the field of V.D. We learnt amongst other things that Henry VIII had ulcers on his legs caused through syphilis – and lots of other things! In the end he gave us all a 'packet' – much to the amusement of all – and told us we should all get 'crabs' before the end of the war – this is only lice really & he said Brasso killed them or else you set yourself on fire. He is a grand lad. His drawing was appalling though.*
*Getting engaged would be certainly a beginning of – on your part collecting 'things' and on my part of saving cash – at least it would be some incentive to try & save cash!*
*Yours forever*
*Stanley*

Was she engaged? She knew that until there was a ring on her finger, it could not be "official", and yet they had now made the commitment to each other. His proposal, rather than a bending of his knee before her, a lengthy campaign, had finally secured her willing surrender. No, it needed both the ring and the declaration to the rest of the world.

"Don't count your chickens, Peg, until you've got his ring on your finger," Brewster said rather ruefully, having admitted to at least three engagements, two of which had actually included the ceremonial sliding of ring onto finger only for it to be removed, unceremoniously, a short time later. "You can't trust them even then. Best to get him up the aisle as soon as possible."

"What about this?" Sally has asked, saddened at the thought of losing her close friend, gesturing with a wafting of her arms in the air to indicate the nurses home, and the hospital. "You've always said that you would finish before getting married."

Peggy felt unable to answer, setting off on the short walk to the hospital for the start of her night duty, her mind, as so often in recent weeks, in a whirl of uncertainty. Once she was in the ward, however, busying with the multitude of tasks, getting the patients settled, she felt calmer and indeed, with the peace which she often found during the night hours, when the patients were asleep, a deep contentment.

As many had anticipated, with the arrival of spring, any remaining tendrils of hope that somehow, all out war might still be prevented, were finally dissipated when Germany invaded Denmark and Norway.

Within the army, there was a new sense of purpose, and, amongst the men in the ranks, of concern as to what was going to be their role. The general assumption was still that they would soon be sent to France, everyone expecting Germany to attack the allies in the West at any moment.

Within the hospital, also, although information was scarce, rumour was rife, that all hospitals were being told to be ready to receive casualties, army medical officers being seen to arrive, closeted for discussions with the hospital senior staff, and on one occasion, a small convoy of army ambulances arriving at Hill End, this, they were told, being part of a training exercise.

Peggy watched from one of the ward windows as the ambulances departed, the red crosses on white roundels, standing out so vividly as the khaki vehicles processed slowly along the driveway, the thought of Stanley being wounded, or worse, making her shudder, her conviction that God would protect him, needing an effort of belief to dispel the moment of alarm.

She felt sometimes, when she was writing to Stanley, that she was needing to give herself the reassurance that her conviction in divine protection would endure, the manifestation of hope, as so often, the beauty she observed, of so much of the world around her, nature providing her with solace, and optimism, the pleasure she found in her work and her friends fortifying her spirits.

*Friday – pay day!*
*Darling heart*
*As you see this is pay day - definitely a red letter day as I am now the proud possessor (for a very short while) of some brand new lovely pound notes. Since coming off duty at 7.0 this morning – besides being paid - I have had dinner, had a cigarette with Sally on the roof, admired the view of a perfect English spring, discussed birth control with her, and had a bath in the most super bathroom right at the top of the house, all white & looking out onto just sky & green trees & blossom with the casement window wide open & the sun streaming in so that it made you feel lovely & warm. Then in uniform again & cycled down to Hill End to a practical class which was very amusing & back here to be paid, then one more rush over to the nurses home to collect some things & back here to bed. So darling sweetheart I am afraid that this will only be a short note, to be continued as I did not have much sleep yesterday.*
*Goodbye for the present darling – don't be browned off – because the world is very beautiful at the moment i.e. nature & our love & all will come right in the end. God willing. I kiss you fondly goodnight darling*
*Peggy*

No sooner had Germany shown its intent, with its occupation of Denmark and Norway, than everything seemed to gather pace, their forces invading the Low Countries and, on 10th May, crossing the border into France. The BBC reported events in sombre tones, the only positive news being the announcement that Chamberlain had resigned, at long last, Winston Churchill appointed as his successor, his first task being the establishment of a coalition, bringing Labour and Liberal MPs into the cabinet, including the Labour leader, Clement Atlee.

That same day, 10th May, Stanley's training at Eastbourne was abruptly curtailed, the cadets and their trainers and officers being recalled to their units, Stanley and his comrades from 514 Company, returning to Kent, where, on arrival, they were told that all leave had been cancelled.

Demand for use of the telephone was such that calls had to be short, Stanley managing to get through to Peggy that evening, to tell her that he would not be able to meet her in two day's time as they had arranged.

"I don't know where I'll be," he said. "They're not telling us much, but everyone thinks we'll be going abroad."

"Do take care of yourself, darling, won't you?" Peggy could not think of anything else to say, the sense of apprehension like a hand clutching the pit of her stomach.

"Yes, darling, I will marry you," she suddenly heard herself saying. "Let's get engaged right away."

There was a moment of silence at the end of the line when she was picturing his expression, a smile of delight spreading across his open, boyish features.

It took the German army little more than a week after crossing the French border, to reach the Channel coast, thus encircling the retreating British Expeditionary Force, accompanied by remnants of the shattered French army.

The news of what was happening was, however, confused, Peggy listening intently, now with a personal interest, certain that, before long, Stanley would be part of the British army trying desperately to halt the German advance. When the reports began to indicate the extent of the advance, it was as if the nation was seized with a sudden realisation that, unthinkable as it had been until that moment, the country itself was in peril.

As she sat in the dining room with several of the other nurses, silently listening to the evening bulletin on the wireless, Peggy stared at her hand, the wedding finger still bare, the absence of the ring which, on the phone, Stanley had vowed to place on it the next time they were together, making her feel dreadfully sad.

"Come on, buck up Peg, my love. It won't be long." Brewster, ever observant and remarkably astute, seemed to be reading Peggy's thoughts.

Amongst the cadets in the rural Kent billet, there was an air of tension, the daily round of drilling and training now more purposeful, the prospect of soon having to face the enemy, energising them. Conversations were more animated, apprehension disguised behind a collective bravado, although in some of the quieter moments, they would confide in each other, many talking of their families and sweethearts, Stanley as effusive as any, proudly showing Peggy's photograph to nods of appreciation.

Having managed to buy the engagement ring some weeks earlier, on one of his visits home, satisfied that he had, rather subtly, he felt, elicited from Peggy, what sort of ring she might like, he was confident he had made the right choice, of gold with three small diamonds. Everyday he would open the small box, inspecting the ring giving him reassurance that their engagement was real, the sight of the shining metal and the glint of the tiny stones, more than satisfying him. All that he needed now, was her finger to take the ring, his imagining of the moment filling him with a frisson of expectancy.

What caused him some concern, however, was the thought of meeting her parents, now that they were his prospective parents-in-law. Respectful of them as he was, her father being such a prominent figure in the parish, it was not only his sense that they did not entirely approve of him. There was something rather austere about them. Peggy assured him that her father did have a sense of humour, which, whilst only displayed infrequently, indicated a warmth beneath the gruff exterior.

"Mummy's a bit of a softy at heart," she had told him. Coming shortly after one of her periodic bouts of complaining at what she felt to be her mother's incessant criticism, most recently, of her lack of seriousness about her studies and her preference to "be going out and enjoying yourself", Stanley had not replied, realising that she was trying to convince herself.

When he received a letter from her mother, he was, therefore, pleasantly surprised by her kind words but at the same time, understood the statement of expectation, that if he was to marry Peggy, he had better make sure he measured up.

*22.5.40*
*Elmcroft, 4 Hove Park Road, Hove 4*
*Dear Stanley*
*I have intended writing to you, but thought you had been moved, so when I knew Peggy was coming home, waited to get your address from her. I am so glad you two are so happy, & trust you will always be so, as I told Peggy, I think married life is the ideal state, if one has the right partner, & each are prepared to give & take. I am sure you will look after Peggy, & work well in your profession when the opportunity comes.*
*I pray God will bless & spare you both to enjoy many years together.*
*I sincerely hope we shall soon have better news, it hasn't been very good lately, has it? I*

*never thought we should have to live through these anxious days again, a little more trying*
*too, when one is older, however we must keep as hopeful & cheerful as possible.*
*With best wishes from your Mother-in-Law (to be).*

How funny, he thought in passing, as he re-read the letter, that she did not sign her name.

# FIVE

For several days, towards the end of May, the men of Stanley's unit, 514 Company, were swept up in a surge of activity, Stanley driving a lorry as part of the convoys which filled the Kent roads, sometimes going further afield into Sussex and up to London and beyond, collecting men from the various ports at which they were deposited by the armada of vessels sent to rescue them from France, the combination of the briefings and news bulletins providing sufficient information of what was happening to enable them to understand the ordeal troops being transported had been through.

Defeat, when it came, had seen the British Expeditionary Force encircled by the vastly superior German army, poised to drive them into the sea, or worse, to annihilate them, the fact that so many of them were able to escape being due in large part to the decision by the German command to pause in their advance, allowing time for the extraordinary array of British vessels, shuttling back and forth across the Channel, to rescue the majority of the beleaguered British forces.

Watching the line of boats, many of them, Stanley thought far too small to be able to cross the Channel, making their orderly way to the jetty to off-load their weary passengers, he was shocked to see the state of the men, many wounded, some walking, others aided by colleagues, the more serious cases on stretchers, uniforms and bandages stained with blood, those without wounds, dirty and dishevelled, faces grimy and stubbled.

As one of the soldiers directing the disembarkation summoned him forward, Stanley edging his lorry as close as possible to the jetty, he got down from the cab, unsure whether to help the arrivals as they crossed the flimsy gang-plank, the boat, a rather well appointed looking motor launch with a sunburnt middle aged man at the helm, and a young lad of perhaps fifteen, Stanley guessed, his son, handling the ropes, the boat rocking in the choppy harbour water, churned up by the heavy nautical traffic, making disembarkation precarious, a couple of civilians on the jetty reaching out hands to guide the soldiers onto firm dry land.

For Stanley, it was a salutary experience, to see the state of the troops, the blank faces, even those without injuries, vivid evidence of what they had been through, although for him, and those only hearing about it second hand, they could only imagine the grim reality, compounded by the knowledge that the Germans had been able, so easily, to inflict such a devastating defeat.

Despite a few of the men managing a smile of relief at having made it back, with an occasional attempt at levity – "we gave Jerry a right bloody nose", one wag said with a hollow laugh as he climbed into the back of the lorry - there was a general sense of shock, the fact that the British Army has been so utterly overwhelmed in such a short space of time, impossible for them to comprehend.

Transport now being required for moving men and equipment to defensive positions established throughout the region, both coastal and inland, the Dunkirk evacuation was quickly followed by an array of orders as preparations were made for the invasion which everyone believed to be imminent.

Although most of the wounded men were taken to military hospitals, some were brought to the London hospitals, several arriving at Hill End. There were also half a dozen civilians, mainly middle aged men, who, Peggy was told when they were brought to her ward, were civilians who had answered the call to join the rescue operation, but whose boats had been damaged or sunk, being rescued by other craft.

At first, they – these gallant mariners who had answered their country's call – were very obviously in a state of shock, communication, even answering simple questions, an effort. After a couple of days, however, they became more cheerful, some of them recounting their experiences, although with little regard for their own injuries, their concern being for the plight of the vast numbers of soldiers, and also, for their boats, a sentiment shared by them being their fondness for the craft and sadness for their loss.

As Peggy came down to the dining room the morning after getting back from a couple of days at home, several nurses were sitting, glum faced, listening to the news.

"Paris," Sally said, her voice hushed. "Paris has fallen."

Peggy felt her stomach contract, as if something had physically winded her. Paris! The fact that it had been expected had not prepared them for the reality. With the Germans occupying Paris, it was obvious that France was defeated.

"They'll be heading our way next," Brewster said, her face set. "Just let them see what we'll do to them. Bleeding Huns!"

A few faces turned towards her, but nobody said anything, preferring instead to hear the rest of the news.

With a spare half hour before the start of her duty, she went back to her room, needing to write to Stanley, if only a short letter. How close to him she felt these days, even when they were apart.

*Darling*
*When I drew back the blackout last night, brilliant moonlight lit the room from the brightest moon I think I have ever seen.*
*Darling, it is grand to think we are all together in England to defend this land we love & that no one will be going abroad. Somehow it is much more just & much kinder to the women, especially one who would have tried very hard to be brave.*
*The more beauty I see around me the more I think of the complete contrast between the glory of the earth & the horror of the things happening in it.*
*Mummy sounds very worried although she doesn't actually say she is, as she has told me what they have done with their papers & documents etc. & says she hopes they won't have to move. They had an air raid warning at home last night & they all got up.*
*Darling as I love you so, it is wonderful to feel that you are not too far away.*
*All my love & kisses*
*Peggy*

For the nurses, as for most of the country, listening to the BBC news became a focal point of each day, the bulletins generally both accurate and sufficiently detailed to enable listeners to obtain a clear picture of what was happening despite the moderation of content at the behest of the Ministry of Information, and the temptation, at times, to try to escape the incessant catalogue of bad news.

The pleasantly warm, still June evening, with the dining room windows open, birdsong drifting in from the hospital garden, seemed a cruel contrast to the news that a troopship, *Lancastria*, had been sunk by a German submarine with the loss of four thousand men, news as shocking as anything they had heard. Peggy noticed the tears rolling down Sally's cheeks, feeling her own eyes prickling, her throat constricted as if she needed to emit a loud sob.

"Those poor souls," Brewster whispered. "Four thousand of them! My God, that is..." She closed her mouth, pressing her lips together, words failing her.

"Come on, buck up," the Ward Sister had told Peggy and Sally when they arrived for the start of their duty an hour later, their faces glum and blotched from crying. "The patients don't want to see you moping around."

As they bustled about their tasks, exchanging small talk with the patients, their despondency soon lifted, and indeed, before long they were engaged in their usual repartee, the fact of having a handful of soldiers on the ward, at times, giving it a positively jolly atmosphere. None of them having major injuries, the more seriously wounded being treated at other hospitals, the soldiers became known as "our small boys", such was their irrepressible humour, and their playing on the nurses' role, of maternally caring for them. "Can I have a drink please, mummy?" one of them had called out one day, the others joining in, the joke running for many days, even some of the other patients getting in on the game, nurses being addressed generally as "mummy', despite the Ward Sister's frowning disapproval.

The camaraderie, both amongst the nurses and with the patients was something that Peggy had come to value, counting herself fortunate to be part of such a wonderful, caring, occupation, thankful that she had decided on nursing.

Worries were, however, always close beneath the surface, both as to the war generally and in relation to Stanley and her family. There seemed to be so much uncertainty, new anxieties cropping up each day, the latest being the possibility that her parents might have to move, everyone living near the south coast being warned about the possibility of invasion, being advised to take various precautions including a readiness to be moved at short notice.

When her mother telephoned, although she described the steps they were taking as "a bit of a nuisance", Peggy could hear the worry in her voice. It was when she remarked, dismissively, that they had been awoken the previous night by an air raid warning, which "kept us up for half the night," that Peggy suddenly felt a jab of a new anxiety, that Brighton and Hove were exposed by reason of their coastal location, and within easy range of enemy aircraft. Bombing, as yet only sporadic, was nevertheless, an all pervading fear, with rumours rife, of dreadful new weapons, bringing devastation to the country's towns and cities.

From Stanley's letters, she could see that he was constantly on the move, the letters sometimes very obviously written in haste, telling her little about what he was actually doing, other than keeping very "busy", a term which, over the months and years ahead, she came to recognised as encompassing the gamut of military activity, one of his handful of stock terms intended to play down the seriousness of what he was involved in.

Increasingly, also, his letters touched upon his concerns about her safety, asking her whether there had been any raids in the St Albans area, and suggesting that she should go home as infrequently as possible.

Despite having agreed that they would tell each other everything – all of their innermost thoughts and worries – she was hesitant to say anything which she felt would fuel his anxiety, instead, keeping her letters bright and newsy. Just occasionally, however, she felt she had to mention things of importance. She paused, undecided whether to tell him of the possibility of her moving back to Bart's main hospital in London, which their Matron had told them about, nurses being expected to rotate between sites, concluding that if she did not say something now, and only told him after she had moved, he would be far more upset. Yes, she would mention it, in passing, in the middle of the letter.

*My darling sweetheart*
*Thanks you so much for a wonderful letter. It was rather begrimed with oil – but it was grand all the same.*
*Please don't worry about me as we seem to be fairly out of range of the air raids. We haven't had any for quite a long time. We have only had two altogether.*
*There is the possibility that we might go back to Bart's soon. I have come to the conclusion that it would not be so bad after all although I should miss the country. If you are still in Kent or within range of town I could come to see you.*
*I have bought an R.A.S.C. regimental brooch to show support for my fiancé. I am wearing it now with some beautiful scented flowers tucked in it.*
*I am glad you have landed in another nice spot although it does sound rather difficult to get out of. Annoying isn't it that you are not allowed visitors – but it really is war now isn't it? I can take it & I am sure you can, darling*
*All my love and many kisses*
*Peggy*

Within a few days, however, the plans had changed, the only move being rotation between wards at the two St Albans hospitals, Hill End and Cell Barnes, Peggy feeling slightly disappointed, the prospect of being back in London rather exciting although she was also relieved that she would not have to cope with Stanley's opposition. He had told her a number of times that it was almost certain that the bombing would get a lot worse and that London would be a prime target.

With the arrival of summer, the war began to increase in its intensity, air attacks becoming more frequent across much of the country, the targets, initially, being airfields and industrial areas. The sight of formations of enemy planes, particularly in southern and eastern counties, criss-crossing the sky, and of dog-fights as they were endlessly harried by RAF fighters, became all too familiar, although when Stanley was posted to Ramsbury in Wiltshire, the aerial battles he witnessed were relatively few.

For Stanley, such relationships with his comrades were the essence of army life. Gregarious by nature, but valuing, in particular, those close associations which enabled him to share confidences, he was able to make friends easily. He thoroughly enjoyed being part of the group, singing songs in the pub, playing impromptu games of rugby or cricket, or simply being part of the general chatter at those moments when they came together, often at the end of an arduous day, sitting on the canvas beds, subjects ranging across the usual territory, of sex, films and music, and always, inevitably, news of the war.

Each of them also harboured their personal anxieties about their families and, for many of them their fiancées and sweethearts, their avid listening to the news as much about the parts of the country affected as the general state of affairs.

Throughout those torrid months, Stanley's closest friend, fellow cadet, Ian Blackford, was a quiet, thoughtful chap, with reddish hair and pale blue eyes. Well read and with an enquiring mind, they initially found that they had much in common in their interest in the world at large, and, inevitably, in music and cinema, comparing notes over their collections of records, bemoaning the difficulty in getting hold of more recent ones.

What they also had in common, was love, Ian's fiancée being with the ATS, having been posted to Yorkshire with the result that he had not been able to see her for several months.

Their conversations would often turn to the subject of marriage, each admitting not only to their virginity, but to their lack of knowledge of sex. Another of the cadets, a Scottish lad, Angus, inevitably known as "Jock", became a sort of third participant in such intimate discussions, the difference being that Jock and his girlfriend "did it", he thus being able to impart his graphic experience.

"It really helps if you get to know how they work," he told them one night when, over a pint of beer in the local, the three of them were huddled at a table in the pub garden, enjoying the warmth of the summer evening, the tranquillity disturbed by the distant sound of aircraft, and somewhere far away, the distinctive "whump" of bombs.

"Probably Swindon," Ian said, being the nearest town which had had several raids.

"You can get some books about it," Jock resumed. "But what we – me and Morag – have learned, is that it's really good to talk about it. We tell each other things. You know, how each other's bits work."

Stanley and Ian glanced at each other, Stanley raising his eyebrows, the idea of talking to Peggy about the sex act, let alone asking her how her "bits worked", quite unthinkable, the conversations which they had had, tending to be couched in terms of feelings and desires, but falling short of the specifics. For Stanley, it was an omission which he was eager to resolve, not only for the enhancement of his knowledge ahead of the eventual consummation of his relationship with Peggy, but because the idea of getting into such graphic matters was decidedly titillating.

"It makes it a damned sight more enjoyable," Jock insisted, "for both of us."

That conversation lodged in Stanley's brain, paving the way, albeit at a much later stage, for him to broach the subject with Peggy.

With the close camaraderie among the cadets, and with such uncertainty about their own futures, discontent would often surface, particularly on the subject of their opportunities to extricate themselves from what, at times, seemed the interminable drudgery of cadetship, quite apart from the meagre pay.

What they aspired to was a place on an officer training course, and of gaining a commission when, as an officer, even a lowly "one-pipper" - a second lieutenant - would bring status of a wholly different order, and a foot on the ladder of the commissioned hierarchy.

The vagary of army management, with the uncertainty as to officer training, was therefore, for Stanley, all the more frustrating, the ambition of getting that pip on his shoulder, being an essential means to the desirous end, of Peggy becoming his wife.

"Don't you think we could fix a date," he ventured when he next phoned her. "I don't mind if it's not for some time. When I can get my pip, and you can get on with your training."

For a moment she seemed to be full of enthusiasm, effusively talking about her "bottom drawer" and getting a wedding dress made, his hopes surging with the prospect of their marrying in a few months time, his hope being that if he could get onto the officer training course, he might get his commission by Christmas.

"Let's aim for 1942," she then said, the suggestion like a sluice of cold water, drowning his expectation.

When her next letter arrived, the fact that she was back at home, the affirmation of the suggestion of their not marrying for two years left him feeling utterly dejected.

*Darling*
*At the moment I am lounging in the garden with Sally & we have just had our result & do you know we have passed – isn't it grand? We have done a war dance round the garden & now are settled down writing like fury to tell all the world. We feel terribly proud of ourselves. We have really got half way through our training and are now on the National Register.*
*Darling sweetheart, I would marry you in 1942 'what'er betide' although I would like peace for preference. Still even though it is war time now I am very happy inside. My darling I hope you are too.*
*Goodbye for the present & all my fondest love.*
*Peggy*

As was invariably the case, his glum mood did not last for long, his spirit revived, to some extent, by the comfort of knowing that they would be married, even if it meant having to wait. What also gave him a lift was the posting on the notice board of their positions, assessed from their training record.

And then, at last, word came that leave was resuming and, better still, he was due for forty- eight hours the following week. To put the icing on the cake, when he phoned, she told him that she was also able to get home for a day.

When it came to it, however, by the time they had arrived at their respective homes and had done their filial duty with their parents, they managed only a few hours together.

But it was just enough for them to endow each other with the re-statement of their love, before he waved her off at the station, her tears adding an extra feeling of reassurance. What disappointed him, however, was that she had somehow managed to divert him from talking about their wedding plans, and whether she might agree to an earlier date. At least, however, the engagement ring was now firmly on her finger.

*My beloved darling*
*I had a good journey back though my thoughts were so much with you. We got back here about 12.30 in the middle of bombs all round and we saw a Jerry plane brought down. The day didn't end quite perfectly as we found we were on cookhouse at 6.30 & that*

*forthwith everything was to be very regimental – tent inspections etc – in fact everything to be inspected.*

*I think the O.C.T.U. course will be about 2 or 3 months which means no pips till probably the end of November.*

*I was terribly happy yesterday darling – even if I should die I thank God for giving such a sweet darling girl to love and be loved by. But please may he grant that that happiness & love may grow even greater & may many years together be ours, my darling Peggy. Goodnight my darling & may God bless you & look after you so carefully always – my heart and love are your tonight as always.*

*Stanley*

With the increasing frequency of bombing raids duty periods were changed to cope with the influx of patients from London, Peggy and Stanley's meeting plans once again thwarted.

Having been told that those with the more serious injuries were treated at London hospitals made Peggy realise how grievous those injuries must have been, judging by the condition of many of those arriving at Hill End, broken limbs and torn flesh being the norm. What the nurses were also becoming familiar with was the shocked state of most of those admitted, often having to comfort them with gentle words as they treated their injuries, the old remedy of tea and sympathy becoming an essential element of nursing care.

It proved to be only a short deferment of their meeting, both managing to get home the following week, Stanley with only one day's leave, Peggy having two whole days and nights. They were able to have the time largely to themselves, walking up to the Devil's Dyke where they sat on the grass, their vantage point giving them a grandstand view of the dog-fights which seemed to fill the sky, particularly away to the east and north towards London.

"You can't believe that there are men up there," Peggy remarked, the patterns – of the planes, small black shapes weaving back and forth like insects, leaving behind several smears of smoke, one issuing from a plane spiralling downward – like a vast work of abstract art. "Dying," she said as a tiny ball of flame marked the demise of the plane, although whether friend or foe they were too far distant to discern.

"No, look!" Stanley said, pointing, as a parachute, its canopy, like a minute falling petal, catching the sun, told of the pilot's survival.

The sound of the battle seemed to float on the light breeze, reaching them as a fluctuating humming of myriad engines, punctuated by the rhythmic tapping of ack-ack fire.

After a while, prizing their gaze from the morbid fascination of the aerial battle, they lay down, embraced, kissing, savoring their all too short time together.

"When are you going to marry me?" He had determined not to raise the subject but was unable to help himself, his longing for her to be his wife pervading his thoughts throughout his waking hours, and invading his sleep with dreams, common to so many of the men, which culminated in damp patches, the sounds of quickened breathing and rhythmic agitating of bedding, part of the nightly dormitory soundscape.

She sat up, holding up her wedding finger, the gold and diamonds glinting, as if the affirmation of their engagement was sufficient response.

How many times each day did she look at the ring, stroking it with her thumb, sometimes pressing it against her lips, loving the touch of the metal and the precious stones, their solidity having a feel of such permanence.

For the formalising of their engagement, three weeks earlier, he had insisted on their meeting at the Cumberland Hotel, the grand, stolid edifice facing Marble Arch which, being a good deal cheaper than many of the better known London hotels, was frequented by many military men, the hotel also having a more relaxed , "blind eye" approach to the status of the many visiting couples, its requirement being a simple record in the register of the couple's name, the fiction prompted by the well practiced receptionists whose invitation to new arrivals to sign the registration book was prefaced with "Would you care to sign, Mr & Mrs...?"

They had a room on the eighth floor, looking down onto Marble Arch, with a view across Hyde Park to the Albert Hall, the wide vista of the City dominated by barrage balloons, tethered to their lines, like watchful sentinels guarding the populace.

The bombing still, at that time, mid June, being more concentrated on places away from the centre of the capital, Stanley felt it was safe enough to stay in town, his heart being set on it as the place where he would do the deed, so long overdue, of putting the ring on her finger.

The dining room of the hotel, with its rather tired décor, nevertheless had a grand feel to it, a five piece band with a less than enthusiastic singer, working their way through their repertoire of popular songs, several couples already circulating the dance floor.

As the waitress removed their plates, Stanley reached into his pocket, extracting the ring, which had felt like a living presence, desperate to be released.

"Would you do me the honour of consenting to be my wife?"

She looked at him, his eyes shining with pleasure, cheeks flushed, his nervous smile suggesting that he was still uncertain of her answer.

"If you don't mind, I won't go down on one knee," he added. "Not with so many people watching."

"I think you should," she replied, laughing softly at him as he glanced around, getting up from his chair. "No, not really," she added hastily. "Yes, I will." She held her hand out to him, splaying her fingers as he slowly eased the ring into place.

"I love you, Peggy Wing, with all my heart and soul." He lifted her hand, inspecting the ring now so gratifyingly in its proper place. "Let's get married as soon as we can."

She had tried to steer the conversation away from the vexed issue of timing, aided by the band which, at that moment played *A Nightingale Sang in Berkeley Square*, Peggy getting to her feet, holding out her hand to him. "My favourite tune. Come on." She led him through the tables to the dance floor.

Lying on the downland grass, lost in their embrace, they both suddenly looked up at the sound of a plane approaching, the distinctive tone of an enemy engine, the Messerschmitt being closely pursued by a Spitfire which it was trying unsuccessfully to shake off, the pursuer seeming to read its quarry's maneuvering, issuing bursts of gunfire.

Stanley was about to pull Peggy flat onto the ground when the planes veered away, out across the Weald, rapidly shrinking, the trail of dark smoke, when it appeared, no thicker than a pencil line, the German slanting downward, its point of impact hidden from view by a rise in the ground, the only evidence of it meeting its end, a small blotch of smoke.

"I really do want to finish my training," she told him as they walked back towards the first houses of the town, at the top of the wide, leafy Dyke Road Avenue. "I would love it if it could be soon, but you know it can't."

Why did he persist when he knew full well that her heart was set on qualifying.

"And you know that Mummy and Daddy will never agree, until you have your commission." She was hesitant to play this card, knowing that if, as he expected, he achieved it by the end of the year, it would no longer work.

On each occasion, the conversation ended with him lapsing into morose silence, although she knew by now, that it would only last a short time, just sufficient for him to register his unhappiness, before brightening up, determined, as always, that their limited time together should not be tainted by argument.

Yet each time, as soon as they parted, her doubts began to cloud her earlier certainty. How she loved the thought of being married; of being back home, away from the demands of patients and study. She imagined having a home, a small flat or cottage, which she could tend, adding her touches, her choice of furnishing and decoration; a place to welcome him home on leave; a marital home. Why was it so difficult to reconcile the two things she wanted so much? It was no wonder he became confused when she was so entangled in her own equivocation.

The discussions amongst the cadets on the subject of sex had the same effect on many of them, of sowing seeds of anxiety amongst the numerous virgins, making many of them realise that despite the fact that excitement at the prospect of satiating their erotic fantasizing was their principal preoccupation, the thought of the act itself was almost intimidating, with so many uncertainties.

Stanley, being no different, dreamt of that moment, when he and Peggy could consummate their love, and yet the longer it remained a matter of lustful imagining, the more the doubts crept in. Did females really enjoy it? What must it be like for them, to have *it* inside them? What did you do when it was inside? Did you keep still, or, as everyone seemed to suggest – Jock having rather too vividly confirmed this with a demonstration of thrusting pelvis – push it in and out? With them – men – the culmination was obvious. But what about the females? How did it end? And how did one know?

If only they – he and Peggy - could discuss it. Several times he was on the verge of broaching the subject, his opening comment forming in his head. But something prevented him. It was as if their intimacy was bound by some sort of parameter of propriety, with certain things being off limits.

With pen and paper, however, such constraints seemed to diminish, his courage much more evident when she was not beside him, and indeed, the idea of her reading his written thoughts he found quite stimulating.

*9.8.40*
*O.C.C. R.A.S.C Russley Park Camp, Nr Lambourn, Berkshire*
*My only sweet darling girl*
*As you see I am back in my stable – and the above is really the correct address.*
*I do hope you don't feel too 'awe inspired' about being married to me.*
*The sexual side of marriage is one that worries nearly everyone, darling, and as we are really quite normal people physically & mentally & terribly in love, we have nothing to worry us unduly. I think if I knew you were giving yourself to me, that feeling of unfulfilled desire which is rather upsetting would be unknown & you would find nothing distasteful about the physical side of love. Please excuse this long oration but I want to be so very close to you, literally, & in understanding too.*
*I will send you my love for your deep understanding & my kisses; gentle they would really be today.*
*Yours for all time*
*Stanley*

He read what he had written, pleased to have been able to articulate these thoughts but still hesitant, wondering if he had gone too far. He had never, until this moment, been so explicit.

His resolve held firm as he addressed and sealed the envelope, touching it to his lips as he placed it in the bag for collection later in the afternoon, knowing that, with the reliability of the postal service, she would be reading his words the next morning.

When he received her reply, he was surprised at its brevity, and perplexed by her comment. Her allusion to matters sexual seemed flippant, and the picture she painted, of riding her bike with her skirt blowing up, filled him with indignation.

*My darling sweetheart*
*Your theories seem to be generally held for as I was cycling up the hill in the village my rather undress dress blew up. I promptly pulled it down again & a quite serious voice beside me said "It is a pity to cover up such lovely knees". The voice belonged as you can guess to a khaki form! Also a lorry went past & someone inside raised a tin hat to me. I think*

*it must have been one of the people you introduced to me, probably the one under the lorry.*
*Yours for ever*
*Peggy*

Through that August, the war in the air continued, as a sort of backdrop to life on the ground, people going about their business, faces turning periodically to the sky, drawn to the endlessly fascinating, grim but strangely remote spectacle. For those closest to the battles, apart from the more frightening moments when planes plummeted to the ground, or an intruder sought to make its escape, hurtling past, seemingly at rooftop height, pursuer on its tail, there was the different and sometimes hazardous experience, of a sort of metallic rain, thousands of spent bullets dropping to earth, thudding onto the ground, and in towns and villages, clattering onto streets and buildings, interspersed with larger fragments of aircraft, torn off when guns found their target, many planes damaged, returning to their airfields displaying the wounds of battle.

For Peggy and Stanley, the struggle to coordinate their off duty times to allow for their meetings became ever more difficult, particularly as, during early September, the German strategy seemed to shift, with ever more frequent raids, particularly on London, although they heard from the news that several other cities were also being targeted.

From the BBC news and the reports in the papers, it was clear that for several weeks, the battle was in the balance, even Churchill's morale boosting oratory failing to disguise the reality, that the country was fighting with its back to the wall, resources, in particular, aircraft, ammunition and, most of all, trained pilots, being in perilously short supply.

It being only the Members and reporters present in the House of Commons on that August day who were fortunate enough to hear the Prime Minister's speech, Stanley, like so many others, had to make do with extracts cited by the newsreader, a lengthier version appearing in the next day's paper.

As he read the report in the *Telegraph,* sitting on his bed, reciting parts of it to the group of cadets around him, he was conscious of a surge of emotion, unsure whether he wanted to weep or to shout out loud. It was as if the words touched something within him, an electric pulse of pride.

*"The gratitude of every home in our island, in our Empire, and indeed, throughout the world, except in those abodes of the guilty, goes out to those British airmen who, undaunted by the odds, unwearied in their constant challenge and mortal danger, are*

*turning the tide of the war by their prowess and by their devotion. Never in the field of human conflict was so much owed by so many to so few."*

"God Almighty!" he exclaimed, lowering the newspaper, "with Winnie in charge, there's no chance of defeat." He looked at the faces around him, several heads nodding in assent.

"Come on, Jerry!" Jock said. "Come over here and we'll show you what we're made of!" His broad Scottish brogue seemed to infuse his words with a fervour that had several of them up on their feet, fists thrusting as if the enemy was about to burst into the dormitory.

Within just a few days, the term which had been the keynote of Churchill's speech, "the few", became a central part of the new vocabulary of the country's defiance, rivalling "we shall fight on the beaches", the phrase similarly adopted from the great man's speech a few weeks earlier, Churchill's name featuring in almost every conversation, revered already, after just a few months in office.

Despite his worries about going to London, Stanley felt that if they avoided the centre of the City – and they certainly would not be going anywhere near the docks or the East End - they should be safe. His main concern was for Peggy, but if they went to the flat in Hampstead, they would be far enough away from the danger areas, it also being relatively easy for her to get there by bus, even though he had to go to Paddington for his train.

This time, both having a full day, they met at the flat mid morning, giving them time for a walk to the Heath where they ate the picnic she had prepared, the day sultry, the view across the city hazy, the barrage balloons hovering like bulbous creatures, their mooring lines invisible. It was a scene of remarkable peace, broken only by the occasional aircraft, patrolling the skies, although it would not be until after dusk that the raiders would be arriving.

"Would you think about giving it up?" he ventured during the afternoon when they were back at the flat, lying on the bed, luxuriating in the knowledge that they had two more hours before having to depart. "I'm not wanting to persuade you," he added quickly, knowing the sensitivity of the subject. "I was just wondering, as you are wanting to get married just as much as I am."

"Oh, I don't know." There was a hint of exasperation in her voice although he felt it was, in this instance, as much to do with her indecision as his persistence. "I just don't think we can. How would we live? I'm sure I could get some sort of nursing work, which might give us a bit more. And where would we live?"

Sitting on the train as it made its way out of Paddington, the blinds pulled down, the blue lights in the carriage tinting the faces of the passengers as if they were submerged in the sea, he was a good deal more encouraged by her apparent willingness at least to consider leaving Bart's.

It was with some trepidation that he opened her letter a couple of days later, his heart plummeting as he came to her suggestion of waiting.

*My darling sweetheart*
*All the time since I left you last night I have been thinking really seriously about the marriage question. Darling, if I did leave & we got married should we really have enough cash to live on? That sounds horribly practical but I know we should have to be to make Daddy agree & your parents too I think. I suppose with a commission we could manage it. If we could possibly manage to wait a year I should have a certificate from here & could do Auxiliary Nursing or something like that.*
*My darling, this all sounds so terribly hard, doesn't it when we love each other so much & are really quite old enough to marry.*
*I am afraid I shan't be able to write very much as I am writing by the red glow of a very much dimmed light due to a warning. We were out for a walk just now & saw flares & what we thought to be A.A. fire. We just got in before the warning. It is a wonderful evening & it seemed such a pity to leave it.*
*All my love, sweetheart*
*Peggy*

For several weeks Stanley and his fellow cadets had been waiting for word as to whether they were going to be selected for officer training, the endless delays having become a subject for much derision of the incompetence of "Fred Karno's army". When the order suddenly came, those chosen – he being one of them – joyfully packed their kit, unsure where they were heading for, other than being told that there would be an interim holding period in Swindon.

But then, as if intent on demonstrating its hapless disorganisation, as soon as the men had climbed down from the lorries after the short journey to Swindon, milling around in a small square, waiting to be directed to their quarters, a young Lieutenant emerged from what appeared to be a rather grand house, telling them tersely and without apology that the order had been countermanded from "someone up the line" and that although they would still be going on the officer training, all candidates would, for the time being, be going back to their units, which for Stanley and his comrades from 514 Company, meant returning to Kent.

"Fucking shambles," Ian said just loudly enough for those close to him to hear, several heads turning, with wry smiles of agreement.

"Don't know their arses from their elbows," was Stanley's contribution, similarly pitched but, unfortunately, just loud enough for the officer to hear.

"Right, you two, with me! Now!" the officer barked, turning smartly away and marching back to building.

The journey to Kent was, however, delayed, the lorries being required for what was evidently some more important purpose than ferrying a bunch of lowly cadets who thus found themselves herded into one of the requisitioned houses, having to sleep on the floor, far too many of them crammed into each room. There was, however, just about enough room for Stanley to prop himself against a wall, and, needing to get things off his chest, to write to Peggy.

*My very darlingest Peggy*
*I'm afraid this is going to be a pretty miserable & hopeless epistle because since I last wrote to things have been getting worse and worse.*
*The first bombshell was that as soon as we arrived we were told that we were all going back to our units. This is really an admittance by this hopeless Army of gross mismanagement. We shan't know till after our lousy Colonel has told us a pack of lies on his parade tomorrow when we'll be coming back.*
*To make matters really worse, there is a flap on, first class this time! All leave has been cancelled. I think you'd better definitely put yours off. Worse to come!*
*Ian and I have been naughty boys! It's easy to say but we've got 7 days confined to barracks. Horrid thought, being in this place for 7 days. But despite all these major disasters, I am happy in my heart darling and very much cheered up by your sweet letters. We must now I suppose put off all idea of getting married as this commission racket seems so far off. If only our living standard didn't demand more than the soldier's fee allowance of 30/- a week, we could get married now.*
*It's terribly worrying hearing stories of 400 dead in London air raids and reading of hospitals being bombed & not knowing where.*
*God bless & keep you safe, darling*
*Your always loving*
*Stanley*

Being confined to barracks felt to Stanley to be an unconscionable insult added to the grievous injury of being held in some bureaucratic limbo, the cancellation of leave rubbing a handful of salt into the smarting wound. And tapping deep into the undercurrent of discontent was the feeling of impotence. Here they were, able-bodied young men, desperate to get to grips with the enemy, rattling around like so many spare parts while, according to the news and the papers, the country was suffering an onslaught of bombing.

How they thought they could engage with the enemy was something they did not give a great deal of thought to other than the conviction that, at any time, every one of them would be called upon to defend the land if – when – the Nazi army attempted to invade; "we shall fight them on the beaches," Churchill's rallying call to the flag they were so eager to serve.

Eventually, in the last week of September, his turn came and he received his posting to the Officer Producing Centre at Boscombe a small town in Dorset, not far from Bournemouth. Having been told that they had 48 hours leave before starting the course, and Peggy being unable to get time off, he and Ian booking in at the Strand Palace Hotel which, rather like the Cumberland, was reasonably priced and hence, popular with servicemen.

Rather rashly, they had decided that they would take the risk of staying in London despite the escalation of the bombing, a decision that, by the next morning, Stanley very much regretted.

*2.10.40*
*Strand Palace Hotel*
*My darling Peggy*
*I survived the batterings of the night safely – it was certainly rather hazardous. The train was nearly half an hour late & got in at five past midnight. We nearly got hit & the whole thing rocked precariously. I had to dodge my way from Charing Cross to here. I was so sleepy I slept through the bombs & everything but awoke when there was a terrific bang nearby.*
*This morning's experience was the worst. The alarm went at 9 & in less than five minutes there was a terrible rushing noise and a crash which rocked the whole building – three times - and I thought we'd been hit. However, we seem to be intact although the water is cut off and some of the lights are out. The bombs were just down the Strand.*
*London seems far more scarred than a fortnight ago but the people are quite cheery. I think this place isn't what it was. The food is lousy & the service bad.*
*I must stop now & go & see the damage – then a haircut.*
*I am yours forever in love*
*Stanley*

# SIX

Having finally escaped the purdah of his long cadetship, the relief Stanley felt at now being on the stepping stone to his commission was marred by the uncertainty about marriage, his anxiety, about Peggy's wavering commitment to curtail her nursing training, becoming magnified, and at times, casting a shadow of doubt across her commitment to him, and to their future.

There were moments when guilt bubbled to the surface, that he was putting undue pressure upon her, but any contrition that he felt was nothing compared with his exasperation with her, and, in particular, with her parents who, at times, seemed intent upon delaying the wedding, and, he suspected, of thwarting them entirely.

His desire to get her to the altar as soon as he got his pip, preoccupied him, the moments of optimism invariably alternating with troughs of despondency as he cajoled and pleaded, her equivocation infuriating him.

Peggy hated herself for being so indecisive, and for allowing her parents to dictate. And yet she also knew that, as they had told her repeatedly, they were only "trying to do what's best" for her.

Whilst they adhered resolutely to the conviction that their daughter's marriage should only be sanctioned if – and when – they were satisfied that she would be properly provided for, they could see that these were exceptional times, which created a new dilemma, of trying to reconcile the inevitable changes in one's expectations which war brought about, not least, the understandable desire of young people to hasten marriage for fear of what the future might bring, with the worrying risk, of a young wife becoming a young widow with all of the consequences that would ensue.

In their private deliberations, they continued to share their lingering reservations about Stanley generally; whether he was really a suitable match for their daughter; whether his prospects, and his character, were likely to measure up to their expectations.

They would sit in their respective armchairs after their supper, their timetable and ritual rarely altered, even when Peggy's brother, Tom, was present, although he would often excuse himself, preferring to spend his time in the study which he was now allowed to share with this father, immersed in his books on surveying and valuing, now being well into his articles at his father's practice.

It was the time when they would talk, for half an hour or so, depending on the subject matter, the conclusion of the conversation marked by Arthur picking up the newspaper, his wife opening her book, the ensuing silence enduring until nine thirty when they would retire to bed.

Peggy's mother, Marion Frederica, known as May, a tall woman with fine, slightly pronounced features, and an air of seriousness, sometimes verging on austerity, was not one for joviality or flippancy. There was too much of that these days, young people rather too intent, for her liking, on enjoying themselves when they should be spending a little more time improving themselves, preparing for their lives ahead.

Her husband, Arthur, generally maintained a set expression, his tufted cheeks giving his round face a certain sternness, his manner, as with his appearance, redolent of the gentlemen of the country's greatest era, that of the Empress Queen, Victoria. Indeed, when he stood, back to the fire, holding forth to his family, one hand resting on the mantelpiece, the other with thumb hooked into this waistcoat pocket, he was every part the figure he aspired to, his practice, as a land agent and surveyor, allowing him frequently to come into contact with those whom he most admired, the landed gentry.

"He does tend to be a little *wayward*," May opined, Stanley regularly the subject of their evening discussions in recent months. She found him perfectly personable; in all honesty, a little too much so, his politeness occasionally verging on over familiarity, as if he were speaking to one of his peers rather than his elders and betters.

"I'm not sure he is a particularly *serious* young man," her husband added, the two of them being in complete agreement that, were it not for the fact that Stanley was the vicar's son, it would have been a very different matter.

But it was too late now. The couple were engaged, the thought of their breaking the solemn commitment that this entailed, quite out of the question, although they still harboured the thought that, by delaying the wedding, with the turbulence of the world, circumstances might change.

There was also the all important matter of Peggy's nursing career. She had made it abundantly clear to them that she was determined, at the very least, to complete her training so as to become a registered nurse. It thus behoved them to use their parental judgment and authority to help her to achieve that admirable goal.

There were moments when Peggy became resentful of Stanley's insistence that they should fix their wedding for the earliest possible date after he gained his expected commission, although it was not her way to confront him, other than in the mildest terms. She would debate with herself, berating him for being so self centred. "Spoiled child!" she hissed under her breath as she paced around the hospital garden, echoing something her mother had said, some years earlier, before they were even courting, the disparagement also levelled at Stanley's mother whom May considered "soft", the result being that Stanley lacked the sort of discipline that had been the cornerstone of their own son, Tom's, upbringing.

Peggy so much wanted to make something of herself, becoming a fully qualified nurse the only route open to her. Why the hospital would not allow her to continue simply because she was married, was quite beyond her. Her father's attempt to persuade the matron, that in this time of war, the rules should be relaxed, foundered on the stolid, obdurate rock of the immutability of the hospital's constitution, the requirement for a nurse to be a spinster, sacrosanct.

But the thought of being married thrilled her. The wife of an army officer, even a lowly Second Lieutenant, would give her a place in the world. And he would, inevitably, rise up the ranks, perhaps becoming a captain. Captain and Mrs Stanley Allen! How splendid it sounded. She imagined being announced as they entered some grand ballroom, or reading their title on an invitation, their status declaimed in copper-plate script.

But then there was the prospect of having to return home. There had been times, not so much in recent months, but still from time to time, when she felt homesick, longing to be back in leafy Hove; to be able to look from her window out across the town to the glistening English Channel; to be able to see her old friends, Paddy, Barbara, Marjorie. But where would she – they – live? And what would she do?

It was all so uncertain. He had mentioned several times, that he expected to be sent abroad, although thankfully, since Dunkirk, much of the British army had become the "Home Forces", relatively safe, away from enemy guns. True, if the Germans invaded, as still seemed very much on the cards, it would be the Home Forces which would confront them. Somehow, however, she could never quite imagine it; German troops on British soil; let alone subjugating the country to their occupation. No, surely Britain would never go the way of the French.

Even with him relatively safe, here in England, their time together would be limited to his short periods of leave. The idea of him staying with her, in her – her parents' – home was quite unthinkable. Yet where else could they stay?

Her mind was in such a muddle. When she was with him, or talking to him on the phone, she was happily swept up in the excitement of being married to him. His suggestion that, if her parents refused to give their consent, they should elope, made her shudder with apprehension and the sheer thrill of it. But her loyalty and duty to her parents were too much a part of her.

So it was that, throughout that autumn, and with the arrival of winter, the question as to when they were to wed, remained up in the air, becoming a source of friction between them, testing the depth of their commitment to each other.

Stanley found the officer training absorbing and not overly demanding, the Dorset surroundings, and the comfort of the accommodation contributing to his enjoyment of it. What caused him most discontent, however, was the restrictions on leave, his meetings with Peggy sporadic.

The first weekend, with the freedom of Saturday night and Sunday off, he went with Ian, Jock and several others, for a visit to Bournemouth, taking in a film, Charlie Chaplin's brilliant satire of Hitler, *The Great Dictator*, a fish and chip dinner, and several pints of beer, before getting the bus back to Boscombe.

His officer training had started remarkably well. If only things could have been as rosy on the marriage front, although when they had last been together, much to his delight, she appeared to have taken a final decision, to leave Bart's in December, clearing the way for them to marry at Christmas.

Yet again however, his was cruelly crushed when he opened her next letter, arriving at the same time as a sombre letter from his mother.

*My darling sweetheart*
*I am afraid my day had a crash yesterday when I receive a long & grim letter from Daddy in completely different frame of mind to the one written earlier in the week.*
*They seem to have made up theirs that I should stay here & you get your commission & go abroad if necessary & then come back and marry me. As you can guess darling, all my hopes of my family's agreeing & everyone being happy went with the wind but all the other girls tried to cheer me up.*
*I have just thought of another very appropriate remark – "the course of true love never did run straight". Still, darling, I am very happily in love despite the world & feel I could*

116

*discard it all for you if necessary.*
*All my love ever yours*
*Peggy*

*My very sweet darling*
*I hadn't intended burdening you with another epistle so soon but as a result of the letters received today I'm feeling rather hopeless & rather beaten in our battle. The first was from Mother: after talking a lot about air raids, it ran something like this — "Mrs Wing came in this morning after church" (they always discuss us then don't they!) "and the subject of your marriage came up: she was very nice about it but she and Mr Wing, I can see, do want Peggy to finish her training so that she can have something to fall back on, especially as she had got on so well." She then they talked about "it being so nice if we could both save a little". The whole thing made me livid & completely fed up, as first of all we're too young, & so it goes on. I suppose it means we'd have to wait till after the war. Then at lunch time the news that Italy & Greece were at war made the war seem far more complicated.*
*Then your letter this afternoon put the cap on Black Monday and now I'm trying to get my thoughts straight by writing to you.*
*Well, darling, if you really want to stay on, that's the end of it all — you talk about 'a few months' — in a few months unless a miracle occurs we shall be in Wanga-Wanga or somewhere remote in topee etc! I dare say soon life will renew the good old cheery outlook but it won't be nearly such a happy one, and this commission business with its eternal spit & polish, parades and not talking, all seems rather aimless & futile when the best inspiration of all is removed.*
*I'm afraid this letter must make your hard life even harder — but if only you'd make your life a little more yours, now that you've done such a grand job by giving up two years of your sweet life to a hospital.*
*Goodnight darling angel*
*Yours ever*
*Stanley*

Was he being unreasonable? Would it really matter if they waited a little longer? No sooner did he ask himself the question than he brushed it aside, his conviction, that they must marry without any further delay, impervious to any possible doubt, and indeed, strengthened the more opposition he faced.

What really irked him was knowing how upset his beloved Peggy was, having to cope with the pressure from her parents, playing, as they were, upon her own residual doubts about giving up her nascent career. What difference did it make anyway, whether she left now, half way through, or when she qualified? Either way, she was not going to continue nursing. Most compelling of all, overriding her considerations, was the prospect of his being sent abroad, to face mortal danger for his country. Surely she, and all of them, must recognise the justice of his cause; that it was right and proper for him to marry the girl he loved, to provide him with the comfort of a home and wife to return to, and to sustain him through whatever he might be called upon to endure.

Yes, there was no doubt at all that he was in the right.

The question of where they would be deployed once they had their commissions was the subject of a great deal of speculation amongst the cadets, the consensus being that the Far East or North Africa were most likely.

"Give me Africa any time," Ian said, during one of the discussions. "From what I've heard, the Far East is pretty grim. All that stuff in the jungle – you know, snakes and spiders, and leeches. And fighting against the Japs. At least with the Hun and the Wops you know your enemy."

"Except the Germans are a bit damned good," Jock said.

"We may have to fight them here," Stanley suggested, "if they do invade."

"Surely they won't be stupid enough." Of all of them, Jock always seemed to have better understanding of the overall situation with the war. "Without first beating us in the air – and they haven't managed that."

The only other subject which featured in virtually every conversation and which, indeed, demanded centre stage, was their loved ones, which, for Jock and now Ian, meant their wives, but for Stanley, the girl for whom he pined and who caused him such anguish.

They shared their intimate thoughts, many of which were, inevitably, with a group of young men deprived of female company, about sex, graphic in the recounting by the married men, and graphically fantasised by Stanley, the carnal aspect alternating with the deep anxiety which they all felt by reason of the bombing which was now almost nightly, inflicted upon towns and cities across the country, the news only exacerbating their worries, their means of ascertaining whether their loved ones were safe being the exasperatingly erratic telephone system, or by letter.

With the closeness between the three of them, as well as sharing confidences, they knew and played upon each other's foibles and weak spots. With Stanley, it was his incessant agonising about his marriage which made him the butt of their humorous goading.

When Peggy's letters arrived, Ian and Jock would look at each other, eyebrows raised in silent enquiry; which version was it going to be? The answer was soon apparent on Stanley's face, a sickly smile spreading across his features, or a knitting of his brow and setting of his jaw.

"For Christ's sake, Stanley!" Jock exclaimed one day, Stanley's name enunciated with a throatful of Scottish phlegm. "If you're so desperate to get your leg over, and she's making you wait, there's plenty available elsewhere. I'm sure you can get a decent twopenny stand-up even in Bournemouth."

Stanley stared at him, shocked at the crudeness of the remark. "It's not a matter of *getting my leg over*," he replied indignantly. "I just love the girl and need her to be my wife."

"So that you can get your leg over!" As the two of them burst out laughing, Stanley's face flushing angrily, he lay down on his bed, turning away from them. "I'm sorry," Jock said quietly, "no offence meant."

"None taken," Stanley said, keeping his back to them. What rattled him was the fact that to an extent they were right. His nights were fraught with his dreams of her; her naked body appearing like a mirage, just out of his reach, disported before his lustful imagining, his carnal craving satiated, for the moment, by hastily self-administered relief.

Unusually, this time, his moroseness endured for nearly a week, with no letter from her. He wasn't sure whether it was better to be left with his gloomy thoughts or to have to endure yet more glum news from her.

When she phoned to say that she was going home the coming weekend and to ask him if he could get away, at least for a day, at first he feared that she was wanting to tell him, face to face, that they were going to have to wait.

"I think it's going to be alright, darling," she said, those words feeling like a warm balm, spreading through him. "But I need to talk to Mummy and Daddy, and I think you do as well. And to your people."

He was able to get away late on the Saturday afternoon, managing to catch the last coastal train, getting home just before midnight, his father waiting up for him, greeting him with a glass of whisky and a plate of sandwiches.

As arranged, he picked Peggy up after breakfast the next morning, with time for a walk around the park before church where they took their place in the front pew with Peggy's parents and Stanley's mother.

When the service was over, they assembled for the planned family meeting, Stanley's father offering glasses of sherry, Stanley feeling decidedly apprehensive despite Peggy's earlier reassurance that she was now confident that her parents had come round.

"Well then," Stanley's father began, all assuming that he would take the lead. After all, he was the vicar and they were holding their meeting in the vicarage. "We, your respective parents, been having a good deal of discussion while you were *in absentia*, and, you'll be happy to hear, are in full agreement that your wedding should go ahead in January." He smiled benevolently at the couple, sitting side by side on upright chairs, as if in readiness for interview. "Assuming that remains your wish," he added, his long, kindly face creasing into a quizzical smile.

"We are delighted to concur," Peggy's father said, glancing sideways at his wife. "As you know, we were a little disappointed that Peggy should not be completing her training, but we understand, and respect, the reasons for her decision."

"These are difficult times," the vicar continued, "with an uncertain future. We were all agreed that it is right and proper for you to find happiness while you can."

"Our consent is on the basis that you obtain your commission, Stanley," Arthur Wing said, looking at his prospective son-in-law in a way which Stanley read as conveying something more than this simple requirement; a hint of a warning that the gaining of a commission needed to mark a new maturity and responsibility, befitting the man who was to marry his daughter.

"I'm confident that I shall marry Peggy as a commissioned officer," Stanley replied, with a certain satisfaction that he would be able to meet this condition.

The meeting concluded, the participants adjourned to the dining room where the aging Mrs Christian served the Sunday lunch, of roast beef, Stanley's father producing a bottle of wine, "one of my finest Clarets", to celebrate the occasion, although afterwards, when Stanley and Peggy were alone in the vicarage study listening to records enjoying what they knew would be there last few hours together probably until their wedding, they thought it rather odd that there should be such a celebration of fixing a date.

For both of them, however, it was an afternoon which they savoured, all of the doubts and tribulations finally laid to rest, or so they believed.

As they stood on the platform, holding onto each other, before catching their respective trains, this parting felt wholly different, with none of the usual weight of sadness, Peggy exuding a glow of happiness, her mind filled with the detail of the wedding which they had discussed for much of the afternoon.

Little did he realise that he was embarking on a journey which would take many hours longer than expected and which he was lucky to survive.

*My darling*
*When I realised I wasn't dreaming and that my wildest dreams were within grasp at last I was so happy. All my friends are too, darling.*
*I had a long journey back and was extremely lucky to get back at all. I had a six hour journey with no lights. There was a terrific raid going on and myself and another cadet thought the end was in sight when two bombs whistled down close to the train in Eastleigh Station. However we survived but ten minutes after our train was through Southampton the line was bombed and we arrived back to an air raid in Bournemouth*
*My love for you is so indescribable. May God grant you such happiness as my wife.*
*Yours forever in love*
*Stanley*

The following days, despite the cold, wet weather, the wind whipping in from the Channel, their exercises miserable, the rain penetrating their clothing, bedraggled cadets returning to their quarters like so many drowned rats, Stanley felt a spring in his step, sustained by the gratification of knowing that, within just a few weeks, he would be a married man, his wonderful, beautiful Peggy his own wife.

"Are you happy, darling?" he asked her when he phoned her, as always, needing her to tell him, yet again, that she was now fully committed, whole-heartedly ready to leave Bart's and to dedicate herself to married life. "No more worries about leaving before Christmas or wanting to stay for another year?"

By way of reply, she chatted enthusiastically about the wedding plans, the lightness in her voice leaving him with his euphoria intact.

In truth, he still harboured a residual shred of anxiety, a consequence of all the months of painful fluctuation, so that when her letter arrived, the blow was not as great as it might otherwise have been.

*My darling sweetheart*

*I am very happy in the thought of getting married but I have to confess that I did not answer exactly truthfully to your question about if I would be happier if it was October. I am afraid that because I did not want to hurt your feelings. I said 'no', but there is just a little something in the bottom of my heart, though I am really happy. I think it may be selfishness on my part that wants to complete an ideal or being too 'sensible', a word I know you dislike. At any rate, my darling, I will try & live it down, I think it will probably fade quite quickly when I get away from here & be with you entirely as I have promised. I hope you are happy, entirely, in our decision. War does make life so terribly hard doesn't it darling?*

*Have you told the Army authorities yet? It has not been broadcast at home yet as I have not given in my resignation. Daddy has written to Helen Day, matron at Barts, re the possibility of me finishing later if you went abroad. I am sure I shouldn't be allowed to but still I said I would wait until he had heard.*

*All the best & all my love*

*Peggy*


*My darling*

*I am afraid I was somewhat shocked by your letter: it was in such a different tone from what I had hoped for inwardly and from what you said on the phone. Darling, why oh why in God's name didn't you tell me the truth before we went to your people with what I thought was our final decision: why did you let me come back here with more false happiness: was it because you wanted to cheer me up for the exam? Now I have told all my friends that we are going to get married, and it seems obvious that if you are half-hearted about it (no other word can describe it) it would really be foolish to go through with it. You remember I told you that your happiness was the prime consideration. I think it's a case of women not knowing their own minds again!*

*I've just rung up home and had another bombshell. That is that after they thought everything was settled last Sunday, on Monday they received a letter from your people asking them to write to me & ask us to put things off as you were very upset at the prospect of not taking the exam.*

*I must stop now darling: for God's sake don't be scared of hurting my feelings if you really hate the idea of leaving Barts. Please let me know very soon.*

*Yours*

*Stanley*


Having finished his exams and with all of the cadets being given an unexpected day's leave, albeit, with the restriction on travel still in place, prohibiting them from going further than Bournemouth, in his desperation he sent her a telegram by way of impatient follow up to his letter.

*VERY SHOCKED. MEET ME AT 11AM TOMORROW. HOLBORN TUBE. STANLEY*

Having persuaded Ian and Jock to cover for him, he set off for London, fully prepared for an outcome which would, he realised, mean having to tell the world that his wedding was off.

"Don't throw the baby out with the bath water!" Jock had said, when, the evening before, he had decided to take them into his confidence. "If you love her, as you clearly do, judging by your bloody moping, then a few months won't make any difference. She's still going to be your wife."

Why did they manage to make things sound so logical, flying in the face of his own determination to stick to his guns.

"Because if we have to wait, we may be God knows where. Or blown to pieces."

"Perhaps that's a good reason to wait them," Ian chimed in.

"It's all very well for you two, when you're both married."

"Fair point," Jock acknowledged. "But keep things in perspective is all I'm saying."

He sometimes felt that she held his heart in her hands, toying with it, tugging mercilessly at his volatile emotions. Thus is was, yet again, that from behind the dark clouds of dejection, the sun emerged with renewed brilliance as, having endured a miserable train journey, contemplating the prospect of having to survive a year or more of engagement, with marriage an ever distant mirage, within just as few minutes of meeting her, walking arm in arm along Kingsway, oblivious to the biting cold wind, she had convinced him that her machinations were finally at an end.

"I'm so sorry, my darling. I never want to cause you so much upset. I've made up my mind, and I'm leaving next week. I've told Matron and Mummy and Daddy."

He wanted to weep with joy, holding her hand across the table in the Cornerhouse, his fingers caressing the engagement ring, looking at her lovely eyes as if searching for the absolute certainty that had, for so long, eluded him. And what gave it to him now – that certainty he craved - was to see her welling tears.

"I didn't really want to go on at Bart's. I think it was being home again last weekend, with Mummy and Daddy on about it again. It's as if they were making me doubt myself. But now I don't. I love you, darling, and in January, I will be your wife."

The return journey, slow as it was with the usual disruptions, although on this occasion, without any immediate danger, could not have been more different, his mood positively euphoric, prompting him to chat to fellow passengers.

When he got back to Bournemouth, sneaking in the back entrance of the hotel, arriving just as the rest of the cadets were assembling for tea, Ian and Jock had no need to enquire as to the outcome, the Cheshire cat grin which greeted them telling them all that they needed to know.

"Are you sure this time?" Jock asked. "We couldn't stand any more of your blathering if it were off again."

"Rock solid," Stanley replied, this time being wholly convinced.

Late on the afternoon of the 5th January, Stanley stepped down from the train at Hove station, Ian behind him, both proudly disporting their dress uniforms, the single pip on their shoulders the mark of their now being commissioned officers of the Crown.

With their kitbags hoisted onto their shoulders, as the light was fading, the mid winter dusk cold and still, they walked across the recreation ground, keeping to the paths where the snow, which covered the grass, had been well trodden, Stanley choosing to take the route up Hove Park Road, pausing outside number 4, ostensibly to show Ian where Peggy lived, but hoping she might be looking out of the window and come out to greet them.

During their last phone call, the evening before, she had reminded him that he must not try to see her before she arrived at the church.

"I thought that was just on the wedding day," he said, although not overly concerned, knowing that he would only be getting home the afternoon before, but, as was his way, wanting to make his point.

"Make sure you're there in good time," she said, ignoring his comment.

He and Ian stood for just a moment, but there being nobody visible inside the house, the cold air prompted them continue, arriving at the vicarage to a warm welcome from Stanley's mother and Mrs Christian.

"This is Ian," Stanley said, as his father also emerged from his study, followed by the aroma of pipe smoke which Stanley always associated with home. "My best man."

"So, the great day is nearly here," his father said with a dry laugh. "After all the hemming and hawing."

"How splendid you look, both of you," his mother said, admiring the two young men in their smart uniforms, buttons shining, Sam Brown's freshly polished, trouser creases still pristine despite the journey.

"So that's your new insignia," his father remarked, studying Stanley's buttons. "I gather your emblem is the Wyvern."

"Yes, the 43rd Division is known as the "Wessex Wyverns," Stanley replied, fingering the button. "I had always thought that Wessex was a bit more to the west, but apparently they are lumping a lot together now, including various of us from Sussex."

Having completed the training and left Dorset as newly commissioned Second Lieutenants, they had to return to Kent, now attached to the Division's Headquarters, although this itself, was spread through several locations, according to its various function, Stanley and Ian both assigned to the Division's RASC.

Familiar as the surroundings had become, as an officer, and with a clear place in the army hierarchy, and a clear function, life suddenly felt very different. And with his marriage just a matter of days away, despite the grimness of the war news in almost every direction, the dawning of 1941, for him, had a new sense of purpose.

The next morning, his wedding day, they awoke to a grey sky with a chill east wind and slight flurries of snow, although by mid morning the snow had stopped.

Stanley had hardly slept, such was his excitement, and indeed, his nervousness, going over his speech in his head, tempted, in the early hours, to take out his notes from the pocket of his uniform hanging on the back of the door but realising that he could not turn the light on without waking Ian, sleeping in the guest bed which had been brought into the room for him.

Now that the day was here, he still found it difficult to believe, after all that had happened over the past few months.

Even when the moment arrived and, with Ian beside him, at the sound of the Michael's deftly gentle opening chords of the *Bridal March,* his brother, a fine young pianist, having been entrusted with the role of organist, as Stanley turned to see Peggy, her hand holding her father's arm, silhouetted in the church doorway, he feared that he would suddenly wake to find that it was but a dream.

At Ian's nudging, he turned back towards the altar, allowing himself only one further quick glance over his shoulder, Peggy, her veil concealing her face, a picture even beyond the imaginings of that dream, floating towards him, her two bridesmaids, her cousin Marjorie and her friend Joan, close behind. She had wanted Sally and Brewster to be her bridesmaids but with the date only being fixed at short notice, neither of them were able to change their duty days.

As she stood beside him, her father stepping away, she glanced up at him, her eyes, through the veil, shining, her smile seeming to say "I'm so sorry for all that I have put you through. Now here I am. I am yours."

Conducted by the Reverend Wilfred Westall, formerly Stanley's father's curate, a heroic figure for the young Stanley when, with his father's blessing, the young clergyman had taken leave of absence to drive the legendary Cornish Riviera Express during the General Strike, Stanley's memory was only of his acute awareness of Peggy's presence at his side and the moment when, as they were directed to do so, they placed the rings on each other's fingers, she having to force his over his knuckle, giving a slight grimace as she did so.

As the congregation processed the short distance to the church hall, Michael and Peggy having spent the previous afternoon decorating it with as much greenery as they could find nearby and a few rather meagre bunches of flowers, the best they could get hold of without spending too much money, Stanley held onto Peggy's hand as if determined never to let it go, but releasing it to take the glass of gin and lime which Michael, as previously instructed, handed to him, the remainder of the guests, immediate family excepted, having a choice of beer, cider cup or orange squash, the liquor helping to calm his apprehension at the imminence of his speech.

When it came to it, however, he found himself basking in the warmth of the response, fifty or so faces looking at him, laughter filling the hall, words seeming to flow from him with consummate ease, his notes no more than an occasional prompt, his effusive thanks to the bridesmaids the stem from which he was able to wax lyrically about his new wife.

"Never has there been a happier man. In these dark days, she lights up my life, offering me a beacon which will guide me through whatever lies ahead."

He paused, looking across the sea of faces, the smiles replaced, briefly, by thoughtful expressions, each person momentarily reminded of their own personal anxieties.

"And when, soon, we hope, we are able to return to a life of peace, with my beloved Peggy I can look forward to a life of happiness, beyond anything I could ever have dreamed of."

He looked down as her, seated beside him, her face flushed with pleasure as the room reverberated with heartfelt applause.

By mid afternoon they were well on their way towards Hampshire, their first night to be spent in a small country hotel, Peggy asleep in the passenger seat, a rug over her knees, her gloved hands folded on her lap. Although he felt tired from the exertions of the day, as well as the effect of several gin and limes, he was wide awake, images of the day filling his head.

For some reason he could not account for, after all the exhilaration of the day – the send off, as they climbed into the car in the vicarage driveway, the guests crowding round the car, confetti, much of it homemade, drifting over the car as they edged out into the road, Stanley holding out his arm, waving, Peggy craning her neck, watching the waving crowd unto they turned the corner – he felt oddly flat. What a day, he said to himself, taking a deep breath, exhaling, as if to dispel the unexpected mood.

"So, this is your wedding night," the middle aged, heavily made up hotel receptionist said with a suggestive smirk. "We've put you in the bridal suite."

The "bridal suite" which, after following her up the creaking stairs and along a dimly lit landing, she showed them into it, was a modest sized room, its large sash window looking out across a wide garden to a scattering of houses and a wood beyond, the leafless trees starkly silhouetted against the low, pallid sun which had broken through the cloud.

"A little welcome," she said, gesturing towards the small box of chocolates on the bedside table. "From us," she added, in case they might have been in any doubt. "Facilities along the landing. Dinner at six."

She handed Stanley the room key, closing the door behind her, her heavy footsteps descending the complaining stairs.

He looked at his watch. "Shall we go for a bit of a wander?" he suggested, feeling the need to do something to fill the hour and half before dinner.

"I think I'll just put my feet up, if that's alright," Peggy said, sitting on the bed. "But you go."

"Are you sure you don't mind? Just need a bit of a leg stretch, and clear the head."

When they entered the dining room, there were two other couples, one elderly, the other a young naval officer with his wife, her wedding ring clearly on display, Peggy wanting to lift up her own hand to show off hers.

"Good evenings" having been formally exchanged, the waitress, a young girl, showed them to a table, thankfully, not too close to the other occupants, half a dozen empty tables separating them. Even with this degree of separation, however, they felt they had to talk almost in a whisper, the room seeming to be filled with a heavy silence, the conversation at the other two occupied tables, similarly *sotto voce*.

A beer for Stanley and a gin and orange for Peggy, followed by a bottle of rather vinegary wine, helped them to feel more relaxed, at one point coming close to a fit of giggles, for no reason other than the awkwardness of the atmosphere, Stanley whispering "it's like being in church", having told Peggy of the occasion three years earlier, when he and a couple of friends had arrived at midnight mass on Christmas Eve, straight from a rather jolly evening at the rugby club, the three of them, in the pew at the back of the church, doing their best to be attentive to the service despite their rather drunken state. It was when Stanley, aware that his friend, Charles's shoulders seemed to be shaking, glanced towards him and noticed that he had stuffed his handkerchief into his mouth in a vain attempt to stop himself from laughing, the corner of the handkerchief protruding from Charles's lips, that Stanley emitted what, to those around him, sounded like a sort of bark, setting off David, on Charles's other side, the three of them having to bolt from the church, stumbling out of the door before convulsing with unconstrained laughter.

"There was absolutely nothing funny," Stanley explained, "other than not being supposed to laugh."

"So, here we are then," Stanley said, the two of them standing rather awkwardly in their room, having lingered over their meal for as long as they could, the other diners having departed, the waitress loitering, obviously eager to be able to clear the last table so that she could get home.

He put his arms around her, kissing her gently.

"That was a very large meal," she said, stepping away. "I feel fit to burst."

"Me too."

She sat down on the bed, taking off her shoes, looking around the room.

"To bed then," he suggested, taking off his sports jacket, having changed out of his uniform after the reception, Peggy wearing a simple dark blue dress, with a string of small pearls and matching clip on earrings, which she unclipped, walking across to the small dressing table, placing them beside her hairbrush.

Taking his hand, she pulled him towards the bed, lying down, both of them fully clothed, arms around each other, faces close together.

"I love you very much, my darling wife," he said softly.

"I'm so glad you persuaded me," she said. "It was such a relief to leave Bart's. I only wish you didn't have to go back so soon. It should be the start of our life together, not just a few days."

"Five whole days," he said, kissing her, trying to sound cheerful. "So we'd better make the best of them."

They both looked across at the window, as a gust of wind rattled the sash, Stanley getting up and closing the curtains before sitting down again on the side of the bed.

"Bit chilly, isn't" he said, the small gas fire, puttering quietly, giving off a meagre warmth if one stood close to it.

"Do you know what to do?" she asked, taking his hand and holding it against her face, instantly regretting the question. For her, having seen more male members than should could possibly count - including a few too many standing up to greet her, aroused by a bed-bath or even, on one occasion, when she was turning an elderly man on his side to wipe his bottom after he had used the bedpan, her surprise that such a usually shrivelled appendage was still capable of such a display – and with the extent of her knowledge of the reproductive organs of both sexes, the process itself was a known quantity, apart from the absence of actually experiencing it. There was also the not inconsiderable matter of it being her first time, and despite the accounts, from Brewster and a few other nurses, she could not help a certain apprehension.

"I'm sorry," she added quickly. "I didn't mean to suggest…" She realised that alluding to the fact that it was also his first time, and that he might be unsure of what to do, could somehow impugn his masculinity.

"Yes, of course I know," he replied with more bravado than he felt.

Several times in recent weeks, they had talked about sex, always at Stanley's instigation, his understanding of female anatomy decidedly hazy, derived as it was from a couple of books which did the rounds amongst the cadets, read more out of salacious fascination than for educational purposes, the academic information he obtained from such texts and diagrams supplemented by what he had managed to glean from the generally lewd references from carnally experienced colleagues, much of this, however, of limited instructive value.

"I'll just go to the bathroom," she said, taking her nightdress and sponge-bag from her suitcase. "Back in a minute."

As she closed the door behind her, he quickly undressed, putting on his pyjamas, taking the Durex packet from his sponge-bag, looking around for a suitable place to conceal it.

When he returned from his trip to the bathroom, she was already in bed. "Can I go that side?" he asked, wanting to be within arm's length of the Durex which he had place in the draw of the small bedside table. She slid across to the other side, holding up the bedding for him to climbed in.

He pulled her towards him, the feel of her body against his engendering a sudden urgency. Through the fabric of her nightie he touched one of her breasts, the nipple hard against his palm.

"Shall I take it off?" she asked in a whisper, pulling the nightie over her head without waiting for an answer. "Now yours."

She moved back slightly while he undid the buttons of his pyjama jacket before pulling the tie of the bottoms, kicking them to the bottom of the bed.

As their bodies came together again, the sensation was such that he feared he was going to erupt instantly. He lay on his back, reaching out to the drawer.

"Better just put this on." As he tore open the foil wrapper, he saw that she was watching. "Don't look!" She looked away as he reached down, becoming flustered when the condom would not unfold, then realising he had it the wrong way round. He had practised a couple of times previously, but without anticipating having to do it if for real in the confined space of the bed, and being unable to see what was doing.

As he rolled on top of her, he was shocked at the touch of pubic hair, and then the wetness, taking hold of himself, manoeuvring to where he assumed it needed to go. But the cocktail of sensations were too much for him, his grunt and the shaking of his body telling her what had happened.

He lay on top of her for a moment, conscious only of the feeling release, the tension instantly dissipated, but also, of deflation, knowing that it shouldn't have been like this.

"Sorry," he said as he lifted himself off her.

"There's plenty of time," she said softly, turning towards him, resting her head on his shoulder, his even breathing telling her that he had already fallen asleep.

The next night, at the hotel he had seen during one of his training exercises, deep in the Dorset countryside, they were able to achieve consummation to the extent that her virginity was committed to history, although the rapidity of the process was such that, for her, it was over almost before it had begun.

"I really am your wife now," she said to him playfully at the breakfast table the following morning. He held his finger to his lips to shush her, looking around at the handful of other guests, the dining room once again, being uncomfortably quiet.

Throughout their five day honeymoon, the weather being unrelentingly grey and cold, occasional light snow showers just enough to keep the ground covered, they managed only short walks, the idea of long daily hikes abandoned in the face of the conditions. Instead they explored more of the area by car with a couple of trips to Bournemouth where he was able to show her his various haunts, taking her for lunch at Bobby's café which was every bit as excellent as he had described in his letters, and a couple of afternoons in the cinema, the first seeing the rather grim James Stewart war film, *The Mortal Storm*, the second visit, for light relief, a news theatre with a series of cartoons.

On the last day, despite their determination to enjoy their truncated honeymoon, the imminence of their renewed separation weighed upon them. For both of them also, there was a feeling of disappointment. It was as if they had had to contrive their enjoyment, the weather, and the hotel which had turned out to be chilly and rather depressing, conspiring to detract from what they had both been so looking forward to; a few days of golden happiness.

For her, in particular, there was also the disappointment that she had found so little pleasure in the sex, although she told herself that at least, by the last night, his staying power was a little improved. She was pleased also, that he was obviously much relieved that, as he put it "things seem to be working better", being the extent of his comment over their last night's dinner. She had noticed also, that his inhibitions, particularly when it came to talking about sex, were loosened when he had had a drop to drink.

During the drive back to Brighton, they struggled to find conversation, other than when, the clouds having now dispersed, they saw, some way off towards the coast, a wide pall of smoke hanging in the sky, a stark reminder of the reality of war they were returning to.

"Must be Portsmouth," he said. "It's been having a pretty bad time."

When she returned home, having driven him to the station, she went to her bedroom, staring out of the window, trying to assemble her thoughts. The feeling of disappointment seemed all encompassing. Here she was, back home, having failed in her ambition to become a qualified nurse, with nothing to do –

no job or occupation, it was as if she had never been away. And being with her parents again, compounded the sense of failure.

She regretted that she had not stuck to her guns and completed the course. What was more, had she done so, and delayed the wedding, they might have avoided having to have their honeymoon in mid winter, although she knew that was not the real cause of her disappointment. The only ray of light in the gloomy outlook was that she was more convinced than ever, that with Stanley, she had made the right choice. She loved him so much, the prospect of having to live apart from him for what people were now suggesting was likely to be years, was almost unbearable, and the thought that at some stage he was almost certain to be going off somewhere to fight, worried her deeply.

She had wanted to talk to him about the sex; to try to explain to him that it did not matter if they did not get it right at first. They had plenty of time. When the war was over, they had the rest of their lives. The regret was as much the fact that there was this barrier; as if some inherent reticence got in the way of the openness which she was convinced they both desired, preventing them from talking about it. But it was more than that. It was as if he did not want to – did not feel the need to – discuss it. He seemed to be satisfied, that he had achieved it, penetration and gratification, with no inkling of the fact that for her it might be different.

It was, however, not in her nature to allow herself to dwell on despondent thoughts, and by the evening, sitting down for supper with her mother and father, her father breaking his usual rules and offering her a glass of sherry despite it being a weekday, she was feeling more positive. Tomorrow she would be meeting Paddy and Marjorie, and visiting Stanley's parents. And her father was due to get a new car which he had promised her she would be able to use.

By the time that Stanley phoned, she was almost back to her usual cheerful self, able to tell him how much she loved him and what a wonderful time they had had. And now that he was back in Kent, they would be able to see each other more regularly.

# SEVEN

Hitler's plan, to neutralise the British air force as a pre-requisite for prospective invasion, having failed, thanks in large part to the extraordinary heroics of "the Few", the three thousand pilots who defended the country from the attacks which continued through the summer and autumn of 1940, at a loss of some five hundred of their number, he, and his henchman, Goering, the less than competent chief of the *Luftwaffe*, embarked on their new strategy, their objective being the destruction of British industrial and transport capability so as to force the country to sue for peace, part of the strategy involving terrorising the populace, particularly of London, demonstrating to them the German capability of inflicting annihilation should their leaders be foolish enough to continue their resistance.

For seven months, the country was battered by incessant bombing, the new German campaign, "the Blitz", pulverising London and several other cities, the capital, during the most intense period, being subjected to consecutive nightly raids for nearly three months, wreaking widespread destruction, particularly of the East End and Dockland, parts of other industrial cities, Liverpool, Southampton and Bristol, each major ports, suffering the onslaught, as were Birmingham, Manchester, Sheffield and many others.

What Hitler and Goering had not anticipated, however, was the resilience of their enemy, the British people demonstrating a capacity to live and function, adversity engendering a determination not only to endure whatever Hitler was minded to throw at them, but to do so with a stoicism which defied his belief that they would be so cowed by the terror he was inflicting upon them, that they would beg Churchill to come, on bended knee, to plead for it to stop.

In spite of the ever mounting death toll, and the disruption, particularly to transport, the country continued about its business, huge efforts being made to repair the damage, or, where factories were destroyed, finding new production capacity, the output of essential military equipment, including aircraft, armaments and ammunition, steadily increasing.

For the men of the British army, by now numbering some two million, the majority being designated "Home Forces", their role, as the threat of invasion receded, became less clear. Endless training, they assumed, was to prepare them for deployment to the various theatres where British forces were actively engaging the enemy, including Crete, South East Asia and, most notably, North Africa.

Far off as it seemed to most of the men, there was a widespread view that if country was able weather the aerial onslaught, and survive the increasingly worrying U-boat menace, sinking ever growing numbers of ships carrying vital supplies to sustain the country's existence, then eventually, it was going to be necessary to return to the European battlefield.

Interminable though the training often seemed, morale fluctuating, affected by boredom as well as the unrelentingly grim news, the same stoicism that instilled the "Blitz spirit" in the civilian population, enabled the men in uniform to continue to apply themselves to the business of preparing to take on the formidable *Wehrmacht*.

As if it were not bad enough to have to endure the German onslaught, for several weeks the country was in the grip of one of the coldest winters for many years, biting winds, sweeping in from the east, blizzards blanketing much of the country with snow.

It was not surprising, amid such adversity at the hands of man and nature, the smallest glimmer of light was thankfully seized upon, lifting morale, inspiring obdurate optimism.

When the BBC first broadcast the opening notes of Beethoven's 5th Symphony as "V" for victory, the four notes representing the "dot-dot-dot-dash" of the Morse Code version of the letter, it instantly resonated with something in the spirit of defiance.

And when, in early January, it was reported that America had agreed to provide support to the country in the form of equipment and supplies by way of a system known as "Lend Lease", an expression which, to most people meant simply that the US was coming to our rescue at the moment when we most needed them, it fed the belief that "we will get through this".

Stanley – Second Lieutenant Allen – found his new role, and army life generally, tolerable through those first few months of that dark year, getting on with the endless instruction and training, his knowledge of the role of the RASC steadily expanding as he recognised how it played such a vital part in enabling the fighting units to function.

What he, along with all of the young men who now served their country had had to learn, was that one had to take the rough with the smooth, the former, for him, being the ever present, nagging pain of being apart from his new wife, each meeting with her seeming to intensify his love for her. Apart from those meetings, cruelly short though many of them were, ending inevitably with the sorrow of parting, Peggy's letters became his lifeline, filled as they were, with news of her life at home, often with snatches of the intimate and sometimes, risqué, and always, with wonderful words of love.

Less frequent though both of their letters had become, reliant as they were on seeing each other on a regular basis, his, in particular, becoming rather sporadic, what was lacking in quantity was more than compensated for in heart warming, and often, for him, stimulating content

His thoughts of her, which, before their wedding had filled his waking hours, continued to do so, but instead of the endless anxiety, his mind was now filled with desire, for the body with which he had become so deliciously acquainted but which, he realised, he still hardly knew, longing for their next time together so that they could resume their voyage of exploration.

During those months, also, and indeed, over the months and years ahead, he developed a love-hate relationship with Kent, the county in which he was compelled to live this new military life, the hatred being partly due to it not being his beloved Sussex, but also its inhospitable climate, in thrall as it seemed to be to its bleak neighbour, the North Sea.

There was undoubtedly a charm to some of its villages, certain of which he became quite fond – Chilham in particular, *The Woolpack* one of his favourite pubs, but the only sizeable towns to which they had access, Canterbury and Ashford, he came to despise for their dourness and the paucity of entertainment, although both had cinemas which thrived on the military audiences.

No sooner had he returned to the county after their honeymoon, than, as they had agreed, he set about finding places where she could stay, their plan being for her to visit him as often as possible, her first stay being in a small pub at Bridge, a village just a few miles from the RASC Headquarters where he was now based.

They arranged her visit when he had twenty-four hours leave, giving them a whole precious day and night together. Although the weather was still cold, the landscape covered in snow, the sun shone from a cloudless sky, the countryside gleaming in its radiant winter mantle.

During the three weeks since their honeymoon, each of them had felt the same sense of disappointment. For Peggy, the reason was self apparent, and something which she was certain was transient, stemming from inexperience and unfamiliarity. For him, it was more difficult to comprehend. It had left him with a feeling of disquiet which he could not define. On the one hand there was the satisfaction that he had, as Jock had rather too loudly proclaimed the moment he was back, "lost your cherry! At last!". But it was not as he had expected, or as he had dreamed about for so long. It seemed so *physical*, as if, when they were having sex, they were somehow separate. And to make matters worse, they had not been able to talk about it, his attempts to say something foundering on his damned inhibition.

Having managed to borrow an army car, he was able to meet her at Ashford station, taking her to a café for lunch before driving up to Bridge.

As soon as he was with her, he felt something was different. There was a brightness about her which, when they were sitting down at the table, seemed to dissipate the anxiousness which had been playing on his mind. Their conversation flowed with such joyful ease that he found himself wanting laugh out loud. And she looked more lovely than ever, her cheeks pink with the chill of the day, her eyes shining, her chatter carefree and affectionate. They held hands across the table, fingers entwined, Stanley feeling a sensation of being connected to her, a current of sheer ecstasy flowing from her.

Even when they were walking in the afternoon, heads down into the teeth of the icy wind, they felt as if they were in a cocoon of their own warmth. Toes and fingers numb with cold, they laughed with delight as they stopped to admire their trail of footsteps imprinted in the fresh powdering of snow on top of the layer, a couple of inches thick, impacted beneath.

Unlike their honeymoon hotel, the pub in Bridge was warm and welcoming, their bedroom tiny but cosy.

Needing no words, of doubt or encouragement, their love-making was unhurried and yet intense, Stanley aware of her in a way which was entirely novel to him, as if their bodies were fusing, her breathing quickening, her fingers digging into the flesh of his back. As she emitted a gasp, followed by a series of moans, rising from deep within her, the fact that he was the cause of such utterances of abandon, excited him, his desire for it to continue defeated by his own explosion of sensation.

They lay there, him still on top of her, her grip telling him that despite his concern that he was weighing upon her, she wanted him to remain, conscious of the light fading, sounds coming from below them, the clatter of pans and plates, and several voices.

At the distant sound of aircraft, he got up and went to the window, glancing up at the sky, now virtually dark.

"Ours," he said, familiar with the distinct difference between defenders, usually fighters, patrolling or on their way to intercept approaching intruders, and the harsher tone of the alien engines. "Apparently they have a shelter close by. They told me when I rang up."

When they went down to the bar, it was full, soldiers mixing with several locals.

"Evening sir." The private greeted him, nodding respectfully to Peggy who smiled, quietly delighted at hearing Stanley's status declared.

"Sir!" Three other privates similarly acknowledged the young officer.

They went to the table reserved for them in the small dining area at the far end of the bar, Stanley wondering if the men might somehow sense the glow he was sure he was giving off, an almost a physical, discernible force.

"You look like a Cheshire cat," Peggy whispered when they were seated and he was quaffing a pint of beer. She sipped her gin and lime, her eyes smiling at him over the rim of the glass.

"Sorry," he replied, the grin spreading across his face.

"Don't apologise. It was lovely."

He glanced around, nodding to the half dozen other diners, his chest swelling with pride, that he was sitting here with this beautiful woman – his wife, her words feeling like a plaudit for what he had accomplished.

They had just been served with their soup when the babble of conversation died away, the low thrumming of multiple aircraft engines rising steadily, the anxious patrons needing no telling that they were enemy. Several people began to move towards the door, as if forming up in readiness to leave, the noise now loud enough to feel it, physically, as if it were emanating from the ground beneath them.

"Should be OK." The landlord appeared from a different door, coming out into the middle of the bar area. "They're over Canterbury way," he said. "Heading for London docks again I reckon. Those poor sods living round there."

The conversation resumed, those diners who had got up from their tables, resuming their seats, Peggy and Stanley having remained, Stanley, now with a good deal of experience of gauging the proximity and direction of enemy aircraft which, almost every night, passed over the county, having concluded that they were not at risk.

A few moments later, the renewed conversation declined again for a few minutes, as ack-ack batteries some miles away, opened up, most of those present, being now used to the regular sounds of aerial warfare, quickly returning to their food and liquor.

"It was different, wasn't it?" Stanley ventured as they finished their meal. Whilst they had had a few discussions about sex before they were married, he had felt them to be slightly embarrassing, particularly when she had asked him if was arranging "protection", it taking him a few moments to realise what she meant, the terms he was familiar with, from army conversation, being "French letter" or "Durex".

"Yes," he had answered, the thought having crossed his mind, although it was only after her prompting that he had steeled himself to go to the shop in Canterbury which Jock had told him about.

"I don't think you'll need that today," she had said that afternoon as they were undressing, reaching into his uniform pocket for the Durex, looking at her questioningly. "I've done my calculation and it'll be quite safe."

During one of their previous conversations she had also explained to him about the menstrual cycle, which, again, he was vaguely aware of, marvelling now as she told him about its following the cycles of the moon and how it was only at certain phases that a woman was ovulating.

The experience of entering her without the barrier of a rubber sheath, was a revelation, exciting sensations which, although he was unaware of it at the time, caused him to grunt, her hushed description, as he returned to their table with refilled glasses, "a bit like a happily snoozing pig!" making him blush, which in turn, made her laugh softly, taking his hand again.

"I've embarrassed you," she said, giving his hand a squeeze before releasing it, picking up and draining her glass of wine.

Partings having become so much part of their lives, they had both come to realise that their determination that each "goodbye" should be accompanied by a smile, was prone to be undone by the emotion of the moment. The imminence of going their separate ways tended to engender a forced, ostensibly light-hearted chatter, Peggy talking about what she had planned as soon as she got home; the friends she would be meeting and the full diary of activities. He hoped each time, that she would be able to contain the tears which he could see, from the set of her face when it came to their final embrace, were close, a tearful parting leaving him with an almost physical hurt. On some occasions also, the lump which constricted his own throat, threatened to reduce him to shedding tears which, his upbringing and his nature had taught him, were not in keeping with one's masculinity.

The next morning, when he drove her back to the station, they sat in the car for several minutes, holding onto each other, their love making, repeated that evening and again the next morning, having taken their relationship to a new level.

"This really has been our honeymoon," she said, as she pulled away from him. "It's been so lovely. I love you, my dearest," she said, her voice tremulous.

She stepped quickly out of the car. "You don't need to come," she told him, but he wanted to stay with her for as long as possible, lifting her small case out of the boot, walking arm in arm to the station entrance where she kissed him, taking the case, making her way hastily onto the platform.

"Go!" she insisted, her eyes now brimming, as he obediently turned back towards the car, his lips pressed tightly together to contain his own stretched emotions.

His role, as a junior officer, now required him to deal with a certain amount of paperwork as he developed his understanding of vast complexity of the business of keeping the army supplied, the training, which he now realised was something which would continue until they were eventually sent to do battle with the enemy, being, as one of the senior officers had described it, being "like running a very big business, the difference being that if you take the wrong decisions, instead of the business going to the wall, you will be responsible for men getting killed."

They were salutary words which Stanley carried in his head for the remainder of his army career and which, many times, he passed on to the junior officers he later commanded.

Their next meeting was less harmonious, Stanley arriving in a black mood, having that morning heard the news of the sinking of *HMS Hood*, the ship which, more than any other, stood for the pride of the Royal Navy, and indeed, of the nation itself. The bulletin had stated with shocking bluntness, that the great ship had been sunk by the German battleship, *Bismark,* which, at that moment, was on the loose in the North Atlantic, putting vital merchant shipping in peril, such was the German vessel's reputation as one of the most powerful in the world.

A few years earlier, Stanley and his father had made the trip to Portsmouth to see the Coronation review of the Fleet, a spectacle unlike anything he had experienced, their vantage point, on Portsmouth waterfront enabling them to see down the avenues of ships stretching the length of the Solent, gathered from every part of the Empire as well as many from other nations, including Japan and Germany which, provocatively, sent the "pocket" battleship, *Admiral Graf Spee,* one of a number of ships which Germany had built supposedly complying with the constraints imposed after the Great War, it being an open secret that the ships were indeed, battleships, flagrantly contravening the spirit and, almost certainly, the letter of the treaty.

But it was the *Hood* which Stanley vividly remembered, a ship of such magnificent grace and potency that one was instilled with absolute confidence that here was probably the greatest fighting ship ever built.

It was that image which was in Stanley's uncomprehending mind when the dreadful news was announced, the fact that there had only been a handful of survivors from its company of some two thousand, making it the grimmest moment of the war to date.

"Did you hear about the *Hood?*" he asked, kissing her briefly. "God Almighty! The *Hood!* I just can't believe it. It's so terrible."

She decided to wait for a bit before broaching the subject which had been on her mind for some time. Thankfully, as they walked in the warm sun through Canterbury's Greyfriars Gardens, the River Stour flowing languidly beside them, his mood changed, his usual joviality returning.

"I thought I might find some work," she said as they sat on a bench to eat the picnic she had prepared, trying to make the remark sound as casual as possible. "Just something part time."

He looked at her blankly, as if not understanding what she was saying.

"What sort of work? Surely you're not going back to nursing?"

"No, of course not. You know they wouldn't have me back even if I wanted to, which I definitely don't." She felt that by sounding so resolute, it would reassure him. "I might be able to a bit a bit of work in a nursing home, or possibly one of the local hospitals. It would only be auxiliary. They need more people, and with the training I have done I would probably be able to find something."

"Just as long as it doesn't involve you going anywhere near London," he said, relieved by her mention of "local".

"Or something completely different. Some sort of clerking perhaps."

"Why do you want to work?" he asked although she sensed that he was not going to stand in her way as she had feared. "I mean living at home with your parents and with what I'm now getting."

"I just want to do my bit," she said, having decided that this was going to be her strongest point. "It's easy for you men. But for us, it's more difficult. And I *need* to be doing something, for the war effort, and to keep me busy."

"But I thought you had plenty to keep you busy, helping your mother and father, and around the house."

She looked at him, a flash of irritation showing in her expression.

"I don't want to be just helping around the house," she said, her tone telling him not to pursue the matter.

"I really don't mind, darling, as long as you don't take on too much. I would hate to think of you wearing yourself out."

What she decided not to tell him, at least not at this moment, was that when she had met up with her Bart's friends, they mentioned that there were openings for auxiliary nurses at several hospitals. It was when Sally told her that she knew that there were some vacancies in Canterbury that her ears pricked up. However, best not to start Stanley worrying unless and until there was something concrete.

As they lay on the grass, conscious of other people nearby, they had to ensure that their conduct remained entirely seemly, without being "naughty", their word for the fondling which was the extent of their sexual activity when they had insufficient time to book into a hotel to enable them to make love. Being naughty became a game which not only gave them a modicum of satisfaction at the time, but which they were able to allude to in their letters.

Peggy had heard the full gamut of terms for the penis, the discussion between the nurses of the terms used by patients the source of a good deal of ribald laughter. When, therefore, he had first referred to his as "John Thomas", she was familiar with the term, nowadays reduced to their shorthand, "JT", whose best friend, in their intimate exchanges, was "Fanny".

"JT's been pretty lonely since he last saw you," he whispered now, as she managed, with suitable discretion, to press her hand against it through the thick fabric of his uniform.

"Poor chap," she said, giving it a gentle pat. "Fanny really wants to welcome him. We'd better make sure they can get together next time."

When it came to it, however, it was not until late summer that she found some suitable work, apart from the occasional days helping out at a couple of local nursing homes and a few times, at the children's hospital.

Apart from the sadness of the partings, despite the lack of the work she aspired to, she found that she was rather enjoying life, were it not for the for the ever present anxiety about the war. The news seemed to be unrelentingly bad, the only positive aspect being the feeling of everyone pulling together, the spirit of community, and of *getting on with it*, universal, the daily round of grumbling and complaint now more of a ritual, often punctuated with wry dismissal, although tragedy was always close, even with the lessening of the intensity of the blitz, death and destruction an almost daily occurrence throughout the country, principally in the cities.

At home, in addition to the daily round of domestic chores, Peggy would often go with her father on his visits to properties around the county, acting as his driver and companion, his initial reservations about being driven by her, resolved as she became more confident, the little Morris 8 he had recently bought for reasons of fuel economy, being so easy to drive, suiting her admirably.

What she has also found, during these domestic months, was that she rather enjoyed the role of wife, shopping for certain of Stanley's requirements – items of clothing, as well as things he found difficult to get hold in Ashford or Canterbury, including his preferred pipe tobacco. There was something oddly intimate about certain of his requests. When he asked her if should could find him some new pants, her trip to the shops revealed that the request was far from simple, such was the range of styles and sizes.

As usual, her letters were filled with her news, her reticence about going on too much about so many trivial parts of her life, allayed by his insistence that she should tell him everything.

"Darling, I love to hear what you've been doing," he insisted. "It makes me feel I'm there with you."

At the end of July Stanley was promoted to captain, and designated as the Brigade RASC Officer – BRASCO - of the 130th Infantry Brigade, part of the 43rd Division, becoming responsible for supplying some three thousand five hundred men with virtually all of their requirements.

The assignment also meant moving from the rather basic accommodation of the past months to the splendour of Milner Court, a large seventeenth century manor house, until recently, a school, before being requisitioned by the army, in the village of Sturry, close to Canterbury, a city which he had already taken against, and which, over the ensuing months, he came to associate with all that he disliked about army life.

*My own darling wife*
*I am feeling much happier than I thought I would this evening as things here are not going to be as bad as we feared.*
*I'll tell you all the bad things first.*
> *You have to be in to dinner roughly three or four nights a week but you can always skip out afterwards.*
> *For 2 hours we have to do PT every other morning (at 7)*
> *Messing is 3/- per day but the food is excellent*
> *You get no day off a week*
*Now the good things.*
> *Saturdays and Sunday (after lunch Sat) are very 'easy' and you do very little work.*
> *This job is a very nice one, as you get out every day.*

*You can bathe anywhere at Herne Bay. I had a most lovely swim today. It's only 6 miles away & there is a bus service.*

*You do 'duty officer' once a week but this only entails sleeping in the office.*

*The mess is about 12 strong and all but 2 appear to be under 35. There are 4 more subalterns, 4 captains & several others whom I'm still a bit hazy about.*

*Lawry says there's no ban on wives, but it's best to say nothing about it.*

*Canterbury is very near – I can see the Cathedral 2 1/2 miles away from my room.*

*Sturry is foul in parts but very pretty this end (Canterbury end) & a lovely river runs through it.*

*The George & Dragon, Forwich, is apparently a very good pub – to stay at too, & is only a few minutes walk away.*

*There are several small houses close by – it would be grand if you could eventually find somewhere there as they are almost on the doorstep of this place (Milner Court) which is a large & rather lovely old school bounded on one side by river & railway & on one by Sturry.*

*There is a railway station close by on the line to Canterbury & Ashford.*

*Leave is good & you get a few hours (even a night) on each one.*

*There is a huge barn in the grounds where they hold dances occasionally.*

*The Brig. is quite nice.*

*I love you.*

*Well, darling, that's roughly the position as I see it after a short while here – not too bad. About the job & promotion – I'm still rather in the dark as I'm 'on probation', but I think that if all goes well & the Brig. doesn't mind me too much, I might just get it alright. Darling sweetheart Peggy, I mustn't get sentimental now – it'd be fatal, but I'll just tell you that I miss you most horribly & love you so terribly utterly & longingly tonight. I have just given JT a pat from you – but he needs more – a big squeeze!*

*Your ever loving husband*

*Stanley*

Coming at the same time as his promotion, when Peggy informed him that she had found some work in Canterbury and would be moving into digs which, although on the far side of the small city, were only a couple of miles from him, notwithstanding his misgivings about her returning to nursing, albeit as an auxiliary, he could not escape the feeling that things were most definitely looking up.

Having become used to the fact that she was the wife of an army officer, Peggy found it particularly amusing when Stanley told her that he had been given a 'batman' whom he described as "a most affable fellow" by the name of Hopkins. "How funny," she said on the phone when he had mentioned it, "that you now have a man to look after you."

# EIGHT

For the next year, Peggy remained in her Canterbury digs, their tentative plan to find a house which they could rent together having been stymied by army red tape, permission for officers to bring their wives to live with them proving to be subject to various conditions which they were unable to comply with. In truth, with the demands of army life and with Peggy's duty hours, they would, as Stanley acknowledged when they finally abandoned the idea, "have passed like ships in the night."

The arrangement, nevertheless, worked out remarkably well, her landlady being generously accommodating of her lodger's husband when he appeared, often staying overnight whenever his absence was permitted, and occasionally, when he managed to creep away undetected, the young officers adept at covering for each other, although in reality, the Military Police were happy to turn a blind eye.

The grimness of war seemed as unrelenting as ever, the bad news incessant. To them, the day to day reality was the aerial battles which, despite the Germans having markedly lessened the intensity of their bombing, particularly of the capital, nevertheless went on, Canterbury being targeted on several occasions.

What the local populace were unaware of was that their small city was one of several selected by German High Command to be attacked by way of retaliation for the RAF raid on Lubeck, an ancient German city, such raids marking an escalation to what was to become known as "total war', civilians being deemed legitimate targets.

For the young couple, and indeed, for most of the population, life went on, the horrors and privations of war becoming something which one simply had to live with. For Stanley, training, in the form of frequent exercises, and the ever expanding body of knowledge necessary to enable the RASC to keep the fighting troops supplied with the wherewithal of warfare as well as their sustenance and welfare, for much of the time, absorbed his attention, although with inevitable spells when boredom or disgruntlement would take hold, such spells generally being short lived, dispelled by being shared with comrades, or, more often, with Peggy who had, by now, acquired the art of placating and soothing away his troubles.

She found her work a good deal more rewarding than her time at Bart's not least because of the absence of the academic side, with its regular exams. Most of her duty periods were at Canterbury hospital although she was also expected to undertake some home visits, the mixture much to her liking.

Her room at her digs quickly became their home, the landlady having found them a double bed, various of Stanley's possessions giving the room a certain something she could never quite put her finger on. Perhaps it was the aroma of the couple of pipes he had left there, or of some of his garments; and a cocktail of brylcreem and leather. It was as if, when he was not there, his essence still inhabited the room.

A number of times they had talked about children, agreeing that they should wait, although each time the subject came up, it was as if they each needed to identify the doubts which, for different reasons, they shared.

The discussions followed a similar route, their reverie, of a future together in a time of peace, in their own house, with two or may be three children; it was so idyllic. And each time, the dream was reduced to the reality, that with such uncertainty about the future, they should not yet consider having a child.

Although they were acutely aware of it, they hated to articulate the reason; that at some stage, Stanley was bound to have to go off to fight.

"Do we want to risk an infant growing up without knowing his Dad?" Stanley tried to make light of it, forcing a laugh, Peggy's expression, for a brief moment, sombre as she contemplated such a dreadful prospect.

"But how long do we wait?" she asked, knowing full well that he could not answer. "Until the war is over, I suppose," she said.

For Stanley, part of his doubt about delaying was for a reason he chose not to allude to, although it constantly played on his mind. If she had a child, she would probably have to live with her parents, in the relative safety of Hove. Whilst he loved having her close by, particularly as their sex life had become so wonderfully fulfilling, for both of them, he hated the fact that she was nursing. He told himself that he wanted her away from the danger of living in Canterbury, even before it was targeted for a major attack, its location on one of the main flight paths for the *Luftwaffe,* making it vulnerable, being hit regularly by what appeared to be random disposal of bombs when aircraft had failed to find their target, quite apart from it serving as one of the revenge targets for the Lubeck raid.

147

He could not admit, even to himself, that he simply wanted his wife at home, there being something about a working wife that grated with a side of him which, despite his embrace of the modern world, harboured a residue of staunch conservatism.

"I don't know, darling. Let's just wait and see how things go," he said doubtfully, adding his answer to hers.

Having agreed, therefore, that they would take precautions, she also taught him the mathematics of the menstrual cycle. Always fascinated by numbers and statistics, he was particularly taken with the notion that a woman's ovulation accorded with the lunar cycle although making the actual connection, that somehow the moon could physically influence the workings of the female physiology, he found hard to accept.

"The changes in the tide are caused by the moon," she pointed out, "so why not us?"

With his interest in figures and patterns, and the way things worked, he would, whenever he could, acquire gadgets, a particular favourite, a barograph which had been his father's, donated to Stanley on his 21st birthday but sadly, having to remain at the vicarage. When he was at home, he would look closely at the graph on the circular drum, the ink line showing the pressure which he could relate to the weather, opening up a new avenue which would prove valuable during the war years, of weather forecasting. He would look up at the clouds, identifying them knowingly – "Mm, nimbo stratus" – as he sniffed the wind before giving his prediction – "a front coming in".

He loved cameras, working out how they functioned, as well as the process of developing film, his affinity with numbers extending his interest to tide times, train timetables, and, to a lesser extent, economics generally, his interest tending to wane when he encountered areas which gave rise to conceptual or academic demands.

It was his "numbers head", as Peggy described it, which made him particularly well equipped for his role as an RASC officer, and indeed, enabled him to take on greater responsibility and to rise up the ranks. Although it was not something he was aware of, and only recognised in himself some years later, he also had a natural authority. Being tall and good natured gave him a certain presence and making him popular was undoubtedly a contributory factor, but it was also his clear sightedness and his ability to analyse and come to a decision.

He could see patterns in the arrangements of army logistics; the correlation of the numbers of troops, the activities they were engaged in, and their requirements, enabling him quickly to move to the next issue, of the mechanisms of supply.

It was also, undoubtedly, his aptitude for organisation, and his evolving ability, recognised by his senior officers, which lead to his acquiring his three pips, being promoted to captain ahead of most of his peers, when he became the Brigade RASC Officer – BRASCO - for 130th Brigade.

"But it's not always exact," Peggy had to explain when, with his diary to hand, he was calculating dates when, as he put it, "we'll be in the clear", for him to try to arrange leave, quickly adding "I don't mean *only* then". "It's sometimes several days early or late. All sorts of things affect it," she cautioned.

Having accepted the connection between the lunar and menstrual cycles, the fact that the former was regular and precisely predictable whereas the latter was subject to variations for all sorts of vague reasons, he found quite baffling.

"Sometimes I just *know*," she said. "Women have a sixth sense."

"I think I would rather rely on a tide table than a *sixth sense*," he replied, although he was more than happy to be guided by her as to when they could make love without the infernal rubber protective.

When, in the middle of September, not having seen him for nearly two weeks as he had been involved in an exercise and she had been on a spell of night duty, they spoke on the phone, she tried to sound unconcerned when she mentioned that she was a couple of weeks late.

"The last one was six weeks ago," he confirmed, now keeping a record in his diary. "You're not thinking…"

"No, don't worry," she interrupted. "I've told you it can vary." But this time, something was telling her that this wasn't the usual fluctuations, sometimes two or three days, but not two weeks. And she was feeling something; it was like the approach of an illness but without feeling ill.

She wished she hadn't told him, knowing that it would set him off, feeding his capacity to worry. What she was thinking, however, was that if it was real, perhaps it was a good thing that the decision would be taken for them. She loved the idea of being a mother. She envied her friend Rosemary, now married and pregnant, although being a full-figured girl with broad hips and a prominent bust, one would not have noticed the swelling of her abdomen had she not pointed it out.

The worry that began to weigh upon her was not about being pregnant, but because she feared that Stanley would be angry with her. He had a tendency to belittle her, in a kindly, slightly condescending way, and now, in this vital matter, she would have to admit that she had got it wrong; her reliance on the combination of timing and instinct proving to be fallible. She needed to see a doctor to find out so that, if it was confirmed, she could at least prepare herself for the consequences.

For Stanley, the prospect of her having to abandon her nursing work and move back home was certainly desirable. There seemed to be no likelihood of him being sent abroad for the foreseeable future, the talk being of a couple of years at least before they, the British army, would be ready to fight their way back into Europe. Did they really need to wait all that time? To be married for possibly three years, or maybe longer, without having a child seemed to fly in the face of nature.

As she had anticipated, he began to worry to the extent that he was phoning her almost every day, his concern ostensibly being about her health despite her insistence that she felt absolutely well.

"But aren't you feeling unwell?" It was almost as if he was wanting her to feel bad, not as a punishment, but because, in his mind, pregnancy was akin to illness.

When, just a few days after telling him that she was late, her period began, she was kicking herself for having mentioned it to him. On the other hand, if it had been real, and she had kept it to herself, she dreaded to think how he would have reacted.

For a couple of days before the period started, she experienced strange sensations, telling her that this was not simply being late, the heaviness of it when it began, making her realise that, almost certainly, it had been real. She could now understand why, a few times, on waking up, she had felt rather queasy.

When she composed the telegram, she was trying to find a form of words which would not make it too obvious what she was saying, conscious as she was that it would be read by others, in particular, the girl at the post office. But she had to let him know straight away, not wanting to wait until later in the evening when he was off duty.

GOOD NEWS. SOMETHING HAS HAPPENED. LOVE PEGGY

As soon as she returned from the post office, having an hour before she was due on duty, she decided to write to him even though she was sure he would try to phone her as soon as he received the telegram.

*My darling sweetheart*
*I hope you have received my telegram & that it has relieved you of all your worries. I am feeling really care free – though not exactly like pushing a bus over – with this 'toothache' which has 'slipped' – but I am so glad it is real now.*
*I realise that I am not going to be a 'Mummy' after all just yet. Aren't you glad you are not going to be a Daddy?*
*It was so strange seeing army lorries going up and down the road today. I felt I ought to be looking out for staff cars which might contain my husband. I am longing to talk to my sweet husband & kiss him & feel warm & comfortable & secure even though he was wearing battledress & it was prickly! I don't think I would mind if he had a bristly chin even!*
*By the way I am so sorry I forgot – congratulations on your 3 pips. We shall have a lot to celebrate when we next meet shan't we?*
*So sweetheart, God bless you & goodnight*
*Peggy*

When they met on Saturday evening, having supper in their regular Canterbury restaurant which offered simple and modestly priced fare, before going on to the cinema to see *The Maltese Falcon*, a film they had heard a great deal about and were both keen to see, instantly, as he walked in, she could see that he was in one of his moods. She had hoped that, with the relief of her not being pregnant, he would be back to his jovial self. Perhaps she had misread the whole situation, and he was actually disappointed.

As soon as he sat down however, the reason for his mood became clear.

"Have you heard about the *Ark Royal*? It's been sunk. God Almighty! As if the *Hood* wasn't bad enough."

It was almost as if he took it personally. Yet she should not have been surprised. A couple of years before the war, he had taken her for a day out to Southampton, insisting that she had to see the ocean liner, the *Queen Mary*.

"Isn't she magnificent?" he had said, breathlessly, as they walked along the quay, the Ocean Terminal being open to visitors until the day the ship was due to sail. He had stood looking up at the vast bow, and high above it, the three red funnels, his expression one of awe. "She's the greatest ship ever built," he had enthused before detailing what seemed to be the ship's full specification, down to crew and passenger numbers, provisions, and the cost of a first class ticket.

"Perhaps I'll take you to America on her one day," he had mused.

So it was with naval ships, his reverence for them and his encyclopaedic knowledge of their dimensions and capabilities, enhanced by what they stood for, his pride in them, as the puissant icons of Britain's status in the world, making the demise of one of them a shattering blow. Against the backdrop of the country seeming to be on the back foot in every theatre of the war, the news of the loss of the *Ark Royal* weighed upon him as much as personal bereavement.

"And the Huns are nearly in Moscow," he said, gripping his mug of tea so tightly she feared he was going to crush it. "It makes my blood boil. All we do it fiddle around, playing war games around the countryside. Why the hell can't we get at them?"

"I'm sure we will at some point," she replied rather feebly, unable to think of anything else to say to placate him.

"I'm sorry, darling," he said, taking her hand. "Sometimes it's just too much to bear. I've been feeling a bit rough as well."

"Not your throat again?" she asked, the frequency of his sore throats and colds causing her some concern. Everyone got colds, particularly in winter, but he seemed to get more than his fair share.

"It's being in Kent," he said with a wry laugh. "Bloody place is so damned cold. And when we're out on exercises, there are times when it gets right to your marrow."

"I'll have to knit you some woolly vests," she suggested, resolving at that moment to try to buy him some, the ones he wore being far too thin. "You must look after yourself a bit better, darling," she said. "Perhaps you need a private nurse to come on the exercises with you."

"She could certainly keep me warm at night!"

"By the way, I've now got a puppy," he said, his face lighting up with his boyish grin.

"How wonderful. What's it called? Are you able to look after it properly?" She was trying to imagine how a puppy would fit in with army life and routines.

Just over a week later, came the news that two more of Britain's most famous capital ships, the *Prince of Wales*, which had played a key part in avenging the loss of the *Hood* by sinking the *Bismark*, and the *Repulse*, one of the Navy's renowned battlecruisers, had been sunk by the Japanese as they advanced across South East Asia, heading for the vital British garrison at Singapore.

The devastating news of the loss of two more of the Navy's proud ships, although it was not generally recognised at the time, marked the ending of the era of naval warfare as gunnery duels between opposing fleets, an era going back several centuries, even before the Armada, the latest – and last – phase seeing mighty "dreadnought" battleships, hurling shells at each other at a distance of twenty miles, having endured for some forty years, its zenith being the inconclusive Battle of Jutland in the Great War. The new era, as so shockingly demonstrated by the destruction of the *Prince of Wales* and *Repulse,* was to be dominated by aircraft, the two ships proving impotent against the onslaught of Japanese bombers.

Within a few months, the great Pacific encounters between the Americans and the Japanese would see opposing fleets engaging while a hundred miles apart, centred around their aircraft carriers, almost overnight becoming the new capital ships, battleships reduced to a supporting role.

In early December, when they had only a couple of hours, squeezed between their respective duty times, having heard the news just before leaving her digs, Peggy was fully prepared for another of his despondent moods. She was pleasantly surprised therefore, when he arrived positively light hearted.

"Bad news," she ventured.

"Pearl Harbour? Yes, it's bloody awful that the Japs have sunk so many ships. But the Yanks are now in. They'll be joining us to take on the Hun as well as teaching the Japs a lesson."

The active theatre of the war which had, in recent months, being getting a good deal of news coverage, was in North Africa where, initially, the British had been able to defeat inferior Italian forces only for the Germans to deploy their own force under the command of one of their most effective generals, Rommel. The focus of the desert war, for some months, was the strategically vital port city of Tobruk which a small British garrison was able to hold onto in the face of repeated attempts by Rommel to capture it.

The breaking of the siege of Tobruk in December, was a rare piece of good news, eagerly seized upon after such a lengthy period of adversity, conflated into a victory rather than the actuality, of avoidance of a critical defeat. It was, only a temporary respite, Tobruk to fall to the Germans the following year, although they were able to retain it for only a short time before the Eighth Army re-took it before surging on to achieve the first significant victory of the war, at the battle of El Alamein.

There was yet more bad news to come just a few weeks into 1942, with the surrender of Singapore to the Japanese, eighty thousand British troops being taken prisoner. The loss of the all important outpost was felt, not only as yet another dreadful defeat, but also as a deep, and possibly mortal wound to the Empire, the Japanese driving Britain out of most of South East Asia, back to Burma and almost to India, the potential loss of which was too awful to contemplate. With the Germans having completed their conquest of Europe, the early weeks of 1942 presented a desperately bleak picture.

What was remarkable, however, was that, as morale had remained unbroken during the worst of the blitz, so the country's capacity to withstand such repeated shocks endured, bolstered by Churchill's inspirational rhetoric and the firm belief that the time would come, sooner or later, to return to the European fray. Perverse as even the most optimistic sometimes had to admit, it seemed the conviction that Britain would prevail, signified by Churchill's now famed "V" sign, was unshakeable.

Stanley's ostensible dismissiveness of any form of ill-health never fooled Peggy, who, by now, had become familiar with his foibles and idiosyncrasies, such bravado thinly veiling yet another facet of his anxious nature, a loathing of all things medical, his self pity when he was suffering any ailment surpassed only by his inordinate concern for her health. Indeed, there were times when she felt like telling him that it was as if he was almost willing her to be unwell.

Over those winter months, she became increasingly worried about him. Whenever they were together, he was either sneezing or sniffling, or complaining of a sore throat, every now and again having to take to his bed with what he described as "a touch of flu". She concluded that army life was having an effect on him, both the living conditions, particularly during exercises, and the diet.

His quarters themselves, which she had visited a few times, were comfortable enough, although Milner Court, a grand seventeenth century manor house, felt chilly and draughty even during warmer weather, the air having a dank smell which sometimes seemed to permeate his clothes, prompting her, whenever there was an opportunity, to insist he took them off so that she could air them properly.

When they were on exercise, they often slept under canvas, his accounts of their mock battles across the Kent countryside, punctuated with references to being endlessly cold and damp, sometimes being unable to change out of wet battledress for several days.

She had met his batman, Hopkins, a few times, taking to him, recognising a kindly man who was clearly dedicated to his officer. She had little idea of the extent of a batman's role, but when Hopkins arrived one day with a letter which Stanley had asked him to deliver, she was delighted, but slightly embarrassed as such personal service. She took the opportunity to offer him a cup of tea and, chatting to him, shared her concerns about his health.

"If you don't mind my saying so, ma'am, I don't think he helps himself. I tell him to let me dry his clothes, and that he should start wearing long coms, but he doesn't want to know."

"Mm, I think I know what you mean," she replied, recognising this description of his tendency to pig-headedness. "And please don't call me "ma'am". It makes me feel like some old dowager."

He had looked at her with some confusion, it being his nature, instilled from his background, that one should know one's place.

"Very well," he said, avoiding using her name.

When Stanley was with her, particularly at her digs, she did her best to feed him well, supplementing the army diet, which, whilst plentiful, lacked the fresh fruit and vegetables which, to her, were absolute essentials, his accounts of his meals describing the vegetables as being "boiled to within an inch of their lives", fresh fruit being a rarity.

Her intervention, in terms of both her healthier offerings, and her scolding him for not looking after himself, particularly after her chat with Hopkins – although, at his anxious request, she had refrained from repeating his concerns to Stanley – was having little effect, and if anything, he seemed to be getting worse.

*My very dear darling*
*The M.O. came at midday and my worst fears were confirmed – he found my temp was 102.6 and said I must stay in bed today. He was about as stupid as a horse – he was a little Yorkshire two pipper and I'm sure you could have done better. He gave me lots of temperature reducers & I got hotter & hotter till I was very sick. I then began to feel better & cooler till I was sick again at 11.30 & again in the night. I feel very much better today though, but very groggy when I stand up. Everyone is very thoughtful & kind & I have a constant stream of callers!*
*Your very loving husband*
*Stanley*

It was her birthday when his letter arrived, although with the general despondency about Singapore, which had affected people more than other setbacks, making them realise that the war was threating British interests and all that they stood for across the globe, and with her own worries, she did not feel in the least like celebrating.

As she had feared, his health deteriorated, the difficulty in obtaining information, communication being erratic at the best of times, compounding her anxiety.

When she was told that there was a phone call for her from someone called Hopkins, she felt a moment of panic. He sounded slightly breathless, as if he had been hurrying, or was reluctant to be the bearer of bad news.

"He asked me to let you know that he's been taken to Leeds Castle," he told her. "He will try to telephone you when he can."

She had seen Leeds Castle once when they had driven past it, a splendid spectacle, straight out of a storybook. Nowadays it served as a military hospital, the accounts she had heard suggesting that it although its medical facilities were as good as any other hospital, in other respects it was not well appointed, the rumours being of cold wards and less than rigorous hygiene. There had even been suggestions that although some of the nursing staff were properly trained civilians, there were also numerous military people – orderlies, nursing assistants and doctors, who were not highly spoken of.

The fact that the day he was admitted was Stanley's birthday entirely past him by, his recollection of the journey, in the passenger seat of an army car with a fretting Hopkins at the wheel, was a series of fragments: lying back in the seat, his head resting on the side window, staring up at the sky, grey clouds scudding from the west, wondering why it was so empty, with not a single aircraft in sight, forgetting that at this time, in the middle of the day, there was generally a lull in aerial activity.

He remembered the unpleasant feeling of sweat inside his clothing, one minute feeling so cold he could not help himself from shivering, the next, so feverishly hot he had to wind down the window prompting Hopkins to tell him to wind it up "or you'll catch your death, sir."

The next twenty four hours he spent languishing in a room which he shared with three other officers, although the extent of his interaction with them was limited to spells of staring at the strange faces, wondering who they were and why they were in his room with its plain whitewashed walls, the light from the window making a rhomboid shape which progressed slowly, elongating as time passed.

If he lifted his head, which he could only do with difficulty as it exacerbated his throbbing headache, he could just see out of the window which offered a view of a rectangle of sky, and in one corner, protruding like bony fingers, branches of a leafless tree.

On the second day, two orderlies arrived, transferring him from his bed to a wheelchair, pushing him along several corridors and into a room full of medical equipment, helping him from the wheelchair onto another bed with a large lamp above it, where a man in a white coat wearing a strange looking hat, and two nurses, started doing things to him, one of the nurses leaning over him, placing a rubber device on his face, the only thing permeating his fading consciousness being the pungent smell of the anaesthetic gas.

It was another full day before he properly regained his senses, a nurse informing him that he had had his tonsils removed. He could not work out why he felt oddly disappointed. Perhaps it was because having one's tonsils out sounded such a small thing. It was like being short-changed; surely, having been as ill as he obviously was, it must have been something more serious that tonsils.

Peggy, having become increasingly frantic in her attempts to find out what was happening to her husband, eventually got through to one of the ward sisters, a rather curt sounding woman, who said that he was "making a normal recovery", which Peggy did not find reassuring, particularly when Hopkins had phoned her to say that "I don't want to worry you, ma'am, but he was in a pretty bad way when I dropped him off."

When, after several further attempts, she was able to speak to someone who described himself as a "superintendent", she was told that civilian visits were restricted and she would need to apply for permission.

"But it's my husband," she pleaded. "I need to know how he is and when I can see him."

"As I said, madam," the unhelpful man repeated, "visits are restricted," although he did enlighten her as to the procedure for arranging a visit. It would be more than two weeks before she was eventually able to see him, having to make do in the meantime with snippets of information she was able to glean from repeated, pestering calls, and with the help of Hopkins, who proved adept as using his "old pals" network, finding that one of the army medical staff was a friend of his from before the war.

When, eventually, she was able to visit him, the army hospital management appearing to be intent upon making it as difficult as possible, she found something in the atmosphere rather unpleasant; the air in the corridors was cold and lifeless, and when she entered Stanley's room, there was a sharp draft coming from the window, the wooden frame decayed and ill-fitting, the four patients all with their blankets pulled up to their chins.

She was shocked at the sight of Stanley, asleep with his head tipped to one side, his face a deathly pallor with dark rings under his eyes, his cheeks hollow as if the flesh had been sucked from them. As she was standing beside the bed he seemed to sense her presence, opening his eyes, blinking for a moment as if trying to recognise her before brightening, the smile spreading across his features seeming an effort.

"Darling, how lovely to see you." He patted the bed, inviting her to sit, taking her hand as she did so, his hand feeling soft and clammy, as if it had been soaked in warm water.

During the hour she sat with him, he seemed to revive, as if her presence was infusing him with new energy.

"God Almighty, I can't wait to get out of this place. I can't tell you how awful it's been."

But it was not until mid March, three weeks after he had been admitted, that he was allowed to leave, Hopkins again chauffeuring him.

"Surely you will be allowed home for a while," Peggy said when they spoke on the phone the evening before he was discharged, after he had told her that the doctor had instructed him he was to return to Milner Court, into the care of the Medical Officer. "You need some proper care. I can get some time off."

"I'm afraid they won't allow it," he said, the idea of a few days of pampering most appealing, and better still if Peggy could be the one ministering to him.

When they met in Canterbury a few days later, she could see straight away, that he was far from being fully recovered, there being a lethargy about him, his conversation flat, devoid of his usual enthusiasm. Her concern proved to be well founded as, two weeks after being discharged he telephoned her to tell her he was back at Leeds Castle.

"The doc reckons it's a touch of septicaemia," he said, "whatever that is. I don't feel as rotten as I did when I came here before. It's like a dose of flu. I get the shivers and sometimes I'm a bit out of breath."

"Septicaemia," she repeated quietly, trying not to let him hear her shock. She had encountered several cases, a few of them proving fatal. "My poor darling. I'm going to get to see you as soon as I can get away from here."

This time, being better acquainted with the army procedures, not only was she able to visit him the following day, but after a forthright discussion with one of the senior doctors whom she waylaid in a corridor, she was given permission to stay overnight, a room being made available for her it the nurses' quarters.

She also found that the ward sister, at first glance a rather stern, "no-nonsense" woman, was a former Bart's nurse, Peggy quickly finding that she was in fact, friendly and caring, admitting that it was sometimes difficult to work with the military management of the hospital.

She resolved to stay for three more nights, departing only when she felt certain that he was improving sufficiently to be left in the hands of the medical staff, the ward sister promising to phone her if he deteriorated.

*Leeds Castle*
*My dearest sweet Funny Bunny*
*We are just expecting the M.O. and all is quite peaceful except for Harry Roy on the wireless. We all had a rather bad night – it was cold and my throat & mouth ached etc. However, I feel OK now.*
*The M.O. has just been round I am allowed up for half a day today which means I can get dressed. I showed him the spots on my tongue and lip and he called it something and now sister has put some 'violet something' on them.*
*I'm afraid I've rather a lot of spots etc: I hope you won't mind them when we go on leave & will help me get rid of them.*
*Darling, you could get a service gas mask couldn't you? The VAD's here have them: do try and get one of some sort & <u>bring it</u> with you to show me!*
*Yours for ever in love*
*Stanley*

# NINE

Having had to spend a further three weeks at Leeds Castle, enduring the discomfort of the ancient and draughty edifice as well as the tedium, alleviated to some extent by Peggy's frequent visits, by the beginning of May he was back to health and army routine.

Shortly before his first spell in hospital, a new Commanding Officer had been appointed to the 43rd Division, Major-General Ivo Thomas. His reputation was as a firm believer in discipline and training, but also as a proponent of modern warfare, his experiences of the Great War having taught him that pitting armies of massed infantry against each other was likely to result in stalemate and the sort of carnage which he had witnessed.

As soon as Stanley was back with his brigade, it was apparent that changes required by the CO's new regime were already under way, particularly with the increase in the number of exercises, each involving carefully planned battle scenarios.

For officers and men, there was also a new feeling of purpose, the CO making it known, through regular briefings with his senior officers, that his aim was to ensure that when – not if – the Wyverns, as he referred to them, proud now to be wearing the Division's insignia – they took on the *Wehrmacht*, probably within the next year or so, they would not only be up to the task, but would be able to prove themselves the most effective fighting force in the British army.

There was something inspirational in the General's conviction, it soon becoming not only the aspiration of every man in the Division, but the goal they were certain they would attain, to be the best, such keenness reflected in their commitment, applying themselves to whatever tasks they were given, even the most gruelling exercises accepted as being an essential part of their preparation.

There were, however, moments when such resolve was tested, the exercise in late May, involving an operation ranging across large swathes of Kent with several "battles" along the way, proving particularly arduous, the week long operation being accompanied by a spell of unseasonably cold, wet weather.

It was after dark on the night of 30th May that Stanley's convoy was making its way back towards Canterbury, the exercise having ended a few hours earlier, the exhausted men looking forwards to getting back to their base for a hot meal and the own beds. They were some five miles from the city when they were stopped by members of the local Home Guard who told them that all roads into Canterbury were closed due to an air raid warning.

As Stanley, being the senior officer of his contingent, stepped down from the cab of the lorry he had been travelling in, ready to pull rank on the sergeant who appeared to be in charge, he stopped, the night filled with the sound of aircraft.

"They're ours," he said, the dark shapes of several formations of bombers clearly visible against the night sky. "Heading for Germany."

"There's a warning for Canterbury," the sergeant insisted.

As Stanley was about to remonstrate with the sergeant, he was cut short by several heavy "whumps", as the sound of enemy aircraft could be distinctly heard, more strident than the hum of the Lancasters, the German planes arcing round at the end of the bomb run, visible as dark shapes against the night sky.

"Got the bastard!" one of the men shouted as a Spitfire wheeled away from its target, a bloom of flame descending rapidly a couple of miles away.

"Christ Almighty!" Stanley muttered at the sound of more detonations, for several minutes, the blasts incessant, the ground beneath them, even with the impacts so far away, reverberating.

Within minutes, fires could be seen, the city's buildings, tiny silhouettes against the glow.

"Peggy, my wife's there," he said, speaking to no one in particular, staring in horror as bombs continued to fall, the fires appearing to spring up across much of the city.

For more than two hours they remained there, helpless spectators, as several waves of bombers delivered their lethal cargoes, the only consolation being the number being hit by the defending fighters, at least a dozen being seen falling to earth, several as balls of fire, one of them, within half a mile of them, exploding as it crashed into a wood, setting fire to several trees.

"I've got to get in there," Stanley said to the sergeant when, at last, it seemed that the raid was dying down.

"I'm sorry, sir, we have orders to keep the road closed until we get word."

Fortunately, word of the all clear arrived shortly after the last of the blasts, Stanley managing to reorganise the convoy, sending it off on a circuitous route back to their base at Sturry, he, with his driver, heading towards the city.

When they reached the outskirts it appeared that it was the centre of the city which had suffered the brunt of the raid, the entire area seeming to be on fire.

"Sir, we can't get any further," the driver said as they came to a road blocked by collapsed buildings, several still burning fiercely, the efforts of the fire engines appearing largely ineffective, Stanley and the driver having got out of the cab, standing staring at the scene of devastation.

"Looks like the cathedral's alright," the driver said, the ancient building appearing to be intact, the light of the flames creating lurid patterns on its graceful structure.

"We have to go to the other side," Stanley said, climbing back into the lorry. "We should be able to get round the north side. Come on!"

Keeping the burning centre of the city on their right and having to navigate several other blocked streets, a number of bombs having fallen away from the centre, they managed to work their way across the river, only to encounter further road closures, this time with police and Home Guard turning them back, a police officer explaining that they had to keep the way clear for ambulances ferrying the injured to the nearby hospital.

"Drop me here!" Stanley said, his panic clear from his shouted command. As soon as he was out of the lorry he began to run, panting as he came to Old Dover Road, his fitness still not fully restored.

Turning into Nackington Road he could see some buildings on fire, not far ahead, in the direction of The Gap, Peggy's digs. He quickened his pace despite the pain in his lungs, pausing as he reached the corner of The Gap, relieved to see that the burning houses were quite a bit further.

As he hammered on the door of number 10, he looked around him before glancing at his watch, realising that although it was now beginning to get light, it was only 4.30. He banged again, becoming impatient, eventually hearing footsteps inside, the front door opening, the landlady, Mrs Donkersly, blinking off sleep.

"Stanley! What...?"

"Is Peggy here?" He looked past her, the kindly landlady stepping aside.

"As far as I know."

"Why aren't you in a shelter?" he asked as he brushed past her, taking the stairs two at a time without waiting for an answer.

As he burst into Peggy's room, she woke with a start, sitting up, her hair dishevelled, a lock lying across one eye.

"Darling!"

He sat on the side of the bed, enfolding her in his arms. "God, I was so worried. Have you seen the state of the place. The whole of the centre of the city is on fire. What are you doing here? Are you OK?"

He continued to hold her against him, his heart thumping in his chest from the exertion of running and of leaping up two flights of stairs.

"I'm fine," she said, pulling back from him. "Look, not even a scratch."

"But why aren't you in a shelter?"

"They've only got an Anderson. And when we heard the warning we all went down stairs and got under the dining table. You've seen it. A big solid oak one. We stayed there till we thought it was dying down and then went back to bed. I was so tired."

"The dining table?" he looked at her, restraining himself from saying what he was thinking. "Darling Pegs, you've got to be more careful."

What she didn't tell him was that five of them, Peggy, two other nurses and Mr and Mrs Donkersly, had huddled together under the dining table, which had been their shelter during several previous raids, it being Peggy who had decided that the worst seemed to be over, despite the fact that bombs were still falling, some not far away. These days, being used to raids, the fear of the earlier days of the blitz had been replaced by a grudging acceptance of the need to retreat to a shelter when the raids were bad, but gauging when they felt it was safe to go about their business. For Peggy, this sometimes meant collapsing into her bed, the long duty hours ensuring that her sleep was much needed and sound. Indeed, her reputation as a solid sleeper had become something of a standing

164

joke with the household, Mrs Donkersly and the other nurses, on several occasions, having had to wake her when she had slept through her alarm clock and, on one occasion, when a raid was underway.

Word of Peggy's sleeping prowess had reached the nurses at the hospital when it was reported that she had managed to sleep through an earlier raid, despite several bombs having fallen in the immediate area, Mrs Donkersly having omitted to wake her and to direct her to the dining table as she had mistakenly believed her to have been on night duty.

"Sorry," Peggy said meekly, laying her head on Stanley's shoulder, inhaling his warmth and his distinctive aroma of pipe smoke and the fabric of his battle dress, its course texture rough against her cheek. There was also something else too, a distinct odour, as if she could breath his very essence.

For several minutes they sat in silence, holding onto each other, the sun now illuminating the floral pattern on the closed curtains. As they kissed, the comforting embrace evolved, Peggy lying back, pulling him down onto the bed, sitting up as she deftly removed his boots and undid this belt before unbuttoning the tunic, stimulated by the odour of his unwashed body.

Their love making was slow, with the deliberation they had learned, acquainted as they now were with each other's bodies, aware of the sources of each other's pleasure.

As they lay, luxuriating in the warmth of the sun now filling the room, having pulled back one of the curtains, she lifted his arm, looking at his watch.

"Darling, I've got to go. I'm on in an hour."

"I've got to get back as well," he said, conscious of the fact that he was supposed to be meeting his fellow officers at that moment, to review the exercise. He was certain, however, that the driver would have reported what had occurred, his absence being put down to extenuating circumstances, as proved to be the case, the meeting, he discovered when he arrived at Milner Hall, having been put back to the afternoon.

What he also learned from one of the other officers, Stanley having missed the morning news, was that the reason for the aerial activity the previous night, apart from the raid on Canterbury, was that the RAF had carried out its biggest raid of the war so far, more than a thousand bombers having destroyed large areas of

Cologne. What was not reported on the news was that the raid killed more than twenty thousand German civilians, marking a significant escalation of the bombing campaign against cities, the German raid on Canterbury, in comparison, being relatively small scale, in terms of aircraft and casualties.

For Peggy and Stanley, there was little change in their lives through those summer months of 1942. He found himself becoming increasingly busy as he took on greater responsibilities, enjoying the organisational side of his role but finding the paperwork rather onerous.

At last there was some slightly more encouraging war news, the German advance towards Cairo having been checked at El Alamein and the Americans turning the tide decisively on the Japanese in the Pacific, following their stemming of the enemy advance across the ocean at the Battle of Coral Sea in May with the ensuing decisive victory at the Battle of Midway.

The news from the east was, however, worrying, with reports of the Russians being up against it at Stalingrad.

*My own darling*
*I have really been ever so lazy today. I do like our little hut. I thought how sweet it was & about coming home to it.*
*After lunch I went in the garden in sun top & shorts & hoped to get sun burnt. I don't think I did though as the sun didn't stay hot for very long & we had to come indoors about three times. One lot of gunfire woke me up from my snooze in the sun.*
*Tuesday 10.50 am*
*My darling*
*In contrast to yesterday it is very grey & wet this morning.*
*The news from Russia doesn't sound too good does it?*
*I am looking forward to seeing my little husband again ever so much for your 48 hours.*
*Lots of love & lots of kisses*
*Peggy*

*My darling*
*This is a grey dark Monday morning and I feel rather like it and am missing you like hell. I hated leaving you yesterday – very much and the rest of the day felt very flat. The train was ¾ hour late getting in and there was a hell of an air battle overhead when I arrived. The ack ack was miles behind as usual. I worked with Howard till 11 last night and went to bed feeling rather exhausted. P.T. at 7.15 this morning was bloody: breakfast at 8, BM's conference 8.45. Into the Brig at 9 as I am A/BTO and he likes to sign work*

*tickets on lean & pointless days. I am duty dog today and the phone has been ringing all morning.*

*The glory of leave is that you get accustomed to being away from the army and living a happy and natural existence. Darling, I'm sure we should get on terribly happily if we lived together always: I think the occasional spars we have are due to the independent lives we live and I get annoyed with you telling me what to do and you think I'm rude and boorish when I grunt at your back! But darling, the happy parts of our leave are far far greater than the quarrelling bits aren't they, and always live dearly in my memory.*

*Ever your loving husband*

*Stanley*

During her visits home she realised how much her parents worried about her brother, Tom, now serving in Burma. They were not people to display their emotions, and when he had told them of his posting, they had expressed their pride at their son doing his duty to God and King, Peggy accompanying them as they saw him off at the station, her mother resolutely holding back the tears Peggy could see she was close to shedding, her father's clenched jaw revealing his determinedly contained feelings.

*My own sweetheart*

*Here I am only a short while after talking to you on the telephone. It is nice to have my own little wireless.*

*Mr Churchill spoke very well didn't he – but only moderately optimistically in saying this was the end of the beginning – no mention of this being six months from the end! But still I hope it is. Six months seems a very short time doesn't it? I think a year will probably be nearer when you think of Germany, Japan & Italy to be dealt with. Sometimes I feel this will be the last Christmas in wartime.*

*A squadron of spitfires are just going over, very high up in formation. There seem to be two missing. I am glad you are not in the RAF darling, although wives do have a better time.*

*Another spitfire has just come over quite low. I think it must be one of the missing ones trying to catch its squadron up.*

*The service on Sunday was lovely. I thought of you very much darling. The church was absolutely full which made it all the more impressive. Your mother, Michael, Mummy & I occupied the back row.*

*I think it will be alright for us to stay in the hut for leave with the weather as warm as this. I have seen your people & told them you will be home.*

*Lots of love & kisses*

*Peggy*

*My darling*

*I was very pleased to hear your voice on the phone last night.*

*We have had a lot of palaver here today but now everything is more or less peace again and I'm trying to get warm in my office. Outside it is a perfect day of early winter – the trees have a very lovely appearance against the hazy sky.*

*Strange to think that this is Armistice Day & of the disillusionment & people who on 11th November 1918 thought that the war was over when in reality it was only a brief truce. This time I really think we are on the path to complete victory.*

*Darling, can we have dinner out in the hut or at Jimmy's next Friday & get a little tiddly? Please lay on some liquor! I hope to home about 3.30. Don't come & meet me as it would mean standing in the cold.*

*I'm duty officer today but don't mind as I sleep in this office which is warm compared with my bedroom which is quite the coldest on earth.*

*Ever your very loving husband*

*Stanley*


News of the war continued to get better, the decisive victory over Rommel at El Alamein just the fillip that was needed, the name of Montgomery now mentioned alongside Churchill and the King as the nation's heroes.

For Peggy and Stanley, the intermittent nature of their relationship was, when they were together, gave it a greater intensity, their love making richly pleasurable, finding now, a far greater openness and depth of intimacy.

"I think it's taken us two years to really get to know each other," she said when, during one of the infrequent occasions when they both managed to get home at the same time, they were lying in bed in the hut, blankets piled on top of them to protect them from the cold, a thick frost covering the vicarage lawn, the moisture given off by the paraffin heater adding to the frozen patterns on the inside of the windows.

Wary of mentioning it, knowing her determination, he was nevertheless, constantly worried about her returning to Canterbury, in spite of her proximity to him.

When he returned from leave, Stanley moved to new quarters in the splendour of Chilham Castle, in terms of grandeur, a definite step up from Milner Hall, taking on a new role at the Divisional HQ.

Once again, the army was responsible for separating him from so many of the friends he had made during his time with 130 Brigade, a time which he looked back on with particular fondness. And as was his habit, it was Peggy to whom he poured out his feelings.

He would, however, be re-joining a handful of old colleagues.

*My very own darling*
*I'm afraid I shall never be happy at the idea of your being in Canterbury. However, darling, while you're there I'll get off whenever I can & after every blitz etc. you must promise to wire, ring, or better still, come & see me. Also promise to go home at Christmas & try not get so many colds though I think that's unavoidable in Canterbury.*
*After I left you yesterday I went back to Bde. HQ feeling very sad at leaving you & then there was dreadful hour saying goodbye to everyone. However at about 11.30 Myles brought me a drink & by 12.45 I was pretty drunk but still sad and eventually I just slipped away, rather drunk but very miserable. Hopkins & I set out & hardly spoke to each other till we reached here. The mess I found was quite pleasant & my billet just above the mess with quite a delightful view. It was so cold though I nearly died.*
*I woke up this morning still cold & had breakfast at 7.30. Then I found my new office which is in a Nissan hut in a field & is quite warm as it has a stove. I share it with a pleasant chap called Captain Larkin who is the best of a pretty lousy selection of officers except Tony & Bill. The O.C. is a horrible type – usually tight.*
*I'd give everything to go back to Bde HQ or better still for the war to end.*
*The trouble is the people at CRASC HQ are all terrified of the stupid Colonel who is an absolute shocker.*
*The one bright spot at the moment is our love, our dog & our home. May God bless & keep save & well, you, my darling Pegs, and the others too.*
*Always your adoring husband*
*Stanley*

What neither of them had anticipated was that as soon as she returned to the hospital she learned that she was to be working as a district nurse, which, although being part of her role previously, had been secondary to working on the wards. It was not something she was happy with, working on wards being what she felt to be proper nursing, not least because she so enjoyed the company of other nurses.

When she told Stanley, on the phone on her first evening back, expressing her disappointment, he did not feel it made a great deal of difference in that she was still going to be living in Canterbury, the experience of the recent raid having shocked him and deepened his concern as to her safety.

Despite her complaining of her change of role, it came as a considerable surprise to him when they met for a few hours a week before Christmas, when she told him she had decided to give up nursing. His relief was, however, short lived, as she explained, with some hesitancy, apprehensive, as always, as to his reaction, that having been to the Labour Exchange to enquire about other nursing jobs, nothing suitable being available, they had given her details of different kind of job.

"It's a sort of clerk," she explained. "Doing some administration and that sort of thing. I've applied for it," she added.

"Where is it?" he asked just as she was about to tell him.

"Would you believe it, it's in Dover Castle! Doesn't that sound grand?"

"My darling girl! Don't you realise that Dover is one of the most dangerous places in the country? It's constantly being shelled. From across the Channel."

She looked at him with the little girl expression he was familiar with when she trying to get round him, or to defuse his anger.

"You can't possibly go to Dover. It's quite out of the question."

"They said something about it being some sort of telephone engineering place and that it's under ground." The man in the Labour Exchange had mentioned to her that there was a note on the paperwork to the effect that it was some form of essential communications centre and was therefore located somewhere "that sounds to be down underneath the Castle, so it should be fine".

The subject blighted their short day together. She knew by now that when he got into one of his moods, it tended to linger, often resulting in a contrite letters, when he went into his *mea culpa* mode. She had also learned that the best thing, when such mood had taken hold, was to skirt carefully around it rather than trying, through charm or persuasion, to pull him out of it.

"Promise me you won't take the job," he said just before they parted. "Please, Peggy, my darling. I can't bear the thought of you being in such danger. It's bad enough you being here in Canterbury. At least speak to me first, before you take a decision."

The letter which arrived the next day, to her surprise, offered her the job, giving her a date for starting – at the beginning of January. She had at least expected to be required to attend for an interview. Perhaps, she surmised, it was such a lowly job that an interview was not considered necessary.

She was dreading phoning him, but, telling herself that it had to be done, she stood with the receiver in hand, waiting while the officer who had answered called him.

"Missus on the blower!" she heard the officer say, his voice only partly muffled by his hand over the mouthpiece.

"I've found out more about the job," she told him, having carefully rehearsed her lines, her phone call a couple of days earlier to the "Staff Manager" whose name appeared on the letter, having given her the information she was seeking about the safety of where she would be working. "It's as they had described it," she said. "Apparently it's as deep down under the Castle as you can go. Far too deep for any shells. Absolutely safe. I'll be doing shifts of four days on and will be staying there during the shifts. They have staff quarters in the same place, so well out of harm's way. And I would be in Canterbury the rest of the time, when not on duty."

She was conscious of having spoken in a gush of explanation, wanting to say it all without giving him the chance to interrupt, feeling relieved that she had got it off her chest.

"I still don't like it," he replied. "Dover really is like being in the front line."

"They said that the shelling is not that bad," she said, not sure whether this was something she should mention, but deciding it might help.

"That's not what I've heard," he replied tersely. "And they're howitzers. So they cause a hell of a lot of damage."

The reality was that the principal target of the German guns, sighted on the French coast around Cap Griz Nez, was shipping passing through the Dover Straits which had become known as "Hellfire Corner", British guns returning fire on an equally regular basis, the German guns appearing to set their sights on Dover when no other targets were available. The effect of the shelling was self apparent from the number of buildings in Dover which had been hit, the size of the shells being such that when a house was hit, the destruction was invariably total.

He knew, as soon as she launched into her explanation, that it was leading to her telling him that she had decided to take the job. In the same way that she had had to come to terms with his fits of ill temper, and his occasional tendency to be almost domineering, he had discovered a streak of obduracy within her make up. And as she had learned to adapt to his foibles, so he had learned to live with hers, albeit, sometimes without the good grace which she was so capable of displaying.

"Well I've decided to give it a go," she said, waiting of the eruption of dissent she was expecting. When he responded with acquiescence, notwithstanding a measure of grumbling, she was much relieved. "I can pack it in if I don't like it or if it feels too risky."

"Please be careful, my darling. I do worry so much about you."

When they met for an evening in Canterbury a few days later, having promised themselves a special dinner before she returned home for Christmas, he seemed reconciled to her decision, or at least, resolved not to let the issue spoil their evening. They had both hoped that he would be able to obtain a day's leave on Christmas day, but the rigours of the CO's regime, extending as it did not only to training, but to instilling an ethos which put dedication and loyalty to the Division above all else, had resulted in a tightening up of leave.

Much as Stanley hated the idea of spending Christmas apart, there was something about such ethos which struck a chord with him, particularly as he now felt himself to be part of the beating heart of the Wyverns, its HQ.

"To our future," he said as they sat at a table in the small restaurant, the cosy, candle-lit atmosphere enhanced by the drawn blackout curtains. "In a time of peace." He held up his glass of wine, she lifting hers, clinking the glasses together, their eyes lovingly looking into each other's, entranced by the dream of finally finding a life together.

"To be a family," she said, their conversations from time to time returning to the question of children, both of them harbouring doubts about their resolve to wait until the war was over.

"May be it wouldn't be so bad," she ventured, "to have a child during the war."

"It'll be bad enough, going abroad and leaving you behind. But imagine with an infant as well."
"I know," she said. "It doesn't bear thinking about." She clasped his hand across

the table, looking intently at him. "But I sometimes think it will give our lives some extra meaning."

He knew what she was trying to say.

"What if I didn't come back."

They continued to look at each other, acutely aware of the awfulness of what they were contemplating.

"What would it be like for the child?" he asked, repeating the reason, aired many times before, for delaying.

"We'll be in God's hands," she said firmly. "I know he will protect you. Deep down, I have this certainty."

On one occasion when she had said something about God's hand in the wonders of nature, he had quipped that she seemed to have a direct line to the Almighty, such was her certainty about his presence and even his mysterious ways. His own faith he realised was what he characterised as being more "flexible", which, whilst never approaching any of the fundamentals of belief, nevertheless enabled it to be applied with a sort of pragmatism, even allowing him to venture, some years earlier, during a rare conversation on the subject with his father when they were sitting on the bank of a river flicking their fishing lines across the surface of the water, that perhaps some aspects of the gospels were not intended to be taken literally.

"Of course that's right," his father had replied, surprising Stanley with such frankness. "A great deal of the catechism is intended as a framework for the way that, as Christians, we should live our lives. We don't need to take it all literally. A parable is a story to illustrate a moral issue."

As always with his father, he found that answers were less than straight forward, often begging further questions, as if he was allowing his son a glimpse of the complexities, and possibly, of the fissures of doubt, within his own mind.

At that moment, in the Canterbury restaurant, however, he experienced a sensation of utter conviction, as if her fervent belief was infusing his being.

"Of course I'll be alright. With you, my darling, and with Good Lord protecting me."

They did not come to any conclusion, the constraints of time and their determination that the evening should be their special Christmas celebration, precluding more serious discussion. For Peggy, however, she was left with little doubt that the time was approaching when their marriage would truly come to fruition.

# TEN

*4.1.43*
*Telephone House*
*My darling*
*Here I am finding myself on the job at 8am & the man I have to report to doesn't arrive*
*until 9.0  I am entertaining myself in the control room. The engineers here seem quite*
*good chaps & the place is very warm.*
*In my first hour I don't seem to have done much work. I am sitting at one of the very*
*modern desks writing this.*
*9.25am*
*Having now met Mr Church & been cheerily greeted by a hand shake & signed numerous*
*forms – all quite harmless though – I have just met one of the head women all dressed*
*up in a navy blue uniform. She seems to drive a rather nice saloon car. She took me round*
*& introduced me to people & then drove me to St Dunstan's where I am working for a*
*week or two.*
*The staff are all quite nice & I have been learning out of an enormous G.P.O. book which*
*was very detailed & I could not concentrate as they had a wireless on. They don't seem to*
*work very hard. I have also been learning about alternating and DC currents etc. The*
*place at St Dunstan's is quite nice & bright & sunny. I only wish we didn't have to start*
*at 8 in the morning.*
*All my fondest love forever*
*Peggy*

Having expected to be spending her days ensconced in the rather stuffy rooms
deep in the bowels of Dover Castle, she was pleasantly surprised to find herself
in a spacious, airy office with a view across a sweep of undulating cliff coast, the
elegant art deco building, St Dunstan's, built just before the war as a home for
the blind, a few miles from Brighton, having been taken over by the army and
now housing a number of operations including communications.

At first it was something of a relief not to have to spend her duty hours dealing
with patients, tending their ailments and injuries, ministering their needs and
bodily functions. The work, although initially rather complicated, with all the
things she had to understand sufficiently to make sense of her clerking role,
proved to be reasonably straight forward, once she had realised that she was not
required to know how all the systems worked. It was more a matter of getting
on top of the terminology so that she could deal with the filing and to enable
her to fill in the various forms correctly, ordering supplies of components. She
had to know what the functions were of the other staff, most of them sitting at
desks with headsets clamped to their heads, each station with its board in front

of it, the operator selecting the appropriate socket to insert the plug, the room filled with the hubbub of conversations.

The staff were a mixture of civilians, the majority female, and forces people, mainly in army or navy uniforms.

It all felt rather convivial, particularly during their breaks when they gathered in the canteen, sometimes taking a short, brisk walk along the cliff tops.

After a couple of weeks however, although she tried not to admit it to herself, she started to find the work a little on the dull side, the tasks given to her mundane and repetitive. She was wondering whether this was the most effective way for her to be "doing her bit" for the war effort, and beginning to regret having given up on nursing. Doing the rounds of patients as a district nurse might not have been particularly to her liking, yet it was still an essential part of nursing.

She resolved, however, to soldier on, looking forward to the three days – and nights – she would shortly be spending with Stanley who had managed to arrange his next leave to coincide with her off duty days. And what was more, they would be in their own home, the hut, having told their respective parents of their intention, declining the suggestions that as it was mid winter, they would be better off in the warmth and comfort of one of their family's homes.

Her father having collected her from the station, she spent what she felt to be a respectable amount of time with her parents, telling them a little about her job, the prohibition on discussing it in any detail quite convenient as she was eager to get to the hut to get it ready for Stanley's arrival later that afternoon.

She felt an excitement she hadn't known for months at the thought that they were going to be alone in their home for three whole days. As soon as she had dropped her small suitcase in the hut and turned on the heater, she hurried to the shops, Gumbrell's grocers a short way along the road, having saved up some of her ration coupons so she could buy a few treats, some extra butter and cheese, and, at Stanley's request, some bottles of beer, and then to the baker's, buying two loaves, Stanley fond of toast, particularly with dripping, Mrs Christian, knowing the tastes of "my young master", having thoughtfully saved a bowl from the previous Sunday lunch.

Her final call, at the butcher's, involved ten minutes queuing, but at least she was able to obtain some bacon and sausages, and, most importantly, two good sized lamb chops.

With her heightened awareness of her husband's demeanour, she could see, as soon as he stepped down from the train, that all was well, his face lighting up as he saw her, chatting as she drove him home – the fact that she allowed him to drive a further indication of his humour, he generally loath to be driven by her – filling her in with his news, listening as she recounted her own, his arm draped along the back of the driver's seat, fingers touching the back of her neck and shoulder.

The first evening, as they had agreed over the phone, they would stay "at home" as they loved to describe it, Peggy cooking, with the blackout blinds closed and the paraffin heater churning out its vaporous warmth, the chops sizzling on the small cooker, the hut quickly becoming delightfully fuggy.

Stanley lay back on the sofa, donated by his mother, drinking his beer, watching Peggy busying with the cooking, his face a picture of rapture. She had put on her best dress, dark blue, its simple design showing off her slender figure, the slightly puffed shoulders and buttons down the front of the bodice giving it a certain allure.

"My God, you look gorgeous," he said, getting up and standing behind her as she tested the potatoes with a fork, encircling her with his arms, inhaling her perfume.

"I'll be spoiling the dinner if you don't leave me be," she said, wriggling her back against him.

After they had eaten, the chops followed by ginger sponge and custard, they reclined on the sofa, Stanley having selected a dozen or so of his favourite records, getting up as Glen Miller's *Elmers Tune* finished, putting on the Andrews Sisters' *Don't Sit Under the Apple Tree,* holding out his hand to Peggy who, inclining her head in acceptance of his offer, slipped into his loose ballroom hold, the two of them rotating around the restricted dance floor.

She looked up at him, his brown eyes gleaming with pleasure, his face flushed with food, liquor and the warmth of the air, his wavy hair beginning to show its usual signs of springing free of its coating of Brylcreem. She was relieved that he seemed so fit, remembering how dreadful he had looked when he had been ill, his tall frame painfully thin. What a difference the intervening months had made. Clearly, the regime he kept telling her about, with the new CO, agreed with him, his arms and shoulders now quite muscular. It was as if his whole body had been expanded, there being a lovely solidity to him.

How different, as well, to see him in civvies. It was as if, in his shirt and tie, and his brown cord trousers, he had left his military persona elsewhere, this version, so much more at ease with himself, and with her.

After several more upbeat tunes, he reached for his current favourite, the Ink Spots' *Whispering Grass,* there being something about the contrast between the strange, almost falsetto of the counter-tenor and the rich bass voice of the lyrically spoken section, the beautiful melody enhanced by the languid guitar.

Their dance reduced to a mere shuffling of their feet as they kissed, floating in a moment of pure love, Stanley breaking away to put the stylus back to the beginning.

"Yes, it is getting a bit warm," she whispered as the record finished, his fingers grappling with the buttons of her dress. "Here, let me." She pushed his hand away, undoing the buttons, then unbuttoning his shirt, pulling it from his belt, tossing it onto one of the chairs. She liked the look of him in his vest, his shoulders, although not broad, rounded, making her want to place her hands on them, feeling the sinews.

"I seem to be down to my socks," he laughed, having shed the rest of his clothes, she having sat down to peel off her nylons before returning to his embrace, the dance hold now abandoned, their arms around each other's backs.

"I never thought I could love you more than I did before," he said, his voice thick. "But I do, my darling Pegs. I love you so much it sometimes hurts."

She turned her face up to him, needing no reply other than the passion of the kiss.

"I assume I don't need..." he said as they lay down on the bed, she understanding instantly that he was referring to Durex.

"No," she replied. "You don't."

Their decision, that they would abandon their agreement to wait until the end of the war, was not something that they could point to with any unequivocal words of intent. Rather, it was the culmination of various conversations, from which a conclusion had emerged. It was something of a relief to both of them, despite the obvious concern about his surviving the war, a concern which would not go away, and which was to become so much more acute over the ensuing months and years. But what mitigated it, was her conviction that they were in God's safe hands, and that she just knew that the time was right; that her body and her heart were telling her that this was her time for motherhood.

For Stanley, the thought of her being back at home, with their families caring for her and the prospective infant, more than offset his worry about the child growing up fatherless. He desperately wanted her to be the mother of his child; to know, wherever the war might take him, that she would be there, at home, nurturing his nascent family for the day when he would be back with her, permanently.

The next night they dined and danced at *Jimmy's*, in the centre of Brighton, their dancing competent if not accomplished, his style rather too flamboyant for his clumsy feet, her toes frequently suffering the consequence, although such was her enjoyment, aided by several cocktails, that she could only laugh at his apologies, the two of them exhilarated, having waited so long for such an evening.

They caught the tram back to Dyke Road, giggling at nothing in particular, their daily worries, just for a short while, put to one side.

"I'm afraid to say that I'm rather sloshed," he said as he stumbled down the narrow stairs from to top deck of the tram, standing swaying slightly as the tram rattled away up Dyke Road towards its terminus.

"I'm a bit squiffy as well," Peggy said, taking hold of his arm just as Stanley turned towards her, taking her in a ballroom hold, twirling her into the middle of the empty road.

"*Pardon me boy, is this the Chatanooga Choo Choo,*" he sang, his voice filling the silence of the road, any lights remaining on in the houses nearby, well concealed behind blackout curtains, the overcast sky, deepening the darkness.

"Shhh!" Peggy looked around, expecting angry people to emerge, unaccustomed to revellers in this select part of the town, particularly at this late hour. But she allowed herself to be swung along the road, twirling with the abandon of the moment, stopping when they were close to the church.

"Right," Stanley said, still holding onto her, manoeuvring back towards the vicarage gateway, "let's go in and make a baby!"

"Darling! Shhh! You don't need to tell the whole neighbourhood."

Her chiding had the reverse effect as he broke into a blaringly discordant rendition of *You Are My Sunshine,* Peggy pushing him hurriedly through the hut door, closing it behind them, glancing back at the vicarage windows, the curtains thankfully remaining static.

When she dropped him at the station early on the Monday morning, their parting embrace felt different, both of them convinced that, with the number of times they had made love over the weekend – Sunday, their last day, once, as they awoke, before going to church, again in Stanley's father's car, windows steamed up, on the top of the Downs, and again in the evening – "something must have happened", Stanley said, laying his hand on her belly, pressing against the thick fabric of her winter coat, a knowing smirk creasing his face.

For Peggy, however, knowing that it would be three months before his next leave got the better of her, her tears suddenly welling, running down her cheeks. He wiped them away with his finger tips.

"Don't be sad, my darling," he said gently, kissing her damp cheeks. "We'll soon be a family."

He found something rather pleasing in being able to provide for her. She might still be earning wages herself – and in reality, what she was getting at the moment from her work with the GPO was more than his captain's pay – but he felt that he was now the breadwinner, measuring up to her father's expectations. Soon, also, all being well, she would have to stop working altogether.

Patience not being his greatest virtue, he watched the days go by, mentally ticking them off on his calendar. He had made his calculations, and even allowing for the two or three days leeway which she had explained to him was the extent of the variance of her usually reliable timing, her next period would be less than two weeks hence.

"I'm going to make a mark on my calendar," he had told her. "A little squiggle so that only I will know what it means," the term "squiggle" thus entering their intimate vocabulary.

"No squiggle," she told him on the phone, just over two weeks later, the date on his calendar having passed, having made himself wait for two days before phoning her. "My tummy feels a bit funny." She did not like to say that it was the familiar pre-menstrual feeling, regretting giving him the idea that it was quite the opposite, making it all the more difficult when she phoned him, two days later.

She should not have been surprised at his disappointment, but what she had not anticipated was that the news would trigger a resurgence of his overbearing insistence that she should give up her job anyway, citing the increased danger which he said that he aware of from "reports" he had been receiving, suggesting that the shelling of Dover and the surrounding area was intensifying.

"But I don't often have to work in Dover," she replied, trying yet again, to reassure him. "And St Dunstan's is miles away. Well out of range of the German guns."

"I just don't like you having to go there at all," he persisted, impervious to her argument. "And may be your working had an effect on, you know...."

"Don't be so daft!" she said sharply. "Of course it didn't. Conceiving is just rather a hit and miss business."

The call ended with him continuing to grumble, his "Goodbye, darling" muted and almost dismissive. How she hated it when he tried to brow-beat her. But yet again, there was something in what he was saying that she agreed with, although for somewhat different reasons. She had become heartily fed up with the job, finding it tedious to the extent that she spent each day watching the clock, longing for the breaks and for the day to end, the work stupefyingly dull.

She surprised herself therefore, not being at all an impulsive person, when, the following week, she handed in her notice. She was smiling as she phoned Stanley, remembering the previous call and the misery it precipitated, this time, picturing his expression of delight.

"Are you sure it's what you want to do?" he asked her. "I know I've been a bit unkind, going on about it. You know I've never made a secret of my worry about you. You can't imagine, darling, how it kept me awake at night when you were at Bart's, knowing how many hospitals were getting bombed. And being anywhere near Dover; it was almost worse."

"I know you were only thinking about me, sweetheart," she said, having resolved to allow no recrimination.

As soon as she was back home, she found that her parents had an even greater need of her support than before, her father being unwell with some stomach condition which the doctor seemed unable to resolve. What she could not have anticipated was that over the months ahead, his health would steadily deteriorate, his constitution, which she had always thought to be so robust, progressively weakened, his condition not helped by his obduracy, refusing to take to his bed unless he was patently too ill to continue his long days at his office and trips around the county. When he did, briefly, retire to bed, he would soon insist on getting up and resuming his routine despite it being obvious to Peggy and her mother, that he was not well enough to do so, their pleading with him falling on deaf ears.

To add to her parents' worries, her brother, Tom, serving in Burma, had told them in a recent letter that he was hoping to be transferred to the "Chindits", commanded by legendary General Orde Wingate who, in the short time he had been in Burma, had carved a reputation as an eccentric, and, to his men, charismatic leader, pitting his tactical wits against the Japanese in the brutal jungle war.

Although Peggy's father spoke of his pride in his son's aspiration, the news reports from the distant theatre, limited and fragmented though they were, nevertheless painted a picture of harsh conditions and gruelling fighting, and of heavy casualties.

When her mother suggested that her husband's health might provide a valid reason for Tom being allowed home, either on compassionate leave, or, better still, to work with his father, land management and surveying in some instances, qualifying as a reserved occupation, he would not hear of it, the very thought of dragging their son back home, particularly when he was on the verge of achieving his ambition of joining the Chindits, quite out of the question.

While Peggy was adapting to, and, surprisingly, enjoying, her resumption of life at home, Stanley was engaged in the longest and most arduous exercise so far, the Division combining with several others in a "campaign" ranging across many parts of the country with several large scale "battles". For him, it was an instructive, and extremely demanding experience, giving him what he felt was the closest yet to a taste of the real thing, the only missing element, as they all knew only too well, being the casualties, apart from a few men injured by the type of accidents which generally occurred – vehicles colliding or men falling over in the dark, and in one sad instance, a soldier getting run over by a tank.

*10.3.43*
*In the field*
*My darling girl*
*Many thanks for your letter. This is my far my most hectic army adventure & includes help to putting out a fire & a mud race through the New Forest at night with no maps & a trip through an air raid. Today I am sitting in a field in the Chilterns. I've had 17 hours sleep since last Wednesday but feel 100% fit but a bit light headed. I do hope your people are better darling girl.*
*We are lucky tonight as we are sleeping in the saloon bar of a little country pub 1000 feet up. We are not allowed to buy anything though. We are beating up the "Huns" & hope will finish at the weekend.*
*Your adoring husband*
*Stanley*

When they had parted at the end of those wonderful three days in January, his next leave seemed so far into the future - ninety-one days he had calculated - and when she discovered she was not pregnant, it felt an unbearably long time to have to wait until they could try again. She had got herself so much into the way of thinking of soon becoming a mother that the disappointment weighed upon her. Having finally come to the decision to have an infant, how cruel of fate then to deny them the consummation of their desire.

And yet now time was positively flying by. She was keeping herself busy, helping her parents, taking on a few tasks for the church, organising some of the socials and generally lending a hand, as well as having plenty of time to spend with Paddy and Barbara. In spite of her pregnancy – Paddy being quite tall and large limbed, her protruding abdomen clearly a considerable burden to her – she and Alan continued to enjoy life, with regular outings and parties at their flat, Alan ever generous with gin, Peggy finding herself, not infrequently, walking back home with feet that didn't seem to be entirely in her control.

She envied her friend, not only for her pregnancy, but having her husband at home although never, for one moment, did she harbour any resentment. She knew full well, that as a builder, his was a reserved occupation, the extent of the damage even around the Brighton area, amply demonstrating the need for builders to undertake repairs.

Ninety-one days! Nearly half it gone. And what a difference it made when the news was no longer all bad. Numerous atlases were poured over, the great expanse of North African terrain across which the desert campaign had unfolded, now familiar, the countries – Algeria, Tunisia, Libya and Egypt – duly located, as were the strategic towns, most notably Tobruk, and of course, the area of apparently empty desert, so precariously close to Egypt and to the great city of Alexandria, El Alamein, where Monty – the general's status as the country's current folk hero evident from his abbreviated name being absorbed into common parlance – had first held, and then resoundingly defeated Rommel, saving the city.

On the Eastern front also, after the long winter months of uncertainty, when the news reports about the seemingly interminable struggle between the Russians and the Germans for control of the strategically vital town of Stalingrad had given little indication of which way it was going, not only was the Russian victory eventually proclaimed, but it was the first time the Germans had been defeated in Europe, their dominance severely dented, the loss of their 6th Army a devastating blow.

Further afield, the Americans, having stemmed the Japanese advance across the Pacific, continued the struggle which, from what one could gather from the news reports, involved a series of battles for islands spread across the huge ocean, much of the fighting now dominated by aircraft operating from aircraft carriers, the land fighting, intense and brutal as the Americans steadily pushed their way forward, inexorably towards Japan.

What was happening in Burma was often difficult to fathom, the reports talking of what, to Peggy and her parents, with their close interest in the distant theatre, seemed a fragmented affair, without any major battles in the way that one could recognise them, the jungle fighting apparently being more a matter of a series of smaller scale encounters. Even the terminology was different, with references to "marches" and "penetration", the situation being more complicated because of the interruption by the monsoon. Worryingly also, the news would sometimes mention the extent of disease affecting the troops; malaria, and other conditions which were prevalent in jungle warfare.

"It all seems so far away," Peggy said, when she was talking to Stanley on the phone, his enquiry, whether she had heard from Tom, prompting her to articulate the thought that had been in her mind for some time, that although there was so much fighting going on, it felt as if the war was not quite real. It wasn't like those early months of the "phoney war", when the protagonists were holding their breath, waiting for the first move. Of course, there was the bombing, which had, in no uncertain terms, brought the war so terrifyingly to much of the country. "I mean, with all the exercises going on, it's like we're endlessly preparing but not actually doing anything," she said.

She realised straight away that it sounded as if she was being critical, suggesting that Stanley, and the Home Forces generally, spent their time playing war games without ever getting to grips with the enemy. Everyone knew that at some point, the war in Europe would have to resume, but there was no indication of anything imminent, the concern being that the war would be dragging on for years.

"I can't say much, darling, as you know," he replied, wanting to divulge something of what he knew, although in reality, it was not a great deal more than anyone else in the country. "It won't be that long before the Second Front opens."

The briefings that he now attended, sometimes with the CO and senior officers, made clear that their time would come, alluding to the planning which as taking place, suggesting that the opening of the Second Front could even be before the end of the year, which, as they all knew, would have to mean summer or early autumn, invading mainland Europe in winter being out of the question.

Sometimes, the discussion was about the possibility of the "soft underbelly" route, North Africa having now been secured, providing the necessary springboard. But one glance at the atlas showed why that was unlikely, of itself, to offer the route to Germany, an invasion of Southern France, across the Mediterranean, involving long distances and major logistical problems, and attacking through Italy requiring the taking of more than a thousand miles of territory before even reaching the Alps.

"We'll certainly be ready," he added, the shared feeling throughout the Wyverns being of eagerness and a firm belief that, particularly since General Thomas had taken over, they had become a fighting force second to none. "We're raring to go!"

"I only wish it was all over," she said gloomily, the ever present worry being that all too soon, he would be "going abroad" as they referred to it, making it sound like some grand tour of Europe.

Quite unexpectedly, in the last week of March, he phoned to tell her that he was able to get a night's "unofficial leave".

"Let's have a night at the Grosvenor," he suggested. "And by my calculations, it would be a good time!"

Most of the phone conversations these days, involved his reckonings of dates, as if he were giving a commentary on her menstrual cycle. His calculations were, as always, reasonably accurate.

One night! But suddenly, here was the chance. She had a strong feeling that this was the moment. If asked, she could not have described what it was that made her so certain; something instinctive; a sense that everything in her body was ripe and ready.

His exercise, now in its final days, had proved to be as tough as any they had had before, testing their endurance and, most importantly, from the point of view of the RASC, their organisational capability. Throughout, they had had to keep track of every part of the division, relying on often rapidly installed and erratically functioning phone lines and radios, at the same time as using the age old method, of dispatches, men, sometimes on foot, but more often on motorbikes, finding the front line units, coming back with the messages as to their requirements.

As always, the salutary part was the debriefings, when the shortcomings were identified, reasons for delays and failures closely examined, changes implemented to ensure improvements.

It was at the end of a long, wearisome day, driving many miles along country lanes and sodden tracks, his battledress wet through in spite of his trenchcoat, culminating in a three hour session with his fellow RASC officers and a handful from other sections, crammed into the dining room of an old requisitioned farmhouse, that "the Old Man", as their immediate CO was universally referred to, lambasted them with his catalogue of complaints, the debriefing ending with his issuing each of them with the requirements for reporting back, to be "on my desk by this time tomorrow!".

Thankfully, when the Old Man had finally departed with a disgruntled "Dismissed!", Stanley was able to drown his sorrows with the two fellow officers who, since he had taken on this HQ role, had become his good pals, Tony and Bill, both, like him, with the three pips although he was the one with the greater seniority, being in charge of their part of the RASC. Miraculously, Bill produced a bottle of Scotch which the three of them polished off, Stanley finding himself feeling pleasantly drunk and, rather surprisingly, wide awake even though it was well past midnight.

As he sat on his bed his thoughts, as so often, turned to Peggy, his lengthy absence from her infusing his fantasising about her with ever more lustful imagining, carnal cravings common to all of the men, engendering shared confidences which had the effect of heightening the longing and stimulation, it being quite normal for one to announce "just off to give myself a seeing to", officers and men alike indulging in the necessity of such relief, their terminology ever inventive: "Meeting Miss Wrist"; "Bashing the Bishop"; "knocking one off for England".

He could picture her body with such vividness it almost hurt, such was his longing. How could he wait for so long? And quite apart from the desperate need to satisfy his pent up physical desire, he knew for certain, his calendar being firmly imprinted in his head, that they would be hitting the critical time when she was most likely to be "fecund" as he loved to refer to it, there being a suggestiveness about the word which appealed to him, smacking of fertility but with something earthier.

Christ, he had to get to see her! Within a couple of days they would be back at Chilham, and joy of joys, the Old Man was going to be off on leave.

He decided he should phone her, managing to get to a phone box the next evening, Peggy's mother answering the phone, sounding surprised to hear his voice.

"I thought you were off on an exercise," she said, a hint of criticism in her tone, suggesting that he should not be phoning. He chose to ignore her comment.

"My darling," he said when Peggy came on the line, "I've worked out that I can get away for the night on Wednesday. Could you get up to London? I've just got to see you, my darling." Sounding breathless, he asked her to make the arrangements, suddenly having to end the call. "Sorry darling, that's Hopkins hooting. The rest of them are already on the road.

When he arrived at the hotel, it was well after seven, the trains having been disrupted by damage from an air raid the night before. Waiting in the room, increasingly worried about the delay, she was relieved when he appeared, looking wonderfully handsome in his dress uniform.

"Darling, I'm so sorry I'm late." He stood staring at her, taking in her appearance. "My God you look stunning!"

She was wearing her blue dress and the string of pearls he so loved, showing off her graceful long neck, her lipstick a brighter red than the one she usually wore.

He took her in his arms, kissing her.

"Now I'll have to re-do it," she laughed, wiping the lipstick from his lips with the back of her hand.

"Let's go and procreate!" Stanley whispered after they had dined and danced, leading her across the hotel foyer and up the grand staircase, their love making purposeful, not only to satiate their physical yearning, but because they were both certain that the time was right.

## ELEVEN

From her experience the previous year, with the bouts of queasiness and that feeling she could not quite put into words – rather like the first signs of an imminent cold or touch of flu, but without being in the least bit ill - she was certain that it had happened. And what was different to the last time was that now it really felt as if it had taken root whereas before, she sensed that it was just a sort of trial run.

Still being only a couple of weeks late, she told herself not to start counting her chickens. Although she could not remember the statistics, that being part of her nursing knowledge that she had not needed to hang on to, she clearly recalled that a pretty large percentage of conceptions did not go beyond the first few weeks. Don't get too excited just yet, she told herself.

For Stanley, the certainty which he felt was tempered by her insistence that it was too soon be definite. But he just knew, in his bones, that it had worked. That night in the Grosvenor – it was as if all of the auguries were with them. And the mathematics made it quite clear. It had been the same last year, he cautioned himself. But this time he just *knew* it was different.

With the arrival of spring, despite living apart, it sometimes felt that the real war, of fighting and dying, was still remote, a dark backdrop to their happiness. Their lives were now fully attuned to wartime conditions; the rationing; the shortages; the disrupted travel. And as one adapted, such changes did not seem like deprivations. It was just the way things were.

They managed to meet quite regularly, every few weeks, telephoning two or three times each week. For both of them, there was a new layer of happiness; as yet, secret between them although they were bursting with eagerness to announce their news.

"Let's wait until we're really certain," Peggy cautioned, Stanley wanting to tell the world.

In April he took another step up the army hierarchy, which, although not changing his rank of captain, gave him the role of Captain Superintendent, attached to the Commander of the Divisional RASC. It also brought him together with two officers who, for very different reasons, were going to play a significant part in his army life, and with one of them, in the remainder of his army career.

His immediate senior, Major Eric Nicholls, was an outwardly reserved, intelligent, thoughtful, quietly spoken man, respected by fellow officers and by the men under his command. His reputation was as a fair minded, effective officer, who saw his own role as getting things done. He expected those around him to share his belief in efficiency, and at times, could dish out forthright censure, rarely shouting yet able to imbue his voice with a force one did not argue with. Unlike many senior officers, those on the receiving end invariably felt that his criticism was fair and fully justified, doing their best to resolve the cause of his complaint.

Stanley soon found, much to his surprise, that he and Eric - getting to the point of using Christian names when off duty within a few weeks of Stanley being assigned – became close friends, a friendship which, combined with their mutual respect as officers, was to result, a year later, in Stanley's promotion and transfer to a different division.

Fellow captain, Philip Mead – his Christian name never used, reduced in Stanley's letters to Peggy to the derisory "P" - for reasons he could never quite explain even to himself, let alone when, as he frequently found himself doing, complaining about him to Peggy, was a man he simply could not abide, what would prove to be his lengthy association with him doing nothing to diminish his antipathy. He put it down to chemistry, as well as to the plethora of the man's shortcomings; questionable competence; unpleasant personal habits; and, after seeing the his performance on their first couple of exercises together, a belief that he was afraid to take responsibility, showing himself to be timid and indecisive; these were just some of the traits which contributed to P. Mead being cast as a "frightful shocker".

In spite of their periodic meetings, a few requiring Stanley to take "unofficial" leave, and of their phone calls, their partings never became any easier. The intensity of their all too short times together heightened the feeling of sadness as they said their farewells, cruelly reminding them, each time, that their marriage was to be like this; a time of longing and sorrow; of pining and partings; and of acceptance, that this was the way it was going to continue for months and probably years ahead.

The joy they shared when they were convinced that she was pregnant, also added a new dimension to their sadness, that their infant would start its life knowing its father only sporadically.

They had, however, like the population generally, learned the art of stoicism.

There was nothing one could do about it, other than hope that peace would not be too far away, and that the end of the war, when it came, would see Britain prevail.

Stanley's official leave, a glorious golden week in April, seemed to pass in a trice. Apart from the obligatory get togethers with respective families and a couple of nights out, they were able to remain in their cocoon of love, embellished now with their new secret. With a spell of early summer weather, they were able to go for walks, sometimes driving to their favourite spots, utterly detached from the war, apart from the regular background hum of aircraft, the RAF raids on German cities and other targets increasing towards their devastating crescendo.

"Only six weeks this time," he reminded her, his voice, as always at these moments, constricted as he kissed her goodbye at the station, she, this time, dry-eyed and bubbling with positivity.

Thankfully, she had to go to work as soon as she had seen him off, having taken a job at a nursing home, not full time, but occupying her for three or four days each week and giving her some welcome extra money.

For Stanley, the equally welcome distraction was his new role, requiring him to move to new quarters assigned to HQ officers. And no sooner had he found his desk and got to know his new colleagues, than the division embarked on its next exercise, the tempo of training continuing to intensify.

*27.4.43*
*In bed in the tent*
*My sweetheart darling*
*It is hard to describe the feeling I have experienced since leaving you, but perhaps you will understand if I tell you I know they were like yours – so very miserable and terribly in need of you my dearest one.*
*I had a few drinks with an MSM friend at the Falstaff, met Stew & Thomas at the Fleur then went & drank some sherry & had some dinner with Bill & his wife at the County. Afterwards back to the Falstaff for more beer.*
*This morning I went to communion at 9. My thoughts and whole being longed for you till I felt quite dazed except that I knew that through God I could get near you my own Pegs.*
*Monday*
*I hope you can read the above darling – it was very dim and windy when I was writing. Darling, I do hope you are not feeling ill and not regretting becoming a mummy. Do write & tell me you are quite happy about it darling.*

*Life has been quite busy since I arrived here on Tuesday, what with getting my kit straight & getting used to my new job. It is rather like a BRASCO's job except that in addition I'm 'stooge' to the S.Sup.O. It is certainly a more gentlemanly existence for breakfast is at 8 to 9, one plays bridge in the evenings etc. It is very alarming bridge though and last night I played with the Colonel and made some awful blunders but he didn't seem to mind.*

*I'm glad you are now happier darling. The more I think about it the more I like it darling – in fact I'm quite thrilled. The only thing I really hate is that you have to see a doctor. I hate you seeing doctors as I like to be there – please tell me all about it darling! – and insist on a nurse being in the room.*

*Darling, will you ask the doctor how long you can go on being naughty without any danger of hurting you or it? Darling I do still want to be naughty!*

*Well darling girl, goodbye and Good bless you*

*Stanley*

As she read the letter she sighed with exasperation. He always seemed to have a bee in his bonnet about something. This new concern, about doctors, surfaced during leave when she had been explaining to him, as delicately as she could, the process of examination to confirm that she was pregnant.

"What? He actually has to put his hand…inside you?" He stared at her, open mouthed with disbelief. "His whole hand? Bloody hell! That's shocking."

"It's alright," she assured him. "It doesn't hurt."

"But a doctor – a male doctor – doing that to you."

It dawned on her at that moment that his concern was not about the invasive nature of the examination but rather the fact that it would be conducted by a man. Back in her Bart's days she had become aware of his thinly veiled jealousy, directed primarily at the hospital doctors, her accounts of their escapades, some involving snippets of Brewster's saucier anecdotes, evoking a reaction quite contrary to the amusement she was expecting, his brow furrowed as he interrogated her until satisfied that she had not been involved in any way which offended his exaggerated sensibility.

She had learned to play along with him, either by editing references to doctors, or indeed, to any other males who might be deemed to present some danger to her – from his distorted perspective – or occasionally, by having a dig at him, in one instance, mentioning a particular young doctor as "one of my boyfriends", instantly regretting doing so as she then had to spend the rest of the day repairing the damage, convincing him that she was having him on and that she was his and his alone.

"It does seem a bit daft that I haven't told Mummy and Daddy," she said when they were discussing her pregnancy on the phone. "I think I should tell them, and that you should tell your people."

"When do you think it will be?" Stanley asked, he and Eric Nicholls enjoying a pint of beer at a table in the yard at the back of the *Falstaff*, which had become a favourite Canterbury watering hole for officers from the 43rd.

Much of the discussion in recent times, following the Allied invasion of Sicily three weeks earlier, had been about the second front which, it was generally assumed, was imminent, although with June having now arrived, and few briefings and no other signs of activity, beyond the ever intensifying training, the consensus was that it would probably be August or September, to avoid the onset of autumn gales, and to allow time, at the very least, to establish a solid bridgehead before winter.

"I've not heard anything," Eric replied, Stanley knowing that not only did his immediate CO attend briefings of senior Division officers, but that he kept his ear to the ground. And he always seemed willing to take Stanley into his confidence. "My own view is that it won't be until the spring. I just don't think we're ready yet. It's going to need preparation on a scale we've never known."

It seemed intensely frustrating that, when the Wyverns felt themselves to be ready and raring to go, all that they were told was that they needed further training, although what they had come to recognise was that each exercise added a new dimension, the most recent one involving their first experience of landing craft, the notoriously nausea inducing, flat bottomed craft designed to get men and equipment onto beaches, the initiation requiring batches of men and officers to carry out trial landings on the beaches of Selsey Bill, another part of the exercise seeing them fighting their way ashore at Pegwell Bay, scaling the cliffs in the face of "enemy" fire.

"I just wish we could get one with it," Stanley said, articulating the frustration of virtually all of the troops, some two million of them, training – and waiting – across the country, "so that we can get it over and done with, and begin to live our lives."

"For those of us who'll come through it," Eric said sombrely. "I don't think many of us have really grasped what it's going to be like. The Germans are the best army in the world even though we are probably now getting close. But believe me, Stanley, their equipment − tanks and guns − are second to none." He sipped his beer thoughtfully, the evening sun slanting into the hotel yard illuminating his fine features, Stanley having described him to Peggy as "rather aristocratic but with no superiority", his fine, light brown hair neatly parted, one side tending to flop across his forehead. "It's going to be a shock when we have our first encounter with death."

"Are you frightened?" Stanley asked, again posing the question which so many of them asked themselves, it being a stupid question when they all knew that fear would go with them throughout the impending campaign.

"Of course I am." He looked at Stanley, his pale blue eyes seeming to be staring inward. "None of us want to die or get wounded, and we know that many of us will. Sometimes I find the thought of Doreen and the girls being without me, quite unbearable."

He had shown Stanley photos of his wife, a slender, fine looking woman, her features similar to her husband's, with strong cheek bones and an air of composure, the two girls, eight and six, very obviously their parents' progeny.

"It's the worst part of the whole thing," Stanley agreed. "I haven't told you, but Peggy's pregnant. So I'll be in a similar situation, and it scares the pants off me."

A smile of genuine delight spread across the major's face. "That's wonderful, Stanley. Congratulations. When did you find out?"

"We were pretty certain a few weeks ago, but Peggy only saw the doctor on Tuesday. It'll probably be January when it's born."

Eric raised his glass. "To wives and children! And to our coming back to them!"

For a few minutes, the two officers sat in silence, each deep in his own thoughts, sipping their beer, the sun finally abandoning the yard, the air quickly becoming cool.

"I've never seen anyone die," Stanley said. "Apart from one time when my father took me to see an old lady, one of the church lot, who, for some reason, doted on me. Apparently she had asked him to bring me to see her. It turned out that she had wanted to give me something − an old silver tie-pin which had been her husband's. She chose the moment when we got there to breath her last. It wasn't what I expected: no spasms or rattle or anything. In fact you hardly noticed it happening. She just stopped breathing." He was picturing the scene, remembering how his heart was thumping in his chest, but as soon as the lady had died, it had reverted to its usual rhythm. "What about you?"

"A couple of times," Eric replied. "Once, when I was a lad, we – my people and me and my sister – we were in the middle of London when a woman was hit by a bus, right in front of us. There was a lot of blood. What I remember, though, was that some of it seemed to be coming from her ears. And as she lay on the road, with people gathering around her, nobody did anything. They – we – all just stared at her. Her body was jerking, as if someone was shaking her. Then she went quite still. I was twelve."

As the summer weeks passed it became obvious that the invasion would not be until the following spring although there were periodic rumours of "something happening", the rumour mill fuelled by announcements of leave being stopped, or of everyone having to have jabs to protect them from some unspecified diseases which, they assumed, were prevalent "abroad".

And yet nothing happened, exercises continuing. Arduous though these were, testing men's fighting capability and their endurance, sometimes involving their going for several days with minimal sleep, they broke the monotony of normal daily life, with its endless square bashing, PT, weapons training, and killing time.

For Peggy and Stanley, little changed other than the swelling of her belly. She was, however, able to continue to work, her determination to do so for as long as possible all the greater for Stanley's nagging her to give it up, her mother's similar suggestion strengthening still further, her resolve.

The war news, for Peggy, seemed less dramatic than it had been previously, probably because the air raids, whilst continuing, were nowhere near as bad as during the Blitz, and had become part of wartime life, the reports from other parts of the world, interesting, but never seeming particularly dramatic.

It was certainly encouraging to hear of the progress the Americans were making in Sicily, although it was just one island way off in the Mediterranean. The news that Mussolini had been ousted was certainly exciting, although it soon became clear that the Germans were effectively taking over in Italy, which was bound to make things much harder for the Allies when, as everyone expected, they crossed from Sicily to the mainland to begin the long march northwards.

Frustratingly, there was very limited news from Burma, the place with which Peggy and her parents were most concerned, the reports which they heard and read, often confusing even when they turned to their well thumbed atlas, searching for places occasionally named, one's impression being of a country swathed in jungle, with protracted, fragmented battles of attrition. Even when there was mention of a battle being won, one had the feeling that it was not a real, strategic victory, as El Alamein had been.

Making matters worse, Tom's letters were infrequent, and when they did arrive, whilst sometimes including passing comments about the conditions, with almost matter of fact references of disease, heat, insects and, albeit rarely, the Japs, they told them little about where he was or what he was doing. It was only from the address on one of his letters that they were able to deduce that he had realised his ambition to join the Chindits, which, as it was known that they were in the thick of the jungle fighting, only added to the family's anxiety.

There were times, though thankfully few, when Peggy found that the grim side of life weighed upon her, testing her determination to remain cheerful. How dreadful it was that the whole world was at war, with no end in sight, and no prospect of Stanley being home for many months – possibly years. Her dream of a happy family existence, with their child, was just a dream, darkened by the knowledge that before it could become a reality, Stanley would be going abroad, with all the danger and implications which that involved.

It was almost unbearable, her despondency affecting her mother who, understanding as she was, nevertheless had a tendency to say the wrong thing.

"Come on, do buck up, Peggy. It's not as bad as all that."

Peggy would grit her teeth, barely able to prevent herself from giving vent to her feelings. Oddly, however, her mother's chiding would generally have the desired effect, Peggy telling herself to "pull yourself together", getting on with her work or some household chores. Whenever she could do so, she would walk down to see Paddy, her friend's company invariably cheering her up, a small glass of gin sometimes administered with a smile and as a "drop of medicine".

Stanley now being quartered in a private house close to HQ, with a landlady, Mrs Finn, who not only loved to look after "my officers", the half dozen of them residing in her small but comfortable house, well fed and mothered by the portly, good natured lady, but who was more than happy to accommodate the wives of the married officers, as well as discretely turning a blind eye to the visits of those she described, generously, as "wives in all but name", Peggy was able to visit, Mrs Finn making her "guest's quarters" – an attic room - available to them, the officers normally sharing their rooms, Stanley's room-mate being a fellow RASC captain, Geoffrey Armitage.

Peggy, at first, found it rather uncomfortable, having to fit into a house full of army officers, particularly as she was the only "other half" staying at the time. And what made matters even more awkward was finding herself alone on her first morning, with Mrs Finn, the officers all having departed early for their day's duties. She soon found, however, that the landlady was remarkably easy to get along with, to the extent that, as she stood beside her in the kitchen, drying the dishes, they were soon chatting like old friends.

"Oh, that's nice dear," seemed to be the landlady's default response to much of what Peggy said, although it was, Peggy felt, quite genuine, indicating a benevolence that not only put Peggy entirely at ease, but was almost maternal in its warmth.

After the first visit, Peggy would make regular trips to Chilham, getting used to both the pretty surroundings of this part of Kent, and to spending days by herself, exploring, sometimes catching the bus to Canterbury, catching up with a few friends from her nursing days, even venturing as far as Whitstable. At times, it almost felt like a semblance of normal married life, with her husband getting up and going to work, the only difference being that after two or three days she had to set off back to Brighton.

Whilst the visits to Kent afforded her the pleasure of such brief spells of married life, what she most enjoyed were the times when Stanley was able to get back home, his few periods of leave when they could stay in the hut, their very own home, joyously happy. Inevitably, however, with such joy, parting was all the harder, the first day of separation always the most miserable before she pulled herself together, setting her sights on their next meeting.

*My darling girl*
*It is 6pm on Sunday and I'm sitting in the hot sun on the terrace at the Pilgrims listening to the news. The extraordinary weather continues and Kent is looking more lovely than I've ever seen before. The animals, birds & country are revelling in it.*
*Yesterday I was on the court marshall all day then did some work. At 5 we went to see 'You Were Never Lovelier'. It was very hot in the cinema and I didn't enjoy it as much as when I saw it with you. We caught the bus back and had a few drinks at the Woolpack. We heard & saw our aircraft going over on Friday night. They went on for ages and were*

*very low. The siren is just going now and I can hear some distant AA fire.*
*Last night we went to see Tommy Trinder in a dreadful film.*
*I hope the infant is behaving itself & not kicking too much during the night.*
*How I wish this was peacetime and I was at home with you.*
*Ever your adoring husband*
*Stanley*

With the exception of the wretched Mead, and, to a much lesser extent, Geoffrey Armitage, who, a relatively recent arrival at HQ, Stanley initially found to be a tolerable chap, apart from certain annoying habits, accentuated by reason of their sharing a room – Armitage spreading his belongings around the room, encroaching well over the invisible yet vital demarcation line; and he muttered in his sleep, as if he was trying to say something, keeping Stanley awake – the rest of the RASC officers were a convivial bunch. Indeed, once again, as with his days at BRASCO, he felt he had found a handful of good friends. The difference with the current group – when compared with previous army pals – was that they shared a sense of fun, once again, Mead being the exception, one of his many shortcomings being his air of disapproval when, often induced by liquor, the rest of them would indulge in "smutty talk", or singing, their repertoire somewhat limited, featuring snatches from a few current popular songs, insofar as they could remember the words, and some of the stock of the seasoned, bawdy songs which could be heard issuing from virtually every part of the British army.

*Three German officers crossed the Rhine*
*Fucked the girls and drank the wine*
*Inky, pinky, parlez vous.*

When they went into town, it was generally a party of them, whoever was off duty, their entertainment - cinema, occasional ENSA and other shows, a few dances, and much drinking – providing necessary relief from military life as well as distraction from their sorrows, most of the men, with the exception of the few who had managed to wangle permission for spouses to live with them, pining for wives or sweethearts, and all of them, to some degree, worrying about the future.

From time to time, for no reason that any of them were aware of, word came from on high that all leave was suspended, reigniting the rumour mill, although nobody now believed that the invasion would take place before the spring.

Quite apart from stymying their plans, the stopping of leave, particularly when it extended to outings to Canterbury, created a good deal of resentment amongst the men, as well as with the officers who, sharing the men's sense of grievance, nevertheless had to appear to tow the party line.

For Stanley, the latest edict, which he later found was part of an exercise aimed at testing morale and mental resilience, was particularly galling, as he had been expecting to get home for twenty-four hours. He was desperate to see Peggy, to find out how she really was, her assurances in her letters and on the phone, that she was fine, never quite convincing him.

*My very dearest Peggy*
*My news in this letter must I'm afraid be limited to general things as it is liable to censorship as are also your letters. As I told you, I don't think there is anything to worry about at the minute, so please keep well & fit so that having the baby will not be too terrible an ordeal. How I long for it to be over for your sake darling and to know that all is well. How I hate the thought that having a baby involves the frightful atmosphere of hospitals and smug doctors. I wish to God husbands were equipped to bring their own children into the world or at least help to.*
*We are going to see an abattoir this afternoon so if I can survive that I could certainly see you have a baby darling. I wish I could if I was on leave.*
*Last night John, Maj Nicholls & I went to the Star & met Bill, Crow and many others and had a pretty hilarious evening. We had to walk home & they tried to remove my trousers, so if Maj Nicholls writes & tells you about how I was walking about with my fly buttons undone at midnight, don't take any notice, darling.*
*Have you ever stripped for gym, darling?*
*I must stop now as I've drunk lots of tea and JT is sending an urgent message.*
*Yours for ever so much love darling girl*
*Stanley*

"Why on earth did you have to go to an abattoir?" she asked him on the phone. "It must have been rather grim."

"It's part of our job, the supply of food," he explained, "and when we're in the field, the assumption is that we'll sometimes have to live off the land. So they reckoned we need to know about the whole process, including slaughtering and butchering. Anyway, it wasn't too bad. A bit like skinning rabbits but on a rather larger scale!" What he did not like to admit was that he found the visit something of an ordeal, for some reason, seeing pigs being dispatched even more disturbing than cattle or sheep. "It's as if they're more aware," he remarked to Armitage when they were back in their car, pleased to be away from the unpleasant sights and smells of abattoir.

"Something a bit different coming up," Eric announced to them when, one evening, the CO returned from one of his regular sessions of senior officers, the invariable product of such meetings, as far the rest of the officers could see, being some additional demands for the next exercise. "Need to keep ratcheting it up," was the usual explanation.

"You're off for a couple of weeks training in chemical warfare."

The game of Monopoly ("about the only decent thing P. Mead has come up with" Stanley reported to Peggy), was instantly suspended, the faces round the table gawping at the major.

"Chemical warfare?" someone repeated.

"Only three of you," the major said. "Allen, Armitage and Crow. You will then give the rest of us a briefing when you get back."

It proved to be an interesting, and at times, daunting, fortnight, Stanley having had little concept of the extent of weaponry categorized as "chemical". Apart from the effects of mustard gas in the Great War, the horrifyingly disfigured faces of the surviving victims all too familiar, they had little idea of the modern arsenal. In fact, other from mustard gas, which had been deployed in readiness for use in the event of a German invasion, the only other chemicals which featured in the training, were anthrax and DM, the latter they were told, not being lethal but used for disabling and subduing attackers, much of the instruction being about the weapons for delivery of the chemicals.

As the army representatives quickly realised, the reason for the larger number of RAF personnel present was that in the event of a decision being taken to use chemicals, delivery of mustard or anthrax would be principally by bombing, the hazard of shelling having been only too apparent in the last war, when changes of wind direction had such devastating consequences.

Much of the course was devoted to the risks of the potential use of chemical weapons by the Germans, a risk that was considered to be very real, particularly if – when – they were fighting to defend their homeland. The role which they, RASC, would have to play, would be vital, necessary supplies including gasmasks, medical equipment, decontaminants and delivery vehicles, which, for obvious reasons, needing to be conveyed rapidly to the affected troops.

"As if it's not bad enough facing the Hun's bloody guns," Armitage said, his comments always seeming to be about the prowess of the enemy, Stanley finding the man increasingly irritating, "now they tell us they're going to poison us as well."

"Don't worry, old boy," Crow replied, Stanley liking his fellow captain's dry sense of humour, "we'll try to ensure you get a bullet rather than a dose of poison." Crow, a small, endlessly chirpy fellow with the nickname "Tick", the origin of which Stanley never fathomed, had become one of his core group of friends, at least for that phase of the interminable training, Crow also being Armitage's successor as his room-mate.

What none of them had anticipated was that they were going to be given doses of both mustard and DM gases. "Just a little taster," a smiling, bespectacled private told them. "Might make you puke a bit but shouldn't kill you." They assumed, hopefully, that this was his standard spiel.

*14.9.43*
*Officers Mess, Army School of Chemical Warfare, Winterbourne Gunner, Salisbury, Wilts*
*My darling girl*
*This place is quite nice – the mess is the best appointed I've been in though the food isn't as good as the surroundings. My ATS batwoman (who is old enough to be my mother) is very neat and quick.*
*The course is interesting and not too boring as I thought it would be. We all smell like swimming baths at the moment – we have been using decontamination ointment – and we have already had one dose of gas. We have two more before the course ends, DM and mustard.*
*Darling, please don't worry too much about being big. I have eyes and I still say that you were not very large when I saw you last week. You looked sweet, and in your breakfast gown no one could tell you were producing an infant. I think you will be a sweet mummy & I'll be so proud of you.*
*Goodbye till tomorrow my sweet girl*
*Stanley*

Nine whole days! Such longer period of leave which Stanley was allowed at the beginning of October, once again gave him the chance to adapt to civilian life, and, more importantly, to married life, albeit now insisting, despite Peggy's assurance that it would be fine "if you're careful", that "I think the time has come for a little celibacy".

Being able to potter around, accompanying Peggy on shopping trips, visiting friends, Paddy and Alan arranging a party in his honour; going to church, surrounded by familiar faces; evenings in the hut with a few bottles of beer, his collection of records and his darling wife; this was the life he dreamed about.

Inevitably, when it came, the parting was so much harder, army life, by the end of leave, seeming so very distant.

"I really don't want to go back," he said gloomily on their last night. "I so love being here, with you, living this proper life. Christ, I wish this bloody war was over."

This time, as they embraced, standing beside the Morris, parked close to the station entrance, it was Peggy who was dried eyed, consoling him, realising that, most unusually, he was close to tears, his voice hoarse with emotion.

"It won't be long till your next leave," she said, kissing him, her arms around his back, his frame so much broader with the thickness of his greatcoat.

As the exercises continued, the weather deteriorated, damp pervading everything – battledress, bedding, almost it felt, one's own body - particularly when, as with the late October exercise, they spent much of the time under canvas. How he detested Kent, once again bearing the brunt, as was its wont, of the foul weather emanating from the inhospitable North Sea. God, how he longed for the warmth and comfort of the hut and Peggy's embrace.

Very soon he was going to be a father. His feelings were so conflicting, the eager anticipating of such fulfilment in sharp contrast with the knowledge that he would be absent when his child was born and for, at the very least, its first months. And to make matters worse, he hated so much the thought that, once again, he and Peggy would be apart at Christmas. It was such a special time. He has always loved it; the atmosphere at home and in church; Christmas dinner; the carol singing; the renewal of one's true valuing of family.

He was well aware of the fact that every so often he had a spell of being "down in the dumps". It just seemed to come over him, his tetchiness and feeling of being browned off, lasting sometimes for two or three days. And when he was in one of his moods, as Peggy described it, even his pals began to grate, with the exception of Eric who, Stanley felt, had a sensitivity about him, understanding how Stanley was feeling, responding with a few gentle words of encouragement.

"Don't worry, old boy. It hits me, just the same, as you know."

Much to Stanley's relief, Peggy finally gave up her nursing. It had been quite a shock, during his leave, to see how swollen her belly had become, the previous visit, it having hardly shown at all. He could see, also, that it was quite an effort for her to carry the extra weight even though she insisted it did not bother her at all apart from having to position herself when lying down, to get comfortable.

The thought of her having to manage the physical work that nursing required, particularly heaving elderly patients around, worried him.

"Is there a risk – that it might do some harm to the infant?" he asked her on the phone, his latest anxiety being about her work, having raised the subject several times since leave.

"You needn't worry, darling," she replied, as always, trying to mitigate his fretting, using her gentlest tone, refraining from challenging his often misplaced assertions.

As well as worrying about her working, his concern was that, being absent, he was not going to be able to "do anything" for the baby. What it was that he thought he would have been doing if he had been at home, she wasn't sure, but she chose not to pose such question.

It had been the doctor who had recommended that she should take it easy during last weeks of her pregnancy, and although she probably still had at least six weeks to go, she felt the time was right. Besides, she had a lot to get ready.

*Sweetheart mine*
*I am glad you are looking forward to 48 hrs despite the fact of having a really expectant motherish wife! I have just been having a bath & thinking how curious it is to have such a large tummy & stranger still when it moves of its own accord. I think the infant must like hot baths!*
*I have had nappies hung all over the garden all day so there can be no doubts left in the neighbourhood now!*
*The hut is all clean & polished now as I spent the afternoon there. It felt gloriously warm this afternoon so I think it will be quite alright as long as we warm it up a bit in the evening.*
*I was sorry to hear that you were freezing darling. At least I will be able to keep you warm. Darling, don't worry about not doing anything for the infant as after all you are having to pay for it which is the largest part I think. I will teach you to bath it etc. later on. Then you will be quite busy.*
*Goodnight darling mine*
*Peggy*

Try as she might to keep cheerful, there were increasingly frequent moments when the sadness which she liked to think that, on the whole, she managed to keep at bay, took hold of her, occasionally leading her to retreat to her room, to lie on her bed, striving to compose herself, but, a few times, surrendering to the tears which she was unable to stem and indeed, which seemed to give her some relief, the outpouring of her emotions leaving her feeling drained but ready to pull herself together.

What a dreadful time to be bringing a child into the world, with no end to the war in sight, with its father absent and, worse still, before long, going to be abroad, facing mortal danger, for who knew how long.

She felt for him, so deeply, his own sadness mirroring her own, and while she did her best to sooth him, she had to struggle to maintain her ostensible fortitude.

How she missed him. Having him home − in their own home, makeshift as it was − made her feel so complete, those glorious nine days giving them such a taste of the life they hoped and prayed that one day, not too far ahead, they would begin together.

She loved being able to look after him, to tend to his needs; his washing and ironing; having his things around; his aroma, that rich mix of pipe tobacco and brylcreem, and the distinctive smell of army clothing. Those evenings in the hut, when he would hum along to his records, or recline on the old sofa, his pipe clamped between his teeth, the sucking sound as he regularly tamped and re-lit it, a smile of contentment on his face as his foot tapped to the rhythm of the song.

It was always her first visit to the hut, after he had departed, which she found hardest, the emptiness intensified by the chill of the air.

More than anything else now, she hoped and prayed that he would be able to get home when the time came. Of course he could not be with her when she was actually having the baby; she knew that that was not permitted. But afterwards, for him to come in to meet their new infant; how wonderful that would be, and how unimaginable for him to be absent.

His exercises seemed to be almost constant these days, and with the onset of winter, she worried about him, his health, she felt, never being as resilient as he liked to think. It had been little more than a year ago that he had been so seriously ill, and although she knew that septicaemia was almost certainly an infection he had contracted in the less than sanitary Leeds Castle, the illness which had resulted in his being admitted in the first place was, she was convinced, caused by the conditions of army life.

*11.12.43*
*In the field*
*My darlingest*
*We are still on exercise which is about the toughest one I've been on for the conditions have been appalling. However we've been lucky on 2 nights for one we spent at John's Company and last night at HQ. The night in between was unspeakably beastly! I am wearing two pairs of socks, two pairs of pants, two pullovers, a sheepskin jerkin, a scarf, and I'm still not very warm. The mud has to be seen to be believed. The road between —*
*— and —— was so thick with mud & two bridges were knocked down & several telegraph poles so they had to close it to lorry traffic. I am at the side of the road writing, in the car. Now the sun is shining and I am gloriously warm after being so cold.*
*Darling girl, how are you really and how is the tummy? I have a mixture of such funny emotions inside me – happiness, quite a lot of worry, an altogether feel 'on hot bricks'.*
*Darling, will you please tell me all about having a baby if you can bear to talk about it afterwards. If you don't I'll feel even more 'out in the cold' and shut off from it than I do already. I'm afraid I've got a fit of awful worry, worse than before. I want to be with you and how I hope you won't have any pains etc.*
*My mother has written & said she understands that we are 'on the move again'. You might put her in the picture will you & tell her we're doing an exercise. You might also tell her that how the hell can I want anything for Xmas when i) you will be having a baby and ii) why fiddle about with Xmas, why not get the war over first. Tell her we are too busy getting ready for 'Der Tag' to worry about it.*
*Goodbye my angel. Oh how I wish I could be with you.*
*Stanley*

*12.12.43*
*Sweetheart of mine*
*Here I am on a very grey afternoon sitting in front of a log fire. My coiffure at the moment is very trim – a lot of little curls as I've just had it permed.*
*I have packed nearly everything so I feel it is OK now if it does decide to arrive. Everybody says that first babies are always late so unless the doctor is right it sounds as though it will be. By the way shall we call it Anthony?*
*Isn't it amazing to think that our baby is due in less than a month? I don't think the time has seemed long at all.*
*Goodbye my sweetheart husband*
*Peggy*

The forty eight hours which he had been hoping for, when it came to it, was a mere twenty four, which, allowing for the journey time through London, meant that he arrived home at lunchtime, having to set off again at the crack of a dark, wet dawn the next day.

They were both aware of the different emotion which, unfamiliar as it was, they skirted around, determined to maintain a brave face. What they understood, however, was that this was the last time they would be together before the baby was born, and before they would begin the phase of their lives which was going to prove so testing. It was this which, when the moment came, Peggy standing inside the hut doorway, her dressing gown pulled tightly over her swollen belly, which defeated them, her tears wetting his face as he held her against him.

There were times when each of them described their feelings as "blank", a word so expressive of the emptiness of their lives apart, the blankness invariably ensuing from their partings.

On this occasion, whilst Peggy was able to preoccupy herself with her preparations, endlessly looking through the baby clothes and the other things she knew she would need – marvelling at how much of it there was, Stanley arrived back at the Divisional HQ with the blankness taking him in its despairing grip.

In the mess, there were all the trappings of Christmas, a decorated tree, streamers on the ceiling, and, when the men assembled in the evening, a jovial atmosphere, all of which compounded his moroseness.

"Here, I think you could do with this," Eric said, handing him a large glass of whisky. "And by the way, it should be OK for you to have forty eight when the time comes. There are no more exercises planned for a couple of weeks."

Stanley gratefully accepted the drink, with several others to follow, and by the end of the evening, he found himself singing carols with his usual gusto, thoroughly caught up in the camaraderie of the mess.

# TWELVE

*27.12.43*
*Usual*
*My sweet darling*
*Here I am back again, and writing my first letter to my wife – and family! So I'll start off by asking how you are, darling, and how Anthony is. I trust he is having regular meals and not taking too poor a view of the world he has arrived in. Has he opened his eyes wide yet? Please tell me all about him each time you write and everything he does.*
*Darling, I'm feeling awfully happy – happier than I've ever been. It's so grand to know that all is well with you – so terribly grand my beloved one – I can't tell you here in a letter how much I'm thanking God that it is really all over. Now I can talk so proudly to everyone about my son, and I've been telling them how you sit them up when they get wind and all about breast feeding!*
*Everybody was very nice when I got back. The Colonel asked how you were. I am very glad that everyone is out now as I like just sitting back & thinking about you & Anthony and realising what a wonderful climax to our love it is to have a son.*
*I hope that you are happy darling. It only makes me wish to be with you more than ever. May God grant you a peaceful night and may all your days be happy in the knowledge that you are so very precious & loved by your ever adoring husband*
*Stanley*

It had not been quite as she had hoped when he arrived to inspect his new son. She had wanted to be sitting up, radiant with the achievement, cradling the baby, the perfect Madonna and Child composition. When it came to it, however, she had been asleep as he had crept quietly into the room.

She woke to find him at her bedside, the broad grin on his face fading for a moment.

"How are you, my darling?" he asked, sitting down cautiously on the side of the bed, taking her hand and holding it against his chest. "Are you in pain?"

"It's not too bad," she said as the midwife arrived, carrying the baby, handing it to Peggy who pulled back the shawl so that Stanley could see his son's face.

"Hello old chap!" Tentatively he touched the baby's cheek, his large finger stroking the soft, pink skin. "He's quite something, isn't he?"

"Yes, he's quite something," she repeated, grimacing as a spasm of pain made her flinch.

"Are you sure you're OK?" Stanley looked at her in alarm. "Shall I call the nurse back?"

"No, it's just things settling down."

There had been several moments during the labour, particularly as it intensified towards its crescendo, when the pain was so acute that she felt it was tearing her body apart. And yet she managed, somehow, to stay on top of it. She was able almost to detach herself, telling herself that this was part of the process and that it would soon be over.

Her labour lasted for more than twenty-four hours, the last part, four or five hours, testing her self control to the extreme. And then, quite suddenly, as if she were collapsing into herself, it was done, the infant she had been carrying for so long, expelled from her body.

A few minutes later, the midwife had placed the baby in the crook of her arm as the doctor who had delivered it, stitched the tear which had been the cause of the most searing pain, the sensation of the stitching, quite tolerable in comparison, particularly as she was now inspecting the strange, miraculous creature which was lying beside her.

For those first two days, it seemed that Stanley was constantly there beside her, although he had been told by the midwife that he needed to let his wife rest and that he should only visit for short periods.

"Bugger that!" he said to himself, resolutely remaining at Peggy's side for two hours or more, returning later in the day and the next morning. And on that second afternoon, he seemed unable to tear himself away.

"I've got to be getting back this evening, my darling," he said as he held the baby which seemed so tiny against him, the white of the wool shawl softly contrasting with the coarse khaki of his uniform. "I'm going straight from here to the station."

"I wish you didn't have to go," she said, instantly regretting it, and, at that moment feeling she just had to speak her mind. "We will so miss you."

"I love you. Both of you. More than I can say." He kissed his son gently on the forehead, handing him back to Peggy, kissing her before turning away, gathering up his kitbag and disappearing through the door.

*28.12.43*
*78 Buckingham Road*
*My dearest darling*
I hope you had a reasonable journey back & that you didn't have too bad a reception
when you got there.
After you left your son & heir made a terrific fuss about being woken up for his second
course! The rest of today he had behaved extremely well & slept all day.
Your father came in this afternoon for about three quarters of an hour. He was very funny
with the baby. He is going to do the registration etc. & also buy some saving certificates for
him.
I now have to lay on my tummy for an hour in the morning & wear a sort of bandage
brassiere all in aid of my figure.
Anthony is going fine now – eating & sleeping well & is opening his eyes a little more.
I have only a week from now to stay in bed which is a very cheering thought. Thursday
week I shall be going home which doesn't seem so long now.
There is a great riot on this evening here as the nurses have been having their Christmas
dinner party & the few that have returned have just roared in, in ordinary clothes, making
a terrific noise & are going back to a show later.
Actually it doesn't seem at all Christmas to me now though I have enjoyed all the time
you were here ever so much. It really was grand, wasn't it?
Now I must say goodnight, sweetheart
*Peggy*

*1 Jan 44*
*Usual*
*My dearest darling*
Good morning Peggy & Anthony, & a very happy New Year to you both and may it bring
you lots of happiness and may God grant that by this time next year I shall be with you
for always.
We spent a very quiet New Year's Eve and listened to some very good wireless programmes.
Have just been up to watch the London barrage in action. It seems pretty heavy and I'm
praying you are OK.
This morning I walked to the office and the first dawn of 1944 was really 'Glorious
Morning'. A mournful medley of soft colours were the prelude to sunrise and these seemed
to fill the whole sky, making me think of the lines –
 For not by Eastern Windows only
 When morning comes, comes in the light
 Westwards, look, comes in the light
Can you supply the necessary corrections and add the missing line?
I hope Anthony is not too greedy, darling, as I'm sure it will sap your strength.
A large pile of bumph has just been put in my 'In' tray so I think I'd better bid you

*goodbye now, darling wife. My love for you is inexpressible on cold paper so I will just say, darling sweetheart, may 1944 be such a happy year for you and may God bless our love and eternal life together.*
*Your adoring husband*
*Stanley*

After the series of exercises in the weeks before Christmas, the ensuing few weeks saw little activity other than the usual routine, the lull in the active training accentuating the irritations and minor conflicts which were an inevitable facet of army existence, with many thousands of men spending their days and nights together, often fractious with boredom, impatient to get on with the job for which they were being trained but at the same time, apprehensive of what lay ahead.

With the dawn of the new year, there was renewed speculation of when it would happen – "Der Tag" as many referred to it, ironically adopting the German term.

"I don't think it will be before the spring," was Eric's considered opinion, Stanley always attaching weight to his friend's views, knowing that he picked up on things, reporting back discretely after his periodic senior officer briefings. "Preparation – the assembly of men and material - will probably start in earnest in a couple of months or so, but it's going to be a hell of a business."

"What do reckon of Eisenhower?" Stanley asked, it having been announced that the American general had been appointed as Supreme Commander of the Allied forces in Europe. "It's a bit of a kick in the teeth for Monty, isn't it?"

"Probably the right man for the job," Eric replied thoughtfully, conscious of Montgomery's revered status since his victory in North Africa. "Of course Monty's proved himself a brilliant tactician and an inspired leader. But the word I hear is that there are some questions about how he gets on with other COs. He's apparently got a bit of a reputation for putting noses out of joint, particularly the Yanks. And he's a bit of a maverick."

"But surely, it should be a Brit, given that it's mainly our show," Stanley said, reflecting the generally held view amongst the British officers and men that, important though the Americans were, theirs was to be a supporting role.

"Don't underestimate the Yanks," Eric replied, again inferring that he knew something that others didn't, or at least, that they did not like to acknowledge. "When it comes to it, they'll probably be providing a good deal more than us in terms of both men and material. Besides, Monty becoming CO of the 21$^{st}$ Army is a pretty clear statement of his worth."

What role to give the British general, his immense popularity throughout the nation obligating Churchill and his war cabinet to ensure that he should hold a post suitable to his standing – Montgomery himself, loudly insistent that he should have a role appropriate for his own self-esteem - was a vexed one, requiring a good deal of negotiation, the trade-off for acquiescing in Roosevelt's determination that an American must have overall command, being for Montgomery to take charge of a major proportion of the Allied forces. The fact that it would be the 21$^{st}$ Army which made the ill-fated attempt to out-flank the German army and to strike into Germany through Holland at Arnhem, would irreparably damage Montgomery's reputation, although his folk hero status would survive the catastrophe.

So the debate as the merits of the generals continued, as did speculation about the location of the invasion, a question that would similarly preoccupy the German high command which, by virtue of an extraordinary act of deception, the Allies were able to delude into making a strategically wrong assumption which would prove critical to the early stages of the campaign.

Despite his despondency at having to leave his wife and child behind, throughout those first days back Stanley found himself buoyed by a sense of euphoria.

"Here comes the cat that got the cream," was the greeting as he entered the mess, the other officers tolerantly listening, yet again, to Stanley proudly reporting on his new son's progress, as recounted during his phone calls with Peggy, now almost daily. What he passed on to the mess was, however, only a small part of Peggy's glowing accounts of their new infant's first steps, Stanley encouraging Peggy to recount even the minutiae, thus receiving a graphic education in the techniques of breast feeding, as well as the discipline, the baby being taught, from day one, that meals were at set times, and, bawl insistently as he might, the midwife and nurses would allow no bending of the rules, dismissive of the consequence, that when feeding time arrived, the baby's voracious sucking would invariably induce regurgitation, hiccups and wind, causing it hours of distress from interrupted his sleep.

No sooner had she returned to the comforts of home than worry about Stanley's health resurfaced. Dismissive as he was of merely having "a bit of a heavy cold', she could discern that he was not at all well. Nevertheless, the phone call she received from Eric Nicholls, and Stanley's letter, came as a considerable shock.

20.1.44
*Officer's Wing, Leeds Castle Hospital, Nr Maidstone, Kent*
*My beloved darling*
*You'll recognise the above address and I expect Major Nicholls will have told you why I was suddenly packed of here – i.e. a diphtheria scare. Well here I am once more in the bloody medical ward of this ———- place. First of all I'll give you a bulletin about myself. As you know, when I rang up, I had a slight cold and during the evening it got a bit worse & I went to bed at 9.30 feeling a bit under the weather. Yesterday morning I still felt under the weather & feverish so I thought that as I had a rather sore throat the doc ought to see me. He duly came and like all blasted doctors he would make no decision. So I had to get out of my nice comfortable bed, get dressed & Hopkins drove me over here.*
*I was looked at by a seedy looking doctor who made me say 'Ah' and asked me what my number was and whether my grandmother had blue eyes. To my delight I am isolated and have a screen round me and that's fine as the other patients are awful old men with permanent wind in their bed pans. They took a dig at my throat with something on a stick which they stuck in a bottle and flew away with.*
*This morning I felt quite well. The doc again made me say 'Ah' and says he doesn't think I've got IT but they won't know until they've got their little be of stuff on the stick back. So here I am stuck in this bloody hole by an incompetent fat doctor who failed to diagnose the last case.*
*So, darling, don't be alarmed because it is very unlikely that I've got diphtheria – all I've got is a touch of tonsillitis I think.*
*As I think I said, all the nurses have gone which is Tragedy No. 1 and have been replaced by gormless, incompetent, impolite, male nursing orderlies who are either conscientious objectors or blasted refugees.*
*Tragedy No. 2 is that all the sisters have gone except the one with glasses whom I didn't like when I was here before (the virginal looking one).*
*They still have the worst papers, i.e. the News Chronicle & Daily Herald.*
*I hope that Anthony is well & that I'll see you both very soon.*
*I am, darling, your very much in love husband.*
*Stanley*

His letters recently having been less frequent, his explanation – one that she had become familiar with - being that as they were speaking so regularly on the phone, he liked to write when he had sometime particular to say, she was surprised when she received two in one day, the later one arriving with the second post.

*Peggy my angel child*

*Still no news of my thing on a stick so I'm still being left having no treatment at all today. What makes me really livid is that this lousy dump costs you 5/5d per day – i.e. 2/6 charges & 3/- loss of Field Allowance. The 2/6 charges are supposed to be towards messing. The food is bloody meagre and the mess lousy, so I'm thinking of writing to my MP, Colonel Marlowe. I think it is an absolute scandal.*

*The place is absolutely dead and everyone here is completely browned off. The Sister is a menace and the orderlies completely dopey. The one who has just been round to take temperatures refused to tell me mine until I ordered him to and threatened him with all kinds of things. It is almost normal tonight so if I've got diphtheria, the temp doesn't seem so bad.*

*If I haven't got diphtheria I'm going to try to persuade old Doc to let me get up tomorrow. You know how he loves keeping people in bed for weeks.*

*Darling they are just about to bring supper.*

*It wasn't supper but treatment in the form of an infernal machine - to use it you disappear under a towel and Breath Deeply.*

*Darling I'm feeling terribly happy tonight because I love you so terribly and love Anthony. I think it is such a grand thought that through war, illness, you having a baby – anything, our love does not and will never change. Being here has given me much needed time to think how terribly lucky I am.*

*Goodnight my angel girl.*

*Stanley*

*Saturday*

*The swab hasn't turned blue or whatever it does. I only had a slight 'streptococcal something' and old Doc seemed as relieved as me. I have also won the Battle of the Bed Pans because I am now allowed up to the lavatory.*

Peggy laughed aloud, both with amusement at Stanley's entertaining way of writing, and with relief. She had been dreading the prospect of his having diphtheria, particularly as it would have been so difficult for her to get to Leeds Castle with the baby.

Twenty five! Peggy could not quite decide whether a quarter of a century was a significant milestone in the ageing process or whether she was, in reality, still as young as she felt. Being a mother added to the recognition of maturity, although living at home with her parents seemed to keep her suspended in a kind of enduring childhood, her parents expectation being that she should continue to know her place as the daughter of the house, baby notwithstanding.

It was a great relief when Stanley phoned to tell her he was out of hospital, the diphtheria scare being nothing more than a throat infection, although she told him, in no uncertain terms, that being required to participate in a week long exercise just a few days later, was "very foolish", her unusually forthright comment indicative of her worrying about his health.

When it came to it, in spite of the cold February weather, he came to no further harm, and indeed, told her when the exercise was over, that he was feeling "fit and raring to go".

During the course of the exercise, the morale of the Division as a whole, and Stanley's in particularly, was raised to a still higher level by a visit from Montgomery himself.

On a bitterly cold day, amid flurries of snow, those parts of the Division which had been in the vicinity, were assembled in a square in the old Sussex town of Rye, the General arriving in a Rolls Royce, standing for a moment on the running board, as if wanting to ensure that the assembly of more than a thousand men had a clear view of him, attired in battledress and his trademark beret, before proceeding with the inspection, ensuring that he passed along every line, pausing frequently for a few words with both officers and men.

Stanley, rigidly at attention, but able to observe out of the corner of his eye, watched the general approach, smartly saluting as he came to the RASC section, stopping in front of Stanley.

"You know how much we will be relying upon you and the RASC, Captain Allen," the general said, his piercing eyes fixed on Stanley who, contrary to protocol, allowed his gaze which had been on some distant point, to move to the man in front of him. He could feel his heart pounding in his chest and, afterwards, he remembered thinking how surprised he had been at Monty's small stature but, despite it, being overwhelmed by the feeling of being in the presence of the most extraordinary force of nature.

"I do, sir," Stanley replied, his voice sounding as if it has come from someone else, his thought, at that moment, being how on earth did the general know his name.

"He's bloody good at that!" Eric told him later with a wry laugh. "You probably didn't see him whispering with the CO as he was doing the inspection." Stanley felt rather disappointed, having, for a short while, had the fanciful notion that somehow, the general knew of him.

It would be a few months later, when he again encountered Montgomery in wholly different circumstances, that he learned that the general did indeed, have a remarkable capacity for remembering names and faces.

As winter slowly gave way to spring, even the North Sea loosening its icy grip on Kent, whilst those in the echelons of high command worked on the dauntingly complex plans for the forthcoming European campaign, lower down the hierarchy there was a feeling almost of limbo. Within the Wyverns, officers and men alike were certain that they were trained to a state of readiness, physically and mentally, to take on the *Wehrmacht,* morale having reached a level that some officers shared their concern as to how they were to maintain it if the invasion were not to take place within the coming weeks.

What sustained them, however, and mitigated any grievance about delay, was the certainty that it was going to happen, the discussion amongst them featuring regular bets on dates as well as locations, their knowledge of the geography of the Channel coast of France enhanced by frequent study of maps and atlases.

In spite of the reduction in air raids, the *Luftwaffe* was still very much in evidence, the raids which did take place tending to be more targeted than the days of blitz, railways, docks, industry and the military bearing the brunt, the increasing build up of troops and equipment throughout the south of the country rendering it more vulnerable to attacks.

Leave was also increasingly limited, generally to twenty-four or occasionally, forty eight hours, Stanley managing a day towards the end of February. When he phoned Peggy the day after he returned to Chilham, he could not help himself from sounding despondent, in part because his next leave would not be for nearly two months. His mood was also affected by the incident which occurred when he was on his way back, which, having mentioned it to Peggy, he brushed aside. "It was nothing much really," he said, his bravado failing to diminish the shock which he had felt.

The picture of the plane, bursting into flames so close to the train and of the helplessness as the train came to a standstill, everyone else in his compartment trying to get down onto the floor, squeezing into the narrow area between the seats, was fixed in his mind, as was the fear, that at any moment the plane, which he recognised as a German Junkers 88, was going to explode, convinced as he was that it must have been carrying bombs. Stupidly, he had not been able to tear himself away from the window, and had thus seen, for a fleeting moment, within the flame filled cockpit, the pilot, arms thrashing against the flames as they engulfed him.

Stanley's dislike of Kent, was, he had to admit to himself, and occasionally to his fellow officers when they were sharing their grievances, derived from his association with the county as a place of unremittingly bitter winters as well as his life of separation from his beloved Peggy, his pining now so much more intense since the arrival of the son who, already, had become a new beacon in his existence.

What he had to admit, however, was that at times the county transformed into an enchanted corner of England, particularly now, with the arrival of the first tendrils of spring.

Whenever he could find a spare hour, he had taken to wandering the lanes and footpaths, finding a new awareness of nature, sometimes standing quite still in a wood or at the side of a field, listening to the birdsong, observing the flittings of the small birds in the hedgerows, increasingly fascinated by the wonder of their plumage; and watching the wild creatures – rabbits and hares, an occasional fox or badger; and most thrilling of all, a barn owl which he had discovered frequented an area of woodland, sometimes sitting on what was clearly its favoured viewing point, the pointed branch of dead oak tree, dropping into its soft, silent flight, gliding across the field.

Invariably, however, the interludes of tranquillity were short-lived, curtailed by formations of aircraft, the drumming of engines drowning the vernally expectant ebullience of nature.

For Peggy, the arrival of spring, delighted as she was with the first blossom and the burgeoning of daffodils, always the harbinger of the changing of the seasons, this year carried the foreboding for what they all knew to be imminent. At times the thought of it caused a tightening of her abdomen, as if someone was physically constraining her, a feeling almost of panic rising inside her.

Austere as her mother could be, she was also well attuned to her daughter's moods and was acutely aware of the depth of her anxiety, her own worries about Tom gnawing at her constantly. It was at such times that Peggy recognised how much she valued her mother. They would rarely touch, in any deliberate way, physical displays always frowned upon. Yet in Stanley's absence, her understated emotional support was deeply gratifying, although not entirely dispelling Peggy's desire to be on her own, thoughts of finding somewhere where she and Anthony could live their own life, and where Stanley could feel at home, becoming a more frequent issue in her mind.

Without any undue sentiment, which was not part of her mother's repertoire, they nevertheless were able to help each other to "buck up", distracting themselves by attending to Anthony's needs and his engaging ways.

If only they – the army – could get on with it, the sooner the war would be over and done with, and her dream of her marriage and family finally becoming whole could become the reality.

Each night she would kneel at the side of her bed, hands clasped in supplication, beseeching the Almighty to protect her husband; solemnly committing him to do his duty, confident that he would do so, but somehow believing that she had to offer such commitment in return for God's watching over the man who was so special, convincing herself that goodness, duty and divine protection were woven together by the power of prayer.

As she concluded with a hasty whispering of the Lord's Prayer, a small muttering from the cot on the other side of the bed reminded her to add a postscript.

"And please, God, watch over our precious son, Anthony."

"Things seem to be happening," Eric Nicholls told Stanley on his return from the senior officer's briefing, speaking in a hushed tone before the meeting with the rest of the RASC officers. "All leave is about to be cancelled."

The pang of anticipation which Stanley felt in his gut was tempered by the bitter pill of having to cancel the leave he had been so looking forward to; again, a mere twenty-four hours, but this time, one that he had been desperately looking forward to.

"I think it will be alright," Peggy had told him on the phone two days earlier. "The doctor has give me the all clear."

"So we'll be able to be naughty?" Stanley did not try to conceal his eagerness. "But only if you are absolutely certain."

"Darling, I can't wait to be naughty!" she replied. "I'm sure Mummy won't mind having Anthony for the night."

*4.4.44*
*My sweetheart husband*
*It is wretched about leave isn't it? I was rather afraid it might be something like that when*

*I heard it was you on the telephone. I did feel awfully miserable for a few minutes, darling, but since then I have pulled myself together & am hoping that there may be some possibility of having it later as you said.*

*I hope you are not too miserable, darling mine. I am going up to the hut tomorrow to tidy your things up just to prove that I am 'always hopeful'.*

*Goodnight my love & God bless you and keep you ever.*

*Peggy*

*8.4.44*

*Usual*

*My sweet darling*

*There has been a lot of gloom flying around as you can well guess although everyone hopes we'll get on with the war and get home quickly to have an unending 'leave'. That's the consoling thought, darling, that the sooner we go the sooner I'm able to be happy with you for ever.*

*The photos are lovely – it's so nice to have a photo of one's son. What I want now is one of you and child together.*

*Darling I have hopes of a day off & will see what I can do but I'm afraid it's doubtful whether I could get as far as Brighton.*

*I might risk coming home – the chief risk is that there might be inquisitive MP's on Brighton Station. Could you pop into the station as some time and see whether there are any by the place where the Hastings train comes in.*

*I do wish I could send you and Anthony an Easter egg but I'm afraid I'll just have to send you a heartful of love & wish you a peaceful and calm Easter.*

*Tomorrow being Easter Sunday, I shall pray so much for you and us: darling, I pray so much these days: do you?*

*There is a dissertation on tits and black men's pricks going on in the mess at the moment which is highly disconcerting!*

*All my love my darling wife*

*Stanley*


"You won't be able to take a car or even a motorcycle," Mead said, with what Stanley discerned to be a hint of satisfaction, the wretched man, being single and, as far as they could gather, not having a girlfriend, sneeringly disapproving of the incessant talk of loved ones and sex. Stanley, having made the mistake of mentioning his plan to "nip down to Brighton for a night", and Eric Nicholls having given his implicit consent in the form of "just keep a weather eye for the MPs", he did not need Mead to remind him that use of all vehicles was now restricted, it therefore being a matter of taking his chances by train, knowing that the Military Police were particularly active on all the major stations as a result of a slight, but, to the army, significant increase in the number of troops going

AWOL, the cancellation of leave and the imminence of the invasion prompting many to arrange what they assumed would be their last assignations with their wives and sweethearts.

Having decided to take the much slower, but, he reckoned, safer cross country route, thus avoiding Charing Cross where the MPs were bound to be out in force, he lingered on the train for several minutes when it arrived at Brighton, peering from the window, seeing only two MPs who appeared to be enjoying a chat and a cigarette on the far side of the concourse, enabling him to cross quickly to the next platform where, fortunately, the train which would take him the one further stop to Preston Park was waiting.

The bottle of gin which Peggy had bought served its purpose, of brightening what otherwise might have been a sombre evening. He sat and watched her as she cooked the meal, the hut's basic "kitchen", the two jet primus sitting on a sideboard so small that one needed to be adept at juggling pots, pans and cutlery, the delicious smell of the sizzling sausages combining with the steam from the boiling saucepan to fill the air, even though the warm spring weather no longer required the paraffin heater.

"It'll be so lovely to have a little sister for Anthony," Peggy said when they had finished eating, the sausage and mash followed by a suet pudding, she having used most of her week's rations on the sausages and suet although she did not mention this to Stanley.

"Or brother!" he added. "But as we agreed, not till the war is over."

"I know," she said sadly. "Definitely a peacetime sister – or brother. Darling, I should be so happy with either, as long as they have a Daddy, to be with us all the time."

"There probably won't be much opportunity anyway," he said, having told her earlier that the word was that "it" would probably be within the next two or three weeks. "Although I should be able to escape again to see you if I play my cards right."

For several minutes they sat at the small dining table, both looking at their hands lying on the surface, fingers interlinked, deep in their respective thoughts.

"But if you happened to have another one while I'm abroad, then, unless it's on the way in the next few weeks, I'll know you've been a bad girl!" He tried to make it sound like a joke although she understood that it was both a warning and, in a strange way, a pained offer of licence, in the event of his failing to return, or even, she surmised, of his long term absence."

"Don't be so daft," she replied, pulling his hand up to her face and holding it against her cheek. "How could you say such a thing?"

In the morning, as they ate their breakfast, the warm sun which filled the hut revived their spirits, their mood lighter, although as always, it was, in part, the imminence of parting which engendered the determined brightness.

It was when Stanley arrived back at Divisional HQ that Eric greeted him with the shattering news that he was being transferred to a different division.

"I've been assigned to 51st Highland Division," Eric told him, the two of them alone in the major's office, Stanley still breathless from hurrying from the station, being told as soon as he arrived that Major Nicholls wanted to speak to him. "And they're making me Colonel."

"Congratulations, sir!" Stanley said with a feigned, half-hearted salute. "Blimey, Eric, it's a bit of a bombshell. I'll miss you."

"I would like to be taking you with me, Stanley," Eric said, his pale blue eyes revealing a hint of sadness. "And in fact, there may just be a possibility, although it could take a little while. The 51st has been in rather poor shape, from what I'm told, since North Africa, and they're having a bit of a shake up."

"So you'll be needing to learn Scottish," Stanley quipped, the unexpected suggestion that there might be an opening for him as well, leading to the curious prospect of becoming part of the famed Scottish division. "I assume you won't be having to wear a kilt!"

"Letters are definitely going to be censored from now on," Stanley said when he phoned Peggy one evening at the beginning of May, the order having been issued the day before, with a directive as to how censorship was to be managed, and what should and should not be allowed. What surprised him was that he was to be one of the officers charged with the task of censoring the men's letters. "I'm not sure who'll be looking at mine, but we'll need to be a bit careful, darling. I'd better refrain from speaking my mind about P – bleeding – Mead!"

"Don't build up your hopes, darling," he told her, "but I might be able to escape for a few hours later this week. It won't be overnight, so you don't need to worry about the hut."

When it came to it, it was the briefest of visits, his free afternoon giving him less than six hours to get to Brighton and back. This time, however, he was able to persuade his fellow officer in charge of vehicles, to allow him to use a motorbike – "bit of a hush-hush mission!", he said, winking as he said it, the journey to Brighton taking him nearly two hours due to a number of checkpoints having been set up across the region, each of which he was able to pass through, having been forewarned that the Military Police were now restricting movement, the brown envelope he brandished with the Divisional insignia stamped on it (having used his own rubber stamp), and the words "confidential despatch", resulting in him being waved through.

The two hours he had at home they spent playing with Anthony in the garden, Peggy having prepared a simple picnic tea. He was desperate to take Peggy in his arms. If only they could have lain down on the picnic rug, just to hold onto each other. Instead, they chatted to Anthony as he sat between them, chirruping happily and playing with a wooden car which Stanley's brother, Michael, had given him.

"I wish we could have just a few minutes alone," he said at one point, conscious not so much of Anthony's presence, but of the feeling that Peggy's mother might be watching from the house. "I don't mean I don't want to be with Anthony. Of course not."

She looked at him, conscious of his apparent reticence to play with his infant son, picking him up and propping him against his father. "Come on, Anthony, give Daddy a kiss. He's a bit sad as he may not see you for a while."

"Wave to Daddy," she whispered to the infant, holding him, standing by the gate as Stanley mounted his motorbike. "He does love you really."

As she turned back towards the house, she was aware of a new anxiety, permeating the familiar despondency of parting. Why was it that Stanley seemed so – what was it - distant? - from Anthony, as if he was somehow disapproving of him, and reluctant for him to be there with them. She could understand that, with so short a time for them to be together, he was wanting to spend it with her, but surely, he would want to be with his son as well. He had seen so little of him in the first few months of his young life. Perhaps that was part of it; he had not had time to be able to truly realise that he was now a father.

She did not blame him; quite the opposite; she felt a deep sadness that her husband had been denied the opportunity to get to know his son. And now it was likely that he would be away for months.

"We love Daddy, don't we," she said to Anthony when they were back in the house, blowing her nose and dabbing her eyes as she deposited him on the floor where he resumed playing with the wooden car which he had been clutching.

Driving back through the country lanes, Stanley felt a similar dejection. What had gone wrong? There had been a distinct discomfort between them. He had felt so *awkward* with Anthony. It was as if she was observing him; the way he behaved to his infant son. And the clear conclusion was that for some reason which he could not fathom, he had been found wanting.

As soon as he was back in his billet, he sat down at the table, looking out of the window for several minutes as he tried to assemble his confused thoughts. He wondered whether he should phone her, wanting to say something straight away. But it was not the same on the phone; he could never quite articulate what was on his mind.

*My very dear darling*
*I have been thinking about you and Anthony since we said goodbye 2 ½ long hours ago. I am feeling quite happy as a result of those wonderful hours together, despite 'the encircling gloom'.*
*Darling, please don't think I 'look down my nose' at Anthony. I'm just terribly fond of him but it is so bloody having just to settle down then go off again. I would be a much nicer popper if I could settle down & adapt myself to home life.*
*Darling, I hope you won't be disappointed in me – get tired of me when you have to put up with my face always!*
*You ever adoring*
*Stanley*

"Did you get my letter?" he asked her when he phoned the following evening, his unease at what had happened – even though he was not clear in his own mind what it was – having been gnawing at his thoughts all day. And the more he dwelt on it, the more he felt a sense of frustration; anger almost; although whether with her or with himself, he wasn't sure.

"Yes, thank you darling. It came in the second post."

"I'm so sorry," he said, his tone conveying the contrition he was feeling. "I know

I'm no good as a father, when I can't be there. It makes be so…I don't know… so bloody cross. Not with you, darling. But with everything. This wretched army. And the war. God how I wish it was over and we could start our life together, properly. I'm so browned off. I just want to get on with the job, get it done, then I can get back to you and Anthony."

She listened as he poured out his grievance, unsure what she could say, making do with a few soothing platitudes.

During the following two weeks he had little time to dwell on such worries, such was the level of increased activity. It was as if, after the long years of preparation, with its periods of boredom and impatience, now, at last, everything was suddenly in motion.

For Stanley, the days required him to be at numerous meetings and briefings, travelling back and forth across Kent and East Sussex, and then spending hours at his desk, attending to the paperwork which, though laborious, was an essential element of ensuring the vast array of supplies were both procured and transported to the designated assembly points.

The briefings, although still not divulging the all important information as to the invasion route, nevertheless, introduced them to places and names which, before long, would become all too familiar: Caen; the rivers Odun and Orne; Mount Pincon.

Stanley had always had a fascination with maps, marvelling at the ingenuity of the cartographers who had invented the array of markings and symbols enabling one to discern not only roads, rivers and such obvious features, but contours and the nature of the terrain, with woods and marshes. Now, however, it was more than a matter of fascination, his familiarisation with Normandy, he knew, being crucial to his role, of establishing supply routes, recognising that the campaign would, almost certainly, require the fighting units to deviate from the planned lines of advance.

On the thirteenth of May, having been required to accompany the new RASC CO on a trip to Rye, he found himself amongst an assembly of senior officers (few other captains being present) on the forecourt of Rye station, wording having been sent that a party of VIPs was due to arrive and that they would be visiting several other places in the area where the 43rd Division was assembling.

As the train came to a stop, a figure whom Stanley vaguely recognised emerged.

"Smuts," someone nearby said, the elderly Field Marshall, with his stiff bearing and goatee beard, a renowned figure from both the Boer and Great Wars, stepping down onto the platform followed by several other figures, none of whom Stanley recognised although, judging by their uniforms and insignia, men of high rank and importance, those in civilian attire, having the appearance of a group of elderly aristocrats leaving an exclusive St James club.

After a theatrical pause, a familiar figure appeared, officers and men instantly saluting as the Prime Minister, donning a rather odd, brown hat as he stood on the platform, looking around him, taking in the scene, the line of senior officers awaiting his inspection, lifting his hand in greeting, brandishing his trademark cigar.

Watching the party as they completed their cursory inspection, all but Churchill climbing into the three Humber staff cars which were to take them on their tour of the Division, the Prime Minister making a point of lingering, chatting to several officers, making sure that they had all had the opportunity of seeing him, as if he knew that his presence amongst them was as inspirational as his oratory, Stanley was eagerly anticipating telling Peggy, when he phoned her that evening, that he had actually met – or at least been inspected by – none other than Winnie!

Even though all leave had been cancelled, within the Division, senior officers allowed final home visits, provided they were limited to twelve hours maximum, with no overnight absences.

When Stanley arrived home, it was only just after eight in the morning, having forewarned Peggy that he would be making a very early start. She greeted him with breakfast in the hut, Anthony, at his insistence, to be with them for the day.

Neither of them needed to say what they knew, that this was to be their last time together before "I set off on my adventure" as he described it, suggesting some sort of voyage of discovery.

They managed, by their shared resolve, to maintain a faux joviality throughout most of the day, spending much of the morning in the park before wandering down to the town for lunch and, as a treat for Anthony, ice-creams, returning to the hut where they listened to records and played with Anthony on the grass, the sun having put in a welcome appearance, the weather generally being cool and showery.

When Peggy put Anthony in his pram for his sleep, they retreated into the hut, lying down on the bed, their love making intense with emotion. For a long time they lay silently, holding onto each other, neither wanting to risk saying anything for fear of breaking their promise, not to let their composure slip.

"Time for me to be hitting the road," he said, looking at his watch. "Can't be hanging around here when I've a war to win."

She lifted Anthony from his pram, handing him to his father, the child's bleary eyes looking at him suspiciously, his face creasing in readiness for a howl of disapproval, Peggy touching his cheek which seemed to reassure him.

"Cheerio, old chap. Look after your mother, won't you. And I'll be seeing you very soon."

As he handed him back to Peggy, he encircled both of them with his long arms, kissing each of them on the cheek before turning quickly away, striding across the grass to the stop just as the tram arrived.

As it moved away, he raised his hand, turning the wave into a salute, Peggy standing, Anthony clasped to her side, remaining for some time after the tram had disappeared from view, the tears which she had been unable to hold back, streaming down her cheeks.

*25.5.44*
*HQ RASC 43 Div APO England*
*My sweet beloved darling*
*I am back in my room sitting on the edge of my bed feeling rather blank & lonely and longing so much to be with you my darling wife and son. Darling you have given me so much wonderful happiness in our days off that I feel that our love and life together is beautiful and sacred.*
*Let us dedicate our lives for each other and for Anthony; that in everything we do our love, blessed by God, may always be present; although physically we may be parted for a little while we shall always feel near each other. I, in my work, shall be so very busy, but in the briefest of days there always comes some moment when my thoughts and heart turn to you, my darling.*
*So I come to wish you goodnight my so precious one.*
*Your ever adoring and loving*
*Stanley*

*My own*
*I just didn't feel that I could write to you before – I felt so very blank and sad that the*

*whole world seemed grey & lifeless. Even Anthony's smiles only made me think again of you saying 'Goodbye' to him which I am afraid spoilt my resolve to be a smiling wife to say goodbye to.*

*Today I feel a little better having made myself just think what a wonderful time we had together. I understood so well that you love your wife very much as I too love my husband very much.*

*This evening I have been happy with your family, though feeling deep down the need for you all the time.*

*Dearest one, I shall always be by your side, wherever you go though it may only be in spirit for a time, God grant that that time may not be too long.*

*Yours for eternity*

*Peggy*

# THIRTEEN

In spite of the requirement for absolute secrecy, it had become an open secret, even amongst the middle ranking officers, that the destination was to be Normandy. Doubtless the high command would have preferred to have delayed the briefings, but, of necessity, the last phase of preparation required detailed study of maps and terrain, the sheer scale and complexity of the operation needing officers in command of units even down to battalion level, to familiarise themselves with their routes of advance and their key objectives.

The name of the operation, "Overlord", was increasingly uttered, hushed tones often arousing the curiosity of those not yet in the know, although, remarkably, an extraordinary degree of secrecy was maintained, most crucially, to enable the elaborate deception aimed at the German high command, to be protected. It surprised even those most closely involved in the ruse – the assembly of a faux invasion force, some of it described in deliberately divulged signals and dispatches, drawing attention to the array of vehicles and craft, mainly flimsy "stage-set" mock-ups – that the enemy had fallen for it, convinced, even when the real invaders appeared off the Normandy coast, that it was to be the Pas de Calais.

With the briefings, and with preparations reaching their final crescendo, the entirety of South East England turned into a vast assembly area, for the uniformed men, now counted in millions, the tension of the last days became almost unbearable. Many of them found they had spare time, leave being allowed, limited to nearby destinations, towns being filled with soldiers mitigating their impatience with liquor and entertainment, mainly in the form of cinemas and a few ENSA shows.

For the RASC however, the pace did not slacken, the logistics of the operation, to equip and support the invading armies, on a scale beyond anything ever previously undertaken, or even conceived. Getting the supplies – of ammunition, fuel, food, and everything else necessary to enable an army to function – to the relevant assembly points in readiness for loading onto the vessels to transport them across the Channel was itself a monumental task, but on top of this, there had to be uninterrupted continuity, taking account of the uncertainties of weather, particularly with the Channel crossing, and of the ensuing unfolding of the campaign.

The grief which Stanley had felt the day after his parting from Peggy, remained as a dull ache which, intensely busy as he was, he did not have time to dwell on, other than at the end of the long days when, in spite of his fatigue, he would allow himself a short interlude, to nurse his emotional wound, grateful for the salve of her letters, managing to write quite regularly to her.

*28.5.44*
*My own dear darling*
*Here I am at the end of a perfect Whit Sunday. It has been an almost too hot day & it is still so hot that I am laying on top of the bed.*
*There is a warning on now & as the guns opened up & I had not put Anthony to bed I have taken him downstairs & am now finishing this sitting in the hall. I have just had a look out and there doesn't seem to be anything happening & it is still quite light.*
*Here I am back in bed as the all clear obligingly went quite quickly.*
*It was so nice to hear your voice for a few minutes again tonight darling, although you can't say much about what you are doing. I keep wanting to ask you questions & then realise it is no good. I like telling you I love you in person even if it is over the telephone. It makes me feel a little less far away though it also always makes me want to be a lot nearer so that I can see if you are smiling or sad or if you have a wicked twinkle in your eye! I can read your thoughts almost from your expressions I think.*
*Sweetheart, I love our telephone talks & shall miss them very much. Strange isn't it but I suppose it was intuition that made me feel somehow that Thursday was the last day without you saying it. I did not work it out or think about it consciously at all but just felt a numbness & something sad inside me. It was that which made me stay in the front garden after we had said goodbye, to waive & just see you for a little longer. The thing that makes me a little sad is thinking of little things to do with Anthony that you won't be able to see or hear, but dearest one, I will tell you all about him & try to take some photos for you.*
*I feel there will be many calls on my resources — though not nearly as much as you will have to endure my beloved one. I feel with God our guide & helper we shall make it.*
*God bless & be with you, darling heart. I love you so terribly.*
*Peggy*

*1.6.44*
*HQ RASC 43 Division APO England*
*My very dear darling*
*After I rang you up I went to the office then this afternoon I have been shopping and had tea at the local tea shop. We had a so called 'pep' talk from the CO but he wasn't a bit inspiring, though everyone is extremely optimistic. Monty is superb, I think he is probably the greatest general of all time and seems almost divinely inspired.*
*Darling I feel it will quite quickly be over & I'll be with you again.*
*I wished you could have been beside me darling, but alas that it not to be for a while: but the sooner our party starts the sooner our dreams will be realised. Monty's words are*

*certainly a tonic on one's spirits – everyone – not only this HQ – seemed much more on top of the world today. Everyone feels so much that it is our lucky lot to be taking part in one of the greatest events in British history. You, too, my darling, are also taking part: your lot is the worse one: to keep the home fires burning and may be put up with enemy actions (though I pray God not) to which you cannot reply.*

*This is the hottest day I remember for ages and I do long for the sea and iced beer - and to be with you looking very cool and voluptuous in a summer frock or bathing dress – anyhow, with little on.*

*Thank you my darling for a very sweet and provoking letter – I could seduce you tonight. I should undress you my sweet and kiss your loveliness from head to toe, and love you so terribly, almost from dusk to dawn, and till we both fell peacefully asleep.*

*My moustache is flourishing. I will show you what it is like to be kissed by one next time unless I forget one morning and shave it off!*

*Darling, I have just had my first telephone conversation with Anthony: he shouted down the telephone and I don't suppose he realised I was at the other end!*

*I love you so much and will ever be your adoring husband.*

*Stanley*

It was a cool, blustery day when they – most of the division's officers – arrived at Hastings, numerous vehicles clogging the seafront and narrow side streets.

Greetings were exchanged as they converged on Cambridge Road, a queue forming outside the Ritz cinema with its striking art deco facade, officers filing through the foyer, looking around as they entered the auditorium, few of them having been there before, the size of it, with capacity for nearly two thousand, surprising them.

"What's the flick tonight?" someone asked, prompting several replies.

"*Casablanca,* I hope," Stanley said. "I haven't seen it yet."

When they were seated, the divisional CO, Major-General Thomas stepped up onto the narrow stage, the ornate Wurlitzer organ behind him, a large map of Normandy pinned to a board beside the organ, the men rising to their feet, the Major-General gesturing to them to resume their seats.

"Do you think he plays?" some wag behind Stanley whispered.

"Right men," the Major-General said, his tone, as always, brisk and peremptory, his reputation being of a man of few words, but those he did utter, he expected to be heard and complied with. "This is the most important briefing any of you have attended." He paused, looking to the back of the auditorium where there was a sound of movement.

The instantly familiar figure started to make his way forward, the men once again rising as one, every one of them rigidly to attention.

As Montgomery mounted the stage, the Major-General saluted him, before climbing down, leaving the General with the stage to himself.

"Officers of the Wessex Wyverns, I salute you!"

The greeting sent a shiver down Stanley's spine, the voice light yet infused with power and authority.

"At ease." He paused again, waiting for his audience to settle. "As your Commanding Officer has rightly said, this is the most important briefing of the war so far. Very soon, you will be embarking on the greatest military crusade in the history of warfare. As you already know, you will be crossing to Normandy as part of the all important second wave, your role then being to translate the bridgehead which will then have been established, into the offensive against our enemy, the German *Wehrmacht*. He, the German, is a formidable opponent. But rest assured, gentlemen, he is no match for the magnificent army which will be confronting him, our mission, our unassailable purpose, being to drive him from the lands he has so cruelly conquered, and thence, to vanquish him in his own land."

As they emerged from the cinema two hours later with a feeling of purposeful elation, it was as if their very souls had been infused with a spirituality flowing from the word of a great guru, the specifics of the invasion now firmly imprinted in their brains in readiness for the innumerable briefings which they, in turn, were now to deliver to their units.

"Whoever is *Mary*?" someone asked the others in the mess after they had returned from Hastings, having been told that they were to await "Codeword *Mary*" which would be the division's notice to move.

"No idea," Tommy replied. "Maybe Queen Mary."

"The old Queen or the ship?" Stanley quipped.

For Stanley, as for so many of them, the only regret was that edict which now precluded any mention of Monty's presence, or indeed, of anything to do with the invasion, meant that he could not tell Peggy when he phoned her that evening. He was bursting to do so, barely able to contain the urge, at the very least, to allude to the event, although the consequences of a breach of secrecy, imparted by endless repetition – "walls have ears" – enabled him to avoid the subject.

"Isn't it wonderful about Rome?" she said, the liberation of the famous city by the Allies as they made their slow and, at times, gruelling advance through Italy, contributing to the momentous nature of those few days. It was also a welcome topic to draw Stanley's thoughts, burgeoning with all manner of preoccupations, away from the invasion and the temptation to tell her at least something about it.

"I do so wish you could tell me where you are and what you are doing," she said, "but I know you mustn't say anything, darling. You'll just have to leave me to guess."

"It won't be long now," was all he could venture, although how long the 43$^{rd}$ would have to wait was dependent on the progress of the first wave, the division's designated date, being 12$^{th}$ June.

"Will you be able to write when you get there?" she asked, repeating the question which had been worrying her, his answer, on that last afternoon they had been together being that the army postal service was deemed to be essential. "Almost as important as ammo and food!" he had said jokingly.

"Make sure you listen to the news, won't you," he told her. "And read the papers. The *Telegraph* will probably be as good as any. You should get a pretty good idea of where we are and how it's going."

She felt oddly restless, unable to get down to anything, her usual distractions of sewing and gardening, offering no solace as she spent her time between feeding Anthony, listlessly playing with him, smoking too many cigarettes and allowing herself to dream about a future which, at that moment, seemed so remote as to be more fantasy than reality.

When Anthony was asleep in his pram, she went up to her bedroom, opening the wardrobe and inspecting her dresses, taking out one, the black evening dress which Stanley's mother had given her and which, after a spot of taking in, fitted her perfectly, and which did not look at all dated, its elegance timeless, showing off her restored slim figure to perfection.

She moved around the room, arms raised, her imaginary husband in ballroom hold, humming as she revolved. Yes, as soon as the war was over, they would go to dances, dressed in their finery, gaily making up for so much lost time.

At that same moment, as she was waltzing dreamily around her bedroom, Stanley was confined to the small HQ office designated for the duty RASC officer. After the unrelenting activity of the preceding days, there was a sudden lull, the phone unusually silent, which was just as well, Stanley feeling extremely drunk, the mess these days, seeming to have a surfeit of liquor, the imminence of their departure giving them licence to indulge.

Drink, and the shared anticipation and anxiety, engendered a new sense of camaraderie, even the generally despicable Mead, now almost tolerable.

Stanley greatly missed Eric, the two men having become genuinely close, unlike the many transient friendships which marked army existence. Once again, however, it being Stanley's nature always to seek out new friends, needing as he did, someone with whom he could share confidences, he found himself drawn to the Medical Officer, Dr Harold Weston, known as "Doc", a reserved, thoughtful, worldly man, formally a hospital registrar.

Doc having only been transferred to the Division a month or so earlier, they were relatively recent acquaintances, getting to know each other during the short interludes in the frantic activity, chatting over a beer, or late at night, when, weary but needing a moments reflection before turning in, they conversed quietly, soon coming to recognise their affinity. It would be the long week on board their ship which would cement their friendship.

When, first thing the next morning, the dispatch arrived, he stared at it, the pit of his stomach churning with excitement. Only yesterday, word was that it had had to be delayed because of the bad weather, the English Channel in typically ragged mood, far too rough for the landing craft and innumerable small vessels which made up so much of the massive invasion armada.

*MESSAGE FROM*
*HQ 43rd (Wessex) Division*
*Royal Army Service Corps*
*6 June 1944 Time 10.50*
*D day today. OPS report to be going satisfactorily. All units informed*

*6.6.44*
*Tuesday 10 am*
*Good morning my darling*
*Terrific excitement – have just heard the great news that D Day is at last here. Well, darling, all I can say is God bless you my darling & don't be too worried about things. Everyone here is frightfully excited and the air seems to have cleared at last from all the waiting and tension of the past few months. We ourselves still have some more waiting but it is not so bad now that things are really happening. Isn't it funny, Eric got the day right? 2 months ago he said it would be today – his birthday. Work still goes on & I'll phone tonight. So goodbye my angel & God bless & keep you safe.*
*Stanley*

There was a palpable mood almost of celebration, that it was finally happening. If only they could get moving now, without having to wait.

For the Wyverns, however, it proved to be an intensely frustrating time; more than a week of waiting, listening to the news, reading between lines to try to work out how well things were really going, word which reached them, affirmed by the evidence in the form of the arrival of increasing numbers of casualties, indicating that some of the landings had been a good deal tougher than expected.

There was something also about being the "second wave" which detracted from their sense of pride in participation in the great crusade, although such disappointment would, within a short time, be well and truly behind them.

The unreality of that period of limbo was accentuated by Peggy's letters, filled as they were with what might have seemed mundane accounts of her days, had it not been for the pleasure they gave him, anchoring him to the wondrous reverie, of life at home – his home – with his beloved wife and son. And running through the letters was the mournful current of heartache, tugging, when he had time to pause in his frenetic activity, at his own forlorn emotions.

*6.6.44*
*HQ RASC 43 Div APO England*
*My beloved*
*D Day is nearly over and now that the excitement of the first news is over and one is more able to appreciate the greatness of the occasion, I feel that I must find the peace and serenity which your arms would give by writing you a few words from my room before sleeping. Our D Day – our own one – has not yet arrived: but it won't be long and during the period of waiting, darling, and on the day itself, my thoughts will be so very near you*

& Anthony & home. It is the thought of your love that fortifies me and urges me to go ahead and help to finish off what must surely be the greatest crusade, and which has started off so marvellously.

I hope that you were listening to the broadcast tonight, from the King's speech, to John Snagge, Howard Marshall, our own Monty, then what I thought the most impressive of all, the Service. I shall never forget that hour and a quarter. We sat in the rather gloomy light of the farmhouse where we're staying, and just quietly listened. All I can say is that we were ever so deeply affected and that my thoughts & love were so close to you, my sweetest one.

And so I come to the present, in my room, on the evening of this great day, the day for which we in this division have been hoping for, preparing for, for so long. You, my angel, are having to play the role that is harder than that of we who have plenty of excitement – just to be the wife of a soldier of the 43$^{rd}$: I hope my darling that you may become just a little proud of us, and that very soon you may read or hear that we have 'done our stuff'. I think God intends us to remain apart for a while, but may He please grant that we may soon be together again in a world at peace.

I am sending you the spoon I used. Please use it for Anthony, with all my love darling. Goodbye & all my love for ever.
Stanley


My dearest one

It is amazing that this has all begun so much more quietly here than I had expected. I have been thinking such a lot about it all day & you, when I listened to the news bulletins. I feel so much that I would like to be in it & doing something too. I think I would be a wren on a ship somewhere – but then I could not look after Anthony & I could not go without him. I should feel quite lost now without our son.

We listened to the King just now. He spoke very well didn't he? The news seems good & Monty was very cheering wasn't he? Howard Marshall has a change from cricket & described it all well didn't he?

It is amazing how little many other people seem to be thinking about all this. I don't think your people realize very much or perhaps it is just hoping as your mother said that she supposes you wouldn't be home this week.

It seems quite cold tonight. I hoped it wouldn't be for all the troops out there. I feel so very much there in spirit & as the King said we at home doing nothing can at least pray for them.

I feel very near you in spirit and so proud despite all other feelings. We certainly have been allowed to live through great events. Pray God we may be allowed to live in a grand peace. Yours for always
Peggy

*11.6.44*

*HQ RASC   43 Div   APO England*

*My darling*

*Sunday morning, and here I am in the office. Last night was what is generally known as a glorious piss-up in the local where we met Hopkins & several other batmen and mess staff. There were 4 of us, Doc, Tony, Dew & myself. My big stick – which you haven't seen – caused quite a sensation and there were many rude remarks about what it looked like! We walked, or rather, tottered home in the twilight.*

*The Doc decided I'd better have the next inoculation when we got in, but although he got the needle, the syringe and the stuff all in a line, he couldn't stand near the table long enough to get them all working in the correct way, and we finished up with me trying to inoculate him in the bottom with a syringe needle full of cold water.*

*I then went to bed with a very stiff Johnnie and very much in love with my darlingest girlfriend Peggy (I like to think of you as a girlfriend sometime as well as a wife, my only girlfriend).*

*Although we want to get cracking, the CO is very uninspiring and P.Mead is just shitting himself at the thought of it. He will pass out if Jerry just say boo to him.*

*I must say goodbye now my angel sweetheart lover.*

*Your adoring lover and sweetheart.*

*Stanley*

"Buzz-bomb? What the hell is that?" Stanley's question was addressed to the eight or nine officers gathered in the mess for breakfast, the radio news, reporting the attack on London by some new form of German weapon, reducing them to silence.

"There've been rumours about some secret weapon," his fellow captain, Jock Dew said, his Scottish accent sometimes almost impenetrable.

"I think it's a pilotless plane," Mead added, as if he had some knowledge of the subject, one of his many aggravating traits being his determination to demonstrate his breadth of knowledge. "I sometimes think he must have spent his youth studying the encyclopaedia so that he can out-do you with this superior knowledge," Stanley had commented to Peggy.

"How the hell do you know that?" Jock's retort was abrupt, indicating his own disdain for Mead's knowingness.

The fact was that Mead was right, as they all soon learned, when, over the ensuing days the weapons, V1 flying bombs, quickly becoming known as "buzz-bombs" or "doodle-bugs", struck various parts of the south east, their targets appearing to be a random selection of civilian and military, the former being by far the most devastating in terms of casualties and the fear they engendered.

"Those bastards!" Stanley's sentiment was shared by the entire mess. "Just wait till we get our hands on them!"

*Mary*! The word was quickly passed around like some party game, although in reality, by the time it was uttered to Stanley, the place was bustling with activity, men hurrying in every direction, kit being loaded onto lorries, engines throbbing into life.

For two days, the various elements of the 43rd Division made their way in convoys, sometimes of as many as thirty lorries, to their allotted destinations in readiness for embarkation, being told when they arrived that, apparently due to the weather conditions - although there was also a suggestion that progress by the first wave was slower than planned – their embarkation was being delayed, rumours about German resistance rife, deepening the increasing anxiety.

The RASC element thus spent a further two days in the sprawling, crowded, encampment at Purfleet on the Thames estuary, its facilities grievously inadequate for the many thousands of occupants. At least, however, there were good supplies of food and, more importantly, of liquor, several of the officers having had the foresight to bring some crates of beer and bottles of whisky.

The only excitement was the air raid warning, in the middle of the morning, many, at first, assuming it was a drill until they heard orders being barked for them to "Take cover!", which meant running to various parts of the camp which had been designated for such purpose, surrounded by sandbags, Stanley finding himself laying on the ground, tightly packed with a hundred or more men.

It was a sound that none of them had heard before, the engine unlike any normal plane, a droning sound more like a motorbike.

"Must be a doodle-bug," someone said just as the engine cut out, everyone, instinctively, pressing themselves against the ground.

The explosion was some way from them, but powerful enough for them to feel it through the ground.

"Missed!" the same voice said as they got to their feet, the all clear sounding as they returned to their quarters.

"Looks like some poor buggers in the town got it," Jock said as they looked across the camp towards the nearby town of Purfleet, a column of dark smoke rising from the point of impact.

Sitting on his camp bed after waking from a welcome doze, induced by several beers in the mess, Stanley felt much refreshed, both physically and emotionally. He dug his notepaper out from his kit bag.

*16.6.44*
*HQ RASC 43 Div APO England*
*My darling*
*We are still in the same place as yesterday & the past 24 hours has been just waiting.*
*I have been to sleep all the afternoon & have just woken at 6 with an enormous stand! As Tommy says, all wasted! The food is not very good but most of us managed to get a bathe in a rather doubtful looking bath.*
*In the mess here there is a fruit machine and I was playing on it before lunch & Tommy had the luck to win the jackpot which was £3-4-6. We had quite a lot of drink to celebrate! We played bridge most of the morning and I had some very lousy hands and lost 1/2d.*
*None of us feel very warlike at the moment & it is hard to realise it although this morning was rather a near reminder with a buzz-bomb coming down quite near to us.*
*I do hope you're not feeling too worried – I shan't get any mail for several days. The thought of you and Anthony John is very sweet and comforting.*
*Goodbye my dearest darling*
*Stanley*

"Looks like we're on our way," Stanley announced on their third morning in the camp, having been summoned to a hastily convened officer's meeting. "France here we come!"

# FOURTEEN

The beach with the dunes behind it, was a scene of apparent chaos, men, many crowded into holding areas, others filing through gaps in the dunes, vehicles – lorries, transporters carrying tanks, field guns towed by artillery tractors, barrels poised as if sniffing the air, many parked, others moving slowly along slatted wooden tracks laid to enable them to cross the expanse of sand, the scene veiled in a haze of exhaust of innumerable engines.

There was, however, remarkable order amid the chaos, signs with the Wyvern and other divisional insignia, marking the routes, the columns directed by the beach marshals, through the dunes, past concrete pill boxes, now empty, pock-marked with the evidence of the recent fighting, the lines of vehicles turning onto the coast road taking them into Courseulles, a small, genteel resort, the new arrivals surprised to see faces peering suspiciously from windows of the few intact, elegant villas lining the promenade.

With Hopkins at the wheel of their khaki Austin 10, the Wyvern insignia mounted on the bumpers, Stanley, Atkins and Dew took their place in the convoy mainly of lorries, making their way to their designated assembly area, close to the historic town of Bayeux, liberated in the first stage of the advance inland after D-Day.

The journey, of a little over two hours, provided them with a salutary introduction to the reality of war, their first sight of burnt out tanks – "brewed up" in the macabre parlance of the tank regiments – two British Churchills and one enemy Tiger, evidence of the battle fought by the first wave as they pushed inland, German resistance have rapidly stiffened as Montgomery's old adversary from the North African desert, Rommel, gathered his forces together, his formidable panzer regiments soon slowing the Allied advance.

In the fields beside the road, swathes of uncut corn lay flattened by the lines of tank tracks, and along the side of the road, as if swept aside to clear the way for the convoys, other debris of battle – shell cases, several broken and twisted field guns, wrecked lorries and personnel carriers.

"Jesus Christ!" Jock Dew muttered as they passed a small farm, the building reduced to rubble, several dead cows in the meadow beside it, lying on their sides, legs stiff, their bodies distended.

The convoy slowed to walking pace as they came to a village, the road partly blocked by a crowd of inhabitants herding half a dozen women before them, two of the women carrying babies, the women's hair roughly cropped.

"What are they going to do to them?" Atkins asked, all of them realising that what they were witnessing was vengeance, the women being publicly shamed for "going" with the Germans.

"Best not to know," Dew replied.

As they edged past the crowd, the faces, instead of smiling with gratitude for their liberation, were surly and suspicious, the expectation that the invaders would be greeted with flags and celebration in stark contrast with such hostility.

"I suppose you can understand it, when we've just been bombing and shelling the crap out of them, but even so," Stanley remarked. It was only later that they learned that the populace in this part of France had been less grievously treated by the German occupiers than in much of the rest of conquered Europe, and whilst many were relieved to have regained their freedom, others had come to value the harsh yet effective regime to which they had been subjected for the past four years. They had been allowed to retain more than sufficient produce to ensure that they were well fed, and with very few Jews amongst their predominantly rural population, they had largely escaped the brutality experienced elsewhere. And now the invaders had come, bringing death and destruction.

The assembly area proved to be a pleasant series of fields and orchards on the fringe of the village of Sommervieu. As with the beaches, the area was well laid out, signs indicating locations for different units, tanks and lorries parked in ordered rows, the only drawback being the state of the roads and network of access tracks, the weight of traffic turning the tracks across the fields, dried by the hot sun, to dust, the poor quality surface of the metalled lanes starting to crumble.

The new arrivals had little time to settle in, let alone to rest, Stanley and a number of his fellow RASC officers being summoned to a briefing, the CO, Major General Thomas, himself officiating, attired as always in his distinctive high, oiled boots, riding breeches and battle dress blouse.

The map which they had previously studied so closely during the recent planning sessions, had now taken on a greater reality as they began to see the lie of the land.

"Operation Epsom," Thomas announced, the name of the first of what would prove to be a series of gruelling engagements, "will be launched at 07.30 on Monday. 26th," he added as if there might be an uncertainty as to which Monday he was referring to. "So we have one day to prepare."

Involving sixty thousand men, the Wyverns joining forces with two other divisions, the assault was to be led by six hundred tanks supported by seven hundred guns.

"We will also have the Navy participating," he said with a nod of satisfaction, "the area we are intending to take," he turned towards the map, his pointer circling an area some four miles wide, extending toward the river which they now knew to be the *Odon,* "being within range of our battleships lying off shore."

"Our objective," he moved the pointer describing a small arc on the map, "is the first stage of the encirclement of *Caen.*" The tip of the pointer tapped the clearly marked town, the roads radiating from it indicating its strategic importance.

So this was it, Stanley thought as he returned to tent which served as the RASC mess. All those months – years – of training, finally coming to fruition.

There was little time for sleep that night as they went about their business of checking with those down the chains of command that every unit was fully supplied, the ammunition dumps positioned for ready access, the units which were to advance following the opening barrage, to be closely followed by their supply vehicles.

Equally important were the lines of supply to maintain the required levels, the quotas based on the assumption of maximum usage of both ammunition and fuel, although the distances to be covered being limited, fuel supplies were a lesser issue.

Communications with those supervising the unloading which was by now a continuous operation on the beaches and in particular, the Mulberry harbours, thankfully, were working well. Remember to complement the REME boys, he mentally noted.

Late on Sunday evening, as daylight faded, the pace of deployment quickened, field guns being towed away to their emplacements, behind the straight road marking the starting line of the attack, men departing for their positions where they would await the tanks which would cross the road to begin the advance as soon as the barrage was lifted.

With timing that could not have been worse, the brief hot spell broke over night, the first light of dawn revealing a grey sky, showers quickly turning the dusty tracks to mud.

At the given hour, the guns opened up, the distinctive howling of the heavy naval shells audible above the cacophony of the hundreds of field guns.

Used as they were, to the sounds of battle from their exercises, the barrages intended to condition them to the actuality of battle, such conditioning had fallen well short, the deafening violence of this overture to the assault beyond anything they had experienced. And to add to the shock of their baptism of real war, shortly after the opening of the barrage, the enemy began to respond, albeit on a far lesser scale, several shells falling within the perimeters of the camp.

Stanley had been present at many gunnery exercises, in one instance, they being required to congregate alarmingly close to the target area to give them a taste of being on the receiving end of shell fire. A particular lesson which they had learned, and which had lodged firmly in Stanley's head, was the fact that when shells exploded, it was the fragments of shrapnel which caused the most harm. At the order, "take cover", they had flattened themselves on the ground, paying attention, as directed, to the fizzing sound of the lethal fragments passing just above them.

Within the first few hours of the attack, Stanley learned another reality which was to be central to his understanding and execution of the function of RASC, that, unlike exercises, however well they had been designed to simulate real battles, they nevertheless, proceeded in accordance with their plans. Now, no sooner had the front line units begun their advance, it became clear that communicating with them, as they made their uneven progress, some moving ahead quite quickly, others halted or having to change course because of opposition, was going to be a serious challenge, radio signals regularly interrupted, the most reliable means of getting word back and forth being the age old use of messengers.

Ensconced in the RASC tent, Stanley and a handful of other officers and men, worked around a table, a map pinned to it, the positions of units, as far as they could ascertain, marked as pencil numbers. The radio operators scribbling on their pads, passed them the updates as they came in every few minutes, the messengers, some motorcycle dispatch riders, others still able to reach the nearer units on foot, passing in and out of the tent, delivering their invariably urgent requests for ammunition.

With their approximate knowledge of locations, the officers then had the task of working out the routes for the vehicles, lorries and some small trucks, to get as close as possible to enable the ammunition to be unloaded and carried to the front line, the task being made more difficult by the fact that many of the units were moving through woods and open country, sometimes a mile or more from the nearest road or track.

The noise of battle began to take on a new dimension, with the rattle of Bren guns, and not much further away, the increasingly familiar rattle of the German Spandaus. Most sinister of all, however, was the eerie sound of incoming mortar fire, the "moaning minnies", which, over the weeks and months ahead, would account for huge numbers of Allied casualties.

Due to the weather, air activity was intermittent, the satisfaction of seeing the RAF doing their stuff, short lived as the clouds closed in.

It was in the middle of the frenetic morning that the very different sound of an explosion, much closer to them drew them out of the tent, the initial "whump", shaking the ground, followed by staccato detonations, one of the ammunition lorries which had just set off, a couple of hundred yards along the road, having suffered a direct hit from an incoming shell, the lorry now a ball of flame, exploding rounds sending men scurrying for cover, a plume of black smoke rising high into the air.

"Fucking hell!" Atkins, standing beside Stanley, muttered, fragments of the body of the lorry raining down just beyond the camp perimeter. "Poor buggers," Atkins added, both of them knowing the two men who, just minutes earlier, they had sent off to convey the ammunition to a number of the twenty-five pounder batteries.

"They won't have known much about it," Stanley said ruefully.

As they ducked back into the tent, shaken at their first encounter with the death of comrades, they quietly got on with their work, the calls for ammunition becoming ever more urgent, the guns having maintained their firing throughout the morning, the initial barrage rolling forward, the gunners responding to the calls for directed targeting of the enemy.

"Right, Hopkins," Stanley said to his batman during the afternoon, communications having become ever more strained, "time to do the rounds."

The place for RASC officers was deemed to be at the point where they could most effectively manage the supply process, this generally being the command position best equipped for communications. However, where the situation dictated, particularly in the event of a breakdown in communications, direct contact with front line officers being the only means of properly assessing the situation, then "doing the rounds" became necessary.

Thus it was that with Hopkins at the wheel of the Austin, they made their way cautiously along the road, soon turning off onto a track which, as far as Stanley could ascertain from the folded map which he was clutching, would take them towards the infantry units which appeared to be having the toughest time, the messages which had come through, confused as they were, suggesting that they were running short of ammunition. And apart from the need to find out what they required, he also had to establish their location and the most effective route to get the ammunition to them.

Within the space of a few minutes, Stanley's cognisance of the brutal reality of war escalated. As they crept along the track, now taking them through a small wood, upon turning a corner they encountered two dead German soldiers, both hanging from a fence as if they had been placed there, like the crows hung up by farmers to warn off others.

Hopkins stopped the car, the two of them horrified at the sight, one of the dead men showing no sign of what it was that had killed him, the other, with one side of his uniform dark with blood and some internal matter, now dried, his eyes open, sunken in their sockets, staring back at them, his expression more surprised than pained.

"Poor sods," Hopkins said. "They've both got mothers and loved ones."

Soon the track joined another narrow lane, the sound of the battle now alarmingly close even though they could not see anything of it, the occasional round whipping through the trees, unleashing cascades of twigs and leaves.

A hundred yards further on, after passing a partly shattered barn, they came upon two tanks, Churchills, skewed off the lane, paintwork blackened, the turret of one of them dislodged from its mounting, its gun pointing down at the ground beside it, and facing them, a mere fifty yards away, the German Tiger which had doubtless been responsible for their demise, before itself meeting its end, the gaping hole in its flank suggesting its nemesis had been an Allied plane or a shell from a twenty-five pounder. Close to the tanks were several mounds of newly dug soil, each with a cross, crudely made of twigs, protruding from the mounds, but with no distinction between friend and foe.

"I don't think we'd better go any further, sir," Hopkins said as they reached the edge of the wood, the scene in the field in front of them, of infantry, lying in firing positions, engaging enemy troops just a few hundred yards in front of them, was enough for him to put the car into reverse, revving hard as they lurched back into the concealment if not the safety of the wood, the two occupants leaping out, lying down on the track, bursts of automatic fire raking the trees about them, splinters of wood dropping around them.

Taking advantage of a fold in the ground, no more than a stream gully, running at a crouch they crossed behind the infantry spread across the field, all of them lying down, several Bren guns and numerous rifles firing towards another wood although Stanley, when he peered cautiously above the bank, was unable to see the enemy.

They found the officer commanding the battalion at the end gully, similarly taking advantage of its protection, a radio operator beside him clearly unable to get his set to work.

"Thank God you're here," the officer said, shouting above the din, before giving Stanley his situation report and requirements. "We need it within the next hour," he added. "Pretty intense as you can see."

The next few units proved easier to locate, each, however, issuing their requirements with similar urgency, such was the fierceness of the fighting across the entire four mile front.

When they got back to the car, they became aware of the ominous rumbling of heavy engines, and a few minutes later, the percussion of several guns firing close to them, a line of six or seven Tiger tanks approaching in line ahead along a track at right angles to their own, their targets, the very units they had just left.

Showing remarkable driving skill, Hopkins swung the heavy Austin around in a full circle, bouncing them across the high verge, rear wheels spinning on the ground softened by rain before thankfully gaining sufficient traction for them to accelerate away.

By the end of the day, Stanley felt that he had truly gone through his baptism of fire, although, despite suddenly feeling exhausted, there was no let up on the calls for ammunition as well as for food and water, lorries coming and going into the night.

After calling at one of the camp supply points to check on the supplies of rations, he decided to make a detour via the field hospital. Although one of the other RASC officers was responsible for medical supplies, certain of the hospital's other requirements, including food, fell to his section.

It was a grim sight which greeted him, every bed occupied, thirty or forty men lying on stretchers on the ground, others, perhaps fifty or more, outside, their only shelter from the now persistent drizzle, some tarpaulins, the rain dripping between them.

He found Doc with a couple of medical orderlies, moving along a row of new arrivals, quickly assessing each one, issuing orders for the most serious cases to be taken to a second tent which served as the operating theatre.

He decided not to disturb the MO, seeing how busy he was, but when Doc caught sight of him he came across, stepping past several of the stretchers.

"What's the latest?" the MO asked. "It's obviously pretty hard going," he added, looking around the tent, the light of the paraffin lamps in the gathering dusk tinting everything yellow, the faces of the wounded taking on the appearance of figures from some nightmarish painting.

"From what I gather, there's some pretty stiff opposition. Apparently we've run into at least two panzer divisions. And making matters worse, I'm told there's some Hitler Youth infantry as well. Fanatical as hell."

"Several hundred wounded so far," Doc said dryly, as if reporting on some routine daily quota. "I've no idea about KIAs. Quite a lot I fear," those killed in action whose bodies could be retrieved, being taken to the morgue, a tent ominously close to the hospital.

It was close to midnight that, leaving Atkins and Dew in charge, Stanley was able to get a few hours much needed sleep, climbing down into the slit trench which had been dug for him the previous day, close enough to the RASC tent if he had to be summoned back.

"Your penthouse, sir," Hopkins had announced, when taking him to the trench which was deep enough to afford protection from shrapnel and all except direct or close hits. "With this tarpaulin over you, you'll be nice and snug," The trench measured some six foot by two foot six, and about five feet deep, its appearance being indistinguishable from a grave, a similarity which Stanley remarked upon.

"Let's hope that it prevents you needing a grave," Hopkins replied, his gallows humour something which Stanley had become used to, and greatly valued.

Wrapped in his blanket, despite the firmness of the ground, Stanley found the trench reasonably comfortable, the sensation of being underground rather pleasant, his feeling being of detachment from what was going on above, and of relative safety.

Although he was tired enough to fall asleep instantly, he had determined to write to Peggy. He propped himself up, leaning against the end of the trench, angling his torch so that he could see what he was writing.

*26.6.44*
*166180 Capt S R Allen  HQ RASC 43 Div BWEF*
*My very dear darling*
*Here I am in my penthouse on a very wet & stormy evening in a field reminiscent of Kent. I will try and tell you what has been happening since we landed on Saturday afternoon — that already seems ages ago. We drove through some terribly dusty roads and eventually arrived at our first place — just a French orchard. We worked till 3.30am on Sunday & got 2 hours sleep & spent Sunday working & washing & brushing up & sorting out our kit & getting off the filth acquired on the ship. It was a lovely summers day & I had no hay fever and slept under the stars in a slit trench on Saturday & last night, but tonight we have rigged up a snug little tarpaulin with our beds in slit trenches. One learns to dig very quickly!*
*Yesterday got pretty hectic at the end and we went to bed about 12 and got up at 6 this morning.*
*The French people are very well fed; we get butter, fresh milk, cheese, etc. easily. They are not friendly as I had first thought & there are many French snipers. There is certainly no feeling of being pleased to see us or of 'liberation'. The Germans apparently behaved very well & the French hate us because we bombed them. It is all very disturbing after all the stories one has heard about days of deliverance etc. Still, whatever the blasted Froggies think, Jerry has got to be knocked for six, & by Jove he is going to be!*
*Darling, I want you to know that I feel so much more deeply in love with you than ever. God knows how much more I and all of us have learnt to feel how precious life is & how much our loved ones mean to us.*

*I am always your adoring husband*
*Stanley*

As he lay down, at first, so full was his head with the myriad images of the day, that sleep would not come to him. He could scarcely believe that this was only his first day of real action, the shocks and intensity of it reverberating through his brain. It was the calming thought of Peggy and little Anthony, and of the tranquillity of home life, which soon lulled him to sleep.

It was, however, a sleep disturbed by the constant sounds of the battle raging only a few miles away, being below ground muffling the noise only to a limited extent. A couple of times, enemy shells falling close to the camp, woke him with a jolt, his first thought being that the sides of his slit trench were going to collapse. He lifted the tarpaulin, peering across the camp, satisfying himself that there was no apparent damage before subsiding once more into deep sleep.

It was still fully dark – three thirty – he could see from his watch, when one of the RASC privates roused him.

"You're needed, sir. Rather a lot going on."

# FIFTEEN

So began the second of what would prove to be seemingly endless days of what he referred to in his letters as "hectic", his terminology, for her consumption, purposely anodyne, "busy" signifying active engagement with the enemy, "hectic" conveying something of the frenetic activity, the hours of processing communications, organising supplies, occasionally shouting down phone lines to procure what was required, and, almost every day, of doing the rounds, the aspect of the role which gave him the full flavour of the front line, and of coming under enemy fire.

The operations came one after another, each with a different name – Jupiter, Express, Bluecoat, Blackwater - although in reality, they were a series of phases of the same increasingly bloody campaign, the named operations denoting the objectives, sometimes an area of terrain, others a town or village, and, as the campaign, subsequently referred to as the Battle for Caen, reached its crescendo, the hills which were of such strategic importance, commanding as they did, so much of the surrounding area: Hill 112, and, latterly, Mont Pincon, infamous for the Wyverns' losses before it was secured.

Throughout July and August, the battle raged, fluctuating in intensity, the Germans refusing to give ground, the panzers out-gunning and superior in all respects to their Allied counterparts, exacting a terrible toll, the Allied tanks "brewed up" in fearful numbers, German weaponry generally proving to be devastatingly effective – the "moaning minnies", endowed with an equally apt alternative name of "sobbing sisters"; the Spandau machine guns; and the 88 millimetre anti tank guns doubling as field guns.

In spite of the opposition, the Allies – in this sector, predominantly British and Canadians – steadily gained ground, the cost in lives measured in many thousands, the field hospitals overwhelmed with the constant influx of wounded, the army ambulances trailing back and forth to the beaches where those badly enough wounded to earn their "Blighty ticket" were embarked.

The villages so fiercely contested, invariably proved to be places of danger, providing concealment for the snipers who became the bane of infantry's lives, often Hitler youth, most of them dying in their vantage points, sometimes having roped themselves to branches of trees, in death, hanging like nightmarish oversized fruit. When taken, many of the villages were virtually obliterated, most of those buildings still standing, badly damaged.

The farms and villages did, however, yield surprising quantities of produce, particularly eggs and cheese, a welcome supplement to the basic army rations, procured, sometimes forcibly, from the grudging populace, albeit, with payment made to them, generally in kind, soap being in particular demand as favoured currency.

Exhaustion became the normal state, sleep, at best, a few hours, inevitably disrupted by the demands of the fighting units or the noise of battle.

From time to time, they, the RASC and other support groups, had to move, following the advance, proximity being essential to enable them to keep closely in touch and to facilitate delivery.

In each location, the tents and phone lines were quickly set up, minimising the interruptions caused by the moves, slit trenches hurriedly dug. In some locations they came under increased fire from both shells and mortars, in one instance having to abandon the selected location, retreating to somewhere less exposed.

Stanley, in common with his fellow officers, and indeed, most of those involved in the battle, came to accept fatigue as a constant, the flow of adrenalin keeping them going.

Never had Stanley experienced anything anywhere near as demanding, the most arduous of the many training exercises, even with live ammunition, bearing no comparison. And with the demands came what at times felt almost like exhilaration. It was as if he was being tested to the absolute extreme; his stamina; his organisational ability; his capacity for being able to keep going. Most testing of all, however, was the trial of his courage. There were moments, particularly during those first few days, when fear would take hold of him, clawing at his gut, making him understand the true meaning of the expression to "crap yourself", the sheer terror of shell and mortar fire occasionally engendering the perverse feeling of wanting to offer oneself up, the hare in the headlights, the wish for death to relieve one from the terror.

Soon, however, familiarity, whilst not quite breeding contempt, did induce an almost instinctive awareness of the danger, enabling one to gauge its level and to react, getting to the ground when necessary, but more often, navigating one's way to the requisite destination.

Always, also, the weather played its part, not merely in its turning the terrain to mud or drying it to dust, but in allowing the RAF to play its vital role, the overcast days so dispiriting, the ground forces having to fight the battle unaided by the all important aerial support, particularly with the panzers, resilient as they were to the infantry's shoulder held PIAT anti tank guns, effective only when hitting a tank from a particular angle, soldiers having to play a lethal game of chasing the tanks on foot, keeping below the lowest depression of their guns as they aimed for their limited weak spots.

With the lifting of the cloud cover, the arrival of aircraft evoked cheers of relief and encouragement, the fighters, most notably the Typhoons, turning the tables on the Tigers, many of which, in their defensive tactics, were dug into emplacements making them exceptionally difficult targets from the ground. From the air, however, they were easy pickings.

Occasionally the *Luftwaffe* would put in an appearance, usually to little effect other than to send men running for cover, the sporadic attacks an indication of the extent to which the Allies now had aerial dominance, the only exception being the V1s, although these, with their lack of accuracy, were limited in battlefield effectiveness, their impact being principally upon the unfortunate civilians of south east England.

There were moments, during those torrid weeks, when Stanley felt that this new mode of existence, with death and destruction, exhaustion and the demands of his role, was not quite real. It was as if he were enduring a nightmare from which, intermittently, he would surface, when reading Peggy's letter, her description of daily life in the remote world back home, becoming like a sort of reverie, distant, yearned for, and desperately unattainable.

The mail delivery became the high point of the day, the days when there was none for him leaving him feeling bereft, but when one – and sometimes two or more together – arrived, he would wait for a suitable moment to open it, conscious of the unopened envelope in his pocket, picturing her lovely, distinctively rounded writing, imagining the flow or her words, and always, her wonderful expressions of her love for him.

Usually, he would wait until he was in his "penthouse", or occasionally, when their camp was equipped with a "thunder box", a portable lavatory, allowing a moment of privacy for a first read although this was invariably interrupted by those in the queue outside, irate at the time he was taking.

Often also, amid his disjointed thoughts, he would visualise her, fantasising, pining, lusting, the images of her naked, beckoning, rousing him, sexual desire pervading the emotions which buffeted him. It was like a sort of derangement, danger, fatigue and lurid images unhinging his mind, it only being in those all too brief interludes that he could find some solace, some semblance of normality, her letters anchoring him to the world beyond this frenzied nightmare through which he was living.

How perverse it seemed, that despite such overwhelming demands on body and mind, sexual fantasies seemed to become ever more vivid, the all too short spells of sleep sometimes disturbed by vividly real imaginings.

There were times when he felt a sudden pang of guilt at divulging some of his most private thoughts about Peggy, although this was largely assuaged by such disclosures being shared, each of them content – compelled – to talk about their loved ones, shared secrets part of the bond forged by fear and fatigue.

*My dearest one*
*I have just wandered in the garden among the flowers in the freshness of this strange &*
*lovely evening. The rain has stopped & the sky has cleared in patches to show clear shades*
*of pale blue & pink. Everything is wet & cool & strangely still now the wind has dropped.*
*The sea looks calm & blue & just over it the most perfect rainbow. There at the end is*
*where my thoughts, dreams & hopes are tonight.*
*I have listened to all the war commentary & tried to decide exactly which parts of it apply*
*to you & hope so very much that some of it may not. It is an indescribable feeling just*
*sitting listening at what seems such a far distance to what must be your world when all*
*instincts make me feel I would be with you & knowing what this awful business of war*
*demands.*
*I am behaving very well really, as I have no "deputy husband" or boy friends! Saturday*
*night was a slight smear on my otherwise clean escutcheon – I just felt rather naughty and*
*wanted you so very much so I had a date with you, imagining that you were very close*
*to me. I loved you so acutely & and then fell into a very deep sleep.*
*I want so very much to be able to stroke the back of your neck and your bottom, in fact,*
*I am longing for you my beloved.*
*Goodnight now my own darling husband. God bless & guard you tonight & always.*
*Peggy*

By the light of one of the candles which Hopkins had managed to get hold of, Stanley lay in his slit trench, the sounds of the incessant fighting and the pulsing flashes of gunfire, muted by the close walls of protective earth, reading the letter, the thrill of the description of her "date" with him, arousing him.

"We could have dates together," she had ventured, during one of his final periods of leave a few weeks before his departure for Normandy. "Be naughty at the same time."

He had seized on the suggestion, carrying it with him not only as the means for gratifying his longing, but for the sheer, delicious knowledge that it was she who had instigated what was to become the sustenance of their distant, yet wonderfully close, sexual relationship. It was as if, at that moment, as she made the suggestion, that the last vestige of – what was it? – certainly not prudishness, more a sort of reserve of propriety instilled by her upbringing – evaporated, their physical and emotional relationship merging with complete openness.

"How do you…you know?" He was suddenly intensely curious as to how she – how women – did it, the question never previously having occurred to him.

"Just like you," she said, laughing at him. "We may be different, but we have similar erogenous bits."

"Erogenous," he had repeated, the word conveying something warmly erotic.

*My own darling Peggy*
*Although the post has been delayed today, I received a very sweet letter from you.*
*There is a terrific thunderstorm on at the moment which may clear the air as it has been very hot & stuffy.*
*Our fighter cover is marvellous – it is grand to see our planes wheeling overhead.*
*I'm afraid we of the 2ⁿᵈ Army are all rather cocky now as we think we are the best Army in the world & we look down our noses at the other troops.*
*The weather has improved after an awful drenching last night – it was absolutely foul & everything got drenched. When I eventually got into a rather a damp bed in a hole in the ground in the middle of the night, Jock Dew who is the next hole & myself drank about half a bottle of whisky to warm ourselves up.*
*I can't tell you much about the battle at the moment but all that I can say is that the good name of Wessex has not been let down and we have already ceased to be known just at the Kent Home Guard.*
*We have great fun trying to make ourselves understood in rather bad French. Avez vous du fromage, du beaurre ou des oeufs are the usual things. The French people will usually exchange things for soap.*
*Naughty girl falling from grace! Darling, I'm so glad you told me that you lay in my arms in imagination – it is a most lovely thought and makes me want to kiss you all over and make you say no, no, darling no.*
*Oh how I sigh wistfully for days & nights of love.*
*I'll bid you goodnight now my darling, and pray that you may be safe tonight.*

*All my love & kisses to you.*
*Stanley*

The sharing of intimate and salacious thoughts and experiences with the small group of fellow officers with whom he now felt such strong bond of friendship did, however, have some bounds, his dates with Peggy being reserved for that special compartment where he secreted what was most deeply personal and special.

The arranging of the dates did also, have a practical difficulty by reason of the delays in the post, the cause of a good deal of discontent. Used as they had been during their years as part of the Home Forces, to the postal service being as consistently reliable as it was for the rest of the nation, with the expectation of delivery of letters the next day, the fact that it was sometimes taking letters four or five days to reach them was considered wholly unacceptable, the increasingly vociferous complaints leading to Montgomery's intervention, who insisted that a regular postal services was "the greatest morale factor in the army".

What those complaining of the delays chose to ignore, was the extraordinary efforts of the relevant section of REME responsible for the postal service, overcoming the not inconsiderable difficulties of conveying large quantities of correspondence and parcels across the Channel, navigating the complications of disembarkation onto beaches or Mulberry harbours and, as the final stage, distribution to the hundreds of thousands of men deployed in their numerous units, tracking them as they made their often deviating progress.

*My own darling*
*Thank you for the wonderful letter which has made life so different for me today as now I feel somehow that I share some of the best of your experiences & feelings though so very small a part until you can tell me all about everything you have done.*
*I have spent the evening with your people telling them as much of your letters as was repeatable – all about the boat, food, weather, landing, etc., in modified terms! They were very glad to hear.*
*This afternoon I went down to the seafront & stood & gazed at the sea that looked so peaceful on this side and thought of the contrast on your side, dearest one.*
*I am hoping to hear again soon to know how things are going with you now you are really in all this. I have a feeling that you are well in it too from some remarks on the news last night.*
*We had rather a noise with the doodlebugs here last night though luckily it was before we had gone to bed as we were quite late. One of our fighters gone one down. It was quite a distance away but still made quite a bang. Most of them just pass over. In fact half the*

*people here don't seem to have ever seen one. Two buzzed over at lunch time yesterday.*
*By the way, you would have liked our Sunday dinner of roast beef & Yorkshire pudding*
*& plum tart & cream – lots of it too.*
*Darling heart, I must say goodnight now & pray God bless you.*
*Peggy*

Amid the maelstrom of emotions, it was the moments of feeling guilty which caught Stanley unawares. There had never been any suggestion that he had heard, that his was a cushy role, out of harm's way. And yet, when doing his rounds, seeing the men in the front line – the infantry, confronting the enemy sometimes at close quarters, protagonists intent on killing each other to avoid being killed; sometimes encountering an unseen enemy, fire unleashed from hidden positions; tanks dishing out death, in some instances, crushing dug-in troops as they drove over their trenches; tank crews, enduring the hell of their own vulnerability, immolated in their metal tombs – when he returned to camp, counting his blessings, the guilt would surface, his means of moderating it to redouble his efforts to ensure that he provided them with everything they needed.

He had also found himself feeling sorry for Mead. It was as if his antipathy towards him was reflecting on himself. The man could not help being who – and how – he was. Mead had become the butt of so much of their derisive humour. It was reminiscent of some of the bullying he had witnessed in his school days, certain boys, usually the least popular, being goaded and sometime brutalised by others, the bullies encouraging each other, baying like a pack of animals.

There was something about Mead which evoked pity. His life seemed so arid and solitary, the few occasions when he spoke about himself, reticent as he was, suggesting loneliness and an inability to make friends.

Stanley resolved to try to moderate his own behaviour towards him. The camaraderie of the mess certainly had an effect, the common purpose and responsibility, both as their unit and, in the greater scheme of things, as part of the historic crusade against the invidious foe, mitigating personal enmity.

During the interludes in their activity, enjoying some rare respite from phones and messengers, they would play bridge or monopoly, Mead tending to participate in the latter, it being his set and he not being a bridge player.

They seemed such strange times, sitting at the table, the cards or monopoly board set out on top of the map bearing the often confused hieroglyphics of the situation in the field, minds temporarily immersed in the game while, just a few miles from them, the battle raged and men were dying.

The games themselves, they took seriously, money, albeit modest amounts, changing hands, their newly acquired French francs rendering their winnings and losses less real, as if using toy money.

The quiet concentration around the table was punctuated with observations on sounds outside; particularly loud detonations or the comforting cacophony of bombers overhead, invariably followed by a succession of deep "whumps" as the bombs rained upon their targets.

The games became an essential part of their comradeship, winning or losing secondary to their collective absorption, immersing themselves in a cocoon of unreality, the games offering something so completely incongruent to the world beyond their thin canvas walls, their determined concentration an antidote to what they were living through.

Used, as he had become over the years of his army career, to transient friendships, in this real cauldron of war, what Stanley felt about these men, the members of his mess, was quite different. It was not so much whether they had interests in common, but rather, they were truly comrades in arms, their fraternity forged by their common purpose and their sense of their place and value in the great scheme of things.

Jock and Tommy were the two he considered to be his closest pals in the RASC mess, although his particular affinity with Doc was different, the two of them sharing a more conventional friendship. His meetings with Doc these days, were few, the MO being fully occupied with the demands of his role, his waking hours being taken up tending the ever increasing numbers of wounded.

Jock, with his wry humour and acerbic remarks, delivered in his broad Scots, the twinkle in his eyes belying the curt delivery, was, Stanley felt, a man of deep humanity, his often brusque manner disguising a soft interior as was evident when, as they were now experiencing on a daily basis, word came to them of the casualties, often men known to them among the dead and wounded. He was a conscientious and effective officer whom Stanley always knew he could rely on.

Tommy was in many ways similar to Jock, although a less forceful character. There was something rather boyish about him, Stanley seeing him rather as a younger brother, reciprocated by Tommy's tendency to defer to Stanley despite their equivalence of rank.

"I wonder what my Morag is up to," Jock said late one evening, he and Stanley now sharing a dug-out, the arrangements in the location they had just moved to, providing for larger trenches, protected by a wall of sandbags, the trench itself large enough for their two camp beds as well as their kit, each of them with photos of their loved ones pinned to the earth wall; Stanley's, a picture of Peggy with Anthony on her knee; Jock's, the smiling, pleasant round face of his fiancée.

"What do you mean?" Stanley asked, assuming he was referring to some form of job.

"I sometimes wonder whether she might be going with some other bloke. It would be understandable, wouldn't it? I suppose it's bound to happen, with some of them."

"Bloody hell, Jock! I would tear my hair out if I thought that Peggy was being unfaithful. And I don't believe for one second, that she would ever dream of it."

"Ach, don't get me wrong, I don't think she would let me down. I'm just wondering how I would feel if she did. Aye, I would tear my hair out as well." Stanley had noticed how, when he was talking about particularly personal matters, Jock would seem to become even more Scottish, his speech and some of his expressions, broader than his more anglicised, operational version.

Stanley had long ago become aware of the fact that jealousy was an element of the package of emotions which were part and parcel of living apart. When Peggy had been at Bart's, he had, at times, become obsessed with the thought that she was playing around with the young doctors. She would talk about them just that bit too often, telling him stories about their japes and what good fun they were.

Of course things were different now, with Anthony, and living at home with her parents. No, not for one minute did he have any worries in that direction. And yet he could not entirely rid himself of the niggling concern.

He hated himself when, with his thing about numbers and statistics, he would do the reckoning of the dates from her last period, "squiggles" in their code, she having, at his suggestion, taken to making a distinctive squiggle in the margin of her letter to let him know it was her time of the month. She had tried, ever since their marriage, to explain to him that she was not that reliable. "You can't set the clock by it," she said. "Sometimes it'll be five or even six weeks," even though she had always been regular within a few days. "And it's been a bit more erratic since having Anthony."

He was, however, unable to help himself from doing the calculations, delays with the post adding to his anxiety, the relief when a "squiggle" letter arrived making him feel a complete fool for allowing himself to become so wound up about it.

*My own darling*
*Life here continues to be much the same as usual, especially the weather which is absolutely terrible. There is a frightful quagmire everywhere and everyone is rather damp and fed up. But we realise it has got to get worse to get better and each place we go to we dig bigger & better holes & try and make ourselves more comfortable.*
*I wish you could have seen me yesterday afternoon, in a few free hours off which luckily coincided with a break in the weather. I had an open air bathe in my canvas bath – which I think you'd probably consider too small even for Anthony, so I had to wash down as far as possible kneeling beside the bath with my legs crossed – a very complicated manoeuvre. Still it was quite effective and provided entertainment for some of the troops and some small French children. They always kiss us on either cheek & babble away at us & ask for 'souvenirs' and 'chocolat'.*
*They've stopped all of the beef purchase at the moment which is damned silly as the inhabitants can't get rid of the stuff now that they can't market it in Paris. How wonderful it would be to have a slice of bread, a potato and an apple and a pint of beer – none of which we have tasted for what seems an eternity.*
*We have one or two radios in the camp but about all we have time to listen to are the news headlines on the Expeditionary Force programme. It is very difficult to get the Home Service or the ordinary Forces programme.*
*Have just heard the news that the Joes have taken Minsk. Jerry has certainly been kicked up the backside on all fronts recently.*
*I take it that the reason that little Peggy felt dopey last Saturday morning was because she had been a naughty girl? Little girls don't have wet dreams do they? By the way, what on earth happened to your monthly? It must be long over due.*
*Darling, will you make another date with me? I love to know that you can find some peace and comfort in being near to being loved as is possible. I would give so much at the moment to kiss you from your lips and eyes down to your toes than to pause in the middle and make you say Oh – then I'd like to turn you round facing he same way as me and pull you close to me, to squeeze your sweet titties, then to love you so utterly and completely my darling.*
*I mustn't go on in that strain or else I shall want to be naughty and circumstances do not permit!*
*All my love and thousands of kisses, darling.*
*Your ever adoring*
*Stanley*

He read through the letter, regretting the mention of her monthly, knowing, full well, the implication. But he decided he could not cross it out and he was not going to start the letter again.

The picture he had evoked of her body, and of making love to her, had the usual effect, but with Jock sitting up on his bed just a couple of feet from his own, he had to restrain himself, at least until the paraffin light was turned off. Used as they were, to hearing each other rhythmically ministering relief, what was acceptable in the dark was one thing, but the idea of seeing each other doing it was quite another.

With daily briefings and frequent situation reports, Stanley, as with officers across the spectrum of the complex structure of a 2nd Army, was kept fully abreast of progress, which had become painfully slow, each objective, sometimes measured in miles or even hundreds of yards, or in villages or hamlets, involving its own plan of attack.

What they now knew was that the strength of the opposition they were encountering was due to Rommel's deployment of no fewer than seven divisions amongst which were some of the *Wehrmacht's* best, including divisions battle hardened on the Eastern front.

From their refusal to concede ground, and from what they learned from the increasing number of prisoners, they had come to recognise also that they were facing a foe imbued with a fanaticism wholly alien to them, driven by an unshakeable belief in the god-like status of their *Fuhrer*, and their determination to protect the Fatherland and the lands which it had conquered, at any cost, the laying down of their lives a price they were willing – and from the interrogation of prisoners, it seemed, almost eager – to pay.

During the first few days, the arrival of prisoners evoked a sort of satisfied curiosity; evidence that some, at least, of the enemy were defeated, the numbers increasing daily, as the Wyverns, in harness with the other elements of the 2nd Army, fought their way forward.

It became a frequent sight when he was out on the road, the lines of prisoners, their grey uniforms dirty and torn, many of them with days of stubble, apart from the younger ones, some clearly being mere boys, shepherded by British soldiers ever watchful of their charges, as if expecting them at any moment, to try to escape or to turn on their captors.

When some of them were brought to the camp to be interrogated, Stanley would sometimes be required to be present, the information gleaned about enemy logistics helping to determine their own choice of ammunition.

His first interrogation was of an SS *Hautpmann*, an officer of his own rank, Stanley's role being that of observer, the questioning being conducted by a German speaking major, although it transpired the prisoner spoke almost perfect English.

The first impression of the man was of what Stanley described, when he was recounting the experience later in the mess, as chilling arrogance.

"He was bristling with hostility," he told them. "It was almost as if he thought we were the prisoners. There was something about him which really told us what we're up against. He refused to answer any questions about his division or anything else useful."

"You will be defeated," the *Hautpmann* had said, with a sneer of certainty that for a moment made Stanley want to strike the man. "You do not know the strength of our *Wehrmacht*. You are – how do you say? – men against boys."

The officer looked at them with steely blue eyes, his belief in what he was saying clearly much more than bravado.

Each question the major put to him elicited the same response, ignoring the question, challenging his interrogators with counter question or assertion.

"Why do you wish your soldiers to die for the French people, a second rate nation. Do you really care about the Jews and mongrel people that we are ridding from Europe?"

The major jotted some notes on his pad, apparently impervious to such provocatively abhorrent retort, Stanley only just managing to contain himself, his senior officer having instructed him to remain silent and to write down any questions he wanted to ask.

"If they're all like that, we really have got one hell of a fight on our hands," he said, Atkins, Dew and a couple of others listening intently to this first hand account of the interrogation.

"I've heard that some of the Hitler Youth are just the same," Jock said. "Like they've been brainwashed."

The fervent belief in their cause was, indeed, a factor which the Allied commanders had underestimated, the SS and the pitifully young Hitler Youth in particular, so ready to lay down their lives for their *Fuhrer*, the fire of their zeal continuing to smoulder even in captivity. In sharp contrast was the sullen defeatism of many others, ordinary soldiers who had, in the early years of their relentless victories, believed in their cause and their invincibility, now accepting the inevitability of defeat, content to be captured by the Allies, a relief for many, their greatest fear being of becoming prisoners of the Russians on the Eastern front.

As the battle continued, the days seemed to merge, almost every hour, the challenge of getting supplies to the fighting units. The only advantage of the slow progress was that most units were within a few miles of the advance supply stores and in particular, the ammunition dumps, the constant struggle being to procure what was needed, the transport arrangements still subject to the problems of unloading onto beaches and temporary harbours, and of lorries having to make their way back and forth along the lanes and tracks, navigating heavy traffic, deep mud and, from time to time, shelling and sporadic air attacks.

The incessant calls up the supply lines, specifying the Division's requirements, were a tortuous business, not so much because of the still unreliable phone lines, but a factor which had not been anticipated, the competing demands from different elements of the 2nd Army. Stanley felt that this battle was almost as demanding as the delivery forward, having to use different strategies and tactics, even resorting to a couple of trips back to the beach-head, where the supplies brought across the Channel were unloaded, his intent being to identify and, if possible, strike up a relationship with the supervising officers. He achieved a degree of success by hitting it off with a fellow captain managing the first ammunition dump, a field, just a short way inland, with vast quantities of ammunition of every size piled up, some in boxes, some — the larger gauges, particularly 3.45 inch shells for the hundreds of twenty five pounders, expending their ammunition day and night — stacked like logs, the ammunition distributed across the field to reduce the risk of a catastrophic explosion in the event of the dump suffering a direct hit.

Steadily, the advance proceeded, but at a cost in killed and wounded that, just a few weeks earlier, would have seemed utterly inconceivable, virtually every regiment of the Wyverns losing hundreds of men as they secured each of their objectives; the villages, until now, mere names on large scale maps, their rural

260

communities, even during the years of occupation, getting on with their lives in relative tranquillity, now giving their names to their local, bloody battles: Cheux, Mouen, La Gaule, Fontaine Etoupefour, Baron. And the rivers, Odon and Orne, meandering gently through the *bocage* country, quite narrow yet both presenting major obstacles to the advance, the Odon, with its steep banks and with its opposing bank being strongly held by the enemy, remembered as "death valley".

Despite having three narrow bridges over the section of the Odon selected for the crossing, none was suitable for tanks, the engineers being called upon to reinforce one of them, themselves suffering several casualties before they had completed their task, the bridgehead then being secured.

Again, much Wyvern blood was spilled taking Hill 112, commanding the network of lanes between the two rivers. Getting across the Orne proved less costly than the Odon, but ahead lay yet more well defended hills and villages.

On the evening of the seventh of July, Stanley emerged from the RASC tent, officers and men standing watching, awestruck, as RAF Lancasters, filling the sky above them, dropped over two thousand tons of bombs on Caen, the spectacle evoking wild cheering. Few of them had ever witnessed anything on such scale, none of them realising – and indeed, even those who had determined to carry out the raid failing to recognise – that reducing the town to rubble, would benefit the German troops who survived – quite extraordinarily, being a significant proportion – streets becoming inaccessible to tanks, and the rubble providing effective defensive positions.

There were no announcements of the casualty figures, the cost to the Wyverns however, being apparent from the steady influx of fresh troops, deployed on an almost daily basis, making up the numbers of the depleted regiments. The extent of the casualties was, however, common knowledge, Stanley's most direct source being Doc with whom, when they found some short respite from their respective tasks, he would drink the whisky which Doc always seemed able to get hold of.

Each time Stanley met the MO, he noticed how progressively wearier he seemed, his face grey with fatigue, his work, unlike most of the Division, being undercover, his pallor contrasting with Stanley's appearance of rude summer health.

For some reason, Doc allocated the toll of dead and wounded to their regiments, as if it gave the numbers some sort of meaning, relating their suffering to their counties, each regiment bearing its county name – Wiltshires, Somersets, Dorsets, Hampshires, designated also by its number – 4th, 5th, 7th.

Apart from the numbers, however, he said little about his work, cutting and sewing human flesh; sawing bones of limbs shattered beyond saving. He was able to gauge, almost at first glance, whether wounds were likely to prove fatal, having to decide whether the most grievously wounded merited his attention, his time, he knew, better spent tending those he had a chance of repairing, leaving it to the nursing staff to comfort the dying.

When Stanley returned to his own work, he counted himself fortunate that he was not incessantly confronted with the carnage of battle, although for all of the men behind the front line, the endless procession of casualties provided them with graphic evidence of the cost of war. For all of them, also, there were sights which remained imprinted in their minds, for some, for the rest of their lives, it being many years before Stanley was free from the recurring image of a man on a stretcher, alive and conscious, with part of his skull missing, his brain exposed, Stanley being unable to tear his gaze away from greyish, offal like substance. Lying on a stretcher outside the hospital tent, awaiting Doc's assessment, the man was talking, his words incomprehensible, as if muttering some incantation. Surprisingly, as he learned from Doc later, the man had survived, Doc explaining that sometimes his decision was almost intuitive. "It's as if you can discern the will that some of them have to survive."

"At least he was still alive when we sent him on his way back to Blighty," Doc added, his tone invariably matter-of-fact when talking about casualties.

Finally, after nearly a month of continuous fighting, and having advanced, it seemed to them just a few miles, the 43rd Division was relieved, withdrawing for much needed respite, to lick its wounds and to re-group, ready for the next call which, it transpired, was less than a week later. And when it returned to the fray, if anything, the fighting became even more intense, the terrain now allowing for some larger scale tank engagements, taking a terrible toll in Churchills and their crews, once again shown to be so inferior in both fire-power and armour plating, to the enemy Tigers.

The operations, designated for the phases of the renewed advance – Jupiter, Express, Bluecoat - set new objectives, again, usually villages, this stage of the campaign reaching its climax with the assault on Mont Pincon, which, even more than Hill 112, dominated the surrounding area and its vital roads.

In spite of the continuing activity, however, Stanley found time to write to Peggy, his letters now a little longer as he filled in some of the gaps from previous accounts. He was also able to re-read some of her earlier letters, most of them read the first time in some haste as well as in less than comfortable circumstances. Indeed, it was a time for him to reflect upon, and to begin to assimilate, the weeks of intense action with its contrasting and conflicting emotions, of fear and exhilaration, grief and shock, emotions tightened by the ever present fatigue.

How could he convey to her what he been through, censorship prohibiting divulging more than the bare bones of the campaign itself, a difficult constraint, with the additional need for sensitivity in his accounts, avoiding overt references to his emotional state, adhering to the anodyne terminology which he had long since settled upon. He wanted to tell her so much of both his experiences and his feelings, unburdening himself to her. He had to hope that she would be able to read between the lines, his obtuse references to "busy" and "hectic" she would realise by now, hinting to her the gradations in intensity of his part in the great battles in which he was playing his part.

*My dearest darling*
*I received your letter this morning and mother's. Thank you both so much.*
*Anthony is becoming a real heavyweight isn't he? I'm sorry he's waking you up at night. I do hope you can knock him off the breast feeds soon.*
*The other night as dusk was approaching, 450 Halifaxes and Lancasters in full view of us all, carried out a 2000 ton raid on the Hun. I have always wanted to see a full scale raid by Bomber Command, but last night's spectacle absolutely took our breath away: it was both awe-inspiring and majestic: the great bombers flew straight through a curtain of flak – completely intent on their purpose, never turning aside or faltering for a moment. We could see the silent bombs coming down and the holocaust they were causing below. The raid was the finest morale raiser we could ever have wished for, and gave one a fine idea of the might of British air power. We all went to bed very excited and cheered up. You can tell people at home what a wonderful effect the RAF bombing has.*
*In the opposite penthouse at the moment is the horrid sight of P.Mead in the canvas bath. I heard a very familiar tune yesterday – 'Somewhere in France' – I suppose we have revived the song.*
*Did you know that the French for a French Letter is Capon d'Anglaise?*
*Those bloody buzz bombs have really roused the Army & those Germans who started them off have provided the finest stimulant to cold blooded hatred since the blitz of 1940. We are all firm believers in the theory that the only good German is a dead one: after the Russians and ourselves have finished the lousy bastards there won't be many left anyhow. If it wasn't for them I wouldn't have to spend this summer camping in the somewhat damp*

*fields of Normandy, with no lovely little wife to snuggle in my arms every night.*
*Some French children are buzzing round me as I write – the only English they have*
*learnt is 'F—k off'!*
*It will be grand to be able to tell you one day the real story of our adventure in the past*
*days. It is much more invigorating when one knows that this is the real thing and that we,*
*the 43ʳᵈ Div, are at least doing our bit toward final victory and homecoming and peace.*
*Please God may that not be too long delayed.*
*I think I'd better stop now and have a wash my lovely darling angel.*
*Your adoring husband and Daddy*
*Stanley*

What he was able to recount to her was the sombre news of the first deaths of colleagues whom he considered his friends, the carnage of the campaign, at that moment, becoming devastatingly personal.

He knew, full well, that it was only a matter of time until one of them - the close-knit group of RASC officers, and indeed, those in the network across the Wyverns with whom they dealt with on a day to day basis, with whom they had established something more than mere working relationships - was killed. The odds were stacked against them, such were the statistics of attrition. But when it occurred, it came as a body blow, affecting him far more deeply than he had anticipated, his belief, until that moment, being that he possessed the inner strength to endure the blows, when they came, with the fortitude he believed to be part of his make-up.

He was in the RASC tent late in the evening, just finishing off a few chores before retiring to his dug-out when word reached him that Jack Atherton, a fellow captain with whom he had felt a particular affinity, had been killed by mortar, two others, John Reid and Johnny Johnson both having been seriously wounded in the same counter attack.

As he slowly unscrewed the top of his pen, he knew only that he needed to pour out his heart to Peggy. How inadequate the blank paper seemed when his emotions were in such turmoil, grief and his ever growing hatred of the barbarous enemy, vying for pre-eminence in his febrile mind.

*My dearest darling*
*Life has become grim. Several friends of mine whom I met yesterday are dead today. Do*
*you remember Jack Atherton? He is dead. John Reid is seriously injured and Johnny*
*Johnson who we met on the train going to Bournemouth last year is critically wounded.*
*I am quite well, darling – don't worry about me. I put myself in God's hands and I know*

*He will look after me and bring me back safely to you my sweet darling.*

*No letter from you today – please try to write every day even if just to say you are alright as I am terribly worried about the buzz bombs. Those bloody Germans, by God, I hope they pay for this war. Why don't we bomb Berlin to hell and all their cities?*

*I feel that you alone will understand what it is like at the moment and will not mind my being honest with you & saying that for the moment life is exceedingly unpleasant. I hope that by the time I write tomorrow our news and life will be better.*

*I will close now my dearest darling.*

*Your adoring husband*

*Stanley*


The following day he was glad to find himself frantically busy, having to go out on his rounds twice to try to resolved problems with different units, coming under some serious mortar fire at one point, he and Hopkins having to leap out of the car, diving into a ditch until the immediate danger had passed, emerging to find the car in one piece save for a small hole in one door where a fragment of shrapnel has struck it, Stanley and Hopkins looking at each other, both realising what a close call it had been.

By the end of the day, the pain of loss had lessened to the extent that he was able to place it in a compartment, to be reopened at a later date. And when, sitting on the grass close to the dug-out, the last of evening sun slanting through the nearby trees, he started to write, he felt a good deal brighter.

*12.7.44*

*Capt S R Allen   HQ RASC   43 Div, BWEF*

*Darling mine*

*I am sitting on the grass after supper just wishing you were keeping me company. It would be a lovely evening for a picnic washed down by bottled beer. As it is the monstrous war goes on day after day.*

*If the weather stays like this it will be grand as we shall get more air support & it is good for morale.*

*The last 24 hours have been pretty momentous here & I'm feeling very sleepy tonight & rather light headed. I expect you can guess that we are all rather pleased with ourselves tonight. Funny to think that we are all 'history' isn't it? For the first time today people cried 'Vive l'Anglais'.*

*I paid my first visit to a French town yesterday and found the shops not bad, but mostly cream, butter & cheese of which we are rather tired. I tried without success to get some scent – the perfume shops were closed. I saw some nice looking clothes but they were very expensive.*

*We are involved in a lot of trouble over dead and stray cows, which the Army have now officially taken in hand. We have our eye on one for consumption as we get no fresh meat at the moment.*

*Is this our longest separation darling? I think it must be. It is horrible isn't it?*

*I have been reading Doc's BMJ . There is a very good letter on birth control and sexual relations which I think the whole mess has read. I wish I could have some sexual relations with you my sweet darling. I'm afraid I shall be extremely naughty when we meet. I wonder if you will have become 'frigid' and will want much rousing? I doubt it! I hope you won't find it strange & a nuisance to have a husband again after being a gay widow for so long!*

*Yesterday turned out to be a red letter day because we had one loaf of bread for the mess – it worked out at half a slice each. I've never tasted such food from heaven in all my life. It is exactly a month since we last had any. I managed to scrounge the loaf from a field bakery.*

*I'm glad to say that both Johnny Johnson and John Reid, though badly wounded, are going to live and have been evacuated to England.*

*I am trying to get myself a German or French car. I think I may get a Citroen by requisition.*

*I am looking forward to getting my tobacco. My stocks will last about another week at present rate of consumption.*

*Did I tell you that we have captured a nunnery complete with nuns & that they found a huge stock of French Letters? (Don't' worry, the nuns have all been evacuated).*

*Stop press news – after 3 majors and umpteen other senior officers have argued for 3 hours over the unfortunate cow, higher authority has decided that we may 'consume' cows. We can have half ourselves & give half to Div HQ. So we are going to have a ceremonial slaughter tomorrow. The lighter side of war, and rather like something out of Punch!*

*Jock Dew and I have decided that our dugout wants some pin-up girls to brighten it up so we have put all our snaps & portraits of our respective families around it. So tomorrow your portrait will be adorning a dugout in France.*

*The weather continues to be most miserable, just grey, overcast & cold. How I would love a hot bath then to go to bed with you. Please write me a naughty letter – I'm due for one!*

*Goodbye my darlings – I send so much love to you and kisses for Anthony from Daddy.*
*Stanley*

Peggy was grateful that the summer days and weeks seemed to pass quickly, hastening what everyone was now certain would be ultimate victory. Although she had become accustomed to the ever present worry about Stanley, having heard on the BBC war reports something about the 2nd Army and occasionally, the 43rd Division, she had to wait, sometimes for two or three days before receiving his letters, the relief of their arrival lifting a great weight from her, although the next report would often be the same day, lowering the weight back onto her anxious shoulders. And always there was the fear of the telegram boy, bringing the news she so dreaded.

The days seemed to be filled with mundane activity; tending to Anthony; passing the time playing with him and chatting to him; and helping her mother with the household chores. There were, however, regular interludes; the outings with her father who enjoyed her company, she happy to drive him around the Sussex lanes, going off for walks while he attended to his business, her mother happy to look after Anthony.

She would also spend a good deal of time with Paddy, their infants playing happily together, Paddy's daughter, Jill, a few months older than Anthony. Peggy found Paddy and Alan's company such a contrast to the rather sombre mood which always prevailed in her own home, her parents, serious minded as they were, and ever anxious about Tom, his letters from Burma infrequent, leaving them to glean what they could from the news, filling in the gaps with their own grim imaginings.

What she found deliciously exciting and at the same time, oddly disquieting, was reading the naughty parts of Stanley's letters, and even more so, of responding in kind. There were moments when, having been rash enough to open his letter at the breakfast table, she had felt her face flushing with alarm that somehow her parents might be able to see what he had written, or even worse, that she might feel compelled to confess a sin, suddenly reading aloud his graphic description of his "date' with her, his letters these days, seeming to leave little to her imagination.

Even in the privacy of her bedroom, the fact of reading, let alone of writing, such lascivious descriptions, engendered a frisson of alarm as if she had wantonly allowed some lewd goings on here under her parents' seemly roof. And yet how liberating she found it, and how richly pleasurable to be able to shed her inhibitions. She had, initially, told herself that it was he who had somehow induced her not only to indulge in such carnal pleasuring, but also to describe it to him. The thought would cross her mind of what she had written being seen by someone else. She knew that letters were censored and yet, perversely, she found the notion of prying eyes upon her most personal revelations added a dash of spice. The truth was that she needed little encouragement. It was as if he had unlocked something which had been latent, firmly repressed within in her, awaiting the spark to ignite it.

*My angel darling*

*We have had lots of excitement recently and made hasty dives into slit trenches.*

*I made my deepest penetration into France so far yesterday & saw lots of Germans, both dead & alive. They are all about 18 years old, completely Nazi & fanatical. They look so odd in full size uniforms. They are hopeless in hand to hand fighting but very good behind a Tiger tank or multi mortar. Mortar fire is quite the worst experience in the world & a quick cure for constipation!*

*Last night we had a film show in a barn – 'Ziegfeld Girl' with Hedy Lamar, Lana Turner and Judy Garland, and lots of lovelies. Everyone was in a frightful state afterwards.*

*The place is full of rumours today – but I'm afraid they are mostly wishful thinking. What a lot of the troops don't understand is that a peace without the completed destruction of the German Army would be fatal for us and just what they want, so that they can rebuild their Army. We all want to get home quickly but we know that the finest thing that can happen is for Germany to be invaded, her cities scorched & burnt down, her people made refugees and the Army pulled to pieces so that it no longer exists. I think our leaders will have the sense to look after this.*

*Things here are going extremely well but a trifle slowly. We are faced by the best of what is left of the German Army, and behind their extremely formidable weapons they are a tough nut to crack, though individually they are not so hot – in fact the miserable bunch of skinny youths of 17 and 18 intermixed with many Russians & Poles of very doubtful character.*

*The weather has improved today but it has been frightful – the roads are in an unbelievable state and everything is damp.*

*I am never tired of hearing about Anthony and your darling self, but I think your idea of writing me some really naughty letters is very sound! I believe that you wrote part of your letter with one hand on Fanny, thinking "I do feel naughty – it is a nice feeling"! Did you? Tell Stanley, please, darling.*

*That reminds me, do you know about the innocent bridegroom? On the first night of his honeymoon he didn't know what to do so the bride starts to play with it. All of a sudden he rushes out of the room. When he came back she asked him what was the matter and he said, well, you know that thing of mine you played with, you shook it about so much that you made it sick!*

*Goodbye my angel*

*Stanley*

It was the following day that Stanley learned that, at the very moment that he had been immersed in his fantasising about Peggy, far to the east in the depths of a Prussian forest, a bomb had been detonated in Hitler's headquarters while the *Fuhrer* and many of his closest associates had been assembled around a table, it being the sturdy structure of the table which had saved Hitler's life, the instigators of the "July Plot", led by *Oberstleutnant* Claus von Stauffenberg, being rounded up and summarily executed.

As the news filtered through, there was a feeling of intense disappointment, the consequence of the plot's failure being the inevitable prolonging of the war with the Allies having to fight their way to the German capital.

Each evening, Peggy and her parents, as with much of the nation, would sit down to listen to the news, the wireless set sitting on a shelf in the corner of the living room, its use being limited, at her father's insistence, that, for his times of relaxation, the "infernal machine" should not be allowed to intrude although, largely at Tom's prompting, before his departure for Burma, certain concerts of classical music were allowed, as were suitably important or uplifting programmes of spoken word, most notably *The Brains Trust* and, of course, speeches by the Prime Minister, Montgomery or such other members of the War Cabinet or the military leadership, the occasional statements by the Labour members listened to with her father's grumbling distaste.

"Why ever do we need to have *socialists* involved in the War Cabinet?" Her father was not looking for a response.

"What a shame they couldn't have done the job properly," was her mother's understated comment at news of the failed attempt on Hitler's life.

At the end of the bulletin, the War Report would provide more detailed information about the campaign in Europe as well as those in other theatres, Peggy listening intently, her atlas open as she endeavoured to interpret the sketchy details of locations, although with her new familiarity with Normandy, knowing the names of many of the villages and rivers, she was able to piece together what proved to be a fairly accurate picture of the Allies' progress, even to the extent of being able to mark, lightly in pencil, what she surmised to be the position of the 43rd Division.

As she listened, her apprehension increased, half expecting to hear some bad news of a setback, censorship intended to mitigate the less palatable news, particularly of casualties, although with the numbers being sent back to British hospitals, Peggy having some direct accounts from a few of her nursing colleagues with whom she was still in touch, the cost of the Allies' progress was well known, as was the scale of the death toll.

Before Stanley had departed, he had insisted that she should have his wireless, which, in spite of her father's mutterings of disapproval – "it's not good for you," he said, without explanation of the potential harm - she now had in her bedroom where she was able to listen to the dance band and popular music which, to a large extent through Stanley's avid interest and his large collection of records, she had come to thoroughly enjoy, as well as comedy programmes and plays. Always, however, she would turn the volume down, not only to avoid disturbing Anthony who seemed to sleep soundly regardless of the volume, but to try to ensure her father could not hear, the result being that she would sit in the chair positioned for the purpose, with her ear a few inches from the set.

With the imminent launch of what would prove to be the climax of the Wyvern's protracted series of battles as they made their painful progress across the *bocage,* the assault on Mont Pincon, the RASC were as busy as they had ever been, the preparation for a new operation, "Bluecoat", the now familiar business of ensuring the ammunition dumps were fully stocked and suitably located, Stanley studying the maps at the briefings, identifying the lanes and tracks which would provide accessible lines of supply, knowing also that operations rarely proceeded as planned, although in this instance, the objective, being no more than a large hill, similar in size to many of the South Downs, the challenge was to move supplies up the steep slopes with few obvious access routes, and to ensure that the RASC drivers were fully aware of the positions – and proximity – of the enemy.

*My angel darling*
*I'm sorry this has to be a brief letter as we're extremely busy.*
*We had some excitement yesterday. We had two Ensa girls to tea, but they were not very attractive and were accompanied by three males. Still it was nice to hear a female English voice and see a pair of silk clad legs again! I wished you could have been here to tea and have come to my dugout afterwards. You'd like it there – it's quite cosy and my bed it quite comfortable although very narrow. We'd have to sleep on top of each other – lovely!*
*I am about to go and have what promises to be a very good visit to nature. The squatting position is very good because one doesn't need so much paper! It is sometimes a little difficult to keep ones balance though. The Doc was sitting in someone's thunderbox yesterday & it collapsed! We are having a new thunderbox erected – it is a glorious green affair with a wyvern on it.*
*Your description of a hot bath and a cosy bed made me very envious & extremely randy! We are all becoming like restive bulls, & the thought of how long it will be before leave starts is filling everyone's minds.*
*The battle is becoming a reality for us now & it is strange to think that some of the arrows on the maps in the morning papers are made by us.*
*This letter was rudely interrupted by my having to go out. I have been out on my motor cycle round the dusty French lanes.*

*Another interruption. I have just had supper of stew, camembert & biscuits, and a whiskey. One feels very cut off from the outside world and just completely absorbed in our bit of the war. That is why your letters are so marvellous to get – they tell me how sweet & lovely the real life is.*
*Your ever adoring*
*Stanley*

*My beloved one*
*This is a grand day as two letters arrived from you. I am glad you have not found anything attractive enough to lead you astray even the ENSA girls. I would have loved to have come to tea – though my legs would not have been silk clad as I haven't worn my stockings for months. I would have loved to have come back to your dugout though I doubt if your camp bed would stand the strain! I never thought that I would ever wish to be living dug in in France as I do now, with the dearest person in the world to me.*
*The news is very good, isn't it?*
*I wish you were here to snuggle in bed with me. I long for you so much, to talk to and to just be with as well as the physical want. I keep looking at your photo and wondering where you are and what you are doing and hoping, above all, that you are fit and well, my dearest one.*
*Yours with all my heart & love.*
*Peggy*

*My very dear darling*
*I had quite an amusing experience with Hopkins yesterday. I was looking for a unit & went a little farther than I had intended and discovered that we were in front of our lines. I think I can claim the furthest penetration into France at that point. We came back in a greater hurry than we went out! I don't think H realised where we were – it was unbelievably quiet. The most alarming experience actually is when you get up in front of our guns – it's far more noise and ear splitting than being on the 'wrong end'.*
*Life is terrifically hectic at the moment and nothing can stop us! It's look out Adolph here we come and everyone is thrilled & excited as we really seem to have broken through.*
*Isn't the news grand tonight. I do wish I could tell you all about it but although our story has got to London it hasn't yet been released to the press & BBC. Also it would exclude the latest & most exciting part. We shall be carrying on and consolidating the good work we have done. Everyone is on their toes, full of confidence, and most terrifically excited and thrilled, especially as the BBC gave the 2nd Army prior place over the Yanks tonight – and incidentally they would have got nowhere if it hadn't been for British Forces.*
*Do you know this story? A man went to see the doctor and complained about feeling constantly tired. The doctor asked him if he was having sexual intercourse with his wife and he said yes, about 4 time a week. The doctor said that sounded OK, was there any other woman and he said well yes, there was his secretary and the doctor said do you do*

*anything with her and he replied yes, as a matter of fact, about 4 times a week. The doctor said that's not really excessive you are a healthy sort of bloke, is there any other reason you can think of and the man said well, we have a very pretty housemaid I've been giving a seeing to about 4 times a week. The doctor was pretty amazed and said Good Lord man, you must knock it off a bit. The man said I do, about 4 times a week!*

*My angel girl, I love you so utterly and so happily tonight, and feel that the happy and wonderful life ahead is beginning to be visible after the dark days of the war.*
*Your ever adoring*
*Stanley*

The fierce resistance which the Wyverns faced in the assault on Mont Pincon continued after the hill itself had been taken, the German forces appearing intent on contesting every village and hamlet, giving no quarter, the fighting as intense as at any stage of the campaign. What the Allies did not know was that Hitler himself, had taken direct control, ignoring the advice of his generals by insisting that his forces stood their ground. By committing them, he offered the Allies the opportunity to engage them rather than leaving them to re-group for a later battle, the enemy also being exposed to the dominant Allied air power.

For the first two weeks of August, the fighting continued, the Allies' advance, slow, costly, but inexorable. And then, finally, the battle for Normandy, this first, vital phase of the invasion, was over. There was, however, little sense of victory beyond the gratifying knowledge that, as General Thomas had assured them during the long months of training, they had not only proved themselves a match for the *Wehrmacht,* but that in this first part of the campaign, they had prevailed.

*Darling sweetheart*
*The circus is just about moving again but Hopkins & I are travelling independently. We both dislike convoys and always try to wangle a job which necessitates travelling in advance to the new location so that we can pick a good spot.*
*It is unbearably hot here. I expect, as I often tell you, that Germany is very far from finished, as far as her army is concerned. The Luftwaffe is non existent but the army is still fanatical and well trained, and fight to the death. The suicide posts have been an awful nuisance & frequently held us up.*
*Our present surroundings are not so nice. We found two dead Germans in the hedge and there are several dead cows lying around and they stink to high heaven. There are mortar holes in the orchard and the country is rather badly knocked about.*
*Though optimistic, it is as well to realise that even if we do polish Jerry off quickly, that unfortunately will not automatically terminate our Army days, or necessarily our service overseas. But we are all very hopeful of being ex-servicemen reasonably quickly.*

*Darling, I'm afraid I ask for something every time I write – this time it's a sponge and a bottle of TCP which is useful for dealing with bites and also disinfecting dugouts. We have a lot of horseflies and wasps.*

*We have acquired a tame white rabbit called Billie which has an ear up and an ear down and looks very quaint. It loves to ride on the passenger seat of Tommy's car. We also have a stray cow which we managed to bring from the last place, and a nearby unit has a thoroughbred racehorse which they rescued, operated on (shrapnel) and now keep with them. A very amusing thing happened just now. A procession of goats solemnly walked right through our location. Daddy goat was leading followed by little goats and Mother goat brought up the rear. It was just like a Sunday school outing.*

*Darling, I keep thinking about your lovely letter and I regret to say that there is a bulge in my trousers and no one to stroke it and eventually to get rid of it!*

*All my adoring love*

*Stanley*

The efficiency of the Divisional RASC was in sharp contrast with what, to them, appeared to be the often chaotic situation up the line, a good deal of Stanley's time spent in cajoling, haranguing and pleading, and occasionally having to make the long journey back to the first supply points, face to face meetings with the relevant officers resolving problems which conversations over the less then reliable phone lines seemed only to exacerbate.

The Division's demands for petrol had not, until then been as acute as those for ammunition although in the weeks ahead, that would change radically. Fortunately, the remarkable feat of engineering, the laying of a pipeline - nicknamed "Pluto" - across the Channel, the pipeline having just become operational, was timely, obviating what, until then had been the onerous business of transporting petrol in drums, not only creating loading and transport difficulties, but slowing the refuelling of vehicles.

The slow progress through Normandy and the sternness of the opposition, never dented the certainty that the Allies would eventually prevail, the only question in the minds of the troops, now numbered in hundreds of thousands, being how long it would take, and at what further cost, the goal for each man being survival, returning home to loved ones, and to live in a time of peace.

For Stanley, however, as with many others, such thoughts brought with them the uncertainties of what their lives would be like, not only in terms of how they were going to earn a living – and what jobs would be available, but what civilian existence would be like. For some, there was already a feeling of perverse apprehension that, after the exhilaration of being part of this great crusade, emotions tested to the extreme, civvy street would be rather dull. It was not just the experience of living with danger, of learning the extent of their capabilities and their courage. There was also the fact that for the time being, they were carried along by this collective endeavour with no concerns about employment or wages, their lives committed to the army which took care of all their needs.

Although, for Stanley, as yet, there was no such worry about adapting to civilian life, the light at the end of this long tunnel of war being the dream of settling down with his beloved wife and son, it would be later, when the moment was growing closer, that a few seeds of doubt would begin to appear.

What did dawn on him was that he needed to decide how he was going to earn his living. Of course the obvious thing would be to return to the law, completing his studies and qualifying as a solicitor. But the thought of being tied to a desk for the rest of his life became increasingly less palatable, this outdoor life suiting him, prompting thoughts of some rural occupation. He knew however, in his heart of hearts, that any such notions were fanciful, and yet he could not help toying with them, mulling them over whilst at the same time, trying to prepare his mind and his resolve, when the moment came, to buckle down and to do what everyone – Peggy, her parents, and his own people – expected of him.

Perhaps he should dip his toe in the water and start reacquainting himself with some law books now, even though the idea of sitting in the mess or his dugout, pouring over some tome on probate or tort seemed utterly incongruous with what was going on around him.

*My darling beautiful one*
*The news at 6 o'c was very good – Alencon is extremely important – far more than Paris from our point of view (at the moment). Have you read today's Telegraph? I'd like you to read the about Mont Pincon.*
*Darling, will you look among my things and see if you can find any law books. You might find Sutton and Shannon's Contract or Underhill's Torts etc. Would you care to send them out to me as I think it would be a good idea to brush up some law in spare moments.*
*At supper tonight we had our first cup of coffee since leaving England. It tasted really good.*
*I have just had a very good game of bridge with Doc and Jock & the CO. We won 6 francs.*
*Darling, can you let me have more photos of yourself and Anthony – particularly some 'pin-up girl' ones. I'm sure you'd make a wonderful pin-up girl – you've got just the right figure – so Peggy get cracking!*
*Life is very interesting – every moment is full of interest and excitement – sometimes a*

*bit too much of the latter: somehow though, in this lovely country it is very hard to realise*
*that there's a hell of a battle on a few miles away.*
*Goodnight my darling wife and goodnight Anthony – god bless you both.*
*Your loving Daddy & husband*
*Stanley*

"There's still an awful long way to go," Peggy's father said, looking across from his armchair at the atlas open, as always during the War Report, on his daughter's lap. "Look at the distance from Caen" – his pronunciation as "Can" common to many British people – "to…" He waved his finger in the general direction of the opposite page, beyond the border, across the great expanse of Germany before reaching Berlin. "But it's certainly a very good start."

Why did he always have to dampen her enthusiasm, the news painting a thoroughly optimistic picture, with the Allies having now taken control of virtually all of Normandy, forcing the Germans to flee across the Seine. On the eastern front also, things were going well, with the Russians advancing across Poland, the Polish uprising in Warsaw adding to the overall positive situation even though there seemed to be some confusion about what was actually happening in the city, the report referring to a German counter attack with an ominous mention of heavy Polish casualties.

"Surely, if the Russians are so close, they will help the Poles," Peggy said, having turned the page of the atlas, finding a name mentioned in the War Report of a town the Russians had taken. "Look how near they are to Warsaw."

How strange that the Russians, so recently a nation deserving only of opprobrium for the treachery of their pact with Germany at the critical moment of the outbreak of war, proving to many that Bolshevism was as offensive to the world order as Nazism, should, almost overnight, when Hitler rashly chose to tear up the treaty and to invade Russia, become Britain's ally, its autocratic and brutal dictator, Stalin, now affectionately known as "Uncle Joe". Never was the maxim "my enemy's enemy is my friend" more apt than for this alliance of necessity, it only being later that the reality of the barbarism of the Russian army would become known. What would also be recognised was that, even more heinous than the callous treatment of the German people by its invading forces, apparently at Stalin's direction, no help was extended to the beleaguered people of Warsaw when they were facing the savage backlash from the Nazi occupiers, resulting in more than fifty thousand deaths within the space of just a few weeks.

*My darling beloved sweetheart*

*Your wonderful letter greeted me when I came in this evening and for the wonderful memories which the beautiful scent brought me. I'm afraid my letter must be a mixture of pipe, earth and sundry other smells. Darling, you've no idea how a little thing like that beautiful spot of perfume makes life so much more real – the thought of you being so sweet makes me adore you all the more. This is a land of bad smells – a lovely one is so rare.*

*The place we are in at the moment has a wonderful view. The smells are as bad as ever though. We found a dead German in the next field and had to bury him. Those smells and the dust have to be seen and smelt to be believed. The putrid stench of dead cows or bodies is something I have not experienced before – it certainly gets right into one's system I had a very unpleasant half an hour tonight in a slit trench. Jerry decided to have a little gunnery practice and the place where I was happened to be his target. All quite OK though, and just part of this life of intense excitement, fear, boredom and pleasant relaxation.*

*By the way, do your cami-knickers stay permanently undone? Gosh I wish I was with you now – they'd certainly be quickly undone and Fanny would quickly be made very naughty! Johnnie could give her a very wonderful time and make it last a long time. Wouldn't it be lovely, darling?*

*I feel so terribly near you this night – God bless you and Anthony, from your ever adoring husband and loving Daddy.*

*Stanley*

By the end of the third week of August, in spite of the hard lesson of the campaign so far, that one had to temper any optimism with a good measure of the harsh reality that the Germans had plenty of fight left in them, everyone recognising that when it came to defending their own country, their determination would be even greater, it was nevertheless clear that the battle for Normandy had indeed been won.

Even when Mount Pincon has been secured, however, there was a growing sense of the scale of the task which still lay ahead, one glance at the map showing the modest extent of the territory taken since D-Day and the vast distance ahead of them across France before they even reached the German border.

There was, however, better news with the progress by the Americans, taking the Cherbourg peninsula, the Allies' object now being to close the "Falaise Pocket", the plan being to encircle the German army, cutting off its line of retreat. The operation was successful to the extent that it resulted in the destruction of the German Army Group B, which had so effectively opposed the Allied advance, inflicting such terrible casualties. However, after the encirclement, US General Patton's Third Army meeting Montgomery's Second Army, German counter attacks enabled a significant proportion of their troops to escape, adding to the numbers which would subsequently oppose the Allies as they moved towards the German Fatherland, although the closing of the "Pocket" was to mark the victorious conclusion of the first, bloody stage of the campaign, opening the way for the Allies advance towards Paris.

# SIXTEEN

"Operation Neptune." Major-General Thomas left the name hanging in the air, allowing the assembled officers of the 43$^{rd}$ Division to speculate as to what was to be their next objective.

After the conclusion of the Caen campaign the Wyverns had been afforded a welcome period of rest, some of their units being dispatched to take part in the great parade to mark the liberation of Paris, the Germans having abandoned the city, their commanding officer, General von Choltitz, in accordance with Hitler's orders that the city should not fall into the Allies hands, having laid charges in readiness for the destruction of its principal bridges and buildings, at the last moment, as the Allies advance reached the suburbs, deciding to ignore the order, thus earning a dubious place in history for his act of defiance.

In August, having been wounded while serving in Italy a year earlier, Lieutenant-General Brian Horrocks, fit to resume duties and being highly regarded by Montgomery under whom he had served with distinction in North Africa, was appointed to command XXX Corps, a key element of Montgomery's Second Army, becoming a valued adviser to the Army commander.

Thus the Wyverns became part of XXX Corps, with their resulting involvement, a few weeks later, in the infamous Arnhem battle.

The next stage of the current campaign, the advance across north eastern France, would, initially, require one major obstacle to be overcome: the River Seine, which, where it flowed through the countryside north of Paris, was a quarter of a mile wide, the intelligence as to the strength of the German forces on the far side being uncertain.

Horrocks shared Montgomery's high regard for Major-General Thomas, his Wyverns having performed particularly effectively throughout the Caen campaign. What was more, Thomas's famously intensive training of his division, not only having paid off during the campaign, but equipping them better than any other for the task ahead, was, for Horrocks, decisive in his recommendation that the 43$^{rd}$ should lead the crossing of the Seine – Operation Neptune.

"Nobody in the British Army," Horrocks said of Thomas, "has given more detailed thought into the problems of crossing rivers in the face of opposition." For more than two years, he added, the Wyverns had practised this complex type of operation, their crossings of several English rivers – Medway, Rother, and the Thames where it was aptly known as the "Reading Sewer" having been carried out in all conditions, including night time, heavy rain and in mid winter. What they had not experienced, however, was a river crossing opposed by the *Wehrmacht*.

It was therefore, a straight forward decision for Montgomery to choose Thomas's Wyverns for the task.

For those few days, however, before the start of the operation, the now battle-hardened men of the 43rd spent their time resting, catching up on the sleep which, for the entire division, had, for nearly two months, been in short supply. After the erratic weather which had so plagued the weeks of fighting, the sun now shone for much of the time, men soaking up its restorative warmth, many of them recalling episodes of the campaign. At this stage, the grim aspects were left to one side, and indeed, for most of those who were to survive the war, remaining packaged away, resurfacing into their memories, sometimes as nightmares, but never leaving them.

Preparation for Operation Neptune required stocks of every type of supply to be replenished, allowing also for reserves, experience of the preceding weeks indicating that over supply, difficult as it was, was a great deal easier to manage than trying to keep up with demands when the division was in action.

"Why can't the buggers be a bit more frugal with the ammo?" Jock Dew had complained, tongue firmly in cheek.

What they were also having to cope with were the lengthening supply lines, the distance from the disembarkation points ever increasing, making for longer round trips by the convoys.

Whilst most of the Division enjoyed its short period of respite, the RASC officers and men were hard at work stock piling supplies at the new encampment set up close to the pretty village of Ecouche, the camp itself spread across several fields and orchards, the dumps of fuel and ammunition, as always, well separated and camouflaged.

It was also a moment for the Division to lick its wounds, although grief for the loss of so many friends and comrades was ameliorated to some extent by the reception they now received from the local populace. It was as if they were among a different race to the surly, often hostile inhabitants of the coastal area in the vicinity of the invasion bridgehead. Indeed, as the advance moved steadily southward, civilians having done their utmost to escape the areas of the fighting, once it passed, they quickly reappeared, their welcome ecstatic as was evident from their inundating the Wyverns with gifts in the form of flowers, wine and a surprisingly rich selection of produce. Everywhere they were greeted with *Vive les Anglais!*, virtually every Wyvern cheek – and many lips – bestowed with kisses of welcome.

*My very dear darling*
*Jerry has certainly taken an awful hiding, but there is still no rout: though he has been completely out manoeuvred and it has been very interesting to see the master plan unfold & to take part in it. I think it can only be a question of a few months to finish them off. I don't think they'll pack up until we and the Russians are both on German soil, though all the rats are getting out – i.e. Romania etc.*
*It is now roses, roses all the way – bundles of flowers, tricolours and waving French people, all very heartening. It has developed into a triumphant march through France. They went mad when they heard about Paris & Marseilles, and we are having a wonderful reception – really being treated like a conquering army.*
*We are now in a new location although I have been out rushing about from early morning. I am feeling very muzzy and I am afraid this may be a rather dopy letter, but until life becomes a bit more settled, I know you won't mind, darling.*
*I am so glad you got the sweets and chocolate. Were they in good condition?*
*All my love and prayers are with you. Give my love to both our parents. Anthony, old boy, lots for you – you write beautifully. Look after Mummy.*
*Yours so very lovingly*
*Stanley*

Stanley was in the RASC tent when word reached him that the convoy he was expecting had arrived. It was a strange sight, many men gathering to watch as the line of transporters edged slowly across one of the fields, parking in line, their loads, the odd looking DUKW amphibian craft – boats with wheels, other lorries carrying the more conventional looking "storm boats". Most of the men had been involved in river crossing exercises as part of their training, some of them having experienced the peculiar sensation of sitting in a boat as it made its way over land towards the river, the occupants perched high up, the spectacle for observers being of some comedic scene, the vessel itself, almost Heath Robinson in its eccentricity.

As Stanley supervised the assembly of the transporters in readiness for the next day's journey, he could not escape the thought that both of the vessels, the DUKWs and storm boats, were devoid of any form of protection. When crossing

English rivers, however arduous the contrived conditions might have been, there had been no mortars or Spandaus on the far bank.

During the course of the evening and throughout the night, more vehicles arrived, the REME contingent with their bridge building equipment, some transporters carrying ready made sections, other with cranes and bulldozers.

Soon after daybreak, the encampment began to reverberate with the starting up of numerous engines as vehicles were manoeuvred into their allotted positions in readiness for departure.

Stanley had been up for most of the night, the scale of the task of assembling and conveying the Division with it array of equipment, beyond anything which any of the logistical support units had previously had to deal with. And before the crossing itself was the matter of travelling a hundred and twenty miles along roads which, despite the advance parties of engineers having done their utmost to render them fit for such a volume of heavy traffic, were nevertheless, in a poor state of repair.

Adding to the logistical complications, the Division had to pass through an area occupied by American troops which had already reached the Seine, the roads in the area they were occupying, busy with their own traffic. Arrangements has been made to clear a route for the 43rd Division to pass through, although there was a good deal of concern about the risk of congestion, the Neptune plan not only requiring the Wyverns to move their entire division such a distance within the space of the morning, but also requiring total secrecy to offer the best chance of minimising the risk of the enemy learning of the intended crossing site, the town of Vernon, and of thus reinforcing his defences.

With a column some five miles in length, of sixteen hundred vehicles, it would only take one passing Messerschmitt to report their presence and for their secrecy to be compromised, quite apart from their having to pass through numerous villages and two towns, their route lined with flag waving French civilians rendering the operation more like that of a travelling circus than an army embarking on one of the most important operations of the campaign to date.

Travelling with Hopkins in a large Citroen which his ever resourceful batman had somehow managed to "requisition", the car being considerably more comfortable than the Army issue Austin, Stanley was a mile or more ahead of the convoy, eager to supervise the setting up of the advance ammunition dumps in the chosen sites in Vernon, sites selected to minimise the risk of shelling from the far bank of the river, although the range, for the highly effective German 88 guns was mere spitting distance, the protection being more a matter of being sufficiently removed and concealed from the crossing sites.

After just a few miles, they came to Argentan, the town lying in ruins with scarcely a building intact. But even here, in spite of such devastation, people emerged from the rubble, looking suspiciously at the Citroen until they saw the small union jack which Hopkins has managed to find, proudly displayed beside the Wyvern insignia, the recognition of the British occupants evoking broad smiles with several hands outstretched with proffered glasses of calvados.

"Rude not to accept," Stanley said, accepting one, Hopkins doing likewise.

The route, then took them across many miles of French countryside, Stanley having to concentrate on the map, navigating complicated by several roads being blocked by vehicles abandoned by the retreating enemy, many of them, including several tanks, damaged they assumed, by air attack.

When they reached Pacy, the small town at the point where they were to cross the river Eure, they encountered their first American checkpoint, the troops manning it having been briefed to give the British 43rd Division clear passage. An officer held up his hand, leaning into the car, breathing a mixture of gum and tobacco to warn them that the river bridge having been partly destroyed by the retreating Germans, the American engineers having been working overnight to make it passable for the heavy British vehicles, work still in progress although he suggested, with a casual laugh, that "it'll probably hold up!".

As they headed towards the bridge, they passed lines of American vehicles, lorries and Jeeps, as well as a column of Sherman tanks, all pulled to the side of the road, GIs waving to them as they passed, many giving their distinctive, casual salute, something between a boy scout salute and a lackadaisical army version.

Stanley had encountered a few US troops, both in England before D-Day and at subsequent joint briefings, but only now did he notice how fit they appeared, with tanned faces and muscular shoulders.

"They look well fed, don't they?" Hopkins remarked.

They covered the last few miles to Vernon without obstruction or incident, arriving in the pleasant, genteel town to find it in festive mode, the streets crowded, the inhabitants lavishing the usual offerings upon them.

Edging their way through centre of the town, keeping well back from the river as instructed, they found their way to the park which had been designated as one for the forward dumps, the advance party and reconnaissance troops - "the recce's" - already having marked out the sites for the ammunition, petrol and other supplies.

Leaving the car, they made their way cautiously towards the river, keeping close to the buildings screening them from binoculars which would, inevitably, be scanning the town, Vernon being one of the likely points at which the Allies would attempt their crossing.

Finding a vantage point beside some trees, they were able survey the scene, one of the two bridges demolished, the other severely damaged but still sufficiently intact, he reckoned, for infantry to get across, although there would be no protection from defenders on the far bank.

"Christ, they're right there," Hopkins said, speaking quietly as if he might be heard, the group of German troops he was referring to being a quarter a mile or so from them, standing beside a pill box, smoking and chatting. "We could pick them off from here," he added, both of them surprised that the enemy should be showing themselves so clearly.

"I think that might tell them we're here," Stanley replied, his own voice similarly hushed.

A short distance beyond the far bank there was a chalk escarpment, two or three hundred feet high, offering even greater advantage to the defenders, and indeed, more German soldiers could be seen on the top, sitting around, apparently enjoying the sun, the earlier rain having now given way to blustery conditions, with spells of broken cloud.

Before long, the sound of the arriving convoy began to fill the midday air, Stanley being certain that the noise and the clouds of exhaust, must alert the Germans to their presence although the heavy rain which had been falling for much of the morning, at least prevented the usual clouds of dust.

Throughout the afternoon, twenty five pounders were positioned and DUKWs and storm boats brought forward into the streets close to the embankment, the launching sites chosen to take advantage of the small island as a staging post, the information gleaned from the local resistance being that the river on the nearside of the island was deep enough for the storm boats to cross.

Concealment of the engineering equipment, which included large rafts, pontoons and ready assembled bailey-bridge sections, was even more difficult, certain of them, mounted on flat-bed lorries, as high as many of the houses, thus having to be held back in the roads at the rear of the town.

While the deployment of men and material was in train, the populace milled around, chatting to the troops, the offering of food and drink unceasing, plenty of liquor being consumed in spite of orders to abstain. The tension amongst the troops was in sharp contrast with the celebratory mood of the inhabitants although once again, there were a few scenes which tainted the atmosphere, several women who had "gone" with the German occupiers, suffering the now familiar shaming, their heads shaved, humiliation being by way of the almost medieval parading through the streets, enduring spitting and execration, the grim processions including several men, collaborators, vengeance against them more obvious from their battered faces, there being reports of widespread killings.

By the end of the afternoon, the assault battalions, the 4th Somersets and the 4th and 5th Wiltshires, were in position, the storm boats close by, each with eight men ready to carry them the last two or three hundred yards down the banks to the launching points, the decision having been taken that the descent to the water was too steep to use the DUKWs.

At 18.45 precisely, the opening barrage erupted, the local populace, now crowding towards the river to witness the crossing, putting their hands over their ears as the plumes of smoke started to appear on the far bank. For fifteen minutes the bombardment continued, the guns then switching to smoke shells, the river quickly blanketed in dark, swirling fog as the troops emerged from the side streets, running towards the river, the boat teams heaving the craft into the water.

The boats seemed to move agonisingly slowly, their outboard motors, even aided by men paddling, hardly up to the task of propelling the weighty vessels, each now carrying fifteen men with their weapons. Those which were making for the island ran aground, the information from the locals proving wholly incorrect, the river at this point having shallows little more than knee depth, the men having to climb out and wade onto the island where, at least for the moment, they were relatively safe from enemy fire.

It was the boats which were heading across the full width of the river which soon began to suffer. A number of them grounded on mud banks close to the far side, offering them as easy targets to the Spandau gunners, fire raking down onto them, the smoke clearing, further smoke shells ineffective, the wind carrying the smoke away along the river.

Stanley was on his way back to the RASC tent, having used a motorbike for his latest visit, to the 4th Wiltshires, assembled on the far side of the town, when he found the road blocked by the throng of spectators trying to get a view from a side street, the river front having been sealed off for military use only. He managed to bypass the crowd, coming out onto the river front a hundred yards further, just as the storm boats were heading out from the near bank. He watched, horrified as the first boat hit the mud bank, several men trying to climb out, only to be mown down, falling into the water, a couple of them floating away with the flow of the river, most of those still in the boat being hit, collapsing on top of one another, a burst of fire splintering the side of the boat.

A handful of men managed to make it to the bank, hurling themselves down onto the mud although still being within the gunners' sights, a few of them were hit where they lay, the survivors belly-crawling forward until they gained the protection of a small section of the river bank.

The scene was the same for most of the boats, several now drifting, some, swinging with the flow, bow or stern stuck on the mud, the relentless spray of gunfire cutting the men down, although by now enough had reached the far bank to enable them to start to edge forward, one of the pill boxes put out of action by a grenade.

Tearing himself away from the grim spectacle, he hurried back to the tent, stopping outside to try to compose himself, swallowing down the nausea rising from his stomach.

When he sat down on one of the canvass chairs in the tent erected as the RASC communications point, picking up the sheaf of messages, his hands were shaking. He realised that although he had seen plenty of dead bodies during the last weeks, he had not, until now, seen men being shot. It was not just the fact of their being killed, but the way in which they were felled, like targets at a shooting gallery, the men in the boat folding over, slumping onto their comrades. He now understood the term "scythed" which had often been used to describe the cutting down of so many men as they climbed out of the trenches in the Great War.

"I saw it as well." Jock was standing beside. "Bloody awful business. Here." He handed Stanley an enamel cup of whisky, Stanley taking a large swig, the liquor quelling the residue of his nausea.

"Barrage didn't do much good," Stanley said ruefully, the extent of the enemy return fire indicating that their gunners had managed to find sufficient shelter during the opening fifteen minute bombardment from the British guns.

Fortunately, the light soon began to fade, the order being given to abandon further attempts to get across in the storm boats. An access point had now been found a short way from the centre of the town where the DUKWs could be launched, it being fully dark when the first four of them entered the water, three of them immediately grounding, only one getting across. The next attempt proved equally unsuccessful, one vessel grounding and another sinking as it entered the water, the occupants of both being able to get back to the shore.

Although a precarious bridgehead had now been established by those who had got across, it was imperative to reinforce them, it being inevitable otherwise, that with daylight, they would be overwhelmed by the defenders.

Stanley, having spent the last hours supervising the movement of ammunition, and overseeing the arrangements for getting fuel to the points where, he had been told, the engineers would shortly be starting work on the bailey bridge, their heavy equipment consuming large quantities of diesel, he now had a brief pause, standing close to the near end of the damaged road bridge, watching with some alarm as the order was given for an infantry platoon to file onto the bridge, the men moving forward in single file along the first section, reaching the part which had collapsed to a steep V shape, climbing gingerly down the steep slope and then up the other side, onto the final undamaged part, at which point, the darkness being insufficient to conceal them, they were met with Spandau fire. As the lead man hesitated, then stepped forward, he triggered a booby trap, the explosion throwing him across the surface of the structure. He managed to get to his feet, obviously wounded, hobbling and waving his arms at the men behind him, all of them hurrying back across the bridge, several of them being hit in the process.

There was little sleep for any of the RASC men that night, the most acute issue being the ferrying of ammunition across the river to the men who were now dug in, protecting their precarious bridgehead, an area no more than a few hundred yards wide, the German positions facing them in every direction.

Fortunately, an attempt by a second company of the 4<sup>th</sup> Somersets, a few hundred yards beyond the town proved successful, a company of more than a hundred men making the crossing in storm boats, quickly establishing a second bridgehead and then managing to clear the area to the first.

Stanley and several of his fellow officers received the calls coming in by radio and brought by messenger, mainly for ammunition, the atmosphere in the tent business like, voices almost conversational, only occasionally raised, and then in frustration usually when some bottleneck caused by the weight of traffic, delayed delivery, several of the streets of the small town now, during the hours of darkness, filled with REME vehicles, moving their equipment towards the river.

At one point in the early hours, an urgent message came through from the Wiltshires, their radio operator dug in on the far bank, speaking in a hoarse whisper, obviously aware of the proximity of the enemy.

"I'll go," Mead said, the call being for 303 rifle and Bren-gun ammunition.

"Don't be stupid," Stanley replied, surprised at Mead's volunteering, the timidity he had shown during the training exercises, having become a standing joke, particularly between Stanley, Dew and Atkins, in the weeks of the campaign. "One of the men can go. It doesn't need an officer."

"I think it does," Mead insisted. "We're going to need to get a lot of boxes across and work out the distribution."

Stanley could see that what Mead was saying made sense, the situation now more complicated with the establishment of the second bridgehead and, according to word reaching them, the two now having joined together. He looked at Mead, the man's narrow, slightly rodent like face set.

"About time I made myself useful," he said, mimicking the derisory comments thrown at him from time to time by the other officers.

"Good luck, man," Stanley said as Mead climbed into the Bedford truck loaded with some thirty boxes of 303 ammunition, the lighter truck being selected to navigate the town's congested roads.

Stanley and Atkins exchange a look, Atkins raising his eyebrows, both of them surprised by Mead's insistence.

"He's going to take it across," Atkins said, shaking his head.

"Yes, I know," Stanley replied, ducking back into the tent, the two radio operators scribbling messages as fast as they could write, dealing them to whoever was nearest to them.

Much of the work throughout the night involved assisting the REME engineers with their complex requirements, their articulated low-loaders damaging a number of buildings as they edged through the streets, several of them carrying the pontoon sections of the bailey-bridge, the site for which had now been selected, the first section to span the narrower part of the river to one of the islands.

Expert as they had become in assembling the bridges, their training having tested them with a variety of rivers, this was the first time they had had to span a river in full view of the enemy, the nature of the operation making it virtually impossible to provide them with any effective protection from enemy positions.

At first light, as some five hundred sappers got to work on the construction, although fire from the enemy on the far bank was reducing partly due to the progress of the troops within the bridgehead, supported by effective fire from British field guns and tanks, several Spandaus and 88 guns continued to operate all too effectively from positions at the top of the escarpment, some twenty sappers being killed and many more wounded. However, with spotters now able to pin-point the firing positions, return fire soon silenced several of the enemy guns although others continued to hamper the operation until the pontoons were assembled across more than half of the width of the river.

It took the whole day for the bridge to be completed, the first vehicles crossing twenty four hours after the initial storm boat assault, and within an hour, tanks were making their way to the eastern bank.

By this time, with many more men able to get across on the damaged bridge, the bridgehead was steadily widened, and although enemy resistance continued, they were steadily pushed back towards the forest which lay beyond the river, the small town on the eastern bank, Vernonnet, now in British hands, enabling most of the rest of the Division to cross.

It was four days before the remaining German forces finally withdrew, the crossing being successfully completed, at a cost of more than five hundred Wyvern casualties.

Filing across the bailey bridge in the opposite direction were a similar number of German prisoners, the bodies of several hundred of their comrades left where they had died.

On the morning of the twenty eighth, Stanley made his first crossing, with Hopkins at the wheel of the Citroen, visiting several surrounding villages now occupied by units of the 43$^{rd}$, the villages – La Queue, Heubecourt, Panilleuse, Pressagny – being remarkably intact, a clear indication that by the time the enemy had been pushed back from the immediate area of the river, they had effectively given up the fight.

Indeed, it soon became apparent that once the Allies were across the Seine, the Germans were already undertaking a major strategic withdrawal of their forces, retreating across most of Northern France, towards their own borders and the low countries.

Such has been the intensity of the activity throughout the days of the operation that it was only now, sitting in the shade of an orchard taken over as one of the forward camps, Stanley found time to write to Peggy. Underlying his fatigue was a deep feeling of satisfaction for a job well done.

Around him the sounds of nature lifted his spirits, the orchard filled with birdsong despite some continuing gunfire a few miles away, as the last, desultory rear-guard German resistance began to peter out.

*28.8.44*
*Capt S R Allen  HQ RASC  43 Div  Brit Lib Army*
*My very dearest darling*
*At last we have a breathing space and life is normal again for a while. I received another sweet letter this morning. I love the 'aroma of Peggy' in some of your letters – it lasts marvellously, darling, and even freshens the earthy smell of my penthouse.*
*I'm glad that Anthony is able to sit up and take notice. I hope I can come home soon as I feel I am missing such an interesting part of his life.*
*As you probably realise, events are moving very swiftly and that means that we are too. The end is now in sight but we are all wondering whether the end of the war will bring release from the Army, or whether we shall click for a long occupation of Germany or a visit to hotter climes. Everyone dreads the latter and would do anything to avoid it, but I don't think it's very likely.*
*The European War should end at the latest by Christmas as the Germans are now in a hopeless plight although still fighting fiercely. It is an amazingly different picture from, say, three weeks ago. We were then just plugging away at them, now we chase them. Anyhow,*

as soon as this war ends we'll certainly get leave, if not immediate discharge.

I would love to tell you more but of course can't. I can say that we are near a very nice river town which I have been into several times. The reception we get is stupendous, so very different to what we used to get. I bought two litres of lovely mushrooms today: it made me feel very homesick and want to take them back to you to cook them in the hut. It would be delightfully cosy there on this dull wet evening.

We visited a little café in one small town whilst halting for 15 minutes & had a memorable meal of duck 'oeufs', tomatoes, chips, cider and black coffee which only cost the Doc & I 80 francs. Wine is given to us everywhere, the French have been digging it out of their secret hiding places, where it had lain for 4 years.

We have had duck for supper tonight – tremendous treat. It was given to us by the wife of Monsieur Le Maire of one of the places we 'liberated'. We use the term liberate quite differently to the BBC. We liberate a place by 'beating it up' – i.e. inspecting its cafes, restaurants and local talent! So far the latter has not really materialised anywhere. A familiar term in the mess is 'Let's go and liberate ——- after supper", though there is usually little time for such pastimes.

My darling, you are a naughty girl! In about my last umpteen letters I have asked why you haven't had a 'squiggle'! Darling, according to my calculations it was six weeks on August 17$^{th}$ – so what has Peggy been up to?!!

Darling, don't think that I'm being fussy or windy, but will you please see to your and Anthony's gas masks? The Germans at the moment are nearly cornered, and they will try and lash out like wild beasts, and might attempt any frightfulness. Travelling through France we have heard so many terrible tales – any doubts about showing any mercy to Germany in the peace have gone for ever, from the Army at least, and I think that if any of you at home could spend half an hour in any of these French villages or towns, you too would have no doubts. They really are utter bastards.

I thank you for the vivid description of cami-knickers and nightdress! It made me want you very much & made JT say hello!

Isn't amazing that in two days I shall complete 5 years of service. Do you remember the night of August 31$^{st}$ 1939? I remember going to the office at the usual time after sleeping very fitfully and dreaming of hordes of great black bombers going overhead and getting out at St James' Park and seeing the fateful placards – 'Warsaw bombed'. It was hard to do any work that day but we all tried hard, until lunchtime, when it became too obvious that we'd finished with civvy street and we saw the placards 'Territorial Army called up', so we packed up and you next saw me at the flat. Do you remember that crazy half hour when I wanted so much to seal our love, because I just thought that I'd be going completely into the unknown & might never see you again? I think on that occasion my feelings were very much deeper than yours, and it was very hard when you were cross, but you didn't know, did you, that I loved you so very much. Then all too soon out into the new horridness of London blackout, and you'd kissed me and had gone. I was left standing there on that dreadful corner, alone, not knowing what to do. For once my usual purposeful life held no *purpose & no hope, and I don't mind admitting, darling, a tear or two sprang from my eye.*

*But now, this week, the purpose I failed to see that grim night has been fully revealed. It has been worth the five years hard training, monotony, often boredom, red tape and the rest. The look on the faces of the French men and women, the smiles & 'mercies' of the children, makes us so proud of our calling and makes this war not a bloody sweat with no purpose but a crusade with a bright & glorious future shining through the clouds as we near the end of the long road.*

*My undying love for ever to you.*
*Stanley*

# SEVENTEEN

*Stanley, my sweetheart*

*Thank you for your very sweet letter which has made me feel so happy on this rather wintery summer day. I am glad you feel you really are a liberation army now & that the people have treated you so well. I wonder if there are any pretty French girls sharing the embracing! I expect there are though I doubt if you have time to think very much about them. Perhaps a good thing!*

*The news tonight is just amazing – British on the Somme, Americans nearing the Belgium border & the Russians in Budapest. There was lots about the 2$^{nd}$ Army – the number of prisoners taken beside equipment & killed is terrific.*

*I have spent the evening since the news doing some mending and sewing buttons on Anthony's romper as he kicks so vigorously they keep coming off. Anthony wants Daddy to come home too, to play with him. He had just waved goodnight & chuckled at his photograph. He always laughs at your photograph.*

*God bless you my beloved one.*

*Peggy*


*My darling Peggy*

*Thank you darling for you letter which arrived this evening.*

*I wish I had been there to be naughty with you, darling. But maybe I will soon if not permanently then at least on leave, then we can be ever so naughty and love and laugh in the hut.*

*We are all anxious to get at the Secret Weapon sites – no mercy will be shown if the British get their hands on the Germans in that quarter.*

*I have just been listening to the 9pm news which must have cheered you folk at home very much. We've even made the Russian advances look small.*

*My mother's last letter sounded as if some Brighton beaches were open. Have you investigated? Do be careful though if you do bathe – especially of mines and hidden obstructions.*

*What we want to hear now is that the Japs have packed up. That's the only qualifying factor to restrain our present great elation. We feel that if we do go on too fast we should be available for Burma – horrid thought, but it's not worrying us unduly.*

*I had the Parish Magazine from my father yesterday. I sat for a moment and looked at the picture of the church on the cover – it looked very dear and suddenly seemed very far away. The path by the church, of which I know every stone and every cement joint, looked empty and I felt that I expected you to come along it, may be pushing Anthony in the pram. How I long for home and your love again.*

*Goodnight my very angel darling.*

*Ever your loving husband & Daddy*

*Stanley*

For nearly two weeks after the Seine crossing, the Wyverns were rested, remaining in the Vernon area, enjoying the generous hospitality of the local populace some of whom, most notably the bar and café proprietors, had good reason to be thankful for the Division's presence, the small town filled, day and evenings, by the Tommies, happy to spend their limited supply of francs, what they could afford often supplemented by the hospitality lavished upon them, many a household welcoming their liberators to their dinner tables.

Stanley and several other RASC officers were amongst those invited to a number of civic receptions, hosted by *Monsieur Le Maire* and other civic figures, the receptions invariably an excuse for much eating and drinking, the mood of the inhabitants one of euphoria that, after four long and painful years, they were finally free from the yoke of occupation and the brutality which the occupiers had visited upon so many of the townsfolk.

"They have such *style*," Tommy Atkins observed rather dreamily, late one evening when they had returned, well fed and watered, from one of the functions. "Even when they're not dressed up, they look so... I don't know."

"*Chic*," is the word, Jock added. "It's the way they walk as well. Always with a bit of "come hither." His Scots brogue was particularly pronounced as her rolled the "R" of "hither".

"It's as if they're offering it all the time," Tommy resumed. "I've had that many kisses. And sometimes you sense they're inviting you to, you know..."

As with all of them, Stanley had been the happy recipient of many kisses and embraces, several from young women, hinting, he had little doubt, at the offers that Tommy was referring to. It was there in the look, the faces brimming with smiles, but the eyes conveying something which any man could read.

"We can only imagine what they've been through," he said, having heard several accounts of the treatment of young women at the hands of the German soldiers whose expectation had been that, as with everything else in the lands they occupied, the women were simply part of their rightful plunder. For the women, it had been an impossibly difficult line between offering themselves in return for the favours they received, both material and, particularly for those who "went" with officers, knowing that they were reserved, not to be molested by other troops, others reduced to the role of prostitutes, and, for those determined to resist, the brutality which was often the consequence, rape being an everyday occurrence.

293

Now, with liberation, had come the reckoning, with those accused of *collaboration horizontale*, pilloried, the opprobrium heaped upon them often encouraged by other women who had managed to avoid such subjugation, and sometimes by those who had secretly succumbed, cheer-leading the rituals of humiliation, drawing attention away from themselves.

"Bloody tempting," Jock said, picturing the girl, probably no more than eighteen who, that very day, had kissed him full on the lips, her arms around his neck, holding onto him for just that bit too long. "If wasn't for my conscience about my Morag," – again the full, celtic purring of the "R", as if the thought of her required him to remind himself of his heritage and loyalty – "I would have given that one a damned good seeing to!"

"Mm," Stanley agreed pensively, the picture of a young woman who, the day before, had suddenly appeared at his side as he was walking through the town, trying to find a shop selling perfume, wanting to send some Peggy, the woman linking his arm and, in a soft, sensuous voice, saying " 'ello Meester Tommy. Do you like?" – giving a suggestive waggle of her hips.

As she pulled his arm against her he could feel the contours of her body, her perfume deliciously exotic. He turned towards her, looking at her pretty, questioning face, the thought suddenly coming to him that she had probably been with German soldiers.

"Non merci," he said, his resolutely English accent accentuating the polite formality of his refusal.

"I wonder what it's going to be like when we get to Germany," Jock said, the thought of being amongst the German population having occurred to all of them.

*My sweetheart darling*
*I have covered lots of new ground. We saw lots of teams of oxen at work – I think it was the first time that I have seen this. France is very much behind England in modern farming equipment and we haven't seen one tractor since we've been here.*
*The armour has gone far ahead very fast though and life is rather dull for us at the moment though no doubt we shall get our excitement again in due course.*
*We all feel like schoolboys on the eve of holiday tonight because Paris has just been put in bounds and tomorrow the CO, Tony Gilson and myself are going in. I'll write & tell you all about it darling.*
*Last night I saw half an Ensa show which included Richard Hearne who was very very*

*funny — one of the funniest acts I've seen for ages.*
*Always your adoring*
*Stanley*

*My sweetheart*
*I wonder if you are having this same windy weather & how you are. I can imagine you*
*and Hopkins in your Citroen — masses of baggage and paraphernalia — rushing along. I*
*should think that snipers must be very nasty.*
*As you say, the end of the road can't be so very far away now. It is incredibly much nearer*
*than I thought could possibly be when we said goodbye.*
*Daddy is not going to the office as he is feeling tired out & is going to spend the rest of*
*the day in bed. I expect he will get up this evening as we are going to have a family game*
*of bridge.*
*Yesterday evening I took Sam out for a walk. As I got to the Recreation Ground & was*
*looking at the sunset sky, I saw a ball of fire in the sky which gradually fell, breaking up*
*as it did so. It must have been a flying bomb blown up in the air as it looked like a*
*firework.*
*The news is still wonderful isn't it, from everywhere. It would be wonderful if Germany*
*were knocked out before the winter. All things like no more compulsory Home Guard and*
*relaxation of the blackout make one feel that it isn't very far away.*
*If you get to Berlin in anything like the speed you got to Brussels, we shall be celebrating*
*victory soon! Actually I think the last lap will be the hardest bit.*
*Wishing you God speed my darling.*
*With all my love*
*Peggy*

As they set off after an early breakfast, wanting to make the most of a full day, Stanley felt a pang of excitement rather as he used to feel at the start of a boyhood holiday, the fact that their divisional RASC CO, Lieutenant-Colonel Reeder, had decided to accompany them, Stanley and his fellow Captain, Tony Gilson, hoping they were going to be able to make the trip by themselves or with another member of their mess, only marginally detracting from the occasion, the positive aspect being that, with the CO joining them, they had use of the large army Humber. It was the first time Stanley had driven the car, the pleasure of being at the wheel of such a luxurious vehicle adding even greater delight.

"*Paree* here we come!" he exclaimed as they turned onto the main road, the *Route Nationale* taking them the fifty or so miles to the heart of the city.

Every town and village they passed through, they were greeted with the familiar reception, waves and smiles and flowers tossed onto the car, many people peering curiously into the car, assuming that the occupants of such a splendid vehicle must be important.

The route into Paris was similarly traffic free, the suburbs, far less sprawling than London, being remarkably undamaged, the areas which had been bombed by the Allies being mainly on the eastern side where inaccurate targeting of railway marshalling yards had caused extensive damage to residential quarters with heavy casualties.

For more than an hour they drove around the city, even the usually dour CO enthusing as they came to famous landmarks, their passage, particularly along some of the better known streets, slowed by crowds, their impression being that the entire population seemed to be continuing the celebration of their liberation by filling the bars and cafes, crowding into shops, or, for many, simply milling around. And each time they slowed, they became the centre of attention, faces appearing through the car's open windows, hands reaching in, many shaking their hands, others bestowing the usual gifts. Several times, also, females of varying ages, leaned through the windows, planting kisses on them, the three occupants soon besmirched with lipstick.

"God, I'm glad Peggy can't see me at the moment!" Stanley laughed, glancing at his reflection in the rear view mirror.

When, after dark, they arrived back at their base in Vernon, weary as he was from the long day of sightseeing, eating and drinking, Stanley was so brimming with exhilaration that he knew he would not sleep until he had recounted part at least of the experience to Peggy.

*My dearest darling*
*Many words have been written about Paris, but I feel that before going to sleep tonight I must add my poor inadequate attempt to describe something of the impressions of this wonderful city.*
*I caught my first sight of the Eiffel Tower when we were some 15 miles away: then before you realise it, you see the Arc de Triomphe standing impressively at the top of a wide magnificent avenue called the 'Rue des Grandes Armees'. You reach the Arc de Triomphe on the top of a slight hill and there stretches in front of you, straight for about 2 miles the gay & colourful Champs Elysees. The first half contains shops and open air cafes, the second half is rather like the Mall.*
*We parked our car in a street about half way down and we walked up the Champs Elysees to look at the shops. But Paris had seen no* British *troops (in service dress too!) for 4 years*

*& we had a grand welcome – the people were marvellous – so terribly pleased to see us. We tried to do some shopping but weren't very successful. Well here we have an amusing adventure – we hired a kind of taxi! A bicycle tows a sort of carriage affair & we drove in great style amidst the smiles & waves of Paris to the Hotel des Invalides: here we saw the tomb of Napoleon and Marshall Foch. Words of mine could not describe the grandeur and wonder of this great building. All this while I was wishing to much that you could be with me & I was making a very determined vow that you are coming to Paris with me après la guerre even if it breaks the bank!*

*We then hired an open carriage to take us to Notre Dame. This cost 100 francs & 50 cigarettes  but included a ride back through a grand stretch of wonderful streets. Notre Dame again has to be seen to be appreciated. It seems somehow to stand aloof from things temporal.*

*We then had some grand iced beer in an open air café, sitting right on the pavement. We were still objects of curiosity, excitement and amazement!*

*Some more shopping followed – oh how you'd love the magnificent boulevards with their cool shady trees, the gay clothes – which even after 4 years of Bosche rule are still gay & chic. The women though seem generally very hard & very much more made up than our girls. Darling without any desire to flatter you, you'd look outstanding amid any of the Paris crowd today & well dressed too.*

*Yes we will visit Paris for a glorious spree. You are going to need your trousseau not just once for our honeymoon but for the one we'll spend in Paris.*

*My undying love is yours so very much for ever.*

*Stanley*


With Anthony playing contentedly on the grass in the warm September sun, a pleasant change after a week of blustery weather, Peggy sat in a deckchair reading the letter which had just arrived.

There was something quite thrilling reading about Stanley's trip to Paris; she could picture it so clearly, so many of the sights he mentioned familiar from pictures she had seen and, more recently, a Pathé news film at the cinema. She tried also, to envisage the reception, the three British officers being greeted like royalty, save that the deference due to royal personages would not allow the hugs and kisses which Stanley had alluded to.

Thrilled as she was, to enjoy, vicariously, what was clearly such a marvellous experience for him, as she finished reading, her hand holding the letter, resting on her lap, she felt unexpectedly flat. There had been moments, thankfully few, when it all felt too much; the strain of having to cope by herself. She told herself not to be so stupid; after all, she had her mother and father, as well as her friends; and of course, Anthony, the centre of her domestic existence. And her situation was no different to that of many thousands of others, with husbands away at the war. At least Stanley wasn't in the front line even though he was obviously still in dangerous situations.

It just seemed so hard. Her longing for him was like a constant ache, made so much worse not only when she knew he was involved in periods of heavy fighting, but – almost more so – when she read of the other side of his "great adventure"; the opportunity to see so much, and the pleasurable experiences, this latest, his visit to Paris, so vivid. How dull her own life was in comparison. If only she could have been doing something useful, or interesting.

It was nearly four years since they were married. It was not simply the thought of having had to live apart for virtually all of that time, but the certainty that it was going to be several months at least, before the war was over, and even then, as he had already mentioned, there was the prospect of him having to stay on in the aftermath.

Adding to her blank mood was her worry about her father. In spite of his determined robustness, he had been so obviously out of sorts for some time with what appeared to be constant chest infections. It was in his nature to shrug off such minor complaints, eschewing the idea of taking to his bed, the fact that several times recently he had done so, making her wonder if there was something more seriously wrong with him. Her nursing experience told her that it was more than the "slight chest cold", his face looking different, the rude health which was so much part of him, seeming to have drained from his ruddy cheeks.

All morning, planes had been passing over almost constantly, Anthony looking up excitedly, pointing, and sometimes copying his mother, waving to them.

"Tell them to say "Hello to Daddy"," she said.

"Da, Da," Anthony said, gesticulating towards them.

Word had been circulating all day that they would be on the move again shortly, possibly even as soon as the next morning, rumours suggesting that they would be following other elements of the Second Army into Belgium. After the gruelling slog through Normandy, the sudden rush to the Seine had marked a dramatic change in the campaign, even though the Allies were still battling the stubborn German resistance in the Channel ports of Calais and Boulogne. Fortunately, however, the garrison at Dieppe proved less determined, the port being taken at the beginning of September, thus providing an entry point for supplies considerably closer to the areas of north-eastern France and Belgium to which the focus of the campaign had now shifted.

It was only that evening, at the briefing held by the Divisional CO, Major General Thomas, that the senior officers, Stanley counted amongst them due to the essential RASC role, learned of the extraordinarily bold plan, hearing for the first time, the name which would haunt many of them for years to come, "Market Garden".

"I have come from a meeting at SHAEF," Thomas told them, referring to the Allied High Command, "where I met General Eisenhower, *Field Marshall* Montgomery," he paused, to ensure that Montgomery's recent promotion to the highest rank in the army was duly noted, "Lieutenant-General Horrocks and other senior officers. I can tell you that the plan which I am about to unveil to you will be the boldest stroke of this campaign to date, taking the Second Army across the Rhine and opening up a route to the heart of the enemy's land."

He nodded to a sergeant who had been standing beside a covered map, the sergeant lifting the covering sheet, the map revealing part of Holland, with several arrows marked on it.

"Here," the Major-General said, jabbing the map with his stick, "is our objective. The town of Arnhem. Once it is in our hands, as you can see, Germany lies open before us." His stick swept down from the Dutch town, drawing a wide arc towards the edge of the map, then tracing an invisible line in the air, which they all realised, was towards Berlin.

As the briefing proceeded, the boldness of the plan became startlingly obvious, requiring the crossing of two major rivers before even reaching the Rhine, Arnhem sitting astride what was certainly, one of Europe's most famous rivers, running through the industrial region, the Ruhr, and effectively the natural moat defending Germany from Western attack.

Thomas handed over to other officers who detailed the different stages of the operation, "Market", comprising no fewer than three airborne divisions, one British and two American, which were to be dropped beyond the bridges at Grave, Nijmegen and Arnhem, holding them until the arrival of the ground forces, "Garden", led by XXX Corps and the 43rd Division, spearheaded by the 5th Guards Armoured Brigade, their task being to advance to each of the bridges, connecting with the airborne division, and thus securing the ultimate bridgehead at Arnhem.

"Speed will be imperative," Thomas said, concluding the briefing. "Tomorrow we will be moving to our starting positions. Good afternoon gentlemen. I'm sure that, once again, the Wyverns will make our nation proud."

The assembled officers rose to their feet as Thomas departed, leaving them looking at each other as they tried to absorb the sheer audacity of the plan, recognising also, the daunting prospect of having to cross three rivers, the experience of the Seine, and the bloody struggles to cross the far smaller rivers of the *bocage*, the Odon and the Orne, all too recent.

"Bloody hell!" Jock sighed as they congregated in the RASC tent.

"Bloody hell indeed!" the RASC CO repeated, entering just behind Jock. "We will certainly have our work cut out, so we'd better get busy."

In fact, the Division did not commence its move until 17th, a day later than expected, the 16th being a day of frenetic activity as they prepared not only for the battle which, they all knew lay ahead, despite the suggestion that the route chosen, a left hook movement through Holland, was likely to be less heavily defended than a direct advance through the Ruhr, such view, they were told, being supported by intelligence reports.

With the map spread in front of them, the group of RASC officers studied the route, the task of moving the entire division to the operational area a challenge in itself, before they even embarked on the business of tackling the crossings and reaching the "Market" airborne divisions.

"Speed will be imperative," Reeder said, echoing the Divisional CO's words. "And we've got a lot of distance to cover."

What they also realised was that with what was, in effect, a single line of advance, at best some six hundred yards wide, astride one road for a crucial sixty mile section, this would also be their only means of supplying the forward units, a scenario which, with the experience they had gained over the previous few months, they knew could be something of a nightmare due to the inevitable congestion.

By the afternoon of 17th, the Division having moved across Belgium, the advance units were meeting stern opposition from the *Luftwaffe*, supposedly largely neutralised, putting in a surprise appearance, some thirty bombers attacking gun positions with devastating accuracy before being driven off by

Allied fighters, the weather then closing in, curtailing further aerial activity.

Now with more than three thousand vehicles making up their long, straggling column, and with attacks coming at them from both flanks, progress was already, within the first critical hours, slowing, reports reaching them that the airborne divisions were also facing far stronger opposition than anticipated, the speed of the land advance becoming even more crucial.

For two days, the Wyverns worked their way forward, hampered by the weather as well as the opposition, some of it from panzer regiments, the terrain well suited for defensive disposition, dug in tanks proving particularly difficult to deal with in the absence of the Typhoons, which had become by far the most effective Allied anti panzer weapon.

How strange, Stanley thought, when, during a brief moment of respite, he was able to write to Peggy, trying to make light of what was going on around him, the twenty five pounders, several of them no more than a quarter of a mile from where he was, firing almost incessantly.

*My angel darling*
*I have often written and told you that life is hectic, but now it is more hectic than it has ever been*
*At the moment I'm in the heart of the country. We have just pulled up for the night: it has just started to rain but it feels very cosy inside my penthouse & the boys are just cooking eggs & chips for tea cum supper. They cooked a wonderful breakfast this morning which reminded me very sharply of the hut and I almost felt the breakfast had been cooked by you. It was egg, sausage and tomato. No toast (that is the one thing we never get in the field) but very nice bread & butter. We also get heaps of peaches given to us by the French. I scrounged potatoes tonight by giving some cigarettes.*
*Lots of things have happened since I last wrote – I'm so sorry you will have such a gap in my letters darling. I will tell you the full story of September 16 – 17 after the war. I expect the 9 o'c news will have given you an inkling of 'great events'.*
*The Belgian people are terrific – we saw nothing like the welcome we've had in Belgium, in France. Even Paris pales compares with Brussels – we have had flowers & Belgian flags put all over the cars, the convoys held up by wildly excited crowds, giving us peaches, apples, pears, tomatoes, ice creams (lovely ones). The whole place is like a huge carnival – the shops are decorated, the trams, everything. Incidentally, this is a land of plenty & the shops are very full – but we are having lots of currency problems! We've had free champagne & wine. This is an all British show. Belgium is ours and the British Army of 1944 will for ever salute and remember happily the very wonderful welcome that we've had.*
*We are going flat out now as we believe we can finish the Hun off very soon.*

*We are all rather stupid through lack of sleep. I am just going to get some – my first since Thursday.*
*I must put my weary head to bed now.*
*Your ever adoring husband*
*Stanley*

Eventually, they reached the Waal bridge at Nijmegen which the US 82nd Airborne Division had captured, it now being the Wyvern's job to secure it in the face of increasingly intensive German counter attacks. With the continuing bad weather, there was negligible air support, leaving the ground forces to deal with the panzers which were now posing a serious threat to the precariously narrow corridor of the Allied advance.

When Stanley arrived in Nijmegen, making the essential trip to try to resolve the confusing messages as to supply requirements, communications were frequently disrupted even to the extent that they had to rely from time to time, on the help of Dutch civilians whose telephones seemed to be in perfect working order, enabling calls to be made to their friends in the various locations, although the messages sometimes came through in a garbled form, having required hasty and rather approximate translation. The large iron arched span of the bridge made a macabre sight, several German snipers having been killed in their ill-concealed vantage points high up in the structure, remaining where they had died.

The firing, from guns of every sort – tanks, field guns, machine guns and rifles – seemed to be in every direction, several panzers dug in in the orchards to the north of the bridge, able to bring their guns to bear on the Wyvern's position, a platoon of PIAT anti-tank gunners being dispatched to deal with them, managing to silence some of them but at a cost of several lives.

Stanley found himself, with Hopkins, sheltering beside a building in the main street of the small, elegant town, numerous troops of the 4th and 5th Wiltshires, most of them sitting in lines along the side of the street least exposed to the incoming fire, surprisingly cheerful, awaiting the order to advance across the bridge as soon as it was deemed sufficiently safe to do so. What they did not know was that at that moment, just as Stanley had located the Wiltshire's CO, the two of them sitting on the pavement, Stanley scribbling notes on his pad as the colonel listed their requirements, the panzers had managed to reach the road behind them, cutting off their means of supply and, if needed, of retreat.

As Stanley was putting his notepad back in his pocket, a private arrived, giving the colonel a quick salute before squatting down beside him, breathlessly informing him of the situation.

Stanley looked at Hopkins, both of them hearing the report, Hopkins' usually imperturbable expression giving way to alarm.

"Looks like we'll be here a while," Stanley told him quietly, when the colonel had hurried off, crouching as he ran along the street.

For several hours they remained in the same place, picking up what they could as to what was clearly a rapidly changing situation, the street itself, crowded with men, many continuing to await their orders, sitting, chatting and smoking, others on the move, the 4th Wiltshires and the 129th Brigade, heading off across the bridge to attempt to advance the half dozen miles to Arnhem, to relieve the now hard pressed 1st Airborne division.

Having sent Hopkins to see what he could find out about the situation at the rear, he arrived back, his battledress and tin helmet covered with a coating of dust clouding the streets, the result of several nearby buildings being hit by German shells.

"No way back," Hopkins reported, several of the troops sitting close by overhearing him, word being passed amongst them.

"We're fucking cut off," Stanley heard a private say. "Whose idea was this crazy party?"

Soon, a straggle of wounded men began to return across the bridge, some walking, others on stretchers, several of both the wounded and the stretcher bearers being hit by Spandau fire or snipers while crossing the exposed bridge.

It was a grim sight, watching the growing procession heading for the temporary field hospital towards the rear of the town, none of the wounded able to be taken back to the main field hospitals a few miles to the rear, beyond the point where the Germans now controlled the road.

Throughout the day and the long, night, sleep snatched in a few short spells, the information which Stanley was able to obtain was confused, with indications not only of the 1st Airborne being in serious trouble, but the Wyvern units trying to reach them being held well short of Arnhem, and with fierce engagements in every direction, Nijmegen threatened from both sides and the rear.

With daybreak, the mood amongst the troops in the centre of the town was palpably different; subdued and anxious, many of the men now realising that something had gone seriously wrong with the entire operation, the fact that their line of retreat had been severed, compounding the situation.

During the morning, Stanley decided to try to find out what was happening towards the rear, assuming that an urgent attempt would be made to clear the route, it being obvious that by now, supplies, particularly of ammunition for the forward units and field guns, as well as the all important PIATs, were running short. He made his way back through streets congested with men and vehicles – parked lorries, a column of Churchill tanks apparently being held back for fear of exposing them to potential lethal fire if they tried to cross the bridge, as well twenty or so DUKWs which had been brought forward in anticipation of the need for crossing the Waal, or the Rhine if they had been able to get that far, in the event of the bridges being destroyed or still in German hands.

He found the Wiltshires' brigade command post, a brigadier and a number of other officers engaged in what sounded to be fierce argument, the brigadier suddenly raising his voice, silencing the others. He looked up as Stanley approached, noting his RASC insignia.

"Just what we need!" he said with obvious bitterness. "I don't suppose you're brought us any ammo!" It was clearly not a question.

"Just trying to find out what's going on, sir," Stanley said, saluting his superior officer.

"We're expecting to have word any time – "Berlin" if you must know – to tell us to get the hell out of here. But at the moment Jerry is up our arses as well as in our faces. So, captain, for the time being, we're staying put."

The brigadier turned back to the group of officers, gathering them round the map laid out on the top of an improvised table of empty ammunitions boxes.

Turning into a narrow side street, Stanley suddenly found himself alone, a few faces peering at him from the windows of the houses, most of the civilians now cowering indoors.

The street led to a small square, houses along three sides, the fourth open, offering a view back toward the east. He could clearly see the road along which they had made their exhilarating dash forward, several Tiger's now positioned on either side of the road a couple of miles away, men in distinctive grey uniforms, he assumed infantry, moving close to the tanks, some arriving across a field, others along a side road, taking up positions, the tanks' guns pointing in both directions in readiness for attacks from front and rear.

Further back, some four miles he gauged, he could see the flashes of the British guns, but the direction of their fire was not apparent. In all directions, however, there was smoke, some from burning buildings and vehicles, much of it gun smoke, the scene reminding him of a painting he had once seen of the Battle of Waterloo, the vista darkened with the fog of battle, the difference being the absence of the vast numbers of cavalry and marching ranks of distinctively coloured uniformed infantry.

He hurried back to the town centre, finding Hopkins, the two of them managing to locate a radio operator who was able to make contact with the RASC HQ, the operator giving Stanley's message, that they were cut off and enquiring as to the situation at the rear.

"They're hoping to get through before too long," the private said, taking off his headphones.

"That's all?" Stanley asked. "Before too long?"

"That's all they told me, sir. It's the same message all the time. It sounds as if there's something happening but they're not saying much at the moment."

Throughout that second, long night, they – he and Hopkins – spent much of the time in the same main street amongst the disconsolate troops, patiently waiting for they knew not what; whether they were going to be thrown into the fighting continuing on the far side of the river, or trying to re-take control of the road to the rear.

Fatigued as they were, sleep was difficult with the noise of the battle, frequent explosions alarmingly close to them, and, from time to time, orders issued for men to move, platoons forming up in the darkness, silhouettes tinted with the light of fires and guns, marching off in different directions.

With the morning came ever more ominous news of the deteriorating situation, the 1st Airborne now clearly trapped and running low on ammunition, the road to the rear still in German hands, the only glimmer of hope being word of the launch of an offensive to regain control of the road.

At one point, several lorries came through carrying storm boats, the "Berlin" code-named operation, a general withdrawal, now underway, with an attempt to establish a rescue route for the remnants of the 1ˢᵗ Airborne and the units of the now hard pressed Wyverns, holding out against progressively stronger enemy forces, the Germans, under the command of Model, one their finest generals, steadily tightening their stranglehold on the Allied forces on the east side of the Waal.

In the wakeful hours of the night, Stanley's thoughts spiralled between longing and nightmare, the pictures of home – the vicarage coming to him in such detail – and of his beloved Peggy and Anthony – all the more vivid with the realisation that all too soon he could find himself a captive, being marched off to a Stalag, festering for the remainder of the war; or worse, of meeting his end here, in this quaint Dutch town, now the scene of what he realised, could prove to be one of the most decisive battles of the war.

At one point he took out his notepad, intending to write to Peggy, but realised the light was insufficient, his feeling, as he returned the pad to his pocket, of relief that he would not have to resort to the usual bland generalisations. What he wanted so desperately to share with her, the only person to whom he could truly express his innermost feelings, was that he was frightened. This was so different to even the most arduous parts of the Normandy campaign when, during the most intense and bloody fighting, there was a sense of being in control, and confidence that, however tough the going, they would succeed. Now there was a feeling of helplessness; sitting, waiting for whatever the outcome might be. It felt like one of those dreams he had had sometimes in his childhood, when he was trying to run from something he couldn't quite make out, but which he knew to be a malevolent force intent on doing him harm, his legs mired in some clawing inertia.

When several shells fell close to them, he could barely restrain himself from shouting out, imploring God to help him, sweat prickling inside his shirt, screams of pain of wounded men echoing along the street. How strange, he thought, his mind briefly deranged by fear, that such screams sounded just the same whatever one's language, there being no way of knowing if they came from wounded British troops or Dutch civilians.

By the middle of the next day, there was better news, the 32ⁿᵈ Guards Brigade, sent back to try to reopen the road, having been successful, several of the panzers having been destroyed, the Brigade reconnecting with the other elements of XXX Corps, the road now secured as the vital line of supply, and of withdrawal.

It was getting dark when Stanley and Hopkins finally arrived back at RASC HQ, Jock welcoming them with a sardonic "You took your time!", the CO nodding at Stanley with a glimmer of sympathy, unusual for the Lieutenant-Colonel, telling him "You'd better get cleaned up before the briefing," looking at his watch and adding "Half an hour."

The CO having returned two hours earlier from a meeting with Horrocks, Thomas and other senior officers, he was able to reveal to his RASC officers, the full extent of the disaster, the "Berlin" withdrawal operation now being underway, the beleaguered units which had managed to get across the Nijmegen bridge now being brought back, some across the bridge under covering fire from the elements of the 43rd on the west side, others ferried by storm boats at a point in the river which was, fortunately, concealed from the German gunners.

Stanley had now reached a state of fatigue which went beyond the desire for sleep, engendering a capacity which many of them found they possessed in such extreme circumstances, to continue to function. Throughout the night, they went about their business of trying to keep abreast of the deployments to enable them to get supplies to the points where they were required, one lorry, filled with ammunition, being destroyed by "friendly fire", British troops mistaking it for a German vehicle, hitting it with a PIAT, the explosion of the ammunition thunderously loud.

It was not until the following evening that he was able to write, the couple of hours sleep he had been able to snatch in the middle of the day having proved remarkably restorative, the art of "cat-napping" being something they had all acquired, the notion of "a good night's sleep" being yet another element of their dreaming of the lives they longed to return to, although for many of them, it would take many years to adjust to the luxury of unbroken nights.

*23.9.44*
*Capt S R Allen HQ RASC 43 Division   British Liberation Army*
*My dearest darling*
*It is very hard to know what to tell you in this letter, but when I am able to tell you the full story of our adventures in the past days it will indeed be a very full story. This has been easily the most adventurous and exciting week since we've been here, and it is one I shall never forget. I don't know how the news is being put at home as we haven't heard any for days, but it should give you a good idea: the Bosche is far from beaten in this particular party, and the fog of war is very thick. As soon as I can I will tell you all about it but I ask you and all at home – please don't worry at the scarcity of letters for a while. I think that the strain of five years of war is having a bit of an effect of everyone. I long*

*for you so terribly that sometimes it hurts. I long for someone to be with always, to whom I can tell everything, funny little things, worries, jokes – to share the beauty of a September evening, the sudden view of a winding river valley; someone to cheer me up on a wet day and say let's go for a walk; someone to look after my clothes for me with that extra touch that only love provides which a batman will never do; someone to be beside me when I wake up in the middle of the night and to kiss sleepily and then to sleep again enfolded in loving arms; to share disturbed nights and not to mind. The someone is only one person – you my darling Peggy.*

*Darling, I am always thinking of you and I'm afraid they are often naughty thoughts – but such lovely ones! I do so much want to play with your titties and press you so close to me, then for some reason I often want to love you with you sitting on top of me. Darling, do let me have your thoughts and naughty letter!*

*Darling, I must now go to sleep but before I do I want to just ask you to pray for us all out here in the last weeks of our job. As you said, they will probably be the worst.*

*Now my angel girl, I will bid you goodnight. I love & adore you so utterly.*

*Yours for ever my own darling.*

*Stanley*

The withdrawal of the remnants of the 1st Airborne and the rescuing of those units of the 43rd which had crossed to the east side of the river, did little to diminish the intensity of the fighting, the German forces intent of pressing the advantage they had gained. For several days engagements continued, this time, however, the Allies managing to hold their ground, the area known as the "Island", the strip of land between the rivers Waal and Waas which, as well as providing some compensation for the failure of the rashly conceived Market Garden operation, maintained the strategic position, close to the frontier of the Third Reich.

At SHAEF, the Allied High Command, the decision was taken to consolidate after the rapid advance across France and Belgium, also opening up the port of Antwerp, which, having remained effectively under German control by virtue of their continued presence on Schelde island, commanding the approaches, now provided a supply route crucial to the next phase of the campaign.

Montgomery's reputation amongst the SHAEF generals, particularly the Americans, already the subject of growing disquiet, as much due to his abrasive manner and what they considered to be insufferable arrogance, having been further tarnished by the Arnhem failure, Eisenhower, now able to attach less weight to the British Field Marshall's opinions, decided to proceed with the caution which was part of his nature, the thrust into Germany which would, inevitably, be the next stage, assuming that the Russians were unable to get to

Berlin beforehand, and effectively finish off the war, to be planned carefully, and almost certainly now, deferred until the spring.

What neither Eisenhower nor any of the High Command anticipated, however, was the shock they were to suffer in the middle of the approaching winter, a shock which at one stage even seemed to threaten the outcome of the war.

For the ensuing weeks, after Arnhem, as the protagonists remained locked in combat for control of the remaining bridges over the Dutch rivers, there was little movement in the front line, it seeming at times as if, despite the continuing pitch of the fighting, both sides recognised that they were now sparring, albeit with the gloves definitely off, limbering up for the decisive battle they knew must come, the Allies intent on shoring up their positions, anticipating the winter months of limited activity.

For Stanley and the RASC, life once again took on the sort of routine they had become accustomed to during the Normandy days, the call for supplies as demanding as ever, but their delivery functioning efficiently, apart from the occasional hold up, usually due to problems in the supply chain behind them.

Indeed, such was the daily routine that they found time for a certain amount of recreation in the form of visits to local towns, Nijmegen itself proving to be a pleasant place, a number of bars and cafes catering for the troops despite the proximity of the fighting, there also being army facilities including a newly established Wyvern Club offering ENSA shows and films. And within the mess, bridge and monopoly, and occasionally poker, became the regular pastime, modest amounts of money changing hands.

Liquor also became more readily available, the strong local beer and the fiery schnapps proving particularly popular, the availability of whisky adding to the selection.

At moments of reflection, Stanley found himself looking around the mess, his feelings towards his fellow officers equivocal. After Arnhem, there was an even closer bond between them, fraternal and, certainly with some of them, intimate, their emotions, so exposed by what they had been through, raw and shared, few secrets withheld. As with families, however, there were also times when they irritated each other, rows short, quickly resolved.

The CO, Lieutenant-Colonel Reeder, like an irascible father figure, presided over them with a firm hand, having earned their respect, albeit punctuated with spells of rancour, short-lived, but part of the fabric of their complex relationship.

Stanley even acknowledged to Jock and Tommy, that the wretched Mead was a good deal more tolerable that he had been, the episode when he had volunteered to take essential supplies of ammunition across the Seine, risking his life, returning many hours later, muddied, dishevelled and unusually garrulous, earning him new respect, although Stanley could still not escape his own antipathy to the man, his personal habits, uninhibited nose-picking in particular, intensely annoying.

It was during those October weeks that, in spite of – or possibly because of – such closeness and combined efficiency, that Stanley came to realise that he was becoming weary of the routine. He was ready for a new challenge and indeed, was somewhat put out when a couple of the other captains were promoted and transferred. Surely his time must come soon.

For Peggy, little changed, her days passing, one very much like the other. She felt generally quite content, enjoying motherhood, the pleasure of tending to Anthony's needs, playing with him and watching him develop, giving a true sense of purpose to her life although always there was the shadow of Stanley's absence.

She followed the news of what was happening in Europe as avidly as ever, the names and voices – John Snagge, Alvar Liddell, Frank Gillard, Richard Dimbleby – becoming familiar, almost like family members, most of her information coming from the evening news and war report, although she would also study the reports in the *Telegraph* and one or two other papers when they were available.

When news began to filter through that the operation to cross the Rhine at Arnhem, initially proclaimed as Monty's bold initiative to open a route striking at the very heart of Germany, was not going according to plan, her heart sank, anxiety keeping her awake. For those few days, as the reports progressively revealed the scale of the "setback", it affected her far more than any of the difficulties encountered during the Normandy campaign. Everyone's hopes had been so high, with much talk of the war being over by Christmas. Not only were such hopes so cruelly dashed, but the certainty that it was only a matter of time before the war was won, was suddenly brought into question.

How infuriating that it was now taking so long – sometime five or six days – for Stanley's letters to reach her, and when they did arrive, he was not able to tell her much more. As always, however, there were sufficient hints and obtuse references, supplementing the news reports, enabling her to form a pretty good idea of what was happening.

Most of all, however, was the incessant worry about him. Well used, as she now was, to his stock of euphemisms, intended, she knew, to prevent her from worrying, it almost had the reverse effect, the references to life being "hectic", and even more so, his being "extremely busy", telling her that he was caught up in the heat of battle.

She gained some solace from talking to Anthony, pouring her heart out to him, the child either ignoring her, continuing to play with his toys, or looking at her blankly. There were, however, moments when she felt certain that he had some instinctive awareness, his expression one morning when something in a letter reduced her to tears, tearing at her heart, as if he was trying to understand her distress, and to comfort her.

27.9.44

*My darling one*

*I feel rather solemn & have an awful blank inside hearing what has actually happened at Arnhem. I felt that it must be something terrible that was happening there though there was very little about it on the news until tonight. I suppose it is inevitable that we should have some bad patches before the end but this seems an awful disaster of the worst kind war can produce.*

*Do you realise that your son & heir is getting quite grown up as he was nine months old yesterday. He celebrated it by standing with the help of his playpen. He was frightfully pleased with himself & looks so tall standing. After a few minutes he collapsed onto the ground but nothing deterred him and he kept pulling himself up to try again. Quite a number of people have said how like you his is.*

*Daddy is coming down as we hope to cheer him up a bit. He seems very depressed & washed out though his temperature is down. He really does look ill & older too. I wish he could be really fit again but he worries about the office all the time which does not help.*

*A whole lot of planes are going over now flying extremely low. I hope they have good hunting and wreak vengeance for Arnhem on Germany tonight. They seem to have been going over for a very long time & I was afraid they would wake Anthony but he is still sleeping.*

*God bless you my dearest one & all my love is yours for ever.*

*Peggy*

*My very precious darling*

*Arnhem was a bit of a disappointment but of course the tremendous write-up given to the*

$1^{st}$ Airborne Division outweighed the rest of the operation. After all this was only part of the big plan which was ¾ successful.

We are really at war at the moment & everybody is a little keyed up. Since we crossed the Seine there has been twice as much feeling about every mile of our advance. I suppose it was realised that the harvest of blood, toils, tears & sweat was being reaped. Everyone somehow felt a desire the cheer or throw one's cap in the air. There was something unbelievable about the tremendous step after the weeks penned up between Bayeux and Caen, where we knew every corner, every smashed village, and where you couldn't move for mines in the verges or booby traps.

Even the speed of our convoys changed after the Seine. They were not crawling along at the old 20 mph. They raced to keep up with the pace. In this irrepressible mood we entered Belgium on top of ourselves − 'old soldiers' if you like − older & wiser, and yet so unchanged really. The same old Army humour, the Cockney & the Yorkshireman joking & wanting to get home, the same trucks & signs, the same fantastic collection of animals we carry − every division carries chicken, rabbits, dogs and the rest − the troops still shouting and whistling at the girls & brazenly saying what they would do to them (most of them are very faithful when it comes to the point): the same old British Army who will work twice as hard & grumble twice as hard as any Army in the world.

So here we are, at the gates of the $3^{rd}$ Reich, and in the same way we shall beat the Huns finally, and Tommy will take victory as he takes everything else, with a grin and he will say "won't be long now before I'm home for good". That's the overriding interest − when it will end. That is the thought which spurs us on to double efforts: each cheering village is a step nearer Berlin & so a step nearer home − to you my darling, to Anthony, the Hut, our parents, friends, possessions, church, everything that really means life.

I was just thinking of the tremendous progress of the last fortnight: Arnhem was not in vain, darling, as I hope I can show you one day and tell you all about the story from my personal experiences.

Well my beloved, I must really say goodnight. Please God I may be with you soon.

For ever your

Stanley


My darlingest angel

Today we had a shopping expedition and tea at a very good officers club. The "shopping" expedition was a visit to the late Gestapo headquarters which is now open to the Army. It is magnificently furnished and we came away with desks, chairs, blotting paper, drawing pins, carpets, paper baskets, electric lamps, and the rest. The chief thing that I was interested in was the carpet which is now a comfortable addition to my penthouse.

The club is quite new and is like a very improved version of the Canterbury one, plus a cinema, showing yesterday 'Fanny by Gaslight', and today, 'This Happy Breed (which I didn't manage to see)'. Darling it was extraordinary to go to a 'Dansant' in a room rather like the restaurant of the Odeon at Ashford, and have a free tea with cream buns. The place is run by Dutch equivalent of the WVS. There were very few girls and about 500 officers so the CO, Doc and I just enjoyed our very good full tea!.

We have certainly done well out of the Bosche for apart from free gin & rum we have captured a vast stock of cigars, and the result is an issue of 17 to every man and officer in the Division.

Darling, it was marvellous of you to buy the low books for me. While on the subject of nude pictures, can you not produce some yourself? You don't keep me at all well supplied in photos of you and Anthony – consider yourself brassed off!

I must see you again soon as it is so unbearable without you. The physical need of a woman is very great, but darling, for me it can only be one woman. Even if one had intercourse with a woman here, it would make no difference. Do you remember how we used to discuss life for me abroad? Well you never need wonder about me as I've never wanted to go with another woman, though to be honest, the chances have been many.

My arm is aching as I am writing in bed, by torchlight, so my darling girl I'll say goodnight and auf wiedersehen

Yours for ever

Stanley

She could never quite understand how, even during his "very busy" times, he still seemed to think about sex. She had realised by now, that there was a sort of undercurrent, pervading the army, of what he referred to as "randiness". She imagined that it stemmed from men being together, without females – apart from those they encountered during their travels, although she was convinced – confidently dismissing the pervasive tendrils of doubt - that Stanley would never partake of what was clearly on offer – and, as with young men congregating anywhere, lewdness was simply part of their discourse.

His declaration of absolute commitment to her made her feel quite elated, suppressing, at least for the time being, the ever nagging knowledge that temptation was ever being thrown into his path. Even the minute strand of niggling cynicism, that made her wonder whether such unabashed frankness might be a clever way of disguising the truth, that he had allowed himself to stray, evaporated in her wave of happiness. Yes, she was certain that he was not capable of such deceit.

She tried to picture him, lying in his "penthouse", which she always imagined to be a sort of deep, damp trench, rather like a grave, writing to her, his mind filled with erotic thoughts about her, undeterred by whatever dreadful things were going on close by. It was as if, once he was down there, below the ground, he could detach himself, thus allowing his mind to turn to "naughty" thoughts – and deeds.

Difficult as it was at times, to comprehend, it nevertheless gave her a particular thrill, the idea of him lying there, safely in his trench, dreaming of her body, conjuring up images of erotic couplings, such thoughts often enhancing her part of their "dates". She wondered as well, how much he told the other officers. Did they share their most private thoughts? There were things he said in his letters which suggested that they had few secrets.

*11.10.44*

*My very dear one*

*I feel so very happy tonight as such a wonderful letter arrived at tea time. Your letters take about six days now.*

*Wouldn't it be fun to have a Gestapo carpet in our home. The cigars and drinks sound good too.*

*Darling, I do like your naughty letters so don't worry about what you write. I think your diagram is ever so funny with me suspended in mid air or doing a balancing trick! I get the idea though and we will certainly try it out one day though I think your tummy might get rather squashed – may be you wouldn't mind! I thought it would be rather a good idea for me to lie on the bed with your legs over the side but I can't think where you would be.*

*I must give up drawing diagrams as they have quite the wrong effect on Peggy – the sort of wrong effect that would be so wonderful if you were here to share it. I so want you in the minutes I have on my own in my wildly busy life!*

*Yours very much in love for ever*

*Peggy*

He awoke with a feeling of panic, the darkness in his dugout, profound, the night silent. For a moment he wondered if he was dead, such was the absence of any sensation he could discern, but reaching out, he pressed his palm against the wall of damp earth, and as he did so, heard Jock's quiet breathing close by.

Yet it was not the fact that a lull in the fighting allowed such unexpected quiet, an owl hooting, some soft footsteps on the grass nearby, presumably the changeover of those on guard duty, which caused his panic, his pulse thumping in his ears. His waking was from a dream – a nightmare – which, as so often, featured Peggy, only this time, as she walked towards him, he could not see her face. Instead, there was simply the shape of her head, like a half finished portrait, the eyes and features absent, awaiting the artist's application. He knew he was trying to say something to her, his desperation rising as he sensed that she was trying to reply but had no mouth to form any words.

As he lay in the dark, staring up at the canvas of the tent which covered the dugout, a glimmer of light now giving it slight texture, he tried to conjure up the image which, until now, had always been there, safely stored in his imagination, enabling him to look at it, to commune with her, whenever he needed to do so. But the image was gone.

He reached for his torch, screwing up his eyes as the beam illuminated the small space, pointing it at the photos pinned to the wall close to his face, his finger tips touching her face.

As he lay on his side, staring at the photo, the silence was shattered by a barrage from what he could gauge to be the closest of the twenty-five pounders, about half a mile from the HQ. Realising that he would not get back to sleep, he climbed up through the tent flap, the flashing of the guns lessened by the approaching dawn.

As he was walking the short distance to the wood which ran along one side of the field in which they were camped, preferring to have his first piss in the open rather than using the rank smelling latrine, it being accepted that the wooden "thunder box" was "reserved for crapping", the unmistakable "whoosh" of incoming shells made him dive onto the ground, just as several explosions erupted a hundred yards beyond the camp, one hitting a parked lorry, lifting it several feet off the ground like a child's toy, the lorry crashing down on its side, one wheel spinning, its fuel tank suddenly igniting, a ball of fire consuming the entire vehicle.

He was about to get to his feet when another salvo fell into the wood just ahead of him, causing him to flatten himself to the wet ground, the shards of shrapnel fizzing far too close to him.

Gingerly, he lifted his head, slowly getting to his feet, seeing the shattered trunks of the trees at the exact spot which he favoured for his morning commune with nature.

"God Almighty!" he gasped, relieving himself in the open field, feeling his heart racing and his hands shaking.

"Christ, man," Jock exclaimed as Stanley climbed back down into the dugout to gather up his cap and belt before making his way to the RASC HQ tent. "I thought you were done for. Why don't you use the lats like the rest of us."

"Just as likely to get it there," he said, hearing the tremulousness of his voice.

"Guess so," Jock conceded, "but at least you've got the lat trench to dive into."

"I think I'd rather risk getting my head blown off than dive into that stinking shit-hole."

Jock gave his throaty laugh, roughened by his taste for the strongest Old Holborn tobacco.

Stanley had an aversion to the latrines, the long, open trenches, with a screen of canvas separating them from rest of the camp but, behind the screen, no privacy between those squatting on the wooden plank, defecating into a communal trench, its foul odour frequently overwhelming the Jayes fluid sluiced into it periodically, the urinal trench, close by, exuding less of stench but equally devoid of privacy.

Although he had become used to performing his bodily functions in such communal facilities, urinating in such circumstances by now second nature, he could not rid himself of what he was sure was some instinctive need to defecate in private.

With his role principally concerned with ensuring the division was fully supplied with ammunition and fuel, he nevertheless had to turn his attention from time to time to the matter of food, considered by most of the troops as of paramount importance, the old adage that "an army fights on its stomach" being as applicable to a division of the Second Army engaged in modern warfare as it had been to fighting men in the days of Agincourt and Waterloo.

For most of the time, the food supply arrangements worked reasonably well, the basics, "M&V" (pre-packed meat and vegetable stew), bully beef, biscuits and tea, arriving in bulk and being easy to store and to distribute. There was, however, great demand for additional produce, the availability of which varied according to the locality, the farmers of the coastal parts of Normandy having been regarded as decidedly stingy, driving hard bargains, unlike their compatriots in the *bocage*, although their greater generosity combined with the duration of that phase of the campaign, resulted in serious supply shortages, the fact that much of the populace had left the area to escape the fighting, and the destruction inflicted on their homes and villages, limiting availability. There had, however, been a degree of compensation by virtue of dead cattle, caught in the crossfire, numerous carcases left to rot in the field, their stench contributing to the miasma, a malodourous mix of decay – human as well as bovine – latrines, exhaust fumes, cordite, as well as hundreds of thousands of unwashed men, certain RASC members acquiring the ability to identify the carcases still sufficiently fresh to be transported to the divisional kitchens.

Here in Holland, a richly productive agrarian country, cattle and pigs were plentiful, the fertile land also producing an abundance of dairy produce and fruit, the problem being the edicts issued from High Command, forbidding their consumption unless they were duly paid for, the Dutch insisting on "market" prices, stretching the paltry army budgets for such additions.

Fortunately, for the troops' stomachs, the death rate amongst farm stock was as extensive as in Normandy, the fact that much of the rural populace had fled the area of most intensive fighting, resulting in the edicts being modified to the allow the consumption of dead animals if the farmers consented, or, in the absence of such consent, the carcases would otherwise be left to rot.

With the Allies now being so proximate to the borders of the Reich, a further proviso was introduced, allowing consumption of German stock which had either been captured – the incidence of capture being limited to the few forays into German territory which succeeded in procuring such bounty – or if the creatures happened to cross into Holland.

"Bit difficult to tell a German pig from its Dutch cousin," Jock quipped, when a platoon returned from patrol with two large dead pigs which they insisted had been loitering close to the border and which they had cunningly enticed across with offerings of apples, the creatures then being hastily dispatched.

"We did not have time to interrogate them!" the platoon sergeant reported, presenting the carcases to the RASC, seeking the necessary authority to deliver them to the division's butchers.

"Permission granted!" the CO said with a nod of acknowledgment of the veracity of the account, his response being widely reported through the camp with the result that the frequency of animals straying across the border noticeably increased, greatly enhancing the divisional diet.

"Jesus effing Christ!" Tommy Atkins exclaimed, clamping his hands over his ears at the eruption of firing, the order having been issued for what was referred to as the "Mad Minute", at seven fifteen in the evening, when every gun – field guns, automatic weapons, rifles – blasted the German lines with as much rapid fire as they could muster for a single minute, invariably invoking a response in kind. The word was that the practice was intended to impress newly arrived reinforcements as much at the enemy, whose often lethal response soon put pay to the practice.

"Waste of bloody ammo," Stanley complained to the CO, who made the same comment to the Divisional CO.

# EIGHTEEN

With the first hints of approaching winter – several clear frosty nights and days of pristine clarity alternating with rain and chill winds blowing in from the North Sea - the 43rd Division remained static, successfully fulfilling its task of retaining the all important "Island" with the bridges over the Waas and the Waal, the Island seen as the essential springboard for the assault on the German Fatherland, when the time was deemed right.

Throughout October, the fighting continued, the enemy being able to hold onto the northern end of the Island, each side making forays into each other's territory but without any substantive change in the front line between them.

It was a strange period, the fighting at times seeming as intense as it had been in Normandy, and yet the absence of movement and of new objectives, making it feel less arduous, notwithstanding the continuing toll of casualties.

The fact that the Divisional CO, Lieutenant-General Thomas, was satisfied that the Division was well able to hold the Island, encouraged him to initiate a new training regime.

In private, he had conceded that he felt that, despite its successes in the campaign so far, the Division was showing signs of fatigue, it being essential to get it back to the necessary levels of fitness, mental and physical, for the rigours of what lay ahead.

On the establishing of the "Battle School" in a large mansion in a suburb of Nijmegen, he addressed his assembled officers in his familiar clipped speech.

"Gentlemen, we must get back to the alert, proud stride of the British soldier who realises he is the conqueror – knows it and knows he has proved it. The motto of the 43rd Division is that "Nothing but the best will do". It still remains true and it is only by sticking to it that we shall be able to maintain the impetus and standard of our battles, at least one of which has already been referred to as a classic victory."

Stanley and Tommy exchanged a glance, sharing the thought that the last thing they wanted was more training, their firm opinion being that they, the divisional RASC, were a well honed unit, delivering every requirement, even during the fiercest of engagements.

"Which battle was that?" Jock asked in a whisper, their assumption being that the CO was probably referring to Mount Pincon although there were certainly other candidates, including the Seine crossing and, despite its failure, Arnhem, the Wyverns having played a key role in the rescue of the 1st Airborne.

Thomas handed over to the designated commandant of the Battle School, a battle-hardened, popular officer, Major Grubb, known for his fervent belief in modern training, far removed from old fashioned square bashing, his determination being to prepare the troops for the type of fighting they were likely to encounter in the months ahead, attuning their tactics to the enemy whose ways had become familiar to them.

Grubb also believed in mental fitness, an unlikely facet of which was to require troops to go into battle in fresh battle dress.

"You are going to get muddied and blooded soon enough, but when you march into battle, I want you feeling fresh, and believing in yourself."

"That's one we didn't see coming," Mead said gloomily, when they returned to the RASC HQ tent.

"Better get on with it then," Stanley replied. "New battle dress for fifty thousand men! Good luck, Mead." The other officers grinned as a crest-fallen Mead slunk away, delegated with the task of procuring the additional uniforms.

"Ridiculous!" he was heard to mutter as he stalked out of the tent.

"I'm afraid we have to be on parade at 10.00 hours tomorrow," the CO announced at one of their evening briefings. "Polished and blancoed. VIP visitors. Can't say more at the moment."

It was only when, with several hundred officers and men drawn up to form three sides of a square encompassing much of the field a mile from Nijmegen, with the three large staff cars slowly drawing up in the middle, chauffeurs climbing out and opening the rear doors, that the identity of their visitors was revealed.

"Christ, it's the Monarch!" Jock gasped.

"And Winnie!" Stanley added. "Bloody hell! And Monty!"

The King, wearing his Field Marshall's uniform, stood for a moment, looking around him as if bemused to find himself the centre of attention, his slightly drooping shoulders and worried expression, suggesting a man less than comfortable with his role, contrasting with the air of self confidence the cigar puffing Churchill exuded, and the self important strut of Montgomery.

The Divisional CO having saluted the arrivals, conducted them to one end of the ranks, King, Prime Minister and Field Marshall, followed by several of their military entourage, processing in front of each phalanx before returning to their cars, all except for Churchill departing for the Divisional HQ, the PM remaining, accompanied by a divisional brigadier and his own aid-de-camp, making for one of the twenty-five pounder emplacements where, as was his habit, like a child eager to play with a new toy, he insisted on being allowed to fire a few rounds, much to the consternation of those accompanying him, fearing retaliatory fire.

"Well that was short and sweet," Stanley said as they resumed their work.

"The Monarch looked pretty knackered, didn't you think?" Jock said. "Not surprising, I suppose, if he's on a conducted tour of the whole Second Army."

*My darling sweetheart*
*I didn't manage to find any lined boots. I think I shall have to get them in town. I want to go up soon for a day so I will go to Simpsons & Lillywhites.*
*I have sent off a parcel to you this afternoon with haircream & soda nuts, notepaper & coffee, besides a styptic pencil which I thought might be useful for cuts or scratches. There is a pound of coffee (2/8 if it is for the mess) & I will send some more next week. It is a bit difficult to pack but I think I will buy it already in tins in future. Boxes are a bit difficult to get so if you could manage to send that one back it would be very useful. I don't expect you have still got the one I sent your hat in, have you?*
*My sweet darling, I was not very serious when I teased you about "if" because I am just not worried. I think I've grown too deep to lack faith or have doubts. I guess if you have survived, or rather refused the offers so far, I don't expect there will be so much in that way from now on. I don't mind you mentally undressing pretty girls as long as it is not actually! Sweetheart mine, I don't mind kisses for conquering heroes. I am glad for it must cheer life up when it has been hard.*
*I am afraid I am not good enough at drawing to draw pin-up pictures. People, especially in the nude, are extremely difficult to draw.*
*Anthony has a nasty cough. I think it may be mild whooping cough although it doesn't seem to trouble him too much.*
*Now my so very dear sweet husband, goodnight.*
*Yours for all time*
*Peggy*

*20.10.44*

*Capt S R Allen HQ RASC 43 Division   British Liberation Army*

*My darling*

*Thank you darling for another sweet letter.*

*Anthony, I hope you won't forget what your old Dad looks like all these months I'm away! Though you probably won't recognise him with a moustache!*

*I expect you have seen that the Monarch has been to see us. I got my closest view of him and he was accompanied by a batch of celebrities. Apparently he was quite amusing, according to the higher officers who shook hands with him. The Prime Minister is very amusing when he visits us – he always insists on doing something peculiar and goes up to some gunner battery and says "What about a few rounds" and then he gives the fire order.*

*Do you remember I told you about the party the other night? The Doc was very amusing and one of his brightest remarks was this – "If friction causes heat, how many fucks would it take to boil a kettle?" He said that this was his sole contribution to science.*

*The last twenty four hours have been the stormiest we've yet had to put up with – terrific squalls and very heavy rain which has just swamped us out. My penthouse has survived well and no rain seems to have come in. Alas, I was duty officer last night & had to sleep in the office penthouse which leaked like a sieve with the result that I spent a bloody awful night! It was a horrid scene everywhere this morning – the mud in places came up over my Wellingtons. Tommy & I both felt browned off so we went to a cinema show – it wasn't bad, called 'Four Jills in a Jeep' – song and dance and lovely little Carole Landis asking for it.*

*Peggy, mine, I'll be yours, loving you utterly for ever.*

*Stanley*


*Dear Anthony*

*I do hope you've stopped whooping cough, old man, and please try and not squeak too much & tire Mummy out. Daddy hopes to be home soon and will then keep Mummy occupied so you must learn not to in advance!*

*Your loving Daddy*


It was in the last week of October that the change which Stanley had been hoping for, suddenly became a reality; a change which would present him with renewed challenges and responsibilities as well as, at times, putting him in the face of considerable danger.

After the exhilaration of the triumphal race across north-east France and Belgium, and the torridly disappointing set back at Arnhem, the ensuing few weeks had felt almost dull in comparison, in spite of the incessant fighting.

When Eric Nicholls paid a visit during the third week of October, Stanley was delighted to see his old friend, now a colonel in the 51$^{st}$ Highland Division which was fighting alongside the 43$^{rd}$ as part of Montgomery's Second Army.

Ostensibly a brief courtesy call following a joint session of senior officers, Stanley was eager to find out whether Eric had been able to find a position for him, as he had long been hinting, offering Stanley the best – and indeed, the only – immediate prospect of moving on and, hopefully, upwards.

"You'll have to wait a few more days before it's confirmed officially," Eric told him when they were alone together, strolling through an orchard close to the fringes of Nijmegen, "but I've got the OK for you to come across to the 51$^{st}$."

Never one to disguise his feelings, Stanley's face lit up with delight.

"Eric, that's the most welcome news."

"It's going to be *Major* Allen, and you'll be my Senior Supply Officer." Stanley noticed the familiar twinkle in his friend's pale blue eyes, the well etched crow's feet creasing into a smile.

For the next week, Stanley could barely contain himself, so desperate was he to break the news to Peggy, Eric having told him that he must treat the matter as strictly confidential until the official announcement.

When it came to it, those few days proved to be exceptionally busy, the Germans launching an unexpected offensive, Model deploying no fewer than four panzer divisions in his determined attempt to drive Horrocks' XXX Corps from the Island and to re-take Nijmegen.

For three days the fighting was frenetic and confused, the enemy managing to penetrate Allied territory, in one instance, a Wyvern reconnoitring detachment, returning to their base, stumbling upon a German patrol digging in, apparently oblivious to the fact that they were well behind the Allied line, the Hampshires being sent to deal with them, managing to winkle them out and secure the line.

For the RASC, the fragmented nature of the fighting presented acute problems, the information reaching them as to the positions of the active units, and of their requirements, sketchy, communications, radio and telephone, erratic, reports from messengers often arriving too late, the situation on the ground changing rapidly.

For nearly two days, Stanley and his fellow RASC officers lived through what they would afterwards refer to as one of their worst nightmares, floundering in the dark, knowing full well that with the intensity of the fighting, some units would inevitably be running short of ammunition, but without knowing their precise positions, they were unable to support them.

"What are you suggesting?" Stanley asked Mead who, as far as he could gather, was offering to take a couple of lorries in the general direction of the main area of engagement. "Just driving around until you find the right place to unload? God Almighty, man, that's sheer madness!"

In reality, it was something they were all considering, such was the extent of their desperation.

Fortunately – for purposes of fighting this battle - it was food rather than ammunition which was in short supply, the Wyverns managing to hold their ground and eventually, to push the Germans back, in the process, capturing several enemy positions, and their stocks of rations, the British troops complaining vociferously about the unpalatable black bread, tinned black pudding and caraway flavoured biscuits, their grievance assuaged to some extent by the capture of a quantity of brandy and Dutch gin.

The expectation was now that they would remain where they were, holding onto the Island, the Divisional HQ and multiple billets spread around Nijmegen and in various locations west of the town. Indeed, there was soon a feeling of being remarkably settled into their new surroundings, their Dutch "hosts" proving to be most hospitable.

Many of the officers, Stanley included, received invitations to visit Dutch homes, becoming familiar with their rather gloomy interiors. The houses here seemed far more foreign than those they had visited in France and Belgium, part of the strangeness being, what to them, was the rather ugly and uncomfortable furniture, many walls hung with pictures just as gloomy as the houses, dark vistas of flat land, even the portraits appearing sombre. And on every surface there were photographs, as if there was a need to display one's entire extended family.

Stanley encountered the tall, middle aged Johan Van Dies when negotiating the purchase of various produce, the Dutchman being the proprietor of a grocery business which, even now, with the devastation of so much of the surrounding farm land, was still able to source produce, the resourceful Van Dies having managed to find ways of transporting products from different areas, less affected by the fighting, the country as a whole remaining highly productive.

Stanley took an instant liking to Van Dies, warming to his courteous, affable manner, the Dutchman similarly recognising an affinity with this pleasantly good natured English officer. The fact that the Dutchman spoke excellent English made a considerable difference both to their business dealings and what was to become a close, if short lived, friendship.

Invited to dinner, Van Dies introduced Stanley to his wife, Hansje, the pronunciation rolling off the Dutchman's tongue, Stanley's repetition of it, "Ansia", causing husband and wife to laugh benevolently.

"Hans-yia". She enunciated slowly, as if to a child.

"And this is our daughter, Eva." Stanley held out his hand, the strikingly beautiful girl, whom Stanley reckoned to be about twenty or so, taking it, holding it lightly, smiling coyly, her eyes, almost duck-egg blue, inspecting his face before glancing away. "Eva speaks a little English but Hansje, I'm afraid does not."

"We have a son, Pieter," Van Dies added, the smile fading from his face. "But he is away somewhere. We have not heard from him for more than a month. We believe he is with the resistance. We only hope…" He looked at his wife who, hearing her son's name, became similarly saddened, her husband gently touching her hand.

In spite of their obvious anxiety about their son, there having been a number of recent reports of Dutch resistance fighters having been captured and summarily executed by the Germans, it was a convivial evening, Van Dries telling Stanley about his family, the history of Nijmegen, and about Dutch art, about which he was clearly well informed. It was towards the end of the evening, Stanley feeling decidedly drunk after good measures of gin and wine, Van Dries now producing an earthenware bottle which he said was a "very good" schnapps, surprised Stanley by putting on a record of Glen Miller.

"You may dance if you wish," he said, gesturing to his daughter. "Eva, I'm sure the Captain would like you to accompany him."

Had it not been for the liquor, Stanley would have found it most embarrassing, to dance in the confines of a small living room, his partner's parents seated, beaming, as if watching an entertaining show, Van Dries nodding with the rhythm of *String of Pearls*, Eva, her ballroom hold at first nervously stiff, relaxing as she sensed his ease of movement and absence of accomplishment.

"So sorry!" he said as he clumsily trod on her foot. "Bit out of practice."

"It does not matter," she replied, the striking eyes looking up at him. She was tall, he guessed five foot ten, an inch or so more than Peggy, with her father's high cheek bones and angular features, her blond hair simply cut, unstyled but suited to her. He could see also, that her skin was perfectly smooth, light olive, with a sheen of health.

With the expectation of remaining in the vicinity for some weeks, possibly months, facilities for the troops were steadily improved, an officer's club being opened in Nijmegen although its opening hours were necessarily intermittent due to enemy shelling. A good deal safer was the Wyvern Country Club, a few miles out of the town, the divisional caterers, with RASC assistance, managing to provide a surprising range of fare, the Club accommodating up to 150 guests at any one time, the residential facilities, basic, yet a definite improvement on the conditions they were used to, notwithstanding the pervasive smell of cow dung from the adjacent farms, and the incessant traffic noise, the Second Army's vehicles passing by day and night.

"I've met a rather nice Dutch girl," Tommy announced a couple of days before they were due to attend a dance at the Officers Club. "I thought I might ask her to come. What about you, Stanley? Are you going to bring the one you were talking about?"

"I hadn't thought about it," Stanley replied with a shrug to suggest he had not considered the possibility. In fact, he had been wrestling with the idea, and with the guilt he already felt, even before coming to a decision, part of which was his conclusion that if he did ask her, he probably wouldn't be able to mention it to Peggy as she would inevitably jump to the wrong conclusion.

"Mm," Jock murmured sceptically. "Anyway, there's a chance they may have to bring their brothers or cousins with them. They don't seem to be allowed to go near a chap, even a British officer with honourable intentions" – he paused to emit his husky laugh – "without a chaperone in tow."

They had learned by now that the Dutch code of morality, rigidly applied by the better families whose company they had been enjoying, insisted that unmarried girls should always be accompanied by a companion, preferably male if available, hence the curious site of trios walking the town's streets and parks, the British soldier, with a local girl on his arm, saddled with the unwelcome chaperone, it having become something of a game, trying various ruses to shake off them off.

"Eva's brother is apparently with the resistance," Stanley said.

"Well, you might just strike lucky then," Jock replied, with another croak of laughter.

When Stanley cautiously broached the subject with Van Dries, the response was unexpectedly enthusiastic, with no mention of a chaperone.

"She will enjoy meeting so many British officers," the Dutchman said, "who I know are men of integrity." He looked at Stanley for a moment, as if to ensure his inference was understood.

Delayed by a small scale but fierce engagement which erupted when a reconnaissance patrol ran into enemy infantry trying to sneak behind the Allied line, resulted in a sudden demand for ammunition, with Stanley, as duty RASC officer, having to remain until the hiatus had died down, he missed the first half of the dance, having had to send Hopkins to the Van Dries house with a message that he would be late. For the remaining two hours, however, he and Eva danced to almost every number played by the remarkably accomplished band, supplied by ENSA, their repertoire comprising most of the current favourites, the modest dance floor being thronged, the girls whom officers had brought with them supplemented by a contingent of waitresses and chambermaids from local hotels and restaurants, the Club staff having extend invitations to ensure a sufficiency of dance partners.

It was when they sat down at a table during the band's interval that Eva told him something of what life had been like during the German occupation, explaining tentatively, that her father had, of necessity, had to have dealings with the occupiers to safeguard his family, and in particular, to protect her. She paused before adding, quietly, that the expectation of the German officers was that families would offer their daughters to them.

Stanley had heard accounts of the level of cooperation of some of the Dutch people, such accounts sitting uneasily with the stories of resistance and of German cruelty and retribution.

"Did you, you know, have to *meet* German officers?" Stanley asked, something in Eva's account suggesting reticence, evoking his curiosity.

"We would sometime go to their club, a bit like this one, or to one of the restaurants which they liked to visit. My father had to be careful to, how to you say…"

"Keep in with them?" Stanley suggested.

"Yes, keep in with them. It was good for his business."

The significance of what she was saying instantly hit him and he was about to pursue the matter, wanting now to find out the extent of Van Dries's cooperation, when the band struck up with *You Always Hurt The One You Love,* Eva standing up, leading him back to the dance floor.

"We walk from here?" she suggested, she and Stanley in the back of the car, the silence between them weighing heavily, Stanley acutely aware of there being unfinished business, there having been no opportunity to resume their conversation, the awkwardness now amplified by Hopkins' presence.

"Drop us here, Hopkins," Stanley said brusquely, he and Eva climbing out of the car. "I'll make my own way back."

It was a clear, cold night, the gunfire relatively sporadic, the night, as so often, filled with the sound of heavy vehicles, movements regularly made under the cover of darkness, not so much because of concern about the occasional *Luftwaffe* raid, but more because of the proximity of the German observation posts, certain of them on higher ground to the north of the town, towards the *Reichswald* forest.

As they began to walk along the street leading towards the area where the Van Dries family lived, Eva took hold of Stanley's arm, pulling him to face her.

"I know it was bad, what my father did. And what I did."

The street was dark, without any streetlights or lights showing in houses, such light as there was being the glimmer from the starry night sky and the flickering of guns. He could see the pain of her expression, tears trickling down her cheeks.

"What was bad?" he asked her gently, putting his hands on her shoulders. Dropping her hands to her sides, she leaned against him, her head resting on his shoulder, facing away from him as if this made it easier for her to offer her explanation.

"Papa only wished for us to be safe. And I knew what I must do." He could feel her shaking with a convulsion of sobbing. "We knew that if I was the *friend* of one officer, and if Papa cooperated with them, that would make us safe."

"*Friend,*" Stanley repeated. "Do you mean you *went* with a German? And that your father was a *collaborator?*" He was picturing Van Dries's face as he had referred to British officers as being men of integrity, now recognising something else in his expression; a hint of conflicting emotions.

By way of answer, she emitted a loud sob, her body pressed against him, her hair against his face. He wanted to push her away yet at the same time, some feeling of compassion compelled him to comfort her. He pulled back, lifting her face towards him, the streaks of tears catching the light.

"I'm sorry," he said, wondering why he was apologising to her. "I cannot begin to understand what it must have been like."

They walked the rest of the way to her house in silence, his arm round her shoulders, she leaning against him. When they came to the house, she turned to him.

"I am sorry to have done such a bad thing," she said, this time, speaking more resolutely, as if making her confession. "I will always have to live with it."

He went to kiss her on the cheek, but as he did so, she turned her face, his lips meeting hers, the kiss brief but fraught with feelings which would linger with him; the wave of affection and pity he felt for her, riven with the guilt which was already weighing upon him.

"You need to be a bit wary of that Van Dries," Mead said to him the next day. "Word is that he was a collaborator and that he's not too popular around these parts."

Stanley could hear the note of satisfaction in Mead's voice but decided not to rise to the pointed comment.

"He had no choice but to deal with them," he replied curtly.

The invitation he received from Van Dries two days later, to dine again with the family, he politely declined when meeting the Dutchman to conclude a transaction for dairy produce.

"I'm afraid we are having a rather busy time," he said, trying to convey the coldness which he knew he should be showing and yet saddened when Van Dries simply bowed his head by way of acknowledgment, the gesture clearly implying that he fully understood the reason for the refusal.

"Eva will be disappointed as well."

When Peggy's letter arrived, he was overwhelmed with such a feeling of love for her that he felt a lump in his throat as he read her accounts of her wonderfully ordinary activities.

*Sweetheart beloved*
*Your lovely letter arrived this morning. I have decided that it had been opened by the censor. It was the one about doing it in the bath. I hope he felt enlightened on the subject! I will try my best to get the boots but they seem to be very scarce as I have had answer from Lillywhites saying that their stocks are sold out.*
*I packed the pillowcases, the socks I knitted & some tins of coffee up today. I hope you get them soon darling. I don't think you can buy thermos flask corks but we had an old one so I have put it in in case it may be better than yours.*
*Darling, Churchill's statement to the Commons made me feel a bit depressed though, saying that the war with Germany would not be over till the end of Spring or even into the Summer. I think we got a bit over optimistic. It really will be good if Germany is finished off in under a year when you think of how momentous a task it sounded.*
*I should have liked to have heard General Horrocks especially about the Wyverns. I feel very proud of my old man.*
*It is an amazing thought about the possibility of leave as I never thought there was a real chance of you getting any. It would be grand to have a party in town, then a few rather homely days in the hut plus Anthony.*
*I am now very sleepy so must say goodnight sweetheart & God bless you darlingest one. Yours with all my love for ever*
*Peggy*

When the formal notification of his promotion and transfer arrived, everything happened quickly, which he felt was just as well, so that he could get on with the new job, and hopefully, avoid any lingering farewells from the Division which had been so much part of his life for those long years of training and, latterly, through the battles of Normandy and Holland.

*30.10.44*
*Capt S R Allen HQ RASC 43 Division, British Liberation Army*
*My own darling*
*This will be the last letter I write from this address because I leave here on Wednesday to join Eric Nicholls in 51ˢᵗ Division. I hope my last letter prepared you for this rather surprising news. Actually it is not so surprising to me as I was recommended for better things in July. This posting is the result of many wangles & Eric has certainly done a fantastic amount to get me. I shall be terribly sorry to leave so many friends in 43rd, but it's nice to know that one's efforts are not entirely unnoticed. Also I've just about had enough of P.Mead & co!*
*I'm taking Hopkins with me I'm glad to say – he's quite excited about it and is trying to scrounge some crowns for me. It will make a slight difference to pay, but of course, the income tax increases as well.*
*Today has been bitterly cold: in fact our first real taste of winter weather. It seems that it was bound to snow this afternoon but it's turned to rain.*
*I wish you were with me tonight darling, to help celebrate. I've only had two or three drinks as it doesn't improve my cold.*
*I don't think I've told you that the job I'm getting is Major, APS (i.e. Ammunition, Petrol and Supplies) – S.Sup.O (Senior Supply Officer) as it is more often called here.*
*Well, darling, your snuffly husband must go to bed now: I shall be very busy tomorrow saying goodbye and packing up. You can imagine my feelings – very elated, mingled with sorrow at leaving this really great division with whom I've been happy, bored, and in every state of human emotion for nearly four years.*
*I am for ever your adoring*
*Stanley*

# NINETEEN

*2.11.44*

*Major S R Allen HQ RASC 51ˢᵗ (Highland) Division, British Liberation Army*

*My own sweet darling*

*Well here I am after a very hectic last day with 43rd. I have never shaken hands with so many people in all my life. We had a colossal drunk – the chief drunks were (as usual) Leslie, Tony, Tommy, Doc, Postey and Ginger. I was pretty lit up by teatime. We sang the usual songs and the night passed quickly. At 11 Leland went and Postey passed out about 12.30 & was carried out with three liquefied candles stuck to him.*

*The party got wilder & wilder – singing, piano quartets, 'horse-play' & the rest. We all went to our tents at 3am.*

*I awoke with a prince of hangovers & Hopkins remarked that whenever we moved I was suffering from one! I rapidly recovered though, and feeling very sad, though fortified with a few more drinks, I left the 43ʳᵈ Division (God bless it) at 5 past one on 1ˢᵗ November and by 4.30 I was S Sup O to Eric Nicholls.*

*So here I am with a lot of Scotsmen. For the first time since Biddenden I'm sleeping with a roof over my head. I'm billeted for tonight in a very nice billet – a lovely comfortable bed & there are 2 other officers also here. The house is owned by four old Dutch ladies who seem very kind.*

*Hopkins is of course, with me. I feel very happy at being with Eric again & not nearly so sad as I feared. I think I must inadvertently be getting used to goodbyes.*

*The first day as a 'new boy' is always the worst, but this one has passed off pleasantly enough and I hope successfully for me. I have met dozens of people, as Eric has been taking me round introducing me to all the people one meets in this job; lots of Scotsmen with 8ᵗʰ Army ribbons but I think I can cope with them though they can never forget the blasted desert. I crack 43rd up to the skies – they've done far far better than this div: this div gets terrific publicity, though, wherever it goes.*

*Give all my love to Anthony and tell him about Daddy's new job! To you, my angel precious, God bless & all my everlasting love and kisses.*

*From your passionately in love husband*

*Stanley*

In terms of distance, Stanley's move was modest, the 51ˢᵗ Highland Division's current area of operation being close to that of 43ʳᵈ, both divisions engaged in the continuing battle for control of the Island and surrounding territory, the features of the area – its great rivers and network of canals – defining the fighting, the waterways providing effective lines of defence for the Germans and challenges for the Allies.

The fighting, however, was by no means one way, with the enemy contesting every inch of territory as well as mounting regular counter-attacks, the overall scenario thus being fragmented and often confused.

The day after his arrival, word reached the RASC HQ of a bizarre incident when a German supply unit mistakenly arrived late one evening in the midst of the encampment of part of the Seaforths, one of the 51$^{st}$ Division's regiments, only realising their mistake when their officer, on entering a tent which he assumed to be the command post, found himself face to face with a group of khaki uniformed Scotsmen, the ensuing exchange of fire lasting a few minutes, several Germans being killed and wounded, the remainder surrendering, the Seaforths presented with a substantial quantity of hot soup, sausage, cigarettes and cigars, and, more gratifyingly, a number of spandaus and mortars.

From the Allies point of view, it remained a matter of holding the ground, thus establishing a firm base for the move into the German Reich which, with the arrival of winter, was now planned for the spring.

Proximate as the two division were, Stanley's first impressions of the Highland Division – HD as it was generally referred to - was markedly different from the 43$^{rd}$, the principal difference being the fact that, unsurprisingly, the division was almost entirely made up of Scotsmen. However, what characterised it, rather more than its national identity and sometimes almost impenetrable accents, at least to the untutored ear, was the badge of pride which it wore as part of Montgomery's now legendary Eighth Army, the victors of El Alamein.

"You'll get used to it," Eric told him as he was taking Stanley on his round of introductions, Stanley's arrival coinciding with a brief interlude in the fighting, the division, having completed a successful operation to take control of an area around the town of s-Hertogenbosch, a name with a plethora of pronunciations, prompting a good deal of ribaldry, not least because of inclusion of "bosch", suggesting some affiliation with the neighbouring Reich, an impression fuelled by the hostility of a significant proportion of the inhabitants to their "liberators", unsurprising given that the local populace was a mixture of Dutch and Germans.

"They're not quite as full of themselves as they were when I arrived," Eric added. "As I think I mentioned before, they've been through a bit of a rough spell, with the morale taking a bit of a battering. They didn't seem to have the same resilience as the Wyverns."

After spending his first night in the house as a guest of the four delightfully warm and welcoming elderly ladies, apparently three sisters and a friend, their ability to communicate with little English but an extensive repertoire of gestures and expressions, making for an entertaining evening as they recounted their experience of their former "guests", a number of German officers, their distaste for them graphically illustrated with grimaces and a sort of charade conveying arrogance and absence of humour, Stanley then found himself billeted with three other officers, in an equally large but depressingly gloomy house, fifteen minutes walk from the mess. The owner of the house, a dour, middle aged man with an equally ill-tempered house keeper, unlike the four ladies, made little secret of his affinity with the Nazis, their antipathy towards the current lodgers such that on more than one occasion, simple requests, for use of a spare bedroom and for clean towels, required the emphasis of a hand placed purposefully on a side-arm, the housekeeper's only redeeming feature being her excellent cooking and well stocked larder.

Fortunately, his time in this particular billet proved to be just a matter of days before the order came to move as the division embarked upon the next phase of the protracted struggle for the Island, the launch of the operation on 4th November resulting in its designation as Operation Guy Fawkes.

No sooner was the round of introductions concluded than Stanley was at work, getting to know his new colleagues as they went about their business, his initial task being to familiarise himself with the network of officers involved in the complex supply arrangements.

How strange it felt to be saluted by other officers including captains, their addressing him as "sir" making him want to grin with an odd combination of pride and disbelief, prompting him to glance down at the crowns on his shoulders, indisputable evidence of his elevation.

Many of the Division's regiments were well known to him, their names part of the rich fabric of the British army's history, certain of them legendary, with their distinct mystique –Black Watch, Die Hards, Buffs, Gordons, Camerons – their part in the North Africa campaign also earning them membership of the heroic club, The Desert Rats.

Stanley's initiation also required him to find his way around the map of the territory in which the division was operating, part of it encompassing an area west of s-Hertogenbosch which seemed to boast more than its fair share of villages with tongue-twisting Dutch names – Waalwijk, Sprang, Waspik, Raamsdonk, and the confusingly similar Raamsdonksveer.

What the names and network of roads shown on the map did not indicate, however, was the conditions on the ground, the flat terrain appearing to be constantly saturated, the traffic, particularly when it involved tanks and other heavy vehicles churning up the soft ground, the clawing, sucking mud as much an impediment to movement as any of the conditions encountered in Normandy.

The Highland Division's equipment as well as its supply requirements, were little different to the those of the 43$^{rd}$ with the exception of "crocodiles" – tanks adapted as flame throwers, often referred to as the "funnies", their reputation being as the weapon most feared by the Germans to the extent that there had been reports of the crews of captured crocodiles being summarily executed.

The transformation of Churchill tanks to these fearsome weapons involved the use of a relatively simple kit, REME carrying out the work in the field, such kits added to the indents.

By the end of his second day, Stanley was feeling surprisingly at home. The mess being in a group of farm buildings a couple of miles from s-Hertogenbosch, some of the buildings severely damaged, but others, including the comfortable and well appointed farmhouse, relatively intact.

*My own lovely girl*
*It is very cold today and a terrific gale has blown for nearly twenty four hours, bringing down trees and stripping off nearly all the leaves. Autumn in this part of Holland had been quite pretty as there are far more trees, and their tints have been very lovely.*
*The owner of this house is a middle aged bachelor who lives alone except for an old housekeeper. He is hostile in attitude like so many of these bloody Dutch. They are about 50% pro Nazi. This one was so rude when we asked to use one of the rooms of this very big house, that our PMC just showed him his gun & said "we will come in". They seemed to respect one far more when you show a little determination. They are very like the Bosche. After all, they are the most similar race in Europe to the Germans, and they live on the German borders.*
*We've had a terrific screed from Monty today – all about the rapid increase in VD. It had a chart attached, and it shows how it's trebled since we started to liberate Belgium and Holland. I'm afraid many silly asses who have had a girl have given themselves a great worry and may have wrecked their whole lives. All because they can't be bothered to go and see the Doc and get that little thing called a French Letter.*
*Darling, I'm still worried about the first time we're together again – it worries lots of people, but there's absolutely nothing one can do about it. All I can do now is ask Peggy, please don't be cross if I come quickly. Sometimes being near you and playing with you*

makes me come without you ever touching John T. It's easier for a girl to stop it as she needs the actual feeling of something hard there to make her come – at least that's nearly always so, isn't it darling, except on occasions when I've almost kissed you into coming. If I go on writing like this I shall come now! I'm all alone with you at the moment, by the light of three candles.

My lovely one, goodnight to you. I'm smiling at you as I write this. Give Anthony a great big kiss from Daddy and lots for Mummy.

So lovely your darling

Stanley

It was not his usual habit to read his letters, the times when he had done so making him doubtful about some of what he'd written, worrying always, whether he had been too explicit in spite of her encouragement for him to say exactly what he was thinking, her response, although perhaps not quite so graphic, leaving him with no uncertainty as to her relishing their wonderfully intimate long distance relationship, almost more carnal in its imagining and description than the real thing, the written word enabling them to cast off the few tendrils of inhibition which still remained when they were together.

This time, however, he read what he had written, shocked – and excited – at his explicitness, quickly writing her address on the envelope, licking and sealing it, his resolve intact.

As always, one infuriating consequence of the time it took for letters to arrive was that their replies were often out of sequence. So it was when, the following day he received her letter, he instantly regretted writing what, just a day earlier, had seemed so deliciously salacious but now, in the light of her news, felt so dreadfully crass.

My dearest one

After your good news I am afraid there is some bad news from here, about Daddy. You know his shoulder has been bothering him for a long time. He had it X rayed & the doctor rang to tell Mummy that there is a malignant growth there which he can do nothing about but he has recommended a specialist in town.

Daddy had an appointment with the specialist yesterday. Mummy went with him.

They came back about 7 having heard the worst & that it was extremely grave. He is going to get Daddy into hospital as soon as possible, probably next week for more X-rays etc. before he decides on the treatment. I am hoping & praying it will not be too late for it to have effect.

This is the one disease that I have always loathed more than anything.

I felt so very sad and wept quite a bit at the thought of life without Daddy.

*My sweet, I'm afraid this is a rather miserable letter but I feel awful because we did not think that there was much wrong with him & wishing I had suggested something earlier. Anthony is full of life & at the moment is roaring around his playpen.*
*Goodbye for now darling.*
*Yours for ever*
*Peggy*

She had suspected for some weeks that what her father pretended to shrug off as "a bit of a chest cold" and a shoulder strain, was more serious, her nursing training telling her that the change in his appearance and his constant weariness were symptoms of something much worse. When the news came, however, it was still a terrible shock. Her father had always been so full of energy, his constitution so robust. Indeed, she could scarcely remember any occasions when he had had to take to his bed; a bout of flu some years earlier, and bad stomach infection caused by a meal of shellfish which he knew to be the culprit, certain other diners at the same restaurant having succumbed to the same complaint.

She had always been slightly in awe of him, knowing her place as his daughter, accepting, without complaint – other than, occasionally, to herself – and to Stanley - that this was simply the way things were, a daughter expected to be part of the home, assistant to her mother until such time as a suitable husband materialised, the mantle of son and heir falling upon the shoulders of her brother, Tom.

The affection which she knew that, at heart, her father felt for her, was rarely displayed in any overt manner, and yet she knew it was there as a sort of unspoken bond between them. But most of all, what she felt towards him was respect; as the solid, reliable head of the household and as a pillar of the community with his place on the parish council and his officiating in matters of the church.

It was only now, when she was so cruelly confronted with his vulnerability, that she truly understood the extent to which he was the rock upon which her life was founded. Certainly, in recent years, Stanley had become the centre of her existence; the person upon whom her dreams of the future were built; yet still it was her father who was her cornerstone.

When her parents arrived home from the visit to the consultant in London, she knew, instantly, from their sombre expressions, that they had had the bad news that she was expecting, although the full extent of the cancer was yet to be diagnosed, the consultant having given his verdict only in relation the tumour in his shoulder. Peggy knew, however, that it was inevitable with this almost invariably untreatable disease, that when one tumour had been found, there would be others, the inexorable spread of the disease to vital organs, corroding the system.

When her father had retired to bed, utterly exhausted, she had sat for a while with her mother, wishing there was some way in which she could comfort her. Displays of emotion were deemed to be signs of weakness; such was the family ethos, instilled into both of her parents, her mother now struggling to maintain her composure when, Peggy could see, she was close to shedding tears, pursing her lips, working her jaw with her determination to remain resolutely composed.

Peggy was tempted to say something to her – "It's alright, Mummy. You don't need to keep it bottled up." But she knew she could not do so, her mother's belief in the virtue of strength, defying any such wavering.

"We will have to look after him," her mother said quietly, this being as close as she was able to go in sharing her constrained sadness. "I will need you with me."

When she lay in her bed, unable to sleep, Anthony's light somnolent breathing, punctuated by his habitual grunts and mutterings, so comforting, she longed for Stanley. If only he could have been with her at that moment, to hold her while she poured out her sorrow, her need for him greater than ever as she contemplated the future without her father.

*My sweet darling*
*Thank you very much for your letter which made me feel so very sad, darling – I'm so terribly sorry to hear of your father's news – and so very helpless. I do wish I could do something to help you and Mother, when you need help most. It seems I can only pray so much that, as you say, it is not as bad as you thought and secondly, that modern medicine will be able to make him better quickly. I shall be waiting so very anxiously for more news, especially of his visit to the specialist.*
*I'm afraid my knowledge of illness is very small but I am sensible enough to realise the gravity of what you describe.*
*I do so hope that your Daddy will decide to try & get Tom released – it would relieve him of much worry.*
*The war just goes on & is rather grim. The weather had been absolutely appalling with terrific snowstorms & intense cold.*
*We are still in Holland, foul country that it is.*
*When things have been 'hot' – i.e. when we were first cut off at Nijmegen, Jerry being*

*very unfriendly, no post in or out, one night I remember I went out under the stars and*
*things temporal, man made war and troubles seemed so small compared with the mighty*
*universe. I then felt in some rather wonderful strange way, completely alone with you &*
*away from this world & that whatever the night might bring, even death, I would always*
*be with you. So darling, I am near you on this night & shall be on so many nights.*
*My darling, your letter bears your tear marks and rends my heart. I wish so much I was*
*home to give you some help & what little comfort I could.*
*Goodbye for now. God bless you.*
*Stanley*

As Operation Guy Fawkes concluded, having attained its objective of removing the enemy from the designated part of the Island, the next operation, Ascot, was launched, to continue the slow and costly advance across the bleak, waterlogged landscape, the objective this time, an area contained by two major canals, the movement of men and armour rendered even more hazardous due to the network of minor waterways, obstacles both as contributors to the sodden terrain and as defensive positions for the enemy.

Most testing for this phase, was the burden upon the engineers, REME being called upon to provide the essential crossings, equipment and ingenuity proving more than equal to the task as bailey bridges and improvised crossings were put in place, often under fire, facilitating the advance, tanks and buffaloes sometimes rolling across as the engineers were still working on the structures, infantry perched precariously on the tanks, transporting them to the ever moving front lines, many others more securely riding inside the buffaloes, tracked transports, capable of carrying lorries and even tanks across the most difficult terrain.

As the Second Army continued its painful struggle in the wetlands of Holland, some way to the south, the American First Army had, since September, been engaged in a bloody and ultimately unsuccessful battle for control of the Hurtgen Forest, an area of rugged, forested hills and deep valleys, unsuitable for tanks and making aerial attack difficult, the burden of the fighting thus falling upon infantry.

Commanded by Lieutenant General Courtney Hodges, one of the Allies' least adept generals, the idea of trying to forge a path into Germany by this route had, to many others, seemed foolhardy, and yet the Supreme Commander, Eisenhower, sanctioned the action, recognising its value in drawing some German forces away from the assault on the adjacent Siegfried line, where the Americans, and to a lesser extent the British, were facing similarly stiff resistance.

American casualties in the two operations amounted to one hundred and forty thousand killed and wounded, over thirty thousand sustained in the Hurtgen Forest, many resulting from the technique which the Germans has adopted, of "air bursts" – detonating shells above ground level amongst the dense forest trees, splintered wood acting like shrapnel with devastating effect.

As the Allies struggled on through November, little did they suspect that Hitler, having returned secretly to Berlin from his *Wolfsschanze* command HQ in East Prussia where he had remained after the failed July attempt to assassinate him, was working on an audacious plan which, when implemented, would present the Allies with their most serious set-back of the European campaign.

For the time being, however, the Allies persevered with their questionable strategy, to bear down upon Germany along a wide ranging front, the adverse terrain of much of its length now compounded by the approach of winter, the weeks of rain turning to snow as the wind from the east and north brought the first taste of what was to be a truly Siberian winter.

Within the 51st Division, in spite of the conditions and the slow progress, morale was now surprisingly high, the changes in senior personnel following the appointment of Major-General Rennie as CO during the Normandy campaign having notably enhanced the division's effectiveness as a fighting force, restoring the self belief of officers and men, many of whom – the veterans of North Africa – had rested on their deserved laurels.

The belief in ultimate victory was never in doubt, the only question, as they fought – and many died – in the flat lands amid the great rivers of Holland, being as to the duration of the war, and, for each individual, whether they would survive to reap the fruits of victory, in particular, the dream of returning, victorious, to their loved ones.

Stanley quickly adapted to his new role, his personality and natural authority, earning the respect of his new RASC colleagues as well as the numerous officers with whom he was now dealing with on a day to day basis.

The real difference from his time with the 43rd, however, was his friendship with Eric Nicholls, his RASC CO. When they were able to find the time to meet, away from the other officers, sometimes in Eric's caravan, or, when the weather allowed, walking along the canals or in the woods, ensuring they were well away from the fluctuating front line, Stanley learning much about the birds which, in spite of the ever present sounds of war, seemed to thrive, Eric's knowledge of ornithology, and of nature generally, something that he was happy to impart, and which Stanley found himself increasingly fascinated by.

One November afternoon, as the light was beginning to fade, the air still and cold, they sat on the trunk of a fallen tree, smoking their pipes, looking across a narrow stretch of grass to a river, Eric identifying various birds which, at first glance to Stanley, appeared to be those anonymous looking small brown ones which one frequently sees darting in and out of woods and hedges.

Handing Stanley his "liberated" German binoculars, he pointed to several small birds which had settled on a tree, Stanley marvelling at the colour of the plumage, with its intricate patterns, a flash of yellow on the folded wing, the face bright red, the overall impression being of a delicate work of art.

"That's beautiful," he said, in hushed whispered.

"Goldfinches," Eric said, as the birds suddenly took off. "Watch their flight. It's as if they dance in the air."

Stanley kept the binoculars on them, Eric's description so apt, the birds looping, as if enjoying some practised, joyous, aerial gavotte.

Their confidences were easily offered, anxieties shared, particularly about their wives and children, the greatest concern being for their welfare should they, their husbands and fathers, fail to survive. Neither of them had any serious doubts as to their wives' fidelity, Eric joking that "fortunately, unlike you, I didn't marry a looker!", his wife, as Stanley had seen from photos, a plain, round faced woman, yet with an appearance which suggested jollity, her expression, as she looked directly at the camera, honest and open. "Unlike you, with your gorgeous Peggy!"

"I never doubt her for a minute," Stanley said, firmly believing in the truth of the statement, but, as always, unable to dispel just the slightest, nagging tendril of doubt. "But I guess that it's the same for all of us. Absent husbands. Temptation thrown in their path."

"For some, yes, undoubtedly. But not Peggy. I might have only met her a few times, but faith and loyalty just shone from her. You're a lucky man, Stanley."

Stanley lowered the binoculars, turning to his friend as he handed them back to him, the kindly blue eyes smiling benevolently at him.

"Thanks Eric. You're a good friend."

Eric turned away, raising the binoculars and scanning the edge of the wood, seeming not to have heard Stanley's remark, or perhaps slightly discomfited by it, friendship something which, though recognised, one did not overtly declare.

*My most beloved sweetheart*
*The war is going very well again now: speculations are again rife about when it will end. Quite a lot of responsible people think that the end is not far off. I think it is everyone's ambition to make a great effort to finish it in 1944. If only it wasn't for those two rivers, the Meuse & Rhine! They are very formidable barriers: in winter the Rhine is very swift running and is ¾ mile to a mile wide.*
*I'm afraid that Xmas is an awful nuisance as far as I'm concerned as I've got to try to 'make' 205lbs sugar, 20lbs sultanas, 240 lbs currants, 60 pints vinegar, 12 lbs salt, 500 lbs suet, 600 lbs fat or marg & 1600 lbs flour. This is so that the Div can have mince pies for Christmas day.*
*Today has been a bloody day – very cold early followed by buckets of biting cold rain: added to this we moved at before 9 and tonight we are in a cluster of unattractive houses near a level crossing. The whole area is badly devastated by shell fire – the worst since Normandy, and the Bosche were in this house the night before last. These people are not pleased at being liberated; we are getting near Germany & I think many of them are 75% German. However, if you just touch your revolver it speaks.*
*God bless you my darling. I hate cold paper tonight.*
*Yours so much in love*
*Stanley*
*PS All my love to that lovely lad.*

The information they received, partly through the news and, somewhat more reliably, by way of briefings and the army network of communication, gave them a reasonably accurate picture of the situation across the entire western front, the overall impression being that the combined Allied armies were now arrayed on the very doorstep of the Reich, steadily pushing the *Wehmacht* back, only the Rhine, and the onset of winter, now standing in the way of the final assault.

Contrary to the expectation of a period of lessened activity, towards the end of November orders came from SHAEF for the 51st Division to relieve the American 101 Airborne Division which was hard pressed in trying to hold the area between Arnhem and Nijmegen, continually disputed since the ill-fated September attempt to take the Rhine crossing at Arnhem.

What particularly concerned Eisenhower and his SHAEF staff, was the danger of the Germans destroying the dykes which protected much of the area, resulting not only in the area becoming inundated, with the consequential risk to large numbers of troops and equipment, but denying the Allies this vital springboard for the advance into Germany.

The rapid planning for what was, for obvious reasons designated Operation Noah, provided for evacuation in the event of the dykes being destroyed, the contingency plan involving deploying storm boats, rafts and DUKWs to transport men across flooded terrain, although the bridge at Nijmegen remained a key route both for deployment on, and, if necessary, withdrawal from, the Island. The main objective of the plan was to drive the enemy from the area in which the all important dykes were located.

For several days, the fighting was as intense as at any time since they had arrived in Holland, the battleground defined by the waterways, the frontline, such as it was, changing rapidly from hour to hour, units of both sides finding themselves caught amongst the enemy, the situation made a good deal more hazardous by the vantage points, the many damaged buildings, available to snipers.

When the Germans destroyed the dyke which contained the River Leck, the withdrawal plan was instantly implemented, working remarkably effectively, the range of available craft moving troops to areas of safety, many others managing to cross the bridge at Nijmegen, which, as so often, was under enemy fire, but, remarkably, remained intact. The worry was that under cover of night, the Germans would send divers to mine it, patrols from the 51st being instructed to be especially vigilant for any movement in the water.

The nature of the operation put additional pressure on RASC, not only because of the need to plan the supply routes around the myriad waterways, trying at the same time, to ascertain the positions of the fighting units, but also, with the additional requirements of boats and amphibious DUKWs, RASC liaising closely with REME colleagues who were similarly stretched, deploying their equipment to facilitate what became, effectively, a marine operation.

As the fighting encompassed areas of farmland still protected by undamaged dykes, the breaching of the River Leck dyke resulting in the flooding of only a part of the Island, most of the rural inhabitants having fled to Nijmegen or further afield, a regular occurrence was the familiar encounters with farm animals, pigs and chicken being prevalent.

"They just ran in front of us," a poker-faced private reported, arriving at the

RASC tent with a trailer bearing a dozen dead pigs. "It was as if they wanted to throw themselves under our wheels, sir."

Stanley surveyed the corpses, noting the obvious flaw in the report, each animal having very obvious bullet wounds.

"Very humane," he said, "to put the poor things out of their misery. Better take them to the butcher."

For some days, the supply of unfortunate creatures caught straying onto the field of battle, supplemented the Division's diet, the smell of roasting meat drifting deliciously across the camp, the tents arrayed around the farm buildings.

With the conclusion of the withdrawal, the Division now found itself rubbing shoulders with 43$^{rd}$, both divisions availing themselves of the amenities of Nijmegen, leave parties being permitted to visit Brussels and Antwerp.

It was on a visit to Nijmegen to attend a dinner for officers from both the 51$^{st}$ and the 43$^{rd}$, hosted by the mayor and a group of the town's businessmen, that Stanley again encountered Johan van Dies. At first, when he found himself standing close to him during the pre-dinner drinks, he was tempted to pretend not to have noticed him, but as soon as Johan saw him, he came up to him, smiling warmly.

"Stanley, it is good to see you again." The Dutchman extended his hand, Stanley taking it but deliberately releasing it after the briefest of handshakes.

"I see you are now with a different division," Johan said, observing the HD badge on Stanley's dress uniform. "And a major! My congratulations."

"Thank you." Stanley tried to maintain his offhand manner, telling himself that this man was branded as a collaborator. Yet here he was, amid the town's business community, there appearing to be none of the brutal ostracism and pillorying that they had seen in France. What made it more difficult was that in spite of this vilifying factor, he still liked the man.

"How are your wife and daughter?" Stanley asked, feeling that, at least, he needed to be civil.

"They are both here," Johan said, looking around the large town hall room. "Over there. They are helping with the drinks as the usual people – the staff –

were not available."

"Please come," he insisted, touching Stanley's arm, guiding him across the room. "They would very much like to greet you."

"Hansje. Eva. Look who is here," he said, his wife and daughter turning towards them, Hansje's expression, momentarily, showing consternation before she managed a nervous smile, Eva's discomfort obvious as she glanced from Stanley to her father.

Stanley could not help himself from thinking how beautiful the girl was, the striking blue of her eyes and her light olive skinned face with such strong features, the blond hair giving her a girlishness, emphasised as she then lowered her gaze, as if coyly unable to look at him.

He remembered that brief kiss, her mouth now set with a sort of pouting truculence, the lips full and inviting.

As they were called to table, he shook hands again with Johan and Hansje, Eva watching him, her eyes fixing him with a look which he found difficult to read except that it seemed to be challenging him and pleading at the same time.

He nodded to her, turning away and taking his seat at the long table, disconcertingly finding that Johan was almost opposite him, next to his fellow officer, Peters, who also seemed to know him, the two greeting each other with obvious familiarity.

Fortunately, Stanley's neighbour on the other side was one of his former colleagues from the 43rd, the two of them spending much of the meal reminiscing although he was conscious of Johan glancing towards him, clearly wanting to converse, Stanley resolutely continuing his close conversation with his neighbour.

It was at the end of the meal that Stanley, feeling quite drunk, their hosts having been generous with wine and schnapps, was standing in the foyer of the old civic building when Eva suddenly appeared in front of him.

"I am sorry you think I am a bad, person" she said, her eyes fixed intently on him, the expression again truculent. "I would like us to have been friends."

"My driver will be here in a minute," Stanley said, moving to the entrance and stepping out into the bracingly cold night. There was no sign of Hopkins. "He will be here in a minute." Eva stood beside him, as if expecting him to offer her a lift.

"You do not understand what it was like," she said, placing her hand on his arm. He looked down at it, unsure whether to remove it or to take hold of it. "We had to do many bad things."

"Giving yourself to a German officer. That's what I certainly call a bad thing. In fact, I could call it a damned sight worse."

As he berated her, her hand continued to rest on his arm, the girl suddenly starting to weep.

"I am sorry," she said again. "I do like you very much."

"And I'm sorry, that we cannot be friends," he replied brusquely. Unable to help himself, he took hold of her hand, turning towards her. "I really am sorry, Eva. I can't think what you must have been through. But all that I know is that you went with a German, and that your father was a collaborator."

As he saw Hopkins approaching in a line of several staff cars, he leaned forward, kissing Eva gently on the cheek. "I am truly sorry," he whispered.

As he sat beside Hopkins in the car, he pondered the vexed question of what he was apologising to her for; the fact that there was an insuperable obstacle between them, or the suffering she had endured. Most of all, however, he was relieved that that obstacle had saved him from what he shuddered to contemplate. Would he really have betrayed Peggy? The fact that he had not done so did little to lessen the guilt which weighed upon him, the thought seeming as bad as the act.

"Good time, sir?" Hopkins asked, glancing at Stanley, putting his silence down to his obvious drunkenness, Stanley now appearing to be nodding off.

"They weren't really collaborators," Peters said when, the next day, they were arguing about their dealings with several local businessmen who were known to have had similar dealing with the Germans. "They did what they had to do to survive. And anyway, it is very different here than in France. More acceptable."

"You mean they got on with the Huns?" Stanley suggested angrily. "You'll be telling me next that they were a bunch of Nazis themselves." What he did not say was that what had really shocked him was the fact that van Dies had, quite clearly, acquiesced in – and possibly even arranged – his daughter's relationship with a German officer. The idea of the man having pimped his own daughter was utterly incomprehensible to him. And yet, in spite of himself, his feeling of such affection towards the girl only served to compound the felony, of flirtation with infidelity.

"You don't see them shaving the heads of women who went with the Huns, or parading them through the streets like the French," Peters said. Although it was only three weeks since Stanley's arrival with the 51st, he had decided that Peters was the one member of the mess he did not take to, the rest of them being a pretty good bunch. With Peters, however, there was something about the man which reminded him of Mead, with a similarly annoying knowingness, as if he was always wanting to score points. "Bleeding medieval, if you ask me. The French."

"So you reckon it was OK for them to deal with the Huns?" Stanley realised that his retort was futile, arguing with Peters never seeming to achieve anything other than a sense of frustration that he could not shake the man's opinions.

"They were just doing what they had to do," Peter repeated. "If that's what most of them were doing, then of course it would be seen as acceptable."

Stanley lapsed into morose silence, his thoughts turning once again to Eva, despite his determination to try to put her out of his mind.

It came as something of a relief when, the following day, Peters announced, rather sheepishly, that he was being transferred to a training role back in England, the decision to transfer him very obviously an indication that the senior officers had decided that he was not an asset to the 51st.

As Stanley read Peggy's letter, he was wracked with self loathing, convinced that he had broken their trust, and yet thankful that the breach had not escalated and become irreparable. How desperately he longed to be with her, to confide in her: yes, he would tell her that temptation had be placed in his path, but that he had resisted it. What he could not say was that it had not been his conscience with had saved him, but the fact that the temptress had been defiled by the enemy.

*My own darling*

*One day I'll tell you why I haven't been able to write to you for three days but perhaps you'll guess if I tell you that I have had a very hectic time, covering great distances and am still in Holland.*

*We have got a new 2 i/c called Stephen Fox. Peters, the fellow I didn't like much, has gone to Army Group. Fox is very much a man about town, aged about 35, tall, horn rimmed glasses, very broad, rather a sharp nose, quiet speaking. I think I like him but perhaps he is a little too smooth.*

*Even though I didn't much like Peters, we had a Scottish farewell party for him. It was a terrific do, the most impressive part was the playing of some very good tunes on the bagpipes by a Major in a kilt. He is very tall & broad & looks a typical Scotch piper. He played some grand tunes – Lily Marlene, Road to the Isles, Skye & the rest. We had lots of Champagne and did Scottish dances rather drunkenly. The party became very gay & very low & all the old songs came out.*

*Although I went to bed at 2 and got up at 6 and drove 90 miles, I felt fine and I had a very excellent shave in Eindhoven. There is an abundance of Champagne just now and I think it is a marvellous drink & I'm just longing to drink it with you & get rather drunk. So, my darling, full of very wicked thoughts (it's a grand moonlight one) I'll kiss you goodnight my lovely young wife.*

*Stanley*

As he slid the letter into the envelope, although he realised that, apart from the account of what he had been doing, he had said little about matters of the heart, constrained both by his awareness of her having to cope with her father's illness and his own guilt, he nevertheless found that just the fact of writing to her, and of his brief restatement of his love for her, had gone some way to appease his troubled conscience.

At the same moment, as he sealed the envelope, writing her address on it, he vowed never again, for as long as he remained absent from her, to allow himself to stray, even to the extent of contemplating succumbing to temptation, crossing the clear line from looking to touching.

He kissed the envelope, ready for posting the next morning, lying down and instantly falling into untroubled sleep.

## TWENTY

*29.11.44*

*My sweetheart husband*

*Thank you so very much for the wonderful letter which arrived this morning.*

*Your letter took six days.*

*I don't think there is any doubt about getting Tom here now as we have heard from the doctor today that Daddy has cancer of the lung. This was rather what I suspected from what I heard of the investigations so it was not so much of a shock to me, but poor Mummy feels that it is almost too much for her especially as people will keep ringing up and enquiring, & when we tell them that it is Daddy's shoulder, they do not understand & think it is quite trivial.*

*We have not told anyone about the lung yet. They think there may be a chance with an operation as Daddy has a strong constitution. I hope they do try it as that at least decides the issue quickly. They are going to treat the arm first though, with deep X ray as that is most urgent.*

*This Christmas that I thought might bring the end of the war looks instead like being a rather sombre one.*

*Darling, please don't let all this worry you in feeling that you ought to be doing anything. It is just a case of waiting to see how things go & none of us can help now.*

*Darling, I too am surrounded by things you have given me – the pen I always write with, my identity bracelet, my watch strap, & even my powder now.*

*I must say goodnight now, darling husband.*

*With all my love*

*Peggy*

After the frequent moves of the previous weeks, with the conclusion of Operation Noah, the 51ˢᵗ set up its HQ in the village of Hooge Heide, halfway between Nijmegen and s'Hertogenbosch with the prospect of a period of relative comfort, the RASC being billeted in a requisitioned monastery, although all but a handful of the monks had either fled or abandoned their calling. It was a relatively modern, well appointed building, and, most importantly, having numerous fireplaces, the surrounding woods offering a plentiful supply of logs, luxuriously warm.

Recent briefings had indicated that the Division would shortly be undergoing a period of specialised training, the nature and purpose of which soon became clear. With a good deal of mention of boats and bridges, and given their location, so close to the German border, it did not take a genius to work out that their next objective was going to be the Rhine, a daunting prospect, particularly for those, like Stanley, who had seen the great river, its width far exceeding any of those they had already had to fight their way across, including the Seine.

At least, however, there was word that the training was going to be interspersed with leave, both Brussels and Antwerp being within bounds, with rumours of the joyous possibility of some being allowed to return home, although the cynics, who, by now, comprised most of the Division, and indeed, of the Second Army, held out little realistic hope of being allowed home for Christmas.

As became apparent from the briefings, there were to be two phases to the next stage of the campaign, the first, designated as Operation Veritable, involving the Division jointly with the 43rd, 53rd Welsh, two armoured divisions and two Canadian, the objective being to remove the enemy from the remaining territory still in his hands west of the Rhine, preparing the way for the second part, the Rhine crossing itself.

When the Operation was to be launched had not been made known to them, the general view being that, as with the advance into Germany, all major offensives would now be deferred until the spring, or at least until they were through the worst of the winter, a season known to be a good deal more severe in this part of the world than in England, the first signs already suggesting that this was shaping up to be a bad one.

In spite of the rumours of home leave, Stanley had long since discounted the prospect, hoping instead, that at least he might get to Brussels, word being that the accommodation provided in the capital city, a number of good quality hotels having been taken over for army leave, the capital also reputed to offer a great deal more in terms of entertainment, the main attraction of Antwerp, at least for those so inclined, being the ready availability of women, the going rate, it was said, being not much more than a couple of pints of beer.

Much to Stanley's surprise, was the indication which, having come that morning from Eric, and thus more reliable than the general rumours, that, contrary to expectations, home leave would starting in a few weeks' time. Suddenly, he felt he could allow himself to dream of that moment he so longed for, of arriving on the doorstep, perhaps even unannounced, rather liking the idea of it being a surprise, imagining Peggy's reaction, opening the door, finding him standing there, their embrace a moment of such ecstasy.

When it came to it, however, writing to Peggy, he was unable to contain himself, deciding that he had to share the news with her.

*My darling angel*

*Reading your letters is quite like reading a chapter of your life. I can see how your spirits rise and fall, how many trials and worries you have and through it all how sweetly in love you are, and I love you more and more after every letter.*

*Darling, I remember that seemingly far off day in Eastbourne in 1940 when you became my fiancée for all the world to see. I felt a curious uneasiness as we listened in the glorious majesty of the night to the foreboding rumbles from across the Channel. It seemed to me then that we both had such hard paths to tread before we should be able to be together in happiness for ever. My darling girl, those paths are leading out into the clear now – and happiness lies so nearby to us.*

*We have plenty of reserve morale, and are certainly not downhearted.*

*I'm afraid my hopes of being at Anthony's first birthday will not be fulfilled: I shall be with you both so much in spirit.*

*I meant to tell you, when writing about that tune, that 'Lily Marlene' is by far the most popular song out here, with both sides, & also the Dutch. It is about the only thing everyone has in common. It is a really grand tune & quite different from all the other so called 'smash hits' of this war.*

*Well the news is out that we are all to get leave and everyone is pretty excited. There is nothing in writing yet but it will be pretty certainly by ballot. There are six officers to go in the hat here so that means I might get leave any time between 1 Jan and the end of February. I shan't believe I'm home on leave until I'm sitting in an English railway carriage, Brighton bound.*

*This leave business is very good for everyone's morale, which had become not low, but a little jaded.*

*Goodbye for now my beloved.*

*Stanley*

*My sweetheart husband*

*My life seems divided in two, the happy part that is so very much in love with you and the sad part that is so very worried for Daddy. I have had a letter from Tom today saying that he will come home if he can manage it.*

*By the way, no one knows the diagnosis of the growth on the lung except Mummy & I so don't mention it if you write to Daddy.*

*Mummy has been up to town today. She spoke to the sister before seeing Daddy & she told her that it was very grave especially as there were two growths. They are treating the shoulder one with deep X ray at the moment & can't tell whether that is going to have any effect for three weeks. There is a possibility that he might be able to come home for Christmas but Mummy thinks that he is quite a bit weaker either from the treatment or the disease. The trouble is that medical science has not yet really found the cause or many details. It is just a case of time – if they get it early enough. That is what we have to wait and see now.*

*Yours in love for ever*
*Peggy*

How it tore at his heart to read her letters, knowing what she was going through and being so helpless, unable to do anything. If only he could speak to her, just to let her know that he was there with her, in spirit. Words on the page seemed so soulless, but he had no alternative but to accept that they were all that he could offer, probably for many weeks, the latest information pointing to home leave starting possibly early in the new year, military matters allowing. He knew however, that when it came to leave, the army were past masters of delay and obfuscation.

Having come so far, and now being poised on the very threshold of the *Reich*, it was so frustrating to feel that they were marking time, eager as they were to get the job done. They fully understood the reasons for waiting, to offer a better prospect of campaigning weather, and yet the thought of spending possibly a couple of months or more, kicking their heels was made even worse by their being unable to get home.

Christmas, for Stanley, was always a special time. He loved every aspect of it; the church services; the conviviality; the Christmas dinner; the carol singing; and now, the illusive wonder of being with his own wife and child. Since the start of the war there had only been two years when he had not managed to get home, if not on Christmas day, then shortly before or after, the visits sometimes cruelly brief, the misery of those years when leave proved impossible only marginally mitigated by the generous quantities of liquor which, for the troops deprived of leave, was *de rigeur*, drunkenness the best antidote to the ache of absence.

This year, already, with Christmas still three weeks away, the weight of despondency of being apart felt so much more painful. The sadness of not being able to see Anthony; to watch him grow; to relish his transformation from baby to toddler, was a constant dull ache, every now and again becoming more acute, a stab of utter misery. Yet he resolved, as always, to maintain his stiff upper lip, allowing himself to complain of being "browned off" but stopping short of out and out self pity.

The fact that the Germans had managed to maintain such an extraordinary level of secrecy, and the shortcomings of Allied intelligence, could not have been more apparent when, on, 15ᵗʰ December, a bitingly cold day with flurries of light snow swirling on an easterly breeze, Montgomery chose to visit the 51ˢᵗ Highland Division, the Field Marshall having no inkling of what the enemy was about to unleash.

As the new Rolls Royce, gleaming pale green paintwork contrasting with the khaki of every man arrayed in ranks around the field close to Hooge Heide, the monotone extending to every tent and vehicle across the extensive camp, drew to a halt to the barked command "Attention!", the Field Marshall climbing out, standing for a minute on the running board, as was his habit, such was his modest stature, before exchanging salutes with the Divisional CO, Major-General Rennie, the two men then proceeding along the ranks, Montgomery stopping frequently to speak to various officers and men before stepping up onto an improvised dais, his distinctive high pitched voice carrying even to the furthest ranks.

"Very soon," his rhotacism – the syndrome which, as Peggy had explained to Stanley, made "r" sound as "w" – seeming more pronounced than ever, "we shall be embarking on the final stage of our great crusade, striking at the enemy's land, and at his very heart; striking him the mortal blow from which he will never be able to rise again."

Stanley, like most of those present, felt the sensation they always experienced in the great man's presence, and even when hearing him on the wireless, the hairs on the back of their necks prickling, the blood stirring in their veins.

"Men of the 51st. Highlanders! You know that you have a very special place in my esteem. We have fought shoulder to shoulder, defeating the Bosch in the desert. And now we will defeat him again, deep inside his own lair."

He allowed a theatrical pause, sensing the frisson, almost of exhilaration, across the temporary parade ground.

"Soon, I can assure you, you will be able to see your loved ones again, when leave commences. We have more work to do beforehand, but I can tell you that you can measure the time now in weeks rather than months. We must pause now, preparing ourselves through these days of deep winter and while we shall be ensuring that, when day comes, we shall be ready for the task, you will be able to enjoy some days of relaxation, which you have thoroughly earned.

And when we begin again, I can assure you that you, men of the 51st, will be to the fore, bearing the standard of our great nation as once again, we join battle with our invidious enemy."

Within twenty-four hours Providence would reveal how fateful were those words.

*Peggy my own*
*We've had a great day today as the C-in-C (Montgomery) has visited us. He was in great form, very optimistic, amusing, and entirely his old self except for a new battledress! He talked a lot about leave and the plan sounds fairly good though I'm not sure that his wishes are being executed quite correctly. He has a grand car – a Rolls painted in peacetime style – pale green. We saw him off and the whole div gave three cheers for the C-in-C.*
*Darling, I've just realised that Xmas is only 10 days off & this will reach you God knows when. I haven't I'm afraid said anything to you to wish you a peaceful and happy Xmas. Those aren't quite my feelings. What I feel is that I shall be missing you more than ever on Dec 25th, longing for you and a little homesick. I am praying very hard that I may be with you and Anthony for his birthday and Xmas 1945, though that is not certain yet, though Monty was very optimistic.*
*Darling, I do hope you are not being bombarded with V1s. Do tell me whether you've had any.*
*So my darling, I shall be thinking of you so vividly, remembering so well last Christmas, strangest and loveliest of all in many ways.*
*In memory and anticipation of our love:*
   *O soothest sleep, if so it please thee, close*
   *In the midst of this thine hymn, my willing eyes*
   *Or wait the Amen ere thy poppy throws*
   *Around my bed its lulling charities*
*My beloved darling, all my love and my heart and live are forever yours.*
*Stanley*

Through the months of the campaign, Stanley had not only learned to distinguish the differences in the sound of friendly and enemy gunfire – the spandaus as distinct from the bren gun as a flute from a trumpet – but also the nature of the fire: the full blooded barrage rolling like a thunderstorm, the regular, daily business of the field guns, more staccato, their single voices discernible.

It was still fully dark when, on the morning of 16th, he was woken by a rumbling which, though far off, was, unmistakably, a heavy barrage, although at distance, one could not determine which side had unleashed it. There had been no indication in recent briefings of any imminent assault, and although they would not necessarily be forewarned of action by the Americans, word of anything on the scale that the barrage indicated would almost certainly have filtered down to them, particularly via his ever reliable conduit, Eric Nicholls.

Having, a few days earlier, been issued with his own caravan, more akin to a small garden shed on wheels, but nevertheless, his own personal quarters, although the walls were more substantial than canvas, they provided little insulation from the sounds of the camp.

He heard men moving around, questions exchanged, but no orders. Pulling back the thick blackout curtain covering the tiny window he could see the distant flashes, a constant flickering of light to the south.

"What do you reckon?" Basil Seymour asked, emerging from his dugout as Stanley climbed down from his caravan. "That's some barrage."

For more than an hour it continued, the camp now fully awake, men staring anxiously at the illuminated pre-dawn sky as if expecting to find some answer, the consensus being that they were German guns, the barrage presaging a counter offensive which, although always anticipated, had certainly not been expected now, with the approach of mid winter, and with the weather becoming colder by the day, the ground already covered with a powdering of snow and with the prospect of more in the air.

By mid morning, reports reached them that their assumption was correct, the attack appearing to be in the area away to the south, known as the Ardennes, which was generally seen as the least likely route, being thickly forested and rugged, particularly adverse terrain for panzers.

It was not until the following day that the Allies realised they were facing a full scale counter-offensive, the still sketchy intelligence indicating that several panzer and other divisions were involved. Caught completed off guard, as the barrage was followed by a rapid German advance through the forest, SHAEF hurriedly set about redeploying a number of divisions, several of which were out of the line or in different sectors of the lengthy front, extending as it now did from the Baltic coast to France's eastern frontier, the numerous senior officers currently on leave, hastily summoned back, fortunately, most of them being relatively nearby, in Brussels, Antwerp or other Dutch or Belgium towns.

For several days, as the enemy began to make serious in-roads into Allied territory to the west of the forest, advancing towards Belgium, confusion continued to reign, the combination of overcast conditions, severely limiting aerial recognisance, and, in the opening days, the density of the forest, making it difficult to gauge the German strength, or, equally importantly, for the Typhoons to get to grips with the advancing panzers.

Having finally obtained a reasonably accurate assessment of the situation, and being able to gauge the considerable strength of the advancing German forces, Eisenhower was able to put in place his defensive deployments. Much to the consternation of most of the American generals, he also decided to appoint Montgomery to command the US 1st and 9th Armies at the same time as retaining command of the British 2nd Army, effectively putting the Field-Marshall in charge of the Allied defence.

For the first week of the offensive, the Allies – particularly the US forces which bore the brunt of the attack – were in retreat, driven out of Holland and well back into Belgium, the concern being that if the Germans could not be held, they could break through into France, their objectives being to divide the Allied armies, and to reach the coast, re-taking Antwerp.

With the Allied redeployments, the 2nd Army was moved to positions which were intended to defend the territory to the north of what was become the "bulge" which later gave its name to the battle, XXX Corps, including the Guards Armoured, 43rd, 51st and 53rd divisions, forming a defensive line across an area south-east of Brussels, Montgomery managing to hold the main German advance along a line between Elsenhorn and Bastogne, the latter town becoming the scene of the most intensive fighting of the battle.

After several days of near constant movement, the 51st division found itself sharing an HQ with the American 9th at the town of Liege. The entire week having been overcast, the cloud finally lifted, allowing the Allies to take advantage of their almost complete air superiority, the Typhoons at last able to set about the panzers which, now being away from the forest, presented themselves as easy targets, over three hundred being destroyed, albeit, having already taken a devastating toll of Allied tanks and men.

For Stanley and for the officers and men of RASC, the first phase of the battle, continuing until after Christmas, presented them with the greatest challenge of the campaign to date, with supply lines already seriously stretched, the task of delivering ammunition and other essential supplies to the fighting units, many of them hard pressed to hold their positions, and with information sketchy and communications erratic, exceptionally difficult. Such was the uncertainty as to the whereabouts of the numerous units dependent upon them, that Stanley found himself frequently on the road, sometimes driven by Hopkins, his decision, a couple of times, to use a motorbike proving to be a mistake, the snow, in some places, now a foot thick, impacted on the roads and lanes, precarious for any vehicles, particularly two wheeled. He was fortunate that when he skidded on a bend, thrown clear of the motorbike, having slid along the road for twenty yards, he ended up in a snow drift. And with the daytime temperature now struggling to get above freezing, a three hour trip on a motorbike left him frozen to the marrow, the pain of thawing his hands telling him that from now on he should travel by car.

It was a frantic and strange week, the countryside now blanketed with snow, weighing on the trees, drifts sometimes several feet deep, a scene of picture postcard beauty, scarred by the detritus of battle; burnt out tanks and vehicles, mostly American, and, all too often, bodies, mainly German, left where they had fallen, rictal faces and distorted limbs protruding from the snow, blood frozen black.

On the occasions when he had to venture close to the ever fluctuating front line, the sounds and sights were similarly distorted by the winter conditions, gunfire, although still thunderously loud, strangely baffled, as if the roar of the guns was partly absorbed by the thick snow, the flashing of thousands of angry barrels reflecting on the brilliant white, the sun now shining, the air itself, bitingly cold but with a remarkable clarity.

The role of the 51st now being to hold the flank of the bulge and, in particular, the bridges over the Maas between Liege and Namur, during this phase of the battle its engagement was on a limited scale, elements of the Sixth Panzer Army seeming to be probing the northern flank, the main thrust, testing the opposition, their intelligence as to the deployment and strength of the defender being similarly poor, it soon becoming apparent that they had, of necessity, abandoned any attempt to force their way to the coast.

For four days after the launch of the offensive Stanley was unable to find time to write to Peggy. The division being on the move most days, it was not until the end of that week that they finally had a solid roof over their heads, short spells of sleep snatched when Stanley was able to climb into his caravan, sleep instant and dreamless, rudely curtailed by Hopkins or one of the duty officers banging on the wooden walls, rousing him from his stupor, it taking several minutes for him surface, the instant of stepping outside into the freezing air, fully waking him like an ice-cold shower.

*Peggy my beautiful darling*
*How are you darling? The post is still haywire and I have only had two letters in a week. The weather has been a bit better lately and morale is high, especially now that the Hun appears to have committed his VI Panzer Army, which is a very good thing and should*

357

*appreciably shorten the war: even if he does penetrate 30 or 40 miles into Belgium: we think that the more he goes in, the more he will eventually get beaten up. Though it was obviously a bit sticky to start with. We are not surprised about his ground forces though he seems to have collected a few aircraft from the junk heap.*

*I'm feeling rather war weary together with the rest for the members of this HQ. It's funny – mass feeling is very common in this Army & occasionally you find a day or an evening when everyone feels the same. Today we've had several chaps killed & one – a sergeant – was a friend of mine & a first class chap. He had come right through most campaigns of this war & he was killed while off duty by a V bomb. It seems so senseless and bloody altogether. By God, the only way to ensure future peace for the next generation is to exterminate Germany as a nation: they are the worst bastards that ever stepped on God's earth. We just loath, detest & despise them – so much more quietly & intensely than on D Day or prior to it.*

*It is often said that the last mile is the hardest, in a race, and this war is certainly proving that to be right. Complete victory seems so elusive, like a lamp post in a dream, that you can never seem to catch.*

*And yet, all the while, that light that burned and shone so brightly in 2nd Army before & after D-Day still shines as brightly as ever. The mud & squalor of Holland, the long days of waiting, the feeling of anti-climax this last few weeks, have not dimmed the steadfastness of that light. The task is clear to all and you can be certain that however big the setback, and the temporary anxiety in England must be considerable, there'll be no faltering at any rate in the 21 Army Group until the job is done and the Third Reich is no more.*

*My dearest dear, all my love is your so much for ever.*

*Stanley*


The Christmas which the division was expecting to spend in Holland, with the prospect of an opportunity for a relatively peaceful spell, allowing for some celebration, was now effectively put on hold, although there were sufficient interludes for a modest semblance of festivity, additional demands coming to RASC for various culinary requirements and liquor, which it did its best to provide.

On Christmas day, Major-General Rennie sent a message to the division: "I am afraid Christmas will not be as organised as it might have been, but I hope the food and drink turn up and that you will have as happy a Christmas as can be under the circumstances. The present German offensive has, to a large extent, been contained, and the flanks of the break-through are firm."

Although the Germans were concentrating mainly on their drive westward into Belgium, being held by the Americans at Bastogne which proved to be the point at which the bulge was finally halted, the sector in which the 51st was deployed was, as with all other sectors, under constant threat from V1s, their targeting lacking precision, but their frequency, at the peak, with thirty or more falling on the sector, and their impact, each one carrying over a thousand pounds of explosive, a matter of considerable concern, several having caused casualties and extensive damage.

Compared to a full scale bombardment, however, the V1s were deemed nothing more than "a bit of a bloody nuisance", the reaction of most of the men being concern about the devastation which the weapons were causing back home, with daily reports of the new blitz and the mounting death toll, particularly in London and across south eastern counties.

At first light on Christmas morning, Stanley, Eric and a number of other officers, drove out of Liege to an area of forest close to the Maas, a Belgian land owner they had met at the hotel in which they were currently billeted, its restaurant continuing to serve civilians alongside it military clientele, having invited them to take part in the traditional *chasse de sanglier* – a wild boar hunt.

It was an experience which Stanley remembered as much for the conditions as for the dozen boars they killed, the snow covering the ground and, as they entered the forest, the clearings, the tracks of boar and other animals imprinted like a boy scout identification test, the air so cold that after half an hour, his face was aching and his eyes stinging, his fingers so chilled he could hardly pull the trigger of his rifle. Their host, however, provided the antidote, of generous measures of schnapps, the liquor instantly warming their spirits and their innards if not their fingers.

He remembered also, with disturbing clarity, the first of his two kills, a large boar, sporting formidable tusks, which suddenly appeared in front of him, seeming to materialise from the frozen forest some thirty yards from him, stopping in a clearing, staring straight at him, sniffing the air as if challenging him, remaining quite still as he raised his rifle. For several seconds, with the beast in his sights, he hesitated, realising that despite the fact that death had been a constant factor over the past months, and with his familiarity with the business of the slaughtering of animals to feed the troops, he had never killed either man or beast, the handful of rabbits he had shot when they were in France, and a few pheasants and pigeons before the war, somehow a different category, this creature exuding such a powerful sentience he felt an overwhelming sense of empathy.

He could feel sweat freezing on his forehead and the back of his neck, his hand gripping the rifle as he forced himself to increase the pressure.

The shot seemed to echo through the forest as the boar lurched in the air, falling backward, its legs shaking as if it were trying to run but without any ground to give it purchase. When it was still, he walked slowly towards it, the patch of blood a livid stain on the snow, the creature even larger now that he was beside it, the bullet hole in the front of its head, a perfect shot.

"Nice one," Eric said, standing beside Stanley, looking at him curiously, sensing the emotion which Stanley was trying not to show. "Right between the eyes."

"I guess it'll be a Christmas treat for a lot of the men," Stanley said, trying to drag his gaze away from the beast, its open eye gazing lifelessly back at him.

*24.12.44*

*My own darling sweetheart*

*When I last wrote to you on the evening of 19th, little did I think that I would be taking part in the greatest military flap since Dunkirk: we have gone from somewhere in Holland to somewhere in Belgium: I cannot tell you where we are spending this strangest of Xmases.*

*There's rather a lot of noise just now, for despite the strange circumstances, various members of the mess have just realised that it's Xmas Eve and not even Von Runstedt and all his blasted 6 Pz Army can stop us remembering that! Yes, strange as it may seem, we are all in great spirits: despite all you've probably heard on the wireless and in the papers, we regard this as terrific: as I believe I said, he has committed VI Pz Army and we are thus saved the job of finding it. So darling, you can tell the folks at home that the BLA has the situation in hand and that your old man is fine.*

*I went for a short walk after breakfast on the banks of a famous river. Ice is beginning to form on it: it looked very lovely today with the misty winter sunshine reflecting on the white frost. The temperature was 20 below freezing last night, so it seems that winter is really here. I've been thinking of you and home such a lot, my darling, and I expect your feelings are as mixed as mine. I'm so glad your father is getting home. Is there any more news of how the first part of his treatment is getting on?*

*We shall probably stay here today & move again first thing tomorrow. That'll make five moves in six days. Yesterday and today have been grand for the RAF − brilliant sun and clear skies. The flap has now died down a bit and we seem to have got the Hun more or less where we want him. His objectives were undoubtedly Brussels & Antwerp, Paris & Dunkirk. So you see he has failed miserably and we all hope he's really committed suicide this time.*

*Darling, I must conclude very abruptly. Will write more when I can. Please don't worry.*

*Yours for ever so much in love*

*Stanley*

By the end of Christmas morning, the rich smell of roasting boar was wafting from the kitchens of several Liege hotels as well as those in certain of the town's buildings which provided temporary homes for the division's troops. The promise of an expected Christmas feast, so tantalising to the nostrils, was, however, suddenly threatened when, less than hour before it was due to be served, the order was received for the division once again to move.

As lorries lined up outside Stanley's hotel, he and his fellow officers, managed to wolf down their portions of roast boar, accompanied by roast potatoes, even managing to gulp a slice of Christmas pudding – RASC having managed to procure the ingredients to cater for the entire division – before grabbing handfuls of cigars, cigarettes and chocolate generously provided by their Belgium hosts and hurrying out to the waiting vehicles.

As they were getting into the car, Hopkins handed him the letter from Peggy which had just arrive, the REME postal service struggling to keep up with the division's frequent changes of location.

Determined as Peggy was, to celebrate both Christmas and Anthony's first birthday, her usually indomitable spirit succumbed to the despondency which, at times threatened to overwhelm her, her only solace being Anthony's blissfully ignorant cheeriness as he played happily with his birthday presents, a toy steam engine from Stanley's parents, a splendid wooden truck from Ted, and a woolly dog from Mrs Christian.

She had hoped that Paddy and Alan would have been able to come for the tea party but Alan was working and Paddy was feeling unwell. At least Michael and Ted were able to bring a little jollity to what would otherwise have been a rather sombre affair, Peggy's father looking sickly and gaunt, her mother unable to hide her anxiety, about both her husband and Tom. Stanley's father seemed uncomfortable, as if he was there to provide spiritual ministration to the sickly Arthur, Stanley's mother on the other hand, contentedly chatting to Anthony, showing him his name which Peggy had written in pink icing on the birthday cake and helping him to blow out the candle.

The last time they had heard from Tom, he had told them that it was likely he was going to be allowed extended leave, in view of his father's inability to manage the business, although he did not know when he would get a definite answer and how long he would be able to stay. When Peggy read his letter, she detected the disappointment that, having finally realised his ambition, of becoming a member of the famous Chindits, he was having to give priority to the call of family duty.

The day after Boxing Day she drove her father back to London, persuading her mother to stay at home as she was feeling under the weather with a heavy cold, Peggy wanting the opportunity to speak to one of the doctors or nurses, to find out how serious her father's condition was, deciding that if, as she expected, the news was going to be bad, she could then decide how to break it to her mother.

It was a bleak journey, the little Morris's heater no match for the cold weather, her father, well rugged up with woollen scarf and a blanket over his knees, trying, intermittently, to make light conversation before lapsing into a lolling sleep, his head jerking up when he realised he had nodded off, thinking he was resuming the conversation, what he was saying in fact being a patchwork of reminiscences, the obvious loosening of his faculties adding to Peggy's sadness, but, with her nursing knowledge as well as her natural intuition, making it even more obvious that his condition was rapidly deteriorating.

Once her father was back in the ward, falling asleep as soon as he was in his bed, she managed to speak to the ward sister, a pleasant woman who took Peggy into a small room, giving her a cup of tea, chatting briefly about nursing careers, Peggy having mentioned her time at Bart's and the curtailment of her training when she got married.

"Damned stupid!" the sister said. "Why on earth, in this day and age, and when there is such a need for SRNs, do they have to dispense with someone just because they're married. Makes no sense."

"I wanted to know how my father is," Peggy said, after a few minutes of lighter conversation. "However bad it is."

"He has a tumour on his lung as well as the one in his shoulder," the sister explained, looking directly at Peggy, gauging that this sensible former nurse should have the full facts. "And I'm afraid it's inoperable. We can try to treat the shoulder. X-ray therapy is still quite new, but it seems to have some benefit in some cases. However, I'm not sure it will be worthwhile given his lung condition. And there are side effects."

After leaving the hospital she drove to Oxford Street, needing something to occupy herself, walking round several shops, picking up items randomly, trying to focus on shop assistants' offers of help, her mind filled with sadness. At one point, she had to hurry out of Selfridges, wandering through side streets, mopping her tears with her handkerchief, before setting out on return journey home.

*My dearest*

*This has been a very quiet Christmas. There was thick white frost & then the sun came out & it was very bright and crisp. I went to the 9 o'c communion and we all went out for a short walk before dinner although Daddy did not feel like walking.*

*In the afternoon Daddy & I sat by the fire & listened to 'The Road Home' & then the King.*

*Darling, I longed for you to be beside me in church & still more later in the evening when I was sitting alone by the fire listening to a concert of Cesar Franck played by Alfredo Campolio.*

*Today I went to London with Daddy. I didn't much like my trip but I was determined to see the sister of the ward about Daddy as I felt that it was time someone knew the exact position. Well, I got what I dreaded hearing − inoperable carcinoma. I think because she knew I was a nurse I got the truth which means that the cancer of the lung is beyond treatment. I just felt stunned & longed to weep very much but I could not. I went into some shops hardly knowing what I asked for but I had to do something.*

*I realised that one day I should come up against the grimness of life but never thought it would be anything like this. It seems so terribly cruel that this terrible disease should have come to Daddy who has always been so fit and strong. O my darling, I just feel awful & incredibly miserable & so completely helpless & knowing too much to even hope. Still I am praying. I feel somehow that God can't let this happen.*

*It has helped somehow writing to you as I can't talk to you. I feel you are near me in spirit, my darling. I just have to keep to myself and bear it on my own.*

*My love to you darling.*

*Peggy*


For more than a week after Christmas the 51st division was constantly on the move although its objectives, beyond holding the Maas crossings, were far from clear, orders and counter-orders arriving at regular intervals. On 28th, heavy snow began to fall, hampering movement of vehicles apart from jeeps and "weasels", the small, tracked transports, the increasing thickness of the snow on the ground and the deepening drifts even making it difficult for tanks, apart from those fitted with special studs. With the temperature dropping to single figures Fahrenheit, everything seemed to freeze, including the electrolyte in the radio batteries, resulting in even greater difficulty with communications, adding to an already confused situation.

Having managed to procure a jeep, Stanley was able to make his essential visits to the active units, although navigating the Belgian lanes in such conditions involved a good deal of trial and error, some being blocked by snow and fallen trees, others taking him alarmingly close to the fluctuating front line. His "doing the rounds" did, however, achieve its objective, of establishing both positions and supply routes and requirements.

Finally, in early January, after brief, generally drunken, but essential celebrations of the New Year, the prospect of not marking Hogmanay, for the Scots troops, quite unthinkable, the greeting of the New Year by pipers, drifting mournfully through the frozen night, the Division was ordered to advance as part of XXX Corps' attack on the northern flank of the bulge.

For Stanley, the next week was somewhere between a surreal dream and a nightmare; winter scenes that in other circumstances would have been enchantingly picturesque, disfigured by devastated villages, blackened buildings starkly contrasting with the surrounding white; everywhere, burnt out tanks and vehicles; and bodies, both Allied and German, left where they had died, frozen, some postured, as if caught by a camera lens, others sitting or reclining, many partly covered by snow.

On a brilliantly clear day, the sky the most perfect blue, he arrived at the village of Ronchamps which the 5th Camerons had taken the previous evening, meeting little resistance. It transpired, however, that the enemy's withdrawal had been tactical, enabling them to take up a position on a ridge a mile from the village from where, just as Stanley, with Hopkins at the wheel of his Jeep, stopped in the centre of the battered village, they were able to subject it to a barrage of shelling.

For more than an hour, he and Hopkins cowered behind a bank at the side of the road, just high enough to afford some protection, several of the buildings close to them receiving direct hits, shrapnel, splintered timber and fragments of masonry filling the air around them, leaving them covered in dust but unharmed.

As the Camerons' officers barked commands, men ran crouching to take up positions, eventually forming up, advancing down into the narrow valley which lay between the village and the German position. As one platoon was moving out of the village, just a hundred yards from where Stanley was sheltering, several shells landed, one close to the platoon, a man hurled into the air, cartwheeling, his rifle flying away from him.

Stanley watched with horrified fascination, the scene, almost in slow motion, the man landing twenty yards along the road, writhing briefly before becoming still. Another man, or what was left of him, was in the middle of the road, sitting up, except that the lower half of his body was missing, the man's head moving from side to side, as if looking for his absent limbs before rolling sideways, leaving

Stanley with the horrifying view of exposed flesh and bone, a mass of entrails flopping onto the road surface, like a string of sausages on a butcher's slab.

During a brief lull in the shelling, he managed to speak to an officer, quickly gauging their requirements and obtaining information as to the locations of other units, the Camerons and Seaforths working closely together.

When the shelling resumed, it was supplemented by the rattle of spandaus, telling him that the troops were approaching the enemy position.

As he and Hopkins were about to return to their Jeep, intent on getting back to HQ, having already visited a number of other units, the familiar whining of incoming shells prompted them to hurl themselves to the ground, belly-crawling behind a partly demolished cottage, its remaining wall offering protection from shrapnel, several shells falling close to them.

After a few minutes, judging it safe to do so, they ran to the Jeep, Hopkins swinging it rounds, sliding on the impacted snow, accelerating away from the village.

When Stanley realised that Hopkins was saying something to him he put his fingers in his ears, wondering if they had become filled with dust, Hopkins' voice faint, as if he was speaking deliberately quietly.

"I can't hear you," he said, massaging his ears with his hands. "Gone a bit deaf."

As they arrived back at the temporary HQ, when the jeep came to a stop, instead of turning off the engine, he saw that Hopkins was sitting quite still, gripping the steering wheel, staring in front of him, a strange expression on his face, as if he was trying not to laugh.

"You alright?" Stanley asked.

As Hopkins turned towards him, Stanley could see that his eyes were wide, his lips sucked tight. He suddenly let out a noise, half sob, half moan, lowering his head onto his hands, still clasping the wheel.

Stanley reached across, placing his hand on his batman's shoulder, realising as he did so, that his own hand was shaking, and that the sensation he had been aware of in his own stomach had become more pronounced, making him fear that he was going to lose control of his bowels.

"I'm sorry, sir," Hopkins said, lifting his head, trying to regain his self control, "but I was shit scared back there." Stanley could see that he was close to tears, his face pale, his eyes bloodshot.

"Me too, old chap. In fact I think…"

Stanley threw his door open, leaning out, vomiting onto the impacted snow, feeling his whole body shaking, sound still seeming to be baffled, his head filled with a noise like a constant gust of wind.

"Are you two OK?" Stanley looked up as Basil Seymour came up to the car. "You in one piece?"

"Think we're both a bit bomb happy," Stanley said, aware of his voice sounding breathless. "Got caught up in it a bit." At least his hearing was returning.

"In Ronchamps? Reports say it's been getting quite a hammering," Seymour told him.

Seymour led the two of them to the mess tent, making an exception to allow Hopkins in as well.

"Here, this'll help." He handed them each a tin cups of brandy. "Best medicine."

Stanley felt the glow of the liquor spreading through him, the shaking abating, leaving him feeling drained, his limbs leaden.

"Thanks Basil."

"I can tell you, Eric, I have never prayed like that in my life," Stanley confided to Eric when, towards midnight, they were in the cosy but confined space of Eric Nichol's caravan, glasses of whisky in hand, Eric having "liberated" a pair of fine crystal glasses from one of the Gestapo buildings they had taken, the former occupants not having had time to removed their possessions, many of which had doubtless been looted from the local inhabitants. "I really thought we'd had it."

"I sometime wish that I could pray," Eric said thoughtfully. "I think what little faith I had has steadily drained away these past months."

"I thought you were C of E, like me," Stanley said, realising how vacuous the remark sounded. "I mean, that you were a regular church goer."

"Yes, a good solid Christian family. Church every Sunday. Pillars of the community."

Stanley detected the note of sarcasm as well as a suggestion of regret.

"I began to have doubts when I was at university. A couple of chaps I was friendly with had actually declared themselves to be atheists. It was rather exciting, being with them, they were so full of new ideas, and weren't afraid to speak their minds. It was as if they were challenging the old order. It made me start thinking for myself."

Sitting side by side on Eric's bed in the caravan, the hurricane lamp filling the confined space with its acrid fumes, they lapsed into silence, Eric staring at the wall in front of him, several photos of his wife and family pinned to it.

"To be honest, when I see something like that, it makes me wonder as well." Stanley could not expel the image of the man sitting on the ground, looking from side to side, keeling over, exposing the ghastly sight of his innards, oozing from his broken body. "How could any half decent God allow such brutality?"

"I sometimes wonder whether we use God to justify and excuse our failings," Eric said, Stanley aware of his friend's tendency, particularly during their quiet chats over a drop of whisky, to become philosophical. "What better recruiting sergeant? Christian Soldiers. Bit of a contradiction."

"Of course, you — we - were brought up with it, weren't we," Eric said, after another pensive interlude. "Steeped in it. Pretty deeply ingrained."

"I think my father has had his moments of doubt." Stanley remembered, a couple of years before the war, when his father went off by himself for a couple of weeks fly fishing, which of itself was not unusual, the difference this time being that it was at rather short notice, Stanley also picking up on an undercurrent of something going on, his mother explaining to him that his father "needs a bit of time to re-charge his batteries", "things having got a bit much recently". What such "things" might have been was not mentioned, his questions brushed aside with vagary about "Parish work".

It had been a few months after the episode that his father, himself, alluded to the episode, albeit in his usual obtuse manner, remarking, when he and Stanley were playing a game of drafts, "the Lord likes to set a test from time to time. Just to make sure that we're measuring up."

Eric's pale, intelligent eyes looked at him sympathetically. "Must be difficult, for an intelligent man like your father, never to have doubts." How curious, Stanley thought, that Eric had gained the impression of his father being an intelligent man, presumably derived from things he had told him, which he could see now could be assembled into a cogent profile.

"He never really rammed it down my throat," Stanley said, his feeling about the family's religiosity being that it was as much about appearance as spirituality. "But I'm not sure I would want to do without him. God, I mean. He can be such a comfort. And for Peggy, it is such a part of her life. I think with her, it was probably laid on quite heavily."

He recalled his father's words of farewell when he was about to set off on his great crusade - "Have faith in the good Lord"- more entreaty than enjoinment, his father-in-law's "Pray to God to safeguard you"- most definitely an edict, implying far more than saying his prayers, imbuing the crusade with Holy purpose, and his own part in it with a morality hinting at his personal conduct as a key element of the Lord's protection.

"She is devoted, but also, I think it is very much a matter of duty. And, knowing her people, a good measure of obeisance."

"The church likes it that way," Eric said, his handsome face creasing into its benevolent smile. "The offer of its embrace in return for subservience."

Stanley pondered Eric's words which, long after, remained in his doubting mind.

*My own*
*It is freezing hard here tonight & everything is white even the gates and the roofs of the houses which are all gleaming in the brilliant moonlight.*
*I am gradually coming to the realisation of the situation with Daddy although I am determined that I will at least try to do something & not to give up all hope though I realise the odds.*
*Last night I wrote to Tom & told him all about it as I don't think he realises that the situation is quite as grave as it is. I am sure he will get home but the red tape seems to be holding things up. He has heard nothing from the War Office yet so he is starting to apply for repatriation from his end with a letter from the General to back him up. Letters are getting through amazingly quickly only taking a week to ten days.*
*Sweetheart, as you can guess I cannot get on with many of my own things now other than looking after Anthony & the essential business. I am glad the news looks good & with some possibility of beating up the Jerries as you said when they are in the open.*

*My darling husband goodbye now.*
*All my love for ever*
*Peggy*

*My very darling girl*
*Thank you too my very dear little girl for a very sweet Christmas card which made your*
*husband rather misty eyed for a few moments and also for the book.*
*I cannot tell you much about my wanderings but we are somewhere in Belgium. I believe*
*my last letter finished in the middle of Xmas Day. Well there was a hell of a flap that day*
*and it was an extraordinary mixture of gaiety and work. Everyone was a bit drunk at*
*lunchtime and the flap that followed was really rather amusing. However we managed to*
*have quite a good Christmas dinner in the evening and it was washed down with*
*Champagne.*
*Boxing day was just a very full day in which we moved. Incidentally we had four or five*
*days of incredibly wonderful weather. The temperature was never above freezing – ice*
*started to form on the rivers, the pine trees carried a very Christmassy coat of silver white*
*frost which combined with a brilliant sun and an unearthly blue sky, seemed like God's*
*own Christmas present to the hard pressed Armies. At night the cold moon shone*
*relentlessly – that did not help us but it did the remnants of the Luftwaffe who did their*
*best to interfere with work & whatever festivities were possible.*
*We saw 1945 in in a large house in Belgium. Today is the Scotsman's great day – it is*
*their Christmas and they had a very inspiring pipe band parade in the local village square.*
*I think the local villagers were most impressed and rather amazed at such strange music.*
*We are now in a dear little town nestling in a valley, through which a lovely river races*
*and gurgles and glides: the town is protected on the North by a great four hundred foot*
*shrub covered cliff. It is grand to be among Belgians again and at least to be able to speak*
*some of the language. You feel you can trust them more than those dullards the Dutch.*
*I think I have driven or been driven about 1500 miles in the past 10 days: 10 days that*
*seem a lifetime.*
*Leave has really started: the first batch went off today: we send our first officer on Jan 7ᵗʰ.*
*We have only one officer vacancy for January and we don't know yet how many we get*
*for February. We ballot monthly so one doesn't know when one will go.*
*Darling I wish so much I could have seen Anthony's Christmas tree. His Xmas card was*
*<u>wizard</u>. Please give him a big kiss and tell him Daddy is very busy but will see him soon.*
*Now my darling, I must say so very lovingly, goodnight – I'll write again tomorrow I*
*hope.*
*I am ever your terribly adoring husband*
*Stanley*

# TWENTY-ONE

He sat in a relatively sheltered corner of the deck as the ship made its way out into the Channel, the sea blue and calm, reflecting the cloudless sky, the white cliffs, catching the morning sun, steadily diminishing as the coast of France with it undulating silhouette, grew more distinct.

The atmosphere amongst the officers and men crowded onto the deck was subdued, each man deep in his own thoughts, all of them sharing the weight of despondency of having to return after leave, the cruelly short interlude from the rigours of the campaign, knowing that it would be months before they would see their loved ones again. They knew also, that they still faced great danger, with the battle for Germany imminent, every indication, based on the fight they had put up so far, being that the *Wehrmacht* remained a formidable force, still, somehow, managing to produce new tanks and guns to replace those which the Allies destroyed.

Stanley's mood was of sheer misery, the pain of parting the previous evening less raw, but leaving a numbness which the memories of the glorious ten days failed to alleviate.

What a contrast with the ecstatic moment when he had stood on the doorstep, knocking on the door, hearing the screech of delight from Anthony before Peggy opened it, her face flushed with excitement, embracing him briefly before turning towards the child, standing in the hall, suddenly wary of this large man in his khaki uniform, his kit-bag on the ground beside him.

Peggy picked him up, allowing his father to wrap the two of them in his arms, kissing the child, inhaling the aroma of Peggy's perfume and Anthony's distinct yet indescribable smell, soap infused with some wonderful essence of the infant.

Peggy's mother appeared in the hall, prompting Stanley to release them from his embrace, kissing his mother-in-law formally on the cheek.

Although Peggy had warned him that her father was much changed, it came as a shock to see how ill he looked, his face, previously full, with his tufted cheeks, now gaunt, the skin sagging and with a sickly pallor, his eyes sunken in shadowed sockets, the tufts absent, having been shaved off when he had been in hospital.

After a rather uncomfortable couple of hours sitting in the living room, making polite conversation, her father asking a few questions before lapsing into a doze,

Anthony, thankfully, playing happily with his toys, delighting Stanley with his chatter and his agility, having grown almost beyond recognition over the past six months, the child entertaining them, distracting them from the strained atmosphere, they made their apologies.

It was only when they got to the hut that Stanley felt that he had truly arrived, the heater giving it the paraffin infused cosiness he remembered.

"Home at last," he said, the embrace this time, uninhibited, Anthony looking at them curiously, but continuing to play with his favourite model boat.

How perfect those ten days had been, much of the time spent in the hut, with a few visits to family and friends, and a lively party thrown by Paddy and Alan, with much liquor flowing.

Peggy's mother had offered to have Anthony for a couple of nights, allowing them to go out, for an essential evening at Jimmy's, eating and dancing – "going gay" as Peggy described it – and a day and a night in London, staying at the Grosvenor, again dining and dancing, but here in the luxury surroundings of the splendid Park Lane hotel which, in later years, would become one of the capital's most prestigious – and expensive.

After the first two or three days, however, they became increasingly conscious of the approaching shadow of his departure, the days passing cruelly quickly, adding an almost desperate intensity to their time together, their love making, particularly on the last days, imbued with a deep passion, each of them, as before, all too aware of the underlying anxiety as to what the future might hold. Afterwards, they would lie, tightly embraced, hanging onto each other, saying little, savouring every moment.

The evenings they spent in the hut were particularly special, Peggy cooking their meal, Anthony sleeping in his cot, oblivious to the records which Stanley played, the volume turned well down but sufficient for them to dance, sometimes sitting on the old sofa, listening to the tunes, Stanley smoking his pipe, Peggy enjoying one of the cigarettes he had brought back, a selection of American and various European, Peggy liking the lighter American ones, finding the darker French tobacco far too astringent.

Several times they became immersed in conversation; about life after the war; what he would do and where they would live; of having a second child; and sometimes about her father, Stanley doing his best to comfort her as she contemplated what she knew to be imminent, of his demise and of life without him.

He recounted to her some of his experiences, determined to keep the reminiscences light, high-lighting the more humorous events and describing the cities and countryside. Only once did he allow himself to reveal something of the darker aspects, mentioning his fear when he had been cut off in Nijmegen during the ill-fated Arnhem episode, and describing the grimness of losing friends and colleagues. He held back, however, as he had decided he would, on the more graphic scenes, and although he wanted to unburden himself, the image of the final moments of the man whose body had been ripped apart, something he was unable to be rid of, surfacing in his dreams and waking thoughts, he withheld.

He wanted to tell her also, about the privations; the cold and the damp; the periods of feeling so cold that one became light headed, as if one's very marrow was turning to ice; and the absence of privacy, alleviated only to a limited extent more recently by his having his caravan. How he hated the very basic communal bathing facilities and latrines, there being something quite repellent about having to defecate with others, sitting on a plank over a foul smelling trench. Had it not been for their periodic billeting in various houses and buildings, some with positively luxurious facilities, he would have found this aspect of military life in the field almost unendurable, particularly in winter, in the summer and autumn months mitigated to some extent by the feeling of being close to nature.

Peggy understood that he was holding back, sometimes encouraging him to tell her about his experiences when she sensed his reticence, yet deciding not to press him.

"I want to know about it all," she said, taking his hand as if to indicate that she could endure anything he wanted to tell her, her resilience being far greater than he gave her credit for. And yet she knew it was part of his make up, to maintain his obdurate fortitude, allusions to the grimmest moments quickly injected with humour, the horrors of shell-fire and mortars rendered almost cartoonish, references to death and injury, anodyne, devoid of the carnage of actuality.

"Bloody good for constipation, those Moaning Minnies!" he said with a laugh, repeating what she remembered from one of his letters.

He had decided that he could not bear to let her drive him to the station, the heart-rending sight of her standing on the platform, her vain attempt to maintain a brave face tearing at his own fraught emotions, her insistence always having been to come to see him off rather than just dropping him outside. He therefore phoned for a taxi, the last minutes, waiting for it to arrive, for both of them, an agony of fragile fortitude. They had put Anthony to bed an hour earlier, Stanley kissing his son gently on the forehead, the child having now become entirely familiar with his father, smiling as Peggy encouraged him to say "night night to Daddy," her voice tightening, Anthony repeating "night night Daddy".

He had learned from previous experience of many partings, the last, shortly before his departure for France the previous June having been so much more painful than any before, that the crescendo of tense anticipation was almost worse than the moment itself, and that once they had got through that dreadful moment, and he was on his way, he could start the process of healing of the raw wound, the first phase, of numbness, giving way, usually after a day or two, to acceptance, and then to looking forward, counting time, planning and dreaming.

This time, however, the taste of the delight of life at home, and of time with the two people whom he adored so utterly, rendered the parting as searingly painful as a knife wound to his soul, knowing also, that he was returning to face the ordeal of what many back home thought would be the relatively straight forward business of finishing off the enemy now that they had him on the back foot, the successful outcome no longer in doubt. For Stanley, as with all of those who had learned of the quality and obduracy of the German army, whilst there was confidence in ultimate victory, the fear was of an arduous and dangerous final phase. And what made matters so much worse, heightening those fears, was that all too short glimpse of the future they all dreamed of, making them so much more acutely aware of their vulnerability.

Having been given an update on the situation, the good news being that the Allies had now pushed the Germans back close to where they had had them before the start of the Ardennes offensive, Stanley was briefed on the preparations for the next stage of the campaign, the 51st Division, as part of XXX Corps, to take part in the delayed Operation Veritable, the major Allied offensive the objective of which was to clear the enemy, finally, from the remaining territory still held on the west side of the Rhine. For the 51st, this included the *Reichswald*, an area of thick forest and rugged terrain not dissimilar to the Ardennes, the forest itself being relatively small but, due to its location, of strategic importance, spread as it was, across the Allies' intended line of advance towards the Rhine and beyond, into the Ruhr, Germany's industrial heartland.

Although not unexpected, an advance through the *Reichswald* being one of the scenarios anticipated, which they now realised was likely to be selected, their experience of the Ardennes, even though the Americans has borne the brunt of counter-offensive, having made them wary of forest fighting, created a good deal of concern.

As soon as the operation began at the beginning of February, it became clear that that their concerns had been well founded, the advance into the dense forest, with its adverse terrain, from the outset, slow and costly.

"It's going to be quite a party," Basil Peters remarked when, while it was still dark at six in the morning, a couple of days into the operation, Eric and several RASC officers were gathered in the mess tent, clutching steaming mugs of tea, warming their hands, standing around the situation map spread on the table, the arrows and hieroglyphics indicating the presumed positions of the division's various units which were currently engaging the enemy. "Buggers have been eating ammo like there's no tomorrow."

"We've been pretty stretched," Eric confirmed. "Twenty-five pounders have been getting through over six hundred rounds per day – each gun. Plus smoke rounds."

"And the Vickers seemed to be enjoying their pepperpots," Peters added, referring to the bouts of intense, coordinated firing by numerous machine guns.

The division's advance was along a fairly narrow front of some three miles, the challenge of an offensive in such terrain made a great deal more difficult due to the snow which, for the past few weeks had lain thick and frozen, now starting to thaw, the forest tracks, few as they were, soon becoming broken up, armour and vehicles getting bogged down, infantry often having to wade through slush and mud.

Despite the strength of XXX Corps, with over two hundred thousand men engaged in the operation, when infantry were advancing through dense forest, they were particularly vulnerable to the defensive tactics of their experienced and resourceful enemy, every track, as well as many forest clearings, mined, it needing the eyes of the ever vigilant veterans to be able to spot the tell-tale signs, sometimes no more than the slightest distortion in the weft of the grass or suspiciously positioned sticks.

With the high casualty rate, most units were reinforced with fresh troops, less familiar with such hazards, not only the mines, but the trees best positioned, and with suitably concealed vantage points, for snipers, the casualty rate amongst the reinforcements a good deal worse than the more seasoned troops.

The fighting was often at close quarters, the night engagements being the worst, actions frequently confused, opponents stumbling into each other, many casualties caused by "friendly" fire, infantry having to fight with little support from artillery, it being impossible to provide targeting information without risking bringing fire down upon themselves.

And as in the Ardennes, even on the days when the sky was clear enough for the Allied aircraft to operate, their targets were only intermittently visible, emerging all too briefly from the shroud of the forest.

In addition to the demands on the RASC for such copious quantities of ammunition and sustenance for troops, they were now having to procure quantities of windproof clothing, the thaw intermittent, with continuing spells of icy winds, as well as rubber boots, white camouflage nets, extra bivouac tents and oil stoves, the supply routes becoming clogged by heavy traffic, progress further impeded by the appalling ground conditions.

Each day Stanley was on the road, direct contact being the only reasonably reliable means of gauging the situation of the ground and of obtaining the essential information as to supply requirements, and working out the locations for forward ammunition dumps. RASC worked closely with REME, the sappers being similarly in demand, improvising repairs to impassable tracks, removing fallen trees, some brought down by shells, others felled by the enemy to cause hold ups, providing opportunities for snipers.

Several times he found himself under fire, coming close enough to enemy positions to be within Spandau and mortar range, the sight of men being killed and wounded still shocking him.

One late afternoon as the light was fading, when he was with a unit of the Black Watch, shells started to fall close to them, followed by more sustained fire, it quickly being realised that it was coming from the rear, frantic radio messages eventually getting word to the gunners that they were firing on their own men, one being killed outright and several wounded.

Just as the firing ceased, a corporal beginning to move cautiously forward from the clearing where Stanley, with Hopkins beside him taking notes, were conversing with two Black Watch officers, stepped on a mine, throwing him backwards, the sten-gun he was carrying flying out of his hands, landing on the track several yards ahead, setting off a second mine, the corporal left sitting against a tree, his eyes closed, a sickening brown liquid oozing from his shattered legs, another man, close by, writhing on the ground, shrapnel from the second mine having ripped into his abdomen.

As other men attended to them, the officers resumed the listing of their requirements, all of them hastily diving to the ground at the sound of incoming shells, this time from the enemy, shattering several trees, branches and jagged shards of wood falling around them.

Having been absent on leave for the first ten days of the Veritable offensive, and hence the first bloody phase of the forest fighting, it would take a further three weeks before the objectives were achieved, the intensity of the fighting during those weeks, if not as confused, still as great, the casualty rate continuing.

As the offensive progressed, the 51st and the other elements of XXX Corps inexorably forcing the enemy back towards the Rhine, confronting and breaching parts of the infamous Siegfried Line with its famed array of fortifications – numerous concrete bunkers and pillboxes, tank-traps, minefields and strategically positioned gun emplacements - each day brought increasing numbers of German prisoners, bedraggled and defeated, traipsing disconsolately to the rear, where they were held in temporary prison pens awaiting transfer to the prison camps.

The majority were the ordinary foot soldiers, men, just like themselves, who were obviously relieved that it was all over, and that, ignominious though it might be to become the vanquished, were accepting of their lot, quietly compliant with orders. As before, the POWs also included many SS officers and men, truculent and arrogant, still professing their zealous belief in their cause and their Fuhrer, such men having to be watched carefully by those guarding them due to the incidence suicide, the ignominy of capture, for the SS, leaving many of them with no alternative but to take their own lives.

For the similarly numerous Hitler Youth, many scarcely more than children, the pity which their appearance might otherwise have evoked – dirty and hungry, torn and muddy uniforms often too big for them – was dispelled by their spiky aggressiveness, sharing with their SS elders, a fanatical belief in the Nazism, indoctrinated as they had been since early childhood.

For several days after Stanley's departure, Peggy found it difficult to lift herself from the despondency which held her in an unrelenting grip, finding herself unable to prevent bouts of weeping, as if her body was having to expel the overwhelming sadness. She tried to put on a brave face for Anthony, and to a lesser extent, for her parents, her mother, sympathetic, in her usual no nonsense way, encouraging her to "buck up", her bland reassurance – "it will soon be over"; and "don't worry about him, I'm sure he'll be fine" – doing little to mitigate Peggy's feeling of loss.

The weather reflected her mood, the Atlantic reasserting its dominance, shouldering out the last wafts of Siberian chill, buffeting the country with strong winds and bursts of rain, dankness seeming to penetrate the very fabric of the country.

*19.1.45*
*My own darling*
*I'm afraid your little wife is at the moment a very different person from the one that welcomed you home. A complete feeling of apathy has got hold of me. I am trying very hard to pull myself together but I never knew how hard it would be or how completely our love could be entangled with everything little thing I do each day.*
*This evening I have been talking to Daddy about that flat & he thinks it is a very good idea & not expensive. I do hope we manage to get it darling, as I would not mind living there on my own for a while.*
*According to the news the Russians are only 165 miles from Berlin this evening. I wonder how long those miles will take.*
*Darling, sailing away from England must have been pretty grim. I imagined it just as you described it on that rather lovely soft morning.*
*My sweet, now I just live for your letters. It is late now so I must say goodnight to my darling, so far away & yet so incredibly near.*
*I am yours forever*
*Peggy*

Strangely, when she woke one morning just a week later, to find that winter had returned, the ground covered with a thick blanket of snow, despite the awful sense of foreboding about her father, the hospital having made it known that no further treatment was worthwhile, the gloom seemed to lift just a little, her resilience again asserting itself.

As she sat on the side of her bed, looking out of the window, the sun just breaking through, reflecting on the snow, Anthony, lying in his cot, muttering to himself as was his morning habit, as if having a confidential chat with his rather dog-eared teddy, she drew breath.

"Pull yourself together," she said, nodding to add emphasis to her determination.

Her last conversation with the sister at the hospital had told her what she already knew, that her father's condition was terminal, although the sister was reluctant to answer the question of how long she thought he had.

"There are some treatments," she said, unconvincingly, "which can help people at this stage, to alleviate pain, and sometimes to ..." she paused, looking at Peggy, once again assessing that she was speaking nurse to nurse, and could therefore be totally honest, "...and sometimes to gain a little extra time. It is strange, but a person who has the will to go on, can sometimes survive for longer that one who gives up. But you shouldn't have any false hopes."

It was so difficult to see her father becoming weaker by the day, his physical decline made so much worse by his worrying about the business, particularly as it was still uncertain whether Tom was going to be allowed home on compassionate leave. Several times he insisted on going to his office, his secretary ringing up one day when he was there, desperately worried as the sick man had fallen asleep at his desk and when she had decided she should wake him, for several minutes finding him incoherent and disoriented.

If only Stanley had been home; and Tom, to help with business, having completed his articles just before the outbreak of war and thus being a qualified surveyor. Having served his articles in his father's firm, he also had a good understanding of the business. But he was still on the other side of the world with the Chindits.

With her experience of reading between the lines of the news, maintaining, as she did, her daily routine of listening to the BBC war report coming after the evening news, and of pouring over her father's *Times*, she could see that although the reports of the Allies' progress in Northern Europe remained upbeat, the going was clearly tough, the mention of casualties being the clearest indication that Germans were continuing to put up stiff resistance.

As always, she would have her atlas open, being quite familiar now with that part of Holland which was closest to Germany, and to the German territory west of the Rhine, although due to the small scale maps in the atlas, only the most significant features and largest towns and cities were marked. She could, however, identify the small smudge of green which, although unnamed on the map, she worked out must be the *Reichswald*, the forest which had been referred to in a few of the war reports, where, as far as she would work out, the 51st

Highland Division was fighting.

Compelled as she was to keep abreast of the news, knowing that the fierce fighting showed no sign of abating, only added to her worries. The fact that daily life was becoming increasingly difficult, in comparison, seemed quite bearable, although there were times when she felt this to be getting her down. Rationing was making it ever more challenging to get so many things, and even with the extra allowance for Anthony, essentials like butter, meat and sugar, were limited to such meagre portions that one was ever having to try alternatives.

Invariably, also, one had to queue, the queues often extending outside shops which, in this weather, meant having to try to keep warm, the line of people, stamping their feet and clapping their gloved hands, their breath exhaled as clouds of steam into the cold air.

With this sudden return of cold weather, the shortage of coal meant that one had to be frugal with heating, even her parents, always having seen parsimony as a virtue, complaining about the difficulty of keeping the living room warm, the fire sometimes just a couple of lumps of coal to supplement the slightly more generous supply of logs, although even these had become more difficult to come by, Peggy herself, having taken to chopping up any suitable wood she could get hold of, several times having dragged branches fallen from the trees in the park, back up the hill to the house, until, one day, being confronted by the irascible park-keeper, telling her that the wood was council property.

They managed to keep reasonably warm by being well rugged up, Anthony swathed in several layers, Peggy's father, now home again, in his armchair, wearing his woollen scarf with a rug over his knees.

In the mornings, the windows were patterned with frost, something which, as a child, Peggy had loved to examine, marvelling at nature's intricate beauty, scratching the ice with her fingernails to create pictures. Now, however, the patterns only served as evidence of the chill which pervaded the house, even hot water being rationed, there only being sufficient coke to heat water for one bath each per week, and even then, with just a few inches of water.

What they had to endure was, she told herself, nothing compared to what Stanley was experiencing, the reports, as well as his letters, mentioning the freezing conditions in Europe. And what was more, he was constantly in danger.

For Stanley, more than ever, Peggy's letters were like rays of warm light amid the all pervading chill, the moment when he climbed into his caravan, snuggling beneath the thick blanket, the paraffin lamp puttering beside him, were like oases in the bleakness of day to day existence, moments when he could detach himself from the pressure of the endless demands, letting his mind stray back to the place he so longed to be, and to the two people who were the cornerstone of his life.

It was not just the tiredness resulting from interrupted nights, sleep disturbed almost nightly by calls requiring his urgent attention. When he was free from such demands, there was invariably the rumble of guns, often accompanied by the ominous rattle of machine guns, the distinctive sound of spandaus indicating the proximity of the fighting, it being difficult to sleep when one was constantly trying to gauge not only the distance to the front lines, but the subtle changes in volume indicating movement.

All of them, RASC officers and men, and, even more acutely, the front line troops, particularly those who had been involved from the outset, suffered the cumulative effect of so many months of fear and fatigue; of the strangely earthy existence of men at war, even in a modern army, day in, day out, living with – depending upon – comrades, sharing an intense, communal life, riven with grim regularity of tragedy and loss.

It hit them every so often, a wave of almost debilitating weariness, their spirit drained from them, when all they wanted was for it to end; to be back home, with loved ones and home comforts. There were even moments when, in the very depths of such black moods, the thought of death as the means of release seemed almost welcome; or better still, a Blighty ticket; a wound bad enough to need a trip to a British hospital, preferably with a sufficiently long period of recuperation to offer the prospect of seeing out the war.

"Battle fatigue," Eric said, when, with a rare moment of daytime respite, the two of them found time for walk away from the direction of the fighting, in an area on the fringe of the forest unblemished by shells or tanks. It was one of those days when, although the air was still bitterly cold, there was just the slightest hint that this resurgence of winter might presage the beginnings of spring, a few birds braving the conditions, practising their songs, flitting through the trees, glimpses of plumage caught in the dazzling, snow enhanced sunlight. "Even though we're not in the front line, in some ways it's the same for us. To be honest, Stanley, I have had some moments myself recently. I don't mind admitting that the other night, when I was woken up by the usual call, I thought I wasn't going to be able to move. It was as if I had turned to lead. It was so warm in my bed, and I just couldn't face, yet again, having to go out into the blasted cold."

"I never really knew before," Stanley said, "what chilled to the marrow meant. Not like this, when there isn't a shred of warmth left in your body. Christ, I can't wait for warm weather."

"And for this bloody war to be over."

They walked on for a while in silence, wrapped in the tranquillity of their surroundings, despite the ever constant background rumbling of gunfire.

"Isn't it funny to think we're walking on German soil," Stanley remarked, still trying to grasp the fact that although the Rhine was seen as Germany's real protective western frontier, they had crossed the actual border some time ago.

"That's probably why they're fighting so bloody hard," Eric said. "God, what's it going to be like when we're across the Rhine."

"And getting across," Stanley added.

Adding to the fatigue was the realisation that, while they had managed to push the enemy back, having now virtually cleared the *Reichswald*, there was still hard fighting ahead, just to gain the remaining territory on this side of the Rhine, with the small matter of some formidable sections of the Siegfried Line yet to be broached. And only then would they be ready to tackle the most daunting obstacle, the Rhine itself.

During final phase of Operation Veritable, Stanley witnessed some of the most savage fighting of the campaign. The objective was the strongly fortified town of Goch, which, standing at the intersection of a number of roads as well as a key element of the Siegfried Line, had obvious strategic importance.

The line of advance required the 51$^{st}$ to take the small town of Kessel as well as a number of villages, clearing the route to Goch itself.

For RASC, compared with the difficulty of supplying units fighting in the depths of the *Reichswald,* the direct advance made life a good deal more straight forward, although such a narrow front also led to congestion of tanks and other vehicles. There was also increasing demand for the highly effective new weapons known as "mattresses"; multiple rocket launchers, some capable of unleashing salvoes of thirty rockets with devastating effect on the enemy. There was no doubt however, that the German defenders' greatest fear was the flame throwing "crocodile".

On the morning when the 51$^{st}$, in conjunction with other divisions including the 43$^{rd}$, launched the main assault on the town, advancing from three directions, Stanley was a few hundred yards behind the mattresses as they unleashed their salvoes, the rockets, their flat trajectory marked by the threads of white trails, their whooshing sound, strangely hushed compared with the bark of the guns, their targets erupting with puffs of dark smoke.

As the barrage continued, a hundred or more twenty-five pounders contributing to the bombardment, beneath the thunder of guns he could now hear the distinctive sound of numerous Churchill tanks, some advancing in line ahead along the road, others spread across the adjacent fields, their guns soon contributing to the cacophony.

Several of the tanks, the adapted AVRE versions, were equipped with devices serving as what were in reality, mechanical catapults, enabling them to hurl forty pound bombs at the concrete bunkers, their thick concrete walls almost impervious to standard shells.

With his binoculars trained on the bunkers, Stanley watched, transfixed, as one of the AVREs flung its bomb, the explosion momentarily obscuring the bunker. As the smoke began to clear, he could see a large gaping hole punched through the concrete, a crocodile, approaching to within less than a hundred yards, squirting fuel through the hole, then firing an incendiary round, flames belching out of the hole and through several vents.

"Christ Almighty," he said under his breath, picturing what it must have been like for the defenders inside.

"Not a nice way to go," Hopkins said, standing beside Stanley.

Several other bunkers were receiving similar treatment, flames erupting from them, the crocodiles following up with further jets of flame.

As the infantry, following close behind the tanks, swarmed amongst the bunkers, lobbing grenades into any bunkers continuing to put up resistance, some of the grenades phosphorus, their lethal effectiveness evident from the screams of the defenders, the searing phosphorus adhering to their skin and clothing, enemy troops began to appear, hands in the air, at first just a trickle, quickly increasing, Stanley's reckoning on there being over a hundred, just from the area within the view of his binoculars.

Having largely neutralised the lines of bunkers, progressing through the other obstacles which formed this section of the Siegfried line, the minefields causing extensive casualties to infantry as well as destroying several tanks, the division's advance units were faced with the consequence of the bombardment, very similar to Caen some months earlier, the streets obstructed by piles of rubble, making it difficult even for tanks to progress and providing effective defensive positions for spandaus and snipers.

The advance into the town was painfully slow with much close quarters fighting, and when the town was effectively under Allied control, it still took several days of mopping up, pockets of stubborn resistance costing yet further British and Canadian lives.

It was just as the 51st believed that they were close to completing their task, requiring one final drive, crossing a small river called the Kendel, that they encountered what was, in effect, a classic ambush, walking into a wall of fire from an arc of well positioned spandaus, the 2nd Seaforths suffering serious casualties.

The division's response, as if in a fit of anger, was to bring down on the defenders, a rain of fire from every weapon which could be deployed, the ambush soon quelled.

The calls which came through to RASC were insistently demanding what, even for the ever ammunition hungry gunners, seemed extravagant, the transports plying their way back and forth, slowed by the mud which, the last of the snow having now thawed, once again hampered the meeting of the demands.

With most of the supplies having to be hauled along the crumbling, mud mired roads, the screening of the forest now far behind them, the RASC vehicles were exposed to enemy shelling which, at certain times became concentrated on certain sections where detours were impossible to find, with the result of the loss of more than twenty vehicles. It was the shells striking the ammunition vehicles which, for obvious reasons, were most dramatic, several large explosions killing crews and leaving craters which the already stretched sappers were called upon to repair, the urgency obvious from the backing up of vehicles heading in both directions.

The only minor consolation for the RASC was that the lesson of the campaign having taught them to convey ammunition to the front line in smaller loads, generally in light trucks or trailers, the impact of a direct hit was lessened.

It was not until the first days of March that the Operation was deemed to have concluded, all of its objectives having been attained, the cost, in lives, vehicles and equipment, apparent from the number of reinforcements arriving, together with many welcome new transports. It would not be for some three weeks that these untried replacements would have their first taste of front line warfare, their initiation to be a veritable baptism of fire.

"This has just come through from the Corps Commander," Eric Nicholls announced to the mess, the officers assembled for once, without the disruptions for the frantic demands of battle. Eric held up Horrocks' message, reading to the now silent mess.

"I have seen the 51st Highland Division fight many battles since I first met them just before Alamein. But I am certain the Division has never fought better than in the recent offensive into Germany. You breached the enemy's defences in the initial attack, fought your way through the southern part of the Reichswald, overcame several strongpoints of the Siegfried Line, and then finally cleared Goch, key centre in the German defensive line. You have accomplished everything you have been asked to do in spite of a number of additional German reserves which have been thrown in on your front. No division has ever been asked to do more and no division has ever accomplished more. Well done Highland Division."

Eric looked around the mess, the faces all turned towards him, several nodding, gratified by such fulsome recognition.

"Just a few months ago," Eric said, "Monty was expressing very real concern – well justified, I might add – that the 51st was no longer the force which had so excelled in the desert, having lost something of its fighting prowess and with its morale down by its boots. I think I can say that this," again he held up the message "…this tells us that we're back where we belong, at the pinnacle of the Allied army. I know that many of you have contributed greatly to the restoration of the division's proud name. Gentlemen, I thank you."

Was it by chance that, as he spoke his final words, Eric was looking directly at Stanley, as if to single him out for special, albeit silent praise? Stanley allowed himself a smile of acknowledgment.

"Are you allowed to tell me now, sir?" Hopkins asked, keeping his eyes firmly on the road ahead, the surface pot-holed, with some sections reduced to muddy rubble, Hopkins steering the Jeep in a slalom to minimise the strain on the vehicle's suspension, and on their own shaken bodies. "I mean, being all done up in dress uniform, I assume there's some bigwigs involved."

In front and following them were numerous other vehicles, including convoys of lorries, the troops having been told only that they were required to assemble for an important parade, news greeted with a good deal of grumbling and not a little ribaldry at the idea of a parade at a time when they were had only just finished the arduous business of winkling out the last of the tenacious German defenders, and were expecting at least a short spell of rest.

"I suppose I can tell you now," Stanley replied, looking round enquiringly at Burrows and Hooper on the back seat, both of whom nodded their assent. "Monty and a few other VIPs are coming to have a look at us. Give us a pat on the back, no doubt."

"Blimey!" Hopkins exclaimed, his face lighting up at the prospect of once again, encountering the great man.

What none of them had expected was that as the convoy of staff cars, two Rolls Royces and their escort of armoured cars drew up in the middle of the field, several thousand troops drawn up on three sides of the field called to attention, from one of the Rolls stepped the instantly recognisable figure of Winston Churchill. As Montgomery, the Chief of the Imperial General Staff, Field Marshall Sir Alan Brooke, and the gaggle of VIPs moved away from the vehicles, the PM stood for a moment, as was his habit, to ensure that the troops had the chance to see him, this time in his full colonel's uniform, raising his arm in his famous salute, two fingers in the "V" for victory, his cigar clasped in the fingers of his other hand.

The fine rain which began to fall did nothing to dampen the enthusiasm of the men who, on one voice, gave three cheers to the two great men.

# TWENTY-TWO

It was with mixed feelings that on a sunny, early spring afternoon, Stanley stood at the edge of a small area of woodland, looking out across the Rhine, the absence of gunfire seeming to make the sounds of nature more pronounced, the bird song positively strident. With his binoculars, he scanned the far bank, more than five hundred yards away, the only movement being a few grey uniformed soldiers apparently strolling in the sun, like their khaki clad opponents on this side of the great river, taking advantage of the lull before the next storm which they all knew to be imminent.

As far as he was aware, his information, as usual deriving from the ever reliable Eric, no decision had yet been taken as to where the crossing was to take place. What was clear, however, was that it would be somewhere along the section of the eastern bank which the Allies now controlled. And what was also obvious was that, with no bridges remaining intact, it was going to be an amphibious operation, reliant upon the ponderous DUKWs and Buffaloes to transport men and materiel across the wide, exposed expanse of water.

He lowered his binoculars, turning away from the river, remaining for several minutes listening to the birdsong, able now to identify even some of the smaller birds, distinguishing the various reedy piping songs as well as the shrill laughing of jays and woodpeckers, against the backdrop of the soft cooing of wood pigeons.

It was good, for once, to be on his own, giving him the opportunity to make a few detours from his rounds, exploring some of the countryside, enjoying the sunshine, particularly when driving in the open Jeep. Inevitably, however, he had to pass through several villages, most of them in ruins, few buildings having escaped the devastation of the battle, the civilians now beginning to return, their faces, as he navigated the rubble strewn streets, staring at him, their blank expressions, he sensed, numbly accepting of their lot rather than hostile.

Although, as always for the RASC, work went on, with the division removed from the front line and with the Germans having now been driven back beyond the Rhine offering a period or respite, Stanley at last found the time to re-read Peggy's letters, lingering over them, the second reading so much more pleasurable although at the same time, making her suffering of her father's decline so much harder for him to bear, knowing that he would not be able to comfort her when, as now seemed inevitable, he lost his struggle with the terrible disease.

Try as he would to expunge Eva from his thoughts, from time to time they would turn to her, unable to rid himself of the image of her tall, slender figure, her beautiful face with its sad expression, and most of all, her eyes, seeming to be pleading for forgiveness and at the same time, offering a window to her sensuality.

No, he would not see her again even though she was close by, although when he went about the town, he half hoped to run into her.

Death being an everyday occurrence throughout the campaign, there were still occasions when it seemed so much more personal. He had spent an hour the previous day with Angus Anderson, a captain he had always got on with, their encounters generally being for business purposes, Anderson being responsible for the indents for his battalion. He was a jovial chap, full of life, the two of them sharing a passion for cricket, managing a chat about some county or test match, their banter involving the all important statistics, the great players of the pre-war era invariably featuring Hobbs and Sutcliffe, Hammond and Duleepsinhji, as well as the man who had become the bane of several English test teams, the legendary Don Bradman.

When Stanley learned of Anderson's death, his Jeep having driven over a mine, he found it difficult to comprehend. How could someone with such a zest for life suddenly have it snuffed out? How perilously fragile was their existence. He wished he could have been with Peggy, not so much to pour out his grief, but simply to hold her, to feel her life affirming presence.

How just it felt, that vengeance was being wreaked on the German people, the reports indicating that Bomber Command had destroyed the city of Dresden, the fact that it was civilians who suffered the terrible firestorm unleashed by the thousands of incendiary bombs rained down on them, evoking little sympathy, the shared view being that they, the German people as a whole, having sowed the wind, were now reaping the whirlwind of their making. Few of the Allied troops were aware of the extent of the city's death-toll, later reckoned at over twenty-five thousand. Had they known, their sentiment, that the nation which had caused the deaths of so many of their friends, compatriots and allies deserved nothing but the iron fist of conquest, would have remained impervious. The brutality of war had inured the fighting men to such assaults on humanity.

*16.2.45*

*Major S R Allen   HQ RASC   51st (Highland) Division   BLA*

*My sweetheart darling*

*I've been out most of today in my jeep. The roads are in a frightful state – it is nothing but mud and potholes and slush. It has been a sad day as one of our officers got killed. He was quite a friend of mine. We are burying him in the field next door tomorrow morning.*

*I went into the first German town I've been to today. It was an absolute shambles, a fine example of the New Order. The few remaining civilians have been told to stay in the cellars till we've time to deal with them & if they come out they don't get a chance to go back. They are fed up with the war and disinterested in anything except getting out of it. The war is certainly being brought home to Germany itself at last: there isn't a house intact anywhere. Of course it may be better further on – I hope so, I want some booty. I'm after a camera, binoculars or watch (German) as my souvenirs, plus a German pistol.*

*We are now out of range of shops and in fact any buildings or villages we come to are shuttered and uninhabited, even worse than bridgehead days. Germany is certainly getting its share of the war on its doorstep at last. As far as we are concerned the more of Germany that is destroyed now, and the more dead Huns, the better. It is a stern and bitter army that now fights for the first time on German soil.*

*I didn't quite know whether to take your remarks on my lack of experience of continental womanhood as condonation of my sowing some wild oats or what! Anyhow, the case no longer arises owing to our present preoccupation with matters military! I am sure that there will be opportunities later on, even if I am detained at the office late!!*

*And so I'll go to sleep, dreaming of so sweet a person, so lovely a person, so utterly loveable, I am yours and you are mine for ever.*

*Stanley*


"You can't possibly think of going to the office. Daddy, please!" Peggy had rarely spoken so forcefully to her father, raising her voice to either of her parents invariably eliciting a stern rebuke for her failure to know her place. But his insistence that he was in a fit state not only to accompany Tom to the office, but to go with him on a farm inspection, caused her exasperation to boil over. He was scarcely able to get up from his chair to shuffle from the room to the toilet, and watching him climb the stairs the previous evening had been just too awful, the effort of mounting each step requiring him to pause, summoning up the energy for the next.

She had always so admired his no-nonsense robustness, shrugging off colds and even a mild dose of flu as a no more than a minor irritation. But what he was revealing now was another of his traits, an obduracy which could make him wholly unreceptive to reason.

Her exasperation was, however, tempered by the realisation that the poor, dear man was desperately worried about the business, even though he now had Tom to help him, although it still remained to be seen how long his son was going to be able remain, the War Office being infuriatingly unresponsive.

"Surely Mr Gladding can manage things," Peggy said, referring to her father's partner, aware however, of her father's less than complimentary view of his senior partner's abilities, both professional and in managing the business. "And with Tom there to help."

"I have to be there," her father replied, lying back in his armchair, closing his eyes, his appearance full justifying Peggy's insistent plea.

What made matters so much worse was the decision which she and her mother had taken, to withhold from her father the full extent of the diagnosis, allowing him to assume that what afflicted him was the cancer he knew he had in his shoulder, combined with the chest condition which had affected him for a year or more, and which he had been unable to shake off.

He was, however, fully aware of the reality, having gleaned the truth from the nurses when he had been in hospital, but deciding to hide it from his wife and daughter to minimise their distress, the thinly veiled mutual deception only serving to exacerbate the undercurrent of tension which pervaded the household.

His determination having prevailed, she helped him out to the car, insisting on wrapping a rug around his legs, ignoring his grumbling. "You don't need to molly-coddle me, girl."

When, late in the afternoon, they returned, her father could scarcely walk, Tom holding him upright, guiding him to his armchair where the sick man, still in his coat and scarf, instantly fell asleep, his wife, son and daughter standing in front of him, as if inspecting him.

"My poor husband," Peggy's mother said quietly.

During the long, gruelling struggle of the *Reichswald* battle, when Stanley was ensconced in his caravan nursing the black mood which had taken hold of him, as always if things were getting on top of him, he longed to be able to pour out his heart to his beloved Peggy, having to make do instead, with trying to articulate something of his feelings in writing, knowing that in doing so, he would have to moderate his despondency, yet certain that she would nevertheless be able to read between the lines. One evening during leave, they had talked about the understanding they had developed of each other's coded references to things they wanted to say, but which, for some reason, not merely concern about censorship, they felt compelled to water down. Increasingly uninhibited in their sexual intimacies, their constraint was in the voicing of their fears and anxieties. It was as if they each felt it necessary to bolster the other's morale by keeping up a brave face.

That moment, however, when such unutterable despondency was weighing upon him, he came close to baring his soul, it only being as he was writing, that the simple fact of being able to express himself to her, enabled him to hold back, the composing of the letter, like the visit to the confessional, drawing some of the darkness from his pained soul.

*My sweetheart darling*
*Thank you darling for writing so often and such lovely letters. I'm so sorry there is not better news of your father. I loved your scented letter in the green envelope and I read it in a more peaceful frame of mind last night before going to sleep.*
*The weather has turned against us today – it is gloomy and cold & starting to rain. One moment we are somewhere in Germany, the next somewhere in Holland. Everywhere is the same though, desolation, floods and ruins, though this field & farmhouse are quite pleasant. We are moving again tonight or tomorrow. There are no civilians at all which is a very good thing as they only get in the way.*
*This war is no longer very interesting really. It's so obvious now it'll finish when we have killed or taken prisoner all the German Army and occupied their country. By fighting on, Germany is thus, we hope, writing herself off as a nation for ever.*
*I'm feeling rather weary, more mentally than physically: that always happens when the pace slackens for a few days as it has done at the moment. You feel unbelievably tired of the whole thing and rather disillusioned and browned off. Death & destruction seem endless. You find that people get on each other's nerves & petty squabbles start.*
*The mud improves one day but it rains for a few hours and the result is worse than ever. How glad we'll be to get away from rivers, flat country and floods. In other words the land between the sea and the central European plateau which forms Holland and parts of north west Germany.*
*The war is going as it should i.e. slowly but steadily, to the finish in a few more weeks. Organised resistance will then be declared over and there'll just be mopping up. There will probably be no end to the war as people expect – it'll just fizzle out – it's probably started to do that already: there are a few signs of lack of control by German High Command.*

*It's all rather dull & unpleasant — no thrill of liberation or rushing advances through sun drenched France & Belgium. Just dull plodding through battered Germany & the remnants of the Wehrmacht.*

*The news that gives us most pleasure is that the Yanks are bashing the daylights out of Tokyo and those bastard Japs. Each raid must surely kill thousands of them as they are very overcrowded.*

*I love you utterly darling, through everything & hope that silver lining may soon appear.*

*God bless you & Anthony*

*Yours for ever & so utterly in love.*

*Stanley*

There was something about the war reports in recent days that troubled her. It was as if they — whoever it was who compiled the accounts of the goings on in the various theatres of the global conflict — were holding back about what was happening on western front. Indeed, she had noticed over the months of avid listening, and of studying the newspapers, that what those familiar announcers were reporting did not quite tally with what Stanley was telling her, even though what he was able to say was necessarily constrained by censorship.

She realised that the events he was referring to were sometimes several days in the past by the time his letters arrived, and then she had to glean what she could from his obtuse references to places and activity. And yet, with her experience of filling in the gaps, gathering shreds of evidence and piecing them together, particularly when, later, she was able to compare her conclusions with his more detailed subsequent recounting, her surmise was remarkably accurate.

Now, as she studied the well thumbed atlas, she stared at the word *Rhine*, imagining Stanley somewhere nearby, the river, even with the scale of the atlas, thickly marked, as if indicating its width as such a formidable obstacle for the Allies to have to overcome.

"I'm sure they do their best to reconcile the desire to be as forthcoming as possible with the need for military secrecy," Stanley's father suggested when, one morning, she was sitting with him and Stanley's mother, sipping a cup of Camp coffee, the substitute which, in fact, tasted nothing like coffee, but which, mixed with plenty of milk, Peggy rather liked. How wise her father-in-law always seemed. It was as if, through his long years of communing with the Good Lord, he acquired a perspective of the world, and of mankind in all its wonder and its failings; an understanding beyond that of others, even her own father, who, although very much a man of the world, she felt to be wilfully shuttered in his outlook, and sometimes overly opinionated.

"It is rather frustrating," Peggy said, "not knowing *exactly* where Stanley is, and what he is doing."

"May be best that we don't know," her father-in-law replied, his gaze out of the window. "I fear it would only make us even more anxious about him."

The impression given by the reports was that, after those deeply worrying few weeks, when the Germans had managed to force their way back into Belgium and were threatening to break through to Antwerp and Paris, the Ardennes offensive eventually having been defeated, there was an interlude, with the Allies consolidating their positions in readiness for the big final push into Germany in the spring. And yet now there seemed to be continuing fighting, the indication being that the Germans remained, in considerable strength, on the west side of the Rhine, the fighting, judging by the mention of casualties, which, even with numbers omitted, were clearly heavy, unrelenting.

"I do so wish it was all over," she said, her determined cheeriness momentarily slipping, her father-in-law reaching across, patting the back of her hand.

"We must all remain cheerful," he said, Stanley's mother, with Anthony now sitting on her knee, her round, soft featured face showing a similar anxiety as she stared at the child, nevertheless, nodding her determined assent.

"I'm sure it will all be over by the summer," she said, stroking Anthony's hair, kissing his cheek. How natural she was with the child, Peggy thought, compared with her own mother's stiffness, always, Peggy felt, wanting to correct or scold him.

When Anthony was in bed, she sat for a while, the notepad on the small roll-top desk in front of her, the fountain pen in her hand, her fingers poised to unscrew the top, her thoughts ranging around the battleground, much of it shrouded in the fog of uncertainty. As she unscrewed the top, as so often, she found the right tone coming to her; her worries placed in their separate compartment.

*28.2.45*
*My sweetest darling*
*Thank you for your letter that arrived today. I was so sorry to hear about the friend of yours being killed. There seem quite a lot of grim patches in life nowadays don't there?*
*It sounds from the news tonight as if you are having a still more trying time. I hope you are not too exhausted & tired & that you are quite cheery.*
*Darling, I want to go on the beach this summer though only one patch of beach is going*

*to be opened & there will be such crowds of people that it will be perfectly safe.*

*If you are in the Army of occupation Anthony & I will be able to come too shan't we?*
*They mentioned that in a parliamentary debate today. It would be quite a good way of*
*seeing Germany cheaply don't you think & grand because we would be together?*

*It is wonderful to hear that you might possibly get another leave sometime from July*
*onwards. It is so grand to be able to look forward to it though I hope the war will end by*
*then.*

*God bless you darling mine.*

*Peggy*

Stanley could not recall a day which had been anywhere near comparable. It was as if the division as a whole had received a shot in the arm of some glorious, morale boosting tonic. Although they had seen Monty a few times before – Stanley having encountered him both at the 43$^{rd}$ and once before since joining the 51$^{st}$ – there was something about a visit from the great man. One felt that even if morale had been down in one's boots, his mere presence would raise it up. He had such a way with words, but it was more than that. It was as if he personified the grit and determination of the British fighting man. And he always left them with their optimism, tested as it was but the knocks they suffered along the way, fully restored.

But when Churchill stepped out of the shining Rolls Royce, one's heart veritably missed a beat. As Monty was the embodiment of the British fighting spirit, so Winnie was the very spirit of the nation, dogged and unbowed in adversity, and now, at last with the upper hand, extending his vision to – and beyond – the glorious moment of victory, rousing them with the sight of the promised land, of returning to their homes and loved ones.

Never had Stanley felt the cheering to be so impassioned, the sense, as they returned to their quarters, that one had been blessed, the feeling almost of joy, despite Churchill's frankness about the hard road ahead, the warning tempered by the certainty of victory.

*4.3.45*

*My lovely sweetheart*

*This has been a very exciting day so I'll confine this letter to telling you as much as I can*
*about it & write a more personal one tomorrow: at the moment I'm so full of today that*
*I must tell you.*

*Picture if you can a large open field on the verge of a forest, somewhere in Germany.*
*Forming four sides of a square are a large gathering of officers & men of the Highland*
*Division. In the centre of one side is a marquee: a microphone stands on the grass outside.*

*You would notice a great air of expectancy over the whole. In one corner of the square are the massed pipes and drums bands of the Div.*

*Suddenly several jeeps and armoured cars appear, then slowly, majestically, two of the most impressive Rolls you've ever set eyes on swing into the field: both fly the Union Jack. The whole gathering stands to attention – some 15,000 men. And slowly out of the front Rolls steps a familiar figure in the uniform of a full colonel, and looking the picture of health – Winston himself. With him is our Div Commander. From the second Rolls jumps Monty & Sir Alan Brooke – Monty wearing his beret & his battle rigout, like an old clothes man.*

*The PM then – obviously very deeply moved – makes a short but very wonderful speech: this is his first in Germany. The Last Post, Retreat & "Flowers of the Forest" are played and the grand old boy stands there alone, a venerable and dignified figure, and all who were near him say that as the Retreat echoed through the forest, in memory of the fallen of this Division, there were tears in those very blue eyes.*

*He stood there in the rain for nearly half an hour. He seemed to us to be so very impressed, so very moved by this scene on German soil. At last Monty stepped up to him & said, very audibly, "Winston, it's time we were on our way. He turned slowly & walked down through a lane of officers and Jocks to his car, smiling now, saying good luck to you all, God bless you, & the famous V sign brought forth the pent up cheers. He looked such a grand figure – one felt so terribly fond of him & proud of being British.*

*And so the great procession moved off and our great and exciting afternoon ended. We came away with our hearts very full and soon the inevitable Winston & Monty stories were in full swing – we were living over again his every gesture & word.*

*So you see, my darling, I'm still rather deeply moved, very happy & very proud of the Highland Division & above all of being an Englishman.*

*Goodnight my very beloved darling who so sweetly, as Winston said, "keeps the home fires burning through the dark years behind us".*

*With so much love*
*Stanley.*


How proud she felt, sitting by the fire, her mother and father either side of her, her mother knitting, her father snoring, the *Times* spread across his lap, Howard Marshall's War Report describing Churchill's visit to the 51st Highland Division, accompanied by Montgomery and Brooke.

"How splendid," her mother said, her approval of Stanley's division's achievements, Peggy felt, never quite fulsome.

"It's the first time Winnie has been on German soil," Peggy said, trying to impress upon her mother both the importance of the occasion and the honour for the 51st to be the Prime Minister's host.

Her father woke up, muttering "In Germany. Mm", as if he had been listening to the report, raising his paper, reading it for a few minutes before again nodding off, the paper settling once again on his knees, this time sliding to the floor.

Peggy looked at him, thinking how pitiful he looked, and how helpless, sitting, waiting as the disease ran the last stage of its inexorable course. For months he had sought to treat it with the disdain he showed for a common cold, defying it from preventing him going about his daily life, it only being within the last week or so that he finally seemed to be accepting the inevitability of defeat.

A sign of his decline was the fact that he would sometimes now stay in bed in the morning, Peggy taking him his breakfast, cutting the top off his boiled egg before placing the tray on the bedside-table, helping him to sit up, adjusting his pillows, feeling the bones of his shoulders and the lightness of his frame.

His last outing with Tom, driving out to some Sussex farm, had exhausted him more than any previous trip, and indeed, since then, he had abandoned the idea of going to the office. Not that this stopped him from fretting, insisting on taking Tom into the small study, Tom filling pages of his notebook as he recorded all the details his father was imparting about the business, and about its, and the family's, finances.

Her father was desperately worried about money. He had done everything to prepare for his demise, fully aware now of the gravity of his condition even though, between them, they maintained the fiction that there was to be some further treatment, and that they must all remain optimistic. Tom, since his return, had remained sceptical about such lack of honesty, and although he went along with it to the extent of refraining from any overt statement of the obvious, his allusions, in his private conversations with his father, to the need to prepare, left no doubt between them that they both fully understood the grim reality.

There was enough in terms of assets and his share of the business – her father and his aging and, nowadays, ineffectual partner, Mr Gladding, being the only two partners - to ensure the family would be well provided for, although this did not prevent him worrying. He instructed Tom on the arrangements which should be made for selling the house, and for a smaller house or a flat to be purchased for his wife, his assumption being that both Tom, and Peggy and Stanley, when he returned from the war, would be able to provide for themselves.

It being in Tom's nature to confide in his sister, he would recount to her what their father had told him, thus enabling her to play her part in planning for the future, although her priority was to find an affordable home for her, Stanley and Anthony, hoping not only that the war would be over within the next year, but that Stanley would be able to return to the law, getting through his finals and settling into a suitable local firm.

She even managed to make some enquires about possible openings for him, a conversation with their old friend, Christopher Mileham, who, for some reason Peggy was not aware of, but she assumed to do with his health, had recently been released from the Navy, and was now a junior partner in a Brighton solicitor's practice. Although he was not able to make any promises, he left her with little doubt that, once Stanley had qualified, Christopher would almost certainly be able to find a position for him. She would have to be cautious, however, in mentioning this to Stanley, fearing that he might think she was wanting to get him settled down when his own thoughts were still ranging around all sorts of fanciful notions; the Colonial Service, farming, or even staying on in the army.

Quite apart from the anxiety emanating from her father's illness, there was also the fact that Tom was in the study, working each night until well after midnight, getting up and leaving for the office in the morning before anyone else had surfaced, wearing himself out in his determination to get on top of the business, his own worry being that he was likely to be recalled to the army at any time, his request for extension of his leave having been rejected, although it seemed unlikely that he was going to be sent back to Burma, the hope being that he would be posted somewhere in England, or possibly, to Europe.

She told herself that there was no point in continually wishing Stanley were there so that she could share her worries with him. What she had come to realise also, was that, even though he was some way from being able to earn a living to support her and Anthony, and that there was still a restlessness about him, fuelled by the combination of army life and a streak of adventurousness of spirit, to her he had come to seem so reliable. He had a way of being able to see the entirety of a situation and to put things into compartments, to cope with and to manage around them.

But he was not going to be here for who knew how long, and she therefore had to get on with it. And of course, he had enough on his plate to worry about; immeasurably more important things that put her own tribulations into perspective.

Even her mother, this time, did her utmost to persuade her husband – "you really must not be so foolish!" – but his old obduracy once more prevailed in spite of his hardly having the strength to walk the length of the hall.

"There are some things I have to attend to," he said with a finality they recognised, Peggy helping him into the car, driving him down to the office, holding onto his arm as she guided him into his room, thankfully on the ground floor, leaving him for a couple of hours, giving her the opportunity to wander around the shops, which, enjoyable though it was to look at what passed as the latest fashions, was also rather depressing with the paucity of what was on offer generally, shortages in recent months seeming so much more obvious.

When she collected him, it was as if spending time at his desk had revived him to the extent that as they drove home he was positively chatty, telling her about some valuation for a wealthy landowner client. And even when they were in the house, his surge of renewed vigour sustained until mid afternoon when, once again, the energy deserted him and he slumped in his armchair.

The next day, he was noticeably worse, appearing to find it difficult to focus his mind, several times speaking incoherently to Peggy's and her mother's consternation.

*My own darling one*
*Daddy is so very much worse today – he can't stay still & he can't remember things sometimes & his breathing is very difficult. I was awfully worried yesterday morning about him going down to the office although he was much better after being there for a while. He gets so very fed up & depressed here all day.*
*I just feel so completely sad inside. I am afraid there is little chance of you seeing your father-in-law again. July seems a very long way off. It all seems so utterly incompatible with spring & all its beauty.*
*July does not sound too terribly distant does it? At least it is something to look forward to if you really think that you will get leave then or soon afterwards.*
*Anthony has been behaving very well at nights lately & has gone off to sleep now with the light on. He is growing so fast & is just on the point of walking on his own I think.*
*God bless you my dearest one.*
*I am yours for ever*
*Peggy*

"I've asked Aunt Bea to come down," her mother told her the next morning. "I telephoned her."

Peggy realised, instantly, from the fact of her mother using the telephone, something which she disliked - availing herself of it rarely, when a letter, even with delivery the next day assured, was not sufficiently quick - the reason her aunt, her father's sister, had been summoned.

Peggy was fond of Aunt Bea, finding her a breath of fresh air with her forthright manner and endless supply of often scurrilous gossip, sometimes about the family – Peggy having thus learned good deal about certainly members of the family, including one or two black sheep whom her own parents avoided ever mentioning.

Aunt Bea was something of a mystery, living in a comfortable flat in a select part of Bloomsbury, a spinster, but with a circle of friends she would talk about, but none of whom Peggy had met. She was a working woman, but the precise nature of her job was also obscure – "sort of Government things" she would explain with deliberate vagueness, Tom, with, for him, a surprising flight of fantasy, suggesting that "she's probably a spy", his surmise being based on nothing more than connecting "Government things" with the fact that she seemed to travel abroad a good deal, even during the war, making several trips to America and once to Portugal. In the first year of the war she had been asked to accompany a party of children being shipped off to safety in Canada, a perfectly plausible explanation for the trip, although causing some surprise by reason of the fact that she had never before had anything to do with children, having confided in Peggy that she was so pleased to remain a spinster as "to be honest, my dear, I can't abide the horrid little things".

It was Stanley who had made the outrageous suggestion that "perhaps she's, you know…one of those", pulling a face, something between grin and grimace, which made his meaning clear, the suggestion chiming with the notion which Peggy had herself harboured since the day when she had been having tea with Aunt Bea at her flat, and while her aunt was in the kitchen, Peggy happened to take photograph album from a shelf, finding herself staring at a photo of her aunt with several other ladies, all wearing men's dinner jackets and black ties, their hair oiled and parted. It could have been a fancy dress party, she told herself, but there was something about the look of them – so comfortable in male attire, which told her otherwise. She hastily returned the album to the shelf.

Aunt Bea was always full of common sense, bustling around, organising, sometimes goading her brother for his stuffy seriousness, risking a backlash by airing her decidedly left wing views. And yet her brother took it in good part, appearing to enjoy the joshing, his sister having the capacity to make him laugh, something of a rarity for the generally serious man.

Peggy felt relieved at her aunt's arrival, even though she fully understood the implication. The previous day, her father had remained in bed, abandoning the previous breathless and painful descent to the living room. As soon as she arrived, Aunt Bea went up to the bedroom, remaining ensconced with her brother for more than two hours.

"I don't think it will long," she said when she came down, Peggy and her mother sitting at the kitchen table, going through the motions of preparing the evening meal.

The next morning, Sunday, Peggy and her mother went to church, Aunt Bea happy to remain to sit with her brother. Although never entirely forthcoming about her faith, she had alluded to the subject a few times in terms which pointed to, at the very least, a degree of scepticism and possibly worse, this being a topic which Peggy preferred to steer away from. When, on previous visits, Aunt Bea had accompanied them to church, Peggy would notice her staring distractedly at the fine stained glass window, her lips scarcely moving with her minimal utterance of the responses and prayers.

As Peggy and her mother entered the house on returning from the service, Aunt Bea came down the stairs, Peggy immediately reading her set expression.

"Come up with me, would you, dear," she said to Peggy. "Take your coat off, May," she told Peggy's mother. "Go and sit in the living room for a few minutes."

Peggy followed her aunt into the bedroom, her father lying on his back, his face a waxy pallor but his expression quite different from the last days, as if he was relieved finally to be free of the pain.

With her aunt standing on the far side of the bed, Peggy touched her father's neck, the nurse in her for the moment, going through the necessary procedure, then pressing her finger tips against his wrist.

She looked across at her aunt, nodding her affirmation.

*19.3.45*
*My dearest one*
*Daddy has just died. Auntie called me & I went to see if I could feel his pulse but he must have died peacefully in his sleep. I will write later. Pop is here now.*
*I'm sorry, my darling, that was all that I could write this morning. I was feeling so lost, but we then had a lot to do.*

*After we had got the worst jobs done this morning, this afternoon I took Anthony out &*
*walked hard in the pouring rain down to Withdean. The walk did me good.*
*Now we have had a quiet evening. Aunt Bea has gone back but is coming down on Friday*
*for the funeral. I don't dread the idea of it now quite as much somehow. Tom has just read*
*the will through & it seems that Mummy has the house, Tom the business & we all have*
*shares in the profits, though in varying sizes.*
*Now I am very tired and must go to bed. How I would like your arms round me tonight*
*but I feel your spirit is near me.*
*God bless you darling.*
*Peggy*
*All my love*

"God Almighty, I hate this war," Stanley exclaimed, Peggy's letter lying on his bed, Eric squeezed into the caravan beside him, the two of them clutching glasses of the whisky which Eric had provided, to help his friend to drown his sorrows, the letter from Peggy having arrived late that afternoon. "To think that it's two days since her father died and I'm only learning of it now. Oh God, I wish I could be there with her. My poor dear Peggy."

With his head hanging down, Eric could see that Stanley was close to tears, as much of anger that he could not be with his wife at such a time as from grieving for his father-in-law.

Eric replenished their glasses, the two men drinking in silence.

When Eric departed, Stanley, feeling quite sober in spite of the quantity of liquor they had consumed, took out his notepaper, trying to think what he wanted to say. He decided that, at this moment, brevity was appropriate.

*My darling*
*I just feel I can't write much tonight to you: I know you'll understand as I received your*
*letter & felt so utterly blank & sad after reading them. Darling, I just can't tell you my*
*feelings — I expect you can guess. Life is so strange, I'm in the midst of the most hectic of*
*all times: fate is cruel to treat you thus when happiness for the world is so near, just round*
*the corner. I can only pray my dear that you may be spared the sadness & sorrows of war.*
*Please don't bother to write except when you really feel like it: & don't worry about me*
*at all.*
*Always your adoring husband*
*Stanley*

*23.3.45*

*My sweetheart*

*Yesterday they came & put Daddy in a rather beautiful all white satin lined coffin. It was so strange to think of all the ordinary little things of life going on around that marble like figure and being able to talk of him without it hurting too much.*

*This day I shall always remember is over. I have never been to a funeral before & was rather dreading it darling – but I found it not quite so grim as I had expected though still something of an ordeal. There were such a lot of people at the church – all kinds of people. I could not believe that they were all there to pay their last respects to Daddy. I think I have grown a little older lately or maybe it is just that I had shed my tears beforehand – but I behaved quite well. Daddy was cremated, but only a few of us went to the Crematorium which was really rather lovely – a beautiful little modern chapel almost on the Downs. Despite all this it is so hard to believe that we shall not see Daddy or hear his voice again. Poor Mummy was so grand although I know she is so sad & lonely although we are here. This alone can help her.*

*My sadness has a serenity about it because I feel that Daddy has found peace although it does seem so very hard that he could not live a little longer to spend some leisure in this home & garden he loved.*

*I wonder where you are this evening. I hope life is not too grim. The field in Germany you described sounded lovely though I guess you have left it by now. I just long to hear from you again & hate tomorrow being Sunday because I know that I can't get a letter. I must say goodnight now as this has been a strenuous day and I feel very tired.*

*God bless you darling heart.*

*You will always have my love for ever.*

*Peggy*

# TWENTY-THREE

"I guess we'd better call him "Plunder" then," Johnnie Hooper said when they – the half dozen RASC officers who had attended the briefing – got back to the mess, the dog bounding up to him, clearly having identified the young – meaning nearly three years Stanley's junior – adjutant as his master.

When Hooper had first joined the 51st, Stanley had taken to him, there being something about the chap's openness and ready humour that he warmed to, his pink cheeked, boyish face sometime seeming out of place amongst the rest of the mess, most of them now campaign hardened and war weary veterans, the young adjutant more suited to a school common room.

It had been as they were driving through Goch, the sappers having by then cleared the rubble from the main street, that the dog ran out from the ruins of a house, Hopkins just managing to stop the Jeep in time, the creature seeming intent on throwing itself under the wheels.

Hooper, having screamed at Hopkins to stop, leapt out, grabbing the dog, petting it, the rather non-descript animal, with perhaps a residue of sheepdog in its mongrel mix, wagging its tale, greeting its new master, licking his face.

None of them – Grant being the other passenger – raised any objection when, with an expression which indicated a readiness to plead with them, Hooper climbed back into the Jeep, the dog, continuing its attempts to lick him, cradled in his arms.

"Join the circus," Stanley remarked with a sigh, but in truth, rather pleased, always having a fondness for dogs.

For the past two weeks the division had been out of the line, engaged in a series of exercises in an area of Belgium chosen for the similarity of terrain to that on the west of the Rhine, and, more importantly, as it bordered the Maas river which, although lacking the Rhine's formidable width, nevertheless, provided a suitable approximation for practising what was recognised as being the most challenging of any of the obstacles of the campaign.

Working closely with the REME engineers, RASC played a central role in assembling the myriad equipment, including the engineers' array of pontoons and bridging components, and, in addition to the usual storm boats, buffaloes and DUKWs, various other craft, some complete with Royal Navy personnel.

They also had to liaise with the Royal Signals who were issuing new crystal radio sets, which were said to be a considerable improvement on those which, until now, the Allies had had to manage with, the shortcomings of the old sets having been a significant factor in many of the more difficult battles, interruptions in communications invariably leading to confusion.

"Biggest show since D-Day," Eric said, scanning a sheaf of indents.

"And just look at the ammo," Burrows added, the sheer quantities of every calibre now supplemented by smoke shells for laying down smoke screens as well as the red smoke marker shells, used to designate targets for aircraft.

Although the full briefing was not until 19ᵗʰ March, there was no doubting the purpose of this period of intense training, the only question being which section of the Rhine was going to be selected.

The answer was given by the Divisional CO, Major-General Rennie, at the briefing for senior officers, the CO, this time wearing battle dress, less distinctive than his usual attire, Tam O'Shanter with the red hackle of the Black Watch and a naval duffle coat which he had acquired on his return to England after his time in the desert, the coat donated by a generous naval officer, Rennie complaining of the bitter cold of the North Atlantic after his months in the heat of North Africa.

"I am proud to tell you, gentleman," the general announced, "that we, the 51ˢᵗ, have been selected to make the initial crossing of the Rhine. Other divisions will be crossing at other points shortly afterwards, but the Highland Division will be the first to strike into our enemy's heartland."

"Operation Plunder," he told them, was the designation, the Division's point of crossing being opposite the town of Rees, its initial objective.

By the time the briefing concluded, a number of other senior officers having provided details of the operation, none of them were in any doubt that this was to be an exercise in the application of overwhelming force, Horrocks' XXX Corps, together with Four and Twelve Corps, to cross at night, the American 18ᵗʰ Airborne Corps, 6ᵗʰ British Airborne Division and Eight Corps to follow in daylight, a simultaneous flanking attack to be made by the American Ninth Army.

"Bloody Hell!" Stanley exclaimed, looking up from his jottings, his endless fascination with numbers prompting his "fag packet" calculation, "I make that about one and a quarter million men."

"Still got to get across the damned river," Bertie Burrows said, ever the down to earth realist. "And it's a safe bet that Jerry is going to be ready to give us a warm reception."

For the next two days, every road leading to the selected marshalling areas were congested with vehicles, rows of tanks, lorries and transports, parking in neat rows. Some way back from the river, several thousand guns were arrayed in their emplacements, barrels pointing eagerly to the east, mattress rocket launchers adding a further weight of fire-power. In total, the Allied forces assembled for the assault on this last great hurdle, were able to deploy over five thousand artillery pieces, the "mattresses", now known as "Stalin's Organs", the weapons similar to the renowned Russian *Katushkas*, the launchers themselves, when loaded with their rockets, reminiscent of church organ pipes, more than compensating for the absence of the heavy naval guns which had played such a vital part in D-Day bombardment.

For the RASC officers, not only were the demands, in terms of sheer quantity, greater than any previous operation, but the range of supplies called for had never been more extensive.

"What the hell do they need Mae Wests for?" Peters asked, addressing his question to the officers and men assembled in the large tent which was to be the RASC command post for the operation.

"In case they get splashed on their boat trip," Grant replied, ever the wag. "I expect they'll want umbrellas as well."

Unbeknown to them, as they worked day and night on the preparations, away in SHAEF HQ, in the French city of Reims, General Dempsey, CO of the Second Army, briefing the press ahead of the launch of the operation, paused to consider a question from renowned war correspondent, Alan Moorhead, the question posed more as a statement, seeking the general's affirmation.

"This might well be the last battle?"

"Yes," the general replied, confident as he did so that although the advance into Germany would still present significant challenges, once over the Rhine, there was no doubting that what followed would be a matter of rolling back the enemy forces, believed now to have been degraded to the extent that they would no longer be capable of serious opposition.

As Rennie gave his briefing, on the eastern banks of the Rhine, the *Wehrmacht* commander, *Generalfeldmarschall* Kesselring was deploying his forces, including two panzer and two parachute regiments, together with the usual SS elements, an army which, over the course of the following days, would demonstrate its continuing capability and resolve, inflicting heaving casualties on the 51st and other divisions leading the assault. Indeed, interrogation of SS prisoners indicated that their adherence to their belief in ultimate victory was as staunch as ever, diminishing reality progressively replaced by a menacing commitment to total destruction – of themselves and of their *Vaterland,* the notion of defeat being utterly unthinkable.

With the scale of the Allied forces being assembled, and with their proximity to the enemy, secrecy was difficult to maintain, the final days before the assault seeing a significant increase in German shelling which, although causing only minor casualties, nevertheless added to the difficulties of assembling men and equipment, sporadic bombardments causing even greater congestion and delay.

The date and time of the assault having been set for the night of 23rd March, the RASC contingent worked tirelessly to ensure that everything was in place.

What was different this time, compared to the Seine and other previous river crossings, was that the first assault was to be soon after dark, the timing aimed at trying to achieve a degree of surprise, the enemy having become familiar with a pre-dawn barrage to preface the assault itself.

Despite the fatigue from days of intensive preparation and sleep being limited to a few hours each night with the occasional cat-nap, Stanley, as with all of his fellow RASC officers, felt the adrenalin of anticipation, not simply at the prospect of breaching this, the ultimate German line of defence, but at the imminent unleashing of the firepower now arrayed.

Throughout the afternoon of 23rd, the river was shrouded by a smokescreen, the wind fortuitously light, the smoke shells dropping continually to maintain the blanket shielding the assault craft as they were brought forward in readiness for launching.

With the fading of daylight, the troops of the first wave began to embark, the buffaloes and naval landing craft taking full platoons, the DUKWs, with the men climbing aboard the amphibious craft while they were still on dry land, as always, a comical sight, like something from a fairground.

As the signal was given for the opening of the barrage, it seemed to Stanley that the very Gates of Hell had been opened, the wild howling of the Stalin's Organs combining with the thunder of thousands of field guns to create a noise that felt like a physical force trying to crush one's flesh and bones.

The smoke and now the darkness, prevented them from seeing the full effect on the far bank, although the incessant bursts of flame painted the smoke a lurid flickering red and orange, tinting the faces of the thousands of men, expressions set, awaiting the order to head out into the mirk of night and smoke, their vessels, looming silhouettes, like mythical beasts bearing warriors onto the field of battle with the dark forces of the underworld.

As Stanley, with Hopkins ever present, moved between the embarkation points, making final checks that each of the assault units was fully equipped and confirming delivery arrangements once they had established the first bridgeheads, he felt his eyes smarting, the acrid smoke, from the smoke shells and the barrage which had been sustained now for more than three hours, getting into his throat, men everywhere coughing and attempting to shield their eyes.

Suddenly, shouts could be heard, officers yelling against the cacophony, whistles blowing, the armada moving away from the bank, the DUKWs lumbering down the gradient, settling into the water, the throbbing of engines adding to the din.

"1st Black Watch is across," a private, seated at a radio set, headphones clamped to his ears, said in an almost conversational tone, it taking a few minutes for the tent to fall silent, Stanley looking at his watch.

"That's less than five minutes," he said. "Surely that can't be right."

"And the 7th Argylls," the private added, with similar understatement.

Having had to return to the RASC tent before the eight o'clock launch, Stanley could only imagine the scene, remembering the dreadful spectacle of the Seine, storm boats being torn to shreds by the merciless Spandau fire, men flailing helplessly as the hail of bullets ripped into their hopelessly exposed bodies. What he could not picture was the actual scene, the flickering of guns and explosions illuminating the craft plying back and forth, those which had deposited their passengers hurrying back for their next load, several German searchlights raking the water through the breaks on the smoke, swirling now with the disturbance of so much movement, the enemy gunners taking full advantage of their intermittent targets.

Fortunately, unlike the Seine, an element of surprise had been achieved, a barrage on a different section of the river having served as an effective ruse, drawing part of the defence force away from the landing area.

By midnight, it was reported that all initial objectives had been attained, the bridge heads being rapidly strengthened, the convoys of craft conveying men and equipment, tanks and crocodiles as well as artillery now enabling the advance units to secure their positions in anticipation of the inevitable counter-attack.

Shortly after midnight, the noise level having quite suddenly declined, the guns on the west side of the river now firing intermittently, responding to targeting calls from the units on the far side, an excited Hooper burst into the tent, his face, in the muted glow of the paraffin lamps, blotched with grime, the young adjutant having managed to get himself too close to one of the embarkation points, tanks spattering those close by with mud as they descended the bank, now thoroughly churned up despite the steel slatted matting laid by the sappers.

"I've just seen them!" he said, barely able to contain his excitement. "Right there beside me. And he spoke to me!"

"Who spoke to you?" Grant asked, "the Lord Almighty?"

"Mr Churchill! And Monty! They were just standing there, with a few others. And he came up to me, looked at my badge and asked if we were managing to get supplies across alright."

"You met the PM and Monty?" Stanley asked, glancing around the tent, other faces as sceptical as his own.

"I was told he was insisting on coming to watch the crossing," Eric said, "But we were told to keep it quiet."

"Some chance," Grant said, "if Winnie and Monty are strolling around chatting to all and sundry."

It had only been after a good deal of argument at SHAEF that, recognising that Churchill was not going to take "No" for an answer, arrangements were made for him to visit the 51$^{st}$ Division's embarkation site, although he was persuaded not to do so until the first units were established on the far side and, hopefully, the enemy guns and mortars trained on the sites, neutralised.

An hour later, Stanley was back at the river for an impromptu meeting with a handful of senior officers, the scene, with the smoke now cleared, one of intense activity, numerous vehicles queuing, waiting to be directed onto the landing craft and buffaloes to take them across, several hundred troops, some in orderly embarkation lines, others in groups, sitting on the ground or standing around, the scene illuminated by the almost constant flashes of the battle raging as the advance units fought their way into the town of Rees.

As he approached, Hopkins, as ever, at his side, he saw a large group of men standing in a circle, he assumed obtaining orders. As he came close to them, however, it was the voice which he instantly recognised, before, peering over the heads, he could see the PM, chatting to the men, the expressions on the faces of those closely encircling him, enraptured.

A few yards away from the group, Montgomery, with several other senior officers, was gesticulating towards the river, although Stanley was unable to hear what he was saying.

Stanley stopped a few feet from the officers, certain of them being those he had to liaise with, the Field Marshall, noticing him, the others similarly turning towards him.

"I'll leave you to get on with the important RASC business," Montgomery said, as he walked towards Stanley. "Keeping you busy, are they, Major?" he asked, Stanley coming to attention and saluting.

"They certainly are, sir. But we're managing to get them everything they require."

"Good man. Allen isn't it?"

Stanley gaped at the Field Marshall, staggered that he knew his name.

"Yes sir."

"Carry on Major."

Stanley saluted again, conscious of a warm glow within him.

Daybreak saw the fighting intensify, Kesselring having now managed to concentrate his forces, the battle for Rees involving many close quarters engagements, once again, a town reduced to rubble providing effective defensive positions, impeding the attackers.

It was during the morning that a message came through to the RASC command post which stunned every man present.

"It's the CO," the radio operator said, taking off his headphones.

For a horrified moment Stanley thought he was referring to Eric, before he turned and saw the RASC CO behind him.

"General Rennie," the radio operator added. "He's been…" The young private swallowed, unable to continue, but not needing to do so.

"Dear God," Stanley hissed, the thought that their larger than life General could have been killed, impossible to comprehend.

"I knew he had insisted on going across to see the situation," Eric said, it being part of the Rennie's reputation that he liked to "lead from the front", often putting himself in danger; unnecessarily so in the view of many other senior officers, yet accepting that this was the nature of the man.

When Stanley made his next trip to the embarkation area, the mood was palpably sombre, it now being known that the General had been in a column of six personnel carriers, moving along one of the roads close to Rees, several mortar bombs falling close to them. Although none of the carriers received a direct hit, the one in which he was travelling was pierced with several splinters of shrapnel, one hitting the General, killing him instantly.

Throughout the 24th the fighting continued, the 51st advancing slowly but relentlessly through the town, the loss of their General instilling a determination to avenge his death, the pain of their own casualties born almost with equanimity as they flushed out the defenders. With each step forward they encountered increasing numbers of German dead, the sound of tanks advancing, some lurching over piles of rubble, prompting others to appear, hands high above their heads, their fear being of the dreaded flame throwing crocodiles.

During the morning, the first flights of the airborne divisions began to appear, the sky soon filling with transports dropping several thousand paratroops, others aboard the ponderous, fat-bellied gliders towed by Stirling bombers, releasing their charges, the gliders dropping towards their landing zones, several being hit, Stanley seeing one break up, men falling from it, small dark shapes, hurtling towards the ground.

Back at the RASC tent, there was the same feeling of personal loss, the General, although a rather dour and aloof figure, nevertheless revered throughout the division, and indeed, one of the British army's most esteemed commanders.

"I heard him just before D-Day," Eric said, remembering vividly the occasion when Rennie, then CO of the 5th Black Watch, addressed his battalion, Eric and several officers from other regiments being present. "It was one of the most honest yet inspiring addresses I've heard. "A soldier must face the possibility of being wounded or killed in action," he said, "but if that was the ultimate price to be paid then he should face death in the knowledge that he had done his duty to King and Country. As a soldier, I can expect to die in battle and I do not ask for any other fate." It was as almost as if he had some premonition."

Into the second night the battle raged, the Germans continuing to put up stern resistance in spite of the inevitability of the outcome, their dead, lying where they fell, now numbered in many hundreds.

At the embarkation points, the returning landing craft and buffaloes now carried the grim cargo of dead and wounded, others crammed with prisoners, most arriving cowed but relieved on the west bank of the river, herded away by troops allocated to guard them, any hint of truculence met with a pointed rifle, the guards, however, fastidious in their treatment, proud to demonstrate the respect that, for many captured allied soldiers, had been sadly absent, word not only of often brutal treatment, but of massacres, adding to the determination to adhere to the moral high ground. Inevitably, however, there was instances when anger spilled over, particularly with the most hated SS prisoners who often received rougher treatment, limited generally, to a few kicks and punches.

By the morning of 25th, with the intense fighting continuing around Rees, but with the bridgehead now expanded to the point where the Allies were in control of most of the town and beginning the task of taking a number of surrounding villages, the sappers had completed two Bailey bridges, a remarkable achievement giving the width of the river and their exposure, until a few hours earlier, to enemy machine-guns, the spandaus directed at them now silenced, although shells from guns beyond the town continued to fall close by, none of them, however, damaging the bridges.

The opening of the bridges, named "Westminster" and "Waterloo", was not a moment too soon, the number of available craft now substantially reduced, many having succumbed to mechanical failure, engines having been operating constantly for some thirty six hours, numerous others destroyed or severely damaged by gunfire.

Quickly, the traffic began to flow, several columns of tanks able to join the battle, much to the relief of the most hard pressed infantry struggling to take certain of the villages crucial to the opening up of the roads, although the Camerons had been able to surge forward, taking the town of Isselberg, one of the key objectives.

During the course of the morning, increasingly frantic calls were being received at the RASC command post, several units running low on ammunition, there even being reports of British troops turning captured spandaus on the Germans.

A further enemy counter-attack, this time in some strength, enabled them to re-take Isselberg, much of the town now in flames as the contest for control continued, it not being until 28th that it was finally in the Division's hands.

Late in the evening of 25th Stanley finally had time to write to Peggy although when he climbed into his caravan, all that he wanted was to collapse into sleep. It was, however, more than his commitment to write regularly which prompted him to take out his notepaper; he was eager to recount to her some, at least, of the events of the past momentous days.

As he picked up his pen, he felt light-headed, he assumed from fatigue, although he could also hear a ringing in his ears, not helped by the continuing noise of the battle, the guns on the west of the river keeping up their fire, waves of aircraft passing overhead, now bombers and fighters, the transports having completed their task of delivering the airborne divisions.

Weighing upon him also, was his sadness for the grief he knew she was suffering for the loss of her father. For his own part, although he had never felt close to his father-in-law, and indeed, had found him a rather austere and, at times, disapproving figure, nevertheless, he respected him. And after all, he was the head of Peggy's family into which he had married.

*My darling*
*I received your letter this morning: darling it was so very sweet of you to write and appreciated more than I can say. I somehow felt and shared so much in your feelings, particularly on the day of the funeral.*
*My darling, for us the last few days have been unforgettable. The dividing line between life & death seems so narrow and one thanks God so often when you find that it is morning again and all is safe and well.*
*As you probably heard, 51st crossed the Rhine in the assault. We had a very great tragedy on the morning of the 24ᵗʰ as our General was killed. He was a very fine man and we all loved him & his loss is very great. The banging is just incredible & one can't sleep a wink as the whole world is just a continuous roar. Fine days mean an awful lot to us as it means continual fighter cover, bombers doing their stuff & no mud.*
*As you can imagine the supply problem for ammo, pet and sups in an assault crossing is pretty colossal, but most of our worries have solved themselves and we now have our bridges. The RASC has enhanced its good name and we have put stuff over under 'great difficulties'.*
*You have been so constantly in my thoughts, my beloved, and as I say, I have felt so deeply, not the acuteness that you must have suffered. Rather something inside making one work all the harder and determined to live up to higher ideas and standards.*
*That must be all my darling. My heart cries and bleeds for you & my prayers are ever with you.*
*Your husband, so very clumsy at writing I'm afraid.*
*Stanley*

He wished he could tell her about Churchill, standing chatting to the men, and about his encounter with Monty, but their presence was still a matter of strict secrecy despite it being known to the entire Division.

When Peggy's next letter arrived, as always, he could tell from its brevity as much as from its content, the depth of her sadness. How he longed to be with her, to be able to comfort her. A surge of anger rose within him, the blood hot in his face.

"Bloody war!" he said, staring at the photos pinned to the earth wall of his dugout.

*25.3.45*
*My darling one*
*Thank you for the sweet note that arrived this afternoon. I know how you feel in your*

*wish to be at my side. I so want to be with you too.*

*The first awful hurt & ache has worn off a little & I can think more widely & as you do, appreciate all I have had & learnt from Daddy.*

*I hope you are fit & happy inside even if not cheerful. Anthony is growing very fast darling & is getting a little 'tough'. Poor Mummy, she gets quite knocked about!*

*I must go to bed now sweetheart. God bless you always.*

*Yours so very much in love.*

*Peggy*

On 28<sup>th</sup>, the order was given for RASC HQ, along with the remainder of the Division, to move, crossing the Rhine, Stanley's feelings as he arrived on the east of the river, mixed, a sense of the great achievement tinged as always, with acute awareness of the cost, the images of so many wounded men, many of them grievously hurt, filling his mind, as well as the dreadful sight of the bodies, lying in the bottom of a landing craft, the medics quickly checking them, presumably to ensure that their lives were extinct, before the stretcher-bearers carried them up bank, lifting them into the waiting lorries, the ambulances, with their prominent red crosses, reserved for the wounded.

By the time they made their move, the Division had advanced out of the bridgehead, joining up with other elements of the 21<sup>st</sup> Army, the initial resistance now diminishing, as if both sides realised that once the Allies had established themselves on the east side of the Rhine, the writing was on the wall, it now only being a matter of time before the war came to its inevitable conclusion.

*My darling*

*My thoughts & feelings have been so terribly deep and sad. They are a bit calmer now as life is more normal: how strange that 23<sup>rd</sup> March should be such a grim day in both our lives.*

*We buried our general, Tom Rennie, simply in our Div cemetery on 25<sup>th</sup>: the pipes played 'Flowers of the Forest' and the words "They shall not grow old" were read. In those few moments my combined feelings and thoughts were so near & with you: I was glad that God had in a different way, made those few days so bloody for me too.*

*But now we of the 51<sup>st</sup> are moving triumphantly alongside the rest of the 21 Army Group and the American Armies towards the swift approaching climax & end of the war. By the time this reaches you it may be over, as organised resistance is beginning to break: who knows: it may drag on for another month even so.*

*Today has been grey & misty but it cleared up this evening & the RAF got cracking.*

*We here have all been drawn nearer together in comradeship during the experiences of the past week. I only wish though that when you needed me most I could have been beside you. Some day, darling, when it doesn't hurt too much, may I gently hold your hand and*

*just talk to you about these awful days, unforgettable to us both.*
*For now & always my darling, my God bless you & give you peace & comfort. I love you beyond words.*
*Stanley*

How soon would they be able to resume their "naughty" letters, he wondered, his desire to do so pricking his conscience, making him feel insensitive at such a time. But he had no control of the way in which his fantasies intruded in his thoughts. He had come to realise that even in the most intense periods of activity, when the need for sleep became like a desperate thirst, his dreams became feverish, lustful images so vivid that for a few moments after waking he almost felt that the dreams had been real. Even more disturbing were the fragmented phantasms of his writhing with naked bodies, sometimes, with delicious familiarity, Peggy, but other times, pervaded with salacious guilt, strangers, faces and figures concocted from some deep recesses of his subconscious. Occasionally, also, it was Eva who appeared, her eyes holding him in their wanton gaze, her athletic limbs drawing him to her.

"It happens to all of us," Eric said when Stanley confided in his friend during a short respite when they were able to spend an hour together, Eric, as usual, supplying the whisky. "I sometimes think it must be something in our make up. Some primitive force that makes one form of excitement lead to another. When we've been scared as hell, it touches some basic force within us, stirring up urges."

"Mm," Stanley murmured doubtfully. "I'm not sure about that. All that I know is that I wake up thinking I've been up to all sorts of filthy stuff. And with a damp patch!"

Not yet, was the obvious answer to his own question. He would have to gauge her mood to judge when he felt they could resume their wonderfully liberating exchanges.

As with the crossing of the Seine, so it was with the Rhine that, once the obstacle had been overcome, the way ahead was wide open. With the Seine, however, it was known that the enemy was withdrawing in reasonable order, to prepare to fight again, whereas now it was clear that he was in hopeless disarray, the Allies advancing in leaps and bounds, sometimes twenty or more miles in a day.

Someone – none of them knew who – had coined the phrase "The Great

Swan" to describe the rush across northern France after the Seine had been crossed, the term suggesting that the Allies were free to go swanning across the great swathe of territory which had been opened up to them after the gruelling grind through Normandy.

Once again, now, the term was being mentioned, although this time, in contrast to the flag waving welcome of the French (after the dourly hostile reception of coastal Normandy) and the Belgians, as they advanced ever further into Germany they were encountering a downtrodden and unwelcoming populace.

"No looting and no fraternisation," was the stern edict, issued in the hope of stemming the natural desire of the conquerors to exact what they considered just in terms of personal reparation, virtually every man acquiring his booty generally in the form of watches and cameras, with many mementos including revolvers and daggers, SS badges ripped from uniforms a particularly macabre prize.

The rules which prohibited fraternisation were widely greeted with scorn, even those, including Stanley, required to enforce them, seeing them as being wholly unrealistic. Whilst one could fully understand the need to ensure that the Allies showed some degree of magnanimity to their defeated enemy, reports of the brutality of the Russians towards civilians filling them with disgust, the ready availability of *frauleins* willing to offer themselves to the invaders, necessitated a good deal of turning of blind eyes.

Lines had to be drawn, however, several reported instances of rape, when supported by clear evidence, being dealt with harshly, offenders being hastily court martialled, periods of custody handed down as "short, sharp shocks", the main objective being to get the offenders back to their units as quickly as possible.

One episode widely reported throughout the Allied divisions, was seen as a salutary warning against the dangers of looting, a platoon from the Black Watch, having captured a number of prisoners, in their eagerness to strip them of watches and valuable, failed to see other German soldiers approaching, the Germans opening fire, killing or wounding every member of the platoon.

As the Allied forces fanned out across northern Germany, the 51st Division, as part of XXX Corps, making towards to the major city of Bremen and it port of Bremerhaven, organised resistance had almost ceased, the only significant engagements resulting from encounters with the German forces pouring out of that part of Holland that the Allies had yet to take, the Germans intent on getting themselves back onto home territory to await whatever fate was to befall them, knowing only that they did not want to face the vengeance of the inhabitants of a foreign country whose people they had treated so brutally.

Such casualties as the Division continued to suffer, although on a minor scale compared with those of the Rhine battle, often resulted from minor ambushes, hastily constructed road-blocks manned often by Hitler Youth or SS troops with spandaus and occasional 88s, the Allies also facing the hazards of mined roads and booby-trapped buildings.

In one village, several rounds fired from a *panzerfurst*, the highly effective anti-tank gun sited in a ruined building, delayed the advance for more than an hour, it being discovered that the gun was being manned by a group of schoolboys, the eldest only thirteen, two of them lying dead in the rubble, the survivors, when captured, as truculent as any of the captured SS, but, when faced with a steely Allied interrogator, truculence turning to tears.

*30.3.45*

*My sweet darling, my beloved*

*The great 'swan' is on and life is very hectic: organised resistance is all but over and we find few Hun on our front though there is still a little shelling and mortaring. The Luftwaffe is non existent and Germany is truly almost down for the count. We all hate the Hun but there is something very pathetic about the collapse of a great power. I think they've learnt their lesson this time as their country is really being destroyed yard by yard. It is a pretty terrible lesson too. It has its sad side for us because very soon we'll probably split up and become a 'district' or something as dull, and the comradeship, the friendship and the Highland Division will be no more. The occupation will be very dull I fear.*

*The news is good & it boils down to this: the Western Front has collapsed completely and the German 15th and 7th Armies have suffered a disastrous defeat. The Rhine did not prove nearly so formidable a barrier as the Hun expected, though they fought bravely & fanatically on our front. However they just could not hold with their very limited and over burdened resources and the break came inevitably and the advance broke out from the bridgehead several days ago. We have been pushing steadily on into the Reich, not meeting any really serious opposition but there is the occasional pocket to hold them up; the well sited roadblock and the blown bridge etc. The Hun is pouring out from N Holland and as he does so he is able slightly to cause these small delays. The 1st and 3rd (with Georgie Patton that very great tank expert) got a much cleaner break and not until they were very deep into Germany did they meet any resistance at all.*

*So summing up, the position is that there is nowhere any organised resistance or defended line at the moment.*

*It looks as if Anthony will definitely be running to the gate to meet Daddy at this rate! I think I'm certain to get leave in July darling but one can't pick the date in this system. Darling, an ideal peacetime job would be for us to have a very nice small country pub – very exclusive plus a small garden and maybe a small farm attached, with emphasis on the country.*

*Unfortunately the orders about looting are a bit hot so you have to be careful, but you often get a chance of getting something off a Jerry prisoner.*

*By the way, including TA service, I've now done six years 'with the colours'. Dreadful isn't it? I'll be qualifying for my old age pension at this rate. Lots of people have been trying to persuade me to take a regular commission but I tell them that I love my wife and family too much and want some happy peaceful days with them. I wish to goodness I'd passed my finals though, then I'd not have a care in the world when the war is over. Darling, don't try & make me work for a week or two, will you?*

*There's a frightful non-stop woodpecker nearby who I'm sure will keep me awake. Otherwise all is quiet & peaceful – it's amazing how quickly this front has collapsed – you ought to see the 'New Order' and 'Master Race' as they are today – what a shambles. Well beloved, with so much love I really must say goodnight. I wish so much I could be beside you, my beloved darling girl.*

*Your adoring husband*

*Stanley*

Once across the Rhine, for the next month the Division was constantly on the move, Stanley's subsequent reckoning being that RASC HQ, generally attached to the Divisional HQ, had moved at least fifteen times. At one level, having to live under canvas for most of the time was not ideal, even though they had all now become accustomed to the make-shift arrangements, the need for digging in still paramount in spite of the reduced risk of attack. They had been spoiled by their brief periods with the luxury of bricks and mortar, of roofs over their heads and, just very occasionally, of running water and hot baths, such indulgences making the spartan outdoor existence all the more wearisome.

The only compensating factor was the arrival of spring, the weather, although by no means settled, nevertheless becoming generally quite warm, the German countryside an unexpected delight despite the damage they were inflicting by their having to fight their way across it, although such damage was modest compared with the devastation of the areas of the earlier battles.

The deeper they drove into Germany, the greater their feeling of being within the domain of their enemy, their dealings with the increasing numbers of civilians they were encountering, engendering a new set of emotions; distaste for a people who had knowingly supported, or at least, accepted, the plague on humanity of Nazism; the pride and discomfort of coming into their midst as conquerors; and, disconcertingly, a degree of pity as they came to realise that so many were just ordinary people, intent upon going about their daily lives.

Their, at times, vexed feelings about the German people became a regular subject of debate in the mess, the consensus being that the entire population was culpable, even those who had abjectly accepted that the arrival of the era of the Nazis was a fait accompli, any grievance kept to oneself for fear of being denounced by the zealots who pervaded the new order.

Yet a glimmer of contrary humanity would intrude on such simplistic denunciation, the pathos, particularly of rural folk, and a surprising recognition of a confusing kinship, complicating the notion of collective damnation.

The harsher view was fuelled, to some extent, by the discovery of how well fed and well dressed the populace was, with little apparent sign of shortages although it was also clear that in recent weeks, supplies of both food and most comestibles had become severely disrupted.

*My very lovely darling girl*
*As I'm feeling fairly talkative tonight, as the result of champagne for dinner, I will try to tell you some of the things about which I meant to tell you last week.*
*I'll tell you about our German farmyard: at one time it consisted of a chicken, a bull calf whose mother was hit by a shell, and which we reared with a bottle with a French letter with a hole in it as a teat, and four fat German pigs. At the time of writing the chicken is the only survivor (if you chase it, it lays a doubtful looking egg on alternate days); the pigs have gone the way of all pork, to the detriment of the waistline, and the bull calf got tired of Army life and deserted. Maybe it's found a more orthodox way of feeding.*
*Next darling, I must tell you about two very good pieces of loot I've acquired. One is an aneroid barometer which I've hung in my caravan: and the other is a pukka adding machine which works and which I've given to the clerks. The barometer unfortunately is marked in centimetres but I've worked out a conversion table to inches.*
*Stephen and I had a grand time in the first fortnight of March when Eric was on leave. We used our aeroplane quite a lot to fly to Corps and did all kinds of things of interest. It was altogether a very interesting and exciting op.*
*I'd like to tell you a bit about our problems with the German people. They are quite the reverse to what we always expected. They are nearly all (or try to be) very friendly & are very subservient. It is a very great problem to prevent the troops from fraternising. (A new expression of doubtful meaning has crept into the Army vocab. – "let's slip into town for a "quick frat""). It is a court martial offence to smile or speak or have any dealings whatever with the German civilian except to give an order or in the ordinary course of*

*duty. Notwithstanding there have been all too many regrettable instances of fraternising*
*with German women.*
*I hope you find some interest in this letter which is rather like a catalogue – I do love*
*writing & telling you all the little things because I love you such lots darling.*
*I'm ever your adoring and loving.*
*Stanley*

With the realisation that the end of the war truly was fast approaching, thoughts
of returning to the delights of home were, however, increasingly tinged with
anxiety. What was he going to do to earn a living? The assumption was that he
would resume his articles, buckling down to try to pass his finals. Yet the prospect
of a life indoors, chained to a desk, filled him with misgiving. This outdoor life
certainly had its drawbacks, but it made one feel so alive and close to nature.

Being part of this great crusade, and the camaraderie of army life, was also
something that, when one contemplated it coming to an end, particularly with
the dreadfully dull prospect of spending the rest of one's life in an office, induced
a feeling of despondency. Even though he was able to share his reservations with
others, the apprehension about returning to civvy street being fairly universal, it
remained like a line of dark cloud beginning to appear over the horizon.

How confusing it felt, to long so much for something but at the same time to
have such a feeling of dread about the mundanity which went with the
delight.★★★★

He was strolling along a track in a wood close to the camp, alone with his
thoughts, past a few apparently deserted houses, when the relative tranquillity
was suddenly shattered by gunfire, alarmingly close, his well trained ear telling
him that it was German 88s; two or three of them. He hurried back along the
track, breaking into a run when, as he was approaching the same few houses, he
spotted a grey uniform, the soldier going round the side of a house. He made a
detour amongst the trees, keeping away from the houses, running the remaining
half mile to the camp, reporting on the presence of what he guessed was a
handful of Germans, several shells having landed close to the camp but without
causing any damage or casualties.

An hour later, a platoon returned with two bedraggled prisoners, their handful
of comrades having died beside their guns.

It sometimes weighed on Stanley's conscience that he had written so
infrequently to his parents although he knew that Peggy would regularly

recount to them his exploits, reading from his letters to her.

He occasionally felt a twinge of disappointment that they rarely wrote to him. He knew that his mother was not much of a letter writer, his father, on the other hand, being an inveterate correspondent, the majority of his letters being parish business, although he also kept up regular exchanges with a few old friends.

When he did write to his elder son, the letters felt rather distant, even when expressing affection, Stanley's surmise being that this stemmed from the constraint instilled into his generation, undue sentiment a sign of weakness of character. He felt certain, however, that, behind the veneer of aloof seriousness, his father was, as Peggy had described him, "a bit of a softy", his love for his family something he found ways of expressing in an obtuse manner.

He, nevertheless, truly valued his father's letters, able to read between the lines, the rather stiff chattiness conveying some deeper message of devotion.

*8.4.45*
*From Rev W J R Allen*
*Good Shepherd Vicarage, 173 Dyke Road, Brighton 5*
*My dear Stanley*
*The splendid news from the battle front cheers us mightily and the end cannot be far off now. You are constantly in our minds and prayers you may be sure. It is more than high time the Germans tasted war in their own towns and villages and we must hope and pray they will have had enough of it when its all over to cure them of their horrid war spirit for ever and anon. Well enough of that for I expect you want some news from here.*
*As you know Ted and Michael were here for Easter. The Vicar of St Barts came for the Three Hours and the attendance was quite good. The church was beautifully decorated on Saturday and I am glad to say Mum was able to do the High Altar. The Easter Offering was well above average, £78 odd. Very encouraging for the old man. I felt very tired after it all but got round to the sick folk during the week.*
*Mike is on his first ship in Portsmouth harbour. He says its rather noisy and crowded but he won't be there many days and when he gets to HMS Raleigh in Devonport he will find things more agreeable. He writes very cheerfully and tells us that he was soon "engaged" for a concert party on board. I expect his piano playing will find him many pals.*
*You doubtless have precious little time for letters but you may be assured any line from you is most heartily welcome.*
*God bless & keep you.*
*Much love from*
*Dad*

"I've just heard that Roosevelt is dead," Eric announced, the mess instantly falling silent, everyone present stopping what they had been doing. For several moments it was like a scene from a photograph, the faces, turned towards the CO, expressions of shock, several mouths open, speechless.

As with General Rennie's death, it felt personal, although with Roosevelt it was knowing that he was an essential part of the leadership which had enabled the Allies to navigate the troubled years and, latterly, to map the path to imminent victory.

His relationship with Churchill, which came across as one of trust and friendship, was the foundation of the great Alliance of the nations standing up to the evil of Nazism. Through those most difficult times before America had entered the war, when many in America were vehemently opposed to getting involved, advocating neutrality, it was Roosevelt who had managed to use his political acumen – and his guile - to provide succour and vital material support to beleaguered Britain.

And when the Japanese attack on Pearl Harbour finally brought America into the war, it was Roosevelt who led the transformation of the American economy into the war machine, the scale of which neither Germany nor Japan could ever hope to match.

Once they had got over the initial shock of his death, there was discussion about the Vice-President, the name, Truman, being known to most of them, few, however, being able to picture him, the sense being of a rather faceless man, rarely emerging from the President's giant shadow.

In Stanley's mind was the photograph of the three Allied leaders, Churchill, Roosevelt and Stalin, at the recent Yalta conference, Churchill looking sideways towards Roosevelt, the President, known then to a be a sick man, with a blanket around his shoulders, Stalin, on the President's left, sitting uncomfortably, as if eager to be away, his face averted from the other two leaders, suggesting that he recognised that the bond between them excluded him.

In reality, there were times when the three leaders engaged in elaborate games, each highly skilled in the art of negotiation, playing one off against the other, even Churchill and Roosevelt occasionally allying with the cunning old fox Stalin, when they felt it served their purpose.

"Thank God we're nearly at the end," Stanley said, the feeling being that the

Allies momentum was now unstoppable, and that passing of the presidential reins to a lesser man would, at his stage, make no difference.

"There's still the Japs to be dealt with," Bertie Grant said, with none of his usual humour. "Buggers'll be every bit as difficult at the bloody Huns."

Although the advance into Germany was continuing at a rapid pace, after the first week or so of encountering little opposition, there was a growing awareness that resistance was again becoming more organised, the reckoning being that the enemy was preparing for a final showdown. Indeed, interrogation of prisoners indicated an assembly of several *Wehrmacht* divisions including the 2nd Army's old and much respected adversary, the 15th *Panzergrenadier Division.*

Of increasing concern also, was the fact that the route to Bremen would involve the crossing of a number of rivers and canals including the Weser which, with its extensive meanders across its wide flood plain south of Bremen, offered potentially effective lines of defence.

Relentlessly, the 51st, operating in harness with the other elements of XXX Corps, and with vital air support, continued to move forward, the rate of casualties greater now from the proliferation of devices ingeniously planted to impede their progress. However warily the troops moved forward, they were frequently caught out by hidden trip wires and mines concealed on the ground and in every conceivable site.

What made such hazards worse was the nature of the injuries they inflicted. The effect of bullets, mortars and shells had, by now, become a known quantity, men soon becoming inured to such grisly sights. With the mines and booby-traps, it was almost as if they were designed to cause the most grievous suffering, limbs frequently blown off, the screams of the wounded punctuating the advance.

Even as they approached the Weser, the enemy continued to fight as if the outcome of the war was still to be decided, managing to put up surprising resistance in spite of the ever growing stream of prisoners, many now choosing to leave their posts, it remaining for the most fanatical, loyal or timorous – those fearful of the consequence of surrender or desertion – to fight on. There were reports of many being shot for desertion or even for trying to surrender.

"Where the hell are they getting their ammo from?" Stanley asked, addressing nobody in particular. "We've bombed the hell out of every damned factory in the Reich, and still the ammo keeps coming."

It was when they captured a small town, upon entering its single factory which produced some type of machine parts, that they had their first encounter with slave labourers, twenty or so emaciated, shabbily clothed men cowering in sleeping quarters at the rear of the factory.

The men, a mixture of nationalities, upon realising that they were being liberated, reacted in a way the troops found strangely disturbing, several of the men collapsing in hysterical tears, a few laughing aloud, as if demented, others remaining stony faced, staring suspiciously at their liberators.

It became clear that when not working in the factory, the men has been confined to their sleeping quarters, never being allowed out into daylight, the squalid facilities comprising a foul smelling latrine and what passed for a kitchen, an area no more than ten square feet with a fireplace made out of loose bricks and a rope from the ceiling for hanging cooking pots.

Not anticipating having to deal with slave labourers, the troops sent word back up the line, a number of HQ officers being asked what should be done with them, the answer, for want of any orders or guidance, being simply to release them.

When the labourers stepped out into the bright sunlight, shielding their eyes, looking around them as if arriving on an alien planet, unsure what was expected of them, eventually, when realising that they were being left to their own devices, taking the food packs which the troops offered them, they set off along the road with little idea of where they were going or of what lay ahead.

Stanley was en route to one of the units when he passed the group, shuffling along, their appearance instantly distinguishing them from the German civilians, the men's clothes hanging from their thin frames, their faces pale and downcast.

"Poor sods," Hopkins said as they edged past.

"You dread to think what they've been through," Stanley said, looking at the pitiful figures, a few of them returning his stare, their eyes blank.

With each day, the numbers of slave labourers steadily increased, pathetic lines making their way westward, some managing to get hold of bicycles, their only desire being to be away from the people who had subjected them to such barbarity, and, with rumours spreading about the treatment they might expect from the Russians, determined to find the relative safety of the territory in the hands of the western allies.

In another town, the scenario was very similar except that several of the factory's German managers were found to be present, continuing to order the labourers to work machinery even when the British troops had entered the building, appearing almost oblivious to their presence.

Within an hour, the factory having been forcibly closed, the slaves realising that they were being released, as if suddenly being presented with the moment they had so long dreamt about, turned on the managers, kicking and punching them, the managers cowering in a corner, the troops standing by, watching what they felt to be entirely justified vengeance, albeit on a very modest level, only intervening when they realised that bones were being broken.

*13.4.45*
*My sweet darling*
*We moved once more today and are again in a very pleasant field.*
*Tonight we are in one of the loveliest places – in Germany or anywhere – we've ever been in. It is beside a famous river whose banks are wooded and beautiful. Germany is certainly a very lovely country – it is so green & clean and the farms are quite picturesque. Did I tell you that I have a grand 12-bore rifle – we have four that we have confiscated from Bosche civilians.*
*It is delightful to release slave workers & allow them to kick their former masters up the arse then cycle off. Many of them are in a pitiable state. This morning we had some fun, we opened up on what we thought was a Hun but it turned out to be an Italian, very scared, a member of Italy 'RAMC' – it must be the lowest of low. We also came across Russians, Czechs, Poles, French and Gringo-Slavs.*
*I found another egg store tonight but quite a small one – only 5000! Most of us are already egg-bound especially Stephen as he had three for breakfast and we had one with steak and chips for last dinner just now. We only moved in here at six after a rather long dusty ride. The roads are appalling unless you are lucky enough to get on an autobahn which are first class.*
*The Hun only left here last night but we are going so fast that he's already about 20 miles away & I expect he'll move on tomorrow.*
*Darling, I'm afraid these bedtime notes are awfully scrappy. I get awfully sleepy through all the fresh air and in the mornings I'm very busy, move afternoons and so on. The days just fly away: but each day is a day nearer leave – and demob!*
*The BBC are very inaccurate these days and 48 hours behind normally. The stiffening resistance may be true in some cases but it's not really organised and controlled. It is the type I told you about previously – the odd battn. or regiment or div of paratroops or SS here and there. Incidentally we are getting 100s of prisoners.*
*Goodnight now my cherie, my beloved darling wife*
*For ever*

*Stanley*
*PS Don't be surprised by the notepaper – we have vast captured stocks in our loot.*

Sliding the letter from the envelope, the sight of the head of the German soldier, crested helmet, distinctive high collared uniform and proud profile, gazing into the distance, gave Peggy a moment of panic, wondering, for just a few seconds, if she was about to read of Stanley's capture – or worse - quickly starting to read, laughing at her own stupidity as soon as glanced down at the postscript.

She opened the atlas, conscious of the fact that she had not looked at it for two or three days, her former, almost religious observance of the daily war reports having similarly lapsed, her following of his movements now being a matter of a rough idea that he was moving across northern Germany.

The feeling seemed to have taken hold generally, that it was all over save for the shouting, although she also knew that there was still a good deal of fighting, the casualty figures, reported in one of the inner pages of the *Telegraph* which she and her mother had decided to continue to have, telling the true story.

The problem was that although he would sometimes mention place names, few of them featured on the small scale atlas maps. The *Telegraph* had told her that the Rhine crossing was at a town call Rees and although it was not marked on the atlas, she could guess roughly where it was. What she did not know, however, was his direction of advance. She had always assumed that once across the Rhine, they would be heading for Berlin, although it now appeared that different parts of the Allied army were fanning out across Germany.

She found Enschede which, confusingly, she saw was in Holland, her assumption being that the 51st Division for some reason had had to deviate back across the frontier. And what was the famous river he referred to? The only one she could find was the Ems, a name she had not heard of before, geography never having been one of her stronger subjects.

In fact, as her finger traced a line in a north-easterly direction, with surprising accuracy she came to the coast near to Bremen, something telling her that the Allies would need to secure the coast and its ports, Stanley having mentioned to her the difficulties of long overland supply lines and the importance of obtaining strategically located ports.

One of her excuses, lame as it might be, for being less diligent in following the news, was her increasing preoccupation with the vexed business of trying to find them a home for when he was demobilised, whenever that might be. It made it so much more difficult to know what to be looking for – somewhere to buy or to rent – when she did not know what their livelihood would be. The only certainty at present was his income as a major which, although just about enough to enable them to buy a property, limited the scope to the lower end of the market, probably a flat rather than a house.

*17.4.45*
*My own darling*
*Such a wonderful letter arrived from you yesterday. I did not like the look of the German soldier on the paper!*
*I read it in the garden while having tea. It made me ever so happy, sweetheart.*
*I put four rows of potatoes in after Anthony was in bed. They should have been in some weeks really & I think we shall probably need them as potatoes are quite difficult to get. Mummy and I managed to see the flats in the Droveway which were both nice and modern. The ground floor one was in rather bad condition but all the same very nice with a little decorating. The top flat would be just ideal for us & was beautifully furnished and decorated.*
*Tom is home on two weeks embarkation leave. He is working overtime at the office – at least he has been. Phil Myers, the other young partner, was in Stalag 79 so we are hoping to see him soon & that he will be able to help Mr Gladding. My cousin Stewart was in the same camp so I expect he will be home. I hope they are not in too bad a state of health. The reports on some of them don't sound very cheering.*
*Yours so deeply in love*
*Peggy*

The answer to his whereabouts, and of his direction of advance, arrived in his next letter, the main towns he mentioned appearing on her atlas. She felt rather pleased with herself that her guess had been correct although she still wondered whether he would have to continue across the rest of northern Germany, her finger arriving at Hamburg which she knew to be one of the country's largest cities. Where would they go from there? South to Berlin, or perhaps along the Baltic coast where she could see there were other ports.

*17.4.45*
*My dearest darling*
*We hear an awful lot about V days etc. I can tell you it's so very galling to read about miners having weeks holidays etc. – there ought to be no V day until the last soldier is home from Japan – then we can have a celebration on a national scale. Anyhow I don't think the official announcement will come much before July as there is still a lot of mopping up to do as we move into our occupation areas. And at the moment in some places the*

*Bosche is putting in some fanatical and vicious paratroops and SS training boys etc. who fight well for a day or two & are then annihilated. But as a coordinated army the Wehrmacht ceased to exist some time ago: likewise the Luftwaffe. But so long as a single German fights on, we cannot say that it is V day in Europe.*

*I had an accident with my gun today. It went off and I killed a German goose!*

*Darling, the flats in the Droveway sound absolutely terrific. I hope they looked as good as they sound.*

*Except for leave, I am sleeping in sheets tonight for the first time since about a year ago. These are made from some German material I got from a huge cotton factory. Hopkins & co have got a very good sewing machine worked by treadle and between them they've cut the linen up and put a hem on some sheets for Eric, themselves and me. This army is very remarkable!*

*Now it is 8.45pm and I am sitting with my caravan door open: Eric's caravan is about 12 foot away & I can hear him playing with Plunder. Signals are in the next field & they have a grand wireless which sounds marvellous in the evening across the field & is playing 'Indian Summer', that so lovely air by Eric Coates. The field and camp look very pleasant and peaceful tonight. Eric has just called my attention to a beautiful & rather wild sunset – very red with blue, light at first becoming very much darker towards the zenith where a new moon is riding.*

*One of the patrols had an amusing experience last evening. They came to a suspicious looking house which they entered with a bright torch. They threw a door open & beheld a lovely fraulein standing there in the nude! They were good soldiers & remembered their non-fraternisation orders, so they ordered her to dress (keeping the torch on her for a while as she did!) & then she had to go round the house to help them search it. The epilogue is that an officer's patrol is going to patrol the same area tonight! Not from this HQ – don't worry!*

*Goodnight now my beautiful darling. So many kisses and a heart full of love for ever.*

*Stanley*

There were rumours that demobilisation was going to begin within weeks of the end of the war, this being in stark contrast with the gloom-mongers predicting that the majority of the Allies forces would be required to remain in occupation of Germany for at least a year, the question of choosing the order for being demobbed being equally vexed, although it did now seem clear that it was to be based on a combination of age and length of service.

For much of the time, however, such thoughts were displaced by the business of war, in some instances, reminding one of the momentousness of the events they were party too, dreams of home and a future of peace almost trivialised in comparison.

Stanley's extensive journeying across the territory into which the 51$^{st}$ was advancing, ministering to the unceasing demands of the fighting units, took him on a road northward from the pretty, historic town of Celle, which, unlike so many others, had been spared any serious damage.

There had been reports a few days previously, of the discovery of a prison camp housing civilian prisoners and POWs, with some mention of appalling conditions, several elements from XXX Corps being dispatched to assist in the assessment of the situation, and of what supplies might be needed.

In an open Jeep with Hopkins at the wheel, the spring air pleasantly warm in their faces, having driven twenty or so miles on the almost empty road, they were flagged down at a checkpoint.

"The camp's just ahead," a fresh faced young lieutenant told them, saluting as he approached the Jeep. "Be prepared for the smell, sir. It's pretty bad."

After about another mile they realised that the young officer's warning had been a serious understatement, the first wafts of something akin to silage filling the air with a cocktail of the most malodorous stench Stanley had ever experienced, even compared with the rotting bodies of men and cattle strewn along their route from the Normandy beaches.

"I don't think you need to go in, sir," another lieutenant said as they came to the entrance, explaining that they were able to do their necessary business in one of the tents set up close to the high perimeter fence which stretched for a mile or so.

Behind the fence were rows of anonymous buildings, several watch towers rising above them. In the open areas near to the fence, there were several groups of people, many of them wearing what looked like baggy pyjamas, others in ill-fitting clothes. Most of them were sitting on the ground, dusty earth littered with detritus, several soldiers and medical orderlies moving amongst the groups, bending over them, appearing to check them, Stanley learning later that one of the main concerns had been identifying the inmates with typhus, trying to separate them to limit the spread of the disease.

"Christ, that's bad!" Hopkins said, holding his hand over his face as Stanley got out of the Jeep, making for the tent, the smell of the paraffin lamps inside the tent going some way to drown the foul stench outside.

The major he had come to meet arrived grim faced, with little to say other than to list immediate requirements, mostly food and medical supplies, the list also including quantities of disinfectant and DDT.

"Pretty grim in there, is it?" Stanley ventured.

His fellow major stared at him as if failing to understand the question.

"Beyond comprehension," he said, his voice flat, Stanley sensing the major's contained anger. "That man is capable of this."

The major stood up. "We need it urgently," he said, pointing to the sheets of paper which Stanley was holding before turning and abruptly leaving the tent.

"Have you seen them?" Hopkins asked as Stanley climbed back into the Jeep. "They're like skeletons. And one of the other squaddies said they've buried hundreds of bodies which were just left lying around."

"Let's get away from here," Stanley said, the stench now clawing at him, nausea rising in his throat.

"Stop!" he said after half a mile, stumbling towards the side of the road, vomiting onto the grass verge.

That evening, as he read Peggy's letter, he found it difficult to concentrate, the images of those pitiful creatures, their emaciated bodies and skull-like faces telling something of the brutality they had suffered at the hands of the Nazis, the full extent of which, when the accounts became increasingly graphic, as the major had said, quite beyond comprehension.

What they had now learned was that, quite apart from the state of the survivors and the hundreds of corpses which had been found in the camp, many simply left lying around like discarded rubbish, others in uncovered mass graves, was that tens of thousands had died of starvation and disease, the camp having served as vast storage facility for people reduced to mere components in the Nazi industrial complex, so much of which was operated with slave labour. Unlike various of the other camps, Belsen's function was not the industrial scale extermination which had become part of Nazi policy. Until more recent months, part of Belsen had been designated as a prison camp for Russian POWs, the distinction between categories, and their inhumane treatment, latterly disappearing as the entirety of the camp's population, swollen by tens of thousands of inmates transported from eastern camps threatened by the advancing Russian forces, being subjected to the same abandonment, the camp's authorities effectively giving up any pretence of feeding or tending their pitiful charges.

Over the long months since the previous June he had seen some grim and at times deeply distressing sights, experiencing also, acute fear and sorrow. Nothing, however, had shocked him as much as his visit to Belsen; and he had not even been inside the camp.

Even when he was back in his caravan, the stench seemed to cling to him. It was as if it has permeated his very being, somehow encapsulating the sheer horror of it.

He began to read Peggy's letter again, trying to focus his mind on what she was saying. Catching him unawares, he suddenly felt tears pricking his eyes, a wave of emotion overwhelming him, his love for her, and his gratitude for her love for him and all that she was doing to prepare for their future, contrasting with the shock of the day's experience.

What he also knew, at that moment, was that the memory of the sight and smell of that awful place would remain with him for the rest of his life. And he recognised at the same moment, that in spite of the need to unburden himself to her, of so much of what he had experienced and which lay as great weight upon him, there were certain things that he could never share with her.

Between fellow officers, and occasionally the men, Hopkins in particular, it had become acceptable to allow a modest admission of emotion, their bond of camaraderie providing a safety net, the horrors cited, sometimes tinged with dark, gallows humour – "Should have taken them some meat pies!" was Grant's response to Stanley's account of what he had witnessed; "and a tanker full of Jayes' fluid by the sound of it!"

Over the years to come, Stanley, like so many of them, would at times wrestle with the nightmares of recollection, although the vow, to place the darkest episodes away in their most secret compartments, would remain intact, with only occasional hints, decades later, to certain of his grandchildren, before steering back to the safer territory of the lighter anecdotes.

*My own darling*
*First I must tell you that we all went to the sale this afternoon & we got the house in the*

*Droveway for £2300. I was amazed that there were not very many people bidding. You*
*can see that there weren't as it opened at £1900. All I did was to stand behind Tom &*
*dig him in the back. It was the first property sale I have been to. It is grand to feel that*
*we have got this place as I know you will like it & it makes the idea of having a home*
*of our own seem much nearer.*
*I am glad you are proud of your family. I am so very proud of my husband & Anthony.*
*He shouts Dad-dad-dad at the top of his voice so he is obviously proud of him!*
*I am sorry you were disappointed by the drawings of Anthony's potty. I will have to try*
*some other kinds of sketching again soon! I'm sorry the pyjamas made you so homesick*
*– sheets must feel like home too. Hopkins is certainly getting very domesticated. Isn't is a*
*pity you can't keep him after the war! He would be very useful!*
*Darling, won't our honeymoon be wonderful with no more goodbyes after it. I don't think*
*I shall ever want to go away on my own as I get fed up & think of all the things we could*
*do together. I should miss Anthony who is very much around these days. Tom says I am*
*a fibbity-gib but I think I am quite sensible really.*
*I am sorry to hear about the episode of the fraulein in the nude. I hope the officers patrol*
*was disappointed. Bad boys, but I suppose they are a bit sex starved.*
*So goodbye my darling. My heart is so much yours with all my love.*
*Peggy*

He held her letter to his face, closing his eyes as he inhaled the indescribably
wonderful aroma of her perfume.

Her mention of sketches, with the obvious hint of some risqué images, and of
her response to his reference to the characteristics of *frauleins*, prompted a
stirring which, due to his preoccupation with military matters, as well as his
determination to allow a suitable period of respectful mourning for her father,
he had resolutely suppressed. With any luck they would soon be able to get back
to their naughty exchanges, a thought which lifted his spirits.

As he finished reading the letter, Eric appeared at his caravan door, holding out
an unopened bottle of whisky.

"Thought a drop might be called for," he said, climbing into the confined space,
sitting down beside Stanley on the narrow bed, tipping a generous measure of
the liquor into Stanley's proffered tin cup before pouring his own. "I've heard
it's pretty grim."

"I didn't even go inside the place," Stanley replied. "Not sure I could stomach it,
although needs must," he added, thinking of the stony expression of the major
who was part of the team sent to assess the scale of the task of ministering to the

inmates, and then of deciding what was to become of them, large numbers of them apparently being Jews rounded up from many parts of Europe understandably wary of being sent back home, not least because so many of their homes had been pillaged by the Nazis. For most of them also, they faced the ordeal of having to search for their scattered families, their own information network indicating that the prospects of finding them were not at all good given that so many had died either in one of the camps or during the long train journeys, prisoners herded into cattle trucks, many of those who failed to survive such "death train" journeys buried in hastily dug pits, others simply discarded at the side of the railway lines.

"We knew we are up against a pretty evil lot, but God Almighty, Eric, this is just...." As his words tailed away he took a long swig of the whisky, the warmth of the liquor quelling the surge of anger and distress rising in his chest.

During the last week of April they – the officers – could see that something had changed. It was as if the fighting units which, throughout the campaign had shown such determination, living up to the Division's reputation for its fierce bravery, had taken their feet off the accelerator. There was a noticeable reticence when it came to taking risks, the preference for flushing out of pockets of continuing resistance being bombardment from a safe distance, calling upon tanks and crocodiles to do their business, and for the RAF to pulverize even the smallest defensive positions, infantry holding back until white flags appeared or they were confident that the defenders had been killed.

Everyone was now certain that they were in the home straight, the only thing they now wanted being to survive to the end and to get back home.

There was also a distinct relaxation in the Division's discipline, particularly when it came to looting and fraternisation. Indeed, after they had crossed the last of the rivers, with the route to Bremen open before them, the spectacle was more akin to a giant travelling circus than the drilled and regimented force which had set out on the roads from the Normandy beachheads. The men themselves, weather-beaten, many of them sprouting beards and moustaches, uniforms showing the wear of the campaign in spite of the availability of replacements, had an air of casual confidence as they swept into German towns and villages.

The convoys now included numerous "liberated" German vehicles, the favourite being Mercedes, renowned for their power and reliability as well as for their comfort, several of them, until recently staff cars, still displaying *Wehrmacht* insignia.

There was a good deal of competition when it came to taking over former Gestapo buildings, which, invariably, were found to be well furnished and equipped, their former occupants having been compelled to abandon many of their luxuries; liquor, cigars, bedding and cars the choice acquisitions of the Division's troops, an informal code of fairness having evolved for distribution of such loot, although this did not prevent frequent disputes.

The fact that most of the officers were to the fore when it came to selecting the booty they felt they were full entitled to, meant that any pretence of enforcement of the "no looting" order was almost entirely abandoned, such discipline as there was, reserved for contravention of the directive on the treatment of civilians. Indeed, even allowing for the requirement of the non-fraternisation orders, precluding all but essential dealings with civilians, there was a determination to demonstrate that, compared to the Nazis, the Allies were intent on showing, if not forgiveness, then at the very least, forbearance and civility.

With Hopkins every bit the chauffeur, proud of his latest acquisition, a fine Mercedes which he spent a good deal of time polishing, Stanley thoroughly enjoyed the luxury, the rear seat offering a copious amount of leg room, the leather seats immeasurably more comfortable than those of the Austin staff car he had been used to, the Mercedes noticeably better appointed even than the Humber.

A less acceptable consequence of this shift in morale, with the erosion of discipline and the determination to survive, was the sharp increase in the rate of desertion, the Division's "cage" holding more than two hundred men who, having left their posts, were quickly caught by the military police as they tried to find their way westward.

One of Stanley's additional roles was having to sit on court martial tribunals, his legal training appearing to qualify him, the fact that he had not yet completed his articles of little importance to those at HQ needing to find officers equipped to deal with the sharp increase in cases.

Fortunately, there was an acceptance amongst the HQ senior staff, as well as those sitting on the tribunals, that, in this last phase of the war, punishments which, according to the army statute, included the death penalty for desertion, should be moderated, the idea of having to put so many men against a wall, or even of locking them up for long periods, bad for the Division's reputation. The risk of defendants pointing to the breaching of discipline by those sitting in judgment of them, virtually all now wearing German watches and enjoying a range of German luxuries, was undoubtedly a further factor in determining leniency.

As they indulged themselves on the fat of the land they were invading, their loved one's back home having to endure greater hardships than at any time before, played on their consciences, their concern manifest by way of a growing anger directed vaguely at the "powers that be", the disquiet at the parlous state of their own country drawing in a range of culprits, the miners coming in for a good deal of blame for the fuel shortages which were a particular grievance, virtually every household having to limit hot water, coal fires tending to be meagre affairs, such privations against the backdrop of ever worsening food shortages.

"Have you heard this bollocks about a "V-Day"?" Grant asked, expressing his indignation to the mess generally, angrily slapping the *Daily Express* he had been reading on the table, there being much press speculation about a day of celebration of victory which was generally anticipated to be imminent.

"Let them get on with it," Stanley replied gloomily, the idea of the country celebrating when the troops who had secured the victory were still engaged in what was expected to be the arduous business of occupying and de-Nazifying Germany, particularly galling. "They would do better to concentrate on getting us demobbed."

"I fear we're going to be stuck over here for months," Eric said, unusually for him, sharing the collective despondency. "I've heard that they probably won't start demob for at least three months, and then it'll be phased over God knows how long."

*23.4.45*
*My dearest darling*
*We are very un-busy today and rather bored. We've looted this district pretty thoroughly and want to move on! We had a marvellous meal of goose for dinner last night & had it cold today for lunch. This does seem so greedy when you are so short of food: I'm so sorry to hear about the potato shortage.*
*I'm very fit and browned off & bored as the war is more or less over for us and we now start to frig about again with much red tape and Army nonsense. I'm glad Winston has squashed the V day balls.*
*I'm delighted to hear your mother has bought the flats. They sound grand.*
*Tonight we can almost say that the wheel has turned full circle and that the long story has*

*begun to approach 'finis': that long story darling, that for us, you and I, began on that night of September 1st 1939. Do you remember that stormy night when our world seemed to be collapsing around us, and how those awful last minutes hung so heavily as we sat in the tawdry gaiety of Marble Arch Cornerhouse. If there ever was a living nightmare it was that night. Now the nightmare is gripping the German people: the heart of Germany, Berlin, is paying the most terrible price of all. And even though there may be quite a long epilogue, in which your husband will have to take part, that great task in Europe is nearing its end. Only the maps and the mounting miles on the speedometers tell the story of the overrunning of Germany: until you come to a large or fair sized town, where the tide of war is passing over and then you see that Germany is learning the hard way. I often think of Mr Churchill's words three years ago, when he promised that though the struggle was long and bitter, we'd see it through and "the mills of God grind slowly, but they grind exceeding small".*

*It is hard to realise that it is Sunday today. I am afraid I haven't been to church for ages – there is a dearth of padres and my communion with God is in his open spaces or under the stars, when I pray for you and Anthony, and our future & that he may give you comfort in your loneliness and that we may be together soon.*

*Darling, at that point this letter was interrupted for half an hour as my petrol can of water arrived for one of our periodical washes! Which reminded me – could Peggy oblige and send me some more Persil please? And as I was washing myself I was thinking of you, darling, laughingly thinking how I wish you could see my antics in a very small space. It is amazing how clean one can keep – I haven't had a sit down bath since February, and only one shower. I had my canvas bath on a warm afternoon last week but it's too cold for that again at the moment and there isn't room in my caravan.*

*And so my beloved girl, I am forever yours.*

*Stanley*


Events seemed, if anything, to gather pace through the last days of April, the sense of the approaching conclusion evoking often conflicting emotions; of exhilaration; of pride; and of anxiety as to what was to follow.

On the 25th news reached them that the Americans had finally met the Russians on the River Elbe, the eastern and western fronts thus coming together, the Russians already fighting close to the centre of Berlin where the enemy was making a final, determined stand.

The news, coming three days later, that Mussolini had been executed by Italian partisans, whilst prompting a modest cheer, seemed an almost secondary occurrence as far greater events unfolded across Europe and in the Pacific where the Americans were tightening their noose around Japan, inflicting upon its cities damage comparable to that wrought upon German cities by the Allies.

*29.4.45*

*My beloved one*

*The news is terrific isn't it? I don't think that much of the peace rumours but it is good that they have got old Mussolini & all the other Fascists finished off isn't it?*

*I am wondering if you are around the Elbe crossing as they have not mentioned any divisions yet. I hope you are well and cheerful at any rate darling.*

*Tom has had a phone call from Philip Myers. He arrived home from a prisoner of war camp today. It is thrilling to hear of these people getting back. It must be absolutely grand to be free again.*

*This war has certainly taught us a lot. How long ago that night at Marble Arch seems when we went out into the blackout & the unknown. The 'finis' is evidently near tonight when we heard of advances in the north and Berlin surrounded. I hope the beginning of our life together won't be too long in coming.*

*Yours with a heartful of love.*

*Peggy*

Having the rare opportunity of getting into his bed at a civilised hour, and of enjoying a spot of reading, the few books he possessed tending to last an inordinately long time due to the limited opportunity for reading, usually resulting in his falling asleep after a couple of pages, Stanley had only just opened his book when a commotion outside his caravan, and several shots fired, caused him to grab his tin helmet and step outside, unsure what to expect.

He heard shouting, not of alarm but more akin to the sounds one heard at a football match or outside a rowdy pub at closing time. Somewhere nearby, there was a rendition of *Scotland the Brave*, initially just of raucous voices, a pipe then taking the lead, several more quickly joining in.

"What the hell's going on?" Stanley asked, as a number of other equally alarmed officers emerged from caravans and tents.

"Adolph's dead!" a private, clutching a bottle of wine, said, raising his left hand in salute. "Sir!" Stanley shook his head as the private held the bottle out to him.

"Word just came through," Eric told him, joining the small group of RASC officers, standing, looking around them. "I guess this calls for a celebration," he suggested, leading the officers to the mess tent, several assorted bottles appearing.

"Good riddance!" Grant said, raising a bottle of beer.

How strange, Stanley thought, that the mood in the tent was so subdued, the feeling being more of a weight being lifted from one's shoulders than of the jubilation which the news should have induced.

He held up the bottle of whisky which Hooper had passed to him, taking a swig before passing it on.

## TWENTY-FOUR

*1.5.45*

*Major S R Allen  HQ RASC  51ˢᵗ (Highland) Division  BLA*

*My sweetheart*

*So Adolf is dead: not that it makes much difference at this stage. It seems a great pity that he's got away without a trial though: also Musso.*

*Phil Myers & Stewart – if he's back – must feel pleased with life. I hope their treatment wasn't too bad. Most of our POW we've see are very fit – it's the displaced persons who've suffered most.*

*I shot a hare tonight. Plunder flourishes, so does 'Boomph', Bertie's fox terrier. Eric and I had a good run on an autobahn today. I am very fit & full of fresh air though utterly dead beat & rather light headed hence what may read like a peculiar letter.*

*I'm so glad you like the chance of a trip to Germany. We shall probably be in an occupation role very soon because the Bosche has deteriorated quite a lot in the past week. It's all over here bar the shouting: it has been really for some time and all we want now is to get home quickly: there's already an awful feeling of anti-climax & boredom.*

*Yesterday Eric and I went to Brigadier Jerry Shield's funeral in a little orchard in the pouring rain. It was short but very moving, especially when General Horrocks quickly walked to the foot of the grave and stood at the salute, & everyone else filed by & did the same. Our General and CRA both killed in such a short time, just when the war is about to end seems such bad luck.*

*For ever I am your own*

*Stanley*

As XXX Corps continued its eastward thrust, still having to deal with some significant pockets of resistance, the crossing of the last two major rivers, the Weiser and the Aller proving remarkably straight forward, they then turned north, bearing down upon their destination, Bremen and Bremerhaven.

With the *15ᵗʰ Panzergrenadier* having now concentrated behind a defensive line south of the city, and appearing to show every intention of fighting to the last, the RAF was called in to deliver what would prove to be one of the last major city raids of the war, inflicting terrible damage on the city, the civilian populace once again paying the price for the Nazi rulers' criminal obduracy.

"Why the hell don't they just throw in the towel?" Stanley asked, articulating the frustration they all felt at the dogged resistance that a few elements of the enemy were still showing, the 51ˢᵗ Division's orders now being to by-pass the city, advancing north towards the coast, the objective being the port of Cuxhaven, thus encircling Bremen and Bremerhaven, still in German hands, other elements of XXX Corps designated with the task of taking the city.

Even with resistance to the Division's advance now crumbling, lives were still being lost, engendering a universal anger at what was seen to be such utterly pointless prolongation of the war.

"What do they think they can possibly achieve?" Stanley said gloomily.

"It's their code of honour," Peters suggested. "Better to die fighting than have the ignominy of capture, let alone of surrender."

Stanley was on a road several miles to the south of Bremen when he told Hopkins to stop the car, the two of them getting out, standing beside the car, the slightly higher ground offering a grandstand view of the raid on the city by several hundred RAF and American bombers. It reminded him of the previous occasion when he had witnessed the awe inspiring spectacle of air power, wielded to such devastating effect when the French town of Caen had been reduced to rubble in the space of just a few hours.

For the people of Bremen, air raids had become a regular occurrence, the city having suffered extensive damage, its nearby port of Bremerhaven also being a strategic target. None of the previous attacks, however, compared with this one, its purpose being to bring the city to its knees in readiness for an attack by land forces poised to move forward as soon as the raid concluded.

It was a breath-taking sight, wave after wave of heavy bombers coming in from the north, black puffs of flak appearing around them although Stanley did not see any planes being hit. Having dropped their loads, the percussion of explosions felt through the ground, even at such distance, each formation turned, climbing back towards the sea, making way for the next wave.

When they climbed back into the car, the city now shrouded in smoke, they continued their journey in silence, their emotions, as so often when witnessing the inflicting of such devastation and death, confusingly mixed, the sheer grandeur of the spectacle, and the knowledge that it was a necessary preamble to the ground attack, tempered by some deep, instinctive misgiving. How many people – how many civilians – must have perished as he and Hopkins were standing there watching? Even with death such an everyday occurrence, bearing witness to hundreds – possibly thousands – of lives being snuffed out - induced some innate sense of common humanity, diminished by the necessities of war, and yet remaining, embedded in one's deepest emotions.

The day after the raid, three German staff cars, white flags prominently displayed, were allowed to pass through the Allied front line, General Horrocks receiving the city's *Burgomeister*, accompanied by several generals and admirals, the brief formal meeting concluding with the signing of the city's surrender.

With the news that the Berlin had finally fallen to the Russians, speculation was now rife as to how the end was going to come about.

In the northern theatre in which XXX Corps was operating, even now, with the *Fuhrer* dead and the capital fallen, resistance continued, the seemingly indomitable *15th Panzergrenadier* even managing a counter-attack, the Gordons suffering casualties with several of their vehicles and guns captured, it taking the best part of a day, with some hard house to house fighting, to repel the attack.

The numbers of prisoners were now rapidly increasing, many appearing with white flags, having abandoned their units, accepting the inevitable, the general sense being of relief that they could finally lay down their weapons, grateful to have survived, particularly when many hundreds of their colleagues were still being killed.

"Major Allen, I'll need you with me," Eric said, addressing Stanley formally as always when giving orders. "There will be a number of logistical issues to be addressed which RASC will need to deal with."

On the morning of 4th April a line of German staff cars arrived, the passengers this time being *Generalmajor* Roth, commanding officer of *15th Panzergrenadier*, with a number of his senior officers.

For several hours, Stanley participated in the detailed negotiations, the complexity of the prospective surrender becoming apparent, not least because what was now involved was a substantial section of the German army, with arrangements needing to be worked out for dealing not only with the surrender of thousands of troops and weapons, but for their subsequent management.

From the statement which Roth insisted on giving at the opening session – that *15th Panzergrenadier* continued to be equipped and intact, and more than capable of continuing to fight – it was clear that this was, for the German general, a necessary face saving declaration.

By now, with Hitler dead, surrender negotiations were in train at different levels, Horrocks and Montgomery dealing with the entirety of the enemy forces in north-west Germany.

As the small group of senior German officers came out of the room where they had been ensconced with Horrocks, the British general remaining seated while the Germans stood, formally saluting him, Horrocks returning a token raising of his hand, more gesture of dismissal than salute, they passed through the room where Stanley and the various other officers had been engaged in their logistical discussions. As he stared at Roth, Stanley's impression of the small, neat man, was of self possession with a certain haughtiness as he surveyed the assembled officers, casting his eye over the British contingent with a look of disdain.

Stanley found something both fascinating and repellent about the man, knowing that he had been responsible for so many of the Division's dead, but at the same time, slightly in awe of him, recognising in him a worthy opponent, commanding one of the *Wehrmacht's* best divisions. Did he feel any sympathy for the man? It was a question which, although he did not even articulate it in his mind, somehow suffused that emotive moment in the way one felt pity for a proud jungle creature caged in a zoo.

By the end of the day a truce having been agreed, fighting quickly discontinued, the last guns to be fired in anger, stuttering into silence, like the final few fireworks of a display, the formalities of surrender to be concluded the following day.

It was a strange evening, the silence seeming profound, such had been the incessant noise of battle, the night sounds now of owls and of men celebrating, singing, voices loosened by quantities of liquor and the exhilaration of the moment, again supplemented by bagpipes, this time less mournful, the pipers' repertoires including various reels as well as the stock army songs, inevitably, the most rousing rendition being of the bawdy favourite, *Inky Pinky Parlez-vous*. And instead of the flashes of guns, the darkness was striated with wildly lurching searchlight beams and arcing flares.

When the German deputation returned the next morning, whilst Horrocks presided over the formal surrender signing, Stanley was required to attend a further series of organisational meetings. Although there had been a good deal of planning for the aftermath of the conclusion of hostilities, when they got down to the detail of it, they realised the scale of the task they were facing, with the prospect of having to manage an occupied country, as well as the immense challenge of taking charge of the German military – men, weapons, vehicles, buildings. There was as good deal of apprehension as to how the civilian population would respond to their new masters and concern about the possibility of some of the more fanatical factions continuing to resist, possibly even resorting to some sort of guerrilla warfare.

The whirlwind of events and the demands of RASC's participation in the preparations for the implementation of the long awaited surrender preoccupied Stanley to extent that it was only when Peggy's letter arrived he realised not only that he had not written to her for four days, but that she had scarcely been in his thoughts, a realisation which, in the privacy of his caravan, pricked his conscience, particularly when he read her letter.

How infuriating it felt, that with the time it took for letters to be delivered, events had moved on. If only he could have spoken to her, to tell her about the momentous couple of days.

*1.5.45*

*My own darling*

*I wonder where you are tonight and how you are. I think you must be busy again as I have not had a letter for some days.*

*It looks as though Germany is at last coming to bits with the surrender of Italy and the presumed death of Hitler doesn't it? I will feel most like celebrating victory when I know that you are not going to Burma. I hope that you will not have to be in the army too long after the end of the war. I expect this all sounds a bit previous when you are still in the middle of it. Your trip to the Baltic must have put the final touch to the collapsing Wehrmacht. I would like to see all the country, it sounds very nice.*

*Sorry my letters have been short darling, but I have written nearly every day. Some must have got lost as I have never missed two days.*

*I think we have been apart a little too long darling as I also feel very much in need of love.*

*God bless you sweetheart.*

*Yours forever*

*Peggy*

Why on earth did she refer to Hitler's death as "presumed"? He could only assume that the powers that be, feeding information to the BBC and the press, were being overly cautious, qualifying the news on the basis that all they had to go on was the report from the Russians who, themselves, were decidedly vague about the evidence, and who were never entirely trusted. From what could be gleaned from the reports, Russian troops had found some charred remains close to Hitler's bunker, the identity of the remains being based upon interrogation of a handful of SS troops who had been part of the *Fuhrer's* personal bodyguard.

Within the Division, however, there was no such uncertainty, Roth himself having acknowledged to Horrocks that Hitler had taken his own life, Horrocks recounting that the German general, steeped as he was in Prussian military culture, voiced disdain for the manner of the *Fuhrer's* demise, seeing a marked, if perverse, distinction between the honourable suicide of an army officer faced with the humiliation of surrender and the act of cowardice of a man unable to face the consequences of his own failings.

Stanley never learnt how it was that Roth had managed to find a justification for avoiding putting his pistol to his own head, in spite of the humiliation of surrender, the German general living, embittered, to old age.

Now, even though he could not speak to Peggy, at least he could tell her something of the part he had played in these great events.

What he also realised was that this was the moment which he had so often thought about, and longed for, when he could tell her that it was over, and that he had survived.

*5.5.45*

*My beloved darling*

*On a grey and wet morning – this morning – four German cars drew up outside our Div HQ and a collection of high ranking German officers stepped out and immediately started a surrender conference with our General. Yes, for us the war is really over: this is the greatest hour for the Second Army. But is seems so incredible that we have really reached our goal. The full meaning of it hasn't really sunk in yet: but we all feel very thankful to God that we have survived, safe and sound.*

*There were some incredible scenes last night – flares, fireworks, searchlights, sirens going off, tracers flying all over the place. It was one of the unsafest nights of the war! Celebrations went on far into the night; and I'm afraid there were many thick heads (including mine!) today. All we are worrying about now is how quickly we can get out of the Army, our task being done. It is really an incredible thought. No more shells, bombs, blackout, dugouts, flaps, screams for ammunition, exercises, camouflage - all the things we have learnt and practised in the past six long years.*

*And for those of you at home – for you my beloved darling: no more worries, & the looking forward to final reunion brought closer than ever.*

*I'm afraid I'm rather sleepy as I drank champagne, rum, whisky, brandy, gin, white and red wine & cocoa, & felt odd this morning – I think I was still under the influence!*

*At the moment our life is unchanged & we are still in the field. The only change is breakfast 9.30 tomorrow – whoopee! I think I want to love my Peggy so utterly tonight.*

*Pegs my darling, I adore you & I'm unbelievably happy.*
*Goodnight little girl, my darling*
*Stanley*

As Horrocks and Roth were signing the deed of surrender of *15th Panzergrendier,* eighty miles away, in a tent erected for the purpose close to his current HQ in the town of Luneburg, Montgomery was conducting similar negotiations with representatives of the *Wehrmacht* and *Kriegsmarine* in northern Europe, the German delegation led by *Generaladmiral* Friedeburg, deputed by Admiral Doenitz, head of the *Kriegsmarine,* Doenitz having been named by Hitler as his successor, declining to attend, considering it inappropriate for the head of state personally to conduct such negotiations.

Friedeburg's initial attempt to limit the extent of the surrender to part only of the German forces, having been firmly rejected by Montgomery with the stark threat, "I will go on with the war and I will be delighted to do so", adding a warning that "All your soldiers and civilians may be killed", Friedeburg, having consulted with Doenitz, returned the following morning with instructions to accede to unconditional surrender.

Seated at the head of the cloth covered table, wearing his battle-dress and beret, Montgomery's clipped speech and brusque manner thinly disguised his relishing of the moment he had for so long and so eagerly anticipated, Friedeburg, in his full length leather greatcoat, listening, grim faced as the British Field-Marshall read through the terms of surrender, paused as the document was placed in front of him, scanning it as if still undecided whether he could bring himself to accept it before signing against his name.

Two days later, at SHAEF headquarters in Reims, *Generaloberst* Jodl, the *Wehrmacht* Chief of Staff, and one of the few military figures within Hitler's inner circle who not only retained his role throughout the war, but who survived the *Fuhrer's* periodic fits of pique which resulted in the expulsion of a number of military leaders, including Rommel, tainted by his involvement in the July 20th plot, signed the document acknowledging the capitulation of the entirety of German forces both in the *Reich* and in every country where their forces were still present, a final ceremony taking place the following day in Berlin, this time with the Russians represented by Zhukov, the Field Marshal who had commanded the Russian army from the defence of Moscow and Leningrad, through the gruelling campaign which included the bloody battle for Stalingrad, to ultimate victory with the taking of Berlin, the German delegation this time lead by Friedeburg, Jodl, and Jodl's fellow survivor of Hitler's inner military circle, *Generalfeldmarschall* Keitel.

Peggy settled into what had been her father's armchair, its fabric still seeming to retain a residue of his distinctive aroma, something difficult to define, his slightly sweet pipe tobacco with a hint of the tweed jacket he so often wore, and perhaps just a suggestion of the outdoors – of farms and old manor houses – although she felt that this was probably her imagining, picturing him so much in his element, striding around farms and country estates, assessing values of fields and woodlands, the depth of the chair enfolding her, like her father's comforting arms, her recollection of his rare embrace, long ago in her childhood, hazy and yet, now, cherished in her memory. She switched on the wireless, her mother, as always, retaining her straight backed posture, in the armchair opposite.

Over the past few days there had been reports first, of the cessation of hostilities across Europe, then of various meetings between the generals, and although it was clear that the war was coming to an end, there still seemed to be some uncertainty as to what the end actually involved. She had, for so long, dreamed about the moment, yet it had never occurred to her that it would be anything other than an instant announcement followed by universal celebration.

What was happening instead, was the news coming in dribs and drabs, the overall situation confusing, there being mention of a surrender in the north of Germany where Stanley was, and then another one at the Allied headquarters in Reims. And now there was yet another one, in Berlin.

For some reason she felt a pang of apprehension, not because she felt any doubt as to the "finis", as Stanley had taking to calling it, showing off the bit of French he had picked up, but because of a strange stirring of her emotions. For so many years she - they – had, as the saying went, been "travelling in hope", and yet now that she was facing the moment of arrival, she was unsure what to expect. Wonderful as it was, to feel the weight of anxiety about Stanley's survival lifting from her, she had no idea how long it would be before he came home, and what he would then be doing. There were also dire warnings about the shortages continuing for many months, and if anything, getting worse before they got better. And although it was not something she articulated, even in her own thoughts, there was a general feeling of exhaustion; for six years the country had given its all; and now, battered and bruised, it was a spent force, in need of rest and recuperation.

As the news came on, she and her mother both stared at the wireless set, a glimmer of light showing in the narrow panel in the polished wood, with the

445

dial and the names of the stations, Peggy reaching forward to adjust the tuning, reducing the crackling, John Snagge's voice becoming clear and precise.

*Germany has signed an unconditional surrender bringing an end to six years of war in Europe, according to reports from France,* Snagge announced, his measured tone as always, endowed with a sort of bedside manner. *This evening the Ministry of Information has confirmed that an official statement declaring the end of the war will be made simultaneously in London, Washington and Moscow tomorrow. The day has been declared a national holiday to mark Victory in Europe Day. The following day will also be a national holiday.*

"Well, here we are then," her mother said, noticing the tears trickling down Peggy's cheeks. "Such a relief."

Peggy looked at her mother, for some unaccountable reason, suddenly feeling irritated. Why did she always need to keep her feelings shut away. Even when standing at the bedside, looking down upon her husband after he had breathed his last, Peggy on the opposite side of the bed, her own tears flowing freely, she was aware of her mother's determined constraint, her only concession to a showing of emotion, the slightest dabbing of her eyes with her lace handkerchief.

"I'll be going up then," her mother said, as soon as the news had finished, the timing of her departure for bed, and its announcement, the same each night, although tonight it added to Peggy's feeling of annoyance. Surely tonight of all nights, she would have wanted to have stayed, to talk, and to share their feelings. It was as if she did not truly appreciate the momentousness of what was transpiring.

Peggy remained in the armchair, her annoyance quickly replaced by a pang of guilt, realising that what must have been playing on her mother's mind was the sorrow that her husband had not survived the war, not only being deprived of the opportunity to enjoy the retirement he had been planning for, but also, to have shared the relief that the conflict was finally at an end. So much of his life had been overshadowed by war; how cruel was fate to have ended his life just when this war was coming to an end.

She went to the writing desk, resuming the letter she had begun before listening to the news.
7.5.45
*My darling*

*I wonder how you are & where you are & how it feels to think that 'finis' has been written to the book you helped to write. It all still seems unbelievable and strange yet to me. I need your nearness to make reality 'live' & the idea sinks in a bit more.*

*I wonder when you will know about your future. I am longing to hear from you.*

*Mr Churchill has announced V.Day tomorrow. It seems so sudden & yet so long awaited & so incredibly wonderful that at least half of the fighting has ended. My feelings are so very many & muddled that I just don't feel capable of expressing them on paper. I think tomorrow will be quite an ordinary day for me in the things I do. My thoughts will be with you darling, & longing more than ever to be with you. We shall at least be able to hang a flag out as we have unearthed our large coronation Union Jack.*

*Anthony has celebrated the eve of V.Day by wetting his pants – the first time for ages! Goodnight now my beloved. We shall be dreaming together of a happy future.*

*Yours for always*

*Peggy*

The fact that there was a church service, it being a Tuesday, added to the feeling of unreality. After having their breakfast, Peggy and her mother had unfolded the old Union Jack which her father had bought for the King's coronation, managing to hang it out of the front bedroom window, the flag, Peggy thought, looking slightly faded with a few moth holes, the mothballs of which it smelt having only been partially effective.

All day, as she went about the usual daily chores, she had to keep reminding herself that it was VE Day. The church was nearly full, and hearing Stanley's father speak of deliverance from the scourge of Nazism, and his sombre call for a minute's silent prayer for those who had given their lives, struck a chord with Peggy's volatile emotions, as did the Archbishop of Canterbury's broadcast.

From somewhere down towards the town she heard a band, and during the evening, there was some cheering, she guessed, from outside one of the pubs. Otherwise, after they returned from church, there was nothing remarkable.

How she wished she could have spoken to Stanley. She could not understand why telephoning was out of the question. People often made overseas calls, although Stanley had told her that that calls, other than strictly on army business, were prohibited. Today of all days, they might have relaxed it just a bit. And what made matters worse was that with two days having been declared public holidays, there was no post.

For Stanley, as for most of the officers and men of the 51st Division, feelings about VE Day were similarly mixed, with a good deal of grumbling about the fact that the nation was being given a public holiday and encouraged to celebrate when they, the men who had brought about the victory, were absent, and indeed, for many of them, hard at work implementing the terms of the German surrender. What Stanley and his fellow officers had also begun to notice, was an increasing groundswell of discontent, ostensibly stemming from the mixed messages coming from the powers that be in London about the arrangements for demobilisation, their one desire, now that the job was done, being to get back home. And feeding the discontent was the anxiety as to what life was going to be like when they were back in civvy street. Everyone knew that the country was in a bad way, and that jobs were going to be hard to come by. The sooner they could get back and get to grips with whatever the peace was going to offer, the better.

For that day, however, apart from the necessities of maintaining discipline - particularly guard duty, there being a good deal of apprehension about observance of the terms of the surrender, several incidents being reported of Hitler Youth firing at Allied troops, it being apparent that many of them had held onto weapons they were required to hand over – the order was given that the Division could celebrate, which, inevitably, meant that many thousands of victorious troops set about getting themselves drunk, with the result that the following morning, many a sore head was being nursed as they assembled for the parades, each regiment to receive their first peacetime orders.

For the RASC however, VE Day was a day of work, it having become clear that, over the days ahead, they were going to be playing a central part in the surrender implementation plan.

*8.5.45*

*My darling*

*VE day – I'll just tell you how the 51ˢᵗ have spent it. It's really been like any other day as far as work is concerned: we are just as busy & life is more or less normal. But today, wherever there are Britons, there is joy & pride and a wonderful feeling of indescribable triumph.*

*We had breakfast half an hour later, at 9am. The morning was a glorious one but I had quite a lot of work to do. However we had champagne for lunch then a spot of cricket in our field (it is a very pleasant field) then we all gathered to hear our own grand old Winston - & he didn't fail us & we loved 'Advance Britannia': we were all very quiet after him: we sat & listened to Howard Marshall outside the Palace & our hearts were glad but we were with you in spirit & could almost see the grand scenes in our own dear England.*

*Eric & I had to go out at tea time: it is so strange to go into towns and villages just full*

*of German troops. We tell then 'Hitler Kaput', 'Deutschland Kaput' & they look what*
*they are — thrashed & thoroughly beaten, I trust for always.*
*We got back to a late dinner: chicken & champagne: then the King: & Stewart Hibbert*
*solemnly reading the weather forecast: Howard Marshall again & I regret to say tears were*
*in our eyes: but tears of pride mingled with unbelievable home sickness.*
*Our new world & our happiness are nearly here: so, through all the unleashed celebrations*
*& speeches & emotions, my one outstanding thought is of you & that so soon we will be*
*together for ever & ever. That will be our day, my day, our greatest happiness & rejoicing,*
*but VE Day, May 8ᵗʰ 1945, is the gateway to happiness & wonder ahead darling. Give*
*thanks to God that you and I have come safely through the long years.*
*I am yours till the end of time and beyond.*
*Stanley*

There was nothing triumphal in their progress through the centre of Bremen
and then onto Bremerhaven, the convoy comprising five personnel carriers as
escorts for the six staff cars, orders having been given for all Mercedes and other
"requisitioned" vehicles to be left behind, quashing Stanley's rather vain hope,
encouraged by Hopkins, that he would be able to hang onto the splendid
Mercedes 260 model with its folding roof and outstanding engineering, the
purring of the engine and solid "thunk" of the closing of the doors, a joy.

At first, as they came into the southern suburbs, the damage, whilst extensive,
was not as bad as he had been led to expect. It was only when they approached
the centre that the true scale of the city's devastation was apparent, with hardly
a building remaining intact, their route along *Bismarckstrasse* having been cleared
just enough to allow them to pass through, most of the side streets appearing to
be blocked.

Already, teams of men, many of them in dirty army or navy uniforms, were hard
at work, the impression being of collective endeavour, most of the work
appearing to be by hand, there being few vehicles other than the occasional
lorry being loaded with rubble.

The northern suburbs were in an even worse state, the area of *Walle* which had
borne the brunt of the recent air raid, a desert of destruction, the few people
around appearing to be wandering aimlessly, as if disoriented by the obliteration
of so many streets.

The scene when they reached the port of Bremerhaven was little different,
military personnel here also being put to good use, aided by numerous civilians,
remarkable progress already having been made, most of the principal streets now

cleared to allow vehicles to pass, even the piles of rubble seeming to have an appearance of order.

With so many of the buildings reduced by air raids, the ocean liner, *Europa,* was not only visible as they came to the town centre, but, with its two huge funnels, their pre-war golden yellow replaced with naval grey camouflage pattern, it seemed to dominate the area. On his several visits to Southampton over the years before the war, Stanley had been awed by the spectacle of the liners towering above the port buildings and nearby houses. Yet here, the single liner's presence seemed so much more striking, partly because of it having survived, intact, but also because it stood imperiously alone, the only other ships nearby being various cargo vessels, diminutive compared with their mighty ocean going companion.

He was well aware of the *Europa* which not only featured in the books about liners which so fascinated him, but also because of its claim to fame as a winner of the coveted *Blue Riband* for the fastest Atlantic crossing previously held by its sister ship, the *Bremen.* But to see it now, even without the distinctive funnel colour he had seen in books and pictures, he still found positively exciting. It was only as their route took them close to the docks that he could see the ships sorry condition, its hull, superstructure and even those proud funnels, discoloured with large patches of rust, the vessel besmirched by the rude daubings of naval camouflage.

Their destination was the barracks which had latterly served at the HQ for *15 Panzergrandier,* and which, surprisingly, appeared undamaged, as did the adjoining building, former Gestapo offices, which the 51st had requisitioned, and which, for the next few weeks, was to be the Division's administrative HQ.

The meeting with a group of German officers, arranged for midday, proved to be remarkably business like, the Germans, although generally rather dour, showing little of the surliness of the surrender negotiations, there now been a greater sense of acceptance and of a desire to get on with the job of getting the town, and their country, back on its feet.

The agenda for the meeting, and for those which ensued through the long day, encompassed not only the handing over of military assets, but the taking over of the food supply, which meant that RASC was to assume management of the food stores and distribution.

As Stanley quickly discovered, the Germans' propensity for good order was of great assistance, inventories of both food and other essential commodities readily available. What came as a surprise was to discover that, for the military at least, food supplies appeared to be plentiful, even the civilian population being reasonably well provided for. In stark contrast the many thousands of slave labourers, most of whom were now being housed in temporary accommodation, had barely survived on their meagre rations, there being widespread reports of many having died of starvation.

Sitting around the table with various German officers, at times Stanley had to remind himself not only that they were, effectively, still the enemy, but of the barbarity which had been the hallmark of the regime in whose name they had been fighting. Already, the British officers, when asking their more pointed questions, particularly about provisions for the labourers, were noticing what seemed to be becoming the party line, of "we were just following orders".

Even though the meetings were conducted through interpreters, Stanley soon began to pick up on certain words, *befolgen* – following orders - trotted out regularly as part of the explanation for the policy of maltreating the unfortunates gathered up from across Europe to serve as the *Reich's* vast, enslaved workforce, a policy which, in spite of their attempts to distance themselves from it, they clearly subscribed to, their allusions, and sometimes, overt references, to lesser beings, the conclusive give away.

Brusquely business-like thus became the default approach, meeting the occasional attempts by certain German officers to lighten proceedings by a sort of forced levity, with a cold, unsmiling response.

As he came away from those first meetings, he was beginning to realise not only the scale of the task they were taking on, but of the authority which he was being given, his dealings that day with a number of German officers of more senior rank, effectively endowing him with higher rank, something which he found rather gratifying with one particular officer, a *Brigadegeneral* whom he had instantly taken against, the man's supercilious disdain for this mere British major riling Stanley so as to add a certain relish to his dishing out of orders, making a point of speaking directly to this senior officer, knowing how this humiliated him in front of his own inferiors.

"It feels as if we're rubbing salt into their wounds," Eric commented when they were enjoying a brief rest and their usual glass of whisky in their newly established mess, the liquor this time served in fine cut glass tumblers, the building coming with the trappings of its former occupants. "But I can't help rather enjoying doing so."

"I know what you mean," Stanley replied. "At times I almost find myself feeling sorry for them, but then I remember what bastards they have been."

"At least they seem to be pretty compliant. I think it's in their nature, to accept orders. Which probably accounts for the fact that they went on fighting even when they knew it was a lost cause, just because of Adolph had told them to."

"I can see why we're having a victory parade," Stanley said, the directive from Horrocks having set the following day for a parade through the centre of Bremerhaven, "but there's something in me which, I don't know, makes me feel a bit doubtful."

"More salt in the wound," Eric replied. "But it's the right thing to do, both from our point of view and theirs. This time they really need to know that they've been defeated."

"I'm afraid to say, gentlemen," Eric said to the RASC officers assembled in their new mess, a spacious, wood panelled room in their newly requisitioned building, the room offering a view across the docks, the bow of the *Europa* just visible, part of the camouflage, an arc of pale grey against the dark grey of hull reminding Stanley of something from a child's colouring in, "that we are to be spectators."

There was some muttering of disappointment although for Stanley, armed with his camera - which Peggy had managed to post to him, the prospect of being able to take photographs was very much his preference, Eric having explained the HQ decision that only the fighting units should participate in the parade, support units, including RASC, to be present as part of the array of troops either side of Horrocks when he took the salute, the arrangement staged for the benefit of the Pathé and other news cameras.

Any misgivings which he had previously were dispelled when, standing with Eric and the group of RASC officers close to the dais which had been erected for Horrocks, looking along the street, the location chosen largely because of the moderate amount of damage, he heard the order, which seemed to echo from the buildings: "Pipes and Drums, Quick March!", the sound of the bagpipes catching the emotions.

For a few minutes they were drowned by the noise of aircraft engines, the fly-past, such as it was, attracting a certain amount of derision, not least from Stanley.

"God Almighty! Is that the best the RAF can do?" he complained to those around him as three rather elderly de Havilland Puss Moths came into view, low over the rooftops, the planes used for taxiing senior officers and other VIPs around. "You would think they could at least have spared us a few Spits," he added, to general nods of assent, although there was still something impressive about these rather old fashioned looking planes flying so low, almost as if they were coming along the street.

When the first of the Highlanders came into view, the skirling of the bagpipes rising to an exhilarating crescendo, he was overwhelmed with a sense of pride as, regiment by regiment, they came along the street, kilts and sporrans swaying in perfect unison, each regiment led by a drum major, maces twirled with practised flamboyance, silver glinting in the sun. In the front rank of the Seaforths the famous "Bearded Piper" stood out, a man with the rather unheroic name of Ashe, his appearance and bearing, the picture book Highlander.

As each regiment reached the dais, to the order "Eyes left!", every head turned towards the General, a solitary figure on the dais, a union jack flying from the flagpole behind him, Horrocks saluting, the crowds of spectating men of the 51$^{st}$, cheering their marching comrades with full-throated enthusiasm.

*My sweetheart darling*
*At last I think I'll be able to write you the sort of letter I've been trying to write since before V day.*
*I've had a very strenuous but quite interesting job of taking over all the food dumps, food ships, petrol, ammo & arms in Bremerhaven docks (including the Europa). It's been quite the biggest job I've ever had: it's all part of taking over the administration of the German army. I must say that they've worked very well for us & been extremely cooperative. The back of the job is now broken and life is a bit more normal. It's been a non stop 24 hour job & I'm feeling a bit jaded & weary, but now we have a bit of leisure.*
*Two days ago we had a magnificent Victory Parade at which General Horrocks took the salute. British Movietone News filmed it & it was much photographed by the press so you may see me with Stephen Fox & Eric if you see the B M News next week. I managed to get some photographs but can't get them developed yet. It was a magnificent and unforgettable morning, but very hot.*
*I heard Winston last night & a bit of the VE day programme. I would love to have been with you in Piccadilly or outside Buckingham Palace making glorious whoopee. I think Howard Marshall made us more homesick than anything. I also heard Winnie & the King on VE day.*

*I'm pretty certain that by this time next year Peggy will have a permanent husband. The first lot of people are already being prepared for going home but there are very few of them. Leave won't be before July & it might be August. That's all I can tell you at the moment. The most amazing thing is the fitness and turn-out of the women – they have all the clothes stocks of Europe & look very smart. Without wishing to be told I've got a dirty mind, they all have very neat breasts & the Jocks are sighing, wishing there was no non-fraternisation. They are a very fit nation & take their sunbathing very seriously. They wear even less than English girls & the men's bathing slips are smaller too. I've got a pair! Goodnight my sweetheart.*
*For ever your adoring*
*Stanley*

There were times, reading Peggy's letters, when her world – the world back home – seemed even more distant; wonderfully simple, if overshadowed by the currents of sadness and hardship. There were moments too when he longed more than ever, to return to that far off life, such longing tinged with anxiety as to how he would be able to adapt to its simplicity.

How mundane some of her descriptions and anecdotes seemed, and yet how sweetly they reminded him of the over-arching purpose of what he was about which, at times, became subsumed in the unfolding of the day to day drama with its demands on stamina and emotions.

His irritation with his father's preoccupation with the trivial hardships he recounted in his infrequent letters left him with another strand of guilt. As Peggy had confirmed, from her regular visits to them, dutiful daughter-in-law that she was, they – his mother in particular – appeared to have an oddly sketchy view of the progress of the war, even their knowledge of the Western Front limited to the headlines. On reflection, however, he could understand that it was their way of coping. Having lived through the horrors of the last war, his father having lost a brother, both his parents having lost many friends, they now had to endure the dreadful anxiety of their son fighting in this war, their semblance of detachment a kind of pretence, as if by averting one's gaze, one's attention would be drawn to some distraction.

When his father's letter arrived, he felt a gush of emotion which caught him unawares; a surge of filial love and gratitude. His father wrote so well. It was almost as if he was in the pulpit, there being something formal in the way he expressed what was clearly, his true sentiment.

*18.5.45*

*Rev W J R Allen, Good Shepherd Vicarage, 172 Dyke Road, Brighton 5*

*My dear Stanley*

*We rejoice to get your letter this morning and now I write to say thank you from our hearts and minds for all the hardships you have borne to save us from the wicked Hun. It is no exaggeration to say he would have devoured us if he had spread his vile sway to our land. The combined services have saved us all under the Mighty Hand of God on High. The sacrifices you have all made will I trust give the Nations a long spell of peace and indeed your generation and the next should have no fear of a major war. It remains to knock out the barbarians in the Pacific and then that portion of the globe will also have good prospect of freedom and decency. We have escaped by the skin of our teeth and there is no doubt the world lived in fools paradise for a spell after the 1914/18 affair. We slept on the edge of a precipice but we turned over the right way and so saved ourselves from falling into the abyss. We thank God and you and all your comrades for all the mercies granted to us but the nations must not fall into such a position again. The rejoicings last week were truly wonderful albeit of a sober nature. We had grand services last Sunday and a £50 collection. We only wish you could have heard the bells ring out and also the people sing. I hope you won't get knocked up with so much on your hands in helping to clear up the mess and get things decent again. The Germans can save themselves by their own exertions and by bringing forth fruits meet for repentance. This side there are a few cranks who wish to be soft and sloppy to the Hun but they would be lynched if they spouted their pernicious ideas in public for the British folk won't stand for it.*

*This Whitsuntide Mum and I will earnestly ask for Guidance by the Holy Spirit for you and Peggy and boy as to the future. 'Lead Kindly Light' must be your text I feel sure. You may rest assured that we shall do all in our power to help you so that you may ere long be on the road to a proper job. Don't worry over much. I feel sure you will do your duty as you have done all along and somehow I feel in my bones that all will come right.*

*I saw Anthony in his push car just now. Bonny wee laddie.*

*Love from us.*

*Dad*


"Don't you find it difficult?" Johnnie Harper asked him when they found themselves together comfortably reclining in the deep leather armchairs also provided at the behest of the building's former occupants, "Trying to live in two places at the same time?"

Stanley stared at his young, fresh faced junior officer, it taking a minute for him to understand what he was alluding to, Harper, ever the light-hearted member of the mess, rarely one to express, yet alone to share, matters of the heart.

"You mean here and back home with other halves?" Stanley asked, slightly surprised that Harper, recently married, was already experiencing what so many of them found difficult to deal with. It was not so much the difference between their existence and that of their loved ones; rather it was their wives' simplistic view that, the war now being over, the army had, almost overnight, transformed from a fighting force to a business, their husbands employed as managers of the concern. "Yes, I know what you mean."

He was kicking himself for mentioning to Peggy the possibility of her and Anthony coming out to join him in Germany, with the subsequent realisation that it was not a viable proposition, the army disinclined to make the necessary arrangements, preferring to encourage officers and men to look forward to demobilisation. But there was something else; an uneasy realisation that much as he desperately wanted to be with her, he could not envisage her being part of this existence. He found himself turning over his mind the scenarios where she might feature. Having her to go home to, in some billet for married officers, and to share his bed at night would make such a difference to his life, or so he told himself. Yet the end of the long days was the time when they, the fraternity of officers, would get together, drinking, eating well, indulging in the talk which had become the invaluable currency of their comradeship, even with its various shades, ranging from antipathy to the closest of friendships. The idea of wives becoming a part of such existence, would inevitably, change, fundamentally, the very nature of that fraternity.

The subject's frequent airing reflected their shared dilemma, as well as the nagging contradiction. How could they possibly not want their wives to be there with them, if the army should relent. However they – and he – tried to justify it, they shared the conclusion, that "this is no life for wives and families".

As he wrote his letter, he hated himself, not because he was in any way deceiving her – which he was not, the army resolute in its no wives policy, at least until things had settled down – but because he was relieved that he could hide behind the decision.

As soon as he had addressed this issue with her, however, he found himself back onto the more familiar territory, of reporting on his life and experiences, and, far more stimulating, the matter of their relationship. As so often, staring at the photos pinned to the wall of the room which now gave him the luxurious alternative to his caravan, all such misgivings were displaced by the reigniting of desire. And, invariably, with such desire came a dose of realism, it being clear to him that notions of an outdoor life, possibly in exotic foreign climes, were entirely fanciful. He was under no illusions about what demobilisation entailed;

the harsh reality of getting down to his legal studies and, with the final exams under his belt, of a life behind a desk.

*My sweetheart darling*
*Reference the question of your coming out here etc. it now seems that demobbing will be very much quicker and I'm pretty certain I'll be home at the latest by March next year - European situation permitting. It is very grave at the moment & I think we are now seeing Russia in her true light. Which is worse, Germany or Russia? We all hope and pray most fervently that we shall not be called to arms again. The Yugoslav situation should be dealt with swiftly by force & the brigand Tito shown where he gets off. I think the Russian blame is 50-50 personally. And also they are on the spot. By the time this reaches you the tension may have eased. It is much too like August 1939 at the moment. I feel certain the politicians can, and must fight this battle.*
*We are still extremely busy and moving from Bremerhaven tomorrow to another field about 50 miles away.*
*Darling, I like the thought of you in well fitting pyjamas & brassiere. O Darling, I simply love you in a brassiere and panties that I can take off.*
*I had a marvellous date with you darling – too marvellous for words is the thought of lying so close and being part of you.*
*And so darling, on that lovely thought, goodnight and please God make the world peaceful & let me live with the girl I adore.*
*For ever your*
*Stanley*

Having by now become used to having his private sleeping quarters in the form of his caravan, there was no longer the need for the pretence which, with shared sleeping accommodation under canvas, in trenches, or in transient billets on the long journey across Europe, had been the accepted convention, that indulging oneself in a spot of solitary sexual activity was notionally discrete with the soft rhythms and gruntings of their room – or tent – mates, often with less than an arms length of proximity between them, but the convention was rigidly adhered to; keep it under wraps.

Now, lying on his bed, modesty blanket dispensed with, the last light of the early summer evening finally fading, the curtain open, allowing him the view across the docks, the *Europa* appearing even grander in silhouette, he was able to pleasure himself without the constraints of such convention, images of Peggy becoming exhilaratingly real with his climactic imagining.

When he was spent, he lay back, the feeling of release tinged, as he had found increasingly in recent days, with a sort of melancholy. It was at such moments that his longing for her became such a gnawing ache. How he yearned to be able to drift off to sleep, their satiated bodies entwined, the emptiness of his bed evoking a void almost as if grieving.

Throughout the campaign, never, for one moment, had any of them thought about the long hours of work, the only objective being to do what had to be done, ensuring that the part of the army they were responsible for was kept fully supplied with all of its requirements, to enable it to fight and to prevail in the most testing trial of strength.

Now, however, with victory secured, the work became increasingly wearing, taking up, as it did, at least for those first weeks after the surrender, most of their waking hours. Fatigue seemed to be constant, their short interludes, for a late night drink and conversation, and occasional games of bridge, generally curtailed when they gave in to the need for sleep.

The scale of the task they faced was challenging; the organisation of food supplies for the populace, as well as for the military and the large numbers of displaced persons, requiring organisational skills very different from the management of the sometimes erratic supply lines of the campaign, the problems of food distribution exacerbated by the active black market, the operators of which would do their utmost to keep their stores out of sight from their new masters.

The attempts to subvert the new regime were, however, limited, the RASC officers quickly becoming adept at tracking down those storage facilities which had not been disclosed as part of the set of inventories which had been readily provided. Indeed, the spirit of compliance, on the whole, was markedly fulsome, the few culprits of non-compliance tending to be small factions of the more recalcitrant military, justifying their defiance on the basis of a self serving assertion of resistance, a convenient pretext for profiteering.

It was with a feeling of grim satisfaction that Stanley, having been assigned to the role of food distribution, was able to issue a directive, the effect of which was to entitle all registered displaced persons to a ration very substantially in excess of the near starvation diet they had received from their former masters, and at the same time to reduce those of the military, all recipients thus placed on an equal footing, a move which resulted in howls of indignation from the German military, their complaints given short shrift by Stanley and his fellow RASC officers.

When the issue escalated to General Roth himself, who took the matter up with Horrocks, the response was similarly brusque. "The matter has been delegated."

One less palatable aspect of his dealings with the numerous German officers who were part of the organisational structure which the newly installed occupying command had imposed, was that, amongst them were a number of SS, who, unlike the generally cooperative regular army officers, maintained a cold, condescending hostility.

Fortunately there were few of them within area under the 51st Division's command, although Stanley found his distaste for them difficult to contain, their arrogant manner needling him, as if they were deliberately trying to get him lose his temper, sensing his rising indignation at their attitude.

In spite of himself, he managed to exercise sufficient self control, ordering them to stand to attention when they entered the room serving as his office, deliberately discomfiting them by continuing to read papers while they stood waiting, before issuing abrupt orders. On one occasion, however, his self control failed him.

He had been assigned an interpreter, a young private, Daniel Goldman, who had only just completed his training when the war ended.

Goldman's father, an Austrian Jewish businessman, had escaped from Vienna in 1936, shortly after the *Anschluss,* when the newly arrived Nazis began the process, initially, of harassing Jews, harassment quickly escalating into outright persecution.

The ten year old Daniel has thus found himself living in East London until the family home was destroyed in the Blitz, his father using an old business contact to find him a position in Glasgow, the result being Daniel's English, fluent as it was, having an accent mixing German with Scots.

There was one of the SS officers whom Stanley had particularly taken against, *Oberst* Krause, a name which, some time later, much to his amusement, Stanley learned translated as "curly", the tall, square shouldered, cold eyed, colonel's hair closely cropped, Stanley liked to think, as a means of disguising any trace of suspect curls.

When Krause arrived, accompanied, as he insisted, by a junior SS officer, both in immaculately tailored uniforms, it took a few minutes for Stanley to realise why, having, as a matter of formality, introduced his interpreter, the SS colonel was staring at Goldman, his sallow face colouring, his entire body seeming to bristle as if he suddenly found himself in the presence of a fierce animal.

"*Jude!*" Krause hissed, his eyes wide with a hatred which Stanley himself, found quite intimidating.

"You will address me only when I invite you to," Stanley instructed Krause, turning to Goldman, the young corporal appearing to be summoning up his courage to deliver the translation.

"I understand you." Krause said in almost perfect English, pre-empting the translation. "I will not take orders from a Jew."

Feeling the heat of anger rising within him, Stanley rose to his feet, finding he was a couple of inches taller than the German.

With as much deliberation as he could muster, he took out his side-arm, keeping his eyes fixed on Krause.

"Guards!" he shouted, without allowing his gaze to falter, the pistol clasped in his hand, barrel pointing at the floor.

Two privates hurriedly entered the room, rifles at the ready, unsure what to expect.

"Take this man to the detention block. I will see him again tomorrow when he will show respect to every British soldier. Dismissed!"

As Krause was marched from the room, his shaken junior officer following uncertainly in his wake, Stanley sat down, conscious of his racing heart and the sweat down his back.

"Thank you sir," Goldman said quietly.

"Don't thank me, lad," Stanley replied, looking up at the corporal's anxious face. "You've just been looking into the face of Nazism. Utter bastards!"

"Bastards indeed," Eric agreed when Stanley was recounting the episode to him later that evening. "Apparently they're discovering that several of the concentration camps were used for mass extermination of Jews. We know the

Nazis are an evil lot, but if the reports are true, it really will take it beyond comprehension."

"I have to admit," Stanley said, as if suddenly feeling he had to confess to his slightly troubling attitude to the Jews he had encountered, few though they might have been, a handful at his school and several within the Hove neighbourhood, "that I've always been a bit wary of them. The Jews, I mean. I can't really say why. I know that my father has always been rather disparaging of them, although he was able to make it sound, well, respectable, as a matter of faith, or rather, their lack of belief in Christ. But I do think that this was something of a convenient façade."

"Stanley, let's be honest," Eric said, looking at Stanley with his serious, rather teacherly expression, "we – English people of our class – never really liked them. It was probably because we saw them as intruders, their success giving them the wherewithal to think they could mix in our circles."

"What I've never understood," Stanley continued, not for the first time mulling over the question which, particularly in the light of recent revelations, he found vexing, "is why, throughout their history, they've always tended to be persecuted. Wherever they fetch up, it's as if they're not wanted."

"They have an almost zealous drive to succeed," Eric suggested. "And they are damned good at everything they turn their hand to."

"I admit that I'm not that keen on them," Stanley said, restating his admission, "but God Almighty, Eric, to treat them like that. It really beggars belief."

"I reckon that, more than anything else they've done, the way they've treated the Jews will damn the Nazis for evermore." Eric had a way of finding a statement which rounded off a conversation with an apt summary.

Stanley nodded, draining his glass of whisky. "Better get our heads down as we on the move again tomorrow."

From their temporary HQ in Bremerhaven, the RASC function required certain of them, Stanley included, to spend time at Cuxhaven, a small harbour town thirty miles to the north, its location strategically important, commanding the entrance to the Kiel Canal, Germany's naval route from the Baltic to the North Sea, as well as the Elbe estuary. Cuxhaven was also an important military communications centre, playing a key role in the guidance systems for the infamous V-bombs which, in the last months of the war, had wreaked such havoc on London and southern England, as well as inflicting numerous casualties amongst the advancing Allied armies.

What Cuxhaven offered, much to Stanley's delight, was a breath of sea air and the chance to swim, even though, with it still being early summer, the water was icily cold.

It was with the wonderful feeling of being thoroughly refreshed, the sensation of salt on his skin positively invigorating, that, at the end another long, but satisfying day, he retired to his tent, the HQ having now been moved to an area of countryside, a patchwork of neat, verdant fields interspersed with clumps of woodland, the setting, and the arrival of early summer weather, more than compensating for their being once again under canvass. At least, there was no longer the need to be dug in, Stanley also enjoying the privilege of a tent to himself, his caravan, for some reason that even Hopkins could not fathom, having been left behind in Bremerhaven.

*My dearest darling*
*Just a short happy note on a lovely Sunday evening. We moved early: I've spent the whole day at Cuxhaven, a pleasant unbombed place, then motored 60 miles to our new place, Harsefeld, about 10 miles West of the Elbe & North of Hamburg. This is a very lovely spot. It is a meadow bordered by a little wood: there is a lovely fresh water lake at the far side where you can swim, full of fish. I haven't had a chance to try it yet. I was also able to bathe in the grand looking sea at Cuxhaven.*
*The tragedy of Germany seems to become greater every day you spend here. It is such a very lovely country. They are a remarkably fit and good looking race. Apparently they start physical exercises — serious ones like eurhythmics — at the age of six, which is why they have such poise & good figures. Both young men & women are very fit: they worship the sun, are almost invariably bare headed and all wear very little clothes. They look such nice people — it would be so easy to be deceived especially in comparison to the frightful Russians we come across.*
*I have to interview many Germans and, with a few exceptions, they are very easy to deal with & take orders easily. The job is quite interesting but far more exacting than our wartime jobs.*
*When I'm demobbed darling, we will have a holiday but then I'll have to start my finals course at Gibsons.*
*Darling, isn't it amazing that the days of separation do really seem to be ending, and nearly a fortnight's leave.*
*You are so much my darling for ever.*
*Stanley*

With the food distribution arrangements in place and working surprisingly well just three weeks from their first being implemented, the RASC officers' role was broadened, requiring them to participate in the programme of "de-Nazification" which was to underpin the initial phase of the occupation.

Even with a degree of relaxation of the non-fraternisation rules, it proved difficult to navigate the fine line between the level of contact with the civilian population necessary for organising the "education" sessions which were a key element of the programme, and the distance which the powers-that-be deemed essential to ensure that the authority of the occupying forces was in no way diminished.

Stanley found the first few sessions he attended quite disconcerting. Indeed, the first occasion had all the trappings of a public meeting, the inhabitants of the designated quarter of Cuxhaven required to assemble in the large hall, absence permitted only for authorised reasons. As Stanley and two other officers stepped up onto the dais, taking their seats at the table, Corporal Goldman took his place, standing to one side, the young man sweating with trepidation at the prospect of having to address such a large gathering, albeit, simply acting as the conduit for the words of others.

Stanley, used as he was to exercising authority over large numbers of men, similarly felt distinctly nervous as he surveyed the assembled citizenry, every one of the four hundred or so seats in the hall filled.

His address was short and to the point, read from a script drawn up at SHAEF, setting out the key points of the de-Nazification programme, summarising the Nazi crimes – against other nations and races, and against elements of the German population – and listing the steps which were to be taken: the identification of Nazi officers and officials; the decision making as to individual culpability; the sweeping changes to civil administration; and the wide ranging programme of education.

"We are now going to show you a film," Stanley announced, a projector having been set up in the aisle with a screen behind the dais, "which shows what atrocities which have been committed by the Nazis. By your fellow Germans." He paused as Goldman translated, many people turning to their neighbours, anxious as to what they were about to see, Stanley wondering how many of them had been aware of the level of inhumanity to which the regime had descended. What had become clear was that the atrocities were not contained within the camps, the country's enslaved workforce serving factories and business in every town and city.

"What you are going to see is truly shocking," Stanley continued. "Steps are already being taken to bring those responsible to justice. For those who share responsibility, by *your* silence, and by *your* benefiting from this evil visited on your fellow human beings," again he allowed a pause for the translation, hoping that Goldman would give the same emphasis to the pointed "*your*"; "for you, you will have to live with the shame of silence."

He nodded to the private who was operating the projector, the spool of film beginning to rotate as the images of Belsen appeared on the screen.

*My dear darling Peggy*
*My life is very hectic still with much travelling about & I'm feeling rather tired out at the moment.*
*We had a grand and amusing talk from General Horrocks yesterday. The troops just loved it. He said that the 51ˢᵗ was magnificent and quite the finest div in the Army. Also that when we went to the local after the war & were discussing the campaign over the first pint we could say 'I was 51ˢᵗ. I did more than my share' without boasting. He also said that though he was getting old he knows that 'summer frocks were most disturbing' but that we'd been very good so far and that we must keep it up and not fraternise. He told us about leave & not to believe that demob would be too quick but that it would be just as quick as he could manage. He said they are opening Welfare (Rest) Centres in the Harz Mountains & Cuxhaven. They should both be very pleasant with boating, sport, cinemas, skiing, hiking etc. – and he said dances. He then explained that there were lots of non German girls who were to wear silk brassards with the Corps sign & that meant you could smile at them! He doesn't quite know how that will work.*
*This is a glorious spot with all kinds of wild life – nightingales, owls, herons, squirrels (brown), hares, frogs, toads, an otter, fish, heaps of birds I don't know.*
*I had a brick thrown at my car today which smashed a window. The culprit was a little bastard of some nine summers, & after boxing his ears and giving him a hiding we gave him to a local guardroom. That is the mentality of the youth of Germany: they are taught Hitlerism from 3 onwards. We have a hell of a job to re-teach them. I hate them more than ever now – they are oily & cringing: I have to spend most of the day interviewing the f——ers.*
*I am so sorry to hear about the rations cut. The meat ration is so appalling compared with ours. I had to work out a ration scale for the German Army today & I took great care not to let it exceed the civilian ones. So we give them 1oz per man per day & 6oz bread. They get a total of 1700 calories which is supposed to be just enough to keep them alive & no more. They have been living on the best Europe can produce for five years. It is amazing by the way how terrific their saluting is (of us I mean) – far better than our own Army –*

*but ours has been brassed up a lot in rivalry!*

*Talking of Huns, there is some undercurrent of something horrible about them all. We have been showing films of Belsen & Buchenwald to everyone in the villages around here. Some cried, some were very moved, but some laughed. That shows what kind of people they are.*

*Darling, the nightingale & this season always call to my mind my favourite poem:*

> *I cannot see what flowers are at my feet*
> *Nor what soft incense hangs upon the boughs*
> *But in embalmed darkness guess each sweet*
> *Wherewith the seasonal month endows*
> *The grass, the thicket, the fruit tree wild*
> *White hawthorn and the pastoral eglantine*
> *Fast fading violets covered up on leaves*
> *And mid May's eldest child*
> *The coming musk-rose, full of dewy wine*
> *The murmurous haunt of flies on summers eve*

*Would that you and I could whisper those so lovely words in a grove as glorious as this. In this dreamy & happy frame of mind, darling, I will kiss your soft lips & if perchance your thoughts are with me this night, they will reach communion with nature in the soft beauty & wonder of this night of coming summer.*

*Goodnight my angel Pegs.*

*Stanley*


*My sweetheart husband*

*I have tried to get a moment to write to you today but it has been a really hectic day with not a spare second between selling at our flower stall and raffling a bottle of old liqueur brandy. This fete business certainly is exhausting but I should think we must have taken piles of cash.*

*I am now recuperating on the settee listening to the Empire Day celebrations in the Albert Hall – all the good old hymns & Pomp & Circumstance.*

*The news seems very short these days & has lost its personal interest for me as it does not have any bearing on your life. A pity Himmler managed to finish himself without a trial isn't it? The Russians would doubtless have thought of a suitable end for him.*

*I am quite disappointed that you don't think that we shall be able to come out as I was looking forward to seeing the country. This does not mean that I am not glad you will be out of the army earlier than you expected but I thought even so we might be able to come out for a time say in the Autumn. I think it would be a good thing if I were with you from what you write about the German woman!*

*I have been talking to some South Africans this afternoon who had been liberated by the Russians in Czechoslovakia & they said that although they hated the Germans they did not like what the Russians did in destroying their homes & treating the women & children badly too, but of course they & their homes have suffered so much more haven't they? They certainly sound rather wild & uneducated.*

*The war against Japan seems to be moving apace doesn't it? I hope they finish them off quickly though there seem to be loads of them so I suppose it can't be so very quick.*

*Isn't it annoying of the Labour Party to insist on an election before the final end of the war. Will you have voting papers over there or do I vote for you?*

*Darling, isn't it wonderful to think that we still feel just happy lovers although we have been married for over four years. Of course I remembered our date, darling!*

*Goodnight sweetheart and God bless you.*

*All my love is yours*

*Peggy*

At the beginning of June, the recently established Allied Control Council formally took over the running of the country, marking the transition from the occupation of the victorious Allied armies, to the instigation of an interim system of government.

The days continued to be full, with much travelling around the region and frequent meetings, these days more with civilians than the military, the majority of the German army having been disbanded, the difference now being that the RASC had more leisure time, the evenings generally being their own, allowing for more serious games of bridge, and a good deal more eating and drinking.

The inevitable consequence of the decline in the level of work was the increasing preoccupation with the question of demobilisation, and growing frustration at what appeared to be the machinations of both Government and army, the information which was disseminated seeming to change with tedious regularity.

Stanley could see now that what both Monty and Horrocks had been saying to them involved an element of "soft soaping"; lavishing them with fulsome praise to divert attention from the prevarication over demobilisation, it also becoming apparent that there was a good deal of political disagreement as to the numbers required to remain in Germany.

In spite of his own voice loudly decrying the apparent debacle, Stanley could see that a new factor was coming into play; the growing threat from the Russians. It was widely known that the dividing of Germany, the Allies each being allocated different sectors of control, was proving to be a vexed process, with negotiations continuing, the concern being that the Russians were intent upon holding onto all of the territory they were currently occupying, including, most controversially, the whole of Berlin.

Monty made no secret of the fact that in the final phase of the war, he had had a serious disagreement with Eisenhower, the British Field Marshall having sought to persuade the Supreme Commander that he should be allowed to lead a thrust for the capital, Eisenhower having rejected the suggestion, preferring instead, the advance along a wide front, thus allowing the Russians to take Berlin.

Talk amongst the officers of a continuation of the war, this time against the Russians, although not something any of them seriously believed likely, nevertheless began to feature regularly in the discussions as to the reasons for the delays in demobilisation.

"We – Britain – couldn't afford another war," Eric said, his view being that what they were seeing was "geopolitical posturing", a phrase which Stanley found rather impressive, subsequently trotting it out a few times himself. "And the Americans won't want it. They've got hundreds of thousands of GIs desperate to get home. They'd have a mutiny if they told them they've got fight another war."

"I suppose we have to show the Joes we're going to stand up to them if they overstep the mark," Stanley suggested. "But honestly, Eric, what's happening about demob is a load of bollocks. They just don't seem to know their arses from the elbows."

"Couldn't have put it better myself," Eric laughed, pouring them both a second glass of whisky. "Found this in the Gestapo place in Cuxhaven," he said, holding up the bottle to inspect the Johnnie Walker label. "Makes you wonder how they got hold of the stuff. There were several cases of it."

"Perhaps they managed to get a U-boat up the Spey. Anyway, glad it's now found its rightful home!"

How good it felt, to be able to retire to his tent, mellowed by liquor, but without the weight of fatigue which had been a constant for as long as he could remember, with the exception of the wonderful week of leave when, satiated by their love making, he and Peggy had been able to enjoy nights of solid sleep, Anthony now having become a good sleeper, waking them with his gentle mutterings at some time after seven.

During those intense and draining days of the campaign, and the first weeks after the surrender, writing at times felt almost a chore, having to put off the moment of much needed sleep, summoning up the energy to put pen to paper, the blank sheet testing his resolve, although once he had got started, his lifeline to Peggy was instantly reignited.

What was also gratifying was that with the relaxation of the censorship rules, he was able to get things off his chest. The grumblings within the mess were never quite the same as sharing his true thoughts and grievances with his beloved Peggy.

*My sweetheart darling*

*Everyone is very disappointed and disgusted about leave. If it wasn't for Winston most us would either not vote at all or better still, try & get into the House ourselves. In our absence, darling, it is you and other girls you know who can really help our cry for early release: you form a very strong & foremost weight of public opinion and by passing the word round, you can do a great deal to bring pressure & help us. I'm afraid at the moment I'll be lucky to get out in March or April next year. I'm just speechless with fury & disgust over the whole thing & completely fed up with the ridiculously slow machinery.*

*Re voting - I don't quite know who to vote for − it depends on the demob & gratuity policies, for most of us.*

*Please send me some more of your drawings, darling. I'm very sex starved.*

*Darling, the scent on your last letter was so wonderful − such a lovely and mysterious perfume.*

*I must say goodnight now, darling.*

*All my love for ever*

*Stanley*

# TWENTY-FIVE

After the great climax to the European war and the exhilaration of victory, once the Allies had begun to implement their plans for the occupation of Germany and for ridding the country of every vestige of Nazism, the mood began to change, the frustration stemming from the uncertainty about demobilisation, and the increasing doubt as to their purpose, feeding off the growing sense of boredom.

Much of the work for the RASC now being routine, their lives were more akin to those of office workers save for the fact that they were in uniform and far distant from the other aspects of such lives – socialising, recreation and, most importantly, the sharing of their lives with their loved ones.

At one level, the absence of any responsibility for earning one's living, and the steady increase in opportunities to see more of the country and to enjoy the leisure facilities which were increasingly being made available to them, went some way to alleviate the boredom, the arrival of summer playing its part, allowing for the outdoor pleasures of swimming in lakes and the sea, fishing, and enjoying the delights of the North German countryside.

Food was plentiful, the occupying forces being at the top of the list when it came to distribution, and although they enjoyed such privilege, their generous rations amply supplemented by local produce, it also fuelled the resentment which most of them felt, the accounts from their families back home being of worse shortages now than at any time during the war, with restrictions on essentials such as coal and electricity as well as food.

Almost every conversation in the mess would, at some point, featured an airing of such grievances, the authorities in their myriad forms – individuals as well as government departments and political parties – pilloried for their scheming and incompetence.

The question of how long it would be before they were demobilised, became something of a game, bets being placed, the problem being that the complexity of the arrangements made it difficult to determine clear outcomes in terms upon which one could wager. The process depended on one's Group, which in turn was determined by age and length of service, although, as with all things to do with the army and the War Office, this was subject to the usual "if and buts", certain individuals being treated differently according to special circumstances such as particular skills or experience which were deemed to be indispensable.

Despite the undercurrent of growing disenchantment which Stanley, as with most of them, fully subscribed to, often being one of the more strident voices in the mess discussions, if he was honest with himself, he rather enjoyed this life of more extensive leisure. There was enough work to make him feel he was justifying his existence – regular meetings with officials and inspection of food storage facilities - but the licence to enjoy the fat of the most productive land, as well as the sport – regular games of cricket, albeit, often the field variety, absent the well tended grass of a proper English pitch – and other recreation was very much to his liking.

What did not change was his pining for Peggy and his longing to be back home, to begin his new life.

The arrival of her letters were, as ever, the highlights of those days, the thrill of slitting open the envelopes, touching the letter to his nose, inhaling the scent, pausing, eyes closed for a moment, before starting to read. As always, her descriptions of her day to day life, with all the delightful minutiae, induced an even greater longing, the ensuing melancholy now, however, something he was well used to and able to manage, the most effective antidote, to head straight off to the mess, and, assuming the sun was past the yardarm – conveniently flexible as this was – to take liquor.

*5.6.45*

*Sweetheart mine*

*It hardly seems possible that D-day is a whole year away does it? How incredibly different the outlook on life is with the war for us ended & knowing that it cannot be so very long till we are together.*

*We are both very fit. Anthony is just bubbling over with energy & thinks everything in the world is for his amusement. He will soon need Daddy to say an even sterner 'no'.*

*Your little wife too leads quite an energetic life. I sold flags at the Dials on Saturday morning & then did gardening in the afternoon.*

*By the way, I hear through my secret service that you have three quarters of an hour's doze in bed after your cup of tea in the morning listening to the wireless. What a life! I expect you can guess that my news came from Hopkins. He arrived about teatime yesterday. It was nice to see him and hear more about you, darling. The German binoculars are terrific aren't they?*

*I have had a glorious bath & I am now in bed feeling very warm. Hot water is quite a luxury these days because the coal ration is so short that we have to let the boiler out for about three or four days a week. It isn't so bad now but it will be wretched in the winter. I am applying for a permit for more but I don't expect we shall get much if any. Still life is pretty comfortable really. You certainly need not worry about our food ration darling.*

*I have just heard the news. Old Winston was in grand form and gave the socialists a good kick didn't he?*
*God bless you for all you are & grant we may be forever one*
*Peggy*

For many months, with the only question relating to the successful conclusion to the European war being as to its timing, there had been the worrying prospect of being sent to the Far East, the general view being that the Japanese war, although inevitably going to end in victory, would take a good deal longer, the difficulty of fighting, island by island, across the vast Pacific theatre, and then of the final, formidable task of invading Japan itself, an even greater challenge than rolling back the German army across Europe.

The possibility of being sent to join the force which was known to be in the process of being assembled for the invasion of Japan, having receded, was, nevertheless, still in the back of the minds of those who realised they might have most to contribute. Indeed, the word was that there was a particular need for RASC officers, which, in spite of Eric's assurances that the 51$^{st}$ Division's role in the occupation of Germany being seen as of vital importance, Stanley felt as a constant worry.

He would listen to reports, the Royal Navy playing its part in the current battle for the island of Okinawa, a strategically vital stepping stone towards the Japanese mainland. The invasion of the island having been launched at the beginning of April, still, after two months, the fighting continued, the Japanese putting up fierce resistance, realising that if the island was lost, they would lose their last defensive outpost, their homeland thus becoming exposed to invasion.

At times, although beginning to enjoy the fruits of peace in Europe, they – the RASC officers amongst many others – found the celebrations of victory – VE Day, the various victory parades, and the solemn speeches and prayers of thankful deliverance – hollow and premature, with a major part of the global conflict continuing, and when, as was evident from the reports, so many men were still dying.

Through those weeks of summer, however, they settled into the routines of the occupation, fears of resistance, which has been widely expected, proving unfounded beyond the hostility they encountered in certain quarters, most notably from those civilians who had so enthusiastically espoused, and benefited from, the Nazi cause, and the occasional more flagrant act of defiance by recalcitrant Hitler Youth.

"Buggers are bloody difficult to tame," Stanley commented ruefully one evening after recounting the incident of the youth throwing a brick at his car.

At the end of the first week of June, his role in the administering of the German forces within the Bremen area, came to an end, which was something of a relief, his dealings with certain of the officers, SS in particular, whose smarting arrogance did not seem to diminish, the most unpalatable part the job. Even without the German military, however, his functions remained wide ranging, including the provisioning of the Division as well as the civilian population, the latter aspect requiring him to liaise increasingly, with the British and American civilians arriving to take up administrative posts with the regional sectors of the Allied Control Council.

*My beloved darling*
*It is now 9.15 on a sultry evening. I've had another swim this evening and two yesterday and a walk in this glorious country which grows lovelier as mid summer approaches. It is too lovely for the Germans to have. I think we shall more or less colonise Germany.*
*I'm glad Hopkins arrived safely plus smuggled binoculars. They are a grand pair worth £50 & cost not a penny.*
*I've handed over the German Army to Herbie now – so I shan't get many trips to Cuxhaven.*
*Eric, Stephen & I went to a hectic party in B Mess last night. We were slightly stinking when we came back and raided Johnnie and Herbie's tent. Stephen & I thought we were parachutists and landed on top of it with disastrous results. Eric drove the jeep up a bank on the way back & finished up inside Johnnie's tent. After some very necessary black coffee I decided a walk was called for but everyone else was too drunk so I went on my own. Darling, it was indescribably beautiful – complete peace & still light at midnight: it was a night of heavenly splendour.*
*When I returned 45 minutes later I found a search party drunkenly going out to look for me! When I woke up this morning I decided a swim would complete my cure so I dragged Bertie out and off we went.*
*Darling, I am longing to see Anthony again, second only to my longing to see you. He sounds a grand lad and must be loving a glorious summer.*
*I have vivid memories of this night a year ago. I was duty officer & lay awake for hours listening first to the beautiful nightingales then later on our bombers going out again. It seemed to last so long. I felt a curious knowledge inside that 'this was it'. Sure enough I looked out and could see the shapes of the Dakotas & gliders: the 6th Airborne on the way to open the biggest adventure of the war. D Day had arrived. It all seems an age ago now. O darling, I would fuck you so much & so long tonight, and come so much with you at just the right moment, then come again and kiss you and bite you and kiss you all over your lovely body. O darling, I'm so desperately passionately in love with you on this still night.*

*Goodnight my beloved darling.*
*Yours for ever in love*
*Stanley*
*PS We have just heard that leave restarts on 1ˢᵗ July so I'm liable to get mine any day from then on.*

*18.6.45*
*My beloved darling*
*Yesterday morning, Eric, Johnnie, Herbie and I went to see our final place near Syke: we have quite a nice farmhouse with two other houses associated. The view is really lovely: it's on a hill, not as high as the Dyke but the view is a broad one rather like the Weald, but instead of the Weald you look over the Weser basin. The house where the mess is is very pleasant except that one or two parts of it have not been finished. It has a modern bathroom & WC. The house where I decided to sleep is about 30 yds away & is also very pleasant if you don't mind the smell of farmyards: & of course there are rather a lot of flies. The Huns have had to give us most of their furniture (and picking the best for ourselves!). We moved sofas, armchairs, wardrobes, washstands & God knows what – I've never seen 4 officers work so hard!*
*Darling now let me tell you about the rest of my time on our trip to Bad Harzburg. We had a hell of a party: dinner was hilarious & the party that followed was too. Darling, you would have loved it. The dance was good fun – you'll be pleased to hear I only danced with British girls (nursing sisters). It was a grand dance because the band, being German, could only play pre 1939 stuff: they were very good though & did a Palais Glide, Lambeth Walk, Chestnut Tree & Hokey-Pokey: it was rather amazing to see German girls doing the Lambeth Walk with British Officers. They all stood to attention for the National Anthem. The party ended at 1pm.*
*Yes, darling, I would like to start another baby when my future is a bit more certain.*
*Goodnight now my beloved girl.*
*Your adoring husband*
*Stanley*


At last, with his dates fixed, he began to feel that sensation which he remembered from his school days with the approach of the end of term, the prospect of the imminent holidays, particularly when it was summer, engendering pangs of eager anticipation. The difference now was that rather than contemplating freedom from the rigours of education, the delight that filled his mind was Peggy; being with her, and with Anthony. What would the little chap be like now, seven months from the last time he had seen him. And filling his lustful imagination, was the imminent prospect of being able to put into practice the erotic techniques which, for so long, had been mere words and fantasy. He found himself floating in sort of euphoric fever, counting down the remaining days of June.

*Sweetheart darling*

*Tomorrow is July 1ˢᵗ and leave will seem even nearer – under three weeks.*

*Darling, last night Eric, Johnnie and I went to see a circus in Hamburg. I haven't seen a circus for ages and it was a grand show, right in the middle of the city. It had performing elephants and a breath-taking trapeze act – by Germans I think. Hamburg must have been a very lovely city – despite the amazing devastation, parts of it still are, but it is really 'kaput'. It felt strange to walk in a city and mix with hundreds of Germans out for their evening walk without being able to talk to them. Non frat has become ridiculous – you can talk to a small boy who is 8 today but if his ninth birthday is tomorrow, officially you can no longer talk to him.*

*I hope the Conservatives will get in purely because I think W.Churchill is the only outstanding man who is capable of leading the country through the difficult days to come. I rather fear it may be a stiff fight as so many of the troops will vote socialist: they've no idea why – it's just class inferiority complex – the usual 'down with the upper classes' feeling. I hope to God no one votes for that frightful little upstart from the Pay Corps who has sent me a piece of paper with 'down with Public Schools' etc. all over it. I've sent it back to him with a few comments.*

*For always your adoring*

*Stanley*

# TWENTY-SIX

For several moments he thought he was still drifting in one of the dreams which, with the luxury of the later alarm call over recent weeks, had been a feature of his surfacing from a full night's sleep, the images of the vicarage and its garden so vivid he could see every detail, even the cracks in the paved path running across to the church which he had trodden innumerable times, from his earliest memories when, as a four year old, he had been taken to the childrens' services in what was then the new church, consecrated in 1922, largely funded by the legendary and rather intimidating, Mrs Moore, wealthy benefactor of the parish.

It was the rattle of trams trundling up and down Dyke Road, and the church bells that made him realise that the chiming of the hour he could hear now was real.

He lifted his head, feeling the effects of the previous evening's alcohol, surveying the interior of the hut, the sun lighting the closed blinds, one of the doors to the narrow veranda ajar, allowing him to hear Anthony burbling contentedly outside.

"Shh. Daddy's still asleep."

"It's alright, I'm awake," he called, Anthony pushing the door open, peering suspiciously at his father, having had less than twenty four hours to get used to the presence of this large man, the child having little recollection of father from January.

"Say good morning to Daddy," Peggy said, her hand on the child's shoulder, guiding him inside.

"Hello, old chap." Stanley held out his hand towards the child who remained by the door, continuing to stare.

"Don't forget he was only just over one when you were last home," Peggy had reminded him the previous day, when, shortly after his arrival, stepping towards his cowering son and picking him up, the child had emitted a howl as if being abducted, stretching his arms towards his mother. "It'll take him a while to get to know you again."

It had been a difficult day, Stanley, weary after nearly two days of travelling, Anthony dissolving into tears whenever his father came too close to him,

475

Peggy busying around, clearly on edge.

Those first few hours, as on the previous leave, at Peggy's request, they had spent at the house, Stanley having to make polite conversation with her mother when all that he wanted was for them – the three of them – to be able to go off to the hut, to be alone together.

In the evening, Anthony, being unsettled by the new presence, renewed his cries of indignation when Peggy put him into his cot, the curtain she had put up around it, at least hiding him from his father. And when, eventually, she managed to get him off to sleep, they had to talk in whispers, Peggy suggesting that it might be best not to put on any records. Stanley had long pictured them on that first evening, drinking, Peggy getting a bit "squiffy" – her favourite term for the giggliness which often came over her after a couple of gin and limes – the two of them dancing to his records before progressing, quite rapidly he imagined, to love making.

Instead, as she cooked their meal, rather meagre looking chops, they conversed in lowered voices. There was so much he wanted to talk about, to unburden himself to her, recounting his experiences, but instead, she seemed to want to tell him about everything she had been doing, speaking as if she were nervous, hardly letting him get a word in.

It was only when they had finished their meal that, relaxed by liquor, her gin and his beer followed by a bottle of wine, that she seemed to become calmer. Peering behind the curtain to check that Anthony was sound asleep, she agreed that he could play some records.

"Keep them a bit quiet. We don't want to wake him, do we?" she said, with her saucy smirk.

He took her in his arms, their slow dance having no form, their feet simply shuffling in circles as they rotated until they abandoned the pretence, shedding their clothing, their love making urgent and soon concluded, Stanley falling instantly asleep.

Sunday morning had also featured regularly in his dreams of life at home; the comforting ritual of church; Sunday roast; an afternoon walk before tea and a quiet evening, with beer and supper. And as they made their way the short distance from the hut to the front of the church, Peggy's arm linked through his, her mother having collected Anthony so that they could go to church together, the child being far too young to attend, it was just as he had imagined; and just as he remembered.

Outside the church, there were effusive greetings from many friends and acquaintances, Peggy smiling proudly, Stanley, imposingly smart in his dress uniform, the gold crowns on his shoulders shining in the bright sun, his status recognised by several people who congratulated him even though his promotion had been many months earlier.

Lunch at the vicarage came a quite a shock to Stanley. He was well aware of the fact that rationing had become even tougher towards the end of the war, but compared with the plentiful fare provided for the army, and, more gallingly, the more than adequate rations available for the German populace – something he was closely acquainted with through his role in its distribution - what he was presented with was far more meagre than at the time of his last leave. There was at least a joint of meat, although it hardly seemed large enough for even a modest portion for each of those around the table; his parents, Peggy's mother, Ted, who was visiting for a few days, and he and Peggy.

The vegetables and potatoes similarly, seemed insufficient, Stanley glancing around the table when everyone had been served, the plates scarcely covered, Anthony, sitting in his high-chair, with a helping of similar size to everyone else.

When the pudding arrived, the aging Mrs Christian rolling into the dining room, her arthritic limbs making her gait even more ungainly than before, she proudly announced "jam and carrot sponge", placing the round, flat, solid looking creation in front of Stanley's mother who set about slicing it, her exertion showing the force she needed to drive the spoon into the ungiving substance. Had it not been for the jam, rather tart as this was, sugar content much reduced, the combination of the solid, doughy texture and the distinctly carroty flavour, would have made it wholly unpalatable, used as he was to proper puddings, unaffected by shortages of flour, butter, or eggs, even sugar seeming to be reasonably plentiful.

"I've a good mind to start kicking up a bit of a stink," he said to Peggy after lunch when they were walking along the seafront, Anthony toddling in front of them.

"What is it now?" Peggy asked, trying not to sigh, Stanley appearing to find fault with almost everything.

"It's nothing about you, darling. But it really does make my blood boil that you have to put up with this when we are getting fat over there. I really don't believe that the shortages are half as bad as they are saying. But that pudding! It was quite ghastly!"

She turned to him, her face colouring.

"We do the best we can," she retorted sharply. "Making do with what we've got."

He decided not to pursue the matter.

The seven days of leave seemed to pass in the blink of an eye, two days in the hut followed by two nights in London, one night, a dinner dance at the Grosvenor hotel where they were staying, the second, dinner in restaurant, the food on both occasions, though somewhat more generous than that available at home, nevertheless, compared with what he was used to, disappointing, both in quantity and flavour, as if rationing extended to salt and herbs, both of which his palate had become accustomed to.

He decided, however, to avoid any further comment, surprised as he had been, at Peggy's vehement response when he had raised the subject after Sunday lunch.

Their love making, however, was most certainly not rationed, lost time being energetically made up for, their two days in London, mostly spent wandering around the parks, enjoying the summer weather, returning to the hotel at regular intervals, the "Do Not Disturb" sign on their door.

The final days, back in the hut, serving perfectly, particularly in the warm summer weather, as their family home, were, as on the previous leave, overshadowed by the approaching day of his departure.

It was, however a happy week, for both of them, with much discussion about their lives when, eventually, he was able to come home permanently, by which time, she was confident, the flats which her mother had bought, would be vacant, the sitting tenants departing, allowing them to move in to the top flat which was to become their home.

He also made a commitment, to her and to himself, to abandon any ideas of the regular army or colonial service, and to get down to what he knew was going

478

to the testing task of getting through his law finals, the prospect of many months of study filing him with despondency. At least he still had, he reckoned, six months of enjoying the, by now, care and responsibility free army existence.

It was only after he was back in Germany, that he could admit to himself, a feeling of slight disappointment that, satisfying as it had been, there had been something about the sex – something which he struggled to define – the word *conventional* coming to mind. After all those months of their written exchanges, exploring the intimate depths of their desires and, certainly for him, erotic fantasies; their openness, as they wrote about their "dates", their pleasurings never seeming solitary, such was their loving joinder of thoughts at the chosen times, the actuality, rather like the food, lacked *spice*. He had so excitedly anticipated their written exchanges flowing into real, face to face, body to body reality, their love making to become more elaborate as they tried the more adventurous positions and techniques which they had so avidly practised on paper.

It was not as if they had not enjoyed a certain amount of variety, she encouraging him to try a few changes of position, the occasion in the hotel when she had taken the lead, pushing down onto the bed, laughing as she straddled him, imprinted deliciously in his brain, the memory stirring his juices now as he pictured her, eyes closed in her climactic ecstasy, arching backward, squeezing and crushing him, causing him to emit a groan of almost painful exaltation, such was the intensity of sensation. Rather, it was the feeling that in spite of the wonderful blatancy of her letters, she was still constrained by tendrils of the inhibitions which, for so long, he had recognised as being embedded from her upbringing, his disappointment now, being that such constraints, while certainly loosened, remained, tethering her to some deeply instilled modesty.

It had, however, been a wonderful week, their love renewed, his conviction, as he set off on the gruelling return journey, that their relationship was deeper and more rewarding than ever, his one overriding thought as he sat, gloomily, on the train back to London, that all that he desired was to begin his life with her.

"When I'm back, I'm never going to be away from you again," he promised her, when, on the morning of the last day, they were sitting on a bench in the park, the weather having changed, grey clouds scudding from the west reflecting their mood, her head resting on his shoulder, their familiarity with the emotions of the hours before his departure failing to mitigate the pain.

He put his arm round her shoulder, his face against her hair, the two of them sitting in silence, watching Anthony running around on the grass, chasing some seagulls which were angrily disputing the territory they were compelled to concede to the shrieking child.

When the moment of his departure finally arrived, the tension of the preceding days building to its heart-rending climax, the perfect summer's morning only served to make their parting so much more painful.

"This should be the last time," Stanley said, trying to keep his voice level, Peggy standing by the front door, holding Anthony. He enfolded them in his arms, touching her cheek with his finger tips. "Be brave, my darling," he whispered, her tears making it difficult for him to maintain his self control.

He turned quickly, hoisting his kit-bag onto his shoulder, striding to the tram stop just as the tram arrived. From his seat on top he waved as he passed them, Peggy, still holding the child, at the gate, his small hand waving as the tram quickly passed from view.

She sat down in the kitchen, her means of coping, learned from long experience, being to occupy herself to help the first few hours pass, going about any mindless tasks.

"I'm sure it won't be too long," her mother said, making them both a cup of Camp coffee, Peggy also well used to the hollow reassurances which her mother had the habit of trotting out, rather like her stock of aphorisms, no longer allowing them to irritate her as they had when she had sought to sooth her daughter's distress as Stanley's departures in the earlier years of the war. "I'm sure they'll all be coming home soon, now that they've won the war. And besides, he's safe now."

"I think I'll go up the hut," Peggy said abruptly when she had finished her coffee. "To do a bit of tidying." She needed to be by herself for a while, away from her mother. "Can you look after Anthony for a bit?" In spite of her momentary annoyance at the inference of her mother's remark – that she should buck up as Stanley was no longer in danger, she recognised that this time, the pain of parting no longer carried the previous depth of anxiety.

Stanley's interest in politics and current affairs was something which had evolved from the occasional discussions which, in his last year or so at school, and subsequently, amongst his group of friends, at the rugger club and other social occasions, would feature amid the more usual topics, sport invariably the predominant subject, cricket to the fore, the test match series, whether home or in one of the far flung test countries involving avid listening to the reports on the wireless and sometimes, late at night or in the early hours, tuning in to a crackling overseas broadcast.

The conversations in those pre-war days could scarcely be characterised as debates, the participants largely sharing a rather simplistic world view, the backdrop being the swathes of pink across the globe, indicative of the extent of the Empire, diminished to some extent since the Great War, but still affirming Britain's sway over so much of the world. The discussions tended to be around the cast of characters making up the body politic, the most animated exchanges relating to the competing factions within the Conservative party, Churchill, renowned maverick that he was, nevertheless, increasingly the voice with which many identified, particularly the younger generation who had not had to live through the Great War, Churchill's strident views about Hitler and the rise of the Nazis, in stark contrast with those who had been intent upon avoiding any future conflict.

It was true that, in the run up to the general election which Stanley and many others felt to have been called with undue haste after the end of the war, he had toyed with the idea of voting for one of the other parties, this almost unthinkable prospect due solely to the government's machinations about demobilisation. He knew, however, that the idea of voting Labour was complete anathema, the Liberals being a pretty ineffectual lot, and hardly in a position to make any difference. And of course, there was Churchill. How could one possibly not vote for the great man, not just because of what he had done for the country during the war, but because of his stature generally. If ever there was a time for strong leadership, it was now, with the country down on its uppers, its morale, since VE Day, having steadily declined.

Stanley also had reservations about the local candidate, Sir William Teeling, an Irish born author and the sitting member for Brighton. His stance on demobilisation, as well as the topical – and vexed – subject of the gratuity to be paid to returning troops, had been annoyingly opaque, it being this more than anything which had caused Stanley to think the unthinkable. When it came to it, however, he marked his cross on the postal ballot paper decisively, casting his vote for Churchill rather than Teeling.

The result, deferred for three weeks because of problems in organising the count, was announced while he was home on leave, Churchill's defeat feeling like a personal affront. How could anybody choose to oust him? And to replace him with the faceless Attlee. For the rest of the day, after hearing the result, he made no attempt to disguise his ill-humour, grumbling about the "damned socialists", castigating the troops for their disloyalty. "I suppose it's only to be expected" he conceded in the evening when, his mood having lightened slightly, ameliorated by a glass of beer, he acknowledged Peggy's hesitant suggestion that "an awful lot of people are in desperate straights, with no jobs and little money."

As he made his way back to Germany for what he sincerely hoped would be the last time, the country now being governed by Labour gave a convenient focus to his growing disenchantment. With Churchill out of government, it made it a great deal easier to lambast the new regime, the fact that certain of the new cabinet had served with Churchill in his War Cabinet, most notably Ernest Bevin and Herbert Morrison, as well as Attlee himself, conveniently forgotten now that they were there for all to see in their true socialist colours.

As the summer slowly passed, the sultry, humid days of July followed by the dryer heat of August, whilst the frustration with the ever changing information about demobilisation would periodically boil over into outright anger, they, the RASC officers and their colleagues throughout the army of occupation, stoically accepted their lot, a great deal of socialising – parties and dinners, with plentiful food and liquor – and the recreation facilities provided, going some way to alleviated the malaise of boredom and the widespread feeling of futility.

The Japanese war was clearly heading towards its climax, the general reckoning being that the Japs were even more determined than the Germans had been, to fight to the bitter end, with the grim prospect of another invasion and the inevitability of thousands more casualties.

"Have you heard the news?" Johnnie Harper asked them excitedly, coming off night duty as the others were arriving in the mess for breakfast. "They've dropped this bomb. The Yanks. Atomic bomb."

The others looked at him, trying to comprehend what he was saying.

"Atomic bomb?" Peters repeated. "What the hell is an atomic bomb?"

"I've no idea other than it bloody big. They said that it had destroyed a whole city." Harper stood there as they all continued to look at him, waiting for further information. "They didn't really say anything else. Apart from the name of the place. But I can't remember it. Some Jap name."

"Hiroshima," Eric said, supplying the name that was to become ever associated with the first use of such a weapon. "I've just been speaking to someone at ACC."

"Will it be enough to make them throw in the towel?" Stanley asked.

"I suppose, if they don't, the Yanks will be able to destroy their cities." Peters suggested thoughtfully, all of them trying to imagine cities, Tokyo included, being obliterated one after the other.

Three days later, the Japanese having declined to surrender, as if needing to prove the point, the Americans dropped a second bomb, this time on the city of Nagasaki, with similar devastating effect. Yet even in the face of such brutally stark evidence of what would occur if they fought on, it took nearly a week for the Japan to surrender.

*13.8.45*
*My dearest darling*
*This is a great day isn't it? It seems unbelievable that war is really finished in all the world. The rounding up of all the Japs will be quite a job I should think even without all the territorial settlements. In celebration I have just hung out our victory flag & now I am listening to the Victory Anthem. The King spoke very well didn't he?*
*It is a quieter day than usual as nearly all the shops are shut. I wish you were here, darling, so that we could celebrate together. I think we celebrated enough on leave for both V days. As it is I shall celebrate by going to bed quite soon.*
*I will be thanking God for peace, for you, for life & love.*
*I love you so utterly.*
*Peggy*

"This has just arrived," Eric said at the briefing which he insisted on continuing to hold, although now only every few days, generally when he decided there was something significant to discuss.

He held up the sheet of paper before handing it to Stanley who, having quickly read it, walked across to the noticeboard, pinning it up, the others gathering beside him, reading in silence.

**SUPREME HEADQUARTERS ALLIED EXPEDITIONARY FORCE TO ALL MEMBERS OF THE ALLIED EXPEDITIONARY FORCE The task which we set ourselves is finished and the time has come for me to relinquish Combined Command.**

**In the name of the United States and the British Commonwealth, from whom my authority is derived, I should like to convey to you the gratitude and admiration for our two nations for the manner in which you have responded to every demand that had been made upon you. At times conditions have been hard and the tasks to be performed arduous. No praise is too high for the manner in which you have surmounted every obstacle.**

**I should like, also, to add my own personal word of thanks to each one of you for the part you have played and the contribution you have made to our joint victory.**

**Now that you are about to pass to other spheres of activity, I say Good-bye to you and wish you Good Luck and God Speed.**

**Dwight Eisenhower**

"So it's OK for him to bugger off home," Basil Seymour said, articulating what most of them were thinking. "What about the rest of us?"

"We still have a job to do," Eric replied, Stanley observing the CO's stern expression. He had noticed, in the last couple of weeks, that something seemed to have changed in his friend. He appeared more aloof and less inclined to join in the general conversations, particularly when, as was almost always the case, the subject of demobilisation came up, prompting the usual deluge of disparagement of both the army and the government.

"All OK, Eric?" Stanley asked him one evening when, having suggested the two of them should have one of their quiet night-caps, the response had been a rather curt "No, not tonight."

"Yes, thank you," Eric replied. "I just need to concentrate on what lies ahead."

Having made it known that he had signed up for a further ten years of service in the regular army, it seemed to Stanley as if his friend had decided that he needed to fit the part, it not being appropriate for a colonel to keep company to the extent he had until now with his junior officers. He had to be looking ahead, showing himself to be a serious contender for promotion, being seen in the right places, mixing with his seniors.

His presence in the mess, particularly during the evenings when games of bridge or monopoly were under way, became distinctly uncomfortable, his habit now being to sit in an armchair, reading the paper or with his head in some military literature.

"Seems the fun has gone out of him," Peters remarked to Stanley, echoing Stanley's own view.

Although from time to time he and Eric would continue to go for walks together, there was no doubt that their relationship had changed, Eric reticent to allow the conversation to turn to anything personal. It was a change which saddened Stanley, Eric, he had always considered, his closest friend within the mess, the two of them having been able to share confidences and matters of the heart.

What Eric did let slip was that his wife, having made known her strong opposition to her husband remaining in the regular army if this should involve overseas posting, which, he had avoided admitting to her was inevitable, he had recently had to tell her that had been informed that he was due to be posted to the British colony of Aden, trying to sell the prospect to her on the basis that it would involve his promotion to brigadier, with the resulting increase in his pay as well as enhanced benefits, most importantly, their two children having their education as a British private school in the colony being paid for by the army.

Eventually, in the face of her escalating resistance to the point of refusal to "ship our children off to some far flung corner of the desert", a reasonably accurate portrayal of the colony based on her own enquiries, he had reluctantly turned the posting town, the consequence being that he could expect to remain in Germany for the foreseeable future.

"Not something I relish," he told Stanley, "although I am keeping my ear to the ground for other possibilities."

For Stanley, and the remainder of the RASC officers, the grumbling about their grievances continued to dominate their conversations, the absence of any clearer information about demobilisation remaining firmly at the top of their list of complaints, followed by their anger at the shortages back home which their families were regularly reporting.

"God Almighty!" Stanley exclaimed in one his fits of indignant anger, "you would think we had lost the bloody war!"

As always, Peggy made light of the shortages, looking on the bright side, her stoical "make do and mend" attitude, at times, Stanley finding distinctly annoying. He encouraged her to "kick up a stink", although, apart from writing to Teeling, he was unable to suggest how she was to do so.

The subject which also, increasingly, pervaded their conversations, was the growing threat from the Russians. With the division of Germany into sectors administered separately by the Allied powers, the tensions which were already apparent at the end of the war when there was a real fear of conflict with the Russians, particularly over the control of Berlin, escalated both in Germany and elsewhere, a new flash-point being the Korean peninsula, the Americans and Russians having, respectively, occupied the South and North as both began to strengthen their positions in what was clearly the beginning of a new, global, geo-political stand-off.

There was a growing realisation that the deterioration in relations with the "Joes" had a bearing on the vexed issue of demobilisation, Eric, with the usual suggestion of his being "in the know", being of the opinion that the Western Allies were already working on deployments across Germany to confront the Russians, should they over-step any of the lines agreed between Roosevelt, Stalin and Churchill at the Tehran and Yalta conferences.

To Stanley, it was a gnawing anxiety, his real worry being that demobilisation might be delayed even further. And in the meantime, they had to pass the time, the administering of the Division's supplies, now requiring a modest amount of work, at most a few hours each day, thankfully, with regular trips to different units and to meetings around the region to break up the monotony.

He had become aware, also, of a change in the mood within the mess. In spite of Eric's tendency to remain detached from their games and from much of their conversation, particularly when it descended to the low levels which was virtually a daily occurrence, there remained a remarkable bond of camaraderie between them. Increasingly, however, their differences began to surface, Stanley finding certain of them grating with him, although the cause of his annoyance tended to be fairly inconsequential – irritating habits – which were reasonably easy to pass over.

Their bond these days was of togetherness in the face of the adversity of being stuck there, not knowing for how long, eating and drinking, their lives unavoidably close. Even with their farm accommodation, their bathing facilities were shared, with limited privacy, they all, through the long months of the campaign, having become familiar with each other's bodies and personal habits. It was perfectly normal for them to wander, naked, from their bedrooms to the shared bathrooms, and, when the weather allowed, to enjoy the outdoor shower they had had rigged up.

When they went to bathe in the nearby lake, they would invariably swim naked, only putting their swimming trunks when the occasional local family appeared.

They enjoyed a school-boyish bawdiness, remarking on each other's appendages, comparing notes on masturbation techniques.

*5.9.45*
*Darling one*
*Hello darling! As I'm feeling in a crazy sort of mood this may be a bit of a crazy letter. The conversation in the mess has reached a new low, especially as we had to give Johnnie a lot of last minute advice before he went on leave. We've tried to persuade him not to use the crate of French letters he seemed to have got, & to have an infant. He went away with an almost visible erection. His JT is famous and is known as the Pride of Godestorf! As Eric once said, it's big enough when it's at anchor, heaven knows what it's like when it's at sea!*
*Darling, I feel that this might develop into a bit of a really rude letter, so I'd better stop. The Highland Games were quite good fun though I get very bored watching Scottish dances: I think they are very dull. The massed pipers are always a moving sight though & I think the Huns admitted to the stadium were duly impressed. Needless to say there was quite a party afterwards & your husband was exceedingly merry. I lost my belt etc. in the car coming back (my drunken brother officers removed my trousers) but I got my own back by giving Bertie a lovely black eye with a straight right & I recovered all my possessions by this morning.*
*We have been very busy today and worked quite late: since then we've played some table tennis and 3 handed bridge. What a waste of time it all is now: how we hate it, how bored we all are, in this bloody monastery. Gosh I'd like to go to a rather drunken revellers dance with you tonight & come home swaying slightly.*
*One of our captains, Harold Moncrieff, is spending his last night in the Army with us tomorrow: we are having quite a party. Harold married this girl in Paris about ten days ago. He tells us that six days of married life just about laid him out – he certainly looks a wreck.*
*Darling I hope you don't disapprove of your low minded old man – he's not so bad really you know, and anyhow he loves you very utterly. As he's so very sleepy I think I'd better put myself to bed and say goodnight.*
*I must stop now my darling child.*
*My sweet I love you*
*Stanley*

In the middle of September, Stanley's name came up for a trip to the Harzburger Hof Hotel, renowned before the war, as one of Europe's most luxurious, now taken over by the recently re-named British Army of the Rhine as a retreat for officers, the hotel located in the spectacular setting of the Harzburg Mountains.

He had a strange feeling of unreality on arriving, he, Johnnie Harper and Stephen Peters, turning into the driveway approaching the hotel, the thick forest opening up to offer a view of the grand building against a backdrop of mountains. The fact that it had, until just a few months ago, been a favourite retreat for high ranking *Wehrmacht* officers and a small number of civilians in the higher echelons of the Nazi hierarchy, added a certain relish to it now being reserved for British officers.

As they walked into the ornate foyer, there was little obvious sign that the German staff were anything other than attentive in the manner of concierges and porters anywhere, it only being later that they discerned the undercurrent of frosty hostility, the formal politeness thinly disguising a distaste for these new guests, displacing those who had rightfully enjoyed the hotel's luxurious facilities.

*My very sweet darling*
*I'm writing this on Sunday afternoon in my room at the Hotel Harzburger Hof. Darling, I can't tell you what a delightful place this is. The first thing that strikes one is the lovely situation of the town – at the entrance to the valley with fir covered mountains on either side & a funicular railway up the mountain opposite the hotel. This hotel is the best in town & is of course now our property & the 30 Corps flag flies over it. The Germans staff – i.e. waiters, boots, etc. greet you in great style with a bowing footman at the front door. I was shown to this lovely room on the first floor: it has a balcony where I am now: a waterfall gushes melodiously nearby & the air is sweet with pine scent.*
*Yesterday afternoon we went up the funicular railway which is quite exciting. From the top of this little mountain you get a superb view of the 'Brocken', the highest mountain in the Harz which usually has cloud over its top. We were lucky & saw all of it. In the other direction you get a view of the picturesque town & the North German plain.*
*We had tea on the terrace & a walk around: there are tennis courts, cinemas, riding, fishing, a wonderful open air swimming pool & of course, the mountains.*
*It is certainly a grand short holiday from the dullness & drabness of life at the moment, & the mountain air makes one feel bubbling with energy.*
*There is a dance tonight – you'd love that too. I shan't be fratting though: if I dance it will be with one of the nurses from the hospitals whom I know vaguely. They are 'nice' types: typical nurses (!) but it's grand that there are some English girls because I think an all German dance would be bad.*
*For ever & always your*
*Stanley*

When they – Stanley, Johnnie and Stephen – made their way into the large, ornate, high ceilinged room where the dance was being held, the first thing they noticed was that there were precious few females, outnumbered substantially by the men in uniform, most of them congregated at one end, close to the bar, some forty or so on the dance floor, having found themselves partners, the uniforms, entirely khaki, contrasting with the colours of the girl's dresses.

The three of them joined the crowd around the bar, getting themselves beers, each of them already feeling decidedly merry having been drinking steadily for the past two or three hours.

"We're never going to get a look in," Stephen said when the number finished, many of the dancers leaving the dance floor, other men swiftly finding partners, almost all of the girls thus whisked straight back onto the floor as the band started the next number.
"Look, there's a couple of them sitting out," Johnnie said eagerly, noticing a couple of girls sitting down close to where they were standing. "I really fancy a dance."

"Go on then!" Stephen said. "You'd better be quick before someone else gets them."

"One of you come with me," Johnnie urged, looking at Stanley and Stephen. "I can't go by myself."

"Come on then," Stanley said, watching the dancers reminding him of the night with Peggy at the Grosvenor.

"Would you ladies care for the next dance with us?" Stanley asked, he and Johnnie standing in front of the two seated girls, one of whom having taken off her shoe, was feeling the inside of it.

"New shoes," she said. "Killing my feet."

"Come on Edie," the other girl said. "Thank you, kind sir." She stood up, laughing, placing her hand on Johnnie's arm with mock formality. "Lead on!"

The second girl put her shoe back on, grimacing as she did so. "German shoes," she said, as if this explained why they were uncomfortable before standing up, Stanley admiring her simple green dress with a rather alluring "keyhole" revealing a small circle of her chest and just the slightest glimpse of cleavage.

"Stanley." He held out his hand to her, by way of introduction and to lead her onto the dance floor.

"Edith. The others call me Edie."

His first impression of the girl was that she bore a certain resemblance to Peggy, with her fresh complexion, blue-grey eyes, and slim figure. What was different, however, was her voice, which had a huskiness, suggesting too many cigarettes, her accent placing her somewhere in the London suburbs.

"So, then, Major Stanley," she said, looking up into his face as they went with the rotating flow of dancers in a slow waltz, "what brings you to this part of the world?" Her laugh was throaty and, Stanley thought, rather sexy.

"Just here on holiday," he replied. "Came over for a spot of fighting and decided to stay on to see a bit of the country. And what about you?"

What he learned was that the nurses were mainly from the military hospital in Hamburg with a few others from Hannover. From what he could gather, there was some arrangement between the military and the hospitals to allow parties of nurses to enjoy certain of the army facilities, the inference being that this was seen as a more acceptable means of providing female company than the more traditional arrangement for armies in foreign lands, with a good deal less risk of the men becoming infected by VD which had become alarmingly widespread.

Edie, as Stanley had surmised, was a Londoner, hailing from Deptford, her father being a stevedore working in London docks, Edie being the youngest of five and the only one to have stayed on at school long enough to obtain her certificate, thus enabling her to pursue her dream of becoming a nurse.

It was when she told him that she had trained at Bart's, and he had mentioned Peggy, that she suddenly stood still, mid dance, gaping at him in amazement.

"Peggy Wing!" she exclaimed. "Well I'm damned. She's famous as the nurse who eloped."

It transpired that although Edie's and Peggy's paths had never crossed, Edie having arrived at Bart's shortly after Peggy's departure, Peggy's story had become something of a talking point, featuring in Bart's rich seam of folklore.

"I became friends with one of Peggy's friends," Edie recounted, "a girl everyone called Brewster. Life and soul, she was. Poor thing was killed just before the end of the war. She was back at Bart's in London. Doodle bug hit the digs she was in. Real tragedy."

"Brewster. Peggy often talked about her. I don't think she knew she'd been killed," Stanley said, unsure whether Peggy was still in touch with any of her former Bart's colleagues.

It felt, to Stanley, as the two of them danced together for most of the evening, that they had known each other for ages, such was the ease of their conversation, and when the dance concluded with "God Save the King", they stayed at the bar for a nightcap, Stanley now feeling intoxicated with both liquor and the disturbingly pleasant company.

"Shall we have a breath of air before turning in?" he suggested with a sheepish smirk.

"Rather," she said, giving him a knowing look.

It was a balmy night, the moon hanging above the black silhouette of the mountains, the sky littered with stars. They stood on the terrace, smoking, both now aware of a tension between them, knowing that they had reached a moment of decision.

She turned towards him, her serious expression just discernible in the moonlight, her back to the hotel and the light spilling from its windows.

"I know you're a married man, but you can kiss me if you like," she said, her voice even huskier. "I'm sure Peggy would understand."

The kiss seemed to suspend time, Stanley eventually looking around, noticing several other couples similarly locked in embrace, most of the hotel lights having now being turned off.

They walked back into the hotel in silence, he leading her by the hand, climbing the grand staircase, making their way along the landing and up a second staircase.

"This is me," he said, unlocking the door, stepping into the room, she following, closing the door behind her.

He opened the French windows leading onto the balcony, the moon now sliding behind the mountains, the stars even more vivid.

He began to name various constellations. "Ursa Major – the Great Bear. Sagittarius. Orion's Belt." As he pointed to each she stood beside him, her arm around his back, her head resting against him.

It was she, this time, who led him by the hand, back into the room, pulling him down onto the bed, their embrace now full of intent, their bodies pressed together, hands stroking, exploring.

"Won't be a minute," she whispered, climbing off the bed and going into the bathroom, an en suite room being something he had never experienced before.

He lay on his back, his inebriation beginning to dissipate, allowing his conscience suddenly to reassert itself.

The bathroom door opened, Edie appearing, naked, standing for a moment, as if allowing him to feast his eyes upon her before lying down again beside him, her fingers expertly undoing his belt and fly buttons.

"I can't," he said, sitting up. "I'm sorry, but I just can't." He looked at her, her naked body the ultimate temptation, so sumptuous, and there, ready and available for him. Peggy need never know. After all, it was something that so many of them, the married men, were doing. They explained it away, absolving their consciences, as necessity; assuaging their physical need without in any way affecting their love for their wives. But he knew in that instant, that he could never live with it; the knowledge that he had failed; broken his vow, to her and to himself, of fidelity. He had adhered to it for so long, the episode with Eva having tested him, a test which he felt had enabled him to prove himself, as having the love and strength to keep to the straight and narrow. If he failed now, not only did he realise that it would weigh on his conscience for the rest of his life, but it would tarnish his relationship with Peggy, their absolute openness fatally compromised.

"I'm sorry," he said again. "I just couldn't live with myself."

"You're a rare man, Stan," She stood up, looking at him, nodding to show her acceptance.
 "Peggy's a lucky girl." Nobody ever called him "Stan", but from Edie, with her throaty voice, it had a sort of earthy intimacy to it.

He watched her as she again got off the bed, walking back towards the bathroom, savouring the final glimpse of temptation resisted; of opportunity spurned.

When she re-emerged in her dress but without lipstick, giving her, he thought, a rather sad appearance, she came to the side of the bed.

"Bye then, Stan," she said, leaning over him, kissing him lightly on the cheek. "My feet are killing me, and it's a pity about the hanky-panky, but I'm glad I met you. I hope I end up with someone like you. There aren't many blokes who would have turned it down. Bloody lucky, that Peggy, to have eloped with you.

"Actually, we didn't elope," he said. "I think that was a story that Brewster put about. We thought about it at one stage, but in the end we didn't need to."

"Ah well, it was a good story." She kissed him again before leaving the room, Stanley quickly getting into his pyjamas and climbing back into bed.

His last thought before falling asleep was that he knew that he would have to place Edie in that same compartment where he had secreted Eva; a compartment tightly and permanently sealed.

A couple of years after the war, when, through the solicitor's practice Stanley had joined, he got to know a client, a local builder, Sam "Dink" Davy, the two of them becoming life-long fishing companions, sharing a sturdy clinker boat for the regular trips out into the Channel, until Dink's death from cancer in his sixties, Dink's use of the same diminutive, "Stan", would often remind him of the that night at the Harzburger Hof, Dink's voice, roughened by the Woodbines which he chain-smoked, even when he was fiddling with the unreliable Seagull outboard motor, evoking Edie's sexy, South London, infused, like Dink's, with something which drew Stanley. Perhaps it was the contrast with the proper enunciation of those who inhabited his day to day world.

In the weeks that followed his short sojourn in the Harzburger Mountains, time seemed to pass even more slowly, the tedium of daily life weighing ever more heavily, even the dinners and parties becoming routine, Stanley relying on his correspondence with Peggy as his life-line to the future he felt sometimes to be getting no closer.

Although demobilisation had begun during the summer, RASC were deemed to be one of the essential units, which, as far as he was concerned, was simply the pretext for the authorities to string them along. The latest reckoning was that it would not be until at least the following spring that they would be released, the prospect of a further six months of this existence almost unendurable.

What he also realised, however, was that, taking a leaf from Peggy's book, he had no alternative but to accept his lot, and to make the best of it, disheartening though it might be. He found the countryside offered him ever greater solace, his walks become a regular feature of his days, often by himself, familiarising himself with the bird life and with the other wild creatures, occasionally coming across deer and wild boar as well as the smaller animals – weasels, stoat, pine martens and red squirrels.

Often also, when he was pondering what to say to Peggy, his mind would wander back through the past years, revisiting their times together; their courtship as well as the more painful moments. Reminiscing became a new strand of their correspondence, the memories, for both of them, enriching their distant relationship, adding a further layer to the foundation for the future which they knew would soon be theirs.

More than ever, he delighted in her accounts of her day to day life; her routines and her socialising; the details of Anthony's achievements and his little adventures; her involvement in the serious business of running the local badminton club. How he longed to be part of such an ordinary existence; to become a true family man, perhaps taking up gardening; going for walks across the Downs and exploring more of the nearby Weald, particularly as he could now see it as a rich habitat for birds.

He lay on his bed, reading her latest letter, another of element of his longing being for the soft spaciousness of a double bed with his beloved nestling beside him, rather than this rather hard yet serviceable single, purloined from the Gestapo HQ in Bremerhaven, it having become something of a joke amongst them that, with all the luxuries that the Gestapo had managed to garner for themselves, their beds left something to be desired, it being assumed that a firm bed had some sort of connotation of Arian manliness.

No longer did he have to read in the dim light of a paraffin lamp, in the blacked out confines of his caravan. Much as he valued his cramped private space, he was much relieved when he had been able to relinquish it, watching the small, shed-like structure, the day before they took up residence in Bremerhaven, being loaded, with several others, onto a transporter, its destination unknown to him.

Nowadays he was able to read her letters properly, dwelling on the parts which most warmed or excited him, sometimes taking down one of her photos, holding it beside the letter, glancing at it as he read as if she were there, speaking to him.

*18.9.45*
*My darling one*
*Today as usual has been wet. I went to church this morning. I was very far away though & not very interested I am afraid. I thought it was rather a poor show that there was not a word about the RAF when this is supposed to be the Battle of Britain Thanksgiving Sunday especially when you think that but for 'those few' we might now be subservient to Germany instead of a victorious nation.*
*Your very happy wife at the moment in just thinking of our love. I feel rather wild and woolly tonight darling. I think you would like my hair. It is long and rather fluffy. I think you would like this jumper too as I have decided that you can see rather a lot through it. As you can guess, Peggy is not feeling very good tonight. If you were here, darling, I would want to love you a lot & prove you were right in saying English girls were passionate – in fact I would want to be on top of you.*
*Goodnight beloved*
*Peggy*

He felt the familiar stirring of his blood, there being something about her explicitness which he found exquisitely arousing. He chose not to remind himself of the slight disappointment he had been left with after his last leave. Several times he had tried to edge their conversation in that direction, alluding to their exchanges, conscious as he did so of a slight embarrassment, as if they had both been overheard talking in their sleep, revealing innermost thoughts, and now, in the light of day, needing to rein them in once more.

But now, once again, she was truly back in such flagrantly uninhibited vein, all shackles of that clawing propriety cast aside. God, how he loved her, and how, at this moment, he longed for her body; to possess it; to explore its every inch and mystery; and most of all, to master the art of arousing her, bringing her to her gasping, whimpering climax.

*My sweet darling*
*It is strange you should mention the RAF. They are not alone, darling, in fading from people's minds. There is a good deal of bitterness out here, for instance, over the cutting of duty free cigarettes. The chaps say, yes, now the war's over people will soon forget. I hate to indulge false heroics, but we feel a little wistful as we think back exactly a year: some of us – including the 43rd Division – were in Nijmegen: we were cut off from the outside*

*world: there was much bombing & shelling. And we say – remember Nijmegen a year ago: and what happens this week? Few remember that hazardous and thrilling operation that might so easily have won the war: all they are worrying about is that soldiers are exchanging cigarettes for a few eggs: but you – you are one of us, and you remember.*

*Darling, I never hated your hospital career. I often speak with pride, that my wife was a nurse through 1939 and 1940. What I did hate was the fact that your hospital life stood as what seem an insurmountable barrier, not only between you and I, but between us and happiness. But then the Walls of Jericho fell. Darling, my life too has, I feel, been all preparation for life with you: ever since I first began to realise years ago that I could never live without you, I felt that there was some rather wonderful if incomprehensible force that would guide our lives, and that our love story would pass through hardship to the stars: that it would be no ordinary story, but one so full of life and colour as to symbolise the story and burning bonds of love and passion ever growing between us.*

*I'll now say goodnight, sweetheart. I love you my darling girl. September evenings always make me want to hold your hand: to take you for a walk before supper & to enjoy the welcome cheerfulness of the heart with you.*

*For always, my darling*

*Yours truly, Stanley*


*My dearly beloved*

*Your letter about the Hartzburger Hof has made me very envious. It sounds so very beautiful. I suppose by the time this reaches you, you will be back to ordinary army life. Yes darling, we must visit. I wonder if you managed to go riding. I really must learn to ride well one day. I hope you behaved well at the dance & did not break too many hearts even if they were nurses. They might be friends of mine.*

*Darling, I have been dreamily thinking of you & wishing I could have been there. It would have saved you having to dance with typical nurses all the time. I don't quite know what 'nice' implies.*

*I love you so much forever.*

*Peggy*


Her unsuspecting comments on his stay at the Harzburger Hof, so precariously close to the reality even in their generous innocence, tugged at the tendrils of guilt which continued to play on his conscience, his own response, with its gaping omission, almost as flagrant an act of deceit as if he had consummated his infidelity. But he had not done so, this bald fact, he told himself, his justification for assuaging his guilt with a contrary, if muted, sense of relief.

# TWENTY SEVEN

Having assumed that the trial would be held in a court similar to the few he had visited during his articles, the most memorable being the neo-gothic grandeur of the Royal Courts of Justice in London, each of the individual courts, oak panelled, with elaborately carved benches, the judges presiding from throne-like seats, raised high above the body of the court, the very air seeming to be infused with the weight of judicial history, it came as a considerable surprise to find that the Belsen trial was being held in a large 19$^{th}$ century gymnasium in the old Saxony town of Luneburg, the building selected to accommodate the large numbers attending.

At this, the first of the trials, there were no fewer than forty-five defendants, each represented by British advocates appointed by the army, the proceedings, being a military tribunal, taking place before a panel of senior officers aided by one British barrister.

It was an extraordinary sight which greeted Stanley as he, Eric and Johnnie filed in, the interior of the building more like a church than a gymnasium, the seating arranged in a large square, the benches which served as the dock facing tribunal, the advocates' benches in front of the dock, several rows of seats on either side for press, military observers – the classification given to the visiting officers – and fifty or so German civilians invited to witness the proceedings, some in the gallery alongside several press photographers and film cameramen.

As they waited, there was a palpable feeling of anticipation, even though this was the third day of the trial, the atmosphere being more akin to that of a show or a boxing tournament, the buzz of expectation as the spectators awaited the actors or pugilists.

The sound of lorries outside the building indicated the arrival of the defendants, Stanley's impression of them, as they filed along their benches, being of fear behind their fixed expressions, some with a veneer of defiance, military police directing them to their allocated places, each defendant having a large number hung around their necks to identify them. None of them spoke, each doubtless immersed in their private thoughts, all aware that they were here, facing the immutable force of British justice, knowing also, that they were on trial for their lives.

The sense of spectacle was heightened by the cameras, several filming the preliminaries, cameramen permitted into the open square in the centre of the hall, pointing their lenses accusingly at the defendants as they took their seats, the films – Pathé News and Movietone – to be shown within a few days in cinemas across much of the world, the names and faces of the most prominent of the defendants recognised as the epitome of evil for which the Nazis would be damned by history.

Having seen films of Belsen, at numerous showings in various towns and cities across the region, each time Stanley found himself unable to comprehend the sheer brutality, and the depths of inhumanity which his species was capable plumbing.

The sight of the mass graves, countless skeletally thin bodies piled up like so much detritus, had a terrible fascination, speaking more than any other image of the extent to which the Nazis had cast themselves adrift from even the most basic tenets of morality. And now, here he was, in the same room with those who had perpetrated not only the suffering of dehumanisation and starvation, but who had treated inmates as no more than laboratory rats, to be used in dreadful medical experiments.

The camp commandant, Joseph Kramer, rightly bearing the number "1" on his chest, earning himself the infamous title *The Beast of Belsen,* sat at the end of the row, nearest to where Stanley was sitting. How could one equate this rather ordinary looking man with the monster described by the prosecuting advocate, and by the witnesses giving their painful evidence. Staring at him, heavy eyebrows, square jawed and eyes slightly too close together, Stanley could imagine him as a street thug or a villain in some gangster film, but it was the gulf from such portrayal of petty criminal to overlord of such an enclave of hell on earth, which, with the man sitting no more than twenty feet from him, he struggled to grasp.

Next to Kramer was Fritz Klein, already, even before the trial, attaining a level of notoriety reserved for the perpetrators of deeds which exceeded even the wanton cruelty of those who ran the camp or the guards who inflicted the daily suffering on the inmates, Klein, a doctor, who, in his own words as recited by the prosecuting advocate, had perverted the Hippocratic oath to its very antithesis: "My Hippocratic oath tells me to cut a gangrenous appendix out of the human body. The Jews are the gangrenous appendix of mankind. That is why I cut them out".

Stanley shifted his gaze to Klein, bearing the number "2", with his rather aristocratic good looks and swept-back hair, unable to equate the man with his most heinous deeds which, as the day's hearing commenced, one of the prosecutors read out, the experiments, some "medical", using inmates to test reactions to diseases and barbaric procedures, others seeming to have no possible medical rationale beyond gauging the response of the human body to extreme pain.

The hall fell utterly silent, no coughing or shuffling of feet, as the prosecutor narrated the catalogue of cruelty.

"God Almighty!" Stanley could not contain his gasp of horror at the account of inmates having petrol forced down their throats, apparently to test the reaction, which was a slow and excruciating death.

Further along the front row of the dock were the several female defendants, one of whom, wearing the number "9", drew his attention. There was something about her which reminded him of Peggy, her pretty face showing the strain of what she was going through, with dark shadows beneath her anxious blue eyes.

Irma Grese, only twenty-two years of age, having graduated from Hitler Youth to concentration camp guard, became known for not only for her exceptional cruelty, the evidence against her a horrifying series of accounts of her brutality, but also of the pleasure she so obviously derived from her sadism, distinguishing her even amongst the assembled enablers and enactors of the camp's horrifying regime, earning her the title *The Beautiful Beast*.

There was, Stanley thought, an almost childlike vulnerability about Grese as she kept glancing around the hall, at one point, her eyes meeting his, holding his stare for a moment. What did he read in that brief moment of connection? Perhaps that appearances can be so utterly deceptive, or that here, in this timid looking girl, was the ultimate example of the extent to which humanity could be corrupted, the innocence of childhood so quickly, and so completely disfigured by the virus of pure evil.

Throughout the morning, the prosecutors continued their opening of the cases against each of the defendants. And then, after the lunch interval, when Stanley, Eric and Johnnie stood outside, eating their sandwiches and smoking their cigarettes in sombre silence, the first of the witnesses gave evidence, a plain, ordinary looking woman, dressed in an ill-fitting blouse and skirt, presumably selected from the supply of second hand clothes made available for the liberated inmates.

She spoke in a quiet, flat, conversational voice, the interpreter's voice a good deal louder but somehow conveying the witness's determined absence of any show of emotion, the crowded hall falling silent as the woman recounted the horrors which she had endured and witnessed, having spent more than a year in the camp, and miraculously survived, as she explained, by making herself known as a good worker, her tasks including the distribution of the rations of food much of it unfit for human consumption, yet all that was available to make the difference between starvation and survival.

Her voice once fell to little more than a whisper, the interpreter quietening his translation, as the woman described another of her roles, of collecting bodies, she and several others doing the rounds each day, carrying those who had died out onto the carts to take them to the burial pits, the bodies light enough for her to carry them with little effort, a detail which added graphic credulity to her account.

As they climbed back into their car for their return journey, Stanley felt emotionally wrung out, the three of them remaining silent for much of the drive save for occasional remarks revealing the impact the day's proceedings had had upon them, the accounts they had heard, and, even more so, coming face to face with those who had committed such atrocities, carved into their memories.

Some two months later, when he heard on the news that eleven of the defendants from the trial, including Kramer, Klein and Grese had been hanged, his reaction of grim satisfaction that justice had been done was tinged with something he could quite put his finger on; a seed of disquiet, not about the executing of such purveyors of evil, but that such a young woman could have become so corrupted by the Nazi ethos. He found himself imagining her on that December morning; being taken from her cell, along the corridors, into the room housing the gallows. Did she have to be dragged, kicking and screaming, or did she maintain her composure? Picturing her face, and her frightened eyes as she had looked at him across the hall where the trial was held, he felt certain that, at that awful final moment she would have collapsed into a state of terror, her writhing body having to be lifted so that the noose could be placed around her neck.

Back in the mess after the day at the trial, the three of them set about getting purposefully drunk, the conversation soon moving away from the events of the day, the liquor helping them to consign the experience to that same compartment, reserved for the experiences too grim for them to recount, where, for each of them, it would remain, inspected occasionally over the years, but, certainly for Stanley, firmly secreted, particularly from the sensibilities of Peggy and others close to him. It was only, in the last years of his life that the memories began to seep from that compartment, although even then, his allusion to them, in conversations with grandchildren, were opaque, with no reference to his having been in the presence of *The Beast of Belsen* or the vivid memory of the young Irma Grese.

The following day he received his dates for his next leave, only just over a month away, which should have filled him with eager anticipation. Delighted as he was with the prospect of again being home with Peggy and Anthony, he found himself feeling unexpectedly flat. How could he possibly feel anything other than joy that, in such a short time he would again be in her arms, and embracing his beloved boy?

Everything seemed so humdrum; so futile. There was no feeling of purpose, stuck here in Germany, their job, of supplying their part of the British Army of the Rhine, undemanding. Throughout the campaign, they had been acutely aware of their role, as the life-blood of the Division as it advanced across Northern Europe. Now, they felt themselves mere workers, clock watching, relying on the distractions on offer to alleviate the tedium.

And what was it going to be like when they eventually got home – not simply on leave, but permanently? How were they going to adapt to working for a living, with none of the demands which had challenged – and excited – them for the year of the campaign?

What he did know, however, was that he had to be away from this existence. He was confident that once he was home, getting to grips with his legal studies, he would become settled, his life – their lives – stretching ahead.

For the moment, however, it was more of the same; games, parties, trips around the country whenever there was the opportunity.

He was becoming increasingly worried about the excess, over eating and heavy drinking having become the norm. Even without the dinners and parties – of which there were at least two every week and sometimes more, the pretext often being simply catching up with former comrades and now, increasingly, farewells to those who were heading home – the daily fare comprised a fried breakfast, and full meals at lunchtime and dinner, lunch accompanied by a few glasses of beer – generally one of the strong German brews – with spirits and wine in the evenings, often rounded off with a beer or two or a brandy.

He was acutely aware of his growing girth, having recently had to loosen his belt yet another notch, his trousers becoming precariously tight across his ample backside.

He was not alone in showing the effects of their life of plenty, only Eric it seemed, of those in the mess, retaining his trim figure, due quite patently, to his relative abstemiousness, another of what, to Stanley, were becoming his increasingly censorious traits.

But he could not help himself from over indulging, and indeed, felt little inclination to show any restraint, the shared view being that they might as well enjoy it while they could.

*My beloved sweetheart*
*I'm recovering from last night's farewell party at Cuxhaven for Ray Wellstead who, as you may remember, is one of our Div officers. I went with Johnnie and Orbell & drove my own car – it's a three hour journey but it was quite a good party & there was much champagne. We had a marvellous dinner – and then everyone made speeches & toasted Ray.*
*We left the party at 12.30 & drove back in record time getting in at 3.15. We all felt pretty ugly this morning but the day has passed alright.*
*Champagne is more expensive now & most of it is terrible stuff. I only drink it when I haven't got to pay.*
*I may go down to Brussels for a couple of days next week with Johnnie. There is very little doing here & I'm bored & fed up with the place, & old Eric is niggly.*
*Bertie goes tomorrow and is giving a small farewell dinner party.*
*From Nov 1ˢᵗ we have to pay for our visits to Brussels, Paris etc. at the ridiculously expensive rate of 15/- per day, so I want to get a trip in before then. This will be a very quiet trip – I want to see the placed and a flick of two.*
*It's now 12 darling & I'm very sleepy so I'll just send you a goodnight kiss.*
*I'm yours so utterly*
*Stanley*

Sitting beside her, his father into his fluent stride from the pulpit, Stanley glanced sideways at her, the sunlight slanting through the high windows making her look even paler. "A bit washed out" she had told him soon after he arrived the day before, deciding to walk up from the station, regretting that he had done so, arriving at the top of the steep hill panting and sweaty in spite of the chill November air.

He had been disappointed when she had told him that this time, it would be preferable for them to stay in the house rather than moving, with Anthony, into the hut. It was clear, however, as soon as he arrived, that she was not well, her face having lost its usual glow of health, her eyes looking tired, her movements, usually so light and nimble, almost laboured.

As she opened the front door to him, her embrace seemed as much of relief as of delight. He was shocked to see how thin she looked, her features appearing drawn.

"I don't seem to have much energy at the moment," she told him as soon as they were sitting down together. "It's been good having Mummy here to help with Anthony."

He always found it uncomfortable, staying in the house, her mother's presence constraining, making him feel he needed to be on his best behaviour. He realised now, however, why Peggy did not want to go to the hut, with the work involved in getting it ready, and having to get in their food and drink.

"Of course it's fine," he said when she repeated the apology from her last letter. "It's far better to be here, what with you feeling under the weather."

As they knelt for the Lord's Prayer, he looked at her again, raising his eyebrows to question how she was feeling, her response, a wan smile.

"The doctor thinks I ought to get it done," she told him when they were alone together, her mother having gone off to bed, a little earlier than her usual bedtime. "And he's arranging it for next month."

"Get what done?" he asked, unclear still as to what was the primary cause of her having been unwell, as she now admitted, for some weeks, although even during his leave in July, he felt that her brightness and determined energy was disguising something wrong.

"Well, he thought they might be able to do my tonsils and wisdom tooth at the same time," she replied cautiously, rightly apprehensive of his reaction. "The tooth has been playing up for some time."

"God Almighty! That sounds dreadful. And why the hell haven't they done something sooner?"

"Don't be cross, darling," she said, reaching across to him, placing her hand on his arm. They were sitting in the two armchairs, which, for so many years, had been reserved for her parents, for their evening relaxation, the fire, of just a few lumps of coal and a couple of logs, flickering in the grate. "It's not the doctors' fault. They are doing their best. It's been difficult for them to work out what's being going on. And anyway, it's only a minor op."

"How long will they keep you in? I must be there? And what about Anthony? I'm sure I'll be able to get compassionate leave."

As she had feared, he was getting himself thoroughly wound up, his face flushed with exasperation. It was as if he needed someone to blame for her being unwell. Why did he always have to want to find fault?

What she knew was that the shortages – of food and fuel – had affected her more than she liked to admit to him, her constitution less resilient to such relatively minor ailments. How perverse it seemed that now, when the war was finally over, she was feeling so down; so worn out.

In contrast to his July leave, this was a dispiriting few days, she breaking it to him on the first night that, "if you don't mind, my darling, I would rather we didn't do it for the moment", his desire which had been growing, feverishly, over the last few weeks, stymied, his ready and sympathetic acceptance belying his disappointment.

"I'm sure it's nothing serious," her mother said the next morning when he found himself alone with her. "She'll be right as rain within a few days. And besides, I'll be here to look after both of them. Peggy and Anthony," she added, as if there might have been some doubt as to who it was she would be looking after.

Did he detect a trace of satisfaction in her voice, that it would be she who would be here to care for them when he was back in Germany? He suspected that she might even doubt the need for his still being there now that the war was long over, as if he were on some extended holiday.

"I'm so grateful, Mother," he replied, confident that there was no trace of resentment or sarcasm in his tone.

The following morning he had arranged to meet Christopher Mileham, who, as Peggy had cautiously mentioned, she had told that Stanley would be looking for a position when he was demobilised, Christopher having suggested there might be an opening in the small practice which he, himself, had recently joined.

It proved to be a convivial meeting, Christopher taking him for lunch at a restaurant just a few yards from the office, the Sussex Grill, an old fashioned establishment known for its wholesome fare although, as with restaurants generally, its current offering decidedly meagre compared with the pre-war years. It was a restaurant which Stanley would come to frequent over the years when, once again, plates were more copiously filled.

"He has offered me a position," he told Peggy when he got back to the house, the lunch, accompanied by a fine bottle of claret and a brandy, having greatly improved his mood.

"That's wonderful, my darling," she said, brightening with obvious relief as she remembered his ideas about staying in the army or seeking some foreign posting with the Colonial Office. "Have you accepted it?".

"Yes, I have." Hearing the decisiveness of his answer, he realised he was drawing a line under those other possibilities and that he was committing himself to the career he had always known, in his heart of hearts, he was destined for.

When it came to the moment of his departure, in spite of the rather muted days of his leave, the familiar sadness caught both of them. As he sat on the train, he told himself that the pain of parting served to remind him of the depth of his love for her. Not for one moment had it been in any doubt; rather, it had seemed, this time, to have lacked its former sheen of sensuality, which, he could see, was revealing to him the underlying depth and value of their relationship, which he grasped unreservedly, as husband, a role which was so much more than lover, and as father.

What he also knew was that he needed to be there to look after her, the strain of what she had been through so evident, although while he had been there, her spirits seemed to have lifted to some extent.

Long and tedious as the journey was, it had now become a known quantity; the delays and detours, not so much now because of war damage to railways and ports, but more the army's insistence that servicemen should use designated routes, often circuitous, the grim, sprawling Purfleet camp continuing to operate as an assembly point, men returning to the continent required to await their turn before being sent off in batches, sometimes on scheduled ferries, and sometimes on the troop ships which continued to ply back and forth across the North Sea and the Channel.

He had learned how to pass the time, chatting to other itinerant servicemen, reading, writing letters, or simply sitting, watching his surroundings and the incessant activity of the ponderous military organisation.

This time, also, it felt different, with the growing certainty that it would now be probably only three or four months before he was finally demobilised.

25.12.45

*My very darling little wife*

*Good morning to you and Anthony and a very happy Xmas to both of you and also a happy 1946. Pray God it may really be the last on which we are miles apart.*

*Darling, it is 9.15 our time – I expect you are just about getting up. We (Tabs, John and I) have been up a long time and followed the time honoured tradition of taking tea round to all the men. I think they appreciate it. Since then I have been for a short walk on this lovely soft morning.*

*Darling, the wireless is a great comfort and is playing Jerusalem. We have no services, which I hate: it makes this seem even less like Xmas. Today in fact is a very busy day for officers. I have to go up to 525 Coy which is 80 miles each way, to take them the CO's Xmas message to read out at their dinner at 1pm. I shan't be back till about 4.30. We shall have our Xmas dinner tonight. Gosh, how I wish you folks at home could have all our food. It is a frightful shame and I don't enjoy any meals – I'm always thinking of the 1/2d worth of meat etc.*

<u>*Boxing day 5.40pm*</u>

*Hopkins has summed up our Christmas by saying that it's just been like two ordinary days. After writing to you I started off on the drive to 525. I thought of you so much as I drove along the deserted roads. It was a soft pleasant day and I quite enjoyed the ride. I arrived there at 12.30 and after a drink we went to their men's messes and read out the Colonel's message. This all took quite a time and after several more drinks and a snack (leg of goose!) I started back at 3.45. It was a lovely evening and I drove down the autobahn with the glorious sunset feeling very near you darling. Through Bremen and home by 6 – a game of table tennis then a far too big meal which I didn't enjoy. I managed to listen to quite a lot of BBC then bed at 11, & that ended Xmas.*

*Today I fished a rather pleasant stream & was quite alone in the peace of the country. Back to lunch – too much again. I've been jawing to Eric (who seems in an unusually good mood!) for a while & now there is an amusing wireless programme with Leslie Henson, Tommy Handley & Hermione Gingold who is singing a doubtful song about trousers.*

*To end on a light note – I forgot to tell you – we had an amusing incident to relieve the*

*monotony after lunch. Plunder was tied to a post outside the mess, and when we looked out he was enjoying a really good post prandial grind! They got stuck, arse to arse, and only Hopkins throwing a basin of cold water on them separated them! Plunder's phallic organ was then revealed as an enormous thing – honestly nearly a foot long!*
*God bless you darling angel. So very many kisses and such an adoring heart full of love.*
*Stanley*

Doing the rounds of RASC troops, acting as representative for the CO, trying not to dwell on his resentment that Eric had managed to arrange his own home leave for the festivities, observing the Highland Division's tradition, taking them tea and delivering Eric's message, the conviviality of chatting with the men, all of them doing their best to contrive some semblance of Christmas spirit, as he read the message to them, he could not help wondering whether the CO knew more than he was admitting about the timing of demobilisation, the reference to their all being home by "Xmas 1946" suggesting that his own expectation of being out by Easter might be overly optimistic.

**Christmas Day 1945**
**Personal Message from Lieut-Colonel E S A Nicholls RASC OBE**
**It is a very great disappointment to me that I am unable to come along and see you on this Xmas Day – the first Xmas festival that we have been able to celebrate with the world at peace, for six long years. Twelve months ago, when we were celebrating Xmas Day in Belgium, as best we could, I told you that it was my sincere hope that you would all be home by Xmas 1945. Some of you still remain in Germany and to you especially, and to those who started at the beginning with you, it is my earnest hope that Xmas 1946 will see you all safely home alongside your families.**
**During the past year you have all done wonders – your work during the closing months of the war, and since, has been quite magnificent, and from the bottom of my heart I want to express to you my deep gratitude for your loyalty to me, and your great devotion to duty, which has played such a great part in helping to make this year of 1945 the year of supreme victory. Nobody has contributed more to our victory than you have.**
**And so, to all of you, officers, NCOs and men, I should like to wish you a very happy Xmas and my very best wishes for the New Year.**
**Eric Nicholls**
**Lieut-Colonel**
**Commander**
**51ˢᵗ Highland Division RASC**

As he read Peggy's letter which arrived three days after Christmas, the feeling of melancholy which had been hovering, took hold of him. He so longed to be with them, his wife and his son for whom he had a found a new depth of love. The prospect of having to spend another three months away from them was bad enough, but with the worry now, of it being a good deal longer was almost unbearable.

*25.12.45*

*Darlingest one of mine*

*Here is just a note to you at the end of what I hope is the last Christmas day we shall have to spend apart. It has been quite a happy one darling, really, though I have missed you so very much. I felt alone without you at church this morning and I do now, sitting by the fire with 'Love old sweet song' on the wireless. Your people and Ted have been down for the evening & I think they enjoyed the results of my last night's cooking. I made some sausage rolls & mince piece & a trifle & chocolate blancmange. The only trouble is that there is a lot left over & sandwiches as well. I wish you were here to help eat it up sweetheart!*

*Now darling I am going to have an early night as it has been quite a hectic day for me although I had a sleep this afternoon (on my own!) after hearing the King.*

*It has been an exciting and strenuous day for Anthony. He has such a lot of parcels. He has now five boats, another truck besides his bicycle & lots of additions to his library.*

*Now I must say goodnight now.*

*Yours with all my love for always.*

*Peggy*

The thought of her, sitting by the fireside, the remains of the fire just the fading embers, the tune on the wireless – *Love Old Sweet Song* – with its heart rending refrain – *Just a song at twilight* – made him feel a helpless yearning, his eyes prickling. And being alone, he made no attempt to contain his sorrow, the tears rolling down his cheeks.

*31.12.45*

*My very angel darling*

*As I write, 1945 has under four hours to go. I am in the mess spending a very quiet evening alone with Tabs and Johnnie.*

*Our thoughts and feelings on Christmas Day seem to have been very alike, darling. I wish so utterly I could have been with you: but now I'm looking forward to days of happiness. Tomorrow it will be January and the days will pass more & more quickly toward our being together again. Anthony seems to have enough toys for a toy shop! I'm glad he was well behaved on Xmas day.*

*It is now 10.15 and I've been listening to the year of Victory programme. I wondered if you were listening. I wish they could have had more of Churchill & Monty.*

*And so 1945 moves to a close – 'Ring out wild bells' comes to mind. A big freeze up seems to be starting here – it's been freezing hard since yesterday evening. I shall start 1946 with a happy heart as I somehow feel that now it's almost January our reunion seems much nearer.*

*Well darling mine, my last letter of 1945 must finish now: may there not be a lot in 1946. I will be thinking so happily of you on our anniversary, January 6<sup>th</sup> – thoughts too deep for words.*

*May God bless you for always & give you great happiness & peace in 1946.*

*All my unending love, darling.*

*Stanley*


As the last hours of 1945 ticked slowly away, Stanley, Tabs and Johnnie the only three officers remaining in the mess, the other three being on leave – their total number now reduced to six by reason of various redeployments and a few who had managed to find posts which gave them a ticket to early demobilisation – did their best to celebrate, liberal with liquor, seeing in the New Year with a raucous rendition of *Auld Lang Syne*, the result being the dawning of 1946 accompanied by aching heads.

When, on New Years Day, he received the printed note, telling him that he was to be "Mentioned in Dispatches", he felt only a glimmer of gratification, the award seeming to count for so little, not least it being one of the more lowly honours. Better than nothing, though, he thought to himself, recognising that it would doubtless count for something with those back home. When, some days later, he got hold of a copy of the *London Gazette,* his view as the value of the award seemed to be borne out by his having to scan the lengthy list, the awards listed by categories, those lower down, a proliferation of names, the print minute, the heading for his category:

*His Majesty the King has been graciously pleased to approve that the following be Mentioned in recognition of distinguished and gallant service in North West Europe.*

He found his name – *Major S R Allen.* So that's what it meant – "Mentioned in Dispatches". To have one's name included in a crowded list in a publication which one only looked at for this very reason – to see one's name, his jaundiced view coloured by his general feeling of disenchantment.

When Peggy told him that he had merited a brief mention in the local papers, the *Evening Argus* and the *Brighton & Hove Herald*, at least this added a modicum of prestige, although in all honesty, it did little to mitigate his feeling of indifference. Surprisingly, his father's note gave him more of a lift than the award itself.

*3.1.46*
*Good Shepherd Vicarage, 172 Dyke Road, Brighton 5*
*My dear Stanley*
*We have heard from Pegs that you have been mentioned in dispatches so we all want to congratulate you very cordially. We must celebrate in due course. Do tell us what it is all for. Naturally we feel proud of you for doing so well. Mum will write tomorrow.*
*Your ever affect.*
*Dad*

When he received her letter, he was reminded of the jealousy which would sometimes rear its ugly head when Peggy had been at Bart's, and from time to time when their long separation engendered the malign seeds of suspicion. Although he could never quite admit it to himself, there were times also, when he felt resentful of the social life she was enjoying without him. Progressively, as he became convinced of not only her absolute fidelity, but her unconditional and untainted dedication to him, such darker thoughts faded, her accounts of her periodic outings and occasional dances and parties, rather now evoking sadness, for her having to put on a brave face, his absence from her side, so clearly detracting from her enjoyment.

He sought to shrug off the unease he felt as he read the letter, imagining the party with her in the embrace of the circle of friends, flushed and laughing, her eyes shining with pleasure, her shyness and her popularity flustering her. The slightest murmur of the old jealousy he brushed aside.

*1.1.46*
*My sweetheart*
*A happy New Year to you. I think this will be the happiest New Year of our lives don't you?*
*Darling, it was a grand party last night but I did so wish you could have been with me. There were a lot of people whom I think you know – the Betts, Stiles, Maisie & Alaistair Ross & numerous other folks in our party although we actually went with Philip and Margaret Myers. We only stayed till 12.30 but it was just long enough to see the New Year in with all the old songs & terrific dancing in circles & to kiss quite a few people & wish them Happy New Year. I hope you don't mind. A very affectionate party altogether! All the other girls seemed to have their husbands there to kiss them fondly first. Still here's to some more parties like this when you are home.*
*I drank dozens of gin & oranges & felt quite sober & this morning I woke up at eight*

*with only a rather dry mouth.*

*I only danced three times, once with Tom, once with Phil Myers and one with Harold Stiles who was there with this wife too. They are a grand couple.*

*I will write again this evening, darling mine*

*All my love*

*Peggy*

*6.1.46*

*My very darling sweetheart*

*I'm glad you seem to be very much better and are leading a gay life again! I hope you liked the dance! Don't worry, darling, I'm only a wee bit jealous, as I always will be of you dancing with other people.*

*I didn't know it was a New Year tradition to kiss everyone – who did you get kissed by darling? Who took you home? Are you trying to make me jealous? I wish I had gone to the dance in the village – I stayed at home thinking of you! Wait till I come home – you'll get a big smack!*

*Happy thoughts today darling – five years ago we were married.*

*I feel a warm glow underneath all this temporary bloodiness as I think of our wedding day. Old Eric has just been in, pulling my leg as usual and insisting on a bottle of champagne to toast my "mention". I'll drink a toast, darling – happy days, to my very wonderful darling lovely desirable girl, & a speedy reunion.*

*For ever your*

*Stanley*

At last, time seemed to gather pace, those early weeks of 1946 passing quickly as the prospect of demobilisation before Easter solidified into pretty near certainty. Indeed, the system, chaotic as it had appeared for so long, now showed consistency, those within specified groups reaching their release dates, packing their bags, the farewell parties coming round with rather tedious frequency.

The conversations amongst those remaining in the dwindling mess, and at the various gatherings, were filled with reminiscing, largely about the great adventure, the year long campaign, and, for those who had been with the 51st for the duration, of their famously victorious desert campaign, anecdotes of battle interspersed, particularly for Stanley and old colleagues from the 43rd when he was invited to their farewells, with memories of the long years of training, the tedium and frustration of that time, distant, the reminiscing mainly about isolated episodes and the characters who had added some colour to the generally drab phase.

Stanley, ever an avid reader of newspapers, and with his interest in goings-on across the world, like many others, had mixed feelings about the value of the newly formed United Nations, replacing its rather hapless predecessor, the League of Nations, the new organisation's inaugural conference, held in London, an occasion for optimistic speeches avowing mankind's good intentions, to work in harmony for the common good, the over-arching commitment being to a future free from global conflict.

Yet, as nations spoke of such high ideals, the dark clouds of a new schism, between east and west, were casting their shadow across the all too brief interlude, the western Allied nations scarcely able to draw breath after the years of war before having to face up to the new threats, the defeat of Germany and Japan, depriving the wartime Allies of the common enemy which had united them.

Churchill, though no longer Prime Minister, nevertheless used his stature as one of the world's great statesmen, to articulate the Russian threat, his forewarning redolent of his recognition of the need to stand up to the advance of Nazism when the more timid voices of government were shying away from confrontation.

Touring America, it was in a speech given at the aptly chosen Westminster College in Missouri that he described the "iron curtain" which was progressively being drawn across Europe, the term instantly characterising the new era, soon to become known as the Cold War, the Russian takeover of large parts of Europe, exerting a stranglehold far beyond the spheres of influence envisaged by the Yalta agreement, engendering increasing hostility when so much blood had been spilt liberating the continent from one oppressor only for it to be occupied by another.

With the gnawing anxiety about the Russians, there was also the stark recognition that Britain was in no state to fight another war, the country being exhausted and close to bankruptcy. What was clear was that if anyone was going to stand up to the Russians, it would be the Americans who were increasingly showing their resolve to do so, their own occupation forces in Germany redeployed with their faces now to the East.

It would be two years before the confrontation escalated to the point where open conflict seemed imminent, the extraordinary logistical feat of the Berlin airlift, America's loud statement of intent to keep the Russians behind the lines drawn on the maps at Yalta and Potsdam, denying them control of Berlin, isolated by the Russian blockade of land routes, the Western Allies thus retaining their designated sectors.

What would ensue, however, would be the escalation of the Cold War, Russia and America, both armed with atomic weapons, squaring up, threatening not only a third world war, but one which would risk the very existence of humanity.

Against such backdrop, Stanley's only desire was to get home to Peggy and Anthony as soon as possible, not only to be with them in the event of any further conflict, his profound hope, shared with so many others, that should there need to be renewed mobilisation, it would fall to a new generation to take on the mantle of defenders of freedom, but also because the future he so longed for, and which was now within touching distance, lay with them, his true loved ones, and with a life, hopefully, of peace.

Having had little communication with his brother-in-law, Tom, since the start of the war, relying on Peggy's reports of his whereabouts, it came as a surprise when a letter arrived, Tom's resolute handwriting immediately recognisable.

*27.1.46*
*Major S R Allen MBE*
*4 Hove Park Road, Hove 4, Sussex*
*Dear Stanley*
*I have for weeks been meaning to write to you to thank you for your share in the tie which Peggy and you were so kind to give me at Christmas.*
*Yesterday though I heard the news about your Mention and the order appended to your name on the address. So now I write this in addition to congratulate you.*
*Peggy is naturally quite excited about it and when yesterday I took her to a dance at the Pavilion she made me point out to her an example of the ribbon.*
*There's one suggestion that you may find helpful is that as clothes these days are very hard to get, if you want a suit soon after your release I should write to the tailor with whom you have most pull and ask him to give you a high place on his waiting list. If you say that you are coming out of the army with no wearable clothes, they may give you additional consideration. The normal time however is 6 months.*
*Please excuse this scrawl but the days now seem all too short & I want to get a job which I have brought home finished before tonight. Your mother had just taken Anthony out. He is in very good form and I think you will notice a considerable improvement in his talking ability when you come back.*
*Yours*
*Tom*

At first, he failed to notice the letters after his name and when he did so, he stared at them, wondering whether Tom had misunderstood his honour, conflating the "Mention" to something grander. But he knew that Tom was not one to make such mistakes, being a stickler for accuracy.

As he sat at the mess table, contemplating the question, unable to suppress a flutter of anticipation, Eric presented him with an envelope, the CO's expression an unusually broad grin.

"I think you will want to see this, Major Allen," he said, the grin remaining fixed, Johnnie and Tabs becoming curious at the CO's strange mood.

Stanley opened the brown envelope, noting the government coat of arms printed on the back.

**31 1.46          WAR OFFICE, HOBART HOUSE,
                   GROSVENOR PLACE, LONDON SW1**
**Sir**
**I am directed to inform you that the following Award to you has been approved by His Majesty the King:-**
**MBE in Recognition of Gallant & Distinguished Service in NW Europe.**
**Authority:- London Gazette Supplement dated 22.1.46.**
**If on receipt of this notification you are still serving on strength of a unit, you should show this memorandum to your Commanding Officer so that the necessary casualty may be published in Orders, and for the Award to be recorded in your personal documents.**
**If you have been awarded a British decoration other than a Mention and on receipt of this letter you are on release leave or have been released, you are advised to communicate with the War Office regarding an invitation to an Investiture.**
**I am, Sir, your obedient servant**
**T Fry**
**Director of Organisation**

He looked up at Eric who remained standing beside the table, Stanley's face creasing into a grin mirroring his CO's.

"Bloody Hell!" he exclaimed, scrutinising the War Office notification again, realising that the announcement must already have appeared in the *London Gazette*, hence Tom's addition of the acronym.

"Champagne's on Stanley tonight!" Eric said, turning to the others. "Member of the Most Excellent Order of the British Empire!" he proclaimed. "Mostly certainly worthy of a bottle of the finest."

*1.2.46*
*My very lovely sweetheart*
*I was amazed to find awaiting for me three letters from you plus the Sussex Daily, one from Tom, one from Mother and Pop! I was also puzzled to see 'MBE' on Tom's letter and 'congratulations' written. I'm feeling very pleased about it — I hadn't heard about it yet as the London Gazette hasn't reached us. I'm glad you are now part of 'Maj & Mrs Stanley Allen MBE' (doesn't look quite right!).*
*For always my lovely angel.*
*Stanley*

As he went about his business over the next few days, he was unable to conceal the glow of satisfaction, in such contrast to his indifference to the Mention. It was not so much pride, although he acknowledged that did certainly feature; rather it was the realisation of the value of the honour not only as the recognition of the part he had played in the campaign, but also in the future, a value which would become apparent when, a few years later, his name was added to the letterhead of his solicitors practice — S.R.Allen MBE.

"I'm afraid you won't be going to the Palace," Eric said, the grin replaced by a faux look of disappointment. "You'll have to make do with Monty instead."

It was a week later that, with Hopkins at the wheel, Stanley set out for the HQ of the 21st Army Group, now BOAR, at the small town of Bad Oeynhausen, being directed to a corridor where he found himself in a short queue of officers and several other ranks, all attired in dress uniform. When a door was opened they filed into a large room, several rows of chairs facing a table raised on a dais.

"Attention!" A sergeant-major barked the order, the assembled company rising, standing stiffly to attention as several senior officers entered from a side door, the small, distinct figure of Montgomery separating from them, stepping up onto the dais, another officer at his side, clip board in hand, handing the Field Marshall a sheet of paper and a medal.

Much to Stanley's surprise, after several higher awards, he was the first to be called of the twenty or so receiving the MBE, the order being alphabetical.

He stood in front of the dais, saluting as they had been directed.

"At ease, Major," Montgomery said quietly, his small, bright eyes observing Stanley intently. "I recall we have met before," he said, maintaining his confidential tone. "Transporting essential supplies of champagne, wasn't it?"

"Indeed it was sir," Stanley replied, staggered that the Field Marshall should not only remember the incident, but that he had been the officer in charge of the consignment of "liberated" champagne.

"You have done your country great service, Major Allen." Montgomery raised his voice for the assembled company to hear. "You are rightly honoured for your contribution, going beyond the call of duty, when the enemy tried his gambit in the Ardennes, and for your sterling work when my Highlanders were given the task of making the first crossing of the Rhine."

Montgomery leaned forward, shaking Stanley's hand, his small, pointed face having a slightly papery appearance, his eyes remaining fixed on Stanley's even as he pinned the medal onto his lapel.

The other officer having handed him the citation, a rolled sheet of thick paper, Stanley stood back, saluting again before making a smart about turn, returning to his seat, elation coursing through his veins not only at receiving the award from the legendary Monty, but at the moment of quite extraordinary connection between them. He knew of the great man's renowned capacity for remembering names and faces, but there was no doubt, in his own mind, that somehow, on that previous encounter – two encounters – something had caused his identity to lodge in Monty's mind. Perhaps he found the champagne episode, in the midst of the great, gruelling military epic, amusing. Perhaps also, the notoriously humourless Field Marshall did, after all, have the capacity to enjoy a moment of whimsy.

Alone in his room late that evening, feeling quite sober in spite of the evening of celebration, he unrolled the document, his first impression being surprise at the length of the citation and the details of the achievements which had earned him the honour.

**Unit: HQ RASC 51st Highland Division**
**Rank: Major**
**Name: ALLEN, STANLEY ROWLATT**
**Honour or Award: MBE**
**Recommended by E.S.A Nicholls, Lieut-Colonel, CRASC 51st Highland Division**

Action for which recommended:

This officer has been Senior Supply Officer of this Division since October of last year and during this period has consistently given determined and distinguished service.

In every operation in which the Division has been engage he has displayed a very high sense of duty in times which severely tested the show of the Divisional RASC.

During the difficult Ardennes campaign he was faced with many major problems affecting food supply of the Division owing to its sudden long move to the Ardennes from Holland. On several occasions a last minute change of plan necessitated his making long journeys by night & in most adverse weather conditions to ensure that the stores that had been asked for were available, before dispatching vehicles.

By his devotion to duty & through his great drive & energy this Officer has to a large extent been responsible for the efficient supply of RASC commodities to the Units of the Highland Division, thus enabling the fighting efficiency of the Division to be maintained at the highest level.

In particular, this Officer displayed great skill & power of organisation during the period immediately prior to the assault on the Rhine. He played a great part in the planning of the dumping programme on the West Bank & the subsequent ferrying across to the East Bank before the bridges were established. This entailed many personal reconnaissances being made, often under mortar & shell fire, & long periods of work; but largely due to his foresight during the planning & by his courage and determination, these essential stores amounting to some 750 tons were ferried across the Rhine immediately following the assault.

This Officer was also largely responsible for the collection and delivery to the guns of 270,000 rounds of 25 pr. during the operation Veritable, an operation which tested the transport & ammunition supply of the RASC to its utmost, & it was largely due to his careful planning, involving very long hours of extra work, that every operation in which the Highland Division has taken part was greatly assisted by the unimpeded flow of ammunition petrol and supplies.

He allowed the document to re-curl itself, holding onto it for a moment, savouring the unexpectedly fulsome plaudit, before placing it on the bedside table. As he drifted off to sleep, he imaged the citation, framed, hanging on a wall in some suitably discrete, yet noticeable part of the house - their home, there on display as a reminder as much to him as to others, of the arduous, and yet now duly recorded part he had played in the great crusade.

# TWENTY-EIGHT

Lying on his back, soaking up the exquisitely hot July sun, he watched a mob of raucous seagulls spiralling against the cloudless sky, his hands resting on the hot shingle either side of his towel. As the seagulls drifted out over the sea, dipping down onto the shoal of small fish ruffling the calm surface, he heard Anthony's voice, chirruping with excitement, Stanley lifting his head, watching Peggy as she held a crab in front of the child, placing it in his metal bucket, Anthony adding some sand and seaweed.

It did not feel quite real, to be here on the beach, luxuriating in the sun, watching the two people who were everything to him. It was the dream of those long months – years - a dream which at times felt fragile, like those which had so often flickered through the long dark nights. He sat fully upright, pinching his thighs to convince himself that this was real, before getting up and walking across the pebbles to the sand.

"Look, here's Daddy," Peggy said, Anthony still studying the crab in his bucket, dropping dollops of wet sand onto it.

"Daddy," Anthony screeched at the sight of his father coming towards him. "Cwab!" He picked up the bucket, holding it up, Stanley peering at the creature, picking it up by its shell, holding it out to the child who recoiled with a scream.

They sat eating their picnic, the beach crowded, several train loads of trippers swelling the numbers, the road down from the station, Queens Road and West Street, a stream of people laden with hampers and bags, children clutching buckets and spades, the trippers, as the locals, taking advantage of this hot day after several weeks of cool, damp weather, the burst of warmth triggering thunderstorms which, as the afternoon progressed, could be seen inland, cumulonimbus clouds building to great burgeoning towers, the air breathless and humid.

"Should we be getting back?" Peggy asked, looking at darkening sky behind them as she ate her sandwich.

"We should be alright here for two or three hours yet," he replied, his knowledge of meteorology, particularly local weather patterns, enabling him to gauge the timing of the imminent storm with some confidence.

"Time for one more paddle," she told Anthony, taking his hand, leaving Stanley to enjoy a renewed doze in the sun.

He could not believe it was four months since had finally been released, his new civilian life almost as unreal as the dreams.

What a joy it had been to come back to their own home, one of two flats in the building which Peggy's mother had bought at last becoming vacant, the tenants, having more than outstayed their welcome, finally departing. The flat was spacious and light, the building's distinctive art deco design including wide windows offering a view across Hove to the sea. His real delight, however, was that they were finally alone, although Peggy's mother was due to move into the ground floor flat as soon as its equally obdurate tenant had moved out.

Those last few weeks in Germany had flown by, his impatience to be on his way mitigated by the succession of farewell parties, which, weary as he had become of them, nevertheless, broke up the weeks and provided an excuse for eating and drinking, which, in spite of his worrying about his ever expanding waistline, he was unable to resist.

There were also a few trips to other units, giving him the opportunity to see a few more parts of northern Germany, including two enjoyable nights in Hamburg. It was, however, his visit to Berlin which truly stood out.

Hamish Macrae, one of the Division's company commanders, whom Stanley had got know well, had invited him to his wedding – to his French fiancée, to be held in the capital. Stanley managed to get hold of a Humber Snipe staff car, thus travelling in comfort with Johnnie and two other officers.

10.2.46
*My sweetheart darling*
*I'll start off right away and give you a description of our Berlin trip.*
*It took a good deal of organising – passes etc. to go through the Russian zone.*
*We left here at 8am Wednesday and I changed cars at Corps and travelled from Nienburg to Berlin in the comfort of a Humber Snipe with Johnny, Ian Thompson and Gabriel Sacher. It is quite an interesting trip – 250 miles of autobahn and 117 miles through the Russian zone which is sinister as well as interesting.*
*We arrived in Berlin about three o'clock; you enter the city quite suddenly – not like English suburbs where you find straggling houses for miles. You come in through Potsdam and Charlottenburg, and into the Kaiserdamm which is where you find the Information Post. We discovered that Frohnau, where the wedding was to be held, was the northernmost suburb, so we set off down Kaiserdamm, Bismark Strasse, past the Franco-Prussian*

memorial, through the Tiergarten, under the Brandenburg gate and down Unter der Linden, & turned off into the Russian sector.

We arrived at 3.30 and had tea, and the party really started with a dinner with much wine etc. which lasted for about two hours. The French seem to eat for hours and hours! The party went on quite late and we found our billet at 2am. – a very nice suburban type house.

Next day was the great day and the Roman Catholic service, despite the fact that it was mostly in Latin and French, was very impressive. Poor old Hamish and Isabelle had to be married twice though, as someone decided at the last moment that a French girl could not legally marry an Englishman under French law on German soil. So they had to have a brief ceremony by the German Burgermeister in another part of town beforehand.

After the ceremony we returned to the club for a lunch party which started at 1 and lasted till 4.15. I've honestly never seen anything like it. When this ended and in view of the fact that the official reception was due to start at 5, a party of us decided to 'do' Berlin, so in Ian's car we set off on a lighting tour & saw the Reich Chancellery (Hitler's bunker, and where Eva 'got up dem stairs' etc.). It was exceedingly interesting and we got back in the middle of the reception.

After the reception we went down into the British sector to the Embassy Club, which you'd love, and where we dined – and danced I'm afraid! Then we went to another place called the Pelican Club – all very well behaved – and then had to drive home through the Russian sector. No sooner had Tabs and I got in than we heard some shots very close. Nothing happened so we fell asleep: next morning, after champagne for breakfast, we had lunch at the Embassy and dinner too. Tabs and I moved our billet to the Gatow Country Club which is a magnificent spot outside Berlin, standing on a lovely lake.

When we got back (via many diversions owing to extensive floods) we found the CO had two Belgian girl friends here for the weekend – a real surprise, Eric being such a moral chap, but we were so tired we went to bed.

Well I'll now say goodnight to my dear, darling little wife.

For always yours

Stanley

The visit had had a marked effect on him, although he found his feelings rather mixed. It was certainly quite something to be there at the very heart of the Nazi empire, the seat of Hitler's power which has caused such a global cataclysm. But there was something else; less tangible; a sense of sadness at seeing a great city so damaged. Nine months from the end of the war, the famous streets remained dreadfully scarred, many buildings damaged and bleakly empty, numerous others demolished, empty sites making way for new construction. What was remarkable was that so much work was going on, although it would be some years before the city was truly restored to anything approaching its former glory.

The people seemed to go about their business purposefully, although one had the impression that they were carrying a great weight, heads bowed, reticent about catching the eye of occupying soldiers, not so much through any resentment but rather as if wearing the burden of their collective shame.

Passing through the Russian sector brought home to him the reality of the growing tension between the erstwhile allies, the Russian soldiers manning the checkpoints, overtly hostile, doing their utmost to be obstructive, glancing at the proffered passes before sauntering off, taking the paperwork into their hut where they could be seen smoking and laughing, one of the guards emerging ten minutes later, handing the passes back, waving the Humber through with a dismissive gesture.

Once they were inside the Russian sector it was as if they had entered a different city, the people noticeably less well dressed, even more downcast than those in the American sector, those shops which were open, as far as they could see, displaying little in the way of clothing or other commodities, the building work, such as it was, appearing to involve the sweeping away of the damaged buildings, several new, faceless ones taking their place, one's impression being of functional ugliness.

It was with a good deal of relief that they entered the British sector, shops and restaurants now back in business, the streets busier with both pedestrians and traffic.

"I'm still not sure what I really made of it," he told Peggy, describing the visit, trying to add something of what he felt to have been the bare bones of the account in his letters. "You wanted to think that they had got their comeuppance, reaping what they had sown. To be honest, though, I was left with a feeling of some sympathy. I know that many – may be most – of them had supported Hitler. But it must have been bloody difficult to do anything else when you risked getting locked up by the Gestapo – or worse."

"You have changed your tune," Peggy said, recalling his scornful comments, particularly when the Allies were first moving into Germany. "I think they thoroughly deserve what they brought upon themselves."

He looked at her, pondering his own equivocal thoughts. "Yes, I know. It's just that… I don't know… imagine it happening here. If we had someone take over, becoming a dictator. Think of Mosely and the support he got."

"Let's not think about it," she replied, content as always, to listen while he recounted his experiences, it feeling sometimes as if he needed to pour it out to her. What she found more difficult was when he started to air his mixed feelings, at times becoming quite philosophical, as if the experiences he had been through were too much for him to assimilate.

She realised, also, that there were some things he did not want to talk about; some of the grimmer experiences. A few times she had encouraged him to do so. "You can tell me anything you want to," she said gently. "I know that you've seen some shocking things. I don't mind. It's good to share things, particularly if they're painful."

She could see from his closed expression, however, that he had resolved to keep some things from her. Over the years, he would occasionally mention – or hint at – those experiences which he had kept hidden away, making it obvious to her that the passage of time did little to diminish the trauma of the worst moments. It was as if, when certain memories came back to him, he had to decide, again, whether to share them, before reasserting his resolve to keep some – the very worst ones - locked away for the rest of his life.

How strange it had felt, sitting at the small table in his room, staring out of the window offering a view across the snow covered German countryside, trying to compose what he was now confident, would be his last letter to her. He had felt a pang of excitement, again rather like that anticipation of breaking up from school at the start of the summer holiday, save that the term that was coming to an end had been six years long, littered with moments of death and destruction; of humour and exhilaration; of close but transient friendships; and ultimately, of victory followed by the decline into the tedium of occupation.

*6.3.46*

*My beloved sweetheart*

*I hope you will have got the news by now and know that my Army days are drawing quickly to an end. I am writing this on Wednesday afternoon – it is still snowing and is very deep.*

*As I prophesied, this is a trying week. The goodbyes are very easy because most of my old friends have gone. I shan't see quite a lot of people including Eric. I'm going to try to leave on Sunday: George Dunst who is also being released, is going by car and I want to go with him. This is a far more comfortable way of travelling than the train, especially in this weather.*

*This week is passing more quietly and soberly than I expected. The next three days will be pretty tough going – but I'll survive ok!*

*We've had lashings of snow in the past fortnight, but green buds are beginning to appear, reminding me that spring is so close.*
*All my love forever*
*Stanley*

It seemed fitting that the day before his departure, the message from Montgomery, in the form of a printed postcard, was disseminated to all of the officers and men of the 21st Army, a message which, for Stanley, touched a strand of affection which they all felt for the often arrogant and irascible Field Marshall, affection and esteem which would be unshaken even when, in his later years, one of Stanley's sons, an avid reader of modern history with a tendency to come to what Stanley felt to be simplistic conclusions, would press him to acknowledge that, great general though he was, Monty was flawed both as a man and a strategist, the debacle of Arnhem so easily cited as compelling evidence.

"What you don't understand," Stanley would reply, patiently, never wanting to put his sons down, "is that we revered him. When we were going through the toughest times, Monty and Churchill were like our gods. With them by our side, we knew we would win."

**I feel I cannot let you leave 21st Army Group on your return to civil life without a message of thanks and farewell. Together we have carried through one of the most successful campaigns in history, and it has been our good fortune to be members of this great team.**
**God bless and God speed.**
**B.L.Montgomery**
**Field Marshall**
**Commander in Chief**

His own farewell, so long anticipated, when it came to it was a subdued affair, a dozen or so officers, with forced jollity, toasting him and wishing him well, Stanley's only wish, as he made his formulaic speech, remembering good times and bad, and many absent friends, to be on his way.

Before turning in for his last night he walked across to the outhouse which had been converted into quarters for batmen and the handful of other ranks who had been part of the residual RASC HQ function.

Hopkins was one of several men sitting round a table playing poker, each with a glass of beer, faces concentrating on their cards.

"At ease!" Stanley said, the men having stood, as one, it being unusual for one of the officers to come into their mess. "Can I borrow you for a moment, Hopkins?"

Hopkins followed him outside, Stanley offering him a cigarette, the flame of the match illuminating his batman's face, looking at him expectantly.

"I'm off first thing," Stanley said, trying to sound matter of fact. "So I just want to say thanks. For everything."

"It's been a privilege, sir," Hopkins replied quietly. "We've been through some stuff, haven't we?"

"We certainly have. And it's been good having you with me."

They stood for a moment, each drawing on their cigarettes, unsure what else there was to say.

"We must meet sometime soon, back in Blighty," Stanley said. "When you're out. And we must keep in touch."

"That would be very nice," Hopkins replied, Stanley noticing the absence of his invariably insistent "sir".

They both new, full well, that their lives would take them in wholly different directions, inhabiting as they would, distinct strata of occupations and society.

"Well, thanks again," Stanley said, the two men shaking hands.

"My best wishes to Peggy," Hopkins said, the use of her first name as opposed to the usual more formal "Mrs Allen", a moment of connection which Stanley recognised, and appreciated.

"And to your Doris," he replied.

It transpired that they did meet a couple of times, once, a few months later, for a beer in a London pub when Stanley was in London studying for his law finals, spending a convivial evening reminiscing, and again, a few years later, at a Highland Division reunion.

Stanley felt no emotion as, the morning after his farewell party, he and fellow major, George Dunst, set off in Dunst's car.

The trip home was a good deal quicker than on previous occasions, their drive to Ostend taking less than two hours, the train from London getting to Preston Park early in the evening.

He walked slowly up the steep hill, not for lack of energy, but rather because of a feeling almost of reluctance. Here it was after so long; the end not only of the great European adventure, but of the years of separation which, at times, had seemed so interminable. And now, as he approached the top of the Droveway, the road where they would live for the next two years, he was confronted with the reality, of the ending of the long phase of his life, dedicated to the army which, in return, had fed and watered him, and kept a roof – of sorts – over his head. Once he crossed the threshold of his new home, he knew that life would change, he becoming responsible for his and his family's livelihood.

Not having a key, he rang the bell which prompted a child's shriek of delight from within.

# TWENTY-NINE

As Stanley, in his dress uniform, stepped up into the carriage, Peggy, her arms around their three boys as if worried they might try to follow their father, vividly remembered those partings through the war years and the all too familiar struggle that she was going through at this moment, to behave, the tears, now as then, welling in her eyes, the children, picking up on the tension, looking up at her, nestling closely against her.

"I'll phone when I get there," Stanley assured her, repeating what he had said more than once, before they left the house.

At the guard's whistle, she craned up to him, the kiss hurried before she stepped back, pulling the children away from the train as it began to move.

Stanley continued to lean out of the window as the train pulled out of the station, watching them until it veered slightly, blocking his view, and even then, he stayed there for a few minutes before taking his seat, several other passengers smiling at him sympathetically.

Peggy, still holding onto her two younger boys, the eight year old Anthony a few steps ahead, walked slowly back along the platform and out of the station into the warm July sunshine, the car parked in a nearby side road.

Back at the house, which had been their home for the past four years since they had left the Droveway flat, she busied herself, clearing away the breakfast things before getting the picnic ready, having promised the boys she would take them to the beach.

For more than six months, this had been hanging over them, ever since that January morning when the letter had arrived.

She had glanced at the brown envelope, noticing the War Office insignia, placing it on the breakfast table beside Stanley who put down his *Telegraph,* turning the envelope over, also looking at the ominous insignia. She watched, conscious of a pang of anxiety as he used his knife to slit open the envelope, taking out the single sheet on which she could see printed writing.

"God Almighty!" He emitted the exclamation under his breath, conscious of the children around the breakfast table, all of them now looking at him, apprehensive that he was cross about something which they were responsible for.

He held the sheet of paper out to Peggy who could see, instantly, what it was.

"I really never thought they'd do it," he said, picking up the newspaper again, as if about to return to the country cricket scores, before flapping it back down on the table, knocking his knife and fork from his empty plate.

For some month there had been speculation in the press, prompted by statements in the House of Commons and, doubtless also, by War Office briefings, that with Britain's increasing involvement in the Korean War, consideration was being given to calling up the "Z men" – soldiers and officers who had served during the war who were under thirty-five, and who were thus on the "Reserve List", eligible for call-up.

"Six years of my life – of our lives – I gave them," he said, shaking his head, the children continuing to look at him uncertainly, sensing that he was not cross with them, but that something else – something unfamiliar – was affecting him. They noticed also, their mother's expression; downcast, as if she were distressed.

"Surely you must be exempt," she said. "I'm sure I heard somewhere that there are all sorts of reasons."

"I'm going to get onto Marlowe. Time to see the metal of the man." Anthony Marlowe, MP for Hove, was not a man in whom Stanley had a great deal of faith, his reputation being as a compliantly line-toing Conservative back-bencher.

"I thought it was the Americans, fighting in Korea," Peggy said. Having no personal interest in this conflict on the far side of the globe. Her avid following of the news having tailed away at the end of the war, she, nevertheless, tended to skim through Stanley's *Telegraph* after he had left for the office and she had walked the two elder boys, Anthony and Martin, up to the bus stop for the short ride to their schools, the youngest, Nick, being tended by the "live in", Cora.

"We seem to be getting dragged in as well," he replied despondently. "Why we can't leave them to get on with it, I really don't know. And we seem to stick our nose into every other damned minor conflict. The latest is some rumblings about a rebellion in Kenya. Farmers getting murdered and that sort of thing."

Proud as he was of the British Empire, the expanse of pink across the maps of the world appearing little diminished in spite of the ructions of the war – the independence of India being the single largest change – he had read and heard enough to realise that, with the increasing dominance of America, and with Russia exerting its pernicious power, Britain's role in the world was declining. Why, therefore, we seemed determined to continue acting as the world's policemen as well as protecting the country's interest, particularly across the Empire, he could not understand.

Marlowe's reply arriving almost by return, its form of words for his explanation as to why he was unable to intervene, reservists being bound by statutory regulations, clearly being fed to him, and, doubtless, to MPs across the country, by the Government, his own Conservative Party now being back in office, Stanley realised that he would have to work out for himself how to get out of the call up which, the notice warned him, could be implemented at any time, requiring him to report for training before possible deployment abroad.

Having got hold of a copy of the *Territorial and Reserve Forces Act* at the local Law Society library, and studied the small print of the *Army Form D407*, being the call-up notice which had arrived so shockingly on his breakfast table, he set about composing his letter which, when concluded, on reading it through, he felt more than adequately stated his case.

*11.1.52*
*26 Hove Park Road, Hove*
*War Office*
*AG8 Branch Registry*
*Sir*
*I have received the enclosed Army Form D407 and.*
*I wish to protest in the strongest possible terms against my selection and to state, in accordance with para 4(e) that it is quite impossible for me to comply with the notice for the following reasons.*
*I joined the TA in March 1939 and was called up in August 1939. I served continuously until March 1946. I was a law student in 1939 and my studies were half completed – I was anxious, as the war was over, to get home and take my final.*
*I eventually qualified as a solicitor in 1947. After a tremendous amount of hard work I have acquired a share in a Brighton firm of solicitors – a new firm. It is utterly impossible for me to leave my business for more than a fortnight a year – and that fortnight represents my annual holiday, with my family. My family consists of my wife, three children and my widowed mother. Two of the boys are at school and I had already arranged my annual holiday in the school summer holiday commencing August Bank holiday. My two partners are also men with large families and my call up would completely wreck the chance of my family and self getting a holiday this year – a holiday for which we have worked damned*

*hard. Quite apart from the holiday angle, I cannot possible leave a new and carefully nursed business for what would be a month in one year, without grave risk of pecuniary loss. What compensation can the Army offer for such losses?*
*My mother was recently widowed, and I look after her affairs entirely as well as my own. She is nearly 70 and has a bad heart.*
*I should point out that last year I had a bad attack of jaundice from which I have not fully recovered as I still get stomach pains which necessitates frequent medical treatment.*
*I trust that in these circumstances you will revoke the notice I enclose herewith. Otherwise great distress will be caused to my wife and family and pecuniary loss to myself.*
*Yours faithfully*
*S R Allen*

He had hesitated when about to include the reference to his mother, wondering whether this might help his cause, concluding that it could do no harm.

This was indeed an important factor, his mother's health having deteriorated since his father's death in 1948, although her weakness for sweets and cakes - with which she would spoil her grandchildren to his and Peggy's exasperation - and her increase in her daily tipple of sherry – "it never did anyone any harm" being her riposte the only time he had mentioned it to her – he was certain didn't help, her weight noticeably increasing, detracting from her mobility.

He had to admit to Peggy, however, that he respected his mother's simple philosophy, that her pleasures were few – her grandchildren, food and drink, and her daily intake of news and gossip from the *Daily Mirror*, Stanley sometimes wondering if she had insisted on taking "that dreadful Labour rag" to vex his father, bringing a bit of scurrilous gossip into the conventionally conservative household, the Vicar's disapproval shared by his elder son as well as by the ever grumbling Mrs Christian, whose firm view was that the *Mirror* was a paper for the "lower orders", being quite unfit to be seen in a respectable home, let alone the vicarage, making it her business to ensure that it was well out of sight whenever there were to be visitors.

As the weeks past, with nothing from the War Office, his exasperation increased, his threats, which he voiced to Peggy on an almost daily basis – to write to the minister, and to go to the papers – he recognised to be quite futile.

When six weeks had passed, he again took up his indignant pen.

*24.2.52*
*26 Hove Park Road, Hove 4*
*Dear Sir*
*It is now over six weeks since I placed before you the reasons why I am quite unable to comply with the Z notice I received that day.*
*Quite frankly I am completely disgusted at the treatment I have received especially in view of the fact that I served continuously from August 31ˢᵗ 1939 having volunteered for TA service earlier that year.*
*To the great distress of my wife and three children I have had to cancel my booking at a farmhouse for our annual holiday and have therefore lost my deposit.*
*Unless I receive a proper answer by Wednesday 27ᵗʰ February, I propose calling my MP and asking him to institute an immediate ministerial enquiry. It seems utterly unfair to treat a family and a business man in this way and I assume that if I had been born one year later, and been over 35, this would not have occurred. This is my reward for volunteering in 1939.*
*I have had more gastric trouble this week, accentuated by the worry over this business.*
*Yours faithfully*
*S R Allen*

"Surely there's no likelihood of them sending you to Korea, is there?" Peggy asked, the thought of him having to off to war again painful enough, but the prospect of him being in such a far distant and unknown place, fighting a war that few people seemed to understand, other than it being to do with the stemming of Russia's expansionist ambition, was quite unbearable.

"Darling, I just don't know!" he replied more brusquely than he had intended. "None of them – the powers that be – are saying much other than that we've got to support the Yanks. I can't think why they don't drop a couple of atom bombs on the damned Ruskies. That would send them scurrying back where they belong."

Unbeknown to anyone outside President Truman's inner circle and the relevant members of the American military, Truman had, many months previously, given his generals the authority to use atomic weapons, a number of which had been transported to the US base on Okinawa in readiness, the reason for their not being used due largely to the difficulty of finding suitable targets, hitting the Russian backed North Korean military, without devastating densely populate civilian areas.

Stanley's second letter brought a reply, although not the one he had been hoping for.

*29.2.52*
*War Office*
*Sir*
*I am directed to reply to your letters of 11ᵗʰ January and 24ᵗʰ February 1952 relating to your training this year.*

*I am to say that it is regretted that your recall this year cannot be cancelled. Cancellation can only be considered in cases of "extreme personal hardship and financial loss". From the evidence so far produced no such hardship would accrue from an absence of fifteen days. Such absence is comparable to that due to sickness or holidays for which alternative arrangements no doubt exist, coupled with the fact that long notice has been given.*

*With regard to loss of holidays I am to point out that if a Reservist is entitled to an annual holiday this must not, unless the reservist so requests, be allowed during any period of training from which he has been summoned by a Warning Notice.*

*In the event of your claim on medical grounds I am to say that all reservists will be examined by a Ministry of Labour Medical Board at least eight weeks prior to recall date. It is not the policy of the War Office to recall reservists who are not fit.*

*I am, sir, your obedient servant*
*Ned Fitzgerald*
*For Director of Personnel Administration*


"It's a complete waste of time!" he said, realising that he was raising his voice, hating the fact that he was taking out his anger on Peggy who suggested he write back, pointing out why he would indeed, suffer the hardship and loss which, as he had explained to her, the regulations were aimed at avoiding. "They're not going to change their tune, it's obvious," he added gloomily.

As he wrote the letter, he knew that he was simply repeating what he had said before, his temptation being to be a good deal more forthright, and yet aware that this would be wholly counter-productive in dealing with some stone-hearted civil servant.

He was in two minds about threatening to involve his MP, Marlowe already having effectively washed his hands of the matter. He was fairly certain, also, that his additional threat, to go to the *Telegraph* was equally fruitless, the venerable paper almost always solidly behind the Conservative government. It was therefore with a heavy heart that he grudgingly accepted that he was now facing the grim prospect of once again donning the King's uniform – the Queen's uniform as he had to correct himself, the King having died a few weeks earlier - his only hope being that the call-up would be for a limited period of training and that the country's current military capability would be sufficient for whatever supporting role was envisage in Korea without having to deploy the Z reservists.

How strange it felt, arriving at Catterick, being directed to his quarters and then finding himself in the RASC mess, where he was greeted by several familiar faces from his days with the 43rd Division as well as 51st.

For two weeks they had to sit through various training lectures, taking part also in a couple of training exercises which, to Stanley, felt quite pointless, bearing little resemblance to the actuality of operating under war conditions. Indeed, the entire fortnight seemed wholly futile although the fact that there were decent pubs nearby made for some convivial evenings.

All that he wanted, however, was to get back home, anxious as he was about the amount of work which he knew would be awaiting him at his office even though his two partners, Christopher Mileham and George Scatliff, would be doing their best to "mind the shop". He was hoping also, that even though they had had to cancel the two week holiday they had booked in a Dorset farmhouse, they might still manage to get a few days away before the end of the school summer holidays.

When he was released at the end of that fortnight, he was confident that his recall was at an end.

It was shortly before midnight when he quietly opened the front door, depositing his suitcase, standing for a moment, listening to the peace and quiet of the house. He heard the slight creaking of the floorboards indicating that Peggy had got out of bed, watching her as she came down the stairs in her silk nightdress, her dishevelled hair telling him that she had been asleep.

As they embraced, he inhaled her intoxicating aroma – her perfume tinged with her own distinct aura which, as they stood there, seemed the very essence of his new life, which he could now resume.

"I think I'm finally done with the army," he said as they went into the kitchen, Peggy putting on the kettle.

Milton Keynes UK
Ingram Content Group UK Ltd.
UKHW021445241124
451413UK00019B/377